The Development Economics Reader

This book collects the most recent and authoritative contributions to the field of development economics and provides a wealth of pedagogical materials that make it ideal for classroom use. As countries such as China and India are experiencing tremendous economic growth, other parts of the world such as sub-Saharan Africa remain mired in poverty and unable to raise standards of living. This volume helps readers understand why poor countries are poor and why designing policies to reduce poverty is such a challenging task.

The book is divided into eight parts and the main themes include economic growth, poverty and inequality, human capital, globalization, and foreign aid. The reader focuses on the most recent and up-to-date contributions to the field of development economics. The articles chosen for the book:

- are understandable to students with a limited background in economics;
- are all written by well-respected development economists or by authoritative scholars and reporters, including Amartya Sen, Jeffrey Sachs, Muhammad Yunus, Hernando de Soto, Dani Rodrik, William Easterly, Joseph Stiglitz, Abhijit V. Banerjee, and Daron Acemoglu;
- include the most recent contributions to the area of development economics, reflecting the latest research and the most promising ideas in the field;
- acquaint students with the wide variety of points of view that generate the controversies and lively debates typical of development economics.

Each part begins with an extensive introduction and a preview of each selection; review and discussion questions follow each reading, and at the end of each part there are suggestions for further reading.

Contemporary and highly accessible, *The Development Economics Reader* is an invaluable resource for all students of the discipline.

Giorgio Secondi is an Associate Professor of Economics at Occidental College in Los Angeles, USA.

The Development

Economics Reader

Edited by

Giorgio Secondi

Routledge
Taylor & Francis Group

LONDON AND NEW YORK

First published 2008
by Routledge
2 Park Square, Milton Park, Abingdon, Oxon OX14 4RN

Simultaneously published in the USA and Canada
by Routledge
270 Madison Ave, New York, NY 10016

Routledge is an imprint of the Taylor & Francis Group, an informa business

Reprinted 2010

Typeset in Perpetua and Bell Gothic by
Keystroke, 28 High Street, Tettenhall, Wolverhampton
Printed and bound in Great Britain by
CPI Antony Rowe, Chippenham, Wiltshire

British Library Cataloguing in Publication Data
A catalogue record for this book is available from the British Library

Library of Congress Cataloging in Publication Data
The development economics reader / edited by Giorgio Secondi.
    p. cm.
    Includes bibliographical references and index.
    1. Economic development.   2. Globalization.   3. Sustainable development.
    4. Poverty.   I. Secondi, Giorgio.
    HD75.D4873 2008
    338.9–dc22   2007042490

ISBN10: 0–415–77156–0 (hbk)
ISBN10: 0–415–77157–9 (pbk)
ISBN10: 0–203–92841–5 (ebk)
ISBN13: 978–0–415–77156–6 (hbk)
ISBN13: 978–0–415–77157–3 (pbk)
ISBN13: 978–0–203–92841–7 (ebk)

To the many students I have taught in the past sixteen years and the many more I look forward to teaching in the years ahead

Contents

PART TWO
Geography, institutions, and governance

PART THREE
Beyond growth: inequality and poverty

PART SEVEN
Globalization and financial crises

PART EIGHT
Foreign aid and debt relief

Notes on contributors

Daron Acemoglu is the Charles P. Kindleberger Professor of Applied Economics at the Massachusetts Institute of Technology.

Kenneth J. Arrow is a Professor of Economics (Emeritus) at Stanford University. He received the Nobel Prize in Economics in 1972.

Abhijit V. Banerjee is the Ford Foundation International Professor of Economics and a Director of the Abdul Latif Jameel Poverty Action Lab at the Massachusetts Institute of Technology.

Robert J. Barro is the Paul M. Warburg Professor of Economics at Harvard University and a Senior Fellow at the Hoover Institution (Stanford University).

Kaushik Basu is the Carl Marks Professor of International Studies, a Professor of Economics, and the Director of the Center for Analytic Economics at Cornell University.

Jagdish Bhagwati is a Professor at Columbia University and a Senior Fellow in International Economics at the Council on Foreign Relations.

Rikhil Bhavnani is a Ph.D. Candidate in Political Science at Stanford University and a former Research Assistant at the Center for Global Development.

Nancy Birdsall is the Founding President of the Center for Global Development and a former Director of the Policy Research Department at the World Bank.

David E. Bloom is the Clarence James Gamble Professor of Economics and Demography and the Chair of the Department of Population and International Health at the Harvard School of Public Health.

Norman E. Borlaug is a Distinguished Professor of International Agriculture at Texas A&M University. He received the Nobel Peace Prize in 1970.

David Canning is a Professor of Economics and International Health at the Harvard School of Public Health.

Michael Clemens is a Research Fellow at the Center for Global Development and an Adjunct Professor in the Public Policy Institute at Georgetown University.

Clive Crook is a senior editor of *The Atlantic Monthly*, a columnist for *National Journal*, and a commentator for the *Financial Times*.

Hernando de Soto is the President of the Institute for Liberty and Democracy in Lima, Peru, and a former Governor of Peru's Central Reserve Bank.

Esther Duflo is the Abdul Latif Jameel Professor of Poverty Alleviation and Development Economics and a Director of the Abdul Latif Jameel Poverty Action Lab at the Massachusetts Institute of Technology.

William Easterly is a Professor of Economics and the Co-Director of the Development Research Institute at New York University.

Eric V. Edmonds is an Associate Professor of Economics at Dartmouth College.

Diana Farrell is Director of the McKinsey Global Institute.

Martin Feldstein is the George F. Baker Professor of Economics at Harvard University and the President of the National Bureau of Economic Research.

Vincent Ferraro is the Ruth Lawson Professor of International Politics at Mount Holyoke College.

Ian Goldin is the Director of the James Martin 21st Century School at the University of Oxford and a former Vice President of the World Bank.

Mahbub ul Haq was the founder of the United Nations' *Human Development Report* and served as a Special Advisor to the United Nations Development Programme Administrator. He died in 1998.

Dean T. Jamison is a Professor of Health Economics in the School of Medicine at the University of California, San Francisco, and an Adjunct Professor in the Peking University Guanghua School of Management and the University of Queensland School of Population Health.

Robert W. Kates is a geographer and independent scholar in Trenton, Maine, and Professor (Emeritus) at Brown University.

Michael Kremer is the Gates Professor of Developing Societies at Harvard University and a Senior Fellow at the Brookings Institution.

Anne O. Krueger is a Professor of International Economics in the Paul H. Nitze School of Advanced International Studies at Johns Hopkins University.

Timur Kuran is a Professor of Economics and Law and the King Faisal Professor of Islamic Thought and Culture at the University of Southern California.

Anthony A. Leiserowitz is the Director of Strategic Initiatives and a Research Scientist in the School of Forestry and Environmental Studies at Yale University.

Susan Lund is a Senior Fellow at the McKinsey Global Institute.

Martha Nichols is a freelance writer and a former associate editor at the *Harvard Business Review*.

Robert Paarlberg is the Betty Freyhof Johnson Class of 1944 Professor of Political Science at Wellesley College and an Associate at the Weatherhead Center for International Affairs at Harvard University.

Thomas M. Parris is a Research Scientist and the Executive Director of the Boston Office at ISciences, LLC.

Nina Pavcnik is an Associate Professor of Economics at Dartmouth College.

Daniel Pearl was the South Asia Bureau Chief of the *Wall Street Journal*. He was kidnapped and murdered by terrorists in Pakistan in 2002.

Michael M. Phillips is a staff reporter for the *Wall Street Journal*.

Steven Radelet is a Senior Fellow at the Center for Global Development.

Dani Rodrik is a Professor of International Political Economy in the John F. Kennedy School of Government at Harvard University.

F. Halsey Rogers is a Senior Economist in the Development Research Group at the World Bank.

Paul M. Romer is the STANCO 25 Professor of Economics Ralph Landau Senior Fellow at the Stanford Institute for Economic Policy Research, and a Senior Fellow at the Hoover Institution at Stanford University.

Vernon W. Ruttan is a Regents' Professor (Emeritus) in the Departments of Economics and Applied Economics at the University of Minnesota.

Jeffrey D. Sachs is the Director of the Earth Institute, the Quetelet Professor of Sustainable Development, and a Professor of Health Policy and Management at Columbia University. He also serves as a Special Advisor to United Nations Secretary-General Ban Ki-moon.

Amartya Sen is the Thomas W. Lamont University Professor and a Professor of Economics and Philosophy at Harvard University. He received the Nobel Prize in Economics in 1998.

Julian L. Simon was a Professor of Business Administration at the University of Maryland. He died in 1998.

Nicholas Stern is the IG Patel Professor of Economics and Government and Director of the Asia Research Centre at the London School of Economics and Political Science. He previously served as the Chief Economist and Senior Vice President of the World Bank.

Joseph Stiglitz is a Professor at Columbia University. He received the Nobel Prize in Economics in 2001.

Arvind Subramanian is a Senior Fellow at the Peterson Institute for International Economics and at the Center for Global Development and a former Assistant Director of the Research Department at the International Monetary Fund.

John Tierney is a columnist for the *New York Times*.

Muhammad Yunus is the Founder and Managing Director of the Grameen Bank. He received the Nobel Peace Prize in 2006.

Preface

SCHOLARLY WORK IN DEVELOPMENT ECONOMICS has been substantial and innovative in the last decade. Development economists have refined their theories to explain the causes of poverty in developing countries and have conducted a tremendous amount of field work to test some of these theories. Information collected on the ground has also helped us gain an increasingly accurate understanding of the features and causes of poverty. This work has fueled a lively debate on the best approaches to raise standards of living in poor countries, making this an exciting and hopeful time to study development economics.

Student interest in development economics is also as strong as ever. As societies become increasingly diverse and connecting with people all over the world becomes easier, students desire a greater understanding of the wide differences in standards of living across countries. But when they try to learn more about the economics of developing countries, they are often faced with a discouraging set of options. The latest scholarship found in professional journals is far too technical and mathematical to be accessible to the average student. Even some of the economic development textbooks currently on the market are aimed at economics majors with intermediate-level theory and calculus under their belt. Students without substantial background in economics may find that the only remaining option is to learn about economic development from sources that lack rigor and oversimplify the issues or from non-specialists who may misunderstand or misrepresent the scholarly work in the field.

This Reader is aimed at students who may have little or no background in economics but want to gain a thorough understanding of what economists have to say about the causes of poverty in developing countries and the best approaches to help these countries raise standards of living. The Reader includes a variety of journal and magazine articles, selections from books and reports, and case studies, most of which I have assigned in the classes I have taught at American University, Wellesley College, Occidental College, and the Phillips Exeter Academy. In assembling this collection, I have strived to choose readings that meet four key criteria:

1   They are understandable to students with very limited background in economics. I did not include readings with equations and complex graphs or readings that assume familiarity with intermediate-level economic theory. The vast majority of the selections will be understandable to students who have never taken any economics; because of their rigor, however, the readings are also appropriate for economics majors or graduate students in fields such as public policy and international affairs.
2   They are written by well-respected development economists or by scholars and reporters with a firm understanding of the scholarly research in development economics. All the key figures in contemporary development economics are represented in the reader – Amartya Sen, Jeffrey Sachs, Muhammad Yunus, Hernando de Soto, Dani Rodrik, William Easterly, Joseph Stiglitz, Abhijit V. Banerjee, Daron Acemoglu, and many others.
3   They include the most recent contributions to the field of development economics, reflecting the latest research and the most promising ideas in the field. Classic contributions to our understanding of development should not be discounted, but they are easily available from a variety of sources, and development economics is a field that continues to move forward and to incorporate new results of recent empirical work. The debate on the role of institutions in development, the idea of "clinical economics" to diagnose obstacles to development, or the use of randomized trials to assess the effectiveness of foreign aid are all explained and explored in the Reader.
4   They acquaint students with the wide variety of points of view that generate the controversies and lively debate typical of development economics. For instance, while the views of free-trade enthusiasts such as Jagdish Bhagwati are presented in the Reader, the critique of free-trade skeptics such as Dani Rodrik and Joseph Stiglitz is presented as well. And while students can read and understand the position of foreign aid advocates such as Jeffrey Sachs, they are also asked to consider the scathing critique of foreign aid put forward by economists such as William Easterly.

The book is divided in eight parts, following what might be a syllabus for a class in development economics. Each part begins with an introduction that familiarizes students with the key issues in a specific area of development economics and helps them see how this area connects to the rest of the discipline. A preview of each selection is included in the introduction. Review and discussion questions follow each reading, helping students focus on specific issues and asking them to think critically about what they just read. At the end of each part there is a section with annotated suggestions for further reading.

Understanding the obstacles to poverty reduction and the challenges faced by developing countries is too important to be limited to students who specialize in economics. It is my hope that this Reader will help a much broader audience move beyond the factoids about development often supplied by the media and gain a much more thorough and rigorous understanding of the latest scholarly work in the field.

I am indebted to the many authors, publishers, and other copyright holders who have agreed to let me reprint their work in this book. I would also like to express my gratitude to Rob Langham, my editor at Routledge, for making this project possible and supporting me throughout its execution, and to Seth Chapman and David Lindauer for bringing to my attention several of the readings that I included in the book. It would be an understatement to say that Michael Kaiser-Nyman provided superb research assistance; his thoughtful and constructive input throughout the process of assembling the Reader went far beyond what could be expected of a research assistant. I am also grateful to my department colleagues for making Occidental College such a wonderful place to work, and, as always, to my family for unwavering support in whatever project I take on. Finally, I want to thank the many students who have given me the opportunity to share my enthusiasm for development economics with them. Their energy, optimism, and desire to play a part in the economic development enterprise make me hopeful that the day will come when "the word 'poverty' will no longer have relevance. It will be understood only with reference to the past" (Muhammad Yunus, *Banker to the Poor: Micro-Lending and the Battle against World Poverty*, New York: PublicAffairs, 1999, p. 236).

Acknowledgements

The publishers would like to thank the following for their permission to reprint their material:

Alfred A. Knopf for permission to reprint Amartya Sen, "Women's Agency and Social Change," chapter 8 from *Development as Freedom* by Amartya Sen, copyright © 1999 by Amartya Sen. Used by permission of Alfred A. Knopf, a division of Random House, Inc.

Aurum Press and PublicAffairs, a member of Perseus Books, L.L.C. for permission to reprint Muhammad Yunus, *Banker to the Poor: Micro-Lending and the Battle against World Poverty*, New York: PublicAffairs, 1999, pp. 43–65.

Blackwell Publishing for permission to reprint Anne O. Krueger, "Why Trade Liberalisation is Good for Growth," *The Economic Journal*, Vol. 108, No. 450 (September 1998), pp. 1513–22. © Royal Economic Society 1998.

Dow Jones & Company, Inc. for permission to reprint Daniel Pearl and Michael M. Phillips, "Small Change: Bank That Pioneered Loans for the Poor Hits Repayment Snag," *Wall Street Journal*, November 27, 2001. Copyright 2001 by Dow Jones & Company, Inc. Reproduced with permission of Dow Jones & Company, Inc. in the format Textbook via Copyright Clearance Center; Joseph Stiglitz, "Social Justice and Global Trade," *Far Eastern Economic Review*, Vol. 169, No. 2 (March 2006), pp. 18–22. Copyright 2006 by Dow Jones & Company, Inc. Reproduced with permission of Dow Jones & Company, Inc. in the format Textbook via Copyright Clearance Center.

Foreign Affairs for permission to reprint Martin Feldstein, "Argentina's Fall," Vol. 81, No. 2 (March/April 2002), pp. 8–14. Reprinted by permission of *Foreign Affairs*. Copyright 2002 by the Council on Foreign Relations, Inc.; Nancy Birdsall, Dani Rodrik, and Arvind Subramanian, "How to Help Poor Countries," Vol. 84,

No. 4 (July/August 2005), pp. 136–52. Reprinted by permission of *Foreign Affairs*. Copyright 2005 by the Council on Foreign Relations, Inc.

Foreign Policy for permission to reprint Dani Rodrik, "Trading in Illusions," No. 123 (March/April 2001), pp. 54–62. Reproduced with permission from *Foreign Policy* www.foreignpolicy.com. Copyright 2001, Carnegie Endowment for International Peace; Jeffrey Sachs, "How to Run the International Monetary Fund," No. 143 (July/August 2004), pp. 60–4. Reproduced with permission from *Foreign Policy* www.foreignpolicy.com. Copyright 2004, Carnegie Endowment for International Peace; William Easterly, "Debt Relief," No. 127 (November/December 2001), pp. 20–6. Reproduced with permission from *Foreign Policy* www.foreign policy.com. Copyright 2001, Carnegie Endowment for International Peace.

Harvard Business School Publishing for permission to reprint Martha Nichols, "Third-World Families at Work: Child Labor or Child Care?" *Harvard Business Review*, Vol. 71, No. 1 (January–February 1993), pp. 12–14.

Hernando de Soto for permission to reprint "The Mystery of Capital," *Finance & Development*, Vol. 38, No. 1 (March 2001), pp. 29–33.

John Tierney for permission to reprint "Fanisi's Choice," *Science 86*, January/February 1986, pp. 26–42.

M.E. Sharpe, Inc. for permission to reprint Kaushik Basu, "International Labor Standards and Child Labor," from *Challenge*, Vol. 42, No. 5 (September–October 1999): 80–93. Copyright © 1999 by M.E. Sharpe, Inc. Reprinted with permission. All Rights Reserved. Not for Reproduction.

Nancy Birdsall for permission to reprint "Inequality Matters," *Boston Review*, March/April 2007.

Oxford University Press for permission to reprint Mahbub ul Haq, "The Human Development Paradigm," in Sakiko Fukuda-Parr and A. K. Shiva Kumar, eds, *Readings in Human Development: Concepts, Measures and Policies for a Development Paradigm*, New York: Oxford University Press, 2003, pp. 17–21; Jagdish Bhagwati, "Poverty: Enhanced or Diminished?" chapter 5 of *In Defense of Globalization*, New York: Oxford University Press, 2004, pp. 51–67.

Princeton University Press for permission to reprint Simon, Julian L., *The Ultimate Resource 2*, pp. xxxi–xxxiii and 491–507. © 1996 Princeton University Press. Reprinted by permission of Princeton University Press.

Robert W. Kates, Thomas M. Parris, and Anthony A. Leiserowitz for permission to reprint "What is Sustainable Development?" *Environment*, Vol. 47, No. 3 (April 2005), pp. 8–21.

Scientific American for permission to reprint Jeffrey Sachs, "Can Extreme Poverty Be Eliminated?", Vol. 293, No. 3 (September 2005), pp. 56–65. Reprinted with permission. Copyright © 2005 by Scientific American, Inc. All rights reserved.

The American Economic Association with acknowledgment to the authors for permission to reprint Timur Kuran, "Why the Middle East is Economically Underdeveloped: Historical Mechanisms of Institutional Stagnation," *Journal of Economic Perspectives*, Vol. 18, No. 3 (Summer 2004), pp. 71–90; Abhijit V. Banerjee and Esther Duflo, "The Economic Lives of the Poor," *Journal of Economic Perspectives*, Vol. 21, No. 1

(Winter 2007), pp. 141–67; Michael Kremer, "Pharmaceuticals and the Developing World," *Journal of Economic Perspectives*, Vol. 16, No. 4 (Fall 2002), pp. 67–90; Eric V. Edmonds and Nina Pavcnik, "Child Labor in the Global Economy," *Journal of Economic Perspectives*, Vol. 19, No. 1 (Winter 2005), pp. 199–220; Vernon W. Ruttan, "Productivity Growth in World Agriculture: Sources and Constraints," *Journal of Economic Perspectives*, Vol. 16, No. 4 (Fall 2002), pp. 161–84.

The Atlantic Monthly for permission to reprint Clive Crook, "The Ten-Cent Solution," *Atlantic Monthly*, March 2007. Copyright 2007 by The Atlantic Monthly. Reproduced with permission of the Atlantic Monthly in the format Textbook via Copyright Clearance Center.

The Economist Newspaper Group for permission to reprint "The Poor and the Rich," *The Economist*, May 25, 1996. Copyright 1996 by Economist Newspaper Group. Reproduced with permission of Economist Newspaper Group in the format Textbook via Copyright Clearance Center; "New Thinking about an Old Problem," *The Economist*, September 15, 2005. Copyright 2005 by Economist Newspaper Group. Reproduced with permission of Economist Newspaper Group in the format Textbook via Copyright Clearance Center; "The Learning Deficit," *The Economist*, April 22, 2004. Copyright 2004 by Economist Newspaper Group. Reproduced with permission of Economist Newspaper Group in the format Textbook via Copyright Clearance Center; "A World of Opportunity," *The Economist*, September 8, 2005. Copyright 2005 by Economist Newspaper Group. Reproduced with permission of Economist Newspaper Group in the format Textbook via Copyright Clearance Center; "The Hidden Wealth of the Poor," *The Economist*, November 3, 2005. Copyright 2005 by Economist Newspaper Group. Reproduced with permission of Economist Newspaper Group in the format Textbook via Copyright Clearance Center.

The Helen Dwight Reid Educational Foundation for permission to reprint Robert Paarlberg, "From the Green Revolution to the Gene Revolution," *Environment*, Vol. 47, No. 1 (January/February 2005), pp. 38–40. Reprinted with permission of the Helen Dwight Reid Educational Foundation. Published by Heldref Publications, 1319 Eighteenth St., NW, Washington, DC 20036–1802. Copyright © 2005.

The Institute for Research on Public Policy for permission to reprint Paul M. Romer, "Beyond Classical and Keynesian Macroeconomic Policy," *Policy Options*, July–August 1994, reproduced with permission of the Institute for Research on Public Policy, www.irpp.org

The International Bank for Reconstruction and Development / The World Bank for permission to reprint "New Directions in Development Thinking," in *Entering the 21st Century:World Development Report 1999/2000*, New York: Oxford University Press, 2000, pp. 13–20 and 24–30; and *Engendering Development: Through Gender Equality in Rights, Resources, and Voice*, Washington, DC: World Bank, 2001, pp. 1–14.

The International Economy for permission to reprint Diana Farrell and Susan Lund, "Unleashing India's Potential: The Key is to Modernize the Financial System," Fall 2006, pp. 42–6; Jeffrey Sachs, "Upstairs, Downstairs," September/October 1999, pp. 30–1, 65.

The International Monetary Fund for permission to reprint Daron Acemoglu, "Root Causes: A Historical Approach to Assessing the Role of Institutions in Economic

Development," *Finance & Development*, Vol. 40, No. 2 (June 2003), pp. 27–30. Copyright 2003 by International Monetary Fund. Reproduced with permission of International Monetary Fund in the format Textbook via Copyright Clearance Center; Dani Rodrik and Arvind Subramanian, "The Primacy of Institutions (and What This Does and Does Not Mean)," *Finance & Development*, Vol. 40, No. 2 (June 2003), pp. 31–4. Copyright 2003 by International Monetary Fund. Reproduced with permission of International Monetary Fund in the format Textbook via Copyright Clearance Center; Jeffrey D. Sachs, "Institutions Matter, but Not for Everything," *Finance & Development*, Vol. 40, No. 2 (June 2003), pp. 38–41. Copyright 2003 by International Monetary Fund. Reproduced with permission of International Monetary Fund in the format Textbook via Copyright Clearance Center; David E. Bloom, David Canning, and Dean T. Jamison, "Health, Wealth, and Welfare," *Finance & Development* Vol. 41, No. 1 (March 2004), pp. 10–15. Copyright 2004 by International Monetary Fund. Reproduced with permission of International Monetary Fund in the format Textbook via Copyright Clearance Center; Kenneth J. Arrow, "New Antimalarial Drugs: Biology and Economics Meet," *Finance & Development* Vol. 41, No. 1 (March 2004), pp. 20–1. Copyright 2004 by International Monetary Fund. Reproduced with permission of International Monetary Fund in the format Textbook via Copyright Clearance Center; Steven Radelet, Michael Clemens, and Rikhil Bhavnani, "Aid and Growth," *Finance & Development*, Vol. 42, No. 3 (September 2005). Copyright 2005 by International Monetary Fund. Reproduced with permission of International Monetary Fund in the format Textbook via Copyright Clearance Center.

The MIT Press for permission to reprint Robert J. Barro, "Democracy and Growth," in Barro, Robert J., *Getting It Right: Markets and Choices in a Free Society*, pp. 1–12, © 1996, by permission of The MIT Press; Ian Goldin, F. Halsey Rogers, and Nicholas Stern, "We must tackle development problems at the level of the economy as a whole," in Abhijit Vinayak Banerjee, *Making Aid Work*, pp. 29–38; Banerjee, Abhijit Vinayak, with Alice H. Amsden, Robert H. Bates, Jagdish Bhagwati, Angus Deaton, and Nicholas Stern, *Making Aid Work*, 5380 words from pages 3–26, © 2007 Massachusetts Institution of Technology, by permission of The MIT Press.

The New York Times Syndication Sales Corp. for permission to reprint Norman E. Borlaug, "The Next Green Revolution," *The New York Times*, July 11, 2003.

Universitätsverlag Göttingen for permission to reprint Amartya Sen, "Perspectives on the Economic Development of India and China," Universitätsverlag Göttingen, 2005.

Vincent Ferraro for permission to reprint "Dependency Theory: An Introduction." July 1996. Mount Holyoke College, South Hadley, MA. Online. Available HTTP: <http://www.mtholyoke.edu/acad/intrel/depend.htm>.

PART ONE

Economic growth, economic development, and human development

INTRODUCTION

BETWEEN 1975 AND 2004, average incomes in Uganda more than doubled. In Chile, they more than tripled, and in Thailand they quadrupled. In China, they rose by nearly eleven times. Not all poor countries, however, experienced such remarkable income growth. In Zambia, average incomes *decreased* by 45 percent between 1975 and 2004. They decreased by more than 60 percent in Sierra Leone and by more than 75 percent in the Democratic Republic of Congo (author's calculations based on UNDP 2006). Other indicators of standards of living show similar disparities across developing countries. Take life expectancy at birth, which gives an indication of health conditions by measuring the number of years that the average newborn child can expect to live. In the thirty years between the early 1970s and the first half of this decade life expectancy increased from 38 to 48 in Mali, from 54 to 68 in Honduras, and from 45 to 64 in Bangladesh, but it decreased from 54 to 47 in Kenya, from 50 to 37 in Zambia, and from 56 to 37 in Zimbabwe (UNDP 2006). Why have some countries experienced dramatic improvements in standards of living at the same time as other countries have stood still or moved backward?

Development economics is the branch of economics that studies relatively poor countries, often referred to as developing countries or less developed countries (LDCs). The "poor" in "poor countries" has no official definition: standards of living vary widely across countries, and picking a line that separates poor from rich countries is no easy task. There is general agreement, however, that three geographical areas are home to a majority of relatively poor countries: sub-Saharan Africa, which includes countries located south of the Sahara Desert such as Nigeria, Ethiopia, Kenya, and Zimbabwe; Central and South Asia, which includes countries such as Tajikistan, Uzbekistan, India, and Bangladesh; and Latin America, which includes Mexico, Central American countries such as Nicaragua and

Haiti, and South American countries such as Brazil and Peru. Even within these three relatively poor areas, differences in standards of living are significant; broadly speaking, poverty is much more widespread and severe in sub-Saharan Africa than in Latin America, which also includes richer countries such as Chile and Argentina. Relatively poor countries are also found in East Asia (e.g., China and Vietnam), Eastern Europe (e.g., Bulgaria and Romania), and the Middle East and North Africa (e.g., Iraq and Algeria). At the other end of the spectrum are the richest countries in the world, sometimes referred to as more developed countries (MDCs): the United States and Canada, most Western European countries (e.g., Germany and the United Kingdom), Australia and New Zealand, several East Asian countries (e.g., Japan and Singapore), and a few Middle Eastern countries (e.g., Kuwait and Bahrain) (see World Bank 2007).

Development economists try to explain why standards of living grow faster in some places than in others. They investigate what promotes economic development and what hinders it, and they work with governments of LDCs to help them formulate economic development policies (government interventions aimed at raising standards of living). The thinking of economists about what does and does not help countries develop has changed over the past several decades. Many of these changes are discussed in the World Bank reading reprinted in Chapter 1. While investing in productive assets such as new machines and factories was at times believed to be paramount, at other times investments in education and health (e.g., building more schools and training more doctors and nurses) were seen as more effective. And whereas many economists used to view government planning of development as essential, in more recent decades economists have emphasized limited government intervention and greater room for free markets. Debates and controversies are a constant feature of development economics. Today, however, there is also substantial agreement on a variety of issues, as the readings in this volume make clear.

A clear trend that has emerged in the past few decades is the movement away from narrow measures of standards of living as indicators of development and toward broader, more comprehensive indicators of quality of life. Measuring economic development, of course, requires a definition of economic development. Most readers will likely agree that economic development should mean an improvement in people's quality of life. But a broad definition such as this one raises more questions than it answers. How do we measure "quality of life"? Do higher incomes necessarily imply a better quality of life? And whose quality of life are we talking about? If some people's standards of living rise while other people's fall, has economic development taken place? These are important questions that development economists have thought about for a long time.

Economists have often been accused of an excessive focus on narrow indicators such as gross domestic product (GDP) per capita (see, e.g., Griffin and Knight 1989). GDP measures a country's total output of final goods and services – essentially the value of all the goods and services an economy produces in a certain period of time. Dividing GDP by the size of the population gives GDP per capita, an approximation of income per person. To understand the connection between GDP and income, think of an economy that produces $1 million's worth of goods in a year. This economy can expect to sell the goods for $1 million. Once the goods are sold, the $1 million earned by the firms that produced the goods becomes income for those who contributed to production – the firms' workers, owners, suppliers, etc. So production turns into sales and sales turn into income. This can also be understood at the level of the worker. If a worker produces $100's worth of goods every day, she allows her employer to sell $100's worth of goods and bring in $100 in revenue, part of which can be used to pay the worker's wage. The more the worker is able to produce every day, the more money the firm earns, and the more the worker can be paid – an increase in GDP or output per person translates into an increase in income per person.[1]

But is income per person a good indicator of quality of life? It can be in some cases: higher incomes allow people to do more of the activities that matter to them, whether that's paying for their education (or their children's education), having access to high-quality health care, buying consumer goods, traveling, or donating money to causes they are interested in. Higher incomes, however, may mean little for quality of life when people live in a country with a repressive government, where they lack basic freedoms and human rights and are prevented from doing things that they care about: voting, speaking freely, criticizing the government, feeling secure from government abuse, assembling with other people who share their interests, or celebrating their native culture. Equating an increase in incomes to an improvement in quality of life, therefore, ignores aspects of quality of life that are not clearly linked to incomes.

Economists have been aware of this problem for a long time, but in early theories of economic growth and development the tendency has been to mention the problem and proceed to ignore it. Because non-economic aspects of quality of life are much more difficult to measure than incomes, it is tempting to focus on GDP per capita. A few economists have also argued that improvements in incomes make it possible to improve other aspects of one's quality of life. It may be that spending quality time with my family is what matters to me rather than material goods, but that in no way implies that a higher income won't improve my quality of life. To the contrary, a higher income may well allow me to cut down on my work hours and have more free time to spend with my family. Of course, there are just as many examples of aspects of quality of life that higher incomes do not affect – if what matters to me is the right to vote, a pay raise at work will do little to improve my life. These examples should make it clear that quality of life is a very complex concept. Not only is there more to it than incomes, it is also a *subjective* concept: different people measure their quality of life in different ways. An economist trying to assess whether a certain country is making progress toward an improvement in quality of life, therefore, is bound to face significant challenges.

The additional problem of determining *whose* quality of life is improving requires figuring out how increases in standards of living are distributed across the population. Economists have investigated at length the issue of distribution, which is discussed in Part Three. It is important to keep in mind, for instance, that an increase in average incomes doesn't say anything about *whose* incomes are improving. A large increase in the incomes of 10 percent of the population and a decrease in the incomes of the remaining 90 percent may still cause an overall increase in average incomes. Yet most people would agree that the country as a whole is not making economic progress if 90 percent of the population experiences a decrease in incomes. The question of whether higher incomes for a minority eventually "trickle down" to the rest of the population, resulting in widespread gains, is controversial and is examined in Part Three.

Because of the limitation of income as an indicator of quality of life, over time economists have expanded the range of measurements used to assess economic development. The most successful attempt at broadening the definition of economic development and recognizing the subjectivity of quality of life has come from the idea of "human development." Mahbub ul Haq, a Pakistani economist, helped pioneer the concept while working at the United Nations Development Program (UNDP) and was responsible for starting the *Human Development Report*, which is now published annually by the UN. His article reprinted in Chapter 2 explains what human development is and how it is connected to narrower indicators of development. Notice especially the focus on the idea of development as a process aimed at expanding people's *choices*. An increase in incomes allows people to have more choices, such as buying expensive goods or acquiring an education. But changes that have little to do with incomes but much to do with quality of life may also expand people's choices. Changes in government that grant people the right to vote, for instance, expand choices and represent a human development achievement in spite of having little to do with income growth.

The idea of economic development as a process that expands people's choices owes much to the work of Amartya Sen, an Indian economist who received the Nobel Prize in Economics in 1998. Sen has written that development is "the expansion of the capabilities of people to lead the kind of life they have reason to cherish" (Sen 1995: 9). In the reading reprinted in Chapter 3, Sen addresses the connections between economic growth (a long-run increase in incomes) and economic development broadly defined (or what Mahbub ul Haq would call human development) (see also Sen 1999). The reading also serves as an introduction to key economic development issues in the two largest developing countries in the world – China and India. Sen shows us the practical challenges of achieving human development, pointing especially to the influence of government choices. He emphasizes that for a long time government policies in India left much to be desired in allowing people to acquire an education and improve their health conditions. Because India is one of the few democracies of the developing world, however, its people were able to enjoy the many rights that go with this form of government – rights that contribute to human development. China, on the other hand, succeeded where India failed and failed where India succeeded. Chinese government policies allowed the achievement of very high levels of education and health even before market reforms were introduced at the end of the 1970s. The political system, however, has not become democratic: the totalitarian government continues to limit people's civil and political rights, taking away from many cherished aspects of human development.

Sen also points out that the lack of democracy prevents China from fully benefiting from its spectacular economic growth. He notes that life expectancy and infant mortality have shown only modest improvements in recent years; in some Indian states like Kerala, on the other hand, improvements in both life expectancy and infant mortality have been much more significant in spite of slower economic growth than in China. Sen believes that China's health improvements have not kept pace with Kerala's because of a decreased public policy focus on health care – a policy change that Chinese people are not in a position to protest because of their lack of political rights.

While economists debate the many different approaches to measuring economic development and human development, they also recognize that economic growth narrowly defined (growth in incomes) can play a crucial role in improving standards of living. Conversely, they note that it is almost impossible to observe substantial and sustained improvements in standards of living in countries where the economy is stagnating. In the past several decades, economists have developed a number of theories to attempt to explain what causes (and what prevents) growth in incomes. The article from *The Economist* reprinted in Chapter 4 gives an overview of the evolution of growth theories since the 1950s. MIT economist Robert Solow was one of the pioneers in this field. He built a model according to which workers produce output by using tools, machines, and factories – what economists refer to as "capital." Income per worker, as we have seen, increases when output per worker increases; and workers are able to produce more output when they have more tools to work with. For example, an office worker with a telephone, a computer, and a printer will get more work done than an office worker who has only a telephone. Solow, therefore, emphasized that growth in incomes requires capital accumulation, or the willingness and ability of firms to invest in the equipment that makes workers more productive. Solow also pointed out, however, that there are only so many machines that a worker can use. At some point, increasing capital becomes less and less helpful in making workers more productive. Therefore, capital accumulation can deliver sustained income growth only if it goes along with technological progress, i.e., with innovations that make resources (labor and capital) more productive over time.

The article from *The Economist* goes on to review more recent advances in the theory of economic growth, including the so-called "new growth theory," also known as endogenous growth theory. Developed largely by Stanford economist Paul M. Romer, this theory is explored in greater detail in the essay reprinted in Chapter 5. Romer addresses specifically Government policies that are likely to promote long-run economic growth, noting that fiscal and monetary policies are unlikely to do so. Fiscal policies – such as greater government spending or tax cuts that promote greater consumer spending – do provide a short-run stimulus to the economy: as the Government or people spend more, firms produce more to satisfy this demand. But more spending implies less saving, and less saving means less money in the bank for firms to borrow; this makes it harder for firms to expand and carry out the capital accumulation that Solow discusses. So the boost in economic activity from the increase in spending is only temporary and may, in fact, hinder long-run growth by making capital accumulation more difficult. Similarly, monetary policies such as increases in the money supply can generate a temporary surge in spending but, in the long run, do nothing to increase an economy's stock of capital or improve technology. Like Solow, Romer emphasizes that long-run economic growth requires improvements in production methods, but he also goes on to explain how such improvements can be achieved. Specifically, he highlights the key role of the accumulation of knowledge that takes place when countries invest in education and firms invest in research and development. Romer's recommendation, then, is that governments focus on subsidizing research and resist supporting dying industries, as innovation inevitably involves replacing old industries with new ones.

The focus that economists place on factors such as capital accumulation or technological progress when explaining economic development is often puzzling to social scientists from disciplines other than economics. These scientists believe that economists are not placing enough weight on political, social, and historical factors that may play a key role in helping a country develop or preventing it from doing so. In the 1970s, the so-called dependency theories of underdevelopment gained significant prominence as a reaction to models of economic growth that seemed to reduce economic development to an engineering problem of sort, or one of finding the best way to combine inputs into output. In the essay reprinted in Chapter 6, Mount Holyoke College political scientist Vincent Ferraro discusses the broad range of theories that fall under the category of dependency theories. He notes that a key feature shared by these theories is the belief that "external forces" play a key role in determining standards of living in poor countries. Specifically, instead of focusing on domestic obstacles to development such as insufficient investment or lack of technological improvement, dependency theories emphasize that the major constraint to development comes from the unequal relation that developing countries have with rich countries. This relation has long historical roots that go back to colonialism. According to these theorists, rich countries are able to exploit developing countries by using their political power to take advantage of the developing countries' resources, as was the case during colonialism. Even though most developing countries today are independent, they tend to be dominated by small elites who benefit from the exploitative relation between poor and rich countries. As a consequence, these elites are able to perpetuate a situation of dependence that benefits them and rich countries at the expense of the vast majority of people in developing countries. Dependency theorists, therefore, see international trade and the integration of developing countries in the global economy as a mechanism that prevents poor countries from escaping an exploitative relation, forcing them into a condition of "underdevelopment" that gets worse and worse over time.

Today, most development economists see as many shortcomings in dependency theories as dependency theorists saw in mainstream development economics. Economists note that so many poor countries have experienced dramatic economic development while becoming increasingly involved in international trade that it is hard to see trade purely as a mechanism of economic exploitation. They also worry that emphasizing the external obstacles to development may conveniently relieve policy-makers in developing countries from the responsibility of looking for domestic solutions to domestic problems. Finally, economists note that dependency theories may help identify historical obstacles to development, but do not have much to say about what developing countries should do today to achieve increases in standards of living (see, e.g., Todaro and Smith 2006: 115–19). In spite of these criticisms, there is no doubt that dependency theories played a role in helping development economics broaden its scope and focus more on issues of inequality and especially on the role of historical and political factors in explaining development. Today, institutions and governance are a key area of inquiry in development economics; they are explored in Part Two.

The challenge of defining economic development serves to remind us of the complexity of this idea and of the difficulty of translating a concept as multidimensional as quality of life into easily measurable indicators. This challenge also helps us understand why economic development policies generate such controversy – if we cannot agree on what we are trying to pursue, we will certainly have a hard time agreeing on how to pursue it! Yet, recognizing the complexity of economic development is also the first step toward approaching the study of development economics with the humility and open-mindedness that it requires. The quest for silver bullets, panaceas, and one-size-fits-all solutions is best abandoned at the outset; free of this burden, we can begin the process of listening to what people want, understanding what prevents them from achieving what they are after, and using the insights of economics to look for practical solutions that move people a step closer to a more fulfilling life.

NOTE

1   What if the firm simply pockets the extra money when output per worker increases and keeps paying the worker the same? This could only happen if firms do not compete with each other for workers, which is rare in most economies. If firms do compete, the ones that underpay will see their workers quit and move to a different firm.

REFERENCES

Griffin, K. and Knight, J. (1989) "Human Development: The Case for Renewed Emphasis," *Journal of Development Planning*, 19: 9–40; reprinted in Jameson, K. P. and Wilber, C. K. (eds) *The Political Economy of Development and Underdevelopment*, 6th edn, New York: McGraw-Hill.

Sen, A. (1995) "Economic Development and Social Change: India and China in Comparative Perspectives," Development Economics Research Programme Working Paper No. 67, STICERD, London School of Economics and Political Science.

Sen, A. (1999) *Development as Freedom*, New York: Alfred A. Knopf.

Todaro, M. P. and Smith, S. C. (2006) *Economic Development*, 9th edn, Boston, MA: Pearson Addison Wesley.

UNDP (2006) *Human Development Report 2006*. Online. Available HTTP: <http://hdr.undp.org/hdr2006/> (accessed 14 June 2007).

World Bank (2007) *World Development Indicators 2007*. Washington, DC: World Bank.

Chapter 1

World Bank

NEW DIRECTIONS IN DEVELOPMENT THINKING

THE PRINCIPAL GOAL OF development policy is to create sustainable improvements in the quality of life for all people. While raising per capita incomes and consumption is part of that goal, other objectives – reducing poverty, expanding access to health services, and increasing educational levels – are also important. Meeting these goals requires a comprehensive approach to development.

The last half-century has been marked by a mix of pessimism and optimism about prospects for development. The Green Revolution held out the prospect of overcoming the Malthusian threat, and countries like India succeeded in achieving food security. But the world's burgeoning population, combined with relatively slow growth in the productivity of food grains in the 1990s, is once again raising fears of food shortages. Some development approaches, such as Brazil's import-substitution policies, appeared to work for a while but then failed. The more recent downturn in the most remarkable economic success story of all – East Asia – has raised new questions about development policies, as has the slow response to market reforms shown by the economies in transition. Yet a consensus is emerging on the elements of future development policy.

- *Sustainable development has many objectives.* Insofar as raising per capita income improves people's living standards, it is one among many development objectives. The overarching aim of lifting living standards encompasses a number of more specific goals: bettering people's health and educational opportunities, giving everyone the chance to participate in public life, helping to ensure a clean environment, promoting intergenerational equity, and much more.
- *Development policies are interdependent.* When a policy does not work well, what is involved may be more than just the individual strategy. Policies require complementary measures in order to work best, and a policy failure can occur because these complements are not in place.

- *Governments play a vital role in development, but there is no simple set of rules that tells them what to do.* There is consensus that governments should adhere to the policy fundamentals, but beyond that, the part the government plays depends on its capacity to make effective decisions, its administrative capabilities, the country's level of development, external conditions, and a host of other factors.
- *Processes are just as important as policies.* Sustained development requires institutions of good governance that embody transparent and participatory processes and that encompass partnerships and other arrangements among the government, the private sector, nongovernmental organizations (NGOs), and other elements of civil society.

The idea that development has multiple goals and that the policies and processes for meeting them are complex and intertwined has provoked an intense debate on the wisdom of traditional development thinking. This introduction draws on the threads of that debate to review perspectives and lessons from past development experiences. It emphasizes the need to reach beyond economics to address societal issues in a holistic fashion. The chapter then turns to the role of institutions in development and points to the institutional changes that will be necessary to ensure sustainable development in the 21st century. While development still faces many challenges, the opportunities waiting to be grasped in the new century hold out just as many exciting prospects.

Building on past development experiences

The evidence of recent decades demonstrates that while development is possible, it is neither inevitable nor easy. The successes have been frequent enough to justify a sense of confidence in the future. But while these successes may be replicable in other countries, the failure of many development efforts suggests that the task will be a daunting one.

One measure of development is per capita GDP, which is often correlated with other indicators of well-being and so serves as a convenient starting point. The average level of per capita GDP in developing countries for which data are available rose at a rate of 2.1 percent per year from 1960 to 1997 – a growth rate that, if it kept rising, would double average per capita GDP every 35 years or so.

But such aggregate data invariably mask an array of variations across times and places. For example, the growth rate of per capita income in developing countries rose relatively quickly in the 1960s and 1970s and leveled out in the 1980s. An optimist might see signs of a return to rapid growth in the first half of the 1990s, but such signs have been less apparent in the aftermath of the East Asian financial crisis that began in 1997. In addition, East Asia is the only region of the world where incomes in low- and middle-income countries are converging toward incomes in richer countries.

Compared to this regional success, the broad picture of development outcomes is worrisome. The average per capita income of the poorest and middle thirds of all countries has lost ground steadily over the last several decades compared with the average income of the richest third (figure 1.1). Average per capita GDP of the middle third has dropped from 12.5 to 11.4 percent of the richest third and that of the poorest third from 3.1 to 1.9 percent. In fact, rich countries have been growing faster than poor countries since the Industrial Revolution in the mid-19th century. A recent estimate suggests that the ratio of per capita income between the richest and the poorest countries increased sixfold

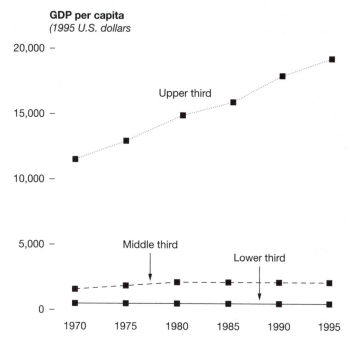

Figure 1.1   The incomes of rich and poor countries continue to diverge

Source: World Bank, *World Development Indicators*, 1999.

between 1870 and 1985.[1] Such findings are of great concern because they show how difficult it is for poor countries to close the gap with their wealthier counterparts.

Standard economic theories predict that, other things being equal, poor countries should grow faster than rich ones. For instance, developing countries arguably have an easier task in copying the new technology and production processes that are central to economic development than industrial countries have in generating them. Capital, expertise, and knowledge should flow from wealthier countries that have these resources in abundance to those developing economies in which they are scarce – and where they should be even more productive.

Both past and present development thinking has devoted much effort to uncovering explanations for why low-income countries have difficulties in following this pattern.[2] A number of studies show that low-income countries can grow faster than high-income countries (by about 2 percent per year), thus catching up gradually over time, if they implement an appropriate mix of growth-enhancing policies.[3] And increasing experience with development outcomes is providing insight into the complexity of the process and the multifaceted approach needed to achieve this growth.[4]

The complexity of the development process has long been recognized. Arthur Lewis's classic 1955 study *The Theory of Economic Growth* includes chapters on profit incentives, trade and specialization, economic freedom, institutional change, the growth of knowledge, the application of new ideas, savings, investment, population and output, the public sector and power, and politics.[5] But over the years, various development processes have been singled out as "first among equals" in terms of their impact. The conceptual frameworks for development of the last 50 years, especially in their popularized versions, tended to focus too heavily on the search for a single key to development. When a particular key failed to open the door to development in all times and places, it was set aside in the search for a new one.

Development models popular in the 1950s and 1960s drew attention to the constraints imposed by limited capital accumulation and the inefficiency of resource allocation.[6] This attention made increasing investment (through either transfers from abroad or savings at home) a major objective. But the experience of recent decades suggests that a focus on investment misses other important aspects of the development process. Investment rates and growth rates for individual countries between 1950 and 1990 varied considerably. Some low-investment countries grew rapidly, while a number of high-investment countries had low growth rates.[7] Although investment is probably the factor that is most closely correlated with economic growth rates in these four decades, it does not fully explain them.[8]

Early theories of development, especially those associated with Simon Kuznets, also argued that inequality generally increases during the early stages of development. Evidence from recent decades has not validated these theories, and it now appears likely that growth, equality, and reductions in poverty can proceed together, as they have in much of East Asia. Many policies promote growth and equality simultaneously. For example, improving access to education builds human capital and helps the poor, and providing land to poor farmers increases not only equality but also productivity. The East Asian countries also showed that countries can have high savings rates without high levels of inequality.

Development theorists of the 1950s and 1960s also offered a wide variety of rationales explaining why open economies and limited intervention would not suffice to spur growth. Many development economists focused on planning as at least a partial solution to the prevailing problems of low investment and slow industrialization, especially as memories of the Great Depression made many policymakers skeptical about the virtues of unconstrained market forces. Two other factors seemed to argue for an aggressive government role in development: the U.S. government's close management of production during World War II, and the investment and GDP levels of the Soviet Union, which was then surging forward under communism despite enormous human costs.

Over time, however, it became clear that while governments do have a vital role in the development process, only a few governments have run state enterprises efficiently. Returns to investment in the Soviet Union fell almost to zero. Governments padded public sector payrolls and the overstaffing, combined with inefficiency, produced large deficits that imposed a fiscal burden and diverted needed revenues. Concerns were also mounting that governments of developing countries were making poor decisions in the macroeconomic sphere, leading to problems such as inflation and the debt crises in Latin America.[9]

In the late 1960s the attention of policymakers began to shift toward an emphasis on human capital, which is often measured in terms of school enrollment (as a proxy for education) and life expectancy (as a proxy for health status). In the last two decades investment in human capital has shown impressive results. Rates of return on primary education in low-income countries have been as high as 23 percent per year.[10] But like investment in physical capital, investment in health and education alone does not guarantee development. In sub-Saharan Africa, for example, life expectancy and school enrollment

- *Macroeconomic policy.* The East Asian countries implemented sound macroeconomic policies that helped contain inflation and avoid recessions. Indonesia and Thailand had positive real GDP growth from 1970 until 1996. Over that same time period Malaysia and the Republic of Korea each had only one year of negative real GDP growth.

Each of these points opens up a number of new issues. For instance, the high savings rate might have been generated by personal preferences, government policies, or a combination of the two. And while these countries invested their savings well, many others do not. Nonetheless these elements of overtly successful policies point the way toward a partial development agenda.

Failures as well as successes can provide positive lessons for development. Among the most recent (and sometimes spectacular) examples of such failures are Russia, some of the economies in transition in Central and Eastern Europe, and several East Asian countries affected by the economic and financial crisis of the mid-1990s. Their experiences point to other factors that can influence economic growth, including corporate and public governance and competition.

- *Legal frameworks.* A sound legal framework helps ensure that managers and majority shareholders in the corporate realm focus on building firms rather than on looting them.
- *Corruption.* Reducing corruption in the public sphere makes a country more attractive to investors. Many privatization efforts have been racked by corruption, undermining confidence in both the government and the market economy. The loans-for-shares scheme in Russia was so widely perceived as raising corruption to new heights that much of the resulting wealth is considered illegitimate.
- *Competition.* Competition is essential. It encourages efficiency and provides incentives for innovation, but monopolies may try to suppress it unless the government steps in.

Studies of World Bank projects illustrate the many elements necessary for successful development.[16] These studies show that projects in countries that adhere to the macroeconomic fundamentals of low inflation, limited budget deficits, and openness to trade and financial flows are more successful than projects in closed countries with macroeconomic imbalances. But the projects need more than a stable macroeconomy in order to succeed. For example, social projects are more likely to succeed if they emphasize beneficiary participation and are responsive to gender concerns. Studies also find that government "ownership" of projects is essential and that measures of government credibility are closely correlated with returns on the projects. In low-income countries stronger institutions are associated with a 20 percent increase in the likelihood that a project will receive a "satisfactory" rating.[17] The role of social capital in project success has also been highlighted – indeed, it is hard to overemphasize the importance of networks of trust and association for sustainable development (box 1.2). Finally, the studies emphasize the importance of coordinated development efforts among governments and donors.[18]

Overall, the impact of World Bank projects depends on a host of factors extraneous to the projects themselves. A recent review of World Bank energy projects in

BOX 1.2   SOCIAL CAPITAL, DEVELOPMENT, AND POVERTY

Social capital refers to the networks and relationships that both encourage trust and reciprocity and shape the quality and quantity of a society's social interactions.[19] The level of social capital has a significant impact on a range of development processes. For example:

- In education, teachers are more committed, students achieve higher test scores, and school facilities are better used in communities where parents and citizens take an active interest in children's educational well-being.[20]
- In health services, doctors and nurses are more likely to show up for work and to perform their duties attentively where their actions are supported and monitored by citizen groups.[21]
- In rural development, villages with higher social capital see greater use of credit and agrochemicals and more village-level cooperation in constructing roads.[22]

Social capital serves as an insurance mechanism for the poor who are unable to access market-based alternatives. It is therefore important to facilitate the formation of new networks in situations where old ones are disintegrating – as, for example, during urbanization.

Social capital can have an important downside, however. Communities, groups, or networks that are isolated, parochial, or counterproductive to society's collective interests (for example, drug cartels) can actually hinder economic and social development.[23] This has led some to make a distinction between vertical social capital (generally negative, as in gangs) and horizontal social capital (generally positive, as in community associations).

sub-Saharan Africa offers some vivid examples of these factors, including governance, human capital, and a good policy framework (box 1.3). What is true of energy projects in sub-Saharan Africa is equally true of privatization programs. The outcome of privatization projects is heavily dependent on governance structures, macroeconomic and structural factors, the competitiveness of the market, social sustainability, regulatory régimes, corporate and commercial law, financial sector reforms, and the state of business accounting.[24] In turn, what is true of power and privatization projects is just as true of efforts to create social safety nets, build schools, or improve the environment.

The many goals of development

The World Bank's experience with large dam projects highlights the importance of taking a broad view of the outcomes of projects. In the 1950s and 1960s large dams were almost synonymous with development. But more recent evidence of their effects on the environment and on the welfare of groups displaced by construction suggests that these projects must be handled with great care if they are to have a positive impact on sustainable development. They require a participatory approach that allows all the potential costs to

BOX 1.3   EXPLAINING POWER PROJECT OUTCOMES IN SUB-SAHARAN AFRICA

Until the mid-1990s the record of World Bank power projects in sub-Saharan Africa was comparatively weak. Out of 44 such projects completed in the region between 1978 and 1996, 64 percent were rated satisfactory, compared with a worldwide average of 79 percent. A recent study analyzing the causes of this poor performance suggested that a wide range of factors influenced project outcomes and sector performance, including:

- *External factors*, such as rising fuel prices, international interest rates, and terms-of-trade shocks
- *Regulatory and legal structures*, including lack of transparency in regulatory processes
- *Low technical capacity*, especially a limited human resource base
- *Lack of private sector involvement*, through either ownership or service contracting
- *Limited government ownership* of reform processes
- *Weak coordination* among donor agencies and little overall government direction.

This list indicates just how complex and intertwined the development process can be in practice.

Source: Covarrubias 1999.

be aired openly and fully.[25] This approach is appropriate for other projects as well. In order to be effective, all projects must be implemented with an awareness of their social, civil, environmental, political, and international implications.

Similar lessons can be drawn from experience with development at the macro-economic level. While increased income is clearly an important component of an improved standard of living, its relationship to other measures of well-being is complex. For example, those living on less than $1 per day are five times more likely to die before age five than those living on more than $1.[26] Nonetheless, recent studies suggest that rates of economic growth over the last 30 years reveal little about the rates of improvement in vital measures of development such as political stability, education, life expectancy, child mortality, and gender equality. Reductions in the mortality rate of children under the age of five, for example, appear to have little to do with the speed of economic growth. While economic performance was poor in many developing countries in the 1980s and early 1990s, only one country in the sample used here (Zambia) saw an increase in infant and child mortality.

One likely reason for this weak relationship is that countries and communities place different priorities on education and health. For example, public expenditures on health care are 63 percent of GDP in Latin American and Caribbean countries and 5 percent of GDP in South Asia, but they account for just 2.7 percent of GDP in sub-Saharan Africa. Sri Lanka is often cited as an example of a poor country that has invested wisely in primary health care and has reaped the benefits. In 1997 life expectancy averaged 59 years in the world's low-income countries, and infant deaths averaged 82 per 1,000 live births. But despite its low level of GDP per capita, Sri Lanka's life expectancy was 73 years, and infant mortality was just 14 per 1,000 live births – not quite the levels of the high-income countries of the world, but not far short either.[27]

Further, like all development endeavors, achievements in health and education are interrelated, and they may also affect other government programs. Countries that pursue egalitarian growth strategies – for example, education or land reform – are more likely to perform well on indicators of human well-being. So, the most effective way to obtain improved health outcomes may be direct spending that improves nutrition and discourages smoking, drugs, and alcohol, rather than direct expenditures on health care. In some areas the most effective way to improve educational outcomes for children may not involve increased expenditure on books or teachers but instead may involve building a rural road or a bridge across a river to facilitate access to schools. Countries that pay attention to such linkages may discover unexpected improvements in their indicators of human well-being.

Improving health is itself one clear case where targeting broad goals is likely to have dramatic spillover effects. Studies suggest that as much as 30 percent of the estimated per capita growth rate in the United Kingdom between 1870 and 1979 might be associated with improvements in health and nutritional status. Microstudies support such findings – in Indonesia, for example, anemia reduced male productivity by 20 percent.[28]

Improvement in gender equality is another important example of a development goal that reinforces other elements of the development agenda. Low levels of education and training, poor health and nutritional status, and limited access to resources depress women's quality of life throughout the developing world. And gender-based discrimination can also be significantly deleterious to other elements of a sustainable development agenda. Women are a major part of the workforce in developing countries – they comprise about 60 percent of Africa's informal sector and 70 percent of the region's agricultural labor, for example. Discrimination reduces their productivity. Estimates from Kenya suggest that if women had the same access to factors and inputs as men, the value of their output would increase nearly 22 percent. Discrimination also has a negative effect on a range of other development indicators. One study has found that a 10 percent increase in female literacy rates reduces child mortality by 10 percent (increased male literacy had little effect).[29] Throughout the developing world, gains in the educational level of women in the 1960–90 period might account for as much as 38 percent of the decline in infant mortality over that time, and for 58 percent of the drop in total fertility rate.[30] Improving gender equality is likely to produce dramatic results, and it is a goal that can be targeted at any level of development.

While the level of income is not necessarily correlated with a higher standard of living, economic growth is linked with some negative outcomes – particularly carbon dioxide and sulfur dioxide output and the production of waste.[31] This suggests the importance of trade-offs in a comprehensive development strategy. Policymakers must sometimes make hard choices when a project or policy supports one development goal while damaging the prospects for another. Such trade-offs are not limited to those involving projects with high economic returns and adverse environmental impacts. In education, for instance, primary schooling may offer the most benefits in terms of increasing equity, but tertiary education may offer the most in terms of closing the knowledge gap with industrial countries.

NEW DIRECTIONS IN DEVELOPMENT THINKING   19

Hence, development must pursue a range of outcomes, such as equality, education, health, the environment, culture, and social well-being, among others. Furthermore, the linkages between these outcomes – both positive and negative – need to be fully understood.

[. . .]

The record and outlook for comprehensive development

What has been the record to date of development? And what does the future hold? Answering these questions involves looking at a range of indicators of economic, human, and environmental welfare. The evidence suggests that while remarkable progress has been made in some areas, in others development has fallen behind. Current trends suggest that even the gains achieved could prove short-lived in the absence of new policies and institutions.

Some parts of the developing world have enjoyed levels of growth high enough to reduce poverty in recent decades. Even in parts of the world where poverty rates remain high, the percentage of the poorest – those living on less than $1 per day (a frequently used poverty line) – has declined. In South Asia, for example, the proportion of the population below the poverty line declined from 45.4 percent in 1987 to 43.1 percent in 1993. But the proportion is rising in some regions. In Latin America it rose from 22.0 percent of the population in 1987 to 23.5 percent in 1993, and in sub-Saharan Africa it increased from 38.5 percent to 39.1 percent (figure 1.2).

The ongoing increase in population levels means that the absolute number of those living on $1 per day or less continues to increase. The worldwide total rose from 1.2 billion in 1987 to 1.5 billion today and, if recent trends persist, will reach 1.9 billion by 2015.

With the recent East Asian crisis, poverty rates have risen again, even in this successful developing region. If the poverty level is set at $2 per day, Thailand is projected to see poverty increase by 19.7 percent between 1997 and 2000.[32] Inequality typically does not reverse itself quickly, so that if average levels of income change, the number of individuals at the bottom – those in poverty – will not move in tandem. An informal rule of thumb is that a per capita growth rate of 3 percent or more is considered the minimum for reducing poverty rapidly.[33] But the average long-term growth rate of developing countries is below that level. Between 1995 and 1997 only 21 developing countries (12 of them in Asia) met or exceeded this benchmark rate. Among the 48 least-developed countries, only 6 exceeded it.[34]

Measures of health and education offer another perspective on development and living standards. By and large, income increases over the last 50 years have been accompanied by improvements in a variety of indicators of human well-being – life span, infant mortality, and educational level. Even many low-income countries with very slow economic growth have been able to manage some significant improvements in the quality of life of their citizens. In the group of low-income countries as a whole, rates of infant mortality have fallen from 104 per 1,000 live births in 1970–75 to 59 in 1996, and life expectancy has risen by four months each year since 1970. Primary school enrollments have shown significant increases, and adult literacy has risen from 46 to 70 percent. Gender disparities have narrowed, with the average ratio of girls to boys in secondary school rising from 70:100 in 1980 to 80:100 in 1993. These trends testify to the enormous gains that

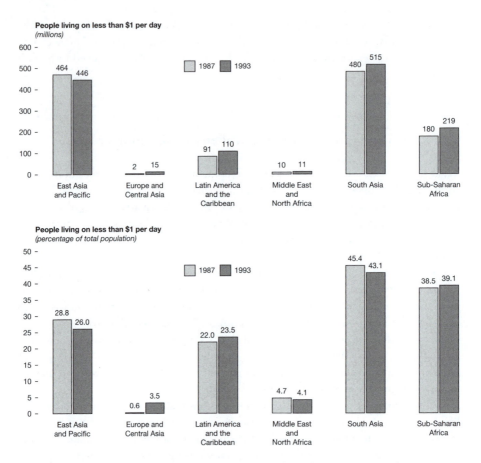

Figure 1.2   The number of poor people has risen worldwide, and in some regions the proportion of poor has also increased

Source: World Bank, *World Development Indicators*, 1998.

have been made in the length and quality of life for billions of the poorest people around the world.[35]

However, some of these gains are proving fragile. A number of factors – notably prolonged economic crises and slumps – have begun to erode previous advances in life expectancy. In African countries burdened with slow economic growth and an increasing number of people with AIDS, life expectancy declined in 1997 to pre-1980 levels. Lower life expectancies are also apparent in countries of the former Soviet Union and in Eastern Europe (figure 1.3).

A number of other fundamental indicators, including adequate calorie intake, reasonable shelter, and access to basic services, remain deeply unsatisfactory. Of the 4.4 billion people in developing countries, nearly three-fifths lack basic sanitation; a third have no access to clean water; a quarter lack adequate housing; and a fifth have no access to modern health services. About 20 percent of children do not complete five years of school, and a similar percentage does not receive enough calories and protein from their diet.

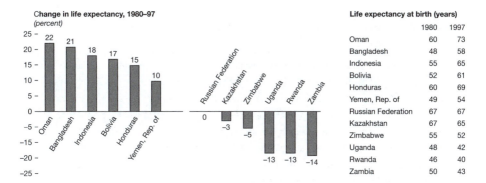

Figure 1.3 Life expectancies have risen greatly in some countries, but others have suffered setbacks

Source: World Bank, *World Development Indicators*, 1999.

Progress on countering infectious diseases over the last 40 years has been dramatic. While the worldwide eradication of smallpox is perhaps the best-known success, polio is also on the retreat. The last-known case of polio caused by wild poliovirus in the Western Hemisphere was on August 23, 1991, and that in the western Pacific was in March 1997. Sadly, the majority of African countries are still exposed to the poliovirus, as well as to malaria and tuberculosis. New diseases such as AIDS have also spread with alarming speed.[36] In 1995 alone more than 9 million children under the age of five in developing countries died from preventable causes.

Population growth is also connected with the success or failure of a sustainable development agenda. Long-term projections show that the world's population may level off around the middle of the 21st century. But before it does, the number of people could rise from the current level of 6 billion to more than 10 billion. This growth will pose difficult issues involving education, worker training, cultural stability, retirement programs, political majorities, and much more.

In parts of the world with fragile ecological systems that are already threatened by water stress and land degradation, increased population pressure could lead to environmental catastrophes. Global food supplies will need to double over the next 35 years because of population (and economic) growth. While food supplies have actually doubled in the last 25 years, agronomists warn that the next doubling will be far more difficult – especially if it is to be environmentally sustainable. In Nepal, for instance, where population growth is reducing average farm size, farmers have been pushed into clearing and cropping hillsides in an attempt to maintain their income, and erosion is becoming an increasingly serious problem.

The doubling of food production will have to occur at a time when 800 million people worldwide are already malnourished, 25 billion tons of topsoil are lost annually, and nearly three-quarters of the ocean's fish stocks are overexploited. The current costs of environmental damage, including such things as erosion and the health and other effects of pollution, have been estimated at 5 percent or more of GNP worldwide – a figure that will increase rapidly if the world does not move toward a sustainable development agenda (box 1.4).

Water scarcity also threatens the potential for continued improvements in the quality of life of the world's poorest people. Today, about one-third of the world is living under

BOX 1.4   SUSTAINABLE DEVELOPMENT

Any sustainable development agenda must be concerned with intergenerational equity – that is, with ensuring that future generations have the same capability to develop as the present generation. A development path is sustainable only if it ensures that the stock of overall capital assets remains constant or increases over time. These assets include manufactured capital (such as machines and roads), human capital (knowledge and skills), social capital (relationships and institutions), and environmental capital (forests and coral reefs). The environment matters not just because of its effect on psychic and noneconomic welfare but also because of its impact on production over the long term.

Environmental sustainability is also closely connected with intragenerational equity. While the wealthy consume more resources overall, the poor tend to rely more heavily on the direct exploitation of natural resources than the rich. If they have no access to nonenvironmental resources – and so have limited capacity to adapt – they may have no choice but to engage in unsustainable uses of environmental resources.

Source: Pearce and Warford 1993; Watson and others 1998.

moderate or severe water stress, with at least 19 countries dependent on foreign sources for more than 50 percent of their surface water. By 2050 the proportion of people living at or above moderate water stress could double. The great majority will be in developing countries where technical, financial, and managerial limitations will complicate attempts to respond.[37] Under conditions of water scarcity, agricultural yields will fall as irrigation supplies dry up, and health will suffer as more people are reduced to using unsafe water sources for drinking and washing. The potential for conflict over riparian rights among states is also likely to increase.

Economic stagnation or collapse, new health crises, continued population growth, and a range of environmental issues all threaten the gains that have been made in the development agenda over the last half century and will be a continuing challenge for development in the new millennium. These issues will have to be faced in a world that is very different from what it is today – a world that will create a new set of challenges and opportunities.

A changing world

The only thing that can be said with certainty about the future is that it will differ from the present. Any list of the most significant changes that the world will undergo in the next few decades is to some degree arbitrary. However, such a list might include the following possibilities.

The spread of democracy. The proportion of countries that are considered democratic has more than doubled since 1974. In a worldwide shift, people are demanding a larger say in the way their governments are run. In addition, demands for increased decentralization of power often accompany democratic trends.

Urbanization. Agriculture accounts for a larger share of production in low-income countries than it does in high-income economies. In sub-Saharan Africa, for example, agriculture today is about one-quarter of GDP – not very different from the level of U.S. GDP in agriculture at the beginning of the 20th century. However, two characteristics of economic development are working together to encourage migration away from rural areas and into cities: increased agricultural productivity (which allows fewer farmers to produce more food) and expanded economic opportunities in the manufacturing and service sectors. The world's urban population is set to rise by almost 1.5 billion people in the next 20 years, and in developing countries the share of the population living in urban areas is likely to rise from one-half to about two-thirds by 2025. This growth will have a significant effect on the political clout of cities and will make getting policy right at the municipal level even more important than it is today.

Demographic pressures. The world's population is likely to increase by at least another 4 billion by 2050 – a huge number of people who will need to be fed, sheltered, and absorbed into the workforce. The age composition of the population will also shift as birthrates decline and life expectancies increase. The transition will be particularly rapid in the industrial world, where in 30 years one in four people will be over 65 – up from one in seven today.[38] This shift will strongly influence global financial flows as an increasing number of retirees stop saving and instead begin to draw down their accumulated assets.

The revolution in information and communications technology. Economic output has traditionally been visualized as commodities and goods – wheat, coffee, shirts, or automobiles. This economic vision grows less accurate each year. In industrial economies the service sector has accounted for more than half of all output for decades, and a similar shift toward services is under way in developing countries. The growing importance of services means that knowledge – how to do things, how to communicate, how to work with other people – is becoming ever more important, overshadowing the natural resource base. It means that investment in human capital, including health and education, might become more urgent than investment in physical capital. It implies that economic output is becoming more "footloose," since many services and information can be shipped over phone wires or fiber-optic cable or even through the radio spectrum, increasing the range of choices for locating production. Improved communications technology – and continued improvements in the efficiency of international transport – have also facilitated the rapid increase in global trade and financial flows.[39]

Threats to the environment. A number of environmental problems will become significant threats to sustainable development if they are not addressed. Climate change from atmospheric concentrations of greenhouse gases and the growing rate of global species extinction are two of the most pressing, but others also demand attention, including disease, water shortages, and land degradation.

This report argues that the changes the world is already experiencing will greatly increase the importance of global and local (or supra- and subnational) institutions. In many cases the responses, to economic, social, and environmental changes will require international cooperation under enhanced or completely new institutional structures. At the same time, governments will increasingly decentralize, devolving greater power to city and regional authorities. While the central authorities will continue to play an important role in coordinating and enforcing cooperative outcomes, decisions affecting people's lives will increasingly be taken at the international and local levels.

The movement toward a globalized and localized world with many more important players and voices from both above and below the national government level offers new opportunities for development and new challenges for governments. Grasping the opportunities and meeting the challenges requires building institutions that will shape and channel the forces of change to best serve the cause of sustainable development.

. . .

Development thinking has followed a circuitous path over the last 50 years. At various times it has emphasized market failures and market successes, governments as active interventionists or passive enablers, openness to trade, saving and investment, education, financial stability, the spread of knowledge, macroeconomic stability, and more. The list of policies accepted as relevant to sustainable development is now longer than it was even 10 years ago, and some of the emphases have changed. Inflation remains a concern, for instance, but little evidence exists showing that low to moderate rates of inflation have significantly adverse effects on growth. On the other hand, increasing recognition is being given to the importance of strong financial institutions, and in the regulatory sphere the focus has shifted from deregulation to building an effective regulatory framework.

It would be presumptuous to predict which of these items will be high on policy agendas one or two decades from now. But even as the general understanding of development grows and evolves, one lesson remains. Understanding the process of development requires acknowledging both its complexity and the context in which it operates. Simple solutions – investments in physical and human capital, for instance, and unfettered markets – will not work in isolation. Governments, the private sector, civil society, and donor organizations need to work together in support of broad-based development.

Notes

1   Pritchett 1997.
2   Among some of the more widely cited papers on why and how convergence is not happening are Bernard and Durlauf 1996; Easterly and Levine 1997; Pritchett 1997, 1998; Quah 1993; and Sachs and Warner 1997b.
3   Some papers that find strong evidence of conditional convergence are: Barro 1991; Mankiw, Romer, and Weil 1992; Sachs 1996; and Sala-i-Martin 1997. Caselli, Esquivel and Lefort (1996) suggest the convergence rate to country-specific steady states could be even faster than the cross-country rate of two percent per year.
4   See Aziz and Wescott (1997) on the need for macro policy complimentarity and Stiglitz (1998a) on the need for a broader approach involving a range of elements.
5   Lewis 1955.
6   Stiglitz 1998b.
7   Devarajan, Easterly, and Pack 1999.
8   Levine and Renelt 1992.
9   Easterly and Fischer 1995.
10 Psacharopoulos 1994.
11 World Bank 1991.
12 Buckley 1999.

13   Stiglitz 1999.

14   Stiglitz 1996.

15   Stiglitz and Uy 1996.

16   Evans and Bataille 1997; Isham, Narayan, and Pritchett 1994; World Bank 1991, 1997.

17   Buckley 1999.

18   Evans and Battaile 1997.

19   This box is drawn largely from the World Bank's Social Capital Web Page
     (http://www.worldbank.org/poverty/scapital/index.htm).

20   Coleman and Hoffer 1987; Francis and others 1998.

21   Drèze and Sen 1995.

22   Narayan and Pritchett 1997.

23   Portes and Landolt 1996.

24   Evans and Bataille 1997.

25   Buckley 1999.

26   WHO 1999.

27   UNDP 1998.

28   WHO 1999.

29   World Bank 1999a.

30   WHO 1999.

31   Easterly 1999.

32   Ravallion and Chen 1998.

33   UNDP 1998.

34   Ravallion and Chen 1998.

35   World Bank 1998.

36   WHO 1999.

37   Watson and others 1998.

38   Peterson 1999.

39   Commentators sometimes downplay the role of technology in globalization, pointing out
     the limited extent of global communications just a hundred years ago. In fact, U.S. exports
     in the late 1900s are only 1 percent higher as a percentage of GDP than they were in the
     late 1800s, and international capital movements are a smaller percentage of output than
     they were in the 1880s (*International Herald Tribune*, May 23, 1999). But the absolute
     levels are clearly much larger. Trade has a much broader base that involves a far larger
     percentage of manufactures and services, and finance includes more short-term investment
     that relies on highly sophisticated information technology.

References

The word processed describes informally reproduced works that may not be commonly
available through libraries.

Aziz, Jahangir, and Robert F. Wescott. 1997. "Policy Complementarities and the
     Washington Consensus." Working Paper 97/118. International Monetary Fund,
     Washington, D.C.

Barro, Robert. 1991. "Economic Growth in a Cross Section of Countries." *Quarterly
     Journal of Economics* 106: 407–43.

Bernard, Andrew, and Steven Durlauf. 1996. "Interpreting Tests of the Convergence
     Hypothesis." *Journal of Econometrics* 71: 161–73.

Buckley, Robert. 1999. *1998 Annual Review of Development Effectiveness*. Washington, D.C.: World Bank.

Caselli, Francesco, G. Esquivel, and F. Lefort. 1996. "Reopening the Convergence Debate: A New Look at Cross-Country Growth Empirics." *Journal of Economic Growth* 1 (September): 363–89.

Coleman, James, and Thomas Hoffer. 1987. *Public and Private High Schools: The Impact of Communities*. New York: Basic Books.

Covarrubias, Alvaro. 1999. "Lending for Electric Power in sub-Saharan Africa." World Bank, Washington, D.C. Processed.

Devarajan, Shantayanan, William Easterly, and Howard Pack. 1999. "Is Investment in Africa Too Low or Too High?" World Bank, Washington, D.C. Processed.

Drèze, Jean, and Amartya Sen. 1995. *India: Economic Development and Social Opportunity*. New York: Oxford University Press.

Easterly, William. 1999. "Life during Growth." World Bank, Washington, D.C. Processed.

Easterly, William, and Stanley Fischer. 1995. "The Soviet Economic Decline." *World Bank Economic Review* 9 (September): 341–71.

Easterly, William, and Ross Levine. 1997. "Africa's Growth Tragedy: Policies and Ethnic Divisions." *Quarterly Journal of Economics* 112 (November): 1203–50.

Evans, Alison, and William Bataille. 1997. *Annual Review of Development Effectiveness*. Washington, D.C.: World Bank.

Francis, Paul A., and others. 1998. *Hard Lessons: Primary Schools, Community, and Social Capital in Nigeria*. Technical Paper 420. Washington, D.C.: World Bank.

Isham, Jonathan, Deepa Narayan, and Lant Pritchett. 1994. "Does Participation Improve Performance? Empirical Evidence from Project Data." Policy Research Working Paper 1357. World Bank, Washington, D.C.

Levine, Ross, and David Renelt. 1992. "Sensitivity Analysis of Cross-Country Growth Regressions." *American Economic Review* 82 (September): 942–63.

Lewis, W. Arthur. 1955. *The Theory of Economic Growth*. Reprint, New York: Harper Torchbooks, 1970.

Mankiw, N. Gregory, David Romer, and David Weil. 1992. "Contribution to the Empirics of Economic Growth." *Quarterly Journal of Economics* 107: 407–37.

Narayan, Deepa, and Lant Pritchett. 1997. "Cents and Sociability: Household Income and Social Capital in Rural Tanzania." Policy Research Working Paper 1796. World Bank, Washington, D.C.

Pearce, David W., and Jeremy J. Warford. 1993. *World Without End: Economics, Environment and Sustainable Development*. New York: Oxford University Press.

Peterson, Peter G. 1999. *Gray Dawn: How the Coming Age Wave Will Transform America — and the World*. New York: Times Books.

Portes, Alejandro, and Patricia Landolt. 1996. "The Downside of Social Capital." *The American Prospect* 26 (May/June): 18–21.

Pritchett, Lant. 1997. "Divergence, Big Time." *Journal of Economic Perspectives* 11 (Summer).

——. 1998. "Patterns of Economic Growth: Hills, Plateaus, Mountains and Plains." Policy Research Working Paper 1947. World Bank, Washington, D.C.

Psacharopoulos, George. 1994. "Returns to Investment in Education: A Global Update," *World Development* 22(9): 1325–43.

Quah, Danny. 1993. "Empirical Cross-Section Dynamics in Economic Growth." *European Economic Review* 37: 426–34.

Ravallion, Martin, and Shaohua Chen. 1998. "Poverty Reduction and the World Bank Progress in Fiscal 1998." Harvard Institute for International Development, Cambridge, Mass.

Sachs, Jeffrey D. 1996. "Growth in Africa: It Can Be Done." *The Economist*. June 29.

Sachs, Jeffrey D., and Andrew Warner. 1997b. "Sources of Slow Growth in African Economies." *Journal of African Economies* 6 (October): 335–76.

Sala-i-Martin, Xavier. 1997. "I Just Ran Four Million Regressions." Working Paper Series 6252. National Bureau of Economic Research, Cambridge, Mass.

Stiglitz, Joseph E. 1996. "Some Lessons from the East Asian Miracle." *World Bank Research Observer* 11(2).

——. 1998a. "More Instruments and Broader Goals: Moving toward the Post-Washington Consensus." The 1998 WIDER Annual Lecture. Helsinki, January 7.

——. 1998b. "Towards a New Paradigm for Development: Strategies, Policies, and Processes." Prebisch Lecture. United Nations Conference on Trade and Development, Geneva.

——. 1999. "Two Principles for the Next Round: Or, How to Bring Developing Countries in from the Cold." Speech delivered in Stockholm, Sweden, April 12.

Stiglitz, Joseph E., and Marilou Uy. 1996. "Financial Markets, Public Policy, and the East Asian Miracle." *World Bank Research Observer* 11(2).

UNDP (United Nations Development Programme). 1998. *Human Development Report*. New York: Oxford University Press.

Watson, Robert Tony, John Dixon, Stephen Hamburg, Anthony Janetos, and Richard Moss. 1998. "Protecting Our Planet, Securing Our Future: Linkages among Global Environmental Issues and Human Needs." United Nations Environment Programme, Nairobi; U.S. National Aeronautics and Space Administration, Washington, D.C.; World Bank, Washington, D.C.

WHO (World Health Organization). 1999. *World Health Report 1999*. Geneva.

World Bank. 1991. *World Development Report 1991: The Challenge of Development*. New York: Oxford University Press.

——. 1997. *World Development Report 1997: The State in a Changing World*. New York: Oxford University Press.

——. 1998. *World Development Indicators 1998*. Washington, D.C.

——. 1999. *World Development Indicators 1999*. Washington, D.C.

——. 1999a. "Africa Regional Gender Action Plan." Washington, D.C. Processed.

REVIEW AND DISCUSSION QUESTIONS

1 According to the authors, how successful have less developed countries (LDCs) been at raising standards of living in the past few decades?

2 Explain what the *focus* of economic development theories was, according to the World Bank, in each of the following periods: 1950s and 1960s; late 1960s and 1970s; and 1980s.

3 Why does the rate of economic growth fail to give an accurate picture of overall improvements in standards of living in LDCs?

4 What does the World Bank mean by "comprehensive development"?

5 What does the World Bank mean by "institutions"?

6 What institutions are deemed important for economic development according to the World Bank? Why?

7 What are some of the major economic development achievements attained by developing countries over the past several decades?

Chapter 2

Mahbub ul Haq

THE HUMAN DEVELOPMENT PARADIGM

"That's very important," the King said, turning to the jury. They were just beginning to write this down on their slates, when the White Rabbit interrupted: "Unimportant, your Majesty means, of course," he said in a very respectful tone, but frowning and making faces at him as he spoke.

"Unimportant, of course, I meant," the King hastily said, and went on to himself in an undertone, "important — unimportant — unimportant — important —" as if he were trying which word sounded best.

— Alice in Wonderland

T HE REDISCOVERY OF HUMAN DEVELOPMENT is not a new invention. It is a tribute to the early leaders of political and economic thought. The idea that social arrangements must be judged by the extent to which they promote "human good" dates at least to Aristotle (384–322 B.C.). He argued that "wealth is evidently not the good we are seeking, for it is merely useful and for the sake of something else". He distinguished a good political arrangement from a bad one by its successes and failures in enabling people to lead "flourishing lives".

Immanuel Kant (1724–1804) continued the tradition of treating human beings as the real end of all activities when he observed: "So act as to treat humanity, whether in their own person or in that of any other, in every case as an end withal; never as means only." And when Adam Smith (1723–1790), that apostle of free enterprise and private initiative, showed his concern that economic development should enable a person to mix freely with others without being "ashamed to appear in publick", he was expressing a concept of poverty that went beyond counting calories – a concept that integrated the poor into the mainstream of the community. A similar strain was reflected in the writings of the other founders of modern economic thought, including Robert Malthus, Karl Marx and John Stuart Mill.

After the belated rediscovery of human development, it is necessary to give this paradigm some firmer conceptual, quantitative and policy moorings – here and in the next six chapters.

The basic purpose of development is to enlarge people's choices. In principle, these choices can be infinite and can change over time. People often value achievements that do not show up at all, or not immediately, in income or growth figures: greater access to knowledge, better nutrition and health services, more secure livelihoods, security against crime and physical violence, satisfying leisure hours, political and cultural freedoms and a sense of participation in community activities. The objective of development is to create an enabling environment for people to enjoy long, healthy and creative lives.

Income and human choices

The defining difference between the economic growth and the human development schools is that the first focuses exclusively on the expansion of only one choice – income – while the second embraces the enlargement of all human choices – whether economic, social, cultural or political. It might well be argued that the expansion of income can enlarge all other choices as well. But that is not necessarily so, for a variety of reasons.

To begin with, income may be unevenly distributed within a society. People who have no access to income, or enjoy only limited access, will see their choices fairly constrained. It has often been observed that in many societies, economic growth does not trickle down.

But there is an even more fundamental reason why income expansion may fail to enlarge human options. It has to do with the national priorities chosen by the society or its rulers – guns or butter, an elitist model of development or an egalitarian one, political authoritarianism or political democracy, a command economy or participatory development.

No one will deny that such choices make a critical difference. Yet we often forget that the use of income by a society is just as important as the generation of income itself, or that income expansion leads to much less human satisfaction in a virtual political prison or cultural void than in a more liberal political and economic environment. There is no automatic link between income and human lives – a theme explored at length in the subsequent chapters. Yet there has long been an apparent presumption in economic thought that such an automatic link exists.

It should also be recognized that accumulating wealth may not be necessary for the fulfilment of several kinds of human choices. In fact, individuals and societies make many choices that require no wealth at all. A society does not have to be rich to afford democracy. A family does not have to be wealthy to respect the rights of each member. A nation does not have to be affluent to treat women and men equally. Valuable social and cultural traditions can be – and are – maintained at all levels of income.

Many human choices extend far beyond economic well-being. Knowledge, health, a clean physical environment, political freedom and simple pleasures of life are not exclusively, or largely, dependent on income. National wealth can expand people's choices in these areas. But it might not. The use that people make of their wealth, not the wealth itself, is decisive. And unless societies recognize that their real wealth is their people, an excessive obsession with creating material wealth can obscure the goal of enriching human lives.

The human development paradigm performs an important service in questioning the presumed automatic link between expanding income and expanding human choices. Such a link depends on the quality and distribution of economic growth, not only on the quantity of such growth. A link between growth and human lives has to be created consciously through deliberate public policy – such as public spending on social services and fiscal policy to redistribute income and assets. This link may not exist in the automatic workings of the marketplace, which can further marginalize the poor.

But we must be careful. Rejecting an automatic link between income expansion and flourishing human lives is not rejecting growth itself. Economic growth is essential in poor societies for reducing or eliminating poverty. But the quality of this growth is just as important as its quantity. Conscious public policy is needed to translate economic growth into people's lives.

How can that be done? It may require a major restructuring of economic and political power, and the human development paradigm is quite revolutionary in that respect. It questions the existing structure of power. Greater links between economic growth and human choices may require far-reaching land reform, progressive tax systems, new credit systems to bank on the poor people, a major expansion of basic social services to reach all of the deprived population, the removal of barriers to the entry of people in economic and political spheres and the equalization of their access to opportunities, and the establishment of temporary social safety nets for those who may be bypassed by the markets or public policy actions. Such policy packages are fairly fundamental and will vary from one country to another. But some features are common to all of them.

First, people are moved to centre stage. Development is analysed and understood in terms of people. Each activity is analysed to see how much people participate in it or benefit from it. The touchstone of the success of development policies becomes the betterment of people's lives, not just the expansion of production processes.

Second, human development is assumed to have two sides. One is the formation of human capabilities – such as improved health, knowledge and skills. The other is the use people make of their acquired capabilities – for employment, productive activities, political affairs or leisure. A society needs to build up human capabilities as well as ensure equitable access to human opportunities. Considerable human frustration results if the scales of human development do not finely balance the two sides.

Third, a careful distinction is maintained between ends and means. People are regarded as the ends. But means are not forgotten. The expansion of GNP becomes an essential means for expanding many human options. But the character and distribution of economic growth are measured against the yardstick of enriching the lives of people. Production processes are not treated in an abstract vacuum. They acquire a human context.

Fourth, the human development paradigm embraces all of society – not just the economy. The political, cultural and social factors are given as much attention as the economic factors. In fact, study of the link between the economic and the non-economic environment is one of the most fascinating and rewarding aspects of this new analysis.

Fifth, it is recognized that people are both the means and the ends of development. But people are not regarded as mere instruments for producing commodities – through an augmentation of "human capital". It is always remembered that human beings are the ultimate end of development – not convenient fodder for the materialistic machine.

A holistic concept

Nor should human welfare concepts or social safety nets or investment in education and health be equated with the human development paradigm, which includes these aspects, but only as parts of the whole. The human development paradigm covers all aspects of development – whether economic growth or international trade, budget deficits or fiscal policy, saving or investment or technology, basic social services or safety nets for the poor. No aspect of the development model falls outside its scope, but the vantage point is the widening of people's choices and the enrichment of their lives. All aspects of life – economic, political or cultural – are viewed from that perspective. Economic growth, as such, becomes only a subset of the human development paradigm.

On some aspects of the human development paradigm, there is fairly broad agreement:

- Development must put people at the centre of its concerns.
- The purpose of development is to enlarge all human choices, not just income.
- The human development paradigm is concerned both with building up human capabilities (through investment in people) and with using those human capabilities fully (through an enabling framework for growth and employment).
- Human development has four essential pillars: equality, sustainability, productivity and empowerment. It regards economic growth as essential but emphasizes the need to pay attention to its quality and distribution, analyses at length its link with human lives and questions its long-term sustainability.
- The human development paradigm defines the ends of development and analyses sensible options for achieving them.

Despite the broad agreement on many of these features, there are several controversies about the human development concept – often stemming from some misunderstanding about the concept itself. Fairly widespread is the mistaken view that human development is anti-growth and that it encompasses only social development.

The human development paradigm consistently takes the view that growth is not the end of economic development – but that the absence of growth often is. Economic growth is essential for human development, but to fully exploit the opportunities for improved well-being that growth offers, it needs to be properly managed. Some countries have been extremely successful in managing their economic growth to improve the human condition, others less so. So, there is no automatic link between economic growth and human progress. And one of the most pertinent policy issues concerns the exact process through which growth translates, or fails to translate, into human development under different development conditions.

There are four ways to create the desirable links between economic growth and human development.

First, emphasis on investment in the education, health and skills of the people can enable them to participate in the growth process as well as to share its benefits, principally through remunerative employment. This is the growth model adopted by China, Hong Kong, Japan, Malaysia, the Republic of Korea, Singapore, Thailand and many other newly industrializing countries.

Second, more equitable distribution of income and assets is critical for creating a close link between economic growth and human development. Wherever the distribution of income and assets is very uneven (as in Brazil, Nigeria and Pakistan), high GNP growth rates have failed to translate into people's lives. The link between distribution of assets and the nature of growth can be:

- Growth-led, with favourable initial conditions in asset distribution and mass education, including the participation of people in economic activities (China, the Republic of Korea).
- Unfavourable initial conditions but high growth with corrective public policy action, including people's participation (Chile, Malaysia).
- Low growth with public policy action to provide basic social services, but normally unsustainable over the long term (Jamaica, Sri Lanka).

Third, some countries have managed to make significant improvements in human development even in the absence of good growth or good distribution. They have achieved this result through well-structured social expenditures by the government. Cuba, Jamaica, Sri Lanka and Zimbabwe, among others, achieved fairly impressive results through the generous state provision of social services. So did many countries in Eastern Europe and the Commonwealth of Independent States (CIS). But such experiments generally are not sustainable unless the economic base expands enough to support the social base.

Fourth, the empowerment of people – particularly women – is a sure way to link growth and human development. In fact, empowerment should accompany all aspects of life. If people can exercise their choices in the political, social and economic spheres, there is a good prospect that growth will be strong, democratic, participatory and durable.

Another misconception – closely related to the alleged anti-growth bias of human development models – is that human development strategies have only social content, no hard economic analysis. The impression has grown that human development strategies are concerned mainly with social development expenditures (particularly in education and health). Some analysts have gone further and confused human development with development only of human resources – that is, social development expenditure aimed at strengthening human capabilities. Others have insisted that human development strategies are concerned only with human welfare aspects – or, even more narrowly, only with basic human needs – and that they have little to say about economic growth, production and consumption, saving and investment, trade and technology, or any other aspect of a macroeconomic framework.

These analysts do scant justice to the basic concept of human development as a holistic development paradigm embracing both ends and means, both productivity and equity, both economic and social development, both material goods and human welfare. At best, their critiques are based on a misunderstanding of the human development paradigm. At worst, they are the products of feeble minds.

The real point of departure of human development strategies is to approach every issue in the traditional growth models from the vantage point of people. Do they participate in economic growth as well as benefit from it? Do they have full access to the opportunities of expanded trade? Are their choices enlarged or narrowed by new technologies? Is economic expansion leading to job-led growth or jobless growth? Are budgets being balanced without unbalancing the lives of future generations? Are "free" markets open to all people? Are we increasing the options only of the present generation or also of the future generations?

None of the economic issues is ignored, but they all are related to the ultimate objective of development: people. And people are analysed not merely as the beneficiaries of economic growth but as the real agents of every change in society whether economic, political, social or cultural. To establish the supremacy of people in the process of development – as the classical writers always did – is not to denigrate economic growth but to rediscover its real purpose.

It is fair to say that the human development paradigm is the most holistic development model that exists today. It embraces every development issue, including economic growth, social investment, people's empowerment, provision of basic needs and social safety nets, political and cultural freedoms and all other aspects of people's lives. It is neither narrowly technocratic nor overly philosophical. It is a practical reflection of life itself.

[. . .]

REVIEW AND DISCUSSION QUESTIONS

1 According to the author, what are the key objectives of development?
2 Under what circumstances might growth in average incomes not translate into greater human development? Explain and give a few examples.
3 Does the human development approach imply that economic growth is unnecessary or unimportant? Why or why not?
4 What policies may help economic growth translate into greater human development?
5 Do you see any possible drawbacks of the human development approach? Explain.

Chapter 3

Amartya Sen

PERSPECTIVES ON THE ECONOMIC DEVELOPMENT OF INDIA AND CHINA

IT IS WONDERFUL FOR ME to become associated with this extraordinary distinguished university in this marvellous way. I feel very honored and extremely grateful. I am also very happy that I can build on the connections I already have with this great university, particularly through my friend and former student, Stephan Klasen. As my subject I have chosen one third of humanity, namely the people of China and India – the two countries that between them have many more than two billion people.

1

China and India are much in the news right now. The attention that they get these days in the West is partly concerned with some kind of a fear that they might take over jobs and work from Europeans and Americans. I shall not address that worry in particular, though I believe it to be largely misguided. Expansion of economic connections hardly ever hurt countries that have the privilege of being already ahead in education, training and socially supportive facilities. Whatever readjustment of trading pattern that the emergence and expansion of new economies may lead to need not worsen the situation of the pre-existing economic powers. Indeed, if these established economic giants (as Germany certainly is) play their cards well and choose economic and social policies that take note of the new economic realities, rather than trying to stick dogmatically to old patterns of trade, there can be much benefit from the economic opportunities of gainful exchange generated by the rapid development of newly industrializing countries, like China and India.

I will, however, concentrate in this speech on some comparative analysis of what is happening in China and India today, seen in the perspective of the people of these countries themselves and the history of their interrelations over the last two thousand years. I begin with citing a question that was asked by a Chinese about India:

Is there anyone in any part of India who does not admire China?

That question could well be asked today given the interest that economic and social achievements of China currently generate in India. The question, however, was actually asked by Yi Jing (or, I-Ching, as the name is sometimes spelt) in the seventh century, on his return to China after spending ten years in India. Yi Jing was one of many Buddhist scholars in the first millennium who spent a decade or more in India. The first Chinese scholar to write an elaborate account of his visit to India was Faxian [Fa-Hsien], who came to India on the difficult land route via Khotan in Central Asia, in 401 AD. After ten active years in India, Faxian returned by sea, sailing from the mouth of the Ganges or Hooghly (not far from present-day Calcutta). Faxian was also particularly interested in studying arrangements for public health care and the art of prolonging life. This was, in fact, a persistent subject of interest for visiting Buddhist scholars from China. It is also not implausible to argue that Buddha's own interest in morbidity, disability and mortality, which initially motivated young Gautama to leave his princely home in search of enlightenment (the word Buddha means 'enlightened') gave the subject of public health a rather special status and standing in Buddhist scholarship.

In the reverse direction too, hundreds of Indian scholars came to China between the first century and the eleventh. Many of them settled there, and were engaged in a variety of activities, varying from translating Sanskrit documents into Chinese to working on mathematics and science. An Indian astronomer called Gautama even became the president of the Board of Astronomy in China in the eighth century.

Although Yi Jing might have been a little rash in doubting that any seventh-century Indian could have failed to admire China, the mutual viewing of each other was indeed a significant feature of the history of the two countries. Sino-Indian cultural relations constitute an oddly neglected part of the heritage of the two countries. The neglect is strange not only because of the light that these relations throw on the nature and evolution of Chinese and Indian civilizations (covering a large fraction of humanity), but also because of what it can tell us on such general subjects of contemporary contention as the history of 'globalization' (how it has been a creative force) and the alleged 'clash of civilizations' (on which, as it happens, more nonsense is said these days than on almost any other subject).

2

Yi Jing's seventh-century question about the general admiration for China in India, with which I began, seemed to many of us, in the second half of the twentieth century, to be extra-ordinarily relevant to our times. Watching from the subcontinent, the emergence of post-revolutionary China appeared to millions of Indians to be the trail-blazing contemporary event, pointing the way to the future. As the early reports of massive gains in living conditions (including life expectancy) in China became widely discussed in India, the comparative picture formed the basis of one line of persistent criticism of Indian public policy in general and its comparative neglect of basic education and basic health care in particular. Even though this criticism was not very successful in getting official attention until very recently, it has been an important part of the intellectual discontent in India over many decades.

Since 1979, China has carried through market-oriented economic reforms in a massive scale, with tremendous success in some fields, such as raising rates of economic growth. This too has not been without impact on India. There is little doubt that India's economic liberalization, starting in 1992, was directly influenced by China's early success in that direction. The Indian reforms have been relatively less extensive so far, though things are changing quickly, but a basic problem is the continued underdevelopment of social opportunities in India, compared with those in China, especially in the field of school education. Indeed, it is often not adequately recognised how much the Chinese economic performance in the 'post-reform' period has benefited from earlier – distinctly 'pre-reform' – expansions of social opportunities (especially in basic education, but also in epidemiology and land reform).

Indian higher education, however, is quite extensive (India still has many more university educated persons, even in absolute numbers, than China does), and its technical training in high technology (from informational analysis to nuclear physics and bio-chemistry) is well developed, which is reflected in India's success in some high-tech sectors in the world economy (such as computer programming and software, information technology, and pharmaceuticals). This has made Indian economic performance quite impressive seen in comparative terms with the rest of the world, but it has still not allowed India to have an economic expansion as fast as China. Developing a wider base of basic education and achieving a further reduction of bureaucratic barriers can make important contributions to making the Indian development even more rapid than it is now.

There is, however, a danger that in trying to identify what India can learn from China, and also the converse (on which more presently), too much focus may be put on the outstanding nature of China's rates of economic growth. Scepticism about growth *per se* is not new, neither in China, nor in India. One can even interpret, in that line, the Chinese writer Wang An-Shah's doubts, expressed in the eleventh century, in his poem, *Casual Inspirations on a Cold Mountain*:

> Having one is to have two,
> Having three is to have four,
> One, two, three, four, and five,
> Having them all, what does it really matter?

Despite these doubts, Wang (a Buddhist administrator in Sung China) worked hard, as a leading reformer, to improve people's lives in ways that goes beyond merely 'having' more and more of ordinary things, and concentrating instead on achievements that 'really matter.'

3

In this light, it is interesting to examine the comparative picture in China and India – and what each can learn from the other – about things that do 'really matter,' in particular what Yi Jing called the art of 'prolonging life.' This is indeed a good focus for some useful comparisons. As I mentioned earlier, Faxian, Yi Jing and other early visitors from China to India were particularly interested in health care, treating diseases, and more generally in the 'art of prolonging life.' Not only has this been one of the historical areas of comparative interest in China and India, but also life expectancy and health are widely recognised these days as good general indicators of comparative success. The most extensive championing of this perspective can be found in the series of yearly reports called *Human Development Reports* produced by the United Nations.

So what is the comparative story in this field in the comparative picture of India and China? In the middle of the twentieth century, post-revolution China and newly independent India had about the same life expectancy at birth, less than 40 years or so. But the Chinese leaders were immediately more successful in expanding health care and life expectancy at birth than their sleepy Indian counterparts were. By the time the economic reforms were introduced in China in 1979, China had a lead of 14 years or more over India, with the Chinese life expectancy at birth at 68 years while the Indian was less than 54.

China did, in fact, experience during this period a disastrous famine, which is estimated to have killed between 23 and 30 million people, whereas India has not experienced any such famine since its independence from British rule in 1947. I have discussed elsewhere that the Chinese famine was strongly linked with a lack of democracy. Even when people were dying by tens of millions each year, the mistaken policies of the so-called Great Leap Forward were not corrected for three years. The government was immune from criticism, since there were no opposition parties, no free elections, no independent newspapers and media, and no free speech. In contrast, it is not hard to see why there have been no famines in India since independence. No democratic government can expect to get re-elected after a famine, and no democratic government can easily face an independent media and the criticism of opposition parties in a famine-ravaged country.

However, the working of democracy, which is almost effortlessly effective in pre-venting famines, is far less immediate in politicizing regular but non-extreme under-nourishment and ill health. The extensive rewards of political freedom and democracy depend very much on the vigor with which it is practised. As far as regular mortality rates are concerned, India has tended to obtain much less – at least until recently – from the opportunity offered by democratic politics than China has been able to get from the political commitment of its authoritarian rulers (including Mao's own general dedication to enhancing living conditions, despite the big policy mistakes he made during the famine). For the decades preceding economic reforms in China in 1979, the trend rate of expansion of life expectancy there (including all the famine years) was more than twice as fast as that in India.

4

I must now continue the comparative story beyond 1979. Over the last two decades China has had an altogether exceptional record of rapid economic growth. The Indian economy has grown rapidly too, but not at all as fast as the Chinese. But how have they fared in terms of promoting life expectancy? Here we run into an odd conundrum. Despite China's much faster rate of growth since the economic reforms, the rate of expansion of life expectancy in India has been about three times as fast, on the average, as that in China. China's life expectancy, which is now about 71 years, compares with India's of 64 years, and the life-expectancy gap in favor of China, which was 14 years before the Chinese reforms, has now been halved to only 7 years.

Note must, however, be taken of the fact that it gets increasingly harder to expand life expectancy further as the absolute level rises, and it could be argued that perhaps

China has now reached a level where further expansion would be very difficult. But that reading is hard to sustain. At the time of economic reforms, when China had a life expectancy of about 68 years, the Indian state of Kerala had a slightly lower life expectancy – around 67 years. By now, however, Kerala's life expectancy is estimated to be around 76 years, which is very considerably above China's 71. While the Chinese cities like Beijing and Shanghai can outmatch the state of Kerala, nearly all Chinese provinces have much lower life expectancy than Kerala.

Indeed, if we look at specific points of vulnerability, infant mortality rate in China has fallen very slowly since the economic reforms (almost none at all in the last decade), whereas it has continued to fall very sharply in Kerala. While Kerala had roughly the same infant mortality rate as China – 37 per thousand – at the time of the Chinese reforms, Kerala's present rate of 10 per thousand is only a third of the Chinese infant mortality rate of 30 per thousand (where it has stagnated over the last decade).

5

Does this indicate that economic growth does not help to enhance life expectancy? There is nothing to suggest this; economic growth does contribute to the enhancing of living conditions, including longevity. However, as China's own pre-reform success shows, other factors, such as public policy of health care and educational expansion, can also make a radical difference. But there is considerable complexity in the experience of China since the economic reforms of 1979. There is clearly some difficulty with the 'reach' of the benefits of economic reform in China, despite its astounding rate of economic growth.

There are three distinct problems of 'reach' here. First, even within the economic field, the poverty-removing character of Chinese economic expansion was much sharper in the early post-reform period than it is today. While the early reforms showed an astonishing jump in rural production and incomes, from the late 1980s the focus of growth has been much more urban, largely related to increasing global integration of China's industrial economy. It cannot, of course, be doubted that this global integration and the related expansion of urban incomes have brought many rewards to the Chinese people. And yet the poverty-reducing character of Chinese economic growth, while still quite firm, has relatively slackened. Furthermore, there has been a big surge in Chinese economic inequality, which is brought out by many empirical studies.

However, China's slow growth in life expectancy and stagnation in infant mortality are not only the result of the worsening reach of its economic growth. It also relates to the social and political reach of the reforms. So, the second factor to note is that along with the political change that ushered in the economic reforms came a slackened social commitment to public health care. It led, in particular, to the eschewal of the automatic and free health insurance provided, before the reforms, by the state, or the collectives or cooperatives in rural areas, which also poured resources directly into public health care. There was now a need to buy a private health insurance at one's own cost (except when provided by the employer, which happens only in a small minority of cases). Interestingly, this significantly retrograde movement in the coverage of health care received little public resistance – as it undoubtedly would have met in any multi-party democracy like India. It is very hard to think that an established public facility of great value to people could be dispensed so easily in a country where the opposition had an effective voice. The denial of that facility certainly has had a role in the slowing down of the progress of longevity.

Third, democracy also makes a direct contribution to health care in bringing social failures into public scrutiny. India's health services are quite terrible – I have discussed how defective they are in my joint books with Jean Drèze, in particular in *India: Development and Participation* (published in 2002), and quite recently, I had the dubious privilege of presenting in a news interview in India the depressing findings of the first health report of the Pratichi Trust (a trust I was privileged to set up with the Nobel money that came my way some years ago). But the possibility of such intense criticism is, of course, also a social opportunity to make amends. Indeed, the persistent reporting of the dreadful state of Indian health services is, ultimately, a source of India's dynamic strength.

The informational and incentive roles of democracy, working mainly through open public discussion, can be pivotally important for the reach of public policy. As was mentioned earlier, even the Chinese famines of 1958–61 reflected the absence of a democratic engagement, but more recently the easy abandonment of public health insurance as well as the immunity from criticism that Chinese health services often enjoy could be linked directly to the lack of multi-party politics.

It is the limitation of this role that came most sharply to attention in the context of the SARS epidemic during 2002–3. Although SARS cases first appeared in Southern China in November 2002 and caused many fatalities, information about this new deadly disease was kept under a lid until April 2003. Indeed, it was only when that highly infectious disease started spreading to Hong Kong and Beijing that the news had to be released, and by then the epidemic had already gone beyond the possibility of isolation and local elimination. The lack of open public discussion evidently played a critically important part in the spread of the SARS epidemic. This is a small example, but the general penalty of the lack of competitive democracy is much more pervasive than that.

6

India has learned much from China about economic policy and also about health care, especially from China's activist public commitment of the early post-revolutionary period. On the other hand, the relevance of public communication and democracy is a general lesson that India can still offer to China.

The comparison with the state of Kerala is particularly interesting here. Kerala seems to have benefitted from its left-leaning democratic politics, having been able to combine (1) the political commitment to social objectives which was typically favored in China and which has helped China to move forward quite early, and (2) the benefits of public criticism – in particular more open scrutiny – that a multi-party democratic system provides in India. The latter, on its own, would seem to have helped India to narrow the gap *vis-à-vis* China quite sharply. Despite all its inadequacies, the Indian health delivery arrangements have to be open to public criticism which a democratic system standardly fosters, and the fact that much is known about these inadequacies from criticisms in the press is itself a contribution to improving things. This opportunity is particularly forcefully seized in a state like Kerala with its high level of basic education and a strong tradition of political appraisal and critique.

The effectiveness of critical public discussion is also reflected in the lower fertility rate in Kerala (without any regulation or compulsion) than in China, and the comparative absence of gender bias against women (the female–male ratio in Kerala's population is 1.06, as in Europe and North America, not 0.94 as in China and 0.93 as in India as a whole). If this diagnosis is correct, then we must conclude that in addition to the direct benefits from democratic practice (related to political freedoms and liberties), China is losing other benefits from not having a vigorous democracy, which could be particularly effective given what China has already achieved in widespread basic education and general health care.

Oddly enough, looking back at history, it is the tradition of public criticism and irreverence, and the defiance of authority, which came with Buddhism from India that was singled out for a particularly strong chastisement in early anti-Buddhist criticisms in China. Fu-yi, a powerful Confucian leader, submitted in the seventh century the following complaint about Buddhists to the Tang emperor (almost paralleling the contemporary ire of the Chinese authorities about the disorder generated by the present-day Falungong):

> Buddhism infiltrated into China from Central Asia, under a strange and barbarous form, and as such, it was then less dangerous. But since the Han period the Indian texts began to be translated into Chinese. Their publicity began to adversely affect the faith of the Princes and filial piety began to degenerate. The people began to shave their heads and refused to bow their heads to the Princes and their ancestors.

Fu-yi proposed not only a ban on Buddhist preaching, but also quite a novel way of dealing with the 'tens of thousands' of activists, rampaging around in China. 'I request you to get them married,' Fu-yi advised the Tang emperor, and 'then bring up [their] children to fill the ranks of your army.' The emperor, we learn, refused to undertake this spirited programme of eliminating Buddhist defiance.

China has embraced the world economy with amazing success, and from this India – like many other countries – has been learning a great deal, particularly in recent years. But there are lessons that can go in the other direction as well. If India has to carry its reforms further, and do better in basic school education and basic health care than it has done in the past, China too has to address the importance of public debating and discussion with a free media and the relevance of democratic politics.

Yi Jing's conclusion that each country has to learn something from the other is as true today as it was in the seventh century when that perceptive Chinese scholar made that remark. There is also a general lesson here about how global contacts can be helpful for different countries. That lesson may have some general relevance, beyond the particular experiences of China and India in particular.

I end by thanking again this distinguished university for making me a member of their academic community. It is a great privilege for me to join this extraordinarily distinguished university – I am tremendously grateful for this opportunity.

REVIEW AND DISCUSSION QUESTIONS

1   Sen points out that while both China and India have carried out dramatic economic reforms over the past few decades, "a basic problem is the continued underdevelopment of social

opportunities in India, compared with those in China." What does Sen mean by "social opportunities," and how exactly is India behind China in this respect?

2   Famines are often believed to be the result of lack of food. Sen, however, believes that famines are really caused by lack of democracy. Explain why lack of democracy may help explain what causes famines.

3   How does Sen explain the fact that life expectancy is significantly longer in the Indian state of Kerala than in China?

4   In the late 1970s China adopted a coercive "one-child policy" to reduce fertility and population growth. While fertility did indeed decline, it did not decline as much as in the Indian state of Kerala, where no coercive policy was used. What is Sen's explanation for this rather puzzling finding?

5   Why does Sen believe that "Yi Jing's conclusion that each country has to learn something from the other is as true today as it was in the seventh century"?

Chapter 4

THE ECONOMIST

THE POOR AND THE RICH

In recent years, researchers have moved closer to answering the most important question in economics: why are some countries richer than others?

UNDERSTANDING GROWTH IS SURELY the most urgent task in economics. Across the world, poverty remains the single greatest cause of misery; and the surest remedy for poverty is economic growth. It is true that growth can create problems of its own (congestion and pollution, for instance), which may preoccupy many people in rich countries. But such ills pale in comparison with the harm caused by the economic backwardness of poor countries – that is, of the larger part of the world. The cost of this backwardness, measured in wasted lives and needless suffering, is truly vast.

To its shame, economics neglected the study of growth for many years. Theorists and empirical researchers alike chose to concentrate on other fields, notably on macroeconomic policy. Until the 1980s, with a few exceptions, the best brains in economics preferred not to focus on the most vital issue of all. But over the past ten years or so, this has changed. Stars such as Robert Lucas of the University of Chicago, who last year won the Nobel prize in economics, have started to concentrate on growth. As he says of the subject, "the consequences for human welfare . . . are simply staggering. Once one starts to think about them, it is hard to think of anything else."

Early economists certainly thought about them. Adam Smith's classic 1776 book was, after all, called an "Inquiry into the Nature and Causes of the Wealth of Nations". Many building-blocks for understanding growth derive from him. Smith reckoned that the engine of growth was to be found in the division of labour, in the accumulation of capital and in technological progress. He emphasised the importance of a stable legal framework, within which the invisible hand of the market could function, and he explained how an open trading system would allow poorer countries to catch up with richer ones. In the early 19th century, David Ricardo formalised another concept crucial for understanding growth – the notion of diminishing returns. He showed how additional investment in land tended to yield an ever lower return, implying that growth would eventually come to a halt though trade could stave this off for a while.

The foundations of modern growth theory were laid in the 1950s by Robert Solow and Trevor Swan. Their models describe an economy of perfect competition, whose output grows in response to larger inputs of capital (ie, physical assets of all kinds) and labour. This economy obeys the law of diminishing returns: each new bit of capital (given a fixed labour supply) yields a slightly lower return than the one before.

Together, these assumptions give the neoclassical growth model, as it is called, two crucial implications. First, as the stock of capital expands, growth slows, and eventually halts: to keep growing, the economy must benefit from continual infusions of technological progress. Yet this is a force that the model itself makes no attempt to explain: in the jargon, technological progress is, in the neoclassical theory, "exogenous" (ie, it arises outside the model). The second implication is that poorer countries should grow faster than rich ones. The reason is diminishing returns: since poor countries start with less capital, they should reap higher returns from each slice of new investment.

Theory into practice

Do these theoretical implications accord with the real world? The short answer is no. The left-hand chart in Figure 4.1 shows average growth rates since 1870 of 16 rich countries for which good long-term data exist. Growth has indeed slowed since 1970. Even so, modern growth rates are well above their earlier long-run average. This appears to contradict the first implication, that growth will slow over time. It may be that an acceleration of technological progress accounts for this, but this should hardly console a

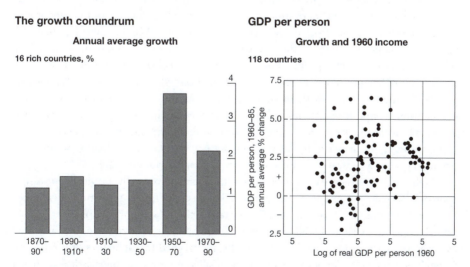

Figure 4.1   The growth conundrum and GDP per person

*13 countries, †14 countries

Source: *Economic Growth* by Robert Barro and Xavier Sala-i-Martin (McGraw-Hill, 1995)

neoclassical theorist, because it would mean that the main driving force of growth lies beyond the scope of growth theory.

What about the second implication – are poor countries catching up? The right-hand chart in Figure 4.1 plots, for 118 countries, growth rates between 1960 and 1985 against their initial 1960 level of GDP per person. If poor countries were catching up, the plots on the chart should follow a downward-sloping pattern: countries that were poorer in 1960 should have higher growth rates. They do not. Indeed, if there is any discernible pattern in the mass of dots, it is the opposite: poorer countries have tended to grow more slowly.

Having arrived at neoclassical growth theory, however, economics by and large forgot about the subject. It had a model that was theoretically plausible, but did not seem to fit the facts. How best to proceed was unclear. Then, after a pause of 30 years, along came "new growth theory".

This new school has questioned, among other things, the law of diminishing returns in the neoclassical model. If each extra bit of capital does not, in fact, yield a lower return than its predecessor, growth can continue indefinitely, even without technological progress. A seminal paper was published in 1986 by Paul Romer (see references at the end). It showed that if you broaden the idea of capital to include human capital (that is, the knowledge and skills embodied in the workforce), the law of diminishing returns may not apply. Suppose, for example, that a firm which invests in a new piece of equipment also learns how to use it more efficiently. Or suppose it becomes more innovative as a by-product of accumulating capital. In either case, there can be increasing, not decreasing, returns to investment.

In this and other ways, new growth theorists can explain how growth might persist in the absence of technological progress. But, they have gone on to ask, why assume away such progress? A second strand of new growth theory seeks to put technological progress explicitly into the model (making it "endogenous", in the jargon). This has obliged theorists to ask questions about innovation. Why, for instance, do companies invest in research and development? How do the innovations of one company affect the rest of the economy?

A further divergence from the neoclassical view follows. As a general rule, a firm will not bother to innovate unless it thinks it can steal a march on the competition and, for a while at least, earn higher profits. But this account is inconsistent with the neoclassical model's simplifying assumption of perfect competition, which rules out any "abnormal" profits. So the new growth theorists drop that assumption and suppose instead that competition is imperfect. Attention then shifts to the conditions under which firms will innovate most productively: how much protection should intellectual-property law give to an innovator, for instance? In this way, and not before time, technological progress has begun to occupy a central place in economists' thinking about growth.

In the latest resurgence of interest in growth theory, however, the original neoclassical approach has enjoyed something of a revival. Some economists are questioning whether the "new" theories really add much. For instance, the new theory emphasises human capital; arguably, this merely calls for a more subtle measure of labour than the ones used by early neoclassical theorists. More generally, it is argued that if factors of production (capital and labour) are properly measured and quality-adjusted, the neoclassical approach yields everything of value in the new theory, without its distracting bells and whistles. So it often proves in economics: the mainstream first takes affront at new ideas, then reluctantly draws on them, and eventually claims to have thought of them first.

The missing link

To non-economists, however, both approaches seem curiously lacking in one crucial respect. Whereas in popular debate about growth, government policy is usually the main issue, in both neoclassical and new growth theory discussion of policy takes place largely off-stage. To the extent that government policy affects investment, for instance, either could trace out the effects on growth – but the connection between policy and growth is tenuous and indirect. Each approach may take a strong view about the role of diminishing returns, but both remain frustratingly uncommitted about the role of government.

An upsurge of empirical work on growth is helping to fill this hole – and, as a by-product, shedding further light on the relative merits of the new and neoclassical theories. The nuts and bolts of this work are huge statistical analyses. Vast sets of data now exist, containing information for more than 100 countries between 1960 and 1990 on growth rates, inflation rates, fertility rates, school enrolment, government spending, estimates of how good the rule of law is, and so on. Great effort has been devoted to analysing these numbers.

One key finding is "conditional convergence", a term coined by Robert Barro, a pioneer of the new empirical growth studies. His research has found that if one holds constant such factors as a country's fertility rate, its human capital (proxied by various measures of educational attainment) and its government policies (proxied by the share of current government spending in GDP) poorer countries tend to grow faster than richer ones. So the basic insight of the neoclassical growth model is, in fact, correct. But since, in reality, other factors are not constant (countries do not have the same level of human capital or same government policies) absolute convergence does not hold.

Whether this is a depressing result for poor countries depends on what determines the "conditional" nature of the catch-up process. Are slow-growing countries held back by government policies that can be changed easily and quickly? Or are more fundamental forces at work?

Most empirical evidence points to the primacy of government choices. Countries that have pursued broadly free-market policies – in particular, trade liberalisation and the maintenance of secure property rights – have raised their growth rates. In a recent paper, Jeffrey Sachs and Andrew Warner divided a sample of 111 countries into "open" and "closed". The "open" economies showed strikingly faster growth and convergence than the "closed" ones. Smaller government also helps. Robert Barro, among others, has found that higher government spending tends to be associated with slower growth.

Human capital – education and skills – has also been found to matter. Various statistical analyses have shown that countries with lots of human capital relative to their physical capital are likely to grow faster than those with less. Many economists argue that this was a factor in East Asia's success: in the early 1960s the Asian tigers had relatively well-educated workforces and low levels of physical capital.

A more difficult issue is the importance of savings and investment. One implication of the neoclassical theory is that higher investment should mean faster growth (at least for a while). The empirical studies suggest that high investment is indeed associated with fast growth. But they also show that investment is not enough by itself. In fact the causality may run in the opposite direction: higher growth may, in a virtuous circle, encourage higher saving and investment. This makes sense: communist countries, for instance, had extraordinarily high investment but, burdened with bad policies in other respects, they failed to turn this into high growth.

The number-crunching continues; new growth-influencing variables keep being added to the list. High inflation is bad for growth; political stability counts; the results on democracy are mixed; and so on. The emerging conclusion is that the poorest countries can indeed catch up, and that their chances of doing so are maximised by policies that give a greater role to competition and incentives, at home and abroad.

But surely, you might think, this hides a contradiction? The new growth theory suggests that correct government policies can permanently raise growth rates. Empirical cross-country analysis, however, seems to show that less government is better – a conclusion that appeals to many neoclassical theorists. This tension is especially pronounced for the East Asian tigers. Advocates of free markets point to East Asia's trade liberalisation in the 1960s, and its history of low government spending, as keys to the Asian miracle. Interventionists point to subsidies and other policies designed to promote investment.

Reflecting the present spirit of rapprochement between the growth models, it is now widely argued that this contradiction is more apparent than real. Work by Alwyn Young, popularised by Paul Krugman, has shown that much of the Asian tigers' success can be explained by the neoclassical model. It resulted from a rapid accumulation of capital (through high investment) and labour (through population growth and increased labour-force participation). On this view, there is nothing particularly miraculous about Asian growth: it is an example of "catch-up". Equally, however, the outlines of East Asian success fit the new growth model. Endogenous growth theory says that government policy to increase human capital or foster the right kinds of investment in physical capital can permanently raise economic growth.

The question is which aspect of East Asian policies was more important which, up to a point, is the same as asking which growth model works best. Although debate continues, the evidence is less strong that micro-level encouragement of particular kinds of investment was crucial in Asia. Some economists dissent from that judgment, but they are a minority. Most agree that broader policies of encouraging education, opening the economy to foreign technologies, promoting trade and keeping taxes low mattered more.

One more heave

There is no doubt that the neoclassical model of the 1950s, subsequently enhanced, together with the theories pioneered by Mr Romer, have greatly advanced economists' understanding of growth. Yet the earlier doubt remains. Both models, in their purest versions, treat the role of government only indirectly. The new empirical work on conditional convergence has set out to put this right. The fact remains that in the earlier theoretical debate between the neoclassical and the new schools, the question that matters most – what should governments do to promote growth? – was often forgotten.

A new paper by Mancur Olson makes this point in an intriguing way. The starting-point for today's empirical work is a striking fact: the world's fastest-growing economies are a small subgroup of exceptional performers among the poor countries. Viewed in the earlier theoretical perspective, this is actually rather awkward. Mr Romer's theories would lead you to expect that the richest economies would be the fastest growers: they are not. The basic neoclassical theory suggests that the poorest countries, on the whole, should do better than the richest: they do not. Neither approach, taken at face value, explains the most striking fact about growth in the world today.

Mr Olson argues that the simplest versions of both theories miss a crucial point. Both assume that, given the resources and technology at their disposal, countries are doing as well as they can. Despite their differences, both are theories about how changes in available resources affect output – that is, both implicitly assume that, if resources do not change, output cannot either. But suppose that poor countries simply waste lots of resources. Then the best way for them to achieve spectacular growth is not to set about accumulating more of the right kind of resources – but to waste less of those they already have.

Marshalling the evidence, Mr Olson shows that slow-growing poor countries are indeed hopelessly failing to make good use of their resources. Take labour, for instance. If poor countries were using labour as well as they could, large emigrations of labour from poor to rich countries (from Haiti to the United States, for instance) ought to raise the productivity of workers left behind (because each worker now has more capital, land and other resources to work with). But emigration does not have this effect.

Data on what happens to migrants in their new homes are likewise inconsistent with the two growth theories. Immigrants' incomes rise by far more than access to more capital and other resources would imply. It follows that labour (including its human capital, entrepreneurial spirit, cultural traits and the rest) was being squandered in its country of origin. When workers move, their incomes rise partly because there is more capital to work with – but also by a further large margin, which must represent the wastage incurred before. Mr Olson adduces similar evidence to show that capital and knowledge are being massively squandered in many poor countries.

This offers a rationale for the pattern of growth around the world – a rationale that, consistent with the recent work on conditional convergence, places economic policies and institutions at the very centre. According to this view, it is putting it mildly to say that catch-up is possible: the economic opportunities for poor countries are, as the tigers have shown, phenomenal. The problem is not so much a lack of resources, but an inability to use existing resources well. It is surely uncontroversial to say that this is the right way to judge the performance of communist countries (those exemplars of negative value-added) before 1989. Mr Olson's contention is that most of today's poor countries are making mistakes of an essentially similar kind.

The question still remains: what are the right policies? One must turn again to the empirical evidence. That seems a frustrating answer because, suggestive though recent work on conditional convergence may be, such findings will always be contested. Citizens of the world who sensibly keep an eye on what economists are up to can at least take pleasure in this: the profession has chosen for once to have one of its most vigorous debates about the right subject.

References

"Increasing Returns and Long-Run Growth". By Paul Romer. *Journal of Political Economy*, 1986.

"Economic Reform and the Process of Global Integration". By Jeffrey Sachs and Andrew Warner. *Brookings Papers on Economic Activity*, 1995.

"The Tyranny of Numbers: Confronting the Statistical Realities of the East Asian Experience". By Alwyn Young. NBER working paper 4680, 1994.

"Big Bills Left on the Sidewalk: Why Some Nations Are Rich, and Others Poor". By Mancur
    Olson. *Journal of Economic Perspectives*, forthcoming [1996].

REVIEW AND DISCUSSION QUESTIONS

1 Why is it that, in the Solow neoclassical growth model, "as the stock of capital expands,
    growth slows, and eventually halts"? Explain.
2 What is the key difference between neoclassical growth models and the "new growth theory"
    developed by Paul M. Romer?
3 What does the empirical evidence tell us about the effects of Government policies on economic
    growth? Give some examples of how, according to the article, different Government choices
    have different implications for economic growth.
4 What are possible explanations for the extraordinary economic growth experienced by some
    East Asian countries?
5 How does Mancur Olson criticize both neoclassical and new growth theories?
6 What conclusions can you draw from the article about what a developing country should do to
    experience faster economic growth?

Chapter 5

Paul M. Romer

BEYOND CLASSICAL AND KEYNESIAN
MACROECONOMIC POLICY

WHEN ADAM SMITH WROTE his treatise on national economic policy, he
observed that monetary tokens do not constitute the true wealth of a nation.
Instead, he pointed to inputs such as tools, structures and improved farm land that can be
used to produce the things we value. He concluded that a nation becomes more wealthy
if its citizens and its government all refrain from excessive consumption today and save
for the future. A high rate of saving will lead to the accumulation of more of these
productive assets. In the classical approach to macroeconomic policy that he initiated,
saving and capital accumulation are the central concerns. Excessive spending on current
consumption, especially by the government, is the most serious threat to sustained
economic growth.

In the early part of this century, John Maynard Keynes argued that the classical fear
of excessive consumption was misplaced, even dangerous. To Keynes and his followers,
the biggest risk was that current spending might be too low, not too high. Classical fears
of government deficits stood in the way of action by the government to increase spending
during a slump in economic activity. By the middle of this century, Keynesians had carried
the day. Since then, macroeconomic policy in many industrialized countries has been based
on the Keynesian strategy of using monetary and fiscal policy to increase "aggregate
demand" and current consumption.

As dissatisfaction with the results from Keynesian demand management grew during
the last decade, the classical approach to macroeconomic policy has made something of a
comeback. Many economists now call once again for smaller government deficits, higher
private savings and more rapid capital accumulation. They argue that excessive government
spending reduces capital accumulation and that capital accumulation is the key to growth.

For someone who is not an economist, this oscillation between calls for more saving
and more spending is more than a little frustrating. When the newspaper reports that
consumer spending has increased – and that private savings has decreased – is this good
for the economy or bad? Moreover, to people who are careful students of business, science

and history, there is also something suspect about this entire discussion. Doesn't the key to economic success lie in a nation's ability to introduce valuable new goods to improve the quality of existing goods and to find more efficient ways to manufacture and deliver these goods? If so, why do economists seem to devote so much attention to monetary and fiscal stimulus on the one hand and purchases of existing capital goods like fork lifts on the other? Where is the discussion of innovation, invention, discovery and technical progress?

A recent branch of work in economics that goes under the label of "endogenous" or "neoSchumpeterian" growth theory validates some of the concerns about competitiveness, innovation and discovery expressed by people who are not economists. It suggests that both the save-more and the spend-more macroeconomic policy prescriptions miss the crux of the matter. Neither adjustments to monetary and fiscal policy, nor increases in the rate of savings and capital accumulation can by themselves generate persistent increases in standards of living. This work suggests that the most important job for economic policy is to create an institutional environment that supports technological change. This sounds simple enough, but policy-makers must also resist the temptation to impede change when it causes temporary disruption. In a modern industrial democracy, achieving a balance between support for economic progress and tolerance of economic change is not a simple task.

Swimming past the competition

Within the economics profession, recent work on the theory of long-run growth is described in terms of mathematical equations and statistical analysis.[1] It is possible, nevertheless, to give an interpretation of this work in terms of a metaphor that is as concrete as the image of a family that needs to save (the metaphor invoked by classical economists) or of a pump that needs priming (the one favored by the Keynesians). This description makes use of the tired rhetorical device of a sports metaphor but relies on an unfamiliar sport. Imagine that an economy is like a swim team. Creating a higher standard of living is like helping swimmers achieve faster times in their races.

Swimming coaches use two approaches to give swimmers a short-run boost just before a race: tapering and blood doping.[2] Blood doping refers to the process of drawing blood from a swimmer weeks or months in advance and then reinfusing the blood just before the race. Hemoglobin is the carrier of oxygen in the blood. Performance falls when blood is withdrawn. As the body replenishes its stocks of hemoglobin, performance returns to its previous level. Then when the withdrawn blood is reinfused, the swimmer will swim faster because she has a temporary excess of hemoglobin and an increased oxygen carrying capacity. But if too much blood is infused, the swimmer can experience serious medical complications from "sludging" and excessive clotting.

The other method for increasing performance in the short run is a taper. A taper refers to the process whereby an athlete follows a training schedule that tapers off in intensity in the weeks before an important race. Most areas of competitive sport are governed by the iron law of athletics: no pain, no gain. The taper, however, seems to exploit a "paradox of training" that parallels the paradox of thrift cited by Keynesians. Training hard just before a race seems to reduce race times, just as saving too much is alleged in some cases to reduce capital accumulation.

Despite the pejorative sound of the term, blood doping can be a valuable medical procedure. If someone knows in advance that he will have to undergo a surgical procedure that has a high risk of blood loss, it is a good idea to store up some blood in advance. If he suffers a major loss of blood, transfusions of his own blood can be a crucial life-saving measure. Symmetrically, injections of money can in some circumstances bring an economy back to life. Economists now understand that a major contributing factor to the depression of the 1930s was the decision by the Federal Reserve Board to stand idly by and watch as the financial system in the United States hemorrhaged. Between 1930 and 1933, the money supply fell by about a third as the banking system collapsed.

Although transfusions are valuable during real emergencies, this does not commend blood doping as a regular part of athletic training. Transfusions can be very effective in averting death, but they cannot permanently raise an athlete's performance by much. In the same way, the power of monetary policy to cause a sharp recession or to speed recovery from one does not imply that we can use frequent adjustments in the supply of money or the level of interest rates to achieve steady increases in standards of living. Our experience with monetary stimulus is like that of a swim team with a medical trainer who has been using blood doping aggressively, achieving some short-run increases in performance. But he pushes the team right up to the limit where the complications from sludging and clotting (i.e., inflation) become unacceptable. Then the trainer withdraws blood, causing a sharp reduction in performance. This creates pressure for more short-run stimulus, and the boom-bust cycle repeats itself.

If blood doping is like monetary stimulus, tapers are like government deficits. A reduction in training may give a short-term boost, but it impedes progress toward better aerobic conditioning and more strength. Conditioning, strength and technique all improve with the total distance that a swimmer covers in practice. Tapers reduce this total. Symmetrically, if government deficits have a positive effect on short-run output, it comes at the cost of a reduction in national saving and the rate of accumulation of capital. In the long run, less capital will translate into few inputs that we can use in production. Tapers and deficits, like injections of blood and money, do have their uses. If you are a coach training a team for an important swim meet, or if you are the leader of a nation that must fight a war, you may be quite willing to give up some future performance to get some short-term gain. But there is no free lunch.

Unfortunately, both coaches and politicians find that their popularity goes up when they institute a taper or undertake fiscal stimulus. As a result, in the politics of macro-economics, both the left and the right have developed their own distinctive versions of fiscal stimulus. Politicians on the left promise an investment-led recovery of growth driven by deficit-financed government spending. Politicians on the right promise a supply side recovery that is driven by deficit-financed tax cuts. Part of the return in the economics profession to a more classical policy stance can be explained as a reaction to these political pressures and the persistent deficits that they have caused.

Stimulative monetary policy and government deficits can both be useful policy tools. But in the long run, they cannot make a nation rich. Unfortunately, neither can the opposite of large deficits – an extremely high rate of savings and capital accumulation. We now know that the classical suggestion that we can grow rich by accumulating more and more pieces of physical capital like fork lifts is simply wrong. The problem an economy faces (but that a family putting its savings in the bank can ignore) is what economists call "diminishing returns." In handling heavy objects, a fork lift is a very useful piece of equipment. When there were few fork lifts in the economy, the return on an investment in an additional fork lift was high. But as we increase the total number of fork lifts the value of each additional fork lift drops rapidly. Eventually, additional fork lifts would have no value and become a nuisance. The return on investment in an additional fork lift diminishes and eventually becomes negative. As a result, an economy cannot grow merely by accumulating more and more of the same kinds of capital goods.

This process of diminishing returns has an exact analog for a swimmer. A swimmer invests in pool time just as an economy invests in capital. She cannot continue to improve her times year after year merely by training harder to improve aerobic conditioning and physical strength. The physics of drag in water and the physiology of the human body impose an upper bound on the speed at which anyone can move through the water using a particular swimming stroke. There is a limit to how far a brute force approach to training can take a swimmer.

In swimming, as in macroeconomics, we nevertheless continue to see steady improvement. From the 1950s up through 1990, the number of world records that were broken in an average year has remained about the same.[3] This improvement derives fundamentally from the same source in both swimming and the economy – cumulative improvements in technique. In swimming, there has been a dramatic improvement in the techniques that swimmers use to propel themselves through the water. They exactly parallel the improvements in the techniques of production that have raised our standards of living.

One of the advantages of using a swimming metaphor to think about the sources of long-run improvement in performance is that it is relatively easy to see what the technical innovations are and why it takes a combination of big breakthroughs and small refinements for real progress to take place. For 400 years (from about 1500 to 1900) a stroke that resembled what we now know as the breast stroke was thought to be the most efficient swimming stroke in the Western world. This stroke, in which the arms remain underwater even during the forward recovery, was used throughout most of the nineteenth century in racing competition. The first person to swim the English Channel did so using the breast stroke in 1875.[4] For readers who do not appreciate how inefficient the breast stroke is, with its underwater recovery of the arms and legs and with the chest plowing through the water like a barge, swimming the Channel with the breast stroke today would be like running a marathon backwards.

Around the turn of the century, English and Australian swimmers copied techniques used by native peoples in Australia and Ceylon and developed what is now known as the free style or crawl stroke. Because the arms recover out of the water, this stroke has inherent efficiency advantages over the breast stroke. As early as 1844, a version of this novel kind of stroke was demonstrated by two native Americans in England, then the center of worldwide swimming competition. But the inherently inefficient breast stroke had been refined, and early attempts to use an overarm recovery of the crawl stroke were crude and awkward. (One of the biggest initial stumbling blocks was the lack of a kick that would work with the new arm stroke.) As a result, the efficiency advantages of having the arms recover out of the water were not generally recognized for more than 50 years.

One of the chronic problems that people have in understanding the potential for discovery is that we extrapolate our current circumstances both forward and backward in time. Most people expect that the basic swimming strokes have been known for centuries and are surprised to learn that something as obvious as the crawl stroke was discovered at about the same time as quantum mechanics. People also tend to under-estimate the enormous gulf that separates the discovery of abstract principles from their effective application. The basic physical laws of fluid dynamics were established in the 1700s but even with all the sophisticated laboratory experiments done today, there is still disagreement among coaches and swimmers about what constitutes the most efficient swimming stroke. New techniques continue to be proposed. Aspects of the stroke are still being refined.

When a new technique like the crawl stroke is discovered, it takes lots of investment in pool-time for the swimming community to uncover these refinements. It also takes lots of pool time for any individual swimmer to master what is already known. In the same way, when a new type of capital goods like the railroad or the digital computer is invented, it takes lots of investment to reap the benefits from these discoveries. But in either case, the return on additional investment falls rapidly in the absence of a steady flow of new techniques and new refinements.

This lesson shows the limitations inherent in the return to a classical emphasis on savings and investment. Especially in discussions of education and human capital accumulation, it is easy to be seduced by a suitably extended version of the family finance metaphor. If I am a high school educated worker and if all of my children become college educated professionals, then their standards of living should be higher than mine. I can invest, therefore, not by putting money in the bank, but by sending my children to college.

This makes sense at the level of the family, but in the economy as a whole, a strategy based on human capital accumulation eventually runs into the same limits from diminishing returns that arise with physical capital accumulation. Suppose that there had been no innovation and no technological change during the nineteenth century. We could have accumulated more human capital by increasing the fraction of the population that was high school educated or even college educated. We could also have accumulated more physical capital in the form of sailing ships, water wheels and ox carts. But eventually we would be forced to admit that we had little use for one more college graduate who is employed driving one more ox cart. The increases in standards of living that we achieved in the last century were possible only because of the discoveries and innovations that let new physical capital and new human capital be put to work in high return activities.

Policy implications

All economists agree that governments need to pay attention to the textbook fundamentals of monetary and fiscal policy. They also agree that governments should encourage, or at least avoid discouraging, the accumulation of capital. But these steps by themselves are not enough. A government must create an environment that fosters change – and progress – in the techniques we use.

For a government, there are two parts to any strategy for creating this kind of environment. The first is the one that most people think of in discussions of technological progress. The government can support the research and training missions of university-based science and engineering. Market incentives by themselves cannot simultaneously solve the problems of discovering and distributing knowledge. But mechanisms like royal patronage and its modern descendent, the government research grant, can. The government pays people to discover new things and to share their knowledge freely.

Subsidies for education and training can indirectly assist in this process. Governments, however, cannot do it all. Market incentives must guide the process of discovery. Some kinds of university-based research and training have a greater likelihood of generating increases in economic value than others. If the private sector and universities are working well together, the market incentives can guide researchers and teachers toward valuable new areas, as happened in the United States when the opportunities in the emerging petroleum refining industry led to the creation of schools of chemical engineering.

For a nation as a whole, an effective institutional arrangement for supporting technological advance must therefore support a high level of exploration and research in both private firms and in universities. Moreover, it must support a high degree of interaction between these two domains. Both people and ideas must move readily between them. If they do not, the university research can become sterile and irrelevant. Private sector efforts can lose the steady flow of new talent and new ideas that sustains its creativity.[5]

In a discussion of macroeconomic policy, it is equally important to emphasize the other part of a government policy that can support progress. Governments must not impede change. Unfortunately, change is disruptive and the citizens of industrial democracies increasingly demand that governments protect them from disruption. From a long-run perspective, the most serious side effect of the Keynesian revolution in macroeconomic policy may have been the intellectual legitimacy it lent to the impulse to blame the government for all economic misfortune. After all, if the government controls powerful levers that can be used to prevent job loss and unemployment, someone who loses a job would seem to have a strong claim of negligence against a government that fails to act.

In economics, the real force of the athletic slogan of "no pain, no gain" lies not in an admonition to consume less and save more. Rather, it comes from the warning that in many cases, things have to get worse before they can get better. If you talk to a swimmer, she will tell you that each time she tries a new variation in her technique, her performance falls. She typically has perfected the details of the old, less efficient stroke, much as the English swimmers had perfected the inherently inefficient breast stroke. When she makes a change, she initially gets many of the details wrong and performance falls. Then slowly the efficiency improves as she adjusts all the details to get the best performance out of the new stroke. If swimmers were never willing to tolerate temporary reductions in performance, they would not be able to experiment and develop better technique.

The equivalent process of experimentation, deterioration and improvement that takes place in an economy was called "creative destruction" by Joseph Schumpeter. A new or improved product typically replaces an existing one. The creation of economic returns for inputs used to make the new good is associated with the destruction of returns for inputs that made the old good. Workers who used to produce the old good have to be shifted into some new activity. At best this results in a spell of unemployment. At worst, it can lead to a permanent loss in income.

If the old activity had been a particularly profitable one (the production of mainframe computers, for example), stockholders of the company engaged in this activity will lose when the new good (the personal computer) comes along. If the company that made the mainframes shared some of its profits with its workers, paying them well above the market wage, these workers may also suffer permanent reductions in income when the new personal computer industry destroys the profits of the mainframe manufacturers. The individual workers who lose their jobs may never again find new jobs that pay them more than the market wage. The job market is therefore characterized by constant turnover, with new hiring at some firms and job losses at others. Much of this turnover takes place during an economic expansion. The rest of it gets concentrated during recessions, when the vulnerability of older firms becomes plainly evident.[6]

Innovation and change create winners and losers. Job losses and pay cuts are the most visible, and politically most powerful symptom of this disruption. But we know that for society as a whole, innovation, discovery and technological change offer large net gains because the new goods or processes are more efficient and more valuable than the old ones. A world with personal computers opens up opportunities that were inconceivable in the era of the mainframe. If we had not tolerated disruption in the past, we would still travel in ox carts.

Macroeconomic policy measures like fiscal or monetary stimulus cannot change the fact that many older firms need to shrink. Aggressive stimulus measures can perhaps change the timing of the job losses that this implies, but they cannot avoid them. If these policy measures delay the process whereby an existing firm comes to terms with new competitive realities, they might make things worse. More aggressive measures like bailouts, government loans, nationalization of failing firms and prohibitions on firing workers are even more likely to have perverse effects in the long run. The ultimate contraction is likely to be associated with more job turnover and income loss than it would if firms had responded sooner.

This perspective suggests that much of the effort expended by governments to prevent recessions and avoid job losses may be misguided. The circumstances of the 1930s may have been exceptional (in part because of government actions that made the contraction so severe). Stimulus measures that were appropriate then may not be useful in the ordinary course of events. Such efforts may only postpone processes of adjustment that are inevitable. There is a growing recognition, for example, that high levels of long-term unemployment in Europe may be the unintended consequence of policies designed to fight unemployment and recessions, not the result of the recessions themselves. A more productive approach to policy would be to make the adjustment process as efficient and painless as possible, and to maintain the conditions that lead to rapid entry of new firms that compete for workers.

The greatest challenge for policy makers may therefore be one of political leadership. Each year, new demands for security and protection from disruption are voiced by the electorate. Meanwhile, evidence mounts that government efforts designed to provide security and prevent disruption have had a corrosive effect on the operation of markets, on the processes of entry and exit by firms and ultimately on the kind of competitive spirit that any successful competitor – in the world of athletics or the world of work – must cultivate. Many workers suffer losses and setbacks during their careers, yet still have access to material advantages that would have been unattainable by even the very rich just two generations ago. Most swimmers lose races, but still benefit from participation in the competition.

To succeed in narrow economic terms, but also in broader human terms, leaders must give people the confidence to compete. They must encourage people to believe that economic change brings real opportunity together with risks that are real, but manageable.

Leaders must not cater to the demands of a generation that seems to believe that each person is entitled to a job, a house in the suburbs and two cars just for serving time in school – as if everyone deserved a trophy just for putting in a specified number of hours in the pool. They must inspire people to dive in, strive for each small improvement in technique, compete to the best of their abilities.

Nations that can sustain a policy stance that tolerates, or perhaps even fosters, the process of creative destruction can count on sustained economic growth that will carry them into the next century. Those that are most successful in creating institutions that foster discovery and innovation will be the worldwide technological leaders. Through mechanisms like free trade and transfers of technology by multinational firms, nations that are less successful in the cultivation and commercial exploitation of science and technology can still follow comfortably along in the wake of the leaders. But nations that try to resist change by protecting inefficient firms, impeding flows of goods and ideas, and making a high level of income an entitlement instead of a reward will slowly be left farther and farther behind.

Notes

1 For technical presentations of this kind of theory, see Philipe Aghion and Peter Howitt, "A Model of Growth Through Creative Destruction," *Econometrica*, Vol. 60 (1992), pp. 323–51; Paul M. Romer, "Endogenous Technological Change," *Journal of Political Economy*, Vol. 98 (October 1990), S71–102; and Gene Grossman and Elhanan Helpman, *Innovation and Growth in the Global Economy* (Cambridge, MA: MIT Press, 1992). For a non-technical discussion, see Peter Howitt, "Endogenous Growth Theory: Taming the Winds of Change, or Tweaking Neoclassical Economics," in Thomas J. Courchene (ed.), *Stabilization, Growth and Distributional Linkages in the Knowledge Economy*, Bell Canada Papers on Economic and Public Policy, no. 2 (forthcoming) or Paul M. Romer, "Economic Growth," in David R. Henderson (ed.), *The Fortune Encyclopedia of Economics* (New York: Time-Warner Books, 1993).

2 The description of training methods is drawn from Ernst W. Maglischo, *Swimming Even Faster* (Mountain View, CA: Mayfield Publishing Company, 1993) and Cecil M. Colwin, *Swimming into the 21st Century* (Champaign, IL: Human Kinetics Publishers, 1992).

3 See Colwin, *Swimming into the 21st Century*, p. 208.

4 See Charles Sprawson, *Haunts of the Black Masseur: The Swimmer as Hero* (London: Jonathan Cape, 1992) for an account.

5 For a discussion of the range of issues that an analysis of economic growth raises for conduct of science and technology policy, see Paul M. Romer, "Implementing a National Technology Strategy with Self-Organizing Industry Investment Boards," *Brookings Papers on Economic Activity: Microeconomics*, no. 2 (Washington, DC: Brookings Institution, 1993), pp. 345–99.

6 Recent work on Canada by John Baldwin and Paul K. Gorecki, *Structural Change and the Adjustment Process* (Ottawa: Economic Council of Canada, 1990) and on the US by John Haltiwanger and Steve Davis, "Gross Job Creation and Destruction: Microeconomic Evidence and Macroeconomic Implications," *NBER Macroeconomic Annual* (1990), pp. 123–186 has demonstrated how important entry and exit by firms are in causing job turnover in good times and bad.

REVIEW AND DISCUSSION QUESTIONS

1   According to Paul M. Romer, how does a team of swimmers trying to achieve faster times resemble a country trying to achieve economic growth?
2   Can fiscal and monetary policies help an economy grow in the long run? Why or why not?
3   Why does Romer believe that high saving and rapid capital accumulation cannot "make a nation rich" in the long run?
4   In what ways does technological progress resemble the invention of a new swimming stroke? What are the short- and long-run effects of technological discoveries? Explain.
5   According to Romer, what is the appropriate role of the Government in promoting long-run economic growth?
6   Do you agree with Romer's policy recommendations? Why or why not?

Chapter 6

Vincent Ferraro

DEPENDENCY THEORY
An introduction

Background

DEPENDENCY THEORY DEVELOPED IN the late 1950s under the guidance of the Director of the United Nations Economic Commission for Latin America, Raul Prebisch. Prebisch and his colleagues were troubled by the fact that economic growth in the advanced industrialized countries did not necessarily lead to growth in the poorer countries. Indeed, their studies suggested that economic activity in the richer countries often led to serious economic problems in the poorer countries. Such a possibility was not predicted by neoclassical theory, which had assumed that economic growth was beneficial to all (Pareto optimal) even if the benefits were not always equally shared.

Prebisch's initial explanation for the phenomenon was very straightforward: poor countries exported primary commodities to the rich countries who then manufactured products out of those commodities and sold them back to the poorer countries. The "Value Added" by manufacturing a usable product always cost more than the primary products used to create those products. Therefore, poorer countries would never be earning enough from their export earnings to pay for their imports.

Prebisch's solution was similarly straightforward: poorer countries should embark on programs of import substitution so that they need not purchase the manufactured products from the richer countries. The poorer countries would still sell their primary products on the world market, but their foreign exchange reserves would not be used to purchase their manufactures from abroad.

Three issues made this policy difficult to follow. The first is that the internal markets of the poorer countries were not large enough to support the economies of scale used by the richer countries to keep their prices low. The second issue concerned the political will of the poorer countries as to whether a transformation from being primary products producers was possible or desirable. The final issue revolved around the extent to which the poorer countries actually had control of their primary products, particularly in the area of selling those products abroad. These obstacles to the import substitution policy led others to think a little more creatively and historically at the relationship between rich and poor countries.

At this point dependency theory was viewed as a possible way of explaining the persistent poverty of the poorer countries. The traditional neoclassical approach said virtually nothing on this question except to assert that the poorer countries were late in coming to solid economic practices and that as soon as they learned the techniques of modern economics, then the poverty would begin to subside. However, Marxists theorists viewed the persistent poverty as a consequence of capitalist exploitation. And a new body of thought, called the *world systems approach*, argued that the poverty was a direct consequence of the evolution of the international political economy into a fairly rigid division of labor which favored the rich and penalized the poor.

How can one define dependency theory?

The debates among the liberal reformers (Prebisch), the Marxists (Andre Gunder Frank), and the world systems theorists (Wallerstein) was vigorous and intellectually quite challenging. There are still points of serious disagreements among the various strains of dependency theorists and it is a mistake to think that there is only one unified theory of dependency. Nonetheless, there are some core propositions which seem to underlie the analyses of most dependency theorists.

Dependency can be defined as an explanation of the economic development of a state in terms of the external influences – political, economic, and cultural – on national development policies (Osvaldo Sunkel, "National Development Policy and External Dependence in Latin America," *The Journal of Development Studies*, Vol. 6, no. 1, October 1969, p. 23). Theotonio Dos Santos emphasizes the historical dimension of the dependency relationships in his definition:

> [Dependency is] . . . an historical condition which shapes a certain structure of the world economy such that it favors some countries to the detriment of others and limits the development possibilities of the subordinate economics . . . a situation in which the economy of a certain group of countries is conditioned by the development and expansion of another economy, to which their own is subjected.
>
> (Theotonio Dos Santos, "The Structure of Dependence," in K.T. Fann and Donald C. Hodges, eds., *Readings in U.S. Imperialism*. Boston: Porter Sargent, 1971, p. 226)

There are three common features to these definitions which most dependency theorists share. First, dependency characterizes the international system as comprised of two sets of states, variously described as dominant/dependent, center/periphery or metropolitan/satellite. The dominant states are the advanced industrial nations in the Organization of Economic Co-operation and Development (OECD). The dependent states are those states of Latin America, Asia, and Africa which have low *per capita* GNPs and which rely heavily on the export of a single commodity for foreign exchange earnings.

Second, both definitions have in common the assumption that external forces are of singular importance to the economic activities within the dependent states. These external forces include multinational corporations, international commodity markets, foreign assistance, communications, and any other means by which the advanced industrialized countries can represent their economic interests abroad.

Third, the definitions of dependency all indicate that the relations between dominant and dependent states are dynamic because the interactions between the two sets of states tend to not only reinforce but also intensify the unequal patterns. Moreover, dependency is a very deep-seated historical process, rooted in the internationalization of capitalism. Dependency is an ongoing process:

> Latin America is today, and has been since the sixteenth century, part of an international system dominated by the now-developed nations. . . . Latin underdevelopment is the outcome of a particular series of relationships to the international system.
>
> Susanne Bodenheimer, "Dependency and Imperialism:
The Roots of Latin American Underdevelopment,"
in Fann and Hodges, Readings, op. cit., p. 157.

In short, dependency theory attempts to explain the present underdeveloped state of many nations in the world by examining the patterns of interactions among nations and by arguing that inequality among nations is an intrinsic part of those interactions.

The structural context of dependency: is it capitalism or is it power?

Most dependency theorists regard international capitalism as the motive force behind dependency relationships. Andre Gunder Frank, one of the earliest dependency theorists, is quite clear on this point:

> . . . historical research demonstrates that contemporary underdevelopment is in large part the historical product of past and continuing economic and other relations between the satellite underdeveloped and the now developed metropolitan countries. Furthermore, these relations are an essential part of the capitalist system on a world scale as a whole.
>
> Andre Gunder Frank, "The Development of Underdevelopment,"
in James D. Cockcroft, Andre Gunder Frank, and
Dale Johnson, eds., Dependence and Underdevelopment.
Garden City, New York: Anchor Books, 1972, p. 3.

According to this view, the capitalist system has enforced a rigid international division of labor which is responsible for the underdevelopment of many areas of the world. The dependent states supply cheap minerals, agricultural commodities, and cheap labor, and also serve as the repositories of surplus capital, obsolescent technologies, and manufactured goods. These functions orient the economies of the dependent states toward the outside: money, goods, and services do flow into dependent states, but the allocation of these resources are determined by the economic interests of the dominant states, and not by the economic interests of the dependent state. This division of labor is ultimately the explanation for poverty and there is little question but that capitalism regards the division of labor as a necessary condition for the efficient allocation of resources. The most explicit manifestation of this characteristic is in the doctrine of comparative advantage.

Moreover, to a large extent the dependency models rest upon the assumption that economic and political power are heavily concentrated and centralized in the industrialized countries, an assumption shared with Marxist theories of imperialism. If this assumption is valid, then any distinction between economic and political power is spurious: governments will take whatever steps are necessary to protect private economic interests, such as those held by multinational corporations.

Not all dependency theorists, however, are Marxist and one should clearly distinguish between dependency and a theory of imperialism. The Marxist theory of imperialism explains dominant state *expansion* while the dependency theory explains *underdevelopment*. Stated another way, Marxist theories explain the reasons why imperialism occurs, while dependency theories explain the consequences of imperialism. The difference is significant. In many respects, imperialism is, for a Marxist, part of the process by which the world is transformed and is therefore a process which accelerates the communist revolution. Marx spoke approvingly of British colonialism in India:

> England has to fulfil a double mission in India: one destructive, the other regenerating – the annihilation of old Asiatic society, and the laying of the material foundations of Western society in Asia.
>
> Karl Marx, "The Future Results of the British Rule in India,"
> *New York Daily Tribune*, No. 3840, August 8, 1853.

For the dependency theorists, underdevelopment is a wholly negative condition which offers no possibility of sustained and autonomous economic activity in a dependent state.

Additionally, the Marxist theory of imperialism is self-liquidating, while the dependent relationship is self-perpetuating. The end of imperialism in the Leninist framework comes about as the dominant powers go to war over a rapidly shrinking number of exploitable opportunities. World War I was, for Lenin, the classic proof of this proposition. After the war was over, Britain and France took over the former German colonies. A dependency theorist rejects this proposition. A dependent relationship exists irrespective of the specific identity of the dominant state. That the dominant states may fight over the disposition of dependent territories is not in and of itself a pertinent bit of information (except that periods of fighting among dominant states affords opportunities for the dependent states to break their dependent relationships). To a dependency theorist, the central characteristic of the global economy is the persistence of poverty throughout the entire modern period in virtually the same areas of the world, regardless of what state was in control.

Finally, there are some dependency theorists who do not identify capitalism as the motor force behind a dependent relationship. The relationship is maintained by a system of power first and it does not seem as if power is only supported by capitalism. For example, the relationship between the former dependent states in the socialist bloc (the Eastern European states and Cuba, for example) closely paralleled the relationships between poor states and the advanced capitalist states. The possibility that dependency is more closely linked to disparities of power rather than to the particular characteristics of a given economic system is intriguing and consistent with the more traditional analyses of international relations, such as realism.

The central propositions of dependency theory

There are a number of propositions, all of which are contestable, which form the core of dependency theory. These propositions include:

1.   *Underdevelopment* is a condition fundamentally different from *undevelopment*. The latter term simply refers to a condition in which resources are not being used. For example, the European colonists viewed the North American continent as an undeveloped area: the land was not actively cultivated on a scale consistent with its potential. Underdevelopment refers to a situation in which resources are being actively used, but used in a way which benefits dominant states and not the poorer states in which the resources are found.

2.   The distinction between underdevelopment and undevelopment places the poorer countries of the world is a profoundly different historical context. These countries are not "behind" or "catching up" to the richer countries of the world. They are not poor because they lagged behind the scientific transformations or the Enlightenment values of the European states. They are poor because they were coercively integrated into the European economic system only as producers of raw materials or to serve as repositories of cheap labor, and were denied the opportunity to market their resources in any way that competed with dominant states.

3.   Dependency theory suggests that alternative uses of resources are preferable to the resource usage patterns imposed by dominant states. There is no clear definition of what these preferred patterns might be, but some criteria are invoked. For example, one of the dominant state practices most often criticized by dependency theorists is export agriculture. The criticism is that many poor economies experience rather high rates of malnutrition even though they produce great amounts of food for export. Many dependency theorists would argue that those agricultural lands should be used for domestic food production in order to reduce the rates of malnutrition.

4.   The preceding proposition can be amplified: dependency theorists rely upon a belief that there exists a clear "national" economic interest which can and should be articulated for each country. In this respect, dependency theory actually shares a similar theoretical concern with realism. What distinguishes the dependency perspective is that its proponents believe that this national interest can only be satisfied by addressing the needs of the poor within a society, rather than through the satisfaction of corporate or governmental needs. Trying to determine what is "best" for the poor is a difficult analytical problem over the long run. Dependency theorists have not yet articulated an operational definition of the national economic interest.

5.   The diversion of resources over time (and one must remember that dependent relationships have persisted since the European expansion beginning in the fifteenth century) is maintained not only by the power of dominant states, but also through the power of elites in the dependent states. Dependency theorists argue that these elites maintain a dependent relationship because their own private interests coincide

with the interests of the dominant states. These elites are typically trained in the dominant states and share similar values and culture with the elites in dominant states. Thus, in a very real sense, a dependency relationship is a "voluntary" relationship. One need not argue that the elites in a dependent state are consciously betraying the interests of their poor; the elites sincerely believe that the key to economic development lies in following the prescriptions of liberal economic doctrine.

The policy implications of dependency analysis

If one accepts the analysis of dependency theory, then the questions of how poor economies develop become quite different from the traditional questions concerning comparative advantage, capital accumulation, and import/export strategies. Some of the most important new issues include:

1. The success of the advanced industrial economies does not serve as a model for the currently developing economies. When economic development became a focused area of study, the analytical strategy (and ideological preference) was quite clear: all nations need to emulate the patterns used by the rich countries. Indeed, in the 1950s and 1960s there was a paradigmatic consensus that growth strategies were universally applicable, a consensus best articulated by Walt Rostow in his book, *The Stages of Economic Growth*. Dependency theory suggests that the success of the richer countries was a highly contingent and specific episode in global economic history, one dominated by the highly exploitative colonial relationships of the European powers. A repeat of those relationships is not now highly likely for the poor countries of the world.

2. Dependency theory repudiates the central distributive mechanism of the neoclassical model, what is usually called "trickle-down" economics. The neoclassical model of economic growth pays relatively little attention to the question of distribution of wealth. Its primary concern is on efficient production and assumes that the market will allocate the rewards of efficient production in a rational and unbiased manner. This assumption may be valid for a well-integrated, economically fluid economy where people can quickly adjust to economic changes and where consumption patterns are not distorted by non-economic forces such as racial, ethnic, or gender bias. These conditions are not pervasive in the developing economies, and dependency theorists argue that economic activity is not easily disseminated in poor economies. For these structural reasons, dependency theorists argue that the market alone is not a sufficient distributive mechanism.

3. Since the market only rewards productivity, dependency theorists discount aggregate measures of economic growth such as the GDP or trade indices. Dependency theorists do not deny that economic activity occurs within a dependent state. They do make a very important distinction, however, between economic growth and economic development. For example, there is a greater concern within the dependency framework for whether the economic activity is actually benefitting the nation as a whole. Therefore, far greater attention is paid to indices such as life expectancy, literacy, infant mortality, education, and the like. Dependency theorists clearly emphasize social indicators far more than economic indicators.

4.   Dependent states, therefore, should attempt to pursue policies of self-reliance. Contrary to the neo-classical models endorsed by the International Monetary Fund and the World Bank, greater integration into the global economy is not necessarily a good choice for poor countries. Often this policy perspective is viewed as an endorsement of a policy of autarky, and there have been some experiments with such a policy such as China's Great Leap Forward or Tanzania's policy of *Ujamaa*. The failures of these policies are clear, and the failures suggest that autarky is not a good choice. Rather a policy of self-reliance should be interpreted as endorsing a policy of controlled interactions with the world economy: poor countries should only endorse interactions on terms that promise to improve the social and economic welfare of the larger citizenry.

REVIEW AND DISCUSSION QUESTIONS

1   According to the author, why did Raul Prebisch recommend import substitution programs for developing countries?
2   What are some common characteristics of the various strands of dependency theories?
3   How are dependency theories different from Marxist theories of imperialism?
4   Why are poor countries poor according to dependency theorists?
5   If relations with rich countries lead to exploitation, why do independent poor countries continue to engage in such relations?
6   What are the policy implications of dependency theories? What should poor countries do to escape underdevelopment?

Suggestions for further reading

Guest, R. (2004) *The Shackled Continent: Power, Corruption, and African Lives*, Washington, DC: Smithsonian Books.

The Africa editor for *The Economist* recounts many of his experiences on the ground in Africa, addressing several of the key obstacles to development – corruption, lack of clearly defined property rights, the AIDS epidemics, lack of infrastructure, etc. The book uses a wealth of anecdotes to help the reader understand some of the realities that the people of Africa face every day.

Helpman, E. (2004) *The Mystery of Economic Growth*, Cambridge, MA: Belknap Press.

The Harvard economist reviews the major strands of theories of economic growth, discussing much of the evidence that supports them (or fails to support them). He addresses both theories that look at traditional sources of growth (capital accumulation, techno-logical progress, etc.) and more recent research (e.g., about the interactions between growth and inequality and the role of institutions and political systems).

Perkins, D. H., Radelet, S. and Lindauer, D. (2006) *Economics of Development*, 6th edn, New York: W. W. Norton.

This is a very comprehensive textbook that covers all the key topics in development economics. The sixth edition includes updates on measuring economic development, the debate over foreign aid, and several other issues. While certain sections of the book assume that the reader is familiar with intermediate-level economic theory, many other parts are accessible to the general reader.

Rodrik, D. (forthcoming in 2008) "A Practical Approach to Formulating Growth Strategies," in J. E. Stiglitz and N. Sierra (eds) *The Washington Consensus Reconsidered: Towards a New Global Governance*, Oxford: Oxford University Press.

Rodrik addresses in this essay the difficulties of formulating growth strategies for developing countries, criticizing the so-called Washington Consensus. He suggests a new approach based on a careful diagnosis of what is hindering growth in each country and the design of policies that target as directly as possible the constraints to growth. He also emphasizes the need for policies that not only jumpstart growth but are also able to sustain it in the long run.

Sen, A. (1999) *Development as Freedom*, New York: Alfred A. Knopf.

In this landmark work, the Economics Nobel Laureate explains why economic development is best seen as "a process of expanding the real freedoms that people enjoy" rather than as an increase in incomes. Sen addresses, among other issues, the relevance of democracy, the role of women, and the causes of famines and other crises, emphasizing the many connections between economic, political, and social aspects of development.

Todaro, M. P. and Smith, S. C. (2006) *Economic Development*, 9th edn, Boston, MA: Pearson Addison Wesley.

This well-known textbook, now in its ninth edition, introduces readers to the field of development economics and covers all major topic areas, including rural-urban migration, the environment, and macroeconomic issues. Certain parts of the book assume that the reader is familiar with intermediate-level economic theory, but most chapters are accessible to the general reader.

United Nations Development Programme, *Human Development Report* (published annually).

The *Human Development Report* has been published since 1990 to provide information about and discussion of the state of human development globally. The report includes a wealth of indicators that attempt to measure people's quality of life in more than 170 countries. Every year the report focuses on a particular human development issue (e.g., climate change, water rights, aid, cultural liberty, etc.).

World Bank, *World Development Report* (published annually).

The *World Development Report* has been published since 1978. Every year it focuses on a specific development aspect chosen by the World Bank president. The report is written by World Bank staff with the contribution of outside consultants. Recent topics include agriculture, the next generation, equity, investment climate, and making services work for the poor.

Geography, institutions, and governance

INTRODUCTION

IN PART ONE WE SAW that economists have developed a variety of theories to explain differences in economic growth and standards of living across countries. Most of these theories point to specific factors that either promote or hinder economic development – saving and investment, population growth, technological progress, and so on. In the article reprinted in Chapter 7 MIT economist Daron Acemoglu writes that all these theories can only identify "proximate causes" of development; they do not help us understand the "fundamental causes." We may agree, for example, that a higher saving rate tends to be associated with more investment and faster growth, but what is the fundamental reason why some countries have higher saving rates than others? The endogenous growth theory tells us that countries that invest more in human capital and research and development will experience greater technological progress and faster growth; but why do some countries make more of these investments than others? Acemoglu's point is that while most traditional growth theories identify the factors that promote or hinder growth, they do not explain why these factors are present in some countries and missing in others.

Acemoglu reviews two common hypotheses about the fundamental causes of economic development: the geography hypothesis, according to which natural resources, climate, and other geographical factors provide the ultimate explanation for development; and the institutions hypothesis, which posits that rules, laws, and organizations devised by people determine whether a country will end up developing or not. According to Acemoglu, institutions that promote growth and development are those that enforce property rights for most people, place constraints on the behavior of people in power, and ensure some degree of equal opportunity for most people. These institutions tend to provide the incentives and the opportunities to engage in profitable economic activity. Acemoglu believes that institutions are more important than geography, and he uses countries' differing experiences with colonization to prove his point. The colonization of many Latin American, Asian, and African countries by European powers changed the institutions in these countries but, of course, did not change their geography. Many countries that were rich before colonization became poor after their institutions were changed, whereas other countries that were poor and adopted different institutions became rich. This "reversal of fortunes" suggests that institutions – not geography – are the ultimate cause of development. Acemoglu also discusses the different kinds of institutions established in different colonies and the thorny issue of what it takes to change institutions.

Harvard economist Dani Rodrik and former IMF economist Arvind Subramanian agree that institutions matter more than geography, but in the article reprinted in Chapter 8 they also emphasize the many interactions between a country's institutional and geographical characteristics. They explain, for example, that there is no one set of institutions that can be considered best for economic development. Countries with equally successful development experiences have had very different institutions, and the specific institutions that lead to development in one country may well depend on geographical and historical factors. The authors' research, however, also shows that institutions can and do change over time, so that historical and geographical factors do not predetermine the course of economic development in the long run. Rodrik and Subramanian argue that the process of institutional change is not well understood and that democracy can play an important role in allowing citizens to pick the institutions they want. In this respect, democracy can be thought of as a "metainstitution," or a mechanism through which all the other institutions are chosen and put in place.

Columbia University economist Jeffrey Sachs provides a different perspective on the debate about institutions and geography. In the article reprinted in Chapter 9 he warns against an oversimplified view in which "institutions explain nearly everything about a country's level of economic development." While Sachs does not believe that geography is the ultimate determinant of development, he emphasizes that geographical characteristics often play an important role in helping or hindering development. Tropical climates where diseases such as malaria are hard to eradicate, geographic isolation that raises transport costs, or poor soil fertility may not doom a country to poverty, but do present obstacles that development policy should not ignore. Developing countries *can* surmount these obstacles, but only through what Sachs calls "special investments" designed to address the geographical handicaps that hold them back. It is Sachs's belief that poor countries with unfavorable geographic characteristics need help from the outside world to overcome their disadvantages (Sachs's perspective on the need for foreign aid is discussed further in Part Eight).

I mentioned earlier that Rodrik and Subramanian refer to democracy as a "metainstitution," or a mechanism that allows people to pick the institutions they want. Does that imply that democracy promotes economic growth? Are democratic countries more likely to experience successful development? Harvard economist Robert J. Barro investigates this question in the essay reprinted in Chapter 10. Barro notes that there are different reasons why democracy may or may not help growth. On the one hand, democracy implies greater political freedoms that may lead to greater economic freedoms and a greater opportunity for people to engage in economic activity conducive to growth. On the other hand, democracy may also imply popular pressure for programs that redistribute resources from the rich to the poor (progressive taxation or welfare systems). Such programs may be desirable from an equity point of view, but Barro emphasizes that they "inevitably reduce the incentives for investment, work effort, and growth." Democracy may also allow powerful interest groups to redistribute resources in ways that hinder growth; e.g., farmers may be able to lobby in favor of agricultural subsidies that make them better off but create inefficiencies that hold back overall economic development. Of course, there is no guarantee that replacing democracies with authoritarian regimes would make things better: dictators may well use their powers in ways that enrich them personally and hinder economic progress. Many developing countries have experienced the devastating effects of authoritarian regimes that enrich the people in power at the expense of the development of the country. Without democracy, there is no effective way to place limits on the absolute power of dictators.

Given that the theoretical link between democracy and development is unclear, Barro turns to the evidence, but fails to find clear support for either the hypothesis that democracy helps growth or the one that democracy hinders growth. As Amartya Sen has also written, there are examples of democratic countries that experienced dramatic growth and poverty reduction (Botswana) and democratic countries that struggled for a long time to make economic progress (India); similarly, one can find examples of authoritarian countries that developed successfully (Singapore) and authoritarian countries that failed to develop (Zimbabwe) (Sen 1995: 23–24). Barro's conclusion is that "more democracy is not the key to economic growth," and that rich Western countries can do more to help developing countries by trying to "export" successful economic institutions (e.g., those that protect property rights) than by trying to export their political systems. By looking at the evidence, however, Barro also finds other interesting connections between democracy and development. For example, it appears that democratic regimes tend to fail and be replaced by authoritarian regimes when economic progress is slow and that authoritarian regimes are more likely to become democratic when economic progress is significant.

There is general agreement among economists that institutions defining and protecting property rights play an especially important role in promoting economic development. Peruvian economist Hernando de Soto has developed a theory of economic development based on the idea that property rights over capital are the key to successful development. More precisely, as de Soto explains in the article reprinted in Chapter 11, property records and titles over assets are what allows these assets to be used in an economically productive way. A house, for example, in and of itself may not be especially useful in helping a country's economic progress. If I have a piece of paper that clearly indicates that I am the owner of this house, however, and if this piece of paper (a title) is a legal document that everyone recognizes, the house suddenly becomes a piece of capital that can be used in productive economic activities in a variety of ways. As the legal owner, I can use it as collateral to borrow money, and I can invest this money in a productive project. Or I can sell the house to purchase something else, and both I and the buyer will be better off (we would not have traded otherwise). If I do own the house but don't have the title to prove it, I will not be able to use the house as collateral or to sell it – I will own an asset that cannot do much to help development.

De Soto notes that one of the major differences between rich and poor countries is that rich countries have a formal property system that allows people to make full use of their assets; in developing countries, on the other hand, the lack of formal records and titles limits people's ability to put property to work. More broadly, the author believes that having one clearly defined and accepted property system promotes development by improving the flow of information, increasing the security of transactions, encouraging people to respect the law, and turning people into "a network of individually identifiable and accountable business agents." Recognized titles also make it easy to combine and divide assets. If I'm able to save some money, I may decide to buy a small piece of a company (i.e., a share of the company's stock) and contribute my money to that company's growth; but I won't do that unless I receive a credible title to a share of the company, so that I'll be able to claim my share of the company's profits and sell my share to someone else at some point in the future. The author estimates that developing countries have some $9.3 trillion of "dead capital," or assets that can't be put to work because of the lack of a clearly defined property system.

An interesting case study of the role of institutions in promoting or hindering economic development is presented by University of Southern California economist Timur Kuran. In the article reprinted in Chapter 12, Kuran explains why the Middle East is relatively poor today even though it was one of the most advanced economic areas in the world around the tenth century. According to the author, explanations sometimes heard in the media regarding the "irrationality" of Islam and its fundamental incompatibility with economic progress are not supported by the evidence; rather, "certain economic institutions of classical Islamic civilization interacted in unintended and unanticipated ways to block adaptations now recognized as critical to economic modernization." Islamic law, for example, allowed people to form partnerships, but did not recognize the concept of a corporation, or a legal entity with rights and responsibilities separate from those of its owners. This made it hard for enterprises to survive their owners and expand in ways that would have promoted economies of scale. Islamic law also constrained inheritance by mandating that two-thirds of every estate be divided among a large number of extended relatives. This rule tended to cause wealth fragmentation and prevent large, long-lasting enterprises from forming.

Kuran believes that institutional differences also help explain why religious minorities living in Middle Eastern countries (e.g., Christians and Jews) were able to advance economically at the same time as the Muslim majority fell behind the West. He argues that the success of these minorities was largely due to the kind of legal pluralism common in the Middle East: whereas Muslims had to observe Islamic law, non-Muslims could choose to acquire the same legal status afforded to foreigners; therefore, they could form corporations, use banks, buy insurance, and enter a variety of business arrangements that Muslim courts may not have approved. The ability to choose these institutions unavailable to Muslims enabled religious minorities to experience faster economic progress than their Muslim counterparts. In concluding his analysis, Kuran notes that if institutions do explain the Middle Eastern development disadvantage, it is unrealistic to expect that things will change quickly – institutional change tends to be a very gradual process. On the other hand, he believes that economic development in the Middle East can be achieved without the need to oppose Islam; several Middle Eastern countries continue to follow Islamic practices but have modified Islamic law to fit the needs of economic development, showing that economic progress can coexist with Islam.

The fundamental causes of – and obstacles to – economic development are elusive. The diversity of successful economic development experiences is such that trying to pinpoint fundamental causes that apply to all countries is bound to be a frustrating exercise. Yet the evidence we have accumulated leads most development economists to recognize what Rodrik and Subramanian refer to as "the primacy of institutions." History and geography do play important roles in determining a country's institutions and the course of its economic development. But experience shows that countries can overcome adverse geographical characteristics and disruptive historical events when they put in place institutions conducive to growth. Unfortunately, we do not have an easy prescription for how to go about changing institutions; if anything, what we know is that institutional change tends to be slow. This helps explain why, as development economists, we cannot limit ourselves to researching institutional change as the ultimate answer to development problems. Rather, we need to ask ourselves how and to what extent poverty can be reduced and people's lives improved even in countries with unsatisfactory institutional frameworks. The next part addresses specifically what we have learned in recent years about poverty reduction in developing countries.

REFERENCE

Sen, A. (1995) "Economic Development and Social Change: India and China in Comparative Perspectives," Development Economics Research Programme Working Paper No. 67, STICERD, London School of Economics and Political Science.

Chapter 7

Daron Acemoglu

ROOT CAUSES
A historical approach to assessing the role of institutions in economic development

TREMENDOUS DIFFERENCES IN INCOMES and standards of living exist today between the rich and the poor countries of the world. Average per capita income in sub-Saharan Africa, for example, is less than one-twentieth that in the United States. Explanations for why the economic fortunes of countries have diverged so much abound. Poor countries, such as those in sub-Saharan Africa, Central America, or South Asia, often lack functioning markets, their populations are poorly educated, and their machinery and technology are outdated or nonexistent. But these are only *proximate* causes of poverty, begging the question of why these places don't have better markets, better human capital, more investments, and better machinery and technology. There must be some *fundamental* causes leading to these outcomes, and via these channels, to dire poverty.

The two main candidates to explain the fundamental causes of differences in prosperity between countries are geography and institutions. The *geography hypothesis*, which has a large following both in the popular imagination and in academia, maintains that the geography, climate, and ecology of a society shape both its technology and the incentives of its inhabitants. It emphasizes forces of nature as a primary factor in the poverty of nations. The alternative, the *institutions hypothesis*, is about human influences. According to this view, some societies have good institutions that encourage investment in machinery, human capital, and better technologies, and, consequently, these countries achieve economic prosperity.

Good institutions have three key characteristics: enforcement of property rights for a broad cross section of society, so that a variety of individuals have incentives to invest and take part in economic life; constraints on the actions of elites, politicians, and other powerful groups, so that these people cannot expropriate the incomes and investments of others or create a highly uneven playing field; and some degree of equal opportunity for broad segments of society, so that individuals can make investments, especially in human capital, and participate in productive economic activities. These good institutions contrast with conditions in many societies of the world, throughout history and today, where the rule of law is applied selectively; property rights are nonexistent for the vast majority of the population; the elites have unlimited political and economic power; and only a small fraction of citizens have access to education, credit, and production opportunities.

Geography's influence

If you want to believe that geography is the key, look at a world map. Locate the poorest places in the world where per capita incomes are less than one-twentieth those in the United States. You will find almost all of them close to the equator, in very hot regions that experience periodic torrential rains and where, by definition, tropical diseases are widespread.

However, this evidence does not establish that geography is a primary influence on prosperity. It is true there is a *correlation* between geography and prosperity. But correlation does not prove causation. Most important, there are often omitted factors driving the associations we observe in the data.

Similarly, if you look around the world, you'll see that almost no wealthy country achieves this position without institutions protecting the property rights of investors and imposing some control over the government and elites. Once again, however, this correlation between institutions and economic development could reflect omitted factors or reverse causality.

To make progress in understanding the relative roles of geographic and institutional factors, we need to find a source of exogenous variation in institutions – in other words, a natural experiment where institutions change for reasons unrelated to potential omitted factors (and geographic factors remain constant, as they almost always do).

The colonization of much of the globe by Europeans starting in the fifteenth century provides such a natural experiment. The colonization experience transformed the institutions in many lands conquered or controlled by Europeans but, by and large, had no effect on their geographies. Therefore, if geography is the key factor determining the economic potential of an area or a country, the places that were rich before the arrival of the Europeans should have remained rich after the colonization experience and, in fact, should still be rich today. In other words, since the key determinant of prosperity remains the same, we should see a high degree of persistence in economic outcomes. If, on the other hand, it is institutions that are central, then those places where good institutions were introduced or developed should be richer than those in which Europeans introduced or maintained extractive institutions to plunder resources or exploit the non-European population.

Historical evidence suggests that Europeans indeed pursued very different colonization strategies, with very different associated institutions, in various colonies. At one extreme, Europeans set up exclusively extractive institutions, exemplified by the Belgian colonization of the Congo, slave plantations in the Caribbean, and forced labor systems in the mines of Central America. These institutions neither protected the property rights of regular citizens nor constrained the power of elites. At the other extreme, Europeans founded a number of colonies where they created settler societies, replicating – and often improving – the European form of institutions protecting private property. Primary examples of this mode of colonization include Australia, Canada, New Zealand, and the United States. The settlers in these societies also managed to place significant constraints on elites and politicians, even if they had to fight to achieve this objective.

Reversal of fortune

So what happened to economic development after colonization? Did places that were rich before colonization remain rich, as suggested by the geography hypothesis? Or did economic fortunes change systematically as a result of the changes in institutions?

The historical evidence shows no evidence of the persistence suggested by the geography hypothesis. On the contrary, there is a remarkable *reversal of fortune* in economic prosperity. Societies like the Mughals in India and the Aztecs and the Incas in America that were among the richest civilizations in 1500 are among the poorer societies of today. In contrast, countries occupying the territories of the less developed civilizations in North America, New Zealand, and Australia are now much *richer* than those in the lands of the Mughals, the Aztecs, and the Incas. Moreover, the reversal of fortune is not confined to this comparison. Using various proxies for prosperity before modern times, we can show that the reversal is a much more widespread phenomenon. For example, before industrialization, only relatively developed societies could sustain significant urbanization, so urbanization rates are a relatively good proxy for prosperity before European colonization. Figure 7.1 shows a strong negative relationship between urbanization rates in 1500 and income per capita today. That is, the former European colonies that are relatively rich today are those that were poor before the Europeans arrived.

This reversal is prima facie evidence against the most standard versions of the geography hypothesis discussed above: it cannot be that the climate, ecology, or disease environments of the tropical areas have condemned these countries to poverty today, because these same areas with the same climate, ecology, and disease environment were richer than the temperate areas 500 years ago. Although it is possible that the reversal may be related to geographic factors whose effects on economic prosperity vary over time – for example, certain characteristics that first cause prosperity then condemn nations to poverty – there is no evidence of any such factor or any support for sophisticated geography hypotheses of this sort.

Is the reversal of fortune consistent with the institutions hypothesis? The answer is yes. In fact, once we look at the variation in colonization strategies, we see that the reversal of fortune is exactly what the institutions hypothesis predicts. European colonialism made Europeans the most politically powerful group, with the capability to influence institutions more than any indigenous group was able to at the time. In places where Europeans did not settle and cared little about aggregate output and the welfare of the population, in places where there was a large population that could be coerced and employed cheaply in mines or in agriculture or simply taxed, in places where there were resources to be extracted, Europeans pursued the strategy of setting up extractive institutions or taking over existing extractive institutions and hierarchical structures. In those colonies, there were no constraints on the power of the elites (which were typically the Europeans themselves and their allies) and no civil or property rights for the majority of the population; in fact, many of them were forced into labor or enslaved. Contrasting with this pattern, in colonies where there was little to be extracted, where most of the land was empty, where the disease environment was favorable, Europeans settled in large numbers and developed laws and institutions to ensure that they themselves were protected, in both their political and their economic lives. In these colonies, the institutions were therefore much more conducive to investment and economic growth.

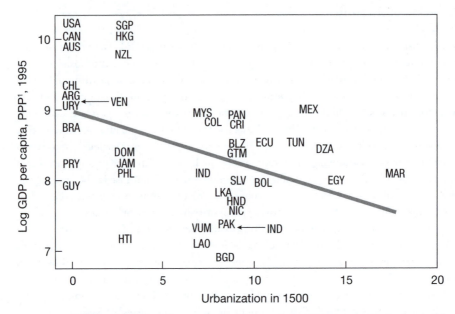

Figure 7.1 Shifting prosperity: Countries that were rich in 1500 are among the less well off societies today

Source: Author.

Note: ARG = Argentina, AUS = Australia, BGD = Bangladesh, BLZ = Belize, BOL = Bolivia, BRA = Brazil, CAN = Canada, CHL = Chile, COL = Colombia, CRI = Costa Rica, DOM = Dominican Republic, DZA = Albania, ECU = Ecuador, EGY = Egypt, GTM = Guatemala, GUY = Guyana, HKG = Hong Kong, SAR, HND = Honduras, HTI = Haiti, IDN = Indonesia, IND = India, LAO = Lao People's Democratic Republic, LKA = Sri Lanka, MAR = Morocco, MEX = Mexico, MYS = Malaysia, NIC = Nicaragua, NZL = New Zealand, PAK = Pakistan, PAN = Panama, PER = Peru, PHL = Philippines, PRY = Paraguay, SGP = Singapore, SLV = El Salvador, TUN = Tunisia, URY = Uruguay, USA = United States, VEN = Venezuela, VNM = Vietnam

[1]Purchasing power parity.

This evidence does not mean that geography does not matter at all, however. Which places were rich and which were poor before Europeans arrived might have been determined by geographic factors. These geographic factors also likely influenced the institutions that Europeans introduced. For example, the climate and soil quality in the Caribbean made it productive to grow sugar there, encouraging the development of a plantation system based on slavery. What the evidence shows instead is that geography neither condemns a nation to poverty nor guarantees its economic success. If you want to understand why a country is poor today, you have to look at its institutions rather than its geography.

No natural gravitation

If institutions are so important for economic prosperity, why do some societies choose or end up with bad institutions? Moreover, why do these bad institutions persist long after their disastrous consequences are apparent? Is it an accident of history or the result of misconceptions or mistakes by societies or their policymakers? Recent empirical and theoretical research suggests that the answer is no: there are no compelling reasons to think that societies will naturally gravitate toward good institutions. Institutions not only affect the economic prospects of nations but are also central to the distribution of income among individuals and groups in society – in other words, institutions not only affect the size of the social pie, but also how it is distributed.

This perspective implies that a potential change from dysfunctional and bad institutions toward better ones that will increase the size of the social pie may nonetheless be blocked when such a change significantly reduces the slice that powerful groups receive from the pie and when they cannot be credibly compensated for this loss. That there is no natural gravitation toward good institutions is illustrated by the attitudes of the landed elites and the emperors in Austria-Hungary and in Russia during the nineteenth century. These elite groups blocked industrialization and even the introduction of railways and protected the old regime because they realized capitalist growth and industrialization would reduce their power and their privileges.

Similarly, European colonists did not set up institutions to benefit society as a whole. They chose good institutions when it was in their interests to do so, when they would be the ones living under the umbrella of these institutions, as in much of the New World. In contrast, they introduced or maintained existing extractive institutions when it was in their interest to extract resources from the non-European populations of the colonies, as in much of Africa, Central America, the Caribbean, and South Asia. Furthermore, these extractive institutions showed no sign of evolving into better institutions, either under European control or once these colonies gained independence. In almost all cases, we can link the persistence of extractive institutions to the fact that, even after independence, the elites in these societies had a lot to lose from institutional reform. Their political power and claim to economic rents rested on the existing extractive institutions, as best illustrated by the Caribbean plantation owners whose wealth directly depended on slavery and extractive institutions. Any reform of the system, however beneficial for the country as a whole, would be a direct threat to the owners.

European colonialism is only one part of the story of the institutions of the former colonies, and many countries that never experienced European colonialism nonetheless suffer from institutional problems (while certain other former European colonies have arguably some of the best institutions in the world today). Nevertheless, the perspective developed in this article applies to these cases as well: institutional problems are important in a variety of instances, and, in most of these, the source of institutional problems and the difficulty of institutional reform lie in the fact that any major change creates winners and losers, and the potential losers are often powerful enough to resist change.

The persistence of institutions and potential resistance to reform do not mean that institutions are unchanging. There is often significant institutional evolution, and even highly dysfunctional institutions can be successfully transformed. For example, Botswana managed to build a functioning democracy after its independence from Britain and become the fastest-growing country in the world. Institutional change will happen either when groups that favor change become powerful enough to impose it on the potential losers, or when societies can strike a bargain with potential losers so as to credibly compensate them after the change takes place or, perhaps, shield them from the most adverse consequences of these changes. Recognizing the importance of institutions in economic development and the often formidable barriers to beneficial institutional reform is the first step toward significant progress in jump-starting rapid growth in many areas of the world today.

Note

This article draws on the author's joint work with Simon Johnson and James Robinson, in particular, on Daron Acemoglu, Simon Johnson, and James A. Robinson, 2001, "Colonial Origins of Comparative Development: An Empirical Investigation," *American Economic Review*, Vol. 91 (December), 1369–1401; Daron Acemoglu, Simon Johnson, and James A. Robinson, 2002, "Reversal of Fortune: Geography and Institutions in the Making of the Modern World Income Distribution," *Quarterly Journal of Economics*, Vol. CXVII (November), pp. 1231–94; and Daron Acemoglu and James A. Robinson, 2000, "Political Losers as a Barrier to Economic Development," *American Economic Review*, Vol. 90 (May), pp. 126–44, as well as on Daron Acemoglu, 2003, "Why Not a Political Coase Theorem? Social Conflict, Commitment and Politics," *Journal of Comparative Economics*, Vol. 31 (December), pp. 620–52.

REVIEW AND DISCUSSION QUESTIONS

1   According to the author, what are the characteristics of institutions that promote economic growth and development? Why are such characteristics conducive to development?

2   What empirical evidence does Acemoglu use to show that institutions are more important than geography in determining a country's economic development?

3   In what ways did geographical characteristics affect the institutions that European colonists established in many of today's developing countries?

4   What might prevent a change from "bad" to "good" institutions? Under what circumstances is such a change more likely to take place?

5   Do you believe that rich countries can help poor countries change their institutions? Why or why not? Explain.

Chapter 8

Dani Rodrik and Arvind Subramanian

THE PRIMACY OF INSTITUTIONS
(and what this does and does not mean)

EXPLAINING THE HUGE DIFFERENCE in average incomes between the world's richest and poorest nations is one of the most fundamental issues in development economics. How did this vast gulf emerge, and can anything be done to reduce it?

To answer these questions, we can seek guidance from three strands of thought. First, there is a long and distinguished line of theorizing that assigns a preeminent role to *geography*. Geography is the key determinant of climate and of natural resource endowments, and it can also play a fundamental role in the disease burden, transport costs, and extent of diffusion of technology from more advanced areas that societies experience. It therefore exerts a strong influence on agricultural productivity and the quality of human resources. Recent writings by Jared Diamond and Jeffrey Sachs [Chapter 9 in this Reader] are among the more notable works in this tradition.

A second view emphasizes the role of international trade as a driver of productivity change and income growth. We call this the *integration* view because it gives participation in the larger global economy – and impediments to participation – a starring role in fostering economic convergence between rich and poor regions of the world. The globalization debate, of course, is to a large extent about the merits of this integration view.

Finally, a third view centers on *institutions* – in particular, the role of property rights and the rule of law. In this view, what matters are the rules of the game in a society, as defined by prevailing explicit and implicit behavioral norms and their ability to create appropriate incentives for desirable economic behavior. This view, associated perhaps most strongly with Nobel Prize winner Douglass North, has recently been the subject of a number of econometric studies, in particular by Daron Acemoglu [Chapter 7 in this Reader], Simon Johnson, and James Robinson.

The idea that one, or even all, of the above deep determinants can adequately explain the large variations in income levels between countries may seem, on the face of it, preposterous. But economists like parsimony, and we were keen to see how these theories would fare when tested simultaneously against each other. Using regression analysis, we came up with some sharp and striking results that have broad implications for development conditionality, discussed below. Our results indicate that the quality of institutions overrides everything else. Controlling for institutions, geography has, at best, weak direct effects on incomes, although it has a strong indirect effect through institutions by influencing their quality. Similarly, trade has a significant effect on institutional quality, but it has no direct positive effect on income. How did we arrive at these findings?

Complex causality

Devising a reasonable empirical strategy for ascertaining how much of the variation in income levels between countries these three deep determinants can explain and whether they are all equally important is not straightforward. The difficulty lies in disentangling the complex web of causality involving these factors and income levels, as Figure 8.1 illustrates.

Geography is the only one of these deep determinants that can be treated as exogenous or not influenced by income. As Figure 8.1 shows, geography can affect income directly (by determining, say, agricultural productivity) as well as indirectly, through its impact on the extent of market integration or on the quality of institutions. With trade integration and institutions, however, causality can run both ways. Integration can raise

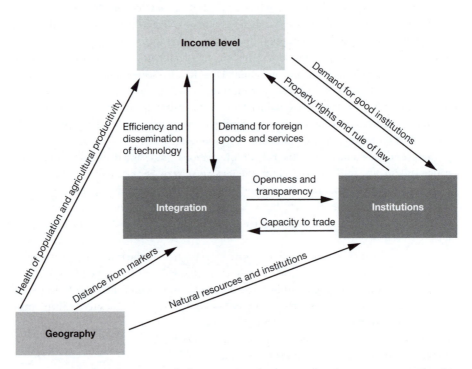

Figure 8.1 The "deep determinants" of income: Development and its determinants are related in multiple and complex ways, making the task of determining and quantifying causality difficult.

incomes, but it is equally possible for trade to be the result of increased productivity in an economy. And, while better institutions and better protection of property rights increase investment and foster technological progress, thereby raising income levels, better institutions can also be the outcome of economic development, not least because the demand for better institutions rises as countries and their citizens become wealthier.

In our research, we adopted a simple yet general research strategy that allowed us to estimate the elements shown in Figure 8.1 simultaneously while taking account of the complex structure of causality. In econometric terms, using an instrumental variables approach, we estimated a series of regressions relating income levels to measures of geography, integration, and institutions. In particular, we employed instruments for the two endogenous determinants – institutions and integration – drawing upon the 2001 work of Acemoglu, Johnson, and Robinson and the 1999 study by Jeffrey Frankel and David Romer, respectively. These instruments allow us to capture the variation in the determinant that is exogenous.

Our results, illustrated in Figure 8.2, show that the quality of institutions (as measured by a composite indicator of a number of elements that capture the protection afforded to property rights as well as the strength of the rule of law) is the only positive and significant determinant of income levels. Once institutions are controlled for, integration has no direct effect on incomes, while geography has at best weak direct effects. These results are very robust. They remain unchanged within a large range of reasonable alterations in our core econometric specification (different samples, alternative measures of geography and integration, different instruments, and additional covariates, among other things).

On the relationship between the determinants, we found that institutional quality always has a positive and significant effect on integration, while integration also has a (positive) impact on institutional quality – suggesting that trade can have an indirect effect on incomes by improving institutional quality. Our results also tend to confirm the 2002 findings of William Easterly and Ross Levine, who found geography to be an important determinant of the quality of institutions.

By how much can good institutions boost incomes? Our estimates indicate that an increase in institutional quality can produce large increases in income per capita. For example, in statistical terms, the difference between the quality of institutions measured

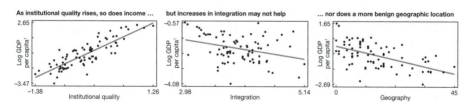

Figure 8.2 Institutional quality scores high: Institutional quality can boost income significantly, while global integration and geography, on their own, do not.

Source: Authors

Note. The graphs capture the causal impact of each of the determinants on income, after controlling for the impact of the others. The indicators of integration and geography used are the ratio of trade to GDP and distance from the equator, respectively. For further details, see Rodrik, Subramanian, and Trebbi (2002).

[1]Expressed in terms of purchasing power parity, 1995.

in Bolivia and Korea is equivalent to one standard deviation, or a 6.4-fold difference. In other words, if Bolivia were somehow to acquire institutions of the quality of Korea's, its GDP would be close to $18,000 rather than its current level of $2,700. Not coincidentally, this is roughly the income difference between the two countries.

Functions of institutions

Most of the recent work on institutions and economic growth has focused on the importance of a particular set of institutions, namely, those that protect property rights and ensure that contracts are enforced. We might call them *market-creating* institutions since, in their absence, markets either do not exist or perform very poorly. But long-run economic development requires more than just a boost to investment and entre-preneurship. It also requires effort to build three other types of institutions to sustain the growth momentum, build resilience to shocks, and facilitate socially acceptable burden sharing in response to such shocks. These institutions might be called

- *market regulating* – namely, those that deal with externalities, economies of scale, and imperfect information. Examples include regulatory agencies in telecommunications, transport, and financial services.
- *market stabilizing* – namely, those that ensure low inflation, minimize macroeconomic volatility, and avert financial crises. Examples include central banks, exchange rate regimes, and budgetary and fiscal rules.
- *market legitimizing* – namely, those that provide social protection and insurance, involve redistribution, and manage conflict. Examples include pension systems, unemployment insurance schemes, and other social funds.

Evidence of some of the stabilizing and legitimizing functions of institutions comes from a study, published by Rodrik in 1999, of the experiences of a number of sub-Saharan African countries. No fewer than 15 such countries grew at rates exceeding 2.5 percent a year before 1973. But, because of weak domestic institutions, few of them, if any, were able to withstand the effects of the oil price increases and other macroeconomic shocks in the 1970s, so growth declined sharply in the subsequent period. Macroeconomic responses to such shocks entail serious distributional implications. For example, in response to a balance of payments crisis, countries need to reduce aggregate demand by tightening fiscal policies. But which ones, and how? Should fiscal tightening take the form of tax increases or expenditure reductions? If the latter, should spending cuts fall on defense, capital, health, or education? Robust domestic institutions, especially those that provide for wide participation, allow these conflicts to be handled at the least possible cost and prevent domestic social and political conflicts from magnifying the initial economic shock.

But form doesn't follow function

Institutions are thus critical to the development process. But for each of the functions performed by institutions, there is an array of choices about their specific form. What type of legal regime should a country adopt – common law, civil law, or some hybrid? What is the right balance between competition and regulation in overcoming some of the standard market failures? What is the appropriate size of the public sector? How much discretion and how much flexibility should there be in arrangements for the conduct of fiscal, monetary, and exchange rate policies?

Unfortunately, economic analysis provides surprisingly little guidance in answering these questions. Indeed, there is growing evidence that desirable institutional arrangements have a large element of context specificity arising from differences in historical trajectories, geography, political economy, and other initial conditions. This could help explain why successful developing countries have almost always combined unorthodox elements with orthodox policies. East Asia combined outward orientation with industrial intervention. China grafted a market system on a planned economy rather than eliminate central planning altogether. Mauritius carved out export-processing zones rather than liberalize across the board. Even Chile combined capital controls with otherwise quite orthodox economic arrangements. Such variations could also account for why major institutional differences – in the role of the public sector, the nature of the legal systems, corporate governance, financial markets, labor markets, and social insurance mechanisms, among others – persist among the advanced countries of North America, Western Europe, and Japan. Moreover, institutional solutions that perform well in one setting may be inappropriate in a setting without the supporting norms and complementary institutions. In other words, institutional innovations do not necessarily travel well.

How then should institutional choices be made? While economic analysis can help by identifying the incentive effects of alternative arrangements and the relevant trade-offs, there is a very large role for public deliberation and collective choice within societies. In fact, political democracy can be thought of as a metainstitution that helps societies make choices about the institutions they want. Indeed, while measures of democracy do not always explain which countries grow faster or slower over selected periods of time, they do explain long-term income levels. That is, while it is possible that growth spurts can be achieved with different political institutional arrangements, as the experience after World War II confirms, it appears that sustaining such spurts and transforming them into consistently higher standards of living are facilitated by democracy.

Are development outcomes predetermined?

Does the strong role of history and geography in shaping institutions mean that current policies have little impact and the trajectory of human development is predetermined? Some researchers say yes. Easterly and Levine, for example, insist that policies have no impact on income levels once institutions are controlled for. But nothing in our work lends support to such a predestinarian view. Indeed, we would argue that the framework employed in recent published research is not really appropriate for testing whether or not policies have an impact. What is explained – levels of income – is a very long term phenomenon, the result of cumulative actions for centuries or longer. To expect that policies, measured over shorter periods, could explain such a long-term phenomenon is unreasonable.

Moreover, although institutions change slowly, they do change. For example, between the 1970s and the 1990s, there were some notable changes in the quality of institutions.

One indicator of institutional quality is the index measuring the constraint on the executive branch of government. Twenty countries improved their institutional quality ratings by more than 40 percent. Of course, how institutional change can be effected is a difficult question – perhaps at the core of many current debates about growth and development – but that institutions can change and that they have a lasting impact on development should not be in doubt.

Implications for development lending

Our findings should raise serious questions about how the IMF and the World Bank set conditions for loans, so-called conditionality. If institutional change is slow, the time horizons for structural adjustment programs need to reflect this. Adjustment that would sustainably improve development prospects simply cannot happen over three or five years – the typical duration of these programs. To believe and plan otherwise risks the near certainty of expectations being unrealized.

Less obviously, if institutions are indeed the deep determinants of development, then we cannot evaluate traditional policies – fiscal, monetary, exchange rates, structural reforms – simply by looking at their intended effects. When the underlying institutions are not being changed in the appropriate way, conditionality on policies is often ineffective. Therefore, the exclusive focus in conditionality on getting policies right needs to be rethought. Take Nigeria, where the policy exhortation to prudently save oil revenues has been systematically ignored. Was it ever realistic to expect Nigeria to meet fiscal policy targets involving the smoothing of expenditure of oil revenues?

The norm in conditionality over the years has been to set what might be called micro targets relating to policies and outcomes. But in countries where the institutional preconditions were missing, conditionality was less likely to succeed. And where the institutional underpinnings existed, micro-conditionality was, in principle, superfluous. It is this recognition of the need to find the right institutional preconditions rather than to micromanage outcomes that is reflected in the recent move – exemplified by the United States' Millennium Challenge account and, to some extent, by the IMF's poverty reduction strategy paper (PRSP) process – of exploring new ways of achieving aid effectiveness.

A shift from current conditionality would have other advantages. Micro, outcome-based conditionality can be inconsistent with the spirit of ownership, which, properly defined, necessarily involves allowing countries a certain measure of freedom to find their own institutional and policy solutions to development problems.

Of course, identifying the appropriate institutional preconditions to ensure the effectiveness of development assistance is challenging. One possibility is to create a list of countries that would be certified as eligible for development assistance based on their fulfilling the requirements for a basic institutional framework: rule of law, independent judiciary, free press, and participatory politics. But such a list would raise a number of difficult questions. How should these requirements be measured? Can they be reasonably objective? What about countries that fail some of these requirements – as Chile, China, Korea, and Uganda would surely have done in the early stages of their growth? Then there is the converse problem. Would today's Nigeria and Indonesia, which would formally meet the requirements of a basic institutional framework, really provide assurances that development assistance would be well spent? Recent cross-country studies on the determinants of development are just a beginning that point us in the right direction, and a wide open and exciting area of research lies ahead.

Note

This article draws upon "Institutions Rule: The Primacy of Institutions over Geography and Integration in Economic Development," by Dani Rodrik, Arvind Subramanian, and Francesco Trebbi, NBER Working Paper 9305, October 2002 (Cambridge, Massachusetts: National Bureau of Economic Research).

References

Acemoglu, Daron, Simon Johnson, and James A. Robinson, 2001, "The Colonial Origins of Comparative Development: An Empirical Investigation," *American Economic Review*, Vol. 91 (December), pp. 1369–1401.

Diamond, Jared, 1997, *Guns, Germs, and Steel* (New York: W. W. Norton & Co).

Easterly, William, and Ross Levine, 2002, "Tropics, Germs, and Crops: How Endowments Influence Economic Development" (unpublished; Washington: Center for Global Development and Institute for International Economics).

Frankel, Jeffrey, and David Romer, 1999, "Does Trade Cause Growth?" *American Economic Review*, Vol. 89 (June), pp. 379–99.

North, Douglass C., 1990, *Institutions, Institutional Change and Economic Performance* (New York: Cambridge University Press).

Rodrik, Dani, 1999, "Where Did All the Growth Go? External Shocks, Social Conflict, and Growth Collapses," *Journal of Economic Growth*, Vol. 4, No. 4, pp. 385–412.

———, 2003, "Institutions, Integration, and Geography: In Search of the Deep Determinants of Economic Growth," in *In Search of Prosperity: Analytic Country Studies on Growth*, ed. by Dani Rodrik, (Princeton, New Jersey: Princeton University Press).

Sachs, Jeffrey D., 2001, "Tropical Underdevelopment," NBER Working Paper 8119 (Cambridge, Massachusetts: National Bureau of Economic Research).

REVIEW AND DISCUSSION QUESTIONS

1 According to the research by Rodrik and Subramanian, how do international trade and participation in the global economy affect income levels in developing countries? Explain clearly.

2 What do the authors mean by "market-legitimizing" institutions? Why do these institutions help economic growth and development?

3 If institutions that lead to development have specific characteristics, does that imply that there is one ideal set of institutions that most or all developing countries should adopt? Why or why not? Explain clearly.

4 According to the authors, how do changes in institutions take place?

5 Loans that international institutions make to poor countries to help them develop are often conditional on the recipient countries putting into effect certain reforms. How does the research by the authors provide guidance on setting such conditions?

Chapter 9

Jeffrey D. Sachs

INSTITUTIONS MATTER, BUT NOT FOR EVERYTHING

The role of geography and resource endowments in development shouldn't be underestimated

THE DEBATE OVER THE ROLE of institutions in economic development has become dangerously simplified. The vague concept of "institutions" has become, almost tautologically, the intermediate target for all efforts to improve an economy. If an economy is malfunctioning, the reasoning goes, something must be wrong with its institutions. In fact, recent papers have argued that institutions explain nearly everything about a country's level of economic development and that resource constraints, physical geography, economic policies, geopolitics, and other aspects of internal social structure, such as gender roles and inequalities between ethnic groups, have little or no effect. These papers have been written by such respected economists as Daron Acemoglu, Simon Johnson, and James Robinson; Dani Rodrik, Arvind Subramanian, and Francesco Trebbi; and William Easterly and Ross Levine.

Indeed, a single-factor explanation of something as important as economic development can be alluring, and the institutions-only argument has special allure for two additional reasons. First, it attributes high income levels in the United States, Europe, and Japan to allegedly superior social institutions; it even asserts that when incomes rise in other regions, they do so mainly because of the Western messages of freedom, property rights, and markets carried there by intrepid missionaries intent on economic development. Second, according to the argument, the rich world has little, if any, financial responsibility for the poor because development failures are the result of institutional failures and not of a lack of resources.

The problem is that the evidence simply does not support those conclusions. Institutions may matter, but they don't matter exclusively. The barriers to economic development in the poorest countries today are far more complex than institutional shortcomings. Rather than focus on improving institutions in sub-Saharan Africa, it would be wise to devote more effort to fighting AIDS, tuberculosis, and malaria; addressing the depletion of soil nutrients; and building more roads to connect remote populations to regional markets and coastal ports. In other words, sub-Saharan Africa and other regions struggling today for improved economic development require much more than lectures about good governance and institutions. They require direct interventions, backed by expanded donor assistance, to address disease, geographical isolation, low technological productivity, and resource limitations that trap them in poverty. Good governance and sound institutions would, no doubt, make such interventions more effective.

When economic growth fails

When Adam Smith, our profession's original and wisest champion of sound economic institutions, turned his eye to the poorest parts of the world in 1776, he did not so much as mention institutions in explaining their woes. It is worth quoting at length from Smith's *Wealth of Nations* on the plight of sub-Saharan Africa and central Asia, which remain the world's most troubled development hot spots:

> All the inland parts of Africa, and all that part of Asia which lies any considerable way north of the Euxine and Caspian seas, the ancient Scythia, the modern Tartary and Siberia, seem in all ages of the world to have been in the same barbarous and uncivilised state in which we find them at present. The Sea of Tartary is the frozen ocean which admits of no navigation, and though some of the greatest rivers in the world run through that country, they are at too great a distance from one another to carry commerce and communication through the greater part of it. There are in Africa none of those great inlets, such as the Baltic and Adriatic seas in Europe, the Mediterranean and Euxine seas in both Europe and Asia, and the gulfs of Arabia, Persia, India, Bengal, and Siam, in Asia, to carry maritime commerce into the interior parts of that great continent: and the great rivers of Africa are at too great a distance from one another to give occasion to any considerable inland navigation. (Book I, Chapter III)

Smith's point is that Africa and central Asia could not effectively participate in international trade because transport costs were simply too high. And, without international trade, both regions were condemned to small internal markets, an inefficient division of labor, and continued poverty. These disadvantages of the hinterland exist to this day.

Smith couldn't know the half of it. The problems of African isolation went far beyond mere transport costs. Characterized by the most adverse malaria ecology in the world, Africa was as effectively cut off from global trade and investment by that killer disease. Although the disease ecology of malaria was not understood properly until two centuries after Adam Smith, what was known demonstrated that Africa's suffering was unique. It had a climate conducive to year-round transmission of malaria and was home to a species of mosquito ideally suited to transmitting malaria from person to person. When Acemoglu, Johnson, and Robinson find that the high mortality rates of British soldiers around 1820 in various parts of the world correlate well with the low levels of GNP per capita in the 1990s, they are discovering the pernicious effects of malaria in blocking long-term economic development.

The ability of a disease to cut off economic development may seem surprising to some but reflects a lack of understanding of how disease can affect economic performance. Thus, in writing that malaria has a limited impact in sub-Saharan Africa because most adults have some acquired immunity, Acemoglu, Johnson, and Robinson completely neglect the fact that the disease dramatically lowers the returns on foreign investments and raises the transaction costs of international trade, migration, and tourism in malarial regions. This is like claiming that the effects of the recent SARS (Severe Acute Respiratory Syndrome) outbreak in Hong Kong SAR can be measured by the number of deaths so far attributable to the disease rather than by the severe disruption in travel to and from Asia.

In an environment in which capital and people can move around with relative ease, the disadvantages of adverse geography – physical isolation, endemic disease, or other local problems (such as poor soil fertility) – are magnified. It is probably true that when human capital is high enough in any location, physical capital will flow in as a complementary factor of production. Skilled workers can sell their outputs to world markets almost anywhere, over the Internet or by plane transport. Landlocked and at a high altitude, Denver can still serve as a high-tech hub of tourism, trade, and information technology. But when countries that are remote or have other problems related to their geography also have few skilled workers, these workers are much more likely to emigrate than to attract physical capital into the country. This is true even of geographically remote regions within countries. For example, China is having great difficulty attracting investments into its western provinces and is instead facing a massive shift of labor, including the west's few skilled workers, to the eastern and coastal provinces.

Recent history, then, confirms Smith's remarkable insights. Good institutions certainly matter, and bad institutions can sound the death knell of development even in favorable environments. But poor physical endowments may also hamper development. During the globalization of the past 20 years, economic performance has diverged markedly in the developing world, with countries falling into three broadly identifiable categories. First are the countries, and regions within countries, in which institutions, policies, and geography are all reasonably favorable. The coastal regions of east Asia (coastal China and essentially all of Korea, Taiwan Province of China, Hong Kong SAR, Singapore, Thailand, Malaysia, and Indonesia) have this beneficent combination and, as a result, have all become closely integrated with global production systems and benefited from large inflows of foreign capital.

Second are the regions that are relatively well endowed geographically but, for historical reasons, have had poor governance and institutions. These include the central European states, whose proximity to Western Europe brought them little benefit during the socialist regime. For such countries, institutional reforms are paramount. And, finally, there are impoverished regions with an unfavorable geography, such as most of sub-Saharan Africa, central Asia, large parts of the Andean region, and the highlands of Central America, where globalization has not succeeded in raising living standards and may, indeed, have accelerated the brain drain and capital outflows from the region. The countries that have experienced the severest economic failures in the recent past have all been characterized by initial low levels of income and small populations (and hence small internal markets) that live far from coasts and are burdened by disease, especially AIDS, tuberculosis, and malaria. These populations have essentially been trapped in poverty because of their inability to meet the market test for attracting private capital inflows.

When institutions *and* geography matter

It is a common mistake to believe – and a weak argument to make – that geography equals determinism. Even if good health is important to development, not all malarial regions are condemned to poverty. Rather, special investments are needed to fight malaria. Landlocked regions may be burdened by high transport costs but are not necessarily condemned to poverty. Rather, special investments in roads, communications, rail, and other transport and communications facilities are even more important in those regions than elsewhere. Such regions may also require special help from the outside world to initiate self-sustaining growth.

A poor coastal region near a natural harbor may be able to initiate long-term growth precisely because few financial resources are needed to build roads and port facilities to get started. An equally poor landlocked region, however, may be stuck in poverty in the absence of outside help. A major project to construct roads and a port would most likely exceed local financing possibilities and may well have a rate of return far below the world market cost of capital. The market may be right: it is unlikely to pay a market return to develop the hinterland without some kind of subsidy from the rest of the world. Nor will institutional reforms alone get the goods to market.

In the short term, only three alternatives may exist for an isolated region: continued impoverishment of its population; migration of the population from the interior to the coast; or sufficient foreign assistance to build the infrastructure needed to link the region profitably with world markets. Migration would be the purest free market approach, yet the international system denies that option on a systematic basis; migration is systemically feasible only within countries. When populations do migrate from the hinterlands, the host country often experiences a political upheaval. The large migration from Burkina Faso to Côte d'Ivoire was one trigger of recent ethnic riots and civil violence.

A fourth and longer-term strategy that merits consideration is regional integration: a breaking down of artificial political barriers that limit the size of markets and condemn isolated countries to relative poverty. In this regard, the recent initiative to strengthen subregional and regional cooperation in Africa should certainly be supported. Yet, given political realities, this process will be too slow, by itself, to overcome the crisis of the poorest inland regions.

A good test of successful development strategy in these geographically disadvantaged regions is whether development efforts succeed in attracting new capital inflows. The structural adjustment era in sub-Saharan Africa, for example, was very disappointing in this dimension. Although the region focused on economic reforms for nearly two decades, it attracted very little foreign (or even domestic) investment, and what it did attract largely benefited the primary commodity sectors. Indeed, these economies remained almost completely dependent on a few primary commodity exports. The reform efforts did not solve the underlying fundamental problems of disease, geographical isolation, and poor infrastructure. The countries, unattractive to potential investors, could not break free from the poverty trap, and market-based infrastructure projects could not make up the difference.

Helping the poorest regions

Development thinking and policy must return to the basics: both institutions and resource endowments are critical, not just one or the other. That point was clear enough to Adam Smith but has been forgotten somewhere along the way. A crucial corollary is that poverty traps are real: countries can be too poor to find their own way out of poverty. That is, some locales are not favorable enough to attract investors under current technological conditions and need international help in even greater amounts than have been made available to them in recent decades.

An appropriate starting point for the international community would be to set actual developmental goals for such regions rather than "make do" with whatever economic results emerge. The best standards, by far, would be the Millennium Development Goals, derived from the international commitments to poverty alleviation adopted by all countries of the world at the UN Millennium Assembly of September 2000. The goals call for halving the 1990 rates of poverty and hunger by the year 2015 and reducing child mortality rates by two-thirds. Dozens of the poorest countries – those trapped in poverty – are too far off track to achieve these goals. Fortunately, at last year's UN Financing for Development Conference held in Monterrey, Mexico, and at the World Summit on Sustainable Development held in Johannesburg, South Africa, the industrial world reiterated its commitment to help those countries by increasing debt relief and official development assistance, including concrete steps toward the international target of 0.7 percent of donor GNP. The extra $125 billion a year that would become available if official development assistance were raised from the current 0.2 percent of GNP to 0.7 percent of GNP should easily be enough to enable all well-governed poor countries to achieve the Millennium Development Goals. Like official development assistance, debt-relief mechanisms have been wholly inadequate to date.

Armed with these goals and assurances of increased donor assistance, the international community, both donors and recipients, should be able to identify, for each country and in much greater detail than in the recent past, those obstacles – whether institutional, geographical, or other (including barriers to trade in the rich countries) – that are truly impeding economic development. For each of the Millennium Development Goals, detailed interventions – including their costs, organization, delivery mechanisms, and monitoring – can be assessed and agreed upon by stakeholders and donors. By freeing our thinking from one-factor explanations and understanding that poverty may have as much to do with malaria as with the exchange rate, we will become much more creative and expansive in our approach to the poorest countries. And, with this broader view, the international institutions can also be much more successful than past generations in helping to free these countries from their economic suffering.

References

Acemoglu, Daron, Simon Johnson, and James A. Robinson, 2001, "The Colonial Origins of Comparative Development: An Empirical Investigation," *American Economic Review*, Vol. 91 (December), pp. 1369–1401.

Bloom, David E., and Jeffrey D. Sachs, 1998, "Geography, Demography, and Economic Growth in Africa," Brookings Papers on Economic Activity: 2, Brookings Institution, pp. 207–95.

Démurger, Sylvie, and others, 2002, "Geography, Economic Policy, and Regional Development in China," *Asian Economic Papers*, Vol. 1 (Winter), pp. 146–97.

Easterly, William, and Ross Levine, 2002, "Tropics, Germs and Crops: How Endowments Influence Economic Development," NBER Working Paper 9106 (Cambridge, Massachusetts: National Bureau of Economic Research).

Gallup, John Luke, and Jeffrey D. Sachs with Andrew D. Mellinger, 1998, "Geography and Economic Development," paper presented at the Annual World Bank Conference on Development Economics, Washington, D.C., April.

Rodrik, Dani, Arvind Subramanian, and Francesco Trebbi, 2002, "Institutions Rule: The Primacy of Institutions over Geography and Integration in Economic Development," NBER Working Paper 9305 (Cambridge, Massachusetts: National Bureau of Economic Research).

Sachs, Jeffrey D., 2002a, "A New Global Effort to Control Malaria," *Science*, Vol. 298 (October), pp. 122–24.

——, 2002b, "Resolving the Debt Crisis of Low-Income Countries," Brookings Papers on Economic Activity: 1, Brookings Institution, pp. 257–86.

——, 2003, "Institutions Don't Rule: Direct Effects of Geography on Per Capita Income," NBER Working Paper 9490 (Cambridge, Massachusetts: National Bureau of Economic Research).

—— and Pia Malaney, 2002, "The Economic and Social Burden of Malaria," *Nature Insight*, Vol. 415 (February), pp. 680–85.

United Nations Development Program, 2003, *Human Development Report* (New York).

REVIEW AND DISCUSSION QUESTIONS

1   In what ways, according to Sachs, do geographical characteristics help explain poverty in sub-Saharan Africa?

2   How does the experience of Denver, Colorado, help us understand what might allow developing countries to overcome geographical disadvantages? Explain.

3   Sachs believes that geography plays a key role in determining development, but he also believes that geographically disadvantaged countries are not doomed to poverty. What does it take, then, for such countries to develop?

4   Why does Sachs believe that economic development in geographically disadvantaged countries requires aid from the rich world?

5   Do you agree with Sachs's recommendations for how to help the poorest countries develop? Why or why not? Explain.

Chapter 10

Robert J. Barro

DEMOCRACY AND GROWTH

IT SOUNDS NICE TO TRY to install democracy in places like Haiti and Somalia, but does it make any sense? Would an increase in political freedom tend to spur economic freedoms – specifically property rights and free markets – and thereby spur economic growth? Is there a reasonable prospect that democratic institutions can be maintained in places with such low standards of living? History provides reasonably clear, even if unpleasant, answers to these questions. More political rights do not have an important impact on growth, but improvements in a broad concept of the standard of living tend strongly to precede expansions of political freedoms. In particular, democracies that arise in poor countries – sometimes because they are imposed from outside – typically do not last.

Theoretically, the effect of more democracy on growth is ambiguous. Some observers, such as Milton Friedman in *Capitalism and Freedom*, argue that political and economic freedoms are mutually reinforcing. In this view, an expansion of political rights – more "democracy" – fosters economic rights and tends thereby to stimulate growth.

But the growth-retarding features of democracy have also been stressed. One such mechanism is the tendency of majority voting to support social programs that redistribute income from rich to poor. These programs include graduated-rate income tax systems, land reforms, and welfare transfers. These activities may be desirable in some circumstances, but the required increases in marginal tax rates and other distortions inevitably reduce the incentives for investment, work effort, and growth.

Another adverse feature of representative democracy is the strong political power of interest groups, such as agriculture, environmental lobbies, defense contractors, and the handicapped. These groups tend to generate policies that redistribute resources in favor of themselves. These transfers create economic distortions that hamper growth, and the programs usually do not benefit the poor.

Authoritarian regimes may partially avoid these drawbacks of democracy. Moreover, nothing in principle prevents nondemocratic governments from maintaining economic freedoms and private property. A dictator does not have to engage in central planning. Recent examples of autocracies that have expanded economic freedoms include the Pinochet government in Chile, the Fujimori administration in Peru, to a lesser extent the shah's government in Iran, and several previous and current regimes in East Asia. Furthermore, most OECD (Organization of Economic Cooperation and Development) countries began their modern economic development in systems with limited political rights and became full-fledged representative democracies only much later.

The effects of autocracy on growth are adverse, however, if a dictator uses his or her power to steal the nation's wealth and carry out nonproductive investments. Many governments in Africa, some in Latin America, some in the formerly planned economies of Eastern Europe, and the Marcos administration in the Philippines seem to fit this model.

Thus, history suggests that dictators come in two types: one whose personal objectives often conflict with growth promotion and another whose interests dictate a preoccupation with economic development. The theory that determines which kind of dictatorship will prevail is missing. Absent this theory, the choice of a dictatorship can be viewed as a risky investment: economic outcomes may be very good or very bad but are surely uncertain.

Democratic institutions may avoid the worst types of results because they provide a check on governmental power. In particular, this check limits the potential of public officials to amass personal wealth and to carry out unpopular policies. Since at least some policies that stimulate growth will also be politically popular, more political rights tend to be growth enhancing on this count.

Overall, there is an abundance of interesting theories that relate democracy to growth, but these theories differ as to whether more democracy is favorable or unfavorable for growth. The net relation is therefore theoretically inconclusive, and we shall have to rely on empirical evidence to sort out the net effect.

The impact of democracy on growth is one thing; the other channel of influence is from economic development to a country's propensity to experience democracy. This issue requires a positive analysis of the choice of political institutions, but theoretical models of this process are not well developed. Nevertheless, a common view – put forward by Seymour Martin Upset in an article in 1959 (and attributed by him to Aristotle) – is that prosperity tends to inspire democracy. Although this "Lipset hypothesis" lacks a fully articulated theoretical foundation, it has been supported by many case studies.

It is possible to quantify and test the various hypotheses about the interaction between democracy and economic growth. Statistical analysis of data for around a hundred countries from 1960 to 1990 reveals a number of variables that systematically influence the growth rate of real per capita gross domestic product (GDP). The growth rate tends to be higher if a country has more human capital in the forms of health and education, a lower fertility rate, and less government spending on consumption. Also helpful are smaller distortions of market prices and an inclination and ability of the government to protect property rights. (The empirical measure of this last variable comes from a subjective index of the degree to which governments maintain the rule of law. These data, prepared for international investors by a consulting firm, were assembled in a study at American University by Stephen Knack and Philip Keefer, "Institutions and Economic Performance: Cross-country Tests Using Alternative Institutional Measures.") An improvement in the terms of trade has a small positive effect on growth, and a high propensity to invest also looks moderately favorable.

For given values of the variables already mentioned, the growth rate tends to be higher if a country starts with a lower level of real per capita GDP. That is, if a poor country can maintain satisfactory government policies and accumulate a reasonable level of human capital, then it tends to converge toward the richer places. Examples of this process are the high growth rates from 1960 to 1990 of some East Asian countries: Hong Kong, Singapore, South Korea, Taiwan, Malaysia, Indonesia, and Thailand. However, one reason that most poor countries remain poor is that their governments distort markets to a high degree and fail to maintain property rights.

A key question is the effect of democracy on growth for given values of the other variables. To address this issue I measured the degree of democracy by the indicator of political rights compiled for nearly all countries by Raymond Gastil and his followers in the serial publication *Freedom in the World*. The Gastil concept of political rights is indicated by his basic definition: "Political rights are rights to participate meaningfully in the political process. In a democracy this means the right of all adults to vote and compete for public office, and for elected representatives to have a decisive vote on public policies" (Gastil, 1986–1987 edition, p. 7). Thus, the definition is a relatively narrow one, which focuses on the role of elections and elected representatives.

Figure 10.1 shows the time path of the unweighted average of the democracy index for the available dates: 1960, 1965, and 1972–1994. (The values for 1960 and 1965 come from an article by Kenneth Bollen in the 1990 issue of *Studies in Comparative International Development*.) The index has been expressed here on a scale from zero to one, with zero indicating essentially no rights and one signifying the fullest rights. The number of countries covered rose from 98 in 1960, to 109 in 1965, and 134 from 1972 to 1994. The figure shows that the average value of the democracy index peaked at 0.66 in 1960, fell

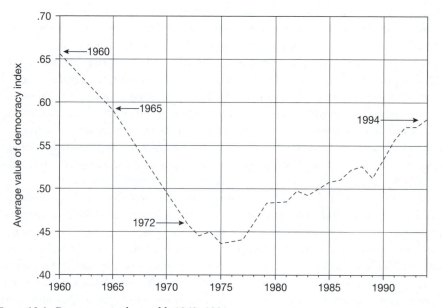

Figure 10.1 Democracy in the world, 1960–1994.

Source: Barro 1996.

to a low point of 0.44 in 1975, and rose subsequently to 0.58 in 1994. An important element behind this pattern is the experience in sub-Saharan Africa. Many of these countries began with democratic institutions when they became independent in the early 1960s, but most had evolved into nondemocratic states by the early 1970s. More recently, the extent of democracy in Africa and elsewhere has increased somewhat.

The net effect of more political freedom on growth is theoretically ambiguous. The quantitative analysis indicates that the overall effect is weakly negative but not statistically different from zero. There is some indication of a nonlinear relation in which more democracy raises growth when political freedoms are weak but depresses growth when a moderate amount of freedom has already been attained.

A story behind this relationship is that limitations on the ruler's power are the critical concern for an absolute dictatorship; hence, in this region, more democracy is positive for growth. When political freedom rises above a certain level – corresponding roughly in the empirical analysis to the situation of Mexico or Taiwan in 1994 – then further expansions of democracy create great pressure for social programs that redistribute wealth. These programs dilute incentives for investment and work effort and are therefore adverse for growth.

Democracy may also influence growth indirectly by affecting some of the variables that the statistical analysis holds constant. For example, democracy might stimulate female education (by promoting equality among the sexes), which in turn reduces fertility and infant mortality and thereby promotes growth. However, if fertility and female schooling are not held constant, then the overall effect of democracy on growth is still negative.

Another possibility is that democracy encourages maintenance of the rule of law. Although tests of this hypothesis are hampered by the limited availability of data on the rule-of-law concept, the information available suggests that, if anything, democracy is a moderate deterrent to the maintenance of the rule of law. This result is not surprising because more democracy means that the political process allows the majority to extract resources legally from minorities (or powerful interest groups to extract resources legally from the disorganized majority).

Good theories of why democracy expands or contracts seem to be missing. A look at the data suggests, however, that countries at low levels of development typically do not sustain democracy. For example, the political freedoms installed in most of the newly independent African states in the early 1960s did not last. Conversely, nondemocratic places that experience substantial economic development have a tendency to become more democratic – for example, Chile, Peru, Korea, Taiwan, Spain, and Portugal.

Formal statistical analysis demonstrates that countries with higher standards of living – measured by real per capita GDP, infant mortality, and male and female schooling – tend to approach higher levels of democracy over time. For example, a nondemocratic place with a high standard of living is predicted to become more democratic in the future. Conversely, a democratic country with a low standard of living is expected to lose political rights over time.

The results can be used to forecast changes in the level of democracy from the last value observed, 1994, into the future. Table 10.1 displays the cases of especially large projected changes in democracy from 1994 to 2000. The group with large anticipated increases, on the left side of the table, includes some countries that had virtually no political freedom in 1994. Some of these are among the world's poorest countries, such as Sudan and Gambia, for which the projected level of democracy in 2000 is also not high. These

Table 10.1   Countries forecasted to experience major changes in democracy: Projected
to be more democratic

Country	Democracy 1994	Democracy 2000
Indonesia	0.00	0.43
Bahrain	0.17	0.52
Hong Kong	0.33	0.67
Algeria	0.00	0.33
Syria	0.00	0.32
Singapore	0.33	0.61
Iran	0.17	0.41
Yugoslavia	0.17	0.41
Sudan	0.00	0.24
Gambia	0.00	0.24
Mexico	0.50	0.72
Tunisia	0.17	0.38
Iraq	0.00	0.21
Swaziland	0.17	0.35
Fiji	0.50	0.69
Sri Lanka	0.50	0.67
Peru	0.33	0.51
Turkey	0.33	0.50
Dominican Republic	0.50	0.66
Japan	0.83	0.98
Malawi	0.83	0.33
Mali	0.83	0.44
Benin	0.83	0.51
Zambia	0.67	0.35
Guinea-Bissau	0.67	0.35
Mozambique	0.67	0.36
Central African Republic	0.67	0.37
Niger	0.67	0.38
Bangladesh	0.83	0.56
Bolivia	0.83	0.58
Hungary	1.00	0.81
Pakistan	0.67	0.48
Mauritius	1.00	0.81
Papua New Guinea	0.83	0.66
South Africa	0.83	0.66
Botswana	0.83	0.66
Congo	0.50	0.36

Source: Barro 1996.

Note: The democracy index in 1994 is the value derived from the categories of political rights
presented in *Freedom in the World*. The value in 2000 is the projection based on the statistical analysis
discussed in the text.

countries are forecasted to raise their levels of democracy from 0 in 1994 to 0.24 in 2000, that is, roughly one-quarter of the way toward a full representative democracy. (Gambia is interesting in that it had maintained democracy for many years before a coup occurred in July 1994.)

Some other countries that had essentially no political freedom in 1994 are more well off economically and are therefore forecast to have greater increases in democracy; for example, the projected value in 2000 is 0.43 for Indonesia, 0.33 for Algeria, and 0.32 for Syria.

Expectations for large increases in democracy also apply to some reasonably prosperous places in which some political freedoms exist, but to an extent that lags behind the standard of living. As examples, Singapore is projected to increase its democracy index from 0.33 in 1994 to 0.61 in 2000, and Mexico is expected to go from 0.50 to 0.72.

The cases of large expected decreases in democracy, shown on the right side of table 10.1, consist mainly of relatively poor countries with surprisingly high levels of political freedom in 1994. Many of these are African countries in which the political institutions recently became more democratic: Malawi, Mali, Benin, Zambia, Guinea-Bissau, Mozambique, Central African Republic, and Niger. The prediction, as with the African experience of the 1960s, is that democracy that gets well ahead of economic development will not last. Two other African countries, Mauritius (which is not actually African) and Botswana, have maintained democratic institutions for some time, but the analysis still predicts that political freedoms will diminish in these places.

South Africa is also included on the right side of the table, with a projected decrease in the democracy index from 0.83 in 1994 to 0.66 in 2000. The political changes in South Africa raised the democracy indicator from 0.33 in 1993 to 0.83 in 1994. The statistical analysis says that this change was in the predicted direction but has likely overshot the long-run level.

To summarize, the interplay between democracy and economic development involves the effect of political freedom on growth and the influence of the standard of living on the extent of democracy. With respect to the determination of growth, the cross-country analysis brings out favorable effects from maintenance of the rule of law, free markets, small government consumption, and high human capital. Once these kinds of variables are held constant, an increase in political freedom has an overall negative (but small) impact on growth. The effect is positive at low levels of democracy but negative at higher levels.

With respect to the impact of economic development on democracy, the analysis shows that improvements in the standard of living – measured by a country's real per capita GDP, infant mortality, and education – substantially raise the probability that political institutions will become more democratic over time. Hence, political freedom emerges as a sort of luxury good. Rich places consume more democracy because this good is desirable for its own sake and even though the increased political freedom may have a small adverse effect on growth. Basically, rich countries can afford the reduced rate of economic progress.

The analysis has implications for the desirability of exporting democratic institutions from the advanced Western countries to developing nations. The first lesson is that more democracy is not the key to economic growth, although it may have a small beneficial effect for countries that start with few political rights. The second message is that political freedoms tend to erode over time if they get out of line with a country's standard of living.

The more general conclusion is that the advanced Western countries would contribute more to the welfare of poor nations by exporting their economic systems, notably property rights and free markets, rather than their political systems, which typically developed after reasonable standards of living had been attained. If economic freedom can be established in a poor country, then growth would be encouraged, and the country would tend eventually to become more democratic on its own. Thus, in the long run, the propagation of Western-style economic systems would also be the effective way to expand democracy in the world.

[. . .]

Reference

Barro, R.J. (1996) "Democracy and Growth." *Journal of Economic Growth* 1 (January).

REVIEW AND DISCUSSION QUESTIONS

1   Why does Barro argue that "theoretically, the effect of more democracy on growth is ambiguous"? Where does the ambiguity come from?
2   What are some of the variables that are associated with faster economic growth according to the evidence reviewed by Barro?
3   Barro finds evidence that there may be a "nonlinear relation" between democracy and growth. Explain what that means and how Barro interprets this evidence.
4   According to the author, in what ways do income levels in a certain country affect the likelihood that democracy will prevail and be sustained over time?
5   What is Barro's recommendation for how rich Western countries can best help poor countries develop? Do you agree with this recommendation? Why or why not?

Chapter 11

Hernando de Soto

THE MYSTERY OF CAPITAL

Why has the genesis of capital become such a mystery? And why have the rich nations of the world not explained to other nations how indispensable a formal property system is to capital formation?

WALK DOWN MOST ROADS in the Middle East, the former Soviet Union, or Latin America, and you will see many things: houses used for shelter; parcels of land being tilled, sowed, and harvested; merchandise being bought and sold. Assets in developing and former communist countries primarily serve these immediate physical purposes. In the West, however, the same assets also lead a parallel life as capital outside the physical world. They can be used to put in motion more production by securing the interests of other parties as "collateral" for a mortgage, for example, or by assuring the supply of other forms of credit and public utilities.

Why can't buildings and land elsewhere in the world also lead this parallel life? Why can't the enormous resources in developing and former communist countries, which my colleagues at the Institute for Liberty and Democracy (Lima) and I estimate at $9.3 trillion of dead capital, produce value beyond their "natural" state? My reply is, dead capital exists because we have forgotten (or perhaps never realized) that converting a physical asset to generate capital – using your house to borrow money to finance an enterprise, for example – requires a very complex process. It is not unlike the process that Albert Einstein taught us whereby a single brick can be made to release a huge amount of energy in the form of an atomic explosion. By analogy, capital is the result of discovering and unleashing potential energy from the trillions of bricks that the poor have accumulated in their buildings.

Clues from the past

To unravel the mystery of capital, we have to go back to the seminal meaning of the word. In medieval Latin, "capital" appears to have denoted head of cattle or other livestock, which have always been important sources of wealth beyond the basic meat, milk, hides, wool, and fuel they provide. Livestock can also reproduce themselves. Thus, the term "capital" begins to do two jobs simultaneously, capturing the physical dimension of assets (livestock) as well as their potential to generate surplus value. From the barnyard, it was only a short step to the desks of the inventors of economics, who generally defined "capital" as that part of a country's assets that initiates surplus production and increases productivity.

Great classical economists such as Adam Smith and, later, Karl Marx believed that capital was the engine that powered the market economy. In *The Wealth of Nations*, Smith emphasized one point that is at the very heart of the mystery we are trying to solve: for accumulated assets to become active capital and put additional production in motion, they must be *fixed and realized in some particular subject* "which lasts for some time at least after that labour is past. It is, as it were, a certain quantity of labour stocked and stored up to be employed, if necessary, upon some other occasion." What I take from Smith is that capital is not the accumulated stock of assets but the *potential* it holds to deploy new production. This potential is, of course, abstract. It must be processed and fixed into a tangible form before we can release it – just like the potential nuclear energy in Einstein's brick.

This essential meaning of capital has been lost to history. Capital is now confused with money, which is only one of the many forms in which it travels. It is always easier to remember a difficult concept in one of its tangible manifestations than in its essence. The mind wraps itself around "money" more easily than "capital." But it is a mistake to assume that money is what finally fixes capital. Money facilitates transactions, allowing us to buy and sell things, but it is not itself the progenitor of additional production.

Potential energy in assets

What is it that fixes the potential of an asset so that it can put additional production into motion? What detaches value from a simple house and fixes it in a way that allows us to realize it as capital?

We can begin to find an answer by using our energy analogy. Consider a mountain lake. We can think about this lake in its immediate physical context and see some primary uses for it, such as canoeing and fishing. But when we think about this same lake as an engineer would by focusing on its capacity to generate electrical energy, by means of a hydroelectric plant, as an additional value beyond the lake's natural state as a body of water, we suddenly see the potential created by the lake's elevated position. The challenge for the engineer is finding out how he can create a *process* that allows him to convert and fix this potential into a form that can be used to do additional work.

Capital, like energy, is a dormant value. Bringing it to life requires us to go beyond *looking* at our assets as they are to actively *thinking* about them as they could be. It requires a process for fixing an asset's economic potential into a form that can be used to initiate additional production.

Although the process that converts the potential energy in the water into electricity is well known, the one that gives assets the form required to put in motion more production is not known. This is so because that key process was not deliberately set up to create capital but for the more mundane purpose of protecting property ownership. As the property systems of Western nations grew, they developed, imperceptibly, a variety of mechanisms that gradually combined into a process that churned out capital as never before.

Hidden conversion process of the West

In the West, this formal property system begins to process assets into capital by describing and organizing the most economically and socially useful aspects about assets, preserving this information in a recording system – as insertions in a written ledger or a blip on a computer disk – and then embodying it in a title. A set of detailed and precise legal rules governs this entire process. Formal property records and titles thus represent our shared concept of what is economically meaningful about any asset. They capture and organize all the relevant information required to conceptualize the potential value of an asset and so allow us to control it.

Any asset whose economic and social aspects are not fixed in a formal property system is extremely hard to move in the market. How can the huge amounts of assets changing hands in a modern market economy be controlled, if not through a formal property process? Without such a system, any trade of an asset, say a piece of real estate, requires an enormous effort just to determine the basics of the transaction: Does the seller own the real estate and have the right to transfer it? Can he pledge it? Will the new owner be accepted as such by those who enforce property rights? What are the effective means to exclude other claimants? This is why the exchange of most assets outside the West is restricted to local circles of trading partners.

Developing and former communist countries' principal problem is clearly not the lack of entrepreneurship: the poor have accumulated trillions of dollars of real estate during the past forty years. What the poor lack is easy access to the property mechanisms that could legally fix the economic potential of their assets so that they could be used to produce, secure, or guarantee greater value in the expanded market.

Why has the genesis of capital become such a mystery? Why have the rich nations of the world, so quick with their economic advice, not explained how indispensable formal property is to capital formation? The answer is that the process within the formal property system that breaks down assets into capital is extremely difficult to visualize. It is hidden in thousands of pieces of legislation, statutes, regulations, and institutions that govern the system. Anyone trapped in such a legal morass would be hard-pressed to figure out how the system actually works. The only way to see it is from outside the system – from the extralegal sector – which is where my colleagues and I do most of our research.

The formal property systems of the West produce six effects that allow their citizens to generate capital.

(1) Fixing the economic potential of assets. Capital is born by representing in writing – in a title, a security, a contract, and other such records – the most economically and socially useful qualities *about* the asset as opposed to the visually more striking aspects of the asset. This is where potential value is first described and registered. The moment you focus your

attention on the title of a house, for example, and not on the house itself, you have automatically stepped from the material world into the conceptual universe where capital lives.

The proof that formal property is pure concept comes when a house changes hands: nothing physically changes. Property is not the house itself but an economic concept *about* the house, embodied in a legal representation that describes not its physical qualities but rather economically and socially meaningful qualities we humans have attributed to the house (such as the ability to use it for a variety of purposes – for example, to generate funds for investment in a business without having to sell the house – by providing security to lenders in the form of liens, mortgages, easements, or other covenants). In advanced nations, this formal property representation functions as the means to secure the interests of other parties and to create accountability by providing all the information, references, rules, and enforcement mechanisms required to do so.

Legal property thus gave the West the tools to produce surplus value over and above its physical assets. Whether anyone intended it or not, the legal property system became the staircase that took these nations from the universe of assets in their natural state to the conceptual universe of capital where assets can be viewed in their full productive potential.

(2) Integrating dispersed information into one system. The reason capitalism has triumphed in the West and sputtered in the rest of the world is because most of the assets in Western nations have been integrated into one formal representational system. This integration did not happen casually. Over decades in the nineteenth century, politicians, legislators, and judges pulled together the scattered facts and rules that had governed property throughout cities, villages, buildings, and farms and integrated them into one system. This "pulling together" of property representations, a revolutionary moment in the history of developed nations, deposited all the information and rules governing the accumulated wealth of their citizens into one knowledge base. Before that moment, information about assets was far less accessible. Every farm or settlement recorded its assets and the rules governing them in rudimentary ledgers, symbols, or oral testimony. But the information was atomized, dispersed, and not available to any one agent at any given moment.

Developing and former communist nations have not created unified formal property systems. In all of these countries I have studied, I have never found just one legal system but instead dozens and hundreds, managed by all sorts of organizations, some legal, others extralegal, ranging from small entrepreneurial groups to housing organizations. Consequently, what people in those countries can do with their property is limited to the imagination of the owners and their acquaintances. In Western countries, where property information is standardized and universally available, what owners can do with their assets benefits from the collective imagination of a larger network of people.

It may surprise the Western reader that most of the world's nations have yet to integrate extralegal property agreements into one formal legal system. For Westerners today, there supposedly is only one law – the official one. Diverse informal property arrangements, however, were once the norm in every nation – the West's reliance on integrated property systems is a phenomenon of at most the last two hundred years. The reason it is so hard to follow the history of the integration of widespread property systems is that the process took place over a very long time.

(3) Making people accountable. The integration of all property systems under one formal property law shifted the legitimacy of the rights of owners from the political context of

local communities to the impersonal context of law. Releasing owners from restrictive local arrangements and bringing them into a more integrated legal system facilitated their accountability.

By transforming people with real property interests into accountable individuals, formal property created individuals from masses. People no longer needed to rely on neighborhood relationships or make local arrangements to protect their rights to assets. They were thus freed to explore how to generate surplus value from their own assets. But there was a price to pay: once inside a formal property system, owners lost their anonymity while their individual accountability was reinforced. People who do not pay for goods or services they have consumed can be identified, charged interest penalties, fined, and embargoed, and can have their credit ratings downgraded. Authorities are able to learn about legal infractions and dishonored contracts; they can suspend services, place liens against property, and withdraw some or all of the privileges of legal property.

Respect in Western nations for property and transactions is hardly encoded in their citizens' DNA; it is rather the result of having enforceable formal property systems. Formal property's role in protecting not only ownership but also the security of transactions strongly encourages citizens in advanced countries to respect titles, honor contracts, and obey the law. Legal property thus invites commitment.

The lack of legal property thus explains why citizens in developing and former communist nations cannot make profitable contracts with strangers and cannot get credit, insurance, or utilities services: they have no property to lose. Because they have no legal property, they are taken seriously as contracting parties only by their immediate family and neighbors. People with nothing to lose are trapped in the grubby basement of the precapitalist world.

(4) *Making assets fungible*. One of the most important things a formal property system does is transform assets from a less accessible condition to a more accessible condition, so that they can do additional work. Unlike physical assets, representations of assets are easily combined, divided, mobilized, and used to stimulate business deals. By uncoupling the economic features of an asset from its rigid, physical state, a representation makes the asset "fungible" – able to be fashioned to suit practically any transaction.

By describing all assets in standard categories, an integrated formal property system enables the comparison of two architecturally different buildings constructed for the same purpose. This allows one to discriminate quickly and inexpensively between similarities and differences in assets without having to deal with each asset as if it were unique.

Standard property descriptions in the West are also written to facilitate the combination of assets. Formal property rules require assets to be described and characterized in a way that not only outlines their singularities but also points out their similarities to other assets, thus making potential combinations more obvious. Through the use of standardized records, one can determine how to exploit a particular asset most profitably.

Representations also enable one to divide assets without touching them. Whereas an asset such as a factory may be an indivisible unit in the real world, in the conceptual universe of formal property representation it can be subdivided into any number of portions. Citizens of advanced nations are thus able to split most of their assets into shares, each of which can be owned by different persons, with different rights, to carry out different functions.

Formal property representations can also serve as movable stand-ins for physical assets, enabling owners and entrepreneurs to simulate hypothetical situations in order to explore other profitable uses of their assets. In addition, all standard formal property documents are crafted in such a way as to facilitate the easy measurement of an asset's attributes. By providing standards, Western formal property systems have significantly reduced the transaction costs of mobilizing and using assets.

(5) Networking people. By making assets fungible, by attaching owners to assets, assets to addresses, and ownership to enforcement, and by making information on the history of assets and owners easily accessible, formal property systems converted the citizens of the West into a network of individually identifiable and accountable business agents. The formal property process created a whole infrastructure of connecting devices that, like a railway switchyard, allowed the assets (trains) to run safely between people (stations). Formal property's contribution to mankind is not the protection of ownership: squatters, housing organizations, mafias, and even primitive tribes manage to protect their assets quite efficiently. The property system's real breakthrough is that it radically improved the flow of communications about assets and their potential. It also enhanced the status of their owners.

Western legal property also provides businesses with information about assets and their owners, verifiable addresses, and objective records of property values, all of which lead to credit records. This information and the existence of integrated law make risk more manageable by spreading it through insurance-type devices as well as by pooling property to secure debts.

Few seem to have noticed that the legal property system of an advanced nation is the center of a complex web of connections that equips ordinary citizens to form ties with both the government and the private sector, and so to obtain additional goods and services. Without the tools of formal property, it is hard to see how assets could be used for everything they accomplish in the West.

(6) Protecting transactions. One important reason why the Western formal property system works like a network is that all the property records (titles, deeds, securities, and contracts that describe the economically significant aspects of assets) are continually tracked and protected as they travel through time and space. Public agencies are the stewards of an advanced nation's representations. They administer the files that contain all the economically useful descriptions of assets, whether land, buildings, chattels, ships, industries, mines, or airplanes. These files will alert anyone eager to use an asset about things that may restrict or enhance its utilization, such as encumbrances, easements, leases, arrears, bankruptcies, or mortgages. In addition to public record-keeping systems, many other private services (escrow and closing organizations, appraisers, etc.) have evolved to assist parties in fixing, moving, and tracking representations so they can easily and securely produce surplus value.

Although they are established to protect the security of both ownership and transactions, it is obvious that western systems emphasize the latter. Security is principally focused on producing trust in transactions so that people can more easily make their assets lead a parallel life as capital. The Western emphasis on the security of transactions allows citizens to move large amounts of assets with very few transactions. In most developing countries, by contrast, the law and official agencies are trapped by early colonial and Roman law, which tilt toward protecting ownership. They have become the custodians of the wishes of the dead.

Conclusion

Much of the marginalization of the poor in developing and former communist nations comes from their inability to benefit from the six effects that formal property provides. The challenge these countries face is not whether they should produce or receive more money but whether they can understand the legal institutions and summon the political will necessary to build a property system that is easily accessible to the poor.

The French historian Fernand Braudel found it a great mystery that at the inception of Western capitalism, it served only a privileged few, just as it does elsewhere in the world today:

> The key problem is to find out why that sector of society of the past, which I would not hesitate to call capitalist, should have lived as if in a bell jar, cut off from the rest; why was it not able to expand and conquer the whole of society? . . . [Why was it that] a significant rate of capital formation was possible only in certain sectors and not in the whole market economy of the time?

I believe the answer to Braudel's question lies in restricted access to formal property, both in the West's past and in developing and former communist countries today. Local and foreign investors do have capital; their assets are more or less integrated, fungible, networked, and protected by formal property systems. But they are only a tiny minority – those who can afford the expert lawyers, insider connections, and patience required to navigate the red tape of their property systems. The great majority of people, who cannot get the fruits of their labor represented by the formal property system, live outside Braudel's bell jar.

The bell jar makes capitalism a private club, open only to a privileged few, and enrages the billions standing outside looking in. This capitalist apartheid will inevitably continue until we all come to terms with the critical flaw in many countries' legal and political systems that prevents the majority from entering the formal property system.

The time is right to find out why most countries have not been able to create open formal property systems. This is the moment, as Third World and former communist nations are living through their most ambitious attempts to implement capitalist systems, to lift the bell jar.

Note

This article is derived from Chapter 3 of the author's book, *The Mystery of Capital: Why Capitalism Triumphs in the West and Fails Everywhere Else* (New York: Basic Books and London: Bantam Press/Random House, 2000).

Reference

Fernand Braudel, *The Wheels of Commerce* (New York: Harper and Row, 1982).
Adam Smith, *The Wealth of Nations* (1776; reprint, London: Everyman's Library, 1977).

REVIEW AND DISCUSSION QUESTIONS

1   How is "capital" different from "money" according to de Soto?
2   What role do titles and formal property records play in turning assets into capital?
3   How does a property system allow assets to "do additional work" according to the author?
4   In what ways are titles "connecting devices" that allow people to network and engage in business transactions?
5   According to de Soto, what does it take for a developing country to put into place a system of titles and property records?
6   The author argues that the lack of a formal property system is the key obstacle to economic development in poor countries. Do you agree with this view? Why or why not?

Chapter 12

Timur Kuran

WHY THE MIDDLE EAST IS ECONOMICALLY UNDERDEVELOPED
Historical mechanisms of institutional stagnation

A **MILLENNIUM AGO, AROUND ROUGHLY** the tenth century, the Middle East was an economically advanced region of the world, as measured by standard of living, technology, agricultural productivity, literacy or institutional creativity. Only China might have been even more developed. Subsequently, however, the Middle East failed to match the institutional transformation through which western Europe vastly increased its capacity to pool resources, coordinate productive activities and conduct exchanges. True, the institutional endowment of the Middle East continued to evolve. But in certain areas central to economic modernization change was minimal, at least in relation to the structural transformation of the West and, for that matter, the Middle East's own evolution during the early Islamic centuries. In eighteenth-century Cairo, credit practices hardly differed from those of the tenth century. Likewise, investors and traders were using enterprise forms essentially identical to those prevalent eight centuries earlier. By the nineteenth century, the entire Middle East was clearly "underdeveloped" relative to western Europe and its offshoots in the new world; and by the twenty-first century, it had fallen markedly behind parts of the Far East as well.

This essay offers reasons why the Middle East became underdeveloped. In particular, it points to certain Middle Eastern institutions, including ones rooted in the region's dominant religion, as past and in some cases also continuing obstacles to economic development. The institutions that generated evolutionary bottlenecks include: 1) the Islamic law of inheritance, which inhibited capital accumulation; 2) the strict individualism of Islamic law and its lack of a concept of corporation, which hindered organizational development and contributed to keeping civil society weak; and 3) the waqf, Islam's distinct form of trust, which locked vast resources into organizations likely to become dysfunctional over time. These institutions did not pose economic disadvantages at the time of their emergence. Nor did they ever cause an absolute decline in economic activity. They turned into handicaps by perpetuating themselves during the long period when the West developed the institutions of the modern economy.

Beginning in the eighteenth century, the Middle East's indigenous Christians and Jews came increasingly to dominate the most lucrative sectors of the local economy. They did so through the choice of law to which they had been entitled since the dawn of Islam. By exercising their choice of law in favor of modern legal systems of the West, they were able to escape the limitations of Islamic economic institutions. Especially in new economic sectors, including banking and insurance, they became decidedly more competitive than the region's Muslims, who lacked choice of law. Muslims began overcoming Islam's legal obstacles to economic development largely through secularizing legal reforms launched from the mid-nineteenth century onward. Until those reforms, Muslims were required to conduct commerce and finance under Islamic law.

In spite of a long string of institutional reforms over the past century and a half, traditional Islamic institutions remain a factor in the Middle East's economic backwardness. For example, weaknesses of the region's private economic sectors and their deficiencies of human capital are rooted in applications of Islamic law. Nothing in this essay implies, however, that Islam is *inherently* incompatible with economic growth, innovation or progress. If the Middle East failed to develop modern economic institutions on its own and was forced to transplant them from abroad, this was not because Islam expressly blocked economic advancement, but because of unintended interactions among Islamic institutions designed to serve laudable economic objectives, such as efficiency and equity.

The term "Middle East" admits many definitions. In the historical sweep of this paper, I am using it in a broad and elastic sense, to comprise not only the entire Arab world and Iran, but also Turkey, along with the Balkan peninsula, which was under Turkish rule during much of the period of interest. Spain belongs to the region up to the Reconquista – its reversion, by the end of the fifteenth century, from Muslim to Christian control.

The Middle Eastern economy, c. 1000

Islam's economic institutions did not emerge all at once, during the lifetime of Prophet Muhammad. Key elements were not present in 661, the end of Islam's canonical "age of felicity," which spanned the helmsmanships of Muhammad and his first four successors. Few economic institutions are even mentioned in the Qur'an, let alone described in detail. The distinguishing economic features of classical Islamic civilization evolved over the next three centuries or so, and not until around 1000 were the central economic institutions of the Middle East firmly in place. These institutions were to remain critical to the region's economy up to the nineteenth century. What follows is a deliberately selective account of the region's economic infrastructure around 1000. As we shall see, each of the identified institutions contributed to the observed delay in economic modernization.

Individually oriented contract law

During the first few centuries following the rise of Islam, Islamic law produced a rich set of principles, regulations and procedures to govern contractual relationships. There were rules to support the joint ownership of property. There were also rules to support the pooling of resources for commercial missions. Commercial partnerships established under Islamic law typically involved one sedentary investor who financed a trading mission run by a single traveling merchant. There could be any number of partners, but in practice the number rarely exceeded six. The cooperative enterprise was limited to a single mission. Nevertheless, compared to other legal systems of the time, this legal structure allowed traders and investors abundant flexibility in circumscribing the mission and setting profit shares (Udovitch, 1970; Çizakça, 1996).

To modern eyes, a striking aspect of classical Islamic law is that it provides no room for corporations – collective enterprises possessing legal rights distinct from those of the individuals who finance or serve it. A corporation can make and remake its own internal rules, possess property, make contracts and file legal claims. Its debts are not owed by its members as individuals. Its decisions do not require the approval of each of its members. It can live on after its founders die or retire. Islamic law recognized only flesh-and-blood individuals. Whereas the members of a partnership could sue one another as parties to a contract, their association had no legal standing of its own. A third party could sue one or more partners, but not the partnership itself.

Finance without banks

At the advent of Islam, money lending was a flourishing pursuit in the Middle East. By one interpretation of the Qur'an, Islam banned the use of interest in loan contracts. However, early Muslims did not achieve a consensus on the scope of this prohibition or even on the definition of "interest." Notwithstanding the persistent controversies, money lending continued, and often it involved transfers recognizable as interest. The jurists of Islam supported credit markets by devising, as in European territories under Christian rule, stratagems that allowed Muslims to circumvent Islam's presumed interest ban without violating its letter (Rodinson, 1966 [1973]).

That interest payments were common does not mean that credit markets resembled those of a modern economy. Uncertainty about the legitimacy of interest, combined with the lack of corporate law, meant that lenders as well as borrowers were usually individuals. Although some loans were provided through small and short-lived partnerships, there were no banks capable of pooling vast resources and of outliving their initial shareholders (Udovitch, 1979).

Arbitrary taxation and weak private property rights

Muslim-governed states of the Middle Ages followed two basic principles of governance: provisionism and fiscalism. Provisionism entails an emphasis on securing steady supplies of critical commodities, usually to keep urban populations content. Often it required the encouragement of imports and the discouragement of exports. Fiscalism signifies the relentless drive to extract resources from one's subjects.[1]

Starting with Muhammad, the earliest Muslim statesmen imposed taxes that were defined in relation to commodities known in the economy of Arabia. Within the span of a generation, as Islam spread to areas whose pre-Islamic civilizations were relatively complex – Palestine, Syria, Iraq, Iran – these policies became obsolete. Precedents thus emerged for adjusting tax rates to suit prevailing needs.

In principle, Muslims paid lower taxes than non-Muslims. In practice, since rulers imposed new taxes and fees wherever possible, faith-based tax discrimination was unsystematic, and Muslims did not necessarily receive more lenient treatment. Any community could also endure expropriation and the corvée – the requirement to contribute labor to state-sponsored projects, for example, road building. In times of crisis, rulers often resorted to confiscation and imposed new taxes.

Egalitarian inheritance system

Of the few economic rules set forth in the Qur'an, the most detailed and most explicit pertain to inheritance. Two-thirds of any estate is reserved according to intricate rules for a list of extended relatives of both sexes, including children, parents, spouse(s), siblings and, under certain circumstances, also more distant relatives. The individual's testamentary powers are limited to one-third of his or her estate. In addition, at least in the Sunni interpretation, no mandated heir may also be included in a will (Fyzee, 1964, chapters 11–13; Powers, 1990).

This inheritance system limited the concentration of wealth. By the same token, it hindered the preservation of successful enterprises, or other assets, across generations. True, one could hold any property undivided by forming a proprietary partnership or having a single heir buy out the rest. Nevertheless, the system's net effect was to fragment property, especially financial wealth.

Private provision of public goods through the waqf system

Before the modern era, states in the Middle East did not seek to micromanage their economy. They intervened only to pursue limited ends. Nor did they seek major roles in such areas as productivity, sanitation, health, welfare and mass education. By modern standards, they were strikingly disinclined to provide public or semipublic goods. Thus, few of the great mosques, libraries, caravanserais and charitable complexes of the time were financed or built by a state.

A vast array of social services, including public and semipublic goods, were supplied through an institution called the waqf, known also as a pious foundation or an Islamic trust. A waqf is an unincorporated trust founded under Islamic law by a person for the provision of a designated service in perpetuity (Çizakça, 2000; Kuran, 2001). One establishes a waqf by turning immovable private property into an endowment to support any social service permissible under Islamic law: a school, a lighthouse, an orphanage, a neighborhood's water supply, a mosque, among innumerable other possibilities. The beneficiaries need not be Muslims. The waqf came to play an increasingly important role in Muslim-governed states. In the memorable words of Marshall Hodgson (1974, p. 124), it became the primary "vehicle for financing Islam as a society." The incentives for founding waqfs were intimately related to certain institutions already presented.

Islam's original institutions did not include the waqf, which the Qur'an does not mention. The waqf was incorporated into Islamic culture a century after the rise of Islam, almost certainly as a creative response to the precariousness of private property rights. The lack of safeguards against opportunistic taxation and expropriation was an enormous source of concern to high officials, many of whom were major landowners. As individuals, they stood to gain from a device to shelter personal assets and enhance the material security of their families. Older civilizations of the eastern Mediterranean had developed various trust-like institutions. From these prototypes, Muslim officials of the eighth and later centuries developed a form of trust suited to their own needs.

Because waqfs were considered sacred, rulers were reluctant to confiscate their assets. Endowing a property as waqf thus gave it substantial immunity against expropriation. But if the founder's goal was to shelter assets for personal or family use, what was gained by converting them into an endowment to finance, say, a soup kitchen? The founder of a waqf enjoyed the privilege of appointing himself – less frequently, herself – its first mutawalli (trustee and manager). The mutawalli of a waqf could pay himself a handsome salary and appoint family members to paid positions. He could also circumvent Islam's inheritance regulations by designating a single child as his successor and disinheriting relatives of his choice. Establishing a waqf was not, then, merely an expression of charity. In addition to enhancing his control over the disposition of his wealth, its founder reduced the risk of losing it all to a revenue-hungry ruler. Could a person found a waqf to support a soup kitchen, and then reserve 99 percent of its revenue for personal use? No formal ceiling existed. Yet the prevailing norms typically required waqf founders to provide meaningful social services.

The waqf system represented, in effect, an implicit bargain between rulers and their wealthy subjects. Rulers made a credible commitment to leave certain property effectively in private hands; in return, waqf founders agreed to supply social services, thus unburdening the state of potential responsibilities. The system was basically decentralized. But rulers used moral suasion to encourage their close relatives and highest officials – two groups that founded most of the largest waqfs – to make choices compatible with the state's strategic objectives. The rule that the designated social service had to be supplied in perpetuity was undoubtedly meant to solve a principal-agent problem. The underlying motive must have been to keep the founder's agents – successive mutawallis – from misusing the resources under their control.

Legal pluralism

From the early days of Islam in the seventh century, Muslims were required to abide by Islamic law in all spheres of life. On commercial and financial matters, therefore, they had no say over the legal system within which they would operate, except insofar as opportunities existed to switch allegiance between Islam's four major schools of law. By contrast, at least in dealing among themselves, Christian and Jewish subjects could choose among co-existing legal systems; thus, they possessed "choice of law." Mixed cases – ones involving both Muslims and non-Muslims – were under the sole jurisdiction of Islamic courts. Islamic judges, or kadis, had to accept every case brought before them, even those strictly among non-Muslims.

Against this background, consider an investor and a merchant, both of the Greek Orthodox faith. They were free to form partnerships under Islamic law and to have any conflicts resolved in Islamic courts. Unlike Muslims, however, they could opt, alternatively, to use contractual forms prevalent in their own community and have disputes litigated in their own ecclesiastical courts. Indeed, non-Muslims could exercise choice of law both before the stage of contract choice (*ex ante*) and after agreeing to conduct a transaction under one particular law (*ex post*).

Merchants belonging to selected western nations – for example, Venice – enjoyed legal privileges that enhanced their incentives to do business in the eastern Mediterranean. These privileges included security of life and property, tax breaks, exemptions from various tolls and fees, and the right to operate special courts that would handle cases among themselves. Initially, such privileges came with reciprocal entitlements for Muslims.

Comparison with the medieval West

The foregoing patterns and institutions shaped the course of the Middle East's economic performance over the subsequent millennium. In western Europe, meanwhile, a generally similar, yet distinct, institutional endowment galvanized an extended transformation that culminated in the modern economy. Which elements of the Middle East's initial economic infrastructure differed from their coeval counterparts in the West, and which were functionally similar? Answering these questions will provide vital clues as to why the Middle East lagged in economic modernization.

To start with the similarities, contract law for individuals was essentially identical, and in neither region did the financial sector include banks. In western Europe, as in the Middle East, governments provided few social services. Legal pluralism was the norm in both regions, in each of which courts competed over the supply of legal services. Also shared was the practice of allowing selected foreigners their own legal jurisdictions.

There were also differences. Whereas Islamic law made no allowance for corporate structures, western cities, religious orders and universities were beginning to get organized as corporations (Berman, 1983, pp. 214–221, 239–240). Partly because of this institutional innovation, certain parts of Europe were developing a tradition of limited government, constrained taxation and secure private property. Merchant-dominated city-states, which had a strong interest in rapid economic growth, were emerging and gaining power (DeLong and Shleifer, 1993). Because the Bible does not specify a system for the disposition of estates, inheritance practices were more diverse and variable in the West than in the Middle East. The western trust developed later than the Islamic waqf. In any case, because private property was becoming more secure in western Europe, the incentives for sheltering wealth through a trust were relatively more limited (Kuran, 2001, pp. 876–883).

The consequences for economic performance did not become noticeable immediately. For the better part of the second millennium, the Middle East's institutional endowment afforded it a remarkable level of prosperity. Around 1200, no city in Christian-governed Europe could match the splendors of Baghdad or Seville. When the Turkish Sultan Mehmet II conquered the last remnants of Byzantium in 1453 and declared Istanbul the new capital of his expanding empire, he had the largest, best-supplied and technologically most sophisticated army in Europe – an achievement that would have been impossible if the Middle East were already an economic laggard. Nevertheless, the two regions were already on divergent institutional paths.

Our challenge, then, is to identify the causal mechanisms that contributed to this divergence and, in particular, to the Middle East's structural stagnation. As a prelude to identifying these mechanisms, I shall draw attention to four puzzling inter-regional contrasts of the nineteenth century. The rest of the article links each of these contrasts to initial differences in economic infrastructure.

Four key contrasts of the nineteenth century

A first contrast is that by the nineteenth century, French, English and other western enterprises established to pursue production or trade were often much larger in size and far more durable than leading enterprises of the Middle East. Established as joint-stock companies or corporations, these enterprises could exploit the economies of scale and scope made possible by new technologies. They also had long time horizons conducive to projects with extended gestation periods. Perpetual financial organizations identifiable as banks were in operation. Joint-stock companies and corporations were being formed through the mobilization of vast resources. Stock markets had been formed, allowing co-owners opportunities for convenient liquidation. The Middle East had not undergone such organizational developments. Although wealthy Middle Easterners invested in production, trade and finance, there were no examples of resource pooling involving mass participation. Pooling on a small scale took place through transient partnerships of the sort common a millennium earlier. There were no stock markets and no banks.

A second salient contrast of the nineteenth century is that the waqf system was failing to supply to the Middle East public services now being provided in the West on a large scale. These included street lighting, piped water, modern sanitation and mass education. The waqf system lacked the flexibility to reallocate its vast resources quickly to meet the emerging demand for these services. Unlike western municipalities and other governmental agencies, which were authorized to tax constituents, change their own budgets and impose new ordinances, the waqf system could not make the necessary adaptations.

Third, at the dawn of the modern global economy there was less material security in the Middle East than in the West. This was not simply a matter of disorder on trade routes. Arbitrary taxation and outright expropriations remained more common in the Middle East, where the state was still considered an extension of the ruler. Bribery was endemic. In the West, there had been successful efforts to make governments respect private property rights, to limit taxation and to curb corruption. Democratic rights had emerged, making governance generally more predictable. Furthermore, because economic growth was more rapid in places where government power was in check, places with relatively secure private property rights had gained social, political and economic importance.

Finally, as the Middle East fell into a state of underdevelopment, west European industrialists, merchants, and financiers came to play a growing role in its economy. In the process, moreover, local Christians and Jews began to register economic advances in relation to the Muslim majority. For example, they came to play highly disproportionate roles in trade with the West, local commerce in the largest cities and the nascent sectors of banking and insurance.

My explanations for these patterns will not presuppose that Islam retarded the Middle East's institutional evolution directly or intentionally. Rather, I shall argue that certain economic institutions of classical Islamic civilization interacted in unintended and unanticipated ways to block adaptations now recognized as critical to economic modernization.

Stagnation of Islamic contract law

The main form of commercial partnership used in the Middle East around 1000, the *mudāraba*, served to pool the capital of one or more investors with the labor of one or more traveling merchants. According to Islamic law, the contract became null and void if any partner died before fulfillment of the selected mission. The assets of the partnership then had to be divided among surviving partners and the decedent's heirs. The greater the number of heirs, the lower the capacity to renegotiate a new partnership aimed at completing the initially contracted mission. The prevailing inheritance system mattered, then, to contractual practices. In mandating the division of estates among a potentially very long list of relatives, the Islamic inheritance system created incentives for keeping partnerships small.

In turn, the prevalence of small partnerships kept the Middle East free of various organizational challenges that proved essential to economic development in western Europe. No need arose, for instance, to develop new accounting techniques, to create hierarchical management practices, to address problems of multipolar communication or to search for organizational forms conducive to resource pooling on a large scale. The Islamic inheritance system was designed to fragment wealth for egalitarian reasons, but it had the unintended effect of stifling organizational innovation (Kuran, 2003). At the end of the first millennium, Islamic contract law was admirably adapted to economic conditions of the time. But another Islamic institution limited its ability to spawn increasingly sophisticated enterprise forms.

As Islamic contract law stagnated, western Europe developed a series of new organizational forms capable of accommodating more members. Eventually they included joint-stock companies, which allowed partners to withdraw without requiring the remaining partners to renegotiate, and business corporations, which, in addition, had lives of their own. Around 1000, contract law was substantially the same in western Europe and the Middle East. For example, an Italian or French partnership, like its Islamic analogue, ended with the death of any partner. But the inheritance practices of medieval Europe showed far greater diversity than those of the Middle East, and because the Bible does not prescribe rules for transferring wealth across generations, Westerners found it relatively easy to vary inheritance practices in response to changing needs. Certain regions of western Europe adopted primogeniture – the practice of leaving all income-producing wealth, if not the entire estate, to the decedent's oldest son. When a partnership had to be dissolved following a death, primogeniture facilitated the mission's resumption by assigning the deceased partner's share to a single heir. In reducing the risk of channeling resources into large enterprises, western inheritance laws thus strengthened the incentive to form them.

Larger commercial and financial enterprises produced new communication and coordination problems, which then stimulated the development of modern forms and instruments of organization. The ensuing innovations include multi-divisional manage-ment, standardized accounting, stock markets and shareholder protection measures. The West thus experienced cumulatively revolutionary organizational advances that bypassed the Middle East.

Primogeniture never became the norm throughout western Europe. Precisely because the Bible provides no clear rule on inheritance, a wide variety of systems could be justified by picking and choosing among scriptures (Thirsk, 1976). However, by the sixteenth and seventeenth centuries, when western merchants controlled most of the trade between the Middle East and the West, primogeniture was the dominant inheritance practice in Britain, the Low Countries, Scandinavia and parts of France and Austria – areas that modernized relatively early. Also significant is that in the late seventeenth century the practice spread rapidly in Germany, over just a few decades (Fichtner, 1989, pp. 14–21 and 72–75; Goody, 1983, pp. 118–25; Platteau and Baland, 2001, especially section 3). In any case, none of the major inheritance systems in western Europe defined the family as broadly as the Qur'an does. As a rule, therefore, it proved much easier in the West than in the Middle East to keep assets intact across generations without resorting to devices such as the waqf.

Early in the second millennium, the promoters of primogeniture could not have imagined the institutions of the modern economy. Likewise, the interpreters and enforcers of Islamic inheritance rules could not have foreseen how these would put future merchants and financiers at a disadvantage in their dealings with Westerners. Although the two evolutionary paths are intelligible with the benefit of hindsight, each is a by-product of numerous adaptations spread across a millennium. This divergence raises, once again, the question of whether Islam somehow imparted rigidity to economic practices of the Middle East. Nothing in the foregoing account points to rigidity across the board, and we know that in some domains, including taxation, there was remarkable flexibility and ingenuity. What caused Islamic contract law to freeze was inflexibility in one specific domain, namely, inheritance.

Dysfunctional waqfs

The vast waqf system of the Middle East produced another set of adverse organizational consequences. A requirement of the implicit bargain that produced this system was that a waqf's functions be fixed in perpetuity. Specifically, neither the founder nor any mutawalli would be authorized to alter its mission or form of management. They had to follow the stipulations in the waqf deed to the letter. If the founder had specified the workforce, one could not add new employees to meet a new need; and if a new technology made it optimal to operate on a large scale, small waqfs could not pool their resources through a merger. A related difficulty lay in the lack of corporate status in Islamic law. The traditional waqf was a partial exception, for it could outlive its founder. Unlike a genuine corporation, however, it lacked legal status as an organization.

At least in principle, by freezing the waqf's functions, the state kept the mutawalli from misusing resources; and, for his part, the founder kept successive mutawallis faithful to his initial intentions. In practice, of course, the waqf system was not totally rigid. For one thing, waqf deeds contained ambiguities that allowed mutawallis some discretion. For another, judges empowered to oversee waqfs sometimes looked the other way as mutawallis made modifications. Ordinarily, however, it was difficult, if not impossible, for a waqf to restructure itself or redefine its mission in the face of new opportunities.

In a relatively fixed economic environment – one with unchanging technologies, demand patterns and supply conditions – this obstacle to change may not have been critical. In the rapidly changing economic conditions of the eighteenth and nineteenth centuries, it proved disastrous. Because the waqf system kept resources locked into uses decided centuries earlier, it became dysfunctional (Kuran, 2001). A glaring manifestation of this inflexibility is the system's slowness in providing new urban services; neighborhoods opted to establish western-style municipalities precisely because of barriers to making the existing waqfs modify their services and procedures.

Everywhere, one might observe, there have existed similar obstacles to resource reallocation. The rigidity of trusts is a salient theme in European economic history; and even today, university endowments contain restricted accounts to support awards in disciplines whose popularity has withered. Yet in the Islamic world, the waqf absorbed far more of society's resources than the trust did in the West, where, in the course of the second millennium, many social services came to be provided by self-governing and, hence, more flexible organizations. Also, the West had a greater variety of organizational forms, which allowed more experimentation in the delivery of services.

Why did the waqf not evolve into a genuine corporation able to remake its rules of operation, change its mission and reallocate resources of its own will? In the absence of corporate models to imitate, the required institutional leap was enormous, and to advocate organizational autonomy would have invited accusations of impiety. In the West, by contrast, as early as the tenth century, there existed organizations chartered as corporations. More important, perhaps, is that the usual responses to waqf rigidity – exploiting ambiguities in the founder's stipulations, waiting for a sympathetic judge, making modifications surreptitiously – dampened pressures for fundamental institutional reform. These essentially illegal practices also generated vast constituencies with a vested interest in the status quo. When their privileges came under challenge, these constituencies mounted heavy resistance. In sum, more or less illicit quick fixes inhibited efforts to find an efficient response to the steady demand for organizational flexibility. By the nineteenth century, many Middle Eastern policymakers understood the rigidities of the waqf system. New constituencies developed for supplying services such as water, sanitation and fire protection through alternative organizational forms, which were to be financed partly by dismantling the waqf system.

The rigidities of the waqf system had additional lasting consequences, also unintended and unanticipated. Given the vast economic weight of the system, efforts to circumvent its rules contributed to the prevalence of corruption, which, especially after the sixteenth century, local and foreign observers of the Middle East stressed ad nauseam as a barrier to trade and investment. When laws are commonly evaded, law breaking brings no major stigma and the costs of enforcement increase. Thus, following the imposition of new legal codes in the nineteenth century, actual practices changed very slowly.

The failure to turn the waqf into a self-governing organization prevented the strengthening of "civil society," which consists of segments of the social system that exist outside of direct state control. Forming an extended network of free associations, civil society serves two functions: it meets the fine-grained needs of diverse and possibly overlapping subcommunities; and it serves as a bulwark against despotism (Tocqueville, 1840 [1945], pp. 94–110). Very early in Islamic history, in the eighth century, the waqf system instituted one element of a strong civil society: the freedom to found nongovernmental organizations of one's choice. At the same time, by inhibiting autonomy, it caused established nonstate organizations to become inefficient, and it also kept them from becoming a political force for democratization. Still another consequence was a mindset inhospitable to political association. Insofar as the available organizational forms hindered effective political movements, people would have been reluctant to take the personal risks necessary for forming a strong civil society.

Retardation of modern rule of law

Limits on the powers of rulers developed more slowly in the Middle East than in western Europe. This is not the place to review the vast literature on the political transformation of the West. However, three observations about this transformation are particularly relevant. First, economic security and democratic rights emerged gradually in western Europe, over many centuries. Second, strengthening the rule of law required epic struggles between rulers and the ruled. The peoples of England, France and their neighbors fought hard and long for democratic rights. In particular, they struggled for judicial independence and for the right to sue royalty in independent courts. They strove also to limit government through institutional checks and balances. Third, many landowners and merchants stood at the forefront of these struggles. They financed and led campaigns to delegitimize and prevent capricious rule.

Why did the Islamic world experience such developments with a long delay and then only partially? Why was the first parliament of the Middle East – the Ottoman parliament in Istanbul – established only in 1876, and under western influences? Why, at the start of the nineteenth century, did taxation remain relatively arbitrary, private property rights generally insecure and the state bureaucracy essentially an extension of the ruler personally (İnalcık, 1994, chapters 1, 3–6; Imber, 2002, chapter 4; Findley, 1989, chapter 2)? Critical parts of the answers lie in the evolutionary mechanisms outlined earlier.

The rule of law is a public good. By the logic of collective action, people will tend to refrain from contributing to measures designed to strengthen it, except if they have an enormous stake in the outcome (Olson, 1971). Therefore, insofar as Islamic law discouraged the emergence of large and durable enterprises, it must also have hindered the advancement of political and economic liberties. Few of the relatively small merchants would have had a sufficient personal stake in democratization, or in stronger property rights, to participate in struggles toward these ends.

The Islamic inheritance system contributed to this limitation. It did so, first of all, by keeping partnerships small and, hence, commercial wealth limited. Secondly, it fragmented private fortunes achieved, against the odds, through concurrent and consecutive partnerships. Typically a successful merchant had many children, often from multiple wives, which increased the likelihood that his wealth would get fragmented. Third, severe restrictions on testamentary freedoms encouraged people to shelter resources within waqfs, which then dampened incentives to fight for individual rights.

Certain particularities of the waqf system compounded these obstacles to advancing personal rights. Unlike commercial wealth, real estate could be preserved intact within waqfs. On this basis, one might expect the waqf to have provided an economic basis for private coalitions aimed at checking the power of rulers. However, the requirement to follow the founder's wishes to the letter limited opportunities to channel resources into broad political causes. Moreover, mutawallis and other waqf beneficiaries lacked a pressing need for strengthening personal economic rights, precisely because their resources were already sheltered against taxation or expropriation. Put differently, by drawing people into structures that preserved some of their wealth, the waqf system dampened the demand for constitutionally enforced private property rights. Like the prevailing inheritance law, it became an institutional trap. Of course, had the Islamic inheritance system been more malleable, or more conducive to keeping fortunes intact, the waqf system would not have been so popular in the first place; and vested interests protecting the system would have been commensurately weaker.

Limited government, legally protected property rights and predictable taxation are known to stimulate economic development. It is not surprising, therefore, that a major empirical study of the determinants of contemporary government performance finds heavily Muslim countries to exhibit inferior government performance (La Porta, Lopez-de-Silanes, Shleifer and Vishny, 1999). In economically critical contexts, such countries were all governed, at least until the nineteenth century and in some cases until more recently, by Islamic law. As we have seen, certain characteristics of Islamic law, all present long before the Middle East became underdeveloped, galvanized extended processes that delayed improvements in governance.

A related literature finds systematic differences in economic practices between countries with legal systems in the common law tradition, which is of English origin, and those with legal systems in the civil law tradition, which goes back to the Romans and relies much more on statutes and comprehensive codes (La Porta, Lopez-de-Silanes, Shleifer and Vishny, 1998). Islamic law does not fit neatly into either tradition. Laws grounded explicitly in the Qur'an, such as inheritance law, resemble the civil law tradition. Yet, only a small fraction of the Islamic laws pertinent to economic development derive from scripture; for example, the Qur'an does not mention partnerships or waqfs, to say nothing of specifying how they shall operate. Many such institutions emerged gradually, as generations of judges reinterpreted existing practices, much like common-law judges who refine, modify and extend laws in the course of resolving specific disputes (Zubaida, 2003, especially chapter 2; Makdisi, 1999). The findings reported in this essay imply, then, that the substance of a legal system is as important to its evolution as its affinities to common or civil law. Institutional traps may block legal evolution in contexts governed by rules imposed from above, in a centralized manner; they may also do so in contexts in which judges decide cases in a decentralized manner, with opportunities for incremental change.

Rise of minorities

By the eighteenth century, western Europe was overwhelmingly better equipped to mobilize and accumulate capital than the Middle East. Western commercial and financial enterprises were much larger, more sophisticated and more durable. Western courts were better suited to handling disputes among modern enterprises. But nothing thus far explains why, as the Middle East became conspicuously underdeveloped, its major religious minorities advanced economically in relation to the Muslim majority. Making sense of why the region's indigenous Greeks, Armenians and Jews made remarkable economic leaps at this particular juncture requires attention to intercommunal differences in legal rights and privileges.

Under Islam's characteristic form of legal pluralism, both Muslims and non-Muslims could do business under Islamic law and appeal to a kadi (an Islamic judge) for adjudication of their disputes. However, only non-Muslims were authorized to have cases decided in a non-Islamic court, by non-Muslim judges. Prior to the eighteenth century, on matters of concern here, minorities tended to exercise their choice of law in favor of Islamic law. Three factors account for this pattern. First, because the decisions of Islamic courts were enforced more reliably, Christian and Jewish subjects were motivated to register property claims, credit contracts and partnerships before a kadi. Second, Islamic law offered substantive advantages to certain groups. For example, Jewish and Christian women found the Islamic inheritance system appealing inasmuch as it grants daughters and wives mandatory shares in any estate. Likewise, under Islamic law, business partners enjoyed relatively broader freedoms in setting profit shares. Not surprisingly, a steady theme in accounts of Jewish economic life under Islamic rule is that of rabbis complaining about merchants doing business "in the manner of Muslims" (Goitein, 1999, chapter 6; Shmuelevitz, 1984, chapter 2). Third, for non-Muslims, choice of law did not end with an agreement made under a non-Islamic legal system; a party to such a contract could opt, at any time, to renegotiate it before an Islamic court. Consequently, contracts made outside of the Islamic legal system lacked full credibility. Christian and Jewish communities used social pressures to limit opportunistic jurisdictional switches. But they could not eliminate the threat of opportunism, which is why they also took pains to anticipate challenges under Islamic law. Thus, in dividing estates, non-Muslim families usually gave women shares sufficiently large to keep them from requesting an Islamic settlement. The courts of the minorities tended to accept such adaptations, for the alternative was to compound the use of Islamic courts.

Prior to the eighteenth century, then, the region's religious minorities usually invested, borrowed and traded under the legal system of the Muslim majority. Accordingly, they enjoyed the advantages and endured the disadvantages of Islamic law, along with Muslims. This observation accords with the lack of major gaps in economic achievement among the principal religious communities. The sharing of legal practices also had far-reaching dynamic consequences. For one, non-Muslims must have found it as difficult as Muslims to accumulate private wealth and to preserve successful business enterprises beyond a single generation. For another, they would have remained as unmotivated to develop large and complex organizations.

With the economic rise of the West, Islamic legal pluralism turned from an obstacle to economic modernization into a vehicle for minority advancement (Kuran, 2004a). Specifically, Jewish and Christian Middle Easterners started using their customary choice of law to access western legal systems. A factor facilitating this access is that western traders had long enjoyed the privilege to settle their internal disputes in local consular courts; these courts began serving indigenous non-Muslims as well. Thus, from the late eighteenth century onward, hundreds of thousands of non-Muslims, including merchants and financiers, switched jurisdiction by obtaining, for a fee, the legal status of a western national. In the process, they became entitled to western tax reductions and exemptions won through bilateral treaties known as "capitulations." They also gained access to consular courts operating in many parts of the Middle East, including all major economic centers. Initially, the ability to use these consular courts was limited to cases involving no Muslims. Eventually, as the balance of military power between the Middle East and the West shifted in favor of the latter, west European diplomats managed to loosen the age-old ban against trying Muslims in non-Islamic courts. The norm came to be for all cases involving even one western citizen or protégé to be tried in a consular court. At least for non-Muslims, the danger of opportunistic jurisdictional switching also diminished, as foreign embassies gained the power to prevent their nationals and protégés from being tried in Islamic courts.

Christians and Jews of the Middle East derived palpable advantages from western legal codes. They could now make agreements involving various new organizational forms, including joint-stock companies and corporations. They could use modern banks. They could purchase insurance without the danger of a judge rejecting the contract as morally repugnant and legally invalid. By the late nineteenth century, practically all bankers and insurance agents in the Middle East were either western expatriates or local non-Muslims operating under a western legal system. Also, local representatives of western companies were drawn almost exclusively from these two groups. The largest and most lucrative businesses in major commercial centers such as Salonika, Istanbul, Izmir, Beirut and Alexandria were disproportionately owned and operated by religious minorities. Moreover, western banks, shipping companies and merchants now preferred dealing with religious minorities over Muslims, largely to avoid lawsuits in Islamic courts.

By the late nineteenth century, many Muslim manufacturers, merchants and financiers recognized the immense handicaps they faced on account of Islamic law. They realized that the region's age-old legal infrastructure precluded permanent organizations and hindered capital accumulation. They saw that Islamic courts were poorly equipped to litigate cases involving recently developed business techniques or organizational forms. Nevertheless, as individuals the vast majority remained reluctant to break with a legal tradition dating back to Islam's earliest period. Thus, practically no Muslims sought foreign legal protection. In any case, foreign consuls were reluctant to protect Muslims, for fear of diplomatic conflict.

For Muslims, the only feasible response to their growing positional losses was to broaden the legal systems under which they could do business. The first major reforms came in the mid-nineteenth century, with the establishment of specialized commercial courts in Istanbul, Cairo and Alexandria. Authorized to try cases without regard to religious affiliation and according to a commercial code largely transplanted from France, these new courts effectively narrowed the jurisdiction of traditional Islamic courts, setting a precedent for later curtailments.[2] In some places, beginning with the Republic of Turkey in the 1920s, Islamic law was abrogated in its entirety. Where it has survived, as in the Arabian monarchies, it has been modified beyond recognition in areas of relevance here (Comair-Obeid, 1996; Wilson, 1983). In most parts of the Middle East, the corporation is now an acceptable and popular organizational form. Insurance contracts are legally enforceable. Banks form an integral component of every economy. Contracts involving interest payments are commonplace, although in certain contexts and places such payments are disguised as "commissions" or "fees."

The persistence of Middle Eastern underdevelopment

For the Middle East, as for the rest of the non-western world, the economic transformation of the West presented both a vexing problem and a golden opportunity. On the one hand, it set the stage for a host of military, political and cultural challenges. On the other, it enabled the region to modernize in a hurry by borrowing institutions that in the West had developed slowly, in fits and starts, over many centuries. It might seem, therefore, that the underdevelopment of the Middle East could have been overcome quickly through institutional transplants. Yet even though key components of the western institutional infrastructure have already been adopted, the region as a whole remains underdeveloped. Why is the catch-up process proving so arduous?

Transplanting a legal code or institution is not the same thing as appropriating the entire social system that produced it. The performance of a legal code depends on the norms, other complementary institutions, and capabilities of the community putting it to use (North, 1990, chapter 5; Platteau, 2000, chapters 5–7). Consider the establishment, starting in the 1850s, of commercial courts modeled after those of France. The judges appointed to serve on these Turkish and Egyptian courts did not become proficient at applying the French commercial code overnight, and it took time to train competent lawyers. Likewise, local norms of fairness, responsibility and procedural correctness did not change instantly. Only slowly has the notion of attributing responsibility for an adverse externality to a judicial person, as opposed to a natural individual or group, taken root in the region's legal culture. Centuries of efforts to overcome the inflexibility of the waqf through illicit means presented yet another source of rigidity. These efforts had spawned a culture of corruption and nepotism, which now undermined campaigns to modify and strengthen the rule of law. In particular, these adverse traits influenced applications of the transplanted commercial code. If nepotism and judicial corruption remain rampant to this day, this is partly because state employees are accustomed to personalizing exchanges involving judicial persons.

The prevalence of corruption is evident in the "Corruption Perceptions Index" of Transparency International, an organization that monitors the business climate in most major countries. According to this index, businessmen consider corruption a significantly greater problem in the Middle East than in western Europe. On a zero to ten scale running from "least clean" to "most clean" government, the five most populated countries of western Europe (France, Germany, Italy, Spain and United Kingdom) received an average score of 7.1 in 2003, as against an average of 3.1 for Egypt, Iran and Turkey (Transparency International, 2003). Modifying the region's business cultures is proving far more difficult than rewriting formal laws.

Because the Middle East began to modernize without a strong civil society, states took the lead in many economic sectors that, in the West, had developed through decentralized private initiatives. The state-centered development programs prevalent in the region are often criticized, with much justification, for limiting private enterprise. Yet, state-centrism gained currency because the states formed after World War I had weak private sectors to start with; and that weakness itself was a legacy of Islamic inheritance practices. Whatever the benefits of state-centered development programs, they reinforced the prevailing infirmity of civil society. Furthermore, they fostered a suspicion of organized dissent and political decentralization, both essential to self-correction and innovation. The commonness of autocratic rule in the region stands, then, among the continuing legacies of traditional Islamic law.

The very condition of chronic economic underdevelopment has created obstacles to reform. By making the region chronically vulnerable to foreign meddling, and many individual countries ever dependent on foreign protection, it has bred complacency toward autocratic rule. The underlying logic is that steps toward democracy, by exposing previously hidden political cleavages and inviting further foreign interference, may cause political instability and, ultimately, economic collapse.

Through mechanisms discussed above, various Islamic institutions had hindered the accumulation of private capital, especially by Muslims. At the start of the twentieth century, almost all large commercial enterprises in the Middle East were owned by either foreigners or local religious minorities. With the departure of most of these entrepreneurs through nationalist movements partial to Muslims, population exchanges (most importantly, the Turkish-Greek population exchange of 1922–1923), and emigrations associated with the founding and Arab rejection of Israel, the Islamic Middle East's private sectors have been accumulating physical and human capital from low bases.

Nothing in my account makes the assumption, common in contemporary writings on the plight of the Middle East, that Islam is hostile to commerce, or that it discourages wealth creation or that it promotes irrationality.[3] Although Islam, like other religions, harbors elements inimical to economic productivity and efficiency, these elements have not formed an absolute barrier to economic growth or creativity. This is easily seen by examining the whole of the Middle East's economic history since the rise of Islam, as opposed to the last quarter-millennium in isolation. It is worth reiterating that only recently has this region qualified as "underdeveloped." What made the Middle East fall economically behind is not only that its own legal infrastructure essentially stagnated but that in the West a similar, but not identical, institutional endowment carried within it the seeds of economic modernization. Likewise, Middle Eastern Muslims fell behind the region's non-Muslims because the latter found it easier, partly as an unintended consequence of Islamic law itself, to overcome the economic handicaps rooted in that stagnation and begin benefiting from advances generated elsewhere.

The region's economic failures, combined with associated political insecurities, have contributed to the rise of Islamism – the diffuse global movement that aims to restore the primacy of traditional Islam by shielding Muslims from the transformative influences of globalization. Oddly enough, Islamists are eager to restore premodern economic relations in only certain areas. They seem to have little quarrel with corporations, joint-stock companies, stock markets or modern accounting, among other economic novelties of the past two centuries. Their opposition to the modern economy focuses on a few pet issues: the immorality of interest and insurance, the unfairness of certain inequalities, and the destructiveness of unregulated advertising and consumerism. Even on these matters, Islamists are divided among themselves, with some displaying acceptance of modern practices that others condemn as un-Islamic (Haneef, 1995; Kuran, 2004b). Yet, even militantly antimodern Islamists have had no notable successes in reversing past economic reforms. Islamism harms development mainly in two ways. In breeding political uncertainty, it lowers investment. It also induces policymakers and business leaders, including secularists, to eschew plans that might subject them to charges of impiety, thus reducing experimentation and discouraging creativity.

Of the institutions identified here as obstacles to indigenous economic modernization, one that remains largely in place is the Islamic inheritance system. Even in countries that have repudiated Islamic law to one degree or another, the prevailing inheritance system shares basic features with the traditional Islamic system, including rules against disinheriting relatives. Yet, now that the corporation and the joint-stock company are widely available organizational options, the Islamic inheritance system no longer poses a problem in regard to enterprise continuity or longevity. If these inheritance practices have any adverse effects today, they involve the monitoring of corporate managers and the fragmentation of agricultural land. They may be compounding the principal-agent problem inherent in the corporate form of organization, because, in fragmenting large blocks of shares, they dampen the incentive to monitor management. They also fragment agricultural land into uneconomically small farms, although the resulting inefficiencies are attenuated by land markets that reconsolidate divided plots.

The foregoing interpretations carry both a pessimistic message and an optimistic one. To start with the bad news, the Islamic Middle East cannot be lifted from its state of underdevelopment in the near term. Even if all the misguided government policies in the region were to disappear today, strong private sectors and civil societies could take decades to develop. The good news is that economic reforms are achievable without opposing Islam as a religion. Whatever the outcome of ongoing struggles over the interpretation of Islam in other areas – education, women's rights, expressive liberties – key economic institutions of modern capitalism were borrowed sufficiently long ago to make them seem un-foreign, and thus culturally acceptable, even to a self-consciously antimodern Islamist. Moreover, given Islam's long tradition of limiting the government's economic role, there is no fundamental conflict between Islam and an economic system based primarily on private enterprise.

Notes

The writing of this essay, which draws on the author's ongoing research projects, was supported by U.S. AID and the Earhart Foundation. Bradford De Long, James Hines, Andrei Shleifer, Timothy Taylor and Michael Waldman offered useful feedback.

1   These are two of the three principles that Genç (2000, chapters 1–4) identifies as the pillars of economic governance in the Ottoman Empire after it reached maturity. But they apply with equal force to earlier Muslim-governed states. The last of Genç's three principles, conservatism, was not yet an identifiable principle around 1000, which followed a period of sustained institutional innovation.
2   For an overview of the region's economic transformation that began in the nineteenth century, see Issawi (1982) and Owen (1993).
3   For a critical survey of these writings, see Kuran (1997).

References

Berman, Harold J. 1983. *Law and Revolution: The Formation of the Western Legal Tradition.* Cambridge, Mass.: Harvard University Press.
Çizakça, Murat. 1996. *A Comparative Evolution of Business Partnerships: The Islamic World and Europe, with Specific Reference to the Ottoman Archives.* Leiden: E.J. Brill.
Çizakça, Murat. 2000. *A History of Philanthropic Foundations: The Islamic World from the Seventh Century to the Present.* Istanbul: Boğaziçi University Press.
Comair-Obeid, Nayla. 1996. *The Law of Business Contracts in the Arab Middle East.* London: Kluwer Law.
DeLong, J. Bradford and Andrei Shleifer. 1993. "Princes and Merchants: European City Growth before the Industrial Revolution." *Journal of Law and Economics.* October, 36:2, pp. 671–702.
Fichtner, Paula Sutter. 1989. *Protestantism and Primogeniture in Early Modern Germany.* New Haven: Yale University Press.
Findley, Carter Vaughn. 1989. *Ottoman Civil Officialdom: A Social History.* Princeton: Princeton University Press.
Fyzee, Asaf A. A. 1964. *Outlines of Muhammadan Law.* London: Oxford University Press.
Genç, Mehmet. 2000. *Osmanlı İmparatorluğunda Devlet ve Ekonomi.* Istanbul: Ötüken.
Goitein, S. D. 1999. *A Mediterranean Society: An Abridgment in One Volume.* Berkeley: University of California Press.
Goody, Jack. 1983. *The Development of the Family and Marriage in Europe.* Cambridge: Cambridge University Press.
Haneef, Mohamed Aslam. 1995. *Contemporary Islamic Economic Thought: A Selected Comparative Analysis.* Petaling Jaya, Malaysia: Ikraq.

Hodgson, Marshall G. S. 1974. *The Venture of Islam: Conscience and History in a World Civilization.* Volume 2. Chicago: University of Chicago Press.

Imber, Colin. 2002. *The Ottoman Empire, 1300–1650: The Structure of Power.* New York: Palgrave.

İnalcık, Halil. 1994. "The Ottoman State: Economy and Society, 1300–1600," in *An Economic and Social History of the Ottoman Empire, 1300–1914.* Halil İnalcık with Donald Quataert, eds. New York: Cambridge University Press, pp. 9–410.

Issawi, Charles. 1982. *An Economic History of the Middle East and North Africa.* New York: Columbia University Press.

Kuran, Timur. 1997. "Islam and Underdevelopment: An Old Puzzle Revisited." *Journal of Institutional and Theoretical Economics.* March, 153:1, pp. 41–71.

Kuran, Timur. 2001. "The Provision of Public Goods under Islamic Law: Origins, Impact, and Limitations of the Waqf System." *Law and Society Review.* December, 35:4, pp. 841–97.

Kuran, Timur. 2003. "The Islamic Commercial Crisis: Institutional Roots of Economic Underdevelopment in the Middle East." *Journal of Economic History.* June, 63:2, pp. 414–46.

Kuran, Timur. 2004a. "The Economic Ascent of the Middle East's Religious Minorities: The Role of Islamic Legal Pluralism." *Journal of Legal Studies.* June, 33:2, pp. 475–515.

Kuran, Timur. 2004b. *Islam and Mammon: The Economic Predicaments of Islamism.* Princeton: Princeton University Press.

La Porta, Rafael, Florencio Lopez-de-Silanes, Andrei Shleifer and Robert W. Vishny. 1998. "Law and Finance." *Journal of Political Economy.* December, 106:6, pp. 1113–155.

La Porta, Rafael, Florencio Lopez-de-Silanes, Andrei Shleifer and Robert W. Vishny. 1999. "The Quality of Government." *Journal of Law, Economics, and Organization.* March, 15:1, pp. 222–79.

Makdisi, John A. 1999. "The Islamic Origins of the Common Law." *North Carolina Law Review.* June, 77:5, pp. 1635–739.

North, Douglass. 1990. *Institutions, Institutional Change and Economic Performance.* Cambridge: Cambridge University Press.

Olson, Mancur. 1971. *The Logic of Collective Action: Public Goods and the Theory of Groups.* Cambridge, Mass.: Harvard University Press.

Owen, Roger. 1993. *The Middle East in the World Economy, 1800–1914.* London: I. B. Tauris.

Platteau, Jean-Philippe. 2000. *Institutions, Social Norms, and Economic Development.* Amsterdam: Harwood.

Platteau, Jean-Philippe and Jean-Marie Baland. 2001. "Impartible Inheritance versus Equal Division: A Comparative Perspective Centered on Europe and sub-Saharan Africa," in *Access to Land, Rural Poverty, and Public Action.* Alain de Janvry, Gustavo Gordillo and Jean-Philippe Platteau, eds. Oxford: Oxford University Press, pp. 27–67.

Powers, David S. 1990. "The Islamic Inheritance System: A Socio-Historical Approach," in *Islamic Family Law.* Chibli Mallat and Jane Connors, eds. London: Graham and Trotman, pp. 11–30.

Rodinson, Maxime. 1966 [1973]. *Islam and Capitalism.* Brian Pearce, trans. New York: Pantheon.

Shmuelevitz, Aryeh. 1984. *The Jews of the Ottoman Empire in the Late Fifteenth and the Sixteenth Centuries: Administrative, Economic, Legal, and Social Relations as Reflected in the Responsa.* Leiden: E. J. Brill.

Thirsk, Joan. 1976. "The European Debate on Customs of Inheritance," in *Family and Inheritance: Rural Society in Western Europe, 1200–1800*. Jack Goody, Joan Thirsk and E.P. Thompson, eds. Cambridge: Cambridge University Press, pp. 177–91.

Tocqueville, Alexis de. 1945 [1840]. *Democracy in America*. Henry Reeve and Phillips Bradley, trans. New York: Alfred A. Knopf.

Transparency International. 2003. "Corruption Perceptions Index 2003." Available at <http://www.transparency.org/cpi/2003/>.

Udovitch, Abraham L. 1970. *Partnership and Profit in Medieval Islam*. Princeton: Princeton University Press.

Udovitch, Abraham L. 1979. "Bankers without Banks: Commerce, Banking, and Society in the Islamic World of the Middle Ages," in *The Dawn of Modern Banking*. Center for Medieval and Renaissance Studies, UCLA, ed. New Haven: Yale University Press, pp. 255–73.

Wilson, Rodney. 1983. *Banking and Finance in the Arab Middle East*. New York: St. Martin's Press.

Zubaida, Sami. 2003. *Law and Power in the Islamic World*. London: I.B. Tauris.

REVIEW AND DISCUSSION QUESTIONS

1 In what ways might Muslim inheritance rules be an obstacle to economic development in Middle Eastern countries?

2 Explain the role of the waqf system in traditional Muslim countries.

3 Why were business enterprises in European countries typically "larger in size and far more durable" than enterprises in the Middle East?

4 Why does the author believe that bribery and corruption were more widespread in Middle Eastern than in European countries?

5 In what ways were governments of Middle Eastern countries less effective at promoting economic development than European governments?

6 How does the author explain the fact that religious minorities in Middle Eastern countries experienced greater increases in standards of living than the Muslim majority?

7 The author argues that the Middle East is unlikely to make swift economic progress in the short run. Do you agree with his assessment? Why or why not?

Suggestions for further reading

Bardhan, P. (2005) *Scarcity, Conflicts, and Cooperation: Essays in the Political and Institutional Economics of Development*, Cambridge, MA: MIT Press.

In this collection of essays Bardhan summarizes and discusses recent research on the role of institutions and governance in economic development. Topics he addresses include democracy and poverty in India, decentralization of governance, corruption, and ethnic conflicts.

De Soto, H. (2000) *The Mystery of Capital: Why Capitalism Triumphs in the West and Fails Everywhere Else*, New York: Basic Books.

The Peruvian economist explains in this book how the lack of formal titles prevents developing countries from turning assets into productive capital. He also explains why governments have not tried to address this problem, why developing countries cannot simply import the Western legal system, and how U.S. history provides clues on solving the mystery of capital.

Hausmann, R. (2001) "Prisoners of Geography," *Foreign Policy*, 122: 44-53.

Hausmann discusses the channels through which a country's geography affects its economic development and cautions that geographical obstacles may prevent poor countries from improving standards of living. He suggests policies that may help such countries overcome geographical disadvantages and benefit from greater integration with the global economy.

North, D. C. (1990) *Institutions, Institutional Change and Economic Performance*, Cambridge: Cambridge University Press.

In this landmark book widely considered a capstone in the field of institutional economics, the Economics Nobel Laureate explains how different economic institutions lead to different economic outcomes and discusses how changes in institutions may affect a country's economic development.

North, D. C. (2005) *Understanding the Process of Economic Change*, Princeton, NJ: Princeton University Press.

Following up on his previous work on the role of institutions, in this book North explains how institutions change over time; he draws on psychology and cognitive science to shed light on economic change and help readers understand why certain countries may fail to develop.

Beyond growth

Inequality and poverty

INTRODUCTION

RECENT DATA SHOW THAT THE RICHEST 20 percent of Americans earns 45.8 percent of total U.S. income, whereas the poorest 20 percent earns only 5.4 percent. This implies that the richest 20 percent makes 8.5 times as much as the poorest 20 percent. This disparity may seem significant, but it pales in comparison to the income gaps found in many developing countries. In Brazil, for example, the richest 20 percent earns 22 times as much as the poorest 20 percent; in Bolivia, the income ratio between richest and poorest 20 percent is 42 to one; and in Namibia it is 56 to one. Such disparities are not found everywhere, however. In India, the income ratio between richest and poorest 20 percent is only 5.6; in Pakistan it is 4.3 (all data are from World Bank 2007).[1] The distribution of income varies widely across developing countries, but, on average, inequality is greater in poor than in rich countries.

How is poverty different from inequality? Inequality is only a relative measurement – it shows how large one person's income is *relative to* someone else's income. It does not tell us, however, how many people can afford to satisfy their basic needs and how many cannot. Poverty is an absolute measurement – it shows whether one person's income is above or below a certain level usually referred to as the "poverty line." Knowing that 58 percent of the population in Tanzania lives below the poverty line (ibid.), for example, tells us the share of the population that is unable to satisfy basic needs.[2] Unlike inequality, however, poverty does not tell us how much people are making relative to each other.

While poverty and inequality are different, they are also related to each other, although often in a complicated manner. In some countries, poverty and inequality may seem completely unrelated. For example, in a country where the average person is quite well off, it is possible to have high inequality but low poverty – the people at the bottom of the distribution make much less than those at the top, but even the relatively poor are above the poverty line (able to satisfy basic needs). Conversely, in a country where average incomes are low, i.e., close to the poverty line, it is possible to observe low inequality but high poverty – many people earn similar incomes, but many of these incomes fall below the poverty line. In developing countries where incomes are similar and the average is close to the poverty line, however, poverty and inequality tend to go hand in hand. That is simply because high inequality implies having a share of the population significantly below average, and if the average is close to the poverty line, being below average must imply being below the poverty line.

There are certainly moral and philosophical reasons to worry about the extent of income inequality; development economists, however, are primarily interested in the connections between inequality, poverty, and economic growth. Specifically, there have been a number of studies to investigate whether greater inequality may hinder or help economic growth and development. Without analyzing data, the nature of the link between inequality and growth is not obvious. One line of reasoning goes as follows. A person's ability to save depends on his or her income. The poor can barely afford to pay for their daily expenditures, but the rich earn enough to be able to save a share of their income. Equality in a poor country means that everyone is equally poor and likely unable to save. If the country has no saving, it has no money to invest in capital, infrastructure, or education, and economic growth is held back. If income distribution is unequal, however, a few people will be very poor and still save nothing, and a few people will have enough to save a share of their income. Inequality, therefore, will help generate some saving and promote growth (see, e.g., Helpman 2004: 91).

Greater inequality, however, may also be expected to hinder economic growth. In the article reprinted in Chapter 13, Center for Global Development President Nancy Birdsall explains why the negative effects of inequality on economic growth are more likely to be observed in developing countries. The share of the population below the poverty line when income distribution is unequal, for example, will largely be unable to contribute to economic growth – because it lacks education, it cannot afford to buy health care, or it may be unable to start new businesses because of difficulties borrowing money. Birdsall also notes that in poor countries inequality often implies a large group of poor people and the absence of a middle class; this situation may decrease support for government policies that would encourage growth. The availability of government-subsidized educational opportunities, for instance, can contribute significantly to economic growth; but high inequality might imply having a few rich families who are not interested in paying for public education (they plan to send their children to private schools anyway) and a large number of poor who do not have enough political strength to push the government to provide these opportunities. Birdsall goes on to consider the impact of globalization on income distribution and to recommend changes in international institutions and policies that would benefit the poor in developing countries.

As indicated above, inequality in developing countries is often connected to poverty. In many respects, poverty has become the key indicator that development economists use to assess progress toward economic development. Whereas it is possible – though unlikely – for economic growth to benefit disproportionately a small and relatively well-off segment of the population, observing changes in poverty means seeing directly whether and to what extent the poor are benefiting from any economic changes. It is difficult, however, to measure poverty adequately and to decide where the line that separates the poor from the non-poor should be. In the article reprinted in Chapter 14, MIT economists Abhijit V. Banerjee and Esther Duflo use data collected recently in several developing countries to try to describe the life of the extremely poor and to identify common threads, as well as differences, across countries. While much of what the data show is not surprising – e.g., the poor own very few durable goods, are often sick, and experience very high infant mortality – other findings are not what one might expect. For example, the authors find that expenditure on food only represents between half and three-quarters of the average family's expenditures; a substantial share of spending is on alcohol, tobacco, and forms of entertainment such as festivals. The poor also often choose more tasty and more expensive food over cheaper food that provides more calories. Banerjee and Duflo also review how the poor earn money, noting that they often run their own business rather than being employed by others. Such businesses, however, tend to be very small given that the poor have limited access to the credit that they would need to expand. The poor also tend to hold multiple occupations, and the authors speculate that this may be both because they are trying to reduce risk and because they lack the capital to expand any one of their activities to the point that all their time is used up by it. The overall picture that emerges points to the poor having and exercising certain choices, but in a context where innumerable constraints make daily life extremely trying and make improvements in standards of living very hard to achieve.

Governments in developing countries have designed over the years a variety of anti-poverty policies, with mixed outcomes. The article titled "New Thinking about an Old Problem," from *The Economist* (reprinted in Chapter 15), investigates a few Latin American poverty reduction programs that provide reason to be optimistic about anti-poverty policies in developing countries. These programs have focused on providing cash transfers to poor families who send their children to school and monitor their health. While fraud and inefficiencies remain, careful studies show that these programs have had a significant positive effect on both school enrolments and health conditions of poor children.

Even in very poor countries, poverty does not affect all people equally. The fact that 58 percent of the population of Tanzania lives below the poverty line suggests widespread deprivation throughout the country. Yet it also tells us that 42 percent of the population is *above* the poverty line. So which of Tanzania's residents live below the poverty line? Which are able to escape poverty in spite of living in a very poor country? Evidence collected in many countries shows that certain groups such as rural residents and ethnic minorities are systematically more likely to be poor (Todaro and Smith 2006: 225–32). Evidence also shows that women are more likely to be poor than men. The reading by the World Bank (reprinted in Chapter 16) summarizes an extensive study of economic development and gender that investigates some of the causes and consequences of gender inequality in developing countries. Gender disparities are shown to be significant in many countries, with women typically having less access to education and health care, fewer legal rights, more limited earning opportunities, and less ability to influence important economic decisions (within the household, the local community, or the country). The World Bank emphasizes the connection between gender inequality and lower standards of living – not just for women but for men as well. There is evidence, for example, that cash transfers directed specifically at women are more likely to be spent in ways that benefit the entire family. A well-known study of Brazilian households, for instance, found that increasing the mother's income has a much greater positive effect on the health of children than increasing the father's income (Thomas 1990).

Amartya Sen, in the chapter from his book *Development as Freedom* (reprinted in Chapter 17), also addresses gender inequality and introduces the concept of women's agency. Sen argues that while gender inequality hurts women's well-being, it also and more importantly stifles the ability of women to be "active agents of change" and "dynamic promoters of social transformations that can alter the lives of *both* women and men." Sen also emphasizes the connection between women's education and child mortality, pointing out that "the effect of female literacy on child mortality is extraordinarily large," and reminding us that male literacy or other general indicators of standards of living, on the other hand, have much smaller effects on the reduction of child mortality.

There is substantial evidence that economic growth and poverty reduction tend to go hand in hand. A study of 92 countries, for example, found that the income of the poorest 20 percent of the population grows as fast as the income of the average person in the population (Dollar and Kraay 2002). But simply assuming that poverty will automatically be reduced when economic growth takes place is dangerous. As the authors of the same study explain, the connection between growth and poverty reduction "does not mean that growth is all that is required to improve the lot of the poorest in society, and that the distributional effects of policies should be ignored" (ibid.: 198). Indeed, a study by World Bank economist François Bourguignon looks at about 50 developing countries and at the changes in poverty that took place over certain periods of time. It finds that "only half of the observed changes in poverty in the sample may be explained by economic growth, the remaining half being the result of changes in the distribution of relative incomes" (Bourguignon 2002: 3–4). Effective economic development policies require an understanding of the interactions between economic growth, income and wealth distribution, and poverty. To the extent that poverty does not affect everyone equally, assessing the distribution of poverty can also play a crucial role in helping governments target poverty reduction programs at the groups whose needs are most severe.

NOTES

1   Please see the notes to Table 2.7 in World Bank (2007) for more details on what these data mean and the extent to which they can be compared across countries. Note especially that numbers in some countries refer to shares of income whereas in other countries they refer to shares of total consumption (money spent on consumption is used as an approximation of standards of living). Also note that the data were collected in different years depending on the country.

2   Picking a poverty line, i.e., a level of income or consumption that separates the poor from the non-poor, is a challenging task. In a landmark 1990 study, the World Bank referred to the poverty line as representing "the expenditure necessary to buy a minimum standard of nutrition and other basic necessities and a further amount that varies from country to country, reflecting the cost of participating in the everyday life of society" (World Bank 1990: 26). The idea, therefore, is that being above the poverty line must mean something more than just being able to feed oneself. For a discussion of where to draw the line separating poor and non-poor see also UNDP (2003: 42) and World Bank (2001: 17).

REFERENCES

Bourguignon, F. (2002) "The Growth Elasticity of Poverty Reduction: Explaining Heterogeneity across Countries and Time Periods," Working Paper No. 2002–03, DELTA; reprinted in Eichler, T. and Turnovsky, S. (eds.) (2003) *Inequality and Growth: Theory and Policy Implications*, Cambridge, MA: MIT Press.

Dollar, D. and Kraay, A. (2002) "Growth is Good for the Poor," *Journal of Economic Growth*, 7: 195–225.

Helpman, E. (2004) *The Mystery of Economic Growth*, Cambridge, MA: Belknap Press.

Todaro, M. P. and Smith, S. C. (2006) *Economic Development*, 9th edn, Boston, MA: Pearson Addison Wesley.

Thomas, D. (1990) "Intra-Household Resource Allocation: An Inferential Approach," *Journal of Human Resources*, 25: 635–64.

UNDP (2003) *Human Development Report 2003*, New York: Oxford University Press.

World Bank (1990) *World Development Report 1990: Poverty*, Oxford: Oxford University Press.

—— (2001) *World Development Report 2000/2001: Attacking Poverty*, Oxford: Oxford University Press.

—— (2007) *World Development Indicators 2007*. Washington, DC: World Bank.

Chapter 13

Nancy Birdsall

INEQUALITY MATTERS

AFTER SPENDING THE LATE 1980s working on Latin America for the World Bank, I became involved in a major study of East Asia's postwar growth. The contrast between the two regions was notable: Latin America was stagnating while East Asian economies were growing rapidly, with tremendously high rates of private and public investment and savings. The emphasis on exports and the pressure to compete in global markets seemed to have worked.

The impressive growth in Taiwan, Korea, Hong Kong, and Singapore, and later in Malaysia, Indonesia, and Thailand, reflected and was reinforced by equally impressive changes in people's behavior and lives: unprecedented gains in small farmers' productivity, high demand for schooling (including schooling for girls), and declines in fertility far steeper and at lower income levels than in industrialized economies. These changes contributed to income gains for households that, in a virtuous circle over many years, fueled further economic growth, demand for education, productivity increases, and declines in fertility. I was familiar with many of the household-level changes through my earlier research in the postwar developing world. What particularly surprised me was that the rapid growth had not led to higher inequality.

Textbook economics describes a tradeoff between growth and equality. Increasing inequality (as in China today) seems to be a natural outcome of the early stages of development, for example as the shift from low-productivity subsistence agriculture to high-productivity manufacturing brings income gains for some people but not for others. In addition, inequality is likely to enhance growth by concentrating income among the rich, who save and invest more. Moreover, inequality reflects a system that rewards hard work, innovation, and productive risk-taking – which ultimately ensures higher output and productivity, and thus higher average income and rates of growth. These inequality-related incentives are the backbone of the argument against tax-financed redistribution: such transfers undermine individual responsibility and the work ethic and thus slow growth.

For economists, then, inequality has typically represented at worst a necessary evil and at best a reasonable price to pay for growth. So, for the most part, they have not been concerned with the apparent trend of rising inequality. Development economists in particular have focused instead on the reduction of absolute poverty. But in East Asia the textbook story seemed altogether wrong. One key to East Asia's success seemed to be its low initial levels of inequality, which were associated with the legacy of postwar redistribution of farm land in the northern economies and with subsequent high public investments in education, agricultural extension, and other programs in rural areas.

In 1993 I left the World Bank to become the executive vice president at the Inter-American Development Bank. By then I was persuaded that Latin America's high inequality was an economic problem, slowing its growth, as well as a social problem. I advocated more research on the issue. By that time – soon after the fall of the Berlin Wall had liberated the mainstream from the taboo of Marxian thought – academic economists were also beginning to study inequality as a possible cause of low growth, and thus as a phenomenon that mattered, at least for understanding growth itself.

Subsequent work by many economists has strengthened my conviction that while inequality may be constructive in the rich countries – in the classic sense of motivating individuals to work hard, innovate, and take productive risks – in developing countries it is likely to be destructive. That is especially true in Latin America, where conventional measures of income inequality are high. It also may well apply in other parts of the developing world, where our conventional indicators are not so high but there are plentiful signs of other forms of inequality: injustice, indignity, and lack of equal opportunity.

Distinguishing between constructive and destructive inequality is useful. To clarify the distinction: inequality is constructive when it creates positive incentives at the micro level. Such inequality reflects differences in individuals' responses to equal opportunities and is consistent with efficient allocation of resources in an economy. In contrast, destructive inequality reflects privileges for the already rich and blocks potential for productive contributions of the less rich.

Inequality of income in an equal-opportunity society would be wholly constructive: there would be high lifetime mobility (up and down) and high intergenerational mobility; children's place in the distribution of lifetime income would be independent of their parents' place. (Income inequality in the United States is higher than in most countries of Western Europe. The perception of the United States as a highly mobile society compared to Western Europe is likely the result of its higher average income growth, which has lifted all boats.)

Since there are no international measures of relative opportunity or mobility, development economists who care about inequality have been measuring "money inequality" – inequality of income, consumption, and wealth. Assessing the effects of money inequality on growth within and across countries can provide a rough indicator of inequality of opportunity and limited social mobility in a particular setting. This brings us to the crux of why inequality can matter, especially in developing countries. Evidence over the last decade and a half suggests that it has a large destructive component: it is associated with unequal mobility and limits economic growth.

Why would this be the case? First, where markets are underdeveloped, inequality inhibits growth through market mechanisms. In developing countries, by definition, markets are relatively weak and governments are less effective in compensating for market failure. When creditworthy borrowers, for example, cannot borrow because they lack

collateral, then their lack of income or wealth limits their ability to invest productively –
in their own farms, small businesses, and in the health and education of their children.

Governments can compensate for market failures; provision of public education is a
classic example. But in developing countries, public systems of all kinds tend to be less
adequately funded and are often poorly managed. That means that public policy is less
likely to correct for the inherent inability of markets alone to compensate for differences
across households in endowments of all kinds.

In fact, some of my own research in Latin America suggests that differences in social
mobility across countries, controlling for other factors, are closely associated with
differences in public spending on primary education and the depth of financial markets.
(Ironically, policies ostensibly designed to address the latter problem and help the poor,
such as repressed interest rates and directed credit programs, generally end up limiting
access to credit in general, except for privileged insiders.)

Land inequality (and unequal access to education) when combined with poor markets
for land and credit may also be destructive for growth itself, and especially for growth
that benefits the poor. Some evidence suggests that large landowners captured most of the
benefits of agricultural growth in Latin America in the 1970s and 1980s. In contrast, in
Indonesia, where small farmers provide the bulk of agricultural production, agricultural
productivity and growth were greater in that period, and were better for the rural poor.

Secondly, where the institutions of government are weak to start with, inequality
makes strengthening them harder, and in general of maintaining accountable government.
That in turn makes it less likely that the government will provide adequate public services,
thus reducing the economy's growth potential. If the rich fail to support public education,
for example, favoring public policy that preserves privileges even at the cost of growth,
inequality not only inhibits growth given government failure (as outlined above), but itself
contributes to government failure. The problem is worse in countries with substantial
poverty at the bottom and without a strong middle class to demand accountability from
government.

Again Latin America and East Asia illustrate the point. In the 1990s in Latin America,
with its high inequality, basic education systems were poor and the children of the rich
attended private school. On average the children of the richest 20 percent of households
in many Latin countries had about six more years of education by age 24 than the children
of the poorest 20 percent; in countries of East Asia, some poorer than their counterparts
in Latin America, the comparable gap was just four and a half years. Why the difference?
In East Asia, public spending on basic education has been higher, school systems have been
better run, and better access and more equal distribution of land have given more
households the assets to send their children to school and the incentives to demand that
their schooling be adequate.

The difference between East Asia and Latin America in educational opportunities for
the poor illustrates the apparent relationship between a high concentration of income in
a society and access to education. The supply of publicly subsidized education is likely to
be limited where the rich resist a large tax burden to finance services they can buy
privately. Targeting services to the poor, an approach encouraged by the World Bank, can
help reduce the fiscal burden of greater public spending, but it easily leads to a loss of
political support from the working and middle classes. Without middle-class interest and
pressure, the quality of schooling deteriorates, and the middle class resorts to private
services. On the demand side, low public spending combined with pressure to maintain

or expand enrollment leads to low-quality schools, reducing for poor families the economic returns of sending children to school who can otherwise help at home or by working. This may explain the high dropout rates throughout much of Latin America, even in the face of high returns on average to those who manage to complete secondary school.

In the case of the poor's extreme political weakness, the privileged can easily exercise sufficient political control – through contributions to political campaigns, access to the media, and even bribes and even extortion – to constitute what Charles Beitz called an "abridgement of liberty." When this kind of influence in turn affects job availability, workplace safety, or local environmental conditions, then large inequalities are having large political repercussions.

But there may be bad political outcomes even when the disadvantaged do have political voice. There are many examples of populist programs designed to attract working-class political support – for example in Garcia's Peru in the 1980s or Perón's Argentina – that hurt workers in the long run. Financed by unsustainable fiscal largesse, they brought the inflation or high interest rates that exacerbated inequality. (The rich can better protect themselves from inflation with indexed financial assets and by placing capital abroad; and from high interest rates by pressing for privileged access to credit.) Price controls imposed on food products hurt rural producers, or end with products disappearing from stores as they are hoarded and resold at prices out of reach of most consumers. A high minimum wage may make it harder for the unemployed to find work. Regulatory privileges, trade protection, and special access to cheap credit and foreign exchange – all bad economic policies – tend to increase the profits of a wealthy minority. Not all bad policy can be blamed on income inequality, but it would be foolish to ignore the risks of inequality to sound policy.

Finally, where social institutions are fragile, inequality discourages the civic and social life that undergirds the collective decision-making necessary to healthy, functioning societies. Robert Putnam defines the asset of social capital in terms of trusts, norms, and networks that can improve the efficiency of society, "facilitating coordinating actions." Social capital has economic value because it is likely to reduce the cost of transactions and contract enforcement and, as Dani Rodrik points out, reduce resistance of the losing groups to political compromises.

There is good evidence from microeconomic analyses that income inequality adversely affects some of the correlates of social capital. In Tanzania, informal insurance is higher in communities where income inequality is lower. Among sugar cooperatives in India, those in which land ownership is more unequal are less productive. Differences across countries in homicide rate are associated with differences in the income gap between the middle class and the rich.

In developing countries, inequality itself is not always so much the problem as is the interaction of inequality with other factors: weak markets or unaccountable or incompetent governments. Weak markets, weak governments, weak institutions – these are the very characteristics that define a country as developing. Reducing inequality might not in itself lead automatically to higher growth or better government or more stable and healthy societies. But development economists should take note: to ignore inequality altogether is to invite setbacks on the development path.

[. . .]

Now globalization is creating pressures that tend to increase inequality. We need to understand what those pressures are and how they operate as today's increasingly integrated global economy raises the bar of competitiveness. How might they best be managed, within countries and at the global level, to avoid their potentially destructive effects on growth?

Proponents of globalization have hailed the rapid economic growth of China, India, and other large and poor countries of Asia. And indeed several decades of rapid growth in some poor countries has moved millions of people out of poverty, shifting a large enough portion of the world's people out of the poorest parts of the world income distribution so that inequality among individuals, regardless of country, has declined. But these successes do not mean, as the title of Thomas L. Friedman's best-selling book suggests, that the world is flat. Globalization is not leveling the global playing field for everyone. Between the average income of the richest countries – those of Europe, North America, and Australia – and the poorest – many in Africa – the gap is increasing. And within China, India and other fast-growing countries where inequality has not been high in the past, it is now rising. It also rose dramatically in most of Eastern Europe and the former Soviet Union in the 1990s, as minimal growth left the poor worse off than they were under communism. And it has remained high in Brazil, Mexico, Panama, and Peru, where there was modest growth.

In other developing countries, income inequality has not changed, and in a few – Bangladesh, Ghana, and the Philippines – it appears to have declined. So it would be an exaggeration to say that rising inequality within countries has been the norm. Nor does it make sense to condemn "globalization" because inequality is rising in countries like China and India. These may be cases of a constructive inequality that reflects new prosperity for some.

But in the case of the poorest countries, we need to explore whether the common assumption always holds: that the pressures of the global economy will enable them to benefit by exploiting the technologies others have developed.

We can start by looking at how the regular workings of the global economy affect inequality.

The market works: global markets reward productive assets. Globalization is shorthand for global capitalism and the extension of global markets. Markets that are bigger and deeper reward more efficiently those who already have productive assets – financial assets, land, physical assets, and perhaps most crucial in the technologically driven global economy, human capital. For countries, the key productive asset seems to be stable and sound institutions. Countries that are already ahead – with stable political systems, secure property rights, adequate banking supervision, reasonable public services, and so on – are better able to cope with market-driven changes in world prices.

Consider the plight of a large group of the poorest countries, including Bolivia and many countries in Africa. Highly dependent on primary commodity and natural resource exports in the early 1980s, their markets have been "open" for at least two decades, if openness is measured by their ratio of imports and exports to GDP. But unable to diversify into manufacturing (despite reducing their own import tariffs) they have been victims of the decline in the relative world prices of their commodity exports, and have, literally, been left behind. These countries have not been xenophobic or in any way closed to the global economy. But despite rising exports, tariff reductions, and, in most of them, economic and structural reforms, including greater fiscal and monetary discipline and the divestiture of unproductive state enterprises, they have been unable to increase their export income, have failed to attract foreign investment, and have grown little, if at all.

What many countries in sub-Saharan Africa – as well as Haiti, Nepal, and Nicaragua – have in common is a vicious circle of low or unstable export revenue, weak and sometimes predatory government, inability to cope with terrible disease burdens (the HIV/AIDS pandemic is only one recent and highly visible example), and failure to deliver to children basic education and other services critical to sustainable growth. Their governments have made, from time to time, fragile efforts to end corruption, to undertake economic reforms, and, more to the point, to enter global markets. But globalization has not worked for them – even those such as Nigeria and Ecuador that are rich in at least one asset, oil, but poor in institutions. In contrast, countries that have the "asset" of strong political and social institutions (Australia and Norway, for example, or among developing countries, Chile and Botswana) have benefited from entering global markets with their natural resources.

William Easterly argues that in the new global economy, we should not expect the convergence between rich and poor countries that conventional economic models based on differences in wealth and other traditional assets predict. He suggests instead that it is existing productivity differences across countries that matter. Productivity differences make "capital" and "skilled labor" economically scarce even in high-productivity settings where they are apparently plentiful, explaining why skilled people continue to move to those settings. This also explains why 80 percent of all foreign investment occurs among the industrialized countries (just 0.1 percent of all U.S. foreign investment went to sub-Saharan Africa last year). The productivity differences arise, presumably, because of differences in physical infrastructure and human capital, themselves a product of long-standing differences in social and political institutions.

The global market for skilled and talented people is a good example of the tendency of markets to benefit the stronger – individuals as well as countries. Advanced economies are now competing with each other in encouraging immigration of highly skilled workers from developing countries. Indian engineers can quadruple their earnings by moving from Kerala to the Silicon Valley, and Indian biochemists by moving from Delhi to Atlanta or Cambridge. More integrated markets thus increase inequality across countries, via emigration from smaller and poorer countries of highly skilled citizens, who naturally are inclined to move to settings where they can deploy their skills productively. For the individuals who emigrate, their mobility is a good thing, and what has been called a "brain drain" can generate offsetting remittances that raise welfare in the sending countries (as migrants send money home). Moreover, if the institutional and policy setting in sending countries improves, as it did in India recently, emigrants are likely to begin investing in their home country and returning permanently. At the same time, however, the ability to emigrate makes tougher the poorer countries' crucial tasks – building institutions and improving policies – if they lose their most talented citizens. (The annual cost to India of its brain drain to the United States is estimated at $2 billion, an amount equal to all the foreign aid it receives.)

Global markets similarly create new pressures for inequality within countries. Healthy global markets can generate unequal opportunities between different individuals. The relative return of a university education has been increasing for years everywhere, despite the fact that more and more people are going to university, including across the developing world. More integrated trade markets, capital flows, and global technology, including the Internet, are increasing the worldwide demand for skills more rapidly than the supply.

Just about everywhere in the world, education is reinforcing initial advantages instead of compensating for initial handicaps among individuals.

Rising wage gaps in open and competitive markets may be a short-term price worth paying for sustainable growth. They create incentives for more people to acquire more education, in principle eventually reducing inequality. The same can be said for the development of institutions at the country level. Many poor countries have responded to global opportunities by strengthening the rule of law, building and strengthening democratic processes, and investing in public health and education. But just as poor families can benefit from public assistance to help them invest in their children's education, so poor countries can benefit from aid and the incentives of a level global playing field to help them build better institutions.

Even when participation in the global market brings growth, as it has in China and India, it is a mixed blessing, bringing political pressures for populist measures and, especially if growth falters, for protectionism. Even Europe and the United States are subject to those pressures – but with more resilient institutions and well-developed social insurance programs they can better afford temporary policy errors. The political risks are greater still when engagement in global markets fails to bring growth.

The market fails: in the global economy, failures hurt the weak most. Global markets are far from perfect. They fail in many domains. The classic example of a market failure is pollution: the polluter captures the benefits of polluting without paying the full costs. The United States, for example, the biggest global polluter per capita, is imposing costs not only on its own future citizens, but also on the children and grandchildren of the world's poor, whose countries have fewer resources to manage or mitigate the effects. Likewise in the case of global financial crises. The financial crises of the late 1990s that rocked Mexico, Thailand, Korea, Russia, Brazil, and Argentina resulted in part from policy errors in those countries. But a healthy portion can be blamed on panic in global markets of the kind that periodically plagues all financial markets. In East Asia many investors reacted by accumulating high reserves for insurance against future crises; the costs of maintaining high dollar reserves (given the low interest rates compared to potential returns) represent a perverse transfer from the developing world to the United States.

The volatility and financial risks that come with participation in global markets tend to increase inequality over the long run within countries. Analysis indicates that trade shocks hurt the bottom 20 percent of the income distribution disproportionately. The evidence is that volatility, whatever its source, is particularly bad for the poor. In Korea, Mexico, and Thailand, financial crises in the 1990s reduced the income shares of the bottom 80 percent of households. During the accompanying recession in Mexico in 1995, many children of the poor dropped out of school – and subsequent studies show that many never returned.

Global financial markets have not only brought instability and reduced growth to the emerging market economies; they have affected their capacity to develop and sustain the institutions and programs that would protect their poor. One culprit has probably been the premature opening of capital markets. In some emerging market economies, premature opening of the capital market – before adequate banking supervision and financial regulation were in place – brought pressures for increased inequality along with volatility, for at least two reasons. First, with global market players doubting the commitment of these countries' governments to fiscal rectitude they were forced to reestablish market confidence by adopting tight fiscal and monetary policy, when ideally in the face of recession they would have implemented macroeconomic measures to stimulate their economies. The austerity policies that the global capital market demands of emerging markets at the time of a shock are the opposite of what the industrial economies implement: for example, reduced interest rates, unemployment insurance, increased availability of food stamps, and public works employment – fundamental ingredients of a modern social contract. The resulting effects of unemployment and bankruptcy can be permanent for the poor, so repeated shocks constitute a structural factor in increasing inequality.

Second, the bank bailouts that followed crises generated high public debt (amounting to ten to 40 percent of annual GDP, compared to two to three percent due to banking crises in advanced economies on average). High public debt still keeps domestic interest rates high in some emerging market countries, stifling investment, growth, and job creation – all bad for the poor – and increases the pressure on those economies to generate primary fiscal surpluses, in the long run reducing their ability to finance sound broad-based investment in health and education – and their ability to spend more on the unemployment and safety-net programs that would protect the poor in bad times.

Global climate change and global financial crises both result from market failures. They are two examples of market failures that hurt poor countries and poor people more. In general, the ability to adjust to change, or to finance mitigation costs, is smaller for poorer countries, and within countries, for poorer people. So market failures tend to increase inequality.

Global rules and regimes tend to favor already rich countries and people. In the end, global markets tend to be disequalizing, because trade, intellectual property, and migration regimes naturally reflect the greater market power of the rich. The battle to reduce rich country agricultural subsidies and tariffs that discriminate against poor countries is a good example. Domestic politics in Europe, the United States, and Japan, as perverse as they are even for those countries themselves, matter more at the negotiating table than unequal opportunities for cotton farmers in West Africa.

As the design of multilateral rules favors the rich, so too does their implementation. In 2003 developing countries finally got clarity on their right to issue compulsory licenses to import and produce generic medicines during public-health emergencies. But the rules for exercising that right are complicated, and many countries eager to maintain or improve their access to the U.S. market for their own exports are acceding to WTO "plus" patent protection, in effect giving up those rights, in bilateral trade with the United States.

The cost and complexity alone of negotiation and dispute resolution processes in the WTO put poor and small countries with limited resources at a disadvantage. About one half of anti-dumping actions are initiated against developing-country producers, who account for eight percent of all exports. These create legal and other costs to current producers in developing countries, and are likely to chill new job-creating investment in sensitive sectors.

International migration is also governed by rules that clearly exacerbate inequality between the richest and poorest – countries and individuals. Permanent migration is small relative to the past because today higher-income countries restrict immigration. In the last 25 years, only two percent of the world's people have changed their permanent country residence, compared to ten percent in the 25 years before the First World War. Yet more movement, especially of less-skilled workers, would reduce world inequality considerably, as did the tremendous movements of Europeans to the Americas in the 19th century. But current policy encourages instead the movement of the highly skilled into the more advanced economies.

Economic power affects the rules and the conduct of those rules by international institutions other than the WTO. The International Monetary Fund is the global institution designed to help countries manage macroeconomic imbalances and minimize the risks of financial shocks. But in the 1990s, the IMF was more enthusiastic about developing countries' opening their capital accounts than subsequent evidence about the costs warranted. This is one example where the IMF and the World Bank have been insufficiently humble in their recipes, perhaps too heavily influenced by their more powerful members. Another is their indiscriminate support for adjustment programs that in some countries, though technically sound on paper, worsened the situation of the poor because transition costs were inadequately considered and safety net programs underfunded.

In advanced market economies there is a well-defined social contract that tempers the inequalities of income and opportunity that efficient markets naturally generate. Progressive tax systems provide for some redistribution, with the state financing at least minimal educational opportunities for all and some social and old-age insurance. Yet in developing countries, where the social contract is less well developed, the economic reforms that competitiveness in global markets require, and the risks to economic stability it brings, tend to exacerbate existing inequality, and in turn generate political pressure for populist redistribution. The political leadership must then manage a delicate balance between enacting the structural reforms that will generate growth and minimizing the short-term political risks they entail.

Politics is local, and the politics of inequality is doubly so. One lesson for the international community is to do no harm as leaders in developing countries cope with the difficult challenges that globalization presents. When donors condition their grants and loans on, for example, less corruption or more open trade regimes, they may complicate the situation – a health program may be cut because of corruption in the oil ministry, or unskilled jobs in local industry or farming may be lost after a reduction in import tariffs. Skepticism and humility about the timing and details of policy reforms pushed from the outside seems warranted.

And in terms of actual resource transfers, the international community needs something closer to a global social contract to address unequal endowments – to rapidly ramp up educational opportunities for the poor in developing countries, and to find ways to help societies build their own sound institutions. Spending by the rich world on the "global social contract," now reflected in the idea of the UN's Millennium Development Goals, is less than one percent of rich-country GDP. That is surprisingly low compared to the typical 20 percent spent on public transfers for education and social insurance within rich countries. The comparison is relevant: we now have a more and more integrated global economy – creating legitimate new demands for more shared prosperity.

The business of foreign aid needs to be reinvented if it is to become reasonably effective – with a premium on financing global public goods such as agricultural research and development, on results or output-based transfers, and on systematic evaluation. And the imperfect record of foreign-aid programs should not be an excuse for the rich countries' minimal spending.

Most important, the global and regional institutions – the most obvious mechanisms for managing a global social contract – need reform. It is ironic that the World Bank and the IMF have together been the lightning rod for anti-globalization protests. In the end they are not too powerful but too ineffective and limited in their resources. To play an effective role in managing a global social contract, they must be more representative. Why should China and India support a World Bank initiative to reduce greenhouse-gas emissions through carbon trading if they have no real power over that use of resources? And they must be more accountable to those most affected by their programs. Why should the financial institutions not share in the costs when the programs they support fail to generate the returns that would warrant those costs – as was almost surely the case in some of the world's poorest countries that ended up with substantial unpayable debt to the official multilateral lenders?

Governments are meant to temper market failures through regulations, taxes and subsidies, and fines, and to share the benefits of such public goods as public security, military defense, management of natural disasters, and public health through their tax and expenditure decisions. Ideally those decisions are made in a democratic system with fair and legitimate representation of all people, independent of their wealth. For the global community, an equivalent system to manage global market failures only barely exists. Because global markets are imperfect, we need global regulatory arrangements and rules to manage the global environment (Kyoto and beyond), help emerging markets cope with global financial risks (the IMF and beyond), and ways to discourage corruption and anti-competitive practices. The Extractive Industries Transparency Initiative, under which countries and multinational firms commit to transparency in their agreements, is a nongovernment initiative created in this spirit. Like this initiative, global agreements on bankruptcy procedures, on reducing greenhouse-gas emissions, on protecting biodiversity and marine resources, on funding food safety and monitoring public health are all development programs in one form or another – because they reduce the risks and costs of global spillovers and enhance their potential benefits for the poor.

The same goes for the provision of global public goods: the returns on spending that benefits the poor have been extraordinarily high. This is the case with tropical agricultural research, public-health research and disease control, and the limited global efforts to protect regional and global environmental resources. The Green Revolution brought shared prosperity to millions of agricultural producers and consumers in India by raising crop yields; a malaria vaccine would save millions of lives in Africa. These sorts of global programs need to be financed by something that mimics taxes within national economies. Proposals for a tax on international aviation or on carbon emissions fall squarely into this category and might be more attractive (even in the anti-tax United States) were they to be used to increase provision of such global public goods.

Within the advanced market economies, democratic politics help temper the inevitable tendency for the rich and powerful to set the rules to their own short-term advantage. There is no equivalent global polity – only the hope that the rich world will resist short-term advantages in favor of long-term enlightened self-interest. Many developing countries – especially smaller and poorer countries – need transfers from rich countries to participate effectively in global trade and other negotiations.

Rich counties would do well to open their doors further to unskilled and not just skilled immigrants, allocating resources at home to ease the adjustment of native workers through job training. Even within political constraints, much more could be done by the rich countries in their own interests to make immigration regimes more consistent with their overall development policies. Sharing of tax receipts of skilled immigrants across sending and receiving countries is one example. Another is the effort to reduce the transaction costs of remittances.

In general the developing countries should be more fully and fairly represented in international institutions; this is especially the case in the international financial institutions, whose policies and programs are so central to their development prospects. The same can be said for other international forums: the UN Security Council, the Basel Committee for Banking Regulation and Supervision, the G-8, and so on.

We have a potentially powerful instrument to increase wealth and welfare: the global economy. But to support that economy we have an inadequate and fragile global polity. A major challenge of the 21st century will be to strengthen and reform the institutions, rules, and customs by which nations and peoples complement the global market with collective management of the problems, including persistent and unjust inequality, which markets alone will not resolve.

Note

This essay is based on Nancy Birdsall's 2005 UNU-WIDER (United Nations University World Institute for Development Economics Research) Annual Lecture. The full lecture is available on the Web site of the Center for Global Development at www.cgdev.org.

REVIEW AND DISCUSSION QUESTIONS

1 How might inequality promote economic growth?
2 What are the channels through which inequality is likely to hinder economic growth in developing countries?
3 Why does Birdsall believe that inequality may lead to political outcomes that hurt the poor?
4 Why is it, according to Birdsall, that certain aspects of globalization hurt the poor more than the rich?
5 What can rich countries do to help reduce inequality in poor countries? Do you agree with Birdsall's recommendations? Why or why not?

Chapter 14

Abhijit V. Banerjee and Esther Duflo

THE ECONOMIC LIVES OF THE POOR

I N WHAT TURNED OUT TO be a rhetorical master-move, the 1990 World Development Report from the World Bank defined the "extremely poor" people of the world as those who are currently living on no more than $1 per day per person, measured at the 1985 purchasing power parity (PPP) exchange rate. In 1993, the poverty line was updated to $1.08 per person per day at the 1993 PPP exchange rate, which is the line we use in this paper. Poverty lines have always existed – indeed $1 per day was chosen in part because of its proximity to the poverty lines used by many poor countries.[1] However the $1-a-day poverty line has come to dominate the conversations about poverty to a remarkable extent.

But how actually does one live on less than $1 per day? This essay is about the economic lives of the extremely poor: the choices they face, the constraints they grapple with, and the challenges they meet. The available evidence on the economic lives of the extremely poor is incomplete in many important ways. However, a number of recent data sets and a body of new research have added a lot to what we know about their lives, and taken together there is enough to start building an image of the way the extremely poor live their lives.

Our discussion of the economic lives of the extremely poor builds on household surveys conducted in 13 countries listed in Table 14.1: Côte d'Ivoire, Guatemala, India, Indonesia, Mexico, Nicaragua, Pakistan, Panama, Papua New Guinea, Peru, South Africa, Tanzania, and Timor Leste (East Timor). We mainly use the Living Standard Measurement Surveys (LSMS) conducted by the World Bank and the "Family Life Surveys" conducted by the Rand Corporation, all of which are publicly available. In addition, we also use two surveys that we conducted in India with our collaborators. The first was carried out in 2002 and 2003 in 100 hamlets of Udaipur District, Rajasthan (Banerjee, Deaton, and Duflo, 2004). Udaipur is one of the poorer districts of India, with a large tribal population and an unusually high level of female illiteracy. (At the time of the 1991 census, only 5

Table 14.1 Description of data sets

Country	Source	Year	Avg. monthly consumption per capita (In PPP$)	Households (HHs) living on less than			
				$1.08 per person per day		$2.16 per person per day	
				Number surveyed	Percent of total surveyed HHs	Number surveyed	Percent of total surveyed HHs
Côte d'Ivoire	LSMS	1988	664.13	375	14%	1,411	49%
Guatemala	GFHS	1995	301.92	469	18%	910	34%
India-Hyderabad	Banerjee-Duflo-Glennerster	2005	71.61	106	7%	1,030	56%
India-Udaipur	Banerjee-Deaton-Duflo	2004	43.12	482	47%	883	86%
Indonesia	IFLS	2000	142.84	320	4%	2,106	26%
Mexico	MxFLS	2002	167.97	959	15%	2,698	39%
Nicaragua	LSMS	2001	117.34	333	6%	1,322	28%
Pakistan	LSMS	1991	48.01	1,573	40%	3,632	83%
Panama	LSMS	1997	359.73	123	2%	439	6%
Papua New Guinea	LSMS	1996	133.38	185	15%	485	38%
Peru	LSMS	1994	151.88	297	7%	821	20%
South Africa	LSMS	1993	291.33	413	5%	1,641	19%
Tanzania	LSMS	1993	50.85	1,184	35%	2,941	73%
Timor Leste	LSMS	2001	64.42	662	15%	2,426	51%

Sources: The Mexican Family Life Survey is documented in Rubalcava and Teruel (2004) and available at <http://www.radix.uia.mx/ennvih/>. The LSMS are available from the World Bank LSMS project page. The IFLS and GFLS are available from the RAND FLS page <http://www.rand.org/labor/FLS/>. The Udaipur data is available from <www.povertyactionlab.org/data>. The Hyderabad data is forthcoming on the same page.

Notes: To compute the $1.08 and $2.16 poverty line for the countries in our sample, we use the 1993 consumption exchange rate provided by the World Bank (available at <http://iresearch.worldbank.org/PovcalNet/jsp/index.jsp>) multiplied by the ratio of the country's Consumer Price Index to the U.S. Consumer Price Index between 1993 and the year the survey was carried out. To compute average consumption per capita and the proportion of households in poverty, observations are weighted using (survey weight * household size).

percent of women were literate in rural Udaipur.) Our second survey covered 2,000 households in "slums" (or informal neighborhoods) of Hyderabad, the capital of the state of Andhra Pradesh and one of the boomtowns of post-liberalization India (Banerjee, Duflo, and Glennerster, 2006). We chose these countries and surveys because they provide detailed information on extremely poor households around the world, from Asia to Africa to Latin America, including information on what they consume, where they work, and how they save and borrow. To flesh out our main themes further, we also draw freely on the existing research literature.

From each of these surveys we identified the extremely poor as those living in households where the consumption per capita is less than $1.08 per person per day, as well as the merely "poor" defined as those who live under $2.16 a day using 1993 purchasing power parity (PPP) as benchmark. In keeping with convention, we call these the $1 and $2 dollar poverty lines, respectively. The use of consumption, rather than income, is motivated by the better quality of the consumption data in these surveys (Deaton, 2004). Table 14.1 provides some background information on these surveys. It lists the countries, and the source of the survey data. It also lists the sample sizes: the numbers and the proportions of the extremely poor and the poor in each survey. The fraction of individuals living under $1 dollar per day in the survey vary from 2 percent in Panama to 47 percent in Udaipur, and the fraction living under $2 per day varies from 6 percent in Panama to 86 percent in Udaipur. All the numbers discussed in this paper and detailed results are available in an appendix that appears with the on-line version of this article at <http://www.e-jep.org>.

The way in which we identify the poor does raise questions. Purchasing power parity exchange rates, which are essential to compute a "uniform" poverty line, have been criticized as inadequate, infrequently updated, and inapplicable to the consumption of the extremely poor (Deaton, 2004, 2006). Prices are typically higher in urban than in rural areas, and even in rural areas, the poor may pay different prices than everyone else. Also, reporting periods vary significantly from survey to survey and this has been shown to affect systematically what people report.

But while these issues are obviously serious for counting the exact number of the poor, they may affect the conclusions of this essay less because instead of counting the poor, we are describing what their lives look like. Misclassifying some households should not change anything very important about the averages we observe in the data, unless both the number affected are very large and those artificially moved into or out of poverty by changes in the poverty line are very different than the other poor. It turns out that most of our conclusions do not change if we look at the poor rather than the extremely poor, which is reassuring. Nevertheless, we cannot entirely rule out the possibility that our results may be different with a different poverty line.

We also assume that the people we are describing as the poor are long-term poor, in the sense that their permanent income is actually close to their observed consumption. If the poor people we observe are just making a brief transition through poverty, then some of the behaviors that we will observe (such as lack of savings) would be less puzzling, and others (like the lack of assets) would be much more so. We feel that this assumption is a reasonable one in most of the countries, since the fraction of the population below $2.16 a day is actually sizeable – 40 percent of the population or more in the median country and more than 70 percent in quite a few. Thus, it is unlikely that many of these people are just temporarily poor. However, for this reason, the poor in Panama, where only 6 percent of the population is poor, or in South Africa, where 19 percent is poor, may not be easily compared to the poor in some of the other countries, where the poor are a much larger share of the population.

The living arrangements of the poor

The typical extremely poor family tends to be large, at least by the standards of today's high-income countries. The number of family members varies between about six and twelve, with a median value (across the different countries) of between seven and eight, compared to 2.5 in the 2000 U.S. census, for example.

Not all surveys report fertility rates, which would be the ideal way to distinguish whether these high numbers result from the average woman having a lot of children, or if it results from an extended family living together. However, the data does give broad measures of the age structure in these families (the number of those below 13, between 13 and 18, above 51, and so on). The number of adults (over age 18) ranges from about 2.5 to about five, with a median of about three, which suggests a family structure where it is common for adults to live with parents, siblings, uncles, cousins, and so on. This finding is common in the literature on developing countries. When every penny counts, it helps to spread the fixed costs of living, like housing, over a larger number of people. Consistent with this view, family size is larger for the extremely poor than for the entire group below $2 a day, on the order of one half of one person or more, though at least some part of this difference is because extremely poor families have more children living with them.

These families also have a large number of children. This fact does not necessarily imply high levels of fertility, as families often have multiple adult women. When we look at the number of children (ages 0 to 18) per woman in the child-bearing age (ages 21–50) we get numbers between two and four in both the rural and the urban sample, though the urban ratios tend to be slightly lower. This ratio cannot be interpreted as a fertility rate, because for example, a 51 year-old could have a child who is now 36, but we only include children who are below age 18. A more useful exercise with this data is to compare the number of young people (those below 18) in these families with the number of older people (those above 51). The ratio varies between three and nine in the rural sample, with a median of six, and between two and eleven in the urban sample, again with a median around six. The corresponding ratio in the United States is around one. The poor of the world are very young.

One reason the population is young is that there are a lot of younger people. A complementary reason is that there are very few older people. The ratio of the number older people (over age 51) to the number of people of "prime-age" (21–50) tends to be between 0.2 and 0.3 in both the rural and the urban sample. The corresponding number in the United States is approximately 0.6. A plausible explanation for this difference might be the higher mortality rates among those who are older and poor in poor countries, but in principle it is possible that it is an artifact of the way we constructed our sample. It could be that older people are underrepresented in our sample because they tend to be richer. But in this case, we might have expected to find more of the older people among the poor (as compared to the extremely poor), whereas the data does not show such a pattern.

How the poor spend their money

A common image of the extremely poor is that they have few real choices to make. Indeed, some people surely work as hard as they can – which may not be particularly hard, because they are underfed and weak and earn barely enough to cover their basic needs, which they always try to fulfill in the least expensive way. Historically, poverty lines in many countries were originally set to capture this definition of poverty – the budget needed to buy a certain amount of calories, plus some other indispensable purchases (such as housing). A "poor" person was essentially defined as someone without enough to eat.

Food and other consumption purchases

Yet the average person living at under $1 per day does not seem to put every available penny into buying more calories. Among our 13 countries, food typically represents from 56 to 78 percent of consumption among rural households, and 56 to 74 percent in urban areas. For the rural poor in Mexico, slightly less than half the budget (49.6 percent) is allocated to food.[2]

Of course, these people could be spending the rest of their money on other commodities they greatly need. Yet among the nonfood items that the poor spend significant amounts of money on, alcohol and tobacco show up prominently. The extremely poor in rural areas spent 4.1 percent of their budget on tobacco and alcohol in Papua New Guinea; 5.0 percent in Udaipur, India; 6.0 percent in Indonesia; and 8.1 percent in Mexico. However, in Guatemala, Nicaragua, and Peru, no more than 1 percent of the budget gets spent on these goods (possibly because the poor in these countries prefer other intoxicants).

Perhaps more surprisingly, spending on festivals is an important part of the budget for many extremely poor households. In Udaipur, over the course of the previous year, more than 99 percent of the extremely poor households spent money on a wedding, a funeral, or a religious festival. The median household spent 10 percent of its annual budget on festivals. In South Africa, 90 percent of the households living under $1 per day spent money on festivals. In Pakistan, Indonesia, and Côte d'Ivoire, more than 50 percent did likewise. Only in some Latin American countries in our sample – Panama, Guatemala, Nicaragua – are festivals not a notable part of the yearly expenditure for a significant fraction of the households. However, in the LSMS surveys, unlike the Udaipur survey, people are not asked to account separately for the food that they bought because of a festival. It is therefore probably no accident that the Udaipur spending on festivals is the highest across the surveys. The LSMS numbers would probably have been higher if data on food spending because of festivals had been directly collected in those surveys.

On the other hand, the under-$1-per-day households spend very little on forms of entertainment common in high-income countries such as movies, theater, or video shows. In all 13 countries in our sample, in the month preceding the survey the average extremely poor household spent less than 1 percent on any of these forms of entertainment. The comparable number for the United States is 5 percent. We can only speculate about the roots of this difference. Has the importance given to festivals and other indigenous forms of entertainment crowded out movie-going? Or is the answer as simple as a lack of access to movie theaters?

The propensity to own a radio or a television, a widespread form of entertainment for American households, varies considerably across low-income countries. For example, among rural households living under $1 per day, ownership of a radio is 11 percent in the Udaipur survey, almost 60 percent in Nicaragua and Guatemala, and above 70 percent in South Africa and Peru. Similarly, no one owns a television in Udaipur, but in Guatemala nearly a quarter of households do, and in Nicaragua, the percentage is closer to a half.

These phenomena of spending on festivals and ownership of radios or televisions appear to be related. In Udaipur, where the share spent on festivals is the highest, radio and television ownership is very low. In Pakistan, the fraction spent on festivals is 3.3 percent and only 30 percent have a radio. By contrast, in Nicaragua where among respectively the rural and the urban poor 57 and 38 percent have a radio and 21 percent and 19 percent own a television, very few households report spending anything on festivals.[3] One wrinkle on this explanation is that the urban poor who are much more likely to own a television than the rural poor (60 versus 33 percent in Indonesia, 61 versus 10 percent in Peru, 38 versus 17 percent in South Africa), do not spend less on festivals than their rural counterparts. While this observation is based on only a few data points, it hints at the possibility of an unmet demand for entertainment among the rural poor – they might like to buy a television, but perhaps the television signal does not reach their neighborhoods.

In either case, the poor do see themselves as having a significant amount of choice, but they choose not to exercise that choice in the direction of spending more on food. The typical poor household in Udaipur could spend up to 30 percent more on food than it actually does, just based on what it spends on alcohol, tobacco, and festivals. Indeed, in most of the surveys the share spent on food is about the same for the poor and the extremely poor, suggesting that the extremely poor feel no extra compulsion to purchase more calories.

This conclusion echoes an old finding in the literature on nutrition: even the extremely poor do not seem to be as hungry for additional calories as one might expect. Deaton and Subramanian (1996), using 1983 data from the Indian state of Maharashtra, found that even for the poorest, a 1 percent increase on overall expenditure translates into about a two-thirds of a percent increase in the total food expenditure of a poor family. Remarkably, the elasticity is not very different for the poorest individuals in the sample and the richest (although nobody is particularly rich in this sample). The Deaton and Subramanian estimate is one of the higher estimates. Thomas and Strauss (1997) found an elasticity of demand for food with respect to expenditure per capita of about a quarter for the poorest Brazilians.

Another way to make the same point is to look at what edibles the extremely poor are buying. Deaton and Subramanian (1996) note that among grains, in terms of calories per rupee, the millets (*jowar* and *bajra*) are clearly the best buy. Yet in their data, only about two-thirds of the total spending on grains is on these grains, while another 20 percent is on rice, which costs more than twice as much per calorie, and a further 10 percent or so is spent on wheat, which is a 70 percent more expensive way to get calories. In addition, the poor spend almost 7 percent of their total budget on sugar, which is both more expensive than grains as a source of calories and bereft of other nutritional value. The same affinity for sugar also shows up in our Udaipur data, in which the poor spend almost 10 percent of their food budget on the category "sugar, salt, and other processed foods" (this does not include cooking oil, which makes up another 6 percent of the expenditures on food). Even for the extremely poor, for every 1 percent increase in the food expenditure, about half goes into purchasing more calories, and half goes into purchasing more expensive (and presumably better tasting) calories.

Finally, the trend seems to be to spend even less money on food. In India, for example, spending on food went from 70 percent in 1983 to 62 percent in 1999–2000, and the share of millet in the food budget dropped to virtually zero (Deaton, 2006). Not surprisingly, the poor are also consuming fewer calories over time (Meenakshi and Vishwanathan, 2003), though this change may also reflect that their work involves less physical effort (Jha, 2004).

The ownership of assets

While all the surveys have some information about assets, the list of assets varies. To obtain a relatively coherent list across countries, we focus on radios, televisions, and bicycles. The share of people who own these particular assets varies significantly across countries.

As we already discussed, ownership of radio and television varies from country to country, but is low in some countries. One reason may be the lack of signal. Another reason may be that a television is an expensive and lumpy transaction for which one has to save if one is born poor. We do see a fairly steep income gradient in the ownership of radio and television: In all countries, the share of rural households owning a television is substantially larger for those who live on less than $2 a day than those living on less than $1 a day. For example, the share owning a television increases from 14 percent for those living on $1 a day to 45 percent for those living on less than $2 a dollar a day in Côte d'Ivoire; from 7 to 17 percent in South Africa; and from 10 to 21 percent in Peru. This pattern has been observed in other contexts (Filmer and Pritchett, 2001) and has been the basis for using the lack of durable goods as a marker for poverty. Our data suggests that this proxy can be appropriate within a country, but it could easily be misleading in a cross-country comparison.

Among productive assets, land is the one that many people in the rural surveys seem to own, although enormous country-to-country variation exists. Only 4 percent of those living under $1 a day own land in Mexico, 1.4 percent in South Africa, 30 percent in Pakistan, 37 percent in Guatemala, 50 percent in Nicaragua and Indonesia, 63 percent in Côte d'Ivoire, 65 percent in Peru, and 85 percent in Panama. In the Udaipur sample, 99 percent of the households below $1 a day own some land in addition to the land on which their house is built, although much of it is dry scrubland that cannot be cultivated for most of the year. However, when the extremely poor do own land, the plots tend to be quite small. The median landholding among the poor who own land is one hectare or less in Udaipur, Indonesia, Guatemala, and Timor; between one and two hectares in Peru, Tanzania, Pakistan; and between two and three hectares in Nicaragua, Côte d'Ivoire, and Panama.

Apart from land, extremely poor households in rural areas tend to own very few durable goods, including productive assets: 34 percent own a bicycle in Côte d'Ivoire, but less than 14 percent in Udaipur, Nicaragua, Panama, Papua New Guinea, Peru, and East Timor. In Udaipur, where we have detailed asset data, most extremely poor households have a bed or a cot, but only about 10 percent have a chair or a stool and 5 percent have a table. About half have a clock or a watch. Fewer than 1 percent have an electric fan, a sewing machine, a bullock cart, a motorized cycle of any kind, or a tractor. No one has a phone. As we will see below, this situation does not mean that most of these households are employees and have little use for such assets. On the contrary, many extremely poor households operate their own businesses, but do so with almost no productive assets.

The pursuit of health and well-being

Should we worry about the fact that the poor are buying less food than they could? According to Deaton and Subramanian (1996), the poorest people – the ones in the bottom decile in terms of per capita expenditure – consume on average slightly less than 1400 calories a day. This level is about half of what the Indian government recommends for a man with moderate activity, or a woman with heavy physical activity (see <http://www.fao.org/documents/show_cdr.asp?url_file=/DOCREP/x0l72e/x0172e02.htm>). The shortfall seems enormous. The Udaipur data, which includes other health indicators, suggest that health is definitely reason for concern.

Among the extremely poor in Udaipur, only 57 percent report that the members of their household had enough to eat throughout the year. Among the poor adults in Udaipur, the average "body mass index" (that is, weight in kilograms divided by the square of the height in meters) is 17.8. Sixty-five percent of adult men and 40 percent of adult women have a body mass index below 18.5, the standard cutoff for being underweight (WHO expert consultation, 2004). Moreover, 55 percent of the poor adults in Udaipur are anemic, which means they have an insufficient number of red blood cells. The poor are frequently sick or weak. In Udaipur, 72 percent report at least one symptom of disease and 46 percent report an illness which has left them bedridden or necessitated a visit to the doctor over the last month. Forty-three percent of the adults and 34 percent of the adults aged under 50 report difficulty carrying out at least one of their "activities of daily living," such as working in the field, walking, or drawing water from a well. Diarrhea is extremely frequent among children. About one-seventh of the poor have vision problems, which may be caused by either poor nutrition, or the diseases that afflict them, or a combination of the two.

Detailed information on health is not available in all the surveys, but most report the incidence over the last month of health episodes that left a household member bedridden for a day or more, or that required a household member to see a doctor. The general pattern is a remarkably high level of morbidity. Among the rural poor living under $1 a day in Peru, South Africa, East Timor, Panama, and Tanzania, between 11 and 15 percent of households report having a member either being bedridden for at least a day or requiring a doctor. The number is between 21 and 28 percent in Pakistan, Indonesia, and Côte d'Ivoire, and between 35 and 46 percent in Nicaragua, Udaipur, and Mexico.

Even these high numbers may be an understatement if the poor are less prone to recall and report such sicknesses than those with higher incomes. The poor generally do not complain about their health – but then they also do not complain about life in general, either. While the poor certainly *feel* poor, their levels of self-reported happiness or self-reported health levels are not particularly low (Banerjee, Duflo, and Deaton, 2004). On the other hand, the poor do report being under a great deal of stress, both financial and psychological. In Udaipur, about 12 percent say that there has been a period of one month or more in the last year in which they were so "worried, tense, or anxious" that it interfered with normal activities like sleeping, working, and eating. Case and Deaton (2005) compare data from South Africa to the data from Udaipur and data from the United States. They find that the answers of poor South Africans and poor Indians about stress look very similar, while reported levels of stress are very much lower in the United States. The most frequently cited reason for such tensions is health problems (cited by 29 percent of respondents), with lack of food and death coming next (13 percent each). Over the last year, in 45 percent of the extremely poor households in Udiapur (and 35 percent of those living under $2 a day) adults had to cut the size of their meal at some point during the year and in 12 percent of them, children had to cut the size of their meals. In the extremely poor households under $1 per day, 37 percent report that, at some point in the past year, the adults in the household went without a meal for an entire day. Cutting meals is also strongly correlated with unhappiness.

Even poor households should be able to save enough to make sure that they never have to cut meals, because as discussed above they do have substantial slack in their budgets and cutting meals is not that common. Additional savings would also make it easier to deal with healthcare emergencies. For these households, saving a bit more would seem like a relatively inexpensive way to reduce stress.

Investment in education

The extremely poor spend very little on education. The expenditure on education generally hovers around 2 percent of household budgets: higher in Pakistan (3 percent), Indonesia (6 percent), and Côte d'Ivoire (6 percent), but much lower in Guatemala (0.1 percent), and South Africa (0.8 percent). The fraction does not really change very much when we compare the poor to the extremely poor, or rural areas to urban areas, though in a few countries like Pakistan, urban families spend substantially more than rural families. This low level of expenditure on education is not because the children are out of school. In 12 of the 13 countries in our sample, with the exception of Côte d'Ivoire, at least 50 percent of both boys and girls aged 7 to 12 in extremely poor households are in school. In about half the countries, the proportion enrolled is greater than 75 percent among girls, and more than 80 percent among boys.

The reason education spending is low is that children in poor households typically attend public schools or other schools that do not charge a fee. In countries where poor households spend more on education, it is typically because government schools have fees, as in Indonesia and Côte d'Ivoire. However, mounting evidence, reported below, suggests that public schools in these countries are often dysfunctional, which could explain why even very poor parents in Pakistan are pulling their children out of public schools and spending money to send them to private schools.

How the poor earn their money

Walking down the main street of the biggest slum in the medium-sized southern Indian city of Guntur at nine in the morning, the first thing one notices are the eateries. In front of every sixth house that directly faced the road, by our count, a woman was sitting behind a little kerosene stove with a round cast-iron griddle roasting on it. Every few minutes someone would walk up to her and order a *dosa*, the rice and beans pancakes that almost everyone eats for breakfast in south India. She would throw a cupful of the batter on the griddle, swirl it around to cover almost the entire surface, and drizzle some oil around the edges. A minute or two later, she would slide an off-white pock-marked pancake off the griddle, douse it in some sauce, fold it in a newspaper or a banana leaf and hand it to her client, in return for a rupee (roughly 15 cents).

When we walked back down that same street an hour later, the women were gone. We found one inside her house, filling her daughter's plate with lunch that she had cooked while making the *dosas*. She told us that later that day, she was going out to vend her *saris*, the long piece of decorative cloth that Indian women drape around themselves. She gets plain nylon saris from the shop and stitches beads and small shiny pieces on them. Once a week, she takes them from house to house, hoping that women would buy them to wear on special occasions. And they do buy them, she said confidently. All the other *dosa* women we met that day had a similar story: once they are done frying *dosas*, they do something else. Some collect trash; others make pickles to sell; others work as laborers.

Entrepreneurship and multiple occupations among the poor

All over the world, a substantial fraction of the poor act as entrepreneurs in the sense of raising capital, carrying out investment, and being the full residual claimants for the resulting earnings. In Peru, 69 percent of the households who live under $2 a day in urban areas operate a nonagricultural business. In Indonesia, Pakistan, and Nicaragua, the numbers are between 47 and 52 percent. A large fraction of the rural poor operate a farm: 25 to 98 percent of the households who earn less than a dollar a day report being self-employed in agriculture, except in Mexico and South Africa where self-employment in agriculture is very rare.[4] Moreover, many of the rural poor – from 7 percent in Udaipur up to 36 percent in Panama – also operate a nonagricultural business.

Many poor households have multiple occupations. Like the *dosa* women of Guntur, 21 percent of the households living under $2 a day in Hyderabad who have a business actually have more than one, while another 13 percent have both a business and a laborer's job. This multiplicity of occupations in urban areas is found in many other countries as well, though not everywhere. Among those earning less than $2 a day, 47 percent of the urban households in Côte d'Ivoire and Indonesia get their income from more than one source; 36 percent in Pakistan; 20.5 percent in Peru; and 24 percent in Mexico. However, in urban South Africa and Panama, almost no one has more than one occupation and only 9 percent do so in Nicaragua and Timor Leste.[5]

This pattern of multiple occupations is stronger in rural areas. In Udaipur district, as we discussed earlier, almost everybody owns some land and almost everybody does at least some agriculture. Yet only 19 percent of the households describe self-employment in agriculture as the *main* source of their income. Working on someone else's land is even rarer, with only 1 percent reporting this as their main source of income. In other words, the poor cultivate the land they own, no less and usually, no more. Yet, agriculture is not the mainstay of most of these households. The most common occupation for the poor in Udaipur is working as a daily laborer: 98 percent of households living under $1 per day in rural areas report doing this, and 74 percent claim it is their main source of earnings.

This pattern is confirmed by data from a smaller survey of 27 villages randomly sampled from eight districts in West Bengal (Banerjee, 2006). In this survey, even households that claim to be the operators for a plot of land spend only 40 percent of their time in agricultural activities on their own land. The fraction is not very different for men and women – women do less direct agricultural work but more animal rearing, along with growing fruits and vegetables. Their other activities include teaching, sewing and embroidery, unpaid household work, and gathering fuel. Strikingly, almost 10 percent of the time of the average household is spent on gathering fuel, either for use at home or for sale. The median family in this survey has three working members and *seven* occupations.

In most of the Living Standard Measurement Surveys, households are not asked their main source of earnings, but the pattern of diversification among rural households is apparent nevertheless. In Guatemala, 65 percent of the rural extremely poor say they get some income from self-employment in agriculture, 86 percent work as laborers outside agriculture, and 24 percent are self-employed outside agriculture. In Indonesia, 34 percent of the rural, extremely poor households work as laborers outside of agriculture, and 37 percent earn income from self-employment outside of agriculture. In Pakistan, 51 percent of the rural, extremely poor earn income from labor outside of agriculture and 35 percent from a business outside of agriculture. Overall, the fraction of the rural extremely poor households who report that they conduct more than one type of activity to earn a living is 50 percent in Indonesia, 72 percent in Côte d'Ivoire, 84 percent in Guatemala, and 94 percent in Udaipur. It is smaller, but not negligible – between 10 and 20 percent – in Nicaragua, Panama, Timor Leste, and Mexico. Once again, an exception to this general pattern is South Africa, where less than 1 percent of the rural poor or extremely poor report multiple occupations.

Temporary migration to work

Where do rural households, which are often a walk of a half-hour or more from the nearest road, find all this nonagricultural work? They migrate.

Temporary migration is rarely documented in surveys, but in the Udaipur survey, which had questions about this activity, 60 percent of the poorest households report that someone from their family had lived outside for a part of the year to obtain work. For 58 percent of the families, the head of the household had migrated. The migrants typically complete multiple trips in a year. However, people do not leave for very long. The median length of a completed migration is one month, and only 10 percent of migration episodes exceed three months. Nor do most of the migrants travel very far: 28 percent stay in the district of Udaipur and only 42 percent leave the state of Rajasthan.

Permanent migration for work reasons is rare, although many women move when they marry. Even if we look at households currently living in urban areas, where the inflow of immigrants is presumably higher than in rural areas, the share of extremely poor households who had one member that was born elsewhere and had migrated for work reasons was just 4 percent in Pakistan, 6 percent in Côte d'Ivoire, 6 percent in Nicaragua, and almost 10 percent in Peru. The 1991 Census of India reports that only 14.7 percent of the male population lives somewhere other than where they were born. Indonesia is the only country in our data where the proportion is higher: 41 percent of the urban households came from elsewhere. Indonesia is also the only country in this sample where migration was explicitly subsidized.

Lack of specialization

A pattern seems to emerge. Poor families do seek out economic opportunities, but they tend not to become too specialized. They do some agriculture, but not to the point where it would afford them a full living (for example, by buying/renting/sharecropping more land). They also work outside, but only in short bursts, and they do not move permanently to their place of occupation.

This lack of specialization has its costs. Many of these poor households receive most of their earnings from these outside jobs, despite only being away for 18 weeks of the year on average (in the case of Udaipur). As short-term migrants, they have little chance of learning their jobs better, or ending up in a job that suits their specific talents, or being promoted.

Even the nonagricultural businesses that the poor operate typically require relatively few specific skills. For example, the businesses in Hyderabad include 11 percent tailors, 8 percent fruit and vegetable sellers, 17 percent small general stores, 6.6 percent telephone booths, 4.3 percent auto owners, and 6.3 percent milk sellers. Except for tailoring, none of these jobs require the high levels of specialized competence that take a long time to acquire, and therefore are associated with higher earnings. In several ways, the poor are trading off opportunities to have higher incomes.

The problem of scale

The businesses of the poor typically operate at a remarkably small scale. As we saw, the average landholding for those who own land is usually quite tiny, and renting land is infrequent. Furthermore, most of this land is not irrigated and cannot be used all year.

The scale of nonagricultural businesses run by the poor also tends to be small. In the 13 countries in our sample, the median business operated by people living under $2 dollars a day either in a rural or an urban location has no paid staff, and the average number of paid employees range between 0.14 in rural Nicaragua to 0.53 in urban Panama. Businesses are operated on average by 1.38 (in Peru) to 2.59 (in Côte d'Ivoire) people – most of them being family members. Most of these businesses have very few assets as well. In Hyderabad, only 20 percent of the businesses operate out of a separate room. In Pakistan, about 40 percent of the businesses of those living under $1 or $2 dollar a day have a vehicle, but only 4 percent have a motorized vehicle and none have any machinery. In other countries, even nonmotorized vehicles are rare. In Hyderabad, where we have an exhaustive list of business assets, the most common assets are tables, scales, and pushcarts.

Many of these businesses are probably operating at too small a scale for efficiency. The women making *dosas* spend a lot of time waiting: having fewer *dosa*-makers who do less waiting would be more efficient. In fact, it might make sense in efficiency terms for the *dosa*-makers to work in pairs: one to make the *dosas* and one to wrap them and make change.

Markets and the economic environment of the poor

The economic choices of the poor are constrained by their market environment. For example, some may save little because they lack a safe place to put their savings. Other constraints result from a lack of shared infrastructure. When the government builds a water line to your neighborhood, for example, you no longer need your own well. This section focuses on markets. The next takes up the issue of infrastructure.

The market for credit and the poor

The data from our 13 countries suggests that the fraction of rural, extremely poor households having an outstanding debt varies between countries, from 11 percent in rural East Timor to 93 percent in Pakistan. But across the surveys, very few of the poor households get loans from a formal lending source.

In the Udaipur sample, about two-thirds of the poor had a loan at the time of the interview. Of these loans, 23 percent are from a relative, 18 percent from a money lender, 37 percent from a shopkeeper, and only 6.4 percent from a formal source like a commercial bank or a cooperative. Lest one suspect that the low share of bank credit is due to the lack of physical access to banks, a similar pattern occurs in urban Hyderabad, where households living below $2 a day primarily borrow from moneylenders (52 percent), friends or neighbors (24 percent), and family members (13 percent), and only 5 percent of the loans are with commercial banks. Indonesia is the one country where a substantial share of loans to the poor is formal: thanks to efforts by the Bank Rakyat Indonesia, one-third of the rural poor Indonesian households borrow from a bank. In the other countries, relatives, shopkeepers, and other villagers form, by far, the overwhelming source of borrowed funds.

Credit from informal sources tends to be expensive. In the Udaipur survey, where we have data on interest rates not available in other surveys, those living on less than $1 a day pay on average 3.84 percent per month for the credit they receive from informal sources. Those who consume between $1 and $2 dollar a day per capita pay a little less: 3.13 percent per month. This lower rate occurs in part because they rely less on informal sources of credit and more on the formal sources than the extremely poor; and in part it reflects that informal interest rates are lower for those with more land – the interest rate from informal sources drops by 0.40 percent per month for each additional hectare of land owned. The monthly interest rate we see in the Hyderabad sample is even higher: 3.94 percent per month for those living under $2 dollars a day. Few of these urban poor borrowers in Hyderabad have any land to use as collateral.

These high interest rates seem not to occur directly because of high rates of default, but rather as a result of the high costs of contract enforcement. While delay in repayment of informal loans is frequent, default is actually rare (Banerjee and Duflo, 2005). For example, a "Summary Report on Informal Credit Markets in India" reports that across four case studies of money-lenders in rural India, default explains only 23 percent of the interest rate charged (Dasgupta, 1989). A well-known study of rural money-lenders in Pakistan found that the median rate of default across money-lenders is just 2 percent (Aleem, 1990).

However, these low default rates are anything but automatic. Contract enforcement in developing countries is often difficult, and courts often fail to punish recalcitrant borrowers. As a result, lenders often must spend resources to assure that their loans get repaid, which drives up interest rates. The fact that lending depends so much on effective screening and monitoring also means that lending to the poor is especially difficult. Again, part of the problem is that the poor lack collateral to secure the loan and therefore lenders hesitate to trust them. Given that the loan amount will in any case be small, the profits from the transaction may not be large enough to cover the cost of monitoring/screening. As a result, many lenders are reluctant to lend to the poor. Moreover, informal lenders located close to the borrowers may be the only ones who are willing to lend to the poor – since monitoring/screening is relatively cheap for them. However, these informal lenders pay more for their deposits than the more formal institutions, since they are less capitalized and regulated and do not have any government guarantees. This higher cost of deposits is passed on to poorer borrowers. The gap can be considerable – in the study by Aleem (1990), the cost of capital for the money-lenders was 32.5 percent in a year when banks were only paying 10 percent for their deposits.

The market for savings and the poor

A main challenge for the poor who try to save is to find safety and a reasonable return. Stashing cash inside your pillow or elsewhere at home is neither safe nor well-protected from inflation. In addition, recent research by Ashraf, Karlan, and Yin (forthcoming) in the Philippines and Duflo, Kremer, and Robinson in Kenya (2006) suggests that the poor, like everyone else, have problems resisting the temptation of spending money that they have at hand.

Few poor households have savings accounts. Except in Côte d'Ivoire, where 79 percent of the extremely poor households under $1 a day have a savings account, the fraction is below 14 percent in the other countries in our data. In Panama and Peru, less than 1 percent of poor households have a savings account. In most countries, the share of households with a saving account is similar in rural and urban areas, and similar for those under $2 a day and those under $1 a day. Here India appears to be an exception, since only 6 percent of the extremely poor households in rural Udaipur have a savings account, while 25 percent of them do in the city of Hyderabad.

A lack of access to reliable savings accounts appears common to the poor everywhere, as documented in Stuart Rutherford's (2000) fascinating book, *The Poor and their Money*. Rutherford describes many strategies the poor use to deal with this problem. For example, they form savings "clubs," where each person makes sure that the others save. Self-Help Groups (SHGs), popular in parts of India and present in Indonesia as well, are saving clubs which also make loans to their members out of the accumulated savings (they are also sometimes linked to banks). In Africa, Rotating Savings and Credit Associations (ROSCAs) allow people to lend their savings to each other on a rotating basis. Others pay deposit collectors to collect their deposits and put them in a bank. Others deposit their savings with local money-lenders, with credit unions (which are essentially larger and much more formally organized self-help groups) or in an account at the local post office. Indeed, one reason why many of the poor respond so well to microcredit is not necessarily because it offers them credit, but because once you take a loan and buy something with it, you have a disciplined way to save – namely, by paying down the loan.

Even participation in semiformal savings institutions (such as self-help groups, ROSCAs, and microfinance institutions) is not nearly as common among the poor as one might have expected. Even in India, despite the high visibility especially of SHGs, less than 10 percent of the poor in our Udaipur and Hyderabad surveys are part of an SHG or a ROSCA. The majority of the households who have any savings deposit it at a bank.

The market for insurance and the poor

The poor have little access to formal insurance. In many surveys, questions about insurance are not even asked. In the six of our seven countries where such data is available, less than 6 percent of the extremely poor are covered by health insurance of any kind. The exception is Mexico, where about half of the extremely poor have coverage. The numbers are not much higher in urban areas. Life insurance is a bit more common in India (and is, essentially, a form of savings). Four percent of the extremely poor in Udaipur and 10 percent in Hyderabad have life insurance.[6]

In principle, social networks can provide informal insurance. For example, Udry (1990) shows that poor villagers in Nigeria experience a dense network of loan exchanges: Over the course of one year, 75 percent of the households had made loans, 65 percent had borrowed money, and 50 percent had been both borrowers and lenders. Almost all of these loans took place between neighbors and relatives. Both the repayment schedule and the amount repaid were affected by both the lender's and the borrower's current economic conditions, underlining the role of these informal loans in providing insurance. Munshi and Rosenzweig (2005) argue that the same process happens in India through the *jati* or subcaste networks.

Yet these informal networks have only a limited ability to protect the households against risk. The consumption of poor households is strongly affected by variations in their incomes, as has been shown by Deaton (1997) in Côte d'Ivoire, Munshi and Rosenzweig (2005) in India, Fafchamps and Lund (2003) in the Philippines, and Townsend (1995) in Thailand. Poor households also bear most health care risks (both expenditures and foregone earnings) directly. For example, Gertler and Gruber (2002) find that in Indonesia a decline in the health index of the head of the household is associated with a decline in nonmedical expenditures. In Udaipur, large expenditures on health ($70 and higher, at purchasing power parity exchange rates) are covered by borrowing or dissaving. Only 2 percent of these expenses were paid for by someone else, and none came from the self-help groups. Twenty-four percent of the households in Hyderabad had to borrow to pay for health expenses in the last year. When the poor fall under economic stress, their "insurance" often means eating less or taking their children out of school. For example, Jacoby and Skoufias (1997) find that poor children leave school in bad years. Rose (1999) finds that the gap in mortality of girls relative to boys is much larger in drought years (but only for the landless households, who are not able to sell land or borrow to weather the crisis). Poor households also are less likely to get medical treatment for themselves or their children. In the Udaipur sample, those who were sick in the last months and did not seek treatment (more than half) cite lack of money more often than any other reason (34 percent). The lack of insurance also leads the poor to underinvest in risky but profitable technologies, such as new seeds (Morduch, 1995).

The weaknesses of informal insurance should not really be a surprise. Ultimately, informal insurance relies on the willingness of the fortunate to take care of those less favored, which limits the insurance provided. Moreover, informal social networks are often not well-diversified. They often spread risk over households who live nearby and have similar incomes and occupations, as Fafchamps and Gubert (2005) show for the Philippines.

Governments in these countries are not very effective at providing insurance either. In most countries, the government is supposed to provide free health care to the poor. Yet health care is rarely free. Government health care providers often illegally charge for their own services and for medicines. Also, as we will see, the quality of care in the public system is so low that the poor often end up visiting private providers.

A number of governments provide a form of income insurance through safety-net "food for work" programs. Under these programs, everyone is entitled to a certain number of days of government employment usually involving physical labor at a pre-announced (relatively low) wage. In Udaipur, where the years leading up to the survey had been particularly arid, 76 percent of the poor had at least one of the household members work on a public employment program of this kind. However, such schemes often offer only a limited number of jobs which can end up being doled out in a way that discriminates against the poor.

The market for land and the poor

For historical reasons, land is the one asset the poor tend to own. But land records in developing countries are often incomplete and many people do not have titles to their land. As many including most famously Hernando De Soto (2003) have emphasized, an unclear title makes it harder to sell the land or mortgage it. This situation is especially troubling for the poor, because they tend to own a lot of the land that was either recently cleared or recently encroached upon, which is typically the land where tilling is incomplete. Erica Field (2006) suggests that, in Peru, the poor spend a lot of time protecting their claims to the land (since they have no tide, they have no legal recourse).

The poor also suffer because where titles are missing or imperfectly enforced, political influence matters. In parts of Ghana, land belongs either to lineages or to the village, and cultivators have only rights of use. In this context, Goldstein and Udry (2005) show that the people who lack the political clout to prevent having their land taken away from them by the village or their lineage (which typically includes the poor) do not leave their land fallow for long enough. Leaving land to fallow increases its productivity, but increases the risk that someone may seize it.

Finally, a long tradition of research in agricultural economics argues that the poor lack incentives to make the best use of the land they are cultivating because they are agents rather than owners (Shaban, 1987). Banerjee, Gertler, and Ghatak (2002) found that a reform of tenancy that forced landlords to raise the share of output going to the sharecroppers and also gave them a secure right to the land raised productivity by about 50 percent.

Infrastructure and the economic environment of the poor

Infrastructure includes roads, power connections, schools, health facilities, and public health infrastructure (mostly water and sanitation). While markets and the government play differing roles in the supply of such infrastructure, all elements of infrastructure are usefully thought of as part of the environment in which people live, with some characteristics of a local public good, rather than something that can be purchased piecemeal by individuals.

The availability of physical infrastructure to the poor like electricity, tap water, and even basic sanitation (like access to a latrine) varies enormously across countries. In our sample of 13 countries, the number of rural poor households with access to tap water varies from none in Udaipur to 36 percent in Guatemala. The availability of electricity varies from 1.3 percent in Tanzania to 99 percent in Mexico. The availability of a latrine varies from none in Udaipur to 100 percent in Nicaragua. Different kinds of infrastructure do not always appear together. In Indonesia, 97 percent of rural, extremely poor households have electricity but only 6 percent have tap water. Some governments provide reasonable access to both electricity and tap water to the extremely poor: in Guatemala, 38 percent of the extremely poor rural households have tap water and 30 percent have electricity. Other governments do very little: in Udaipur, Papua New Guinea, East Timor, and South Africa, the share of the rural, extremely poor with tap water or electricity is below 5 percent.

Generally, access to electricity and tap water is greater for the urban poor than the rural poor (which is probably fortunate since lack of sanitation in very dense surroundings can be particularly dangerous from the public health point of view). The only exception to this pattern in our 13 countries is Côte d'Ivoire, where rural households seem to have better access. Moreover, access to both tap water and electricity is typically higher for those under $2 a day than those under $1 a day.

Most low-income countries have made some attempt to ensure that poor households have access to primary schools and basic health centers. For example, most Indian villages now have a school within a kilometer, and a health subcenter exists for every 10,000 people. However, the quality of the facilities that serve the poor tends to be low, even when they are available, and it is not clear how much they actually deliver. Chaudhury, Hammer, Kremer, Muralidharan, and Rogers (2005) report results on surveys they conducted to measure the absence of teachers and health workers in Bangladesh, Ecuador, India, Indonesia, Peru, and Uganda. They found that the average absence rate among teachers is 19 percent and the average absence rate among health workers is 35 percent. Moreover, because not all teachers and health workers are actually working when at their post, even this picture may be too favorable. Moreover, absence rates are generally higher in poor regions.

In an innovative study on health care quality, Das and Hammer (2004) collected data on the competence of doctors in Delhi, India, based on the kinds of questions they ask and the action they say they would take faced with a hypothetical patient, suffering from conditions they are likely to encounter in their practice. Every Delhi neighborhood, poor or rich, lives within 15 minutes of at least 70 health providers. However, the gap in competence of the average health practitioner between the poorest and richest neighborhoods is almost as large as the gap between the competence of a health provider with an MBBS degree (the equivalent of an MD in the United States) and a provider without such a qualification. In fact, an expert panel found that the treatments suggested by the average provider in their sample are slightly more likely to do harm rather than good, due to a combination of misdiagnosis and overmedication.

These differences in health care and basic sanitation infrastructure can affect mortality. Several surveys ask women about their pregnancies and the outcomes, including whether the child is still alive. We compute an infant mortality measure as the number of children who died before the age of one divided by the number of live births. The numbers are startling, especially because they are likely to be underestimates (not all children are remembered, especially if they died very early). Among the rural, extremely poor, the lowest infant mortality that we observe is 3.4 percent in Indonesia. At the high end, infant mortality among the extremely poor is 8.7 percent in South Africa and Tanzania, 10 percent in Udaipur, and 16.7 percent in Pakistan. The rates are lower, but not much lower, in urban areas. The rates also remain high if the definition of poverty is expanded to include those who live under $2 a day. Wagstaff (2003) uses data from the demographic and health surveys to estimate prevalence of malnutrition and child mortality among those living under $1 a day in a number of countries. He finds very large difference between survival chances of poor children in different countries, and shows that they are correlated with health spending per capita in these countries.

The low quality of teaching in public schools has clear effect on learning levels as well. In India, despite the fact that 93.4 percent of children ages 6–14 are enrolled in schools (75 percent of them in government schools), a recent nationwide survey found that 34.9 percent of the children age 7 to 14 cannot read a simple paragraph at second-grade level (Pratham, 2006). Moreover, 41.1 percent cannot do subtraction, and 65.5 percent cannot do division. Even among children in grades six to eight in government schools, 22 percent cannot read a second-grade text.

In countries where the public provision of education and health services is particularly low, private providers have stepped in. In the parts of India where public school teacher absenteeism is the highest, the fraction of rural children attending private schools is also the highest (Chaudhury, Hammer, Kremer, Muralidharan, and Rogers, 2005). However, these private schools are less than ideal: they have lower teacher absenteeism than the public schools in the same village, but their teachers are significantly less qualified in the sense of having a formal teaching degree.

A similar but more extreme pattern arises in health care. Again, private providers who serve the poor are less likely to be absent and more likely to examine the patient with some care than their public counterparts, but they tend to be less well qualified (for example, Das and Hammer, 2004). However, unlike in education, where most poor children are still in the public system, even in countries and regions where public education is of extremely poor quality, where the public health care system has high levels of absence, most people actually go to private providers. For example, in India, where absence of health care providers is 40 percent, 58 percent of the extremely poor households have visited a private health care provider in the last month. By contrast in Peru, where the absentee rate for health care providers is fairly low at 25 percent (Chaudhury, Hammer, Kremer, Muralidharan, and Rogers, 2005), only 9 percent of the rural extremely poor households have been to a private health provider in the last month. Within the Udaipur District, Banerjee, Deaton, and Duflo (2004) also found that the rate of usage of the public health facility is strongly correlated with the absence rate at the public health facilities in the areas.

Understanding the economic lives of the poor

Many facts about the lives of the poor start to make much more sense once we recognize that they have very limited access to efficient markets and quality infrastructure. The fact that the poor usually cultivate the land they own, no more and no less, for example, probably owes a lot to the agency problems associated with renting out land. In part, it must also reflect the fact that the poor, who typically own too little land relative to the amount of family labor, suffer from lack of access to credit. This pattern is reinforced by the difficulties that the poor face in getting any kind of insurance against the many risks with which a farmer needs to deal: A second job outside agriculture offers security against some of that risk.

Why so little specialization?

Risk-spreading is clearly one reason why the poor, who might find risk especially hard to bear, tend not to be too specialized in any one occupation. They work part time outside agriculture to reduce their exposure to farming risk, and keep a foot in agriculture to avoid being too dependent on their nonagricultural jobs.

Another reason for a second job is to occupy what would otherwise be wasted time. When we asked the *dosa*-sellers of Guntur why they did so many other things as well, they all said: "[We] can sell *dosas* in the morning. What do we do for the rest of the day?" Similarly, farmers who do not have irrigated land can only farm when the land is not too dry. Finding some work outside agriculture is a way for them to make productive use of their time when the land is unusable. However, this argument is incomplete. We also need to explain what made the women opt to sell *dosas*: After all they could have skipped the *dosas* and specialized in whatever they were doing for the rest of the day. Risk spreading remains a possible answer, but many of them seem to be in relatively safe occupations. Given the fact that almost everyone owns the cooking implement that one needs to make a *dosa* and entry is free, it does not seem that *dosa*-making is an extraordinarily profitable activity.

A final, more compelling reason for multiple jobs is that the poor cannot raise the capital they would need to run a business that would occupy them fully. As we saw, most businesses operate with very little assets and little working capital. Likewise, some poor farmers might be able to irrigate their lands and make them useable for a larger part of the year, but they lack the necessary access to funds. Of course, in agriculture, some downtime will always remain, justifying some amount of diversification of jobs. But such downtime would be much more limited than what the data actually reveals.

Why so many entrepreneurs?

Once we draw this link between the tendency of the poor to be in multiple occupations and their access to financial markets, it is clear why so many of the poor are entrepreneurs. If you have few skills and little capital, and especially if you are a woman, being an entrepreneur is often easier than finding an employer with a job to offer. You buy some fruits and vegetables or some plastic toys at the wholesalers and start selling them on the street; you make some extra *dosa* mix and sell the *dosas* in front of your house; you collect cow dung and dry it to sell it as a fuel; you attend to one cow and collect the milk. These types of activities are exactly those in which the poor are involved.

It is important not to romanticize these penniless entrepreneurs. Given that they have no money, borrowing is risky, and no one wants to lend to them, the businesses they run are inevitably extremely small, to the point where there are clearly unrealized economies of scale. Moreover, given that so many of these firms have more family labor available to them than they can use, they do very little to create jobs for others. Of course, this pattern makes it harder for anyone to find a job and hence reinforces the proliferation of petty entrepreneurs.

Why don't the poor eat more?

Another puzzle is why the poor do not spend more on food both on average and especially out of the marginal dollar. Eating more and eating better (more grains and iron-rich foods, less sugar) would help them build their body-mass indices to healthier levels.

One possibility is that eating more would not help them that much, or not for long, because they would become weak again at the first attack of disease, which will invariably occur. For example, Deaton, Cutler, and Lleras-Muney (2006) argue that nutrition is at best a very small part of what explains the tremendous gains in health around the world in the past few decades. However, some improvements in nutrition (reduction of anemia in particular) have been linked to increased productivity (Thomas et al., 2004). Moreover, as we saw, not having enough to eat does, at a minimum, make the poor extremely unhappy.

Provided that eating more would increase their productivity, it is unlikely that the low levels of good consumption can be explained by a simple lack of self control (that is, the poor cannot resist temptations to spend on things other than food). As we noted above, the poor also spend surprisingly large amounts on entertainment: televisions, weddings, or festivals. All of these involve spending a large amount at one time, which implies some saving unless they happen to be especially credit-worthy. In other words, many poor people save money that they could have eaten today to spend more on entertainment in the future, which does not immediately fit the idea that they lack self-control.

The need to spend more on entertainment rather than on food appears to be a strongly felt need, not a result of inadequate planning. One reason this might be the case is that the poor want to keep up with their neighbors. Fafchamps and Shilpi (2006) offer evidence from Nepal in which people were asked to assess whether their level of income as well as their levels of consumption of housing, food, clothing, health care, and schooling were adequate. The answers to these questions were strongly negatively related to the average consumption of the other people living in the same village.

Why don't the poor invest more in education?

The children of the poor are, by and large, going to primary school. However, parents are not reacting to the low quality of these schools, either by sending their children to better and more expensive schools or by putting pressure on the government to do something about quality in government schools. Why not?

One reason is that poor parents, who may often be illiterate themselves, may have a hard time recognizing that their children are not learning much. Poor parents in Eastern Uttar Pradesh in India have limited success in predicting whether their school-age children can read (Banerjee et al., 2006). Moreover, how can parents be confident that a private school would offer a better education, given that the teacher there is usually less qualified than the public school teachers? After all, researchers have only discovered this pattern in the last few years. As for putting pressure on the government, it is not clear that the average villager would know how to organize and do so.

Why don't the poor save more?

The arguments based on lack of access to credit and insurance or labor market rigidities, by themselves, do not help very much in understanding why the poor are not more interested in accumulating wealth. After all, the poor could easily save more without getting less nutrition, by spending less on alcohol, tobacco, festivals, and food items such as sugar, spice, and tea.

It is true that the poor typically have no bank accounts or other financial assets with which to save, but many of them have their own businesses, and these tend to be chronically underfunded. So why not save up to buy a new machine, or increase the stock in the shop? Moreover, as we saw above, a very substantial fraction of the poor have debt, and the interest rate on the debt often exceeds 3 percent per month. Paying down debt is therefore a very attractive way to save. Even if you have no business to grow, and have no debt to repay, just holding some extra stocks for the proverbial rainy day (or "the drought") can save both worry and the misery of watching your children go hungry. In other words, precautionary motives for saving should be especially strong for the poor.

Part of the answer is probably that saving at home is hard. The money may be stolen (especially if you live in a house that cannot be locked) or grabbed by your spouse or your son. Also, if you have money at hand, you are constantly resisting temptation to spend: to buy something, to help someone to whom you find it difficult to say "no," to give your child a treat. Such temptations may be especially hard for the poor, because many of the temptations they are resisting are things that everyone else might take for granted.

The poor seem aware of their vulnerability to temptation. In the Hyderabad survey, the respondents were asked to name whether they would like to cut particular expenses, and 28 percent of the poor named at least one item. The top item that households would like to cut is alcohol and tobacco (mentioned by 44 percent of the households that want to cut on items). Then came sugar, tea, and snacks (9 percent), festivals (7 percent), and entertainment (7 percent).

Self-knowledge does not help in addressing self-control problems; in fact, self-knowledge about a lack of self-control means that you know your saving will probably just end up feeding some future indefensible craving, and the machine for which you are trying to save will never actually be bought. Being naïve might actually help – you might be lucky and save enough to buy the machine before the temptation gets to you.

Beyond market failures and self-control problems

An interesting example that spans many of the arguments we have used above is a study by Duflo, Kremer, and Robinson (2006) on investment in fertilizer in Kenya. According to surveys conducted over several years, just 40.3 percent of farmers had ever used fertilizer, and just 25 percent used fertilizer in any given year. Conservative estimates suggest that the average return to using fertilizer exceeds 100 percent, and the median return is above 75 percent. Duflo, Kremer, and Robinson conducted field trials of fertilizer on the farms of actual randomly selected farmers, which were meant to teach the farmers how to use fertilizer and the rewards of doing so. They found that the farmers who participated in the study are 10 percent more likely on average to use fertilizer in the very next season after the study, but only 10 percent more likely – and the effects fade after the first season.

When farmers were asked why they did not use fertilizer, most farmers replied that they did not have enough money. However, fertilizer can be purchased (and used) in small quantities, so this investment opportunity seems accessible to farmers with even a small level of saving. The main issue, once again, appears to be that farmers find it difficult to save even small sums of money. The program in Kenya offered to sell farmers a voucher right after the harvest, which is when farmers have money in hand, which would entitle them to buy fertilizer later.

This program had a large effect: 39 percent of the farmers offered the voucher bought the fertilizer; the effects are as large as a 50 percent subsidy on the cost of fertilizer. The voucher seemed to work as a commitment device to encourage saving. But a puzzle remains: farmers could have bought the fertilizer in advance on their own. Indeed, a huge majority of the farmers who bought the vouchers for future delivery of fertilizer requested immediate delivery, and then stored the fertilizer for later use. Moreover, almost all of them used the fertilizer they bought. They apparently had no self-control problems in keeping the fertilizer, even though they could easily exchange the fertilizer for something more immediately consumable.

Why don't the poor migrate for longer?

A final puzzle is why the poor do not migrate for longer periods, given that they could easily earn much more by doing so. Munshi and Rosenzweig (2005) argue that the lack of long-term migration reflects the value of remaining close to one's social network in a setting where the social network might be the only source of (informal) insurance available to people. Those who migrate for short periods of up to a few months leave their entire family, who presumably can maintain their social links, behind. However, the ultimate reason seems to be that making more money is not a huge priority, or at least not a large enough priority to experience several months of living alone and often sleeping on the ground in or around the work premises.

In some ways this puzzle resembles the question of why the Kenyan farmers do not buy fertilizer right after the harvest even though they are happy to buy (and use it) if someone made the (small) effort to bring it to their farm. In both cases, one senses a reluctance of poor people to commit themselves psychologically to a project of making more money. Perhaps at some level this avoidance is emotionally wise: thinking about the economic problems of life must make it harder to avoid confronting the sheer inadequacy of the standard of living faced by the extremely poor.

Notes

We thank Andrei Shleifer for motivating us to undertake this exercise. We thank him and the editors of this journal for detailed suggestions on the previous draft of this paper. We thank Danielle Li, Marc Shotland, and Stefanie Stancheva for spectacular assistance in assembling the data, and Kudzai Takavarasha for carefully editing a previous draft. Special thanks to Angus Deaton for extremely useful advice and guidance and extensive comments on the previous draft and to Gary Becker for helpful comments.

1   For example, the "All India Rural" poverty line used by the Indian Planning Commission was 328 rupees per person per month, or $32 in purchasing power parity (PPP) dollars in 1999/2000.

2   The fact that the share spent on food, which is often seen as a physiological necessity, varies so much across countries is itself interesting. One possibility is that this represents the fact that the poor have more choice in some countries than in others, because consumption goods are cheap relative to food in some countries. For example, India, a large economy with a long history of being relatively closed, has evolved a large menu of low-cost and lower-quality consumer goods that are produced almost exclusively for the domestic market, examples include tooth-paste, cigarettes, and clothing. Other countries must buy

these goods at higher prices on the global market. If the manufactured consumer goods that the average person buys in India tend to be inexpensive relative to their traded counterparts, the ratio between the consumption exchange rate at purchasing power parity and the official exchange rate ought to be relatively low in India. More generally: the lower this ratio, the lower is the share of the consumption that should be made up of food. In our data, it turns out that the correlation between the ratio of the PPP exchange rate for consumption to the official exchange rate in 1993 and the share of expenditure spent on food is 0.33 among these 12 countries, although this sample is of course too small to support a definite conclusion.

3   The ultimate source of variation here might be the relative prices of radios and televisions. There is a strong correlation between the ratio of the purchasing power exchange rate for consumption to the official exchange rate, and the probability that a household owns a radio (the correlation is 0.36). The logic is probably quite similar to the argument presented earlier in the context of food consumption in footnote 2. Radios are tradable (they are essentially all made in China). Nontradable goods are much less costly in some countries than others, while traded goods tend to be more similarly priced, so people at the same expenditure levels at purchasing power parity can have widely differing levels of purchasing power in terms of traded goods.

4   The low level of agriculture among the extremely poor in South Africa is easily explained. The black population, which contains almost all of the extremely poor people, was historically under the apartheid regime not allowed to own land outside the "homelands," and most of the land in the homelands was not worth cultivating.

5   This result may reflect a data problem. Anthropologists do claim that they observe multiple occupations in South African households (Francie Lund, verbal communication to Angus Deaton).

6   Surprisingly, weather insurance is also essentially absent everywhere the world over (Morduch, 2006), although it would seem straightforward to provide insurance against observed weather patterns.

References

Aleem, Irfan. 1990 "Imperfect Information, Screening and the Costs of Informal Lending: A Study of a Rural Credit Market in Pakistan." *World Bank Economic Review*, 4(3): 329–49.

Ashraf, Nava, Dean Karlan, and Wesley Yin. Forthcoming. "Tying Odysseus to the Mast: Evidence from a Commitment Savings Product in the Philippines." *Quarterly Journal of Economics*.

Audretsh, David. *The Entrepreneurial Society*. Oxford: Oxford University Press, Inc., 2005.

Banerjee Abhijit, Angus Deaton, and Esther Duflo. 2004. "Wealth, Health, and Health Services in Rural Rajasthan." *American Economic Review*, 94(2): 326–30.

Banerjee, Abhijit, and Esther Duflo. 2005. "Growth Theory through the Lens of Development Economics," Handbook of Economic Growth, Volume 1A, ed. Steve Durlauf and Philippe Aghion, 473–552. Amsterdam: Elsevier Science.

Banerjee, Abhijit, Esther Duflo, and Rachel Glennerster. 2006. "A Snapshot of Micro Enterprises in Hyderabad," Unpublished paper, MIT.

Banerjee, Abhijit, Paul Gertler, and Maitreesh Ghatak. 2002 "Empowerment and Efficiency: Tenancy Reform in West Bengal." *Journal of Political Economy*, 110(2): 239–80.

Banerjee, Abhijit, and Rohini Somanathan. 2005. "The Political Economy of Public Goods: Some Evidence from India." http://econ-www.mit.edu/faculty/download_pdf.php?id=1144.

Banerjee, Abhijit, Rukmini Barnerji, Esther Duflo, Rachel Glennerster, Daniel Keniston, Stuti Khemani, and Marc Shotland. 2006. "Can Information Campaigns Raise Awareness and Local Participation in Primary Education? A Study of Jaupur District in Uttar Pradesh." http://econ-www.mit.edu/faculty/download_pdf.php?id=1425.

Banerjee, Nirmala. 2006. "A Survey of Occupations and Livelihoods of Households in West Bengal," Sachetana. Unpublished paper.

Case, Anne, and Deaton, Angus. 2005. "Health and Wealth among the Poor: India and South Africa Compared." *American Economic Review Papers and Proceedings*, 95(2): 229–33.

Chaudhury, Nazmul, Jeffrey Hammer, Michael Kremer, Karthik Muralidharan, and F. Halsey Rogers. 2005. "Teacher Absence in India: A Snapshot." *Journal of the European Economic Association*, April–May 3(2–3): 658–67.

Das, Jishnu, and Jeffrey Hammer. 2004. "Strained Mercy: The Quality of Medical Care in Delhi." *Economic and Political Weekly*, (February 28), 39(9): 951–65.

Dasgupta, A. 1989. *Reports on Credit Markets in India: Summary. Technical Report*. New Delhi: National Institute of Public Finance and Policy.

Dasgupta, Partha, and Debraj Ray. 1986. "Inequality as a Determinant of Malnutrition and Unemployment: Policy." *Economic Journal*, 96(384): 1011–1034.

Deaton, Angus. 1997. *The Analysis of Household Surveys: A Microeconometric Approach to Development Policy*. Baltimore: Johns Hopkins University Press for the World Bank.

Deaton, Angus. 2004. "Measuring poverty." In *Understanding Poverty*, ed. Abhijit Banerjee, Roland Benabou, and Dilip Mookherjee. Oxford University Press.

Deaton, Angus. 2006. "Purchasing Power Parity Exchange Rates for the poor: Using Household Surveys to Construct PPPs." http://www.princeton.edu/~rpds/downloads/Deaton_PPPP_version_aug_06.pdf

Deaton, Angus, and Shankar Subramanian. 1996. "The Demand for Food and Calories." *Journal of Political Economy*, 104(1): 133–62.

Deaton, Angus, David Cutler, and Adriana Lleras-Muney. 2006. "The Determinants of Mortality." *Journal of Economic Perspectives*, Summer, 20(3): 97–120.

Duflo, Esther, Michael Kremer, and Jonathan Robinson. 2006. "Why Don't Farmers use Fertilizer: Evidence from Field Experiments." Unpublished paper, MIT.

Fafchamps, Marcel, and Susan Lund. 2003. "Risk-Sharing Networks in Rural Philippines." *Journal of Development Economics*, 71(2): 261–87.

Fafchamps, Marcel, and Flore Gubert. 2005. "The Formation of Risk Sharing Networks." DIAL (Développement, Institutions & Analyses de Long terme) Working Papers DT/2005/13.

Fafchamps, Marcel, and Forhad Shilpi. 2006 "Subjective Welfare, Isolation, and Relative Consumption." http://www.economics.ox.ac.uk/members/marcel.fafchamps/homepage/nepwel.pdf.

Field, Erica. 2006. "Entitled to Work: Urban Property Rights and the Labor Supply in Peru", http://www.economics.harvard.edu/faculty/field/papers/Field_COFOPRI.pdf.

Filmer, Deon, and Lant Pritchett. 2001. "Estimating Wealth Effects without Expenditure Data – or Tears: An Application to Educational Enrollments in States of India." *Demography*, 38(1): 115–32.

Gertler, Paul, and Jonathan Gruber. 2002. "Insuring Consumption against Illness." *American Economic Review*, 92(1): 50–70.

Goldstein, Markus, and Christopher Udry. 2005. "The Profits of Power: Land Rights and Agricultural Investment in Ghana." (Yale University) Economic Growth Center Working Papers 929.

Jacoby, Hanan G., and Emmanuel Skoufias. 1997. "Risk, Financial Markets, and Human Capital in a Developing Country." *Review of Economic Studies*, 64(3): 311–35.

Jha, Raghavendra. 2004. "Calories Deficiency in Rural India in the Last Three Quinquennial Rounds of the NSS." http://eprints.anu.edu.au/archive/ 00001701/.

Meenakshi, J.V., and Brinda Vishwanathan. 2003. "Calorie Deprivation in Rural India, 1983–1999/2000." *Economic and Political Weekly*, January 25, pp 369–75.

Morduch, Jonathan. 1995 "Income Smoothing and Consumption Smoothing." *Journal of Economic Perspectives*, 9(3) :103–114.

Morduch, Jonathan. (2006). "Micro-Insurance: The Next Revolution?" In *What Have We Learned About Poverty?*, ed. Abhijit Banerjee, Roland Benabou, and Dilip Mookherjee. Oxford University Press.

Munshi, K. and M. Rosenzweig. 2005. "Why is Social Mobility in India so Low? Social Insurance, Inequality, and Growth." BREAD [Bureau for Research and Economic Analysis of Development] Working Paper 097.

Prathman. 2006. *Annual Status of Education Report, 2006*. Mumbai: PRATHAM.

Ravallion, Martin. 2004. "Pessimistic on Poverty?" *The Economist*, April 7, 2004.

Rose, Elaina. 1999. "Consumption Smoothing and Excess Female Mortality in Rural India," *Review of Economics and Statistics*, 81(1): 41–49.

Rubalcava, L., and Teruel, G. 2004. "The Mexican Family Life Survey Project (MxFLS): Study Design and Baseline Results." CIDE & UIA working paper.

Rutherford, Stuart. 2000. *The Poor and Their Money*. New Delhi: Oxford University Press.

Sala-i-Martin, Xavier. 2004. "More or Less. Equal." *The Economist*, March 11, 2004.

Shaban, Radwan. 1987. "Testing between Competing Models of Sharecropping." *Journal of Political Economy*, 95(5): 893–920.

De Soto, Hernando. 2003. *The Mystery of Capital: Why Capitalism Triumphs in the West and Fails Everywhere Else*. Basic Books.

Thomas, D., and J. Strauss. 1997. "Health and Wages: Evidence on Men and Women in Urban Brazil." *Journal of Econometrics*, 77(1): 159–85.

Thomas, Duncan, *et al.* 2004. "Causal Effect of Health on Labor Market Outcomes: Evidence from a Random Assignment Iron Supplementation Intervention," Mimeo, UCLA, http://www.ccpr.ucla.edu/ccprwpseries/ccpr_022_04.

Townsend, Robert. 1995. "Financial Systems in Northern Thai Villages." *Quarterly Journal of Economics*, 110(4): 1011–1046.

Udry, Christopher. 1990. "Credit Markets in Northern Nigeria: Credit as Insurance in a Rural Economy." *World Bank Economic Review*, 4(3): 251–69.

Wagstaff, Adam. 2003. "Child Health on One Dollar a Day." *Social Science & Medicine*, 57(9): 1529–38.

World Health Organization Expert Consultation. 2004. "Appropriate Body-Mass Index for Asian Populations and Its Implications for Policy and Intervention Strategies." *Lancet*, 363(9403): 157–63.

REVIEW AND DISCUSSION QUESTIONS

1   What do the data collected by the authors show about the consumption patterns of the poor? What goods do the poor spend most of their money on?

2   What kind of assets and durable goods do the poor own?

3   What kind of work do the poor typically do?

4   Why do the poor tend to have multiple occupations? In what ways does having several jobs instead of just one impose costs on the poor?

5   What do the authors find about the behavior of the poor when it comes to borrowing money, saving money, and buying insurance?

6   On the basis of what you learned from the article about the economic situation and behavior of the poor, suggest a few government policies that you believe would be effective at improving the lives of the poor. Explain clearly.

Chapter 15

THE ECONOMIST

NEW THINKING ABOUT AN OLD PROBLEM

Cash transfers, with strings attached, are a better way of helping the poor than many previous social programmes, as experience in Brazil and Mexico shows

PLENTY IS A SEASONAL CROP in Ocara, a parched district of Ceará, a state in Brazil's north-east. Most of its inhabitants piece together a living from odd jobs and family gardens until September, when the annual harvest of cashew nuts brings relief like a long-awaited rain. Recently, the contrast between fat months and lean ones has become less marked, for Ocara's poorest citizens are now drawing a year-round stipend from the government. It is not much, 120 reais ($52) a month at most for a family of five or more. But for Maria Rita Albino da Silva, a "farmer" and cheerful mother of two, it makes the difference between too little food and enough.

Mrs da Silva, along with most of Ocara's population, is a beneficiary of *Bolsa Família* ("family fund"), a scheme set up in 2003 that provides a basic income to 7.5m of Brazil's poorest families, or 30m people. The goal is to reach all with a monthly income per head of less than 100 reais – 11.2m families, or about a quarter of the population – by the end of next year. The success of *Bolsa Família* is almost as vital to Brazil's left-wing president, Luiz Inácio Lula da Silva, as the cash is to Mrs da Silva (no relation). Lula, himself born poor in the north-east, casts himself as a crusader against poverty and corruption. But his government is mired in a party-financing scandal and its first stab at fighting poverty was "Zero Hunger", a feeding programme ridiculed as outmoded and inefficient. *Bolsa Família*, officially part of Zero Hunger, is a chance for redemption.

It is the biggest of a new generation of social programmes across Latin America, known as "conditional cash transfer" schemes (CCTs). The aim is to alleviate today's poverty, in Brazil's case by transferring up to 95 reais a month to poor families (which states and districts can top up, as Ceará does), and to short-circuit tomorrow's, by making the transfers conditional: beneficiaries must have their children vaccinated, and their health monitored, and keep them in school.

Although CCTs are a Brazilian invention, the first large-scale programme began in Mexico. Originally called *Progresa* and now *Oportunidades*, it now provides government cash transfers to 5m Mexican families, or nearly a quarter of the population. As in Brazil, there are conditions attached. The payments are made every two months, to female heads of household. One element, of around $10 per month, is to help with food. A larger element is to help buy school supplies and pay for transport to and from school. If a child misses more than 15% of class days, or fails a grade twice, these payments are suspended. The payments are also made conditional on the family's regular visits to health clinics.

Spending better on the poor

Similar schemes now exist in half a dozen Latin American countries, though the details vary. For example, Argentina's programme, expanded to cope with mass unemployment that followed the economy's collapse in 2001–02, has fewer conditions, higher benefits and has been in part sub-contracted to political leaders. By contrast, the Chilean scheme is the only one to focus specifically on the very poorest, and involves much input from social workers who try to ensure that beneficiaries make use of a range of social programmes.

Some Latin American governments spend too little to make any serious dent in poverty and social disadvantage (Brazil and Uruguay are exceptions). Worse, most of what they have spent has been on social insurance (see Figure 15.1). This goes disproportionately to the better off. Compared even with most social assistance schemes, the CCTs are much more closely targeted to the poor (see Figure 15.2). They are not confined to those with formal-sector jobs, which would largely exclude the poor, says Kathy Lindert of the World Bank. The fiscal cost is relatively modest: Brazil's *Bolsa Família* costs the federal government 0.36% of GDP, far less than social insurance schemes. Not only do the poor get cash, but

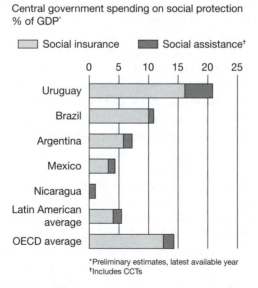

Central government spending on social protection
% of GDP*

*Preliminary estimates, latest available year
†Includes CCTs

Figure 15.1   All belt and no braces

Source: World Bank

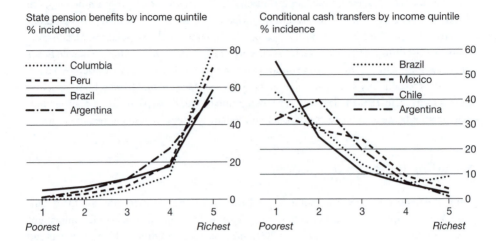

State pension benefits by income quintile
% incidence

Conditional cash transfers by income quintile
% incidence

Figure 15.2 Hitting the right target

Source: World Bank

an incentive to use government services. Prior to *Oportunidades*, says John Scott of CIDE, a university in Mexico City, it was the middle class that would take advantage of health services, rather than the poor. Now poor people go to the doctor more than in the past.

Traditionally, too, each government in Latin America has torn up its predecessor's social programmes. No longer. In Mexico, when Vicente Fox's government took office in 2000, its officials were sceptical of *Progresa*, which covered 2m rural families that year. But the politicians were convinced by the technocrats – whom Gladys López Acevedo of the World Bank describes as exceptionally skilled. The programme not only survived, but was expanded, both to urban areas and in size. This new social safety-net has thus been "successfully institutionalised", as Ms López Acevedo notes.

In Brazil, when Lula took office in 2003 he inherited a clutch of CCTs spread across various ministries, with different lists of beneficiaries and conditions. His accomplishment has been to turn these into a single, expanded programme while improving their quality. "We didn't start from zero," says Patrus Ananias, the minister of social development, giving the previous government more credit than is customary among Lula's officials. "We integrated and consolidated" the earlier CCTs and pushed up the value of the benefit.

The success of the new schemes turns on effective administration. In Mexico, a visit to a government office is normally a far from efficient process. Simple tasks, like getting a driving licence, can take hours in apparently overstaffed offices. By contrast, in an *Oportunidades* regional office in Apan, a town of 40,000 people in the state of Hidalgo, it takes less than ten seconds for each woman in a queue which snakes out into the street to pick up her allotment of cash. Communities line up in turn. As names are called, each woman appears before the window with an identity card and a difficult-to-forge holographic stamp. All this would have been impossible without computerisation, notes Rodrigo García-Verdú, a researcher at Mexico's central bank. The ability to crunch numbers on a massive scale, he says, is part of what has allowed the programme to be better than any previous social spending in reaching the people it is intended to reach. It also has made it possible to evaluate the effects.

From confusion to consolidation

In Brazil – whose unruly federal structure encompasses 5,561 autonomous municipal districts, ranging from rural outposts like Ocara to the metropolis of São Paulo – setting up *Bolsa Família* has been far from simple. At first Lula produced confusion rather than consolidation. He created two anti-poverty ministries and yet another CCT. Under a storm of criticism, the government rethought. Four CCTs were merged into *Bolsa Família* (a fifth is soon to join). Mr Ananias's ministry was created to run it, replacing the two stillborn ministries. The transition, unsurprisingly, was "chaotic", says an official involved. Quality control was forgotten. Government auditors and the media found fraud in the distribution of benefits and laxity in the monitoring of conditions. With millions of beneficiaries joining the rolls and benefits tripling to an average of 65 reais, *Bolsa Família* looked like a blatant bid for popularity rather than serious social policy.

With a new team of career bureaucrats in charge and advice from the World Bank, which is lending $572m to help expand and improve the programme, *Bolsa Família* is righting itself. That means fine-tuning an elaborate system in which federal agencies, municipalities, NGOs and the beneficiaries themselves all play a part.

The task starts with accurate targeting and identification of the beneficiaries. At a church hall in Ocara on a recent Friday the pews were filled with women. They came to enrol in the "single registry" of potential beneficiaries, which replaces the separate rolls of earlier schemes. Three registrars hired by the municipality asked each of the women their family incomes and details such as whether or not their houses had plumbing. But it is the ministry in Brasília that will decide which of them deserves *Bolsa Família*. As in Mexico, women are preferred because they are more likely than their husbands to spend the money on their children. Those who qualify draw benefits from the local branch of a government bank through an electronic card.

With a single registry of potential beneficiaries, the government can check them against its data on employees in the formal sector of the economy. That exercise, conducted for the first time this year, will result in 50,000 people losing their benefits, says Rosani Cunha, who manages *Bolsa Família*. District quotas for beneficiaries, which fostered favouritism, have been dropped; now anyone below a certain income level can register, though they may not qualify for a benefit. Under new contracts with the federal government, municipalities must establish "social councils" composed of local officials and representatives of NGOs to monitor implementation. They will also gain more leeway to block and unblock benefits. Municipalities will get federal money to keep the register up to date.

Incentives and evaluations

The government is driving a harder bargain with beneficiaries, as well. An earlier programme, *Bolsa Escola*, offered families 15 reais per child for keeping up to three children in school; now all of a family's children must attend classes. Under *Bolsa Escola*, just 19% of schools reported that children from beneficiary families were regularly attending classes; now 79% do, according to Ms Cunha. The ministry is readying a scale of sanctions, culminating in the total withdrawal of benefits, to promote compliance.

Another advantage of *Bolsa Família*, say its boosters, is that objective criteria for conceding benefits are supplanting what Brazilians call "clientelism" – the doling out of favours by local potentates in return for political loyalty. In Ocara, these claims ring true, partly because the long-time mayor, who had governed for most of the district's 19-year history, lost an election last year. According to the local manager of *Bolsa Família*, Maria de Sousa Brasil, the re-registration at the church hall will weed out the 20–30% of beneficiaries who were enrolled undeservedly by the old regime.

The evidence from Mexico, where more evaluation has been done, is that CCTs do work. A June 2004 paper in the Journal of the American Medical Association found improvements in the size and health of children participating in the programme. Drop-out rates among secondary-school students are also down – by roughly 5% for boys and 8% for girls, according to a study by Paul Schultz of Yale University. That may be an underestimate: a simulation done by Jere Behrman and his colleagues at the Penn Institute for Economic Research in Philadelphia suggests that *Oportunidades* could increase secondary-school enrolment by 19%.

On their own, the cash-transfer schemes can alleviate but not abolish poverty. Even *Oportunidades* does not reach the poorest of Mexico's rural poor, who live in communities so small that they do not have schools or health clinics within reach – a number that Mr Scott estimates at 500,000 people. Secondly, getting more children to attend school is only as effective as the schools themselves. Mexico spends a fairly large percentage of GDP on education, but its students still lag badly on standardised tests. The same goes for Brazil. Schools that Ocara's education secretary calls "apathetic" are unlikely to teach much, even if students stay until age 15, as *Bolsa Família* requires.

Thirdly, cash transfers might generate some jobs, but in Ocara locals say that employment will come only when water does, and that depends on investment by the hard-pressed federal government. Indeed, according to Ms de Sousa Brasil, some beneficiaries stop working entirely, content to live off the benefit, meagre though it is. Avoiding such dependence will require further changes to *Bolsa Família*. There is talk of "complementary programmes" to shepherd people into productive work, a strong point of Chile's programme. Teenagers could get bonuses for graduating from school, as they do in Mexico, rather than dropping out after their benefits expire, as happens now. There is more to be done in co-ordinating federal, state and local programmes. It will be a long time before Ocara blooms year-round. But a start has been made.

REVIEW AND DISCUSSION QUESTIONS

1   Explain how conditional cash transfer schemes work.
2   Why has the effectiveness of poverty reduction programs differed widely across Latin American countries? What makes programs more or less likely to have an impact on poverty?
3   How has Brazil's *Bolsa Família* program changed over time?
4   What are some of the limitations of conditional cash transfer programs as tools to reduce poverty?

Chapter 16

World Bank

ENGENDERING DEVELOPMENT
Through gender equality in rights, resources, and voice

[. . .]

Despite progress, gender disparities remain in all countries

THE LAST HALF OF THE 20TH CENTURY saw great improvements in the absolute status of women and in gender equality in most developing countries.

- With few exceptions female education levels improved considerably. The primary enrollment rates of girls about doubled in South Asia, sub-Saharan Africa, and the Middle East and North Africa, rising faster than boys' enrollment rates. This substantially reduced large gender gaps in schooling.
- Women's life expectancy increased by 15–20 years in developing countries. With greater investments in girls and women and better access to health care, the expected biological pattern in female and male longevity has emerged in all developing regions; for the first time, in the 1990s, women in South Asia are living longer than men, on average.
- More women have joined the labor force. Since 1970 women's labor force participation has risen on average by 15 percentage points in East Asia and Latin America. This growth was larger than for men, thus narrowing the gender gap in employment. Gender gaps in wages have also narrowed.

Despite the progress significant gender inequalities in rights, resources, and voice persist in all developing countries – and in many areas the progress has been slow and uneven. Moreover, socioeconomic shocks in some countries have brought setbacks, jeopardizing hard-won gains.

Rights

In no region do women and men have equal social, economic, and legal rights (figure 16.1).[1] In a number of countries women still lack independent rights to own land, manage property, conduct business, or even travel without their husband's consent. In much of sub-Saharan Africa, women obtain land rights chiefly through their husband as long as the marriage endures, and they often lose those rights when they are divorced or widowed. Gender disparities in rights constrain the sets of choices available to women in many aspects of life – often profoundly limiting their ability to participate in or benefit from development.

Resources

Women continue to have systematically poorer command over a range of productive resources, including education, land, information, and financial resources. In South Asia women have only about half as many years of schooling as men, on average, and girls' enrollment rates at the secondary level are still only two-thirds of boys'. Many women cannot own land, and those who do generally command smaller landholdings than men. And in most developing regions female-run enterprises tend to be undercapitalized, having poorer access to machinery, fertilizer, extension information, and credit than male-run enterprises. Such disparities, whether in education or other productive resources, hurt

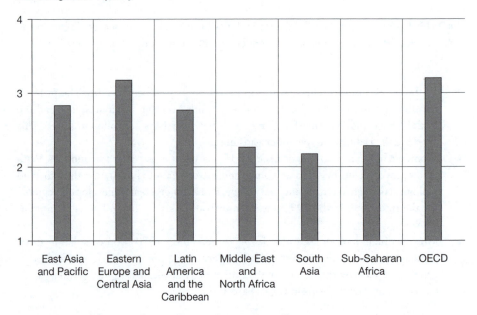

Index of gender equality

Figure 16.1   Gender inequalities in basic rights persist in all regions

Note: A value of 1 indicates low gender equality in rights, a value of 4 high equality (see note 1 at the end of the chapter for more information).

Source: Rights data from Humana (1992); population weights from World Bank (1999).

women's ability to participate in development and to contribute to higher living standards for their families. Those disparities also translate into greater risk and vulnerability in the face of personal or family crises, in old age, and during economic shocks.

Despite recent increases in women's educational attainment, women continue to earn less than men in the labor market – even when they have the same education and years of work experience as men. Women are often limited to certain occupations in developing countries and are largely excluded from management positions in the formal sector. In industrial countries women in the wage sector earn an average of 77 percent of what men earn; in developing countries, 73 percent. And only about a fifth of the wage gap can be explained by gender differences in education, work experience, or job characteristics.

Voice

Limited access to resources and weaker ability to generate income – whether in self-employed activities or in wage employment – constrain women's power to influence resource allocation and investment decisions in the home. Unequal rights and poor socioeconomic status relative to men also limit their ability to influence decisions in their communities and at the national level. Women remain vastly underrepresented in national and local assemblies, accounting for less than 10 percent of the seats in parliament, on average (except in East Asia where the figure is 18–19 percent). And in no developing region do women hold more than 8 percent of ministerial positions. Moreover, progress has been negligible in most regions since the 1970s. And in Eastern Europe female representation has fallen from about 25 to 7 percent since the beginning of economic and political transition there.

Gender disparities tend to be greatest among the poor

Gender disparities in education and health are often greatest among the poor. A recent study of boys' and girls' school enrollments in 41 countries indicates that within countries gender disparities in school enrollment rates are commonly greater among the poor than among the nonpoor. Similar patterns across poor and nonpoor households are seen with respect to boys' and girls' mortality rates for children under 5.

Similar patterns also emerge when comparing poor and nonpoor countries. While gender equality in education and health has increased noticeably over the past 30 years in today's low-income countries, disparities between females and males in school enrollments are still greater in those countries than in middle-income and high-income countries. And despite the links between economic development and gender equality, women's representation in parliaments remains minimal. A few low-income countries, such as China and Uganda, have made special efforts to open parliamentary seats to women, achieving levels of female representation even higher than those in high-income countries. They demonstrate the potential impact of a social mandate for gender equality.

It is important to note that these indicators are only a few measurable markers of gender equality. More systematic information is needed on other dimensions – from control of physical and financial assets to autonomy – to better understand how much has been accomplished and how far there is to go.

Gender inequalities harm well-being, hinder development

Gender inequalities impose large costs on the health and well-being of men, women, and children, and affect their ability to improve their lives. In addition to these personal costs, gender inequalities reduce productivity in farms and enterprises and thus lower prospects for reducing poverty and ensuring economic progress. Gender inequalities also weaken a country's governance – and thus the effectiveness of its development policies.

Well-being

Foremost among the costs of gender inequality is its toll on human lives and the quality of those lives. Identifying and measuring the full extent of these costs are difficult – but a wealth of evidence from countries around the world demonstrates that societies with large, persistent gender inequalities pay the price of more poverty, malnutrition, illness, and other deprivations.

- China, Korea, and South Asia have excessively high female mortality. Why? Social norms that favor sons, plus China's one-child policy, have led to child mortality rates that are higher for girls than for boys. Some estimates indicate that there are 60–100 million fewer women alive today than there would be in the absence of gender discrimination.
- Mothers' illiteracy and lack of schooling directly disadvantage their young children. Low schooling translates into poor quality of care for children and then higher infant and child mortality and malnutrition. Mothers with more education are more likely to adopt appropriate health-promoting behaviors, such as having young children immunized. Supporting these conclusions are careful analyses of household survey data that account for other factors that might improve care practices and related health outcomes.
- As with mothers' schooling, higher household income is associated with higher child survival rates and better nutrition. And putting additional incomes in the hands of women within the household tends to have a larger positive impact than putting that income in the hands of men, as studies of Bangladesh, Brazil, and Côte d'Ivoire show. Unfortunately, rigid social norms about the appropriate gender division of labor and limited paid employment for women restrict women's ability to earn income.
- Gender inequalities in schooling and urban jobs accelerate the spread of HIV. The AIDS epidemic will spread rapidly over the next decade – until up to one in four women and one in five men become HIV infected, already the case in several countries in sub-Saharan Africa.
- While women and girls, especially the poor, often bear the brunt of gender disparities, gender norms and stereotypes impose costs on males, too. In the transition economies of Eastern Europe men have experienced absolute declines in life expectancies in recent years. Increases in male mortality rates – the largest registered in peacetime – are associated with growing stress and anxiety due to rapidly worsening unemployment among men.

Productivity and economic growth

The toll on human lives is a toll on development – since improving the quality of people's lives is development's ultimate goal. But gender inequalities also impose costs on productivity, efficiency, and economic progress. By hindering the accumulation of human capital in the home and the labor market, and by systematically excluding women or men from access to resources, public services, or productive activities, gender discrimination diminishes an economy's capacity to grow and to raise living standards.

- Losses in output result from inefficiencies in the allocation of productive resources between men and women within households. In households in Burkina Faso, Cameroon, and Kenya more equal control of inputs and farm income by women and men could raise farm yields by as much as a fifth of current output.
- Low investment in female education also reduces a country's overall output. One study estimates that if the countries in South Asia, sub-Saharan Africa, and the Middle East and North Africa had started with the gender gap in average years of schooling that East Asia had in 1960 and had closed that gender gap at the rate achieved by East Asia from 1960 to 1992, their income per capita could have grown by 0.5–0.9 percentage point higher per year – substantial increases over actual growth rates. Another study estimates that even for middle- and high-income countries with higher initial education levels, an increase of 1 percentage point in the share of women with secondary education is associated with an increase in per capita income of 0.3 percentage point. Both studies control for other variables commonly found in the growth literature.

Governance

Greater women's rights and more equal participation in public life by women and men are associated with cleaner business and government and better governance. Where the influence of women in public life is greater, the level of corruption is lower. This holds even when comparing countries with the same income (figure 16.2), civil liberties, education, and legal institutions. Although still only suggestive, these findings lend additional support for having more women in the labor force and in politics – since women can be an effective force for rule of law and good government.

Women in business are less likely to pay bribes to government officials, perhaps because women have higher standards of ethical behavior or greater risk aversion. A study of 350 firms in the republic of Georgia concludes that firms owned or managed by men are 10 percent more likely to make unofficial payments to government officials than those owned or managed by women. This result holds regardless of the characteristics of the firm, such as the sector in which it operates and firm size, and the characteristics of the owner or manager, such as education. Without controlling for these factors, firms managed by men are twice as likely to pay bribes.

Why do gender disparities persist?

If gender inequalities harm people's well-being and a country's prospects for development, why do harmful gender disparities persist in so many countries? Why are some gender inequalities much more difficult to eliminate than others? For example, improvements have been rapid in such dimensions as health and access to schooling, but much slower in political participation and equal rights to property. What factors stand in the way of transforming gender relations and eliminating gender inequalities? Institutions, households, and the economy.

Societal institutions – social norms, customs, rights, laws – as well as economic institutions, such as markets, shape roles and relationships between men and women and

Corruption index

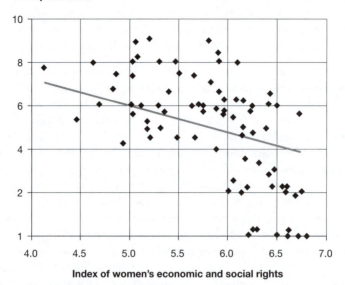

Figure 16.2 More equal rights, less corruption

Note: The corruption index uses data from the International Country Risk Guide (ICRG) and transforms it: corruption index = 10 – (ICRG Index – 1) x 2. A value of 0 indicates low levels of corruption; a value of 10 indicates high levels. The women's rights variable is the Women's Economic and Social Human Rights (WESHR) Indicator developed by Purdue University's Global Studies Program. A score of 7 is interpreted as gender equality in economic and social rights. The figure controls for per capita GDP in each country. See appendix 1 in the full report for included countries.

Source: World Bank staff estimates; see also Kaufmann (1998).

influence what resources women and men have access to, what activities they can or cannot undertake, and in what forms they can participate in the economy and in society. They embody incentives that can encourage or discourage prejudice. Even when formal and informal institutions do not distinguish explicitly between males and females, they are generally informed (either explicitly or implicitly) by social norms relating to appropriate gender roles. These societal institutions have their own inertia and can be slow and difficult to change – but they are far from static.

   Like institutions, households play a fundamental role in shaping gender relations from early in life and in transmitting these from one generation to the next. People make many of life's most basic decisions within their households – about having and raising children, engaging in work and leisure, and investing in the future. How tasks and productive resources are allocated among sons and daughters, how much autonomy they are given, whether expectations differ among them – all this creates, reinforces, or mitigates gender disparities. But families do not make decisions in a vacuum. They make them in the context of communities and in ways that reflect the influence of incentives established by the larger institutional and policy environment.

   And because the economy determines many of the opportunities people have to improve their standard of living, economic policy and development critically affect gender inequality. Higher incomes mean fewer resource constraints within the household that force parents to choose between investing in sons or in daughters. But how precisely women and men are affected by economic development depends on what income-generating activities are available, how they are organized, how effort and skills are rewarded, and whether women and men are equally able to participate.

Indeed, even apparently gender-neutral development policies can have gender-differentiated outcomes – in part because of the ways in which institutions and household decisions combine to shape gender roles and relations. The gender division of labor in the home, social norms and prejudice, and unequal resources prevent women and men from taking equal advantage of economic opportunities – or from coping equally with risk or economic shocks. Failure to recognize these gender-differentiated constraints when designing policies can compromise the effectiveness of those policies, both from equity and efficiency perspectives.

So, societal institutions, households, and the broader economy together determine people's opportunities and life prospects, by gender. They also represent important entry points for public policy to address persistent gender inequalities.

[. . .]

Note

1   The rights indicator used in figure 16.1 is an average of three indexes of gender equality in rights collected for more than 100 countries by Humana (1992). The individual rights indexes focus on gender equality of political and legal rights, social and economic rights, and rights in marriage and in divorce proceedings. The indexes are constructed using a consistent methodology across countries in which the extent of rights is evaluated (on a scale from 1 to 4) against rights as specified in several human rights instruments of the United Nations.

References

Humana, Charles. 1992. *World Human Rights Guide*. 3rd ed. New York: Oxford University Press.

ICRG (International Country Risk Guide). 1999. Syracuse, NY: Political Risk Services, Institutional Reform and Informational Sector.

Kaufmann, Daniel. 1998. "Challenges in the Next Stage of Anti-corruption." In *New Perspectives on Combating Corruption*. Washington, D.C.: Transparency International and World Bank.

World Bank. 1999. *World Development Indicators 1999*. Washington, D.C.

REVIEW AND DISCUSSION QUESTIONS

1   In what ways has the status of women improved in developing countries over the past few decades?

2   According to the World Bank, what are some areas in which gender disparities in developing countries are still significant?

3   How do persistent gender inequalities reduce the well-being of both men and women?

4   Through what channels might gender inequalities hinder overall economic development?

5   Why do gender inequalities appear to persist in spite of their adverse effects on development?

6   Do you believe it is possible to remove the obstacles to greater gender equality? If so, how? Explain.

Chapter 17

Amartya Sen

WOMEN'S AGENCY AND SOCIAL CHANGE

MARY WOLLSTONECRAFT'S CLASSIC BOOK *A Vindication of the Rights of Woman*, published in 1792, had various distinct claims within the general program of "vindication" that she outlined. The rights she spoke about included not only some that particularly related to the well-being of women (and the entitlements that were directly geared to promote that well-being), but also rights that were aimed mainly at the free agency of women.

Both these features figure in the agenda of women's movements today, but it is, I think, fair to say that the agency aspects are beginning to receive some attention at last, in contrast to the earlier exclusive concentration on well-being aspects. Not long ago, the tasks these movements faced primarily involved working to achieve better treatment for women – a squarer deal. The concentration was mainly on women's *well-being* – and it was a much needed corrective. The objectives have, however, gradually evolved and broadened from this "welfarist" focus to incorporate – and emphasize – the active role of women's *agency*. No longer the passive recipients of welfare-enhancing help, women are increasingly seen, by men as well as women, as active agents of change: the dynamic promoters of social transformations that can alter the lives of *both* women and men.[1]

Agency and well-being

The nature of this shift in concentration and emphasis is sometimes missed because of the *overlap* between the two approaches. The active agency of women cannot, in any serious way, ignore the urgency of rectifying many inequalities that blight the well-being of women and subject them to unequal treatment; thus the agency role must be much concerned with women's well-being also. Similarly, coming from the other end, any practical attempt at enhancing the well-being of women cannot but draw on the agency of women themselves in bringing about such a change. So the *well-being aspect* and the *agency aspect* of women's movements inevitably have a substantial intersection. And yet they cannot but be different at a foundational level, since the role of a person as an "agent" is fundamentally distinct from (though not independent of) the role of the same person as a "patient."[2] The fact that the agent may have to see herself as a patient as well does not alter the additional modalities and responsibilities that are inescapably associated with the agency of a person.

To see individuals as entities that experience and have well-being is an important recognition, but to stop there would amount to a very restricted view of the personhood of women. Understanding the agency role is thus central to recognizing people as responsible persons: not only are we well or ill, but also we act or refuse to act, and can choose to act one way rather than another. And thus we – women *and* men – must take responsibility for doing things or not doing them. It makes a difference, and we have to take note of that difference. This elementary acknowledgment, though simple enough in principle, can be exacting in its implications, both for social analysis and for practical reason and action.

The changing focus of women's movements is, thus, a crucial *addition* to previous concerns; it is not a rejection of those concerns. The old concentration on the well-being of women, or, to be more exact, on the "ill-being" of women, was not, of course, pointless. The relative deprivations in the well-being of women were – and are – certainly present in the world in which we live, and are clearly important for social justice, including justice for women. For example, there is plenty of evidence that identifies the biologically "contrary" (socially generated) "excess mortality" of women in Asia and North Africa, with gigantic numbers of "missing women" – "missing" in the sense of being dead as a result of gender bias in the distribution of health care and other necessities (on this see my essay "Missing Women" in *British Medical Journal*, March 1992).[3] That problem is unquestionably important for the well-being of women, and in understanding the treatment of women as "less than equal." There are also pervasive indications of culturally neglected needs of women across the world. There are excellent reasons for bringing these deprivations to light and keeping the removal of these iniquities very firmly on the agenda.

But it is also the case that the limited role of women's active agency seriously afflicts the lives of *all* people – men as well as women, children as well as adults. While there is every reason not to slacken the concern about women's well-being and ill-being, and to continue to pay attention to the sufferings and deprivations of women, there is also an urgent and basic necessity, particularly at this time, to take an agent-oriented approach to the women's agenda.

Perhaps the most immediate argument for focusing on women's *agency* may be precisely the role that such an agency can play in removing the iniquities that depress the *well-being* of women. Empirical work in recent years has brought out very clearly how the relative respect and regard for women's well-being is strongly influenced by such variables as women's ability to earn an independent income, to find employment outside the home, to have ownership rights and to have literacy and be educated participants in decisions within and outside the family. Indeed, even the survival disadvantage of women compared with men in developing countries seems to go down sharply – and may even get eliminated – as progress is made in these agency aspects.[4]

These different aspects (women's earning power, economic role outside the family, literacy and education, property rights and so on) may at first sight appear to be rather diverse and disparate. But what they all have in common is their positive contribution in adding force to women's voice and agency – through independence and empowerment.

For example, working outside the home and earning an independent income tend to have a clear impact on enhancing the social standing of a woman in the household and the society. Her contribution to the prosperity of the family is then more visible, and she also has more voice, because of being less dependent on others. Further, outside employment often has useful "educational" effects, in terms of exposure to the world outside the household, making her agency more effective. Similarly, women's education strengthens women's agency and also tends to make it more informed and skilled. The ownership of property can also make women more powerful in family decisions.

The diverse variables identified in the literature thus have a unified empowering role. This role has to be related to the acknowledgment that women's power – economic independence as well as social emancipation – can have far-reaching impacts on the forces and organizing principles that govern divisions *within* the family and in society as a whole, and can, in particular, influence what are implicitly accepted as women's "entitlements."[5]

Cooperative conflict

To understand the process, we can start by noting that women and men have both *congruent* and *conflicting* interests that affect family living. Decision making in the family thus tends to take the form of pursuing cooperation, with some agreed solution – usually *implicit* – of the conflicting aspects. Such "cooperative conflict" is a general feature of many group relations, and an analysis of cooperative conflicts can provide a useful way of understanding the influences that operate on the "deal" that women get in family divisions. There are gains to be made by both parties through following implicitly agreed patterns of behavior. But there are many alternative possible agreements – some more favorable to one party than others. The choice of one such cooperative arrangement from the set of alternative possibilities leads to a particular distribution of joint benefits.[6]

Conflicts between the partially disparate interests within family living are typically resolved through implicitly agreed patterns of behavior that may or may not be particularly egalitarian. The very nature of family living – sharing a home and leading joint lives – requires that the elements of conflict must not be explicitly emphasized (dwelling on conflicts will be seen as a sign of a "failed" union), and sometimes the deprived woman cannot even clearly assess the extent of her relative deprivation. Similarly, the perception of who is doing how much "productive" work, or who is "contributing" how much to the family's prosperity, can be very influential, even though the underlying "theory" regarding how "contributions" and "productivity" are to be assessed may rarely be discussed explicitly.

Perceptions of entitlement

The perception of individual contributions and appropriate entitlements of women and men plays a major role in the division of a family's joint benefits between men and women.[7] As a result, the circumstances that influence these perceptions of contributions and appropriate entitlements (such as women's ability to earn an independent income, to work outside the home, to be educated, to own property) can have a crucial bearing on these divisions. The impact of greater empowerment and independent agency of women thus includes the correction of the iniquities that blight the lives and well-being of women vis-à-vis men. The lives that women save through more powerful agency will certainly include their own.[8]

That, however, is not the whole story. There are other lives – men's and children's – also involved. Even within the family, the lives affected may be those of the children, since there is considerable evidence that women's empowerment within the family can reduce child mortality significantly. Going well beyond that, women's agency and voice, influenced by education and employment, can in turn influence the nature of the public discussion on a variety of social subjects, including acceptable fertility rates (not just in the family of the particular women themselves) and environmental priorities.

There is also the important issue of *intrafamily* division of food, health care, and other provisions. Much depends on how the family's economic means are used to cater to the interests of different individuals in the household: women and men, girls and boys, children and adults, old and young.[9]

The arrangements for sharing within the family are given, to a great extent, by established conventions, but they are also influenced by such factors as the economic role and empowerment of women and the value systems of the community at large.[10] In the evolution of value systems and conventions of intrafamily division, an important role can be played by female education, female employment and female ownership rights, and these "social" features can be very crucial for the economic fortunes (as well as well-being and freedom) of different members of the family.[11]

In the context of the general theme of this book, this relationship is worth considering a bit more. As has already been discussed, the most useful way of understanding famines is in terms of the loss of entitlement – a sharp decline in the substantive freedom to buy food. This would lead to a collapse in the amount of food the family as a whole can buy and consume. While distributional problems within the family can be serious even in famine situations, they are particularly crucial in determining the general under-nourishment and hunger of different members of the family in situations of persistent poverty, which is "normal" in many communities. It is in the continued inequality in the division of food – and (perhaps even more) that of health care – that gender inequality manifests itself most blatantly and persistently in poor societies with strong antifemale bias.

This antifemale bias seems to be influenced by the social standing and economic power of women in general. Men's relative dominance connects with a number of factors, including the position of being the "breadwinner" whose economic power commands respect even within the family.[12] On the other side of the coin, there is considerable evidence that when women can and do earn income outside the household, this tends to enhance the relative position of women even in the distributions within the household.

While women work long hours every day at home, since this work does not produce a remuneration it is often ignored in the accounting of the respective contributions of women and men in the family's joint prosperity.[13] When, however, the work is done outside the home and the employed woman earns a wage, her contribution to the family's prosperity is more visible. She also has more voice, because of being less dependent on others. The higher status of women even affects, it appears, ideas on the female child's "due." So the freedom to seek and hold outside jobs can contribute to the reduction of women's relative – and absolute – deprivation. Freedom in one area (that of being able to work outside the household) seems to help to foster freedom in others (in enhancing freedom from hunger, illness and relative deprivation).

There is also considerable evidence that fertility rates tend to go down with greater empowerment of women. This is not surprising, since the lives that are most battered by the frequent bearing and rearing of children are those of young women, and anything that enhances young women's decisional power and increases the attention that their interests receive tends, in general, to prevent over-frequent childbearing. For example, in a comparative study of nearly three hundred districts within India, it emerges that women's education and women's employment are the two most important influences in reducing fertility rates.[14] The influences that help the emancipation of women (including women's literacy and women's employment) do make a major difference to fertility rates. I shall return to this presently in the context of assessing the nature and severity of the "world population problem." General problems of environmental overcrowding, from which both women and men may suffer, link closely with women's specific freedom from the constant bearing and rearing of children that plagues the lives of young women in many societies in the developing world.

Child survival and the agency of women

There is considerable evidence that women's education and literacy tend to reduce the mortality rates of children. The influence works through many channels, but perhaps most immediately, it works through the importance that mothers typically attach to the welfare of the children, and the opportunity the mothers have, when their agency is respected and empowered, to influence family decisions in that direction. Similarly, women's empowerment appears to have a strong influence in reducing the much observed gender bias in survival (particularly against young girls).

Countries with basic gender inequality – India, Pakistan, Bangladesh, China, Iran, those in West Asia, those in North Africa and others – often tend to have higher female mortality of infants and children, in contrast with the situation in Europe or America or sub-Saharan Africa, where female children typically have a substantial survival advantage. In India, male and female death rates in the 0–4 age group are now very similar to each other in terms of the average for the country as a whole, but a heavy disadvantage persists for women in regions where gender inequality is particularly pronounced, including most states of northern India.[15]

One of the most interesting studies of these issues – presented in an important statistical contribution by Mamta Murthi, Anne-Catherine Guio, and Jean Drèze – deals with data from 296 districts in India in the census of India of 1981.[16] There have been follow-up studies by Mamta Murthi and Jean Drèze dealing with later evidence, particularly the 1991 census, which broadly confirm the findings based on the 1981 census.[17]

A set of different – but interrelated – causal relations are examined in the studies. The variables to be explained include fertility rates, child mortality rates, and also female disadvantage in child survival (reflecting the *ratio* of female-to-male mortality in the 0–4 age group) in interdistrict comparisons. These variables are related to a number of other district-level variables with explanatory potential, such as female literacy rates, female labor force participation, incidence of poverty (and levels of income), extent of urbanization, availability of medical facilities and the proportion of socially underprivileged groups (scheduled castes and scheduled tribes) in the population.[18]

What should we expect to be the impact on child survival and mortality of the variables that may link most closely to women's agency – in this case women's participation in the labor force and women's literacy and education? It is natural to expect this connection to be entirely positive as far as women's literacy and education are concerned. This is strongly confirmed (more on this presently).

However, in the case of women's labor force participation, social and economic analyses have tended to identify factors working in different directions. First, involvement in gainful employment has many positive effects on a woman's agency roles, which often include greater emphasis being placed on child care and greater ability to attach more priority to child care in joint family decisions. Second, since men typically show great reluctance to share the domestic chores, this greater desire for more priority on child care may not be easy for the women to execute when they are saddled with the "double burden" of household work and outside employment. Thus the net effect could go in either direction. In the Murthi et al. study, the analysis of Indian district-level data does not yield any statistically significant, definite pattern on the connection between women's outside employment and the survival of children.[19]

Female literacy, in contrast, is found to have an unambiguous and statistically significant reducing impact on under-five mortality, even after controlling for male literacy. This is consistent with growing evidence of a close relationship between female literacy and child survival in many countries in the world, and particularly in intercountry comparisons.[20] In this case, the impact of greater empowerment and agency role of women is not reduced in effectiveness by problems arising from inflexible male participation in child care and household work.

There is also the further issue of *gender bias* in child survival (as opposed to *total* child survival). For this variable, it turns out that the female labor force participation rate and female literacy rate *both* have very strong ameliorating effects on the extent of female disadvantage in child survival, with higher levels of female literacy and labor force participation being strongly associated with lower levels of relative female disadvantage in child survival. By contrast, variables that relate to the *general* level of development and modernization *either* turn out to have no statistically significant effect, *or* suggest that modernization (when not accompanied by empowerment of women) can even *strengthen*, rather than weaken, the gender bias in child survival. This applies to, inter alia, urbanization, male literacy, the availability of medical facilities, and the level of poverty (with higher levels of poverty being associated with *higher* female-male ratios among the poor). In so far as a positive connection does exist in India between the level of development and reduced gender bias in survival, it seems to work mainly *through* variables that are directly related to women's agency, such as female literacy and female labor force participation.

It is worth making a further comment on the impact of enhanced women's agency through greater female education. Murthi, Guio and Drèze's statistical analysis indicates that, in quantitative terms, the effect of female literacy on child mortality is extraordinarily large. It is more powerful an influence in reducing child mortality than the other variables that also work in that general direction. For instance, keeping other variables constant, an increase in the crude female literacy rate from, say, 22 percent (the actual 1981 figure for India) to 75 percent reduces the predicted value of under-five mortality for males and females combined from 156 per thousand (again, the actual 1981 figure) to 110 per thousand.

The powerful effect of female literacy contrasts with the comparatively ineffective roles of, say, male literacy or general poverty reduction as instruments of child mortality reduction. The increase in male literacy over the same range (from 22 to 75 percent) only reduces under-five mortality from 169 per thousand to 141 per thousand. And a 50 percent reduction in the incidence of poverty (from the actual 1981 level) only reduces the predicted value of under-five mortality from 156 per thousand to 153 per thousand.

Here again, the message seems to be that some variables relating to women's agency (in this case, female literacy) often play a much more important role in promoting social well-being (in particular, child survival) than variables relating to the general level of opulence in the society. These findings have important practical implications.[21] Both types of variables can be influenced through public action, but respectively require rather different forms of public intervention.

Agency, emancipation and fertility reduction

The agency role of women is also particularly important for the reduction of fertility rates. The adverse effects of high birthrates powerfully include the denial of substantial freedoms – through persistent childbearing and child rearing – routinely imposed on many Asian and African women. There is, as a result, a close connection between women's *well-being* and women's *agency* in bringing about a change in the fertility pattern. Thus it is not surprising that reductions in birthrates have often followed the enhancement of women's status and power.

These connections are indeed reflected in interdistrict variations of the total fertility rate in India. In fact, among all the variables included in the analysis presented by Murthi, Guio and Drèze, the *only* ones that have a statistically significant effect on fertility are female literacy and female labor force participation. Once again, the importance of women's agency emerges forcefully from this analysis, especially in comparison with the weaker effects of variables relating to general economic progress.

The negative linkage between female literacy and fertility appears to be, on the whole, empirically well founded.[22] Such connections have been widely observed in other countries also, and it is not surprising that they should emerge in India. The unwillingness of educated women to be shackled to continuous child rearing clearly plays a role in bringing about this change. Education also makes the horizon of vision wider, and, at a more mundane level, helps to disseminate the knowledge of family planning. And of course educated women tend to have greater freedom to exercise their agency in family decisions, including in matters of fertility and childbirth.

The particular case of the most socially advanced state in India, viz., Kerala, is also worth noting here, because of its particular success in fertility reduction based on women's agency. While the total fertility rate for India as a whole is still higher than 3.0, that rate in Kerala has now fallen well below the "replacement level" (around 2.0, roughly speaking two children per couple) to 1.7, which is also considerably lower than China's fertility rate of 1.9. Kerala's high level of female education has been particularly influential in bringing about a precipitate decline in birthrate. Since female agency and literacy are important also in the reduction of mortality rates, that is another – more indirect – route through which women's agency (including female literacy) may have helped to reduce birthrates, since there is some evidence that a reduction of death rates, especially of children, tends to contribute to the reduction of fertility rates. Kerala has also had other favorable features for women's empowerment and agency, including a greater recognition of women's property rights for a substantial and influential part of the community.[23] There will be an opportunity to further probe these connections, along with other possible causal linkages, in the next chapter.

Women's political, social and economic roles

There is plenty of evidence that when women get the opportunities that are typically the preserve of men, they are no less successful in making use of these facilities that men have claimed to be their own over the centuries. The opportunities at the highest political levels happen to have come to women, in many developing countries, only in rather special circumstances – often related to the demise of their more established husbands or fathers – but the chances have been invariably seized with much vigor. While the recent history of the role of women in top leadership positions in Sri Lanka, India, Bangladesh, Pakistan, the Philippines, Burma or Indonesia may be very well recognized, there is a need to pay more attention to the part that women have been able to play – given the opportunity – at diverse levels of political activities and social initiatives.[24]

The impact of women's activities on social life can be similarly extensive. Sometimes the roles are well known and well anticipated or are becoming so (the impact of women's education on the reduction of fertility rates – already discussed – is a good example of that). However, there are also other connections that call for greater investigation and analysis. One of the more interesting hypotheses concerns the relation between men's influence and the prevalence of violent crimes. The fact that most of the violent crimes in the world are committed by men is well recognized, but there are possible causal influences that have not yet received the attention they may deserve.

An interesting statistical finding in India relates to extensive interdistrict contrasts that show a strong – and statistically very significant – relation between the female-male ratio in the population and the scarcity of violent crimes. Indeed, the inverse connection between murder rates and the female-male ratio in the population has been observed by many researchers, and there have been alternative explanations of the causal processes involved.[25] Some have looked for causal explanations running from the incidence of violent crimes leading to a greater preference for sons (taken to be better equipped to encounter a violent society), whereas others have seen it running from a larger presence of women (less inclined toward violence) to a consequently lower rate of crime.[26] There can also be some third factor that relates both to violent crime and to the male dominance of the sex ratio. There are many issues to be sorted out here, but the importance of gender and the influence of women's agency vis-à-vis men's are hard to overlook under any of the alternative explanations.

If we turn now to economic activities, women's participation can also make a big difference. One reason for the relatively low participation of women in day-to-day economic affairs in many countries is a relative lack of access to economic resources. The ownership of land and capital in the developing countries has tended to be very heavily biased in favor of the male members of the family. It is typically much harder for a woman to start a business enterprise, even of a very modest size, given the lack of collateral resources.

And yet there is plenty of evidence that whenever social arrangements depart from the standard practice of male ownership, women can seize business and economic initiative with much success. It is also clear that the result of women's participation is not merely to generate income for women, but also to provide the social benefits that come from women's enhanced status and independence (including the reduction of mortality and fertility rates, just discussed). The economic participation of women is, thus, both a reward on its own (with associated reduction of gender bias in the treatment of women in family decisions), and a major influence for social change in general.

The remarkable success of the Grameen Bank in Bangladesh is a good example of this. That visionary microcredit movement, led by Muhammad Yunus, has consistently aimed at removing the disadvantage from which women suffer, because of discriminatory treatment in the rural credit market, by making a special effort to provide credit to women borrowers. The result has been a very high proportion of women among the customers of the Grameen Bank. The remarkable record of that bank in having a very high rate of repayment (reported to be close to 98 percent) is not unrelated to the way women have responded to the opportunities offered to them and to the prospects of ensuring the continuation of such arrangements.[27] Also in Bangladesh, similar emphasis has been placed on women's participation by BRAC, led by another visionary leader, Fazle Hasan Abed.[28] These and other economic and social movements in Bangladesh have done a lot not merely to raise the "deal" that women get, but also – through the greater agency of women – to bring about other major changes in the society. For example, the sharp decline in fertility rate that has occurred in Bangladesh in recent years seems to have clear connections with the increasingly higher involvement of women in social and economic affairs, in addition to much greater availability of family planning facilities, even in rural Bangladesh.[29]

Another area in which women's involvement in economic affairs varies is that of agricultural activities related to land ownership. There too the economic opportunities that women get can have a decisive influence on the working of the economy and the related social arrangements. Indeed, "a field of one's own" (as Bina Agarwal calls it) can be a major influence on women's initiative and involvement, with far-reaching effects on the balance of economic and social power between women and men.[30] Similar issues arise in understanding women's role in environmental developments, particularly in conserving natural resources (such as trees), with a particular linkage to women's life and work.[31]

Indeed, the empowerment of women is one of the central issues in the process of development for many countries in the world today. The factors involved include women's education, their ownership pattern, their employment opportunities and the workings of the labor market.[32] But going beyond these rather "classic" variables, they include also the nature of the employment arrangements, attitudes of the family and of the society at large toward women's economic activities, and the economic and social circumstances that encourage or resist change in these attitudes.[33] As Naila Kabeer's illuminating study of the work and economic involvement of Bangladeshi women in Dhaka and London brings out, the continuation of, or break from, past arrangements is strongly influenced by the exact economic and social relations that operate in the local environment.[34] The changing agency of women is one of the major mediators of economic and social change, and its determination as well as consequences closely relate to many of the central features of the development process.[35]

A concluding remark

The focus on the agency role of women has a direct bearing on women's well-being, but its reach goes well beyond that. In this chapter, I have tried to explore the distinction between – and interrelations of – agency and well-being, and then have gone on to illustrate the reach and power of women's agency, particularly in two specific fields: (1) in promoting child survival and (2) in helping to reduce fertility rates. Both these matters have general developmental interest that goes well beyond the pursuit specifically of female well-being, though – as we have seen – female well-being is also directly involved and has a crucial intermediating role in enhancing these general achievements.

The same applies to many other areas of economic, political and social action, varying from rural credit and economic activities, on the one hand, to political agitation and social debates, on the other.[36] The extensive reach of women's agency is one of the more neglected areas of development studies, and most urgently in need of correction. Nothing, arguably, is as important today in the political economy of development as an adequate recognition of political, economic and social participation and leadership of women. This is indeed a crucial aspect of "development as freedom."

Notes

1. I have discussed this issue in some previous works, including: "Economics and the Family," *Asian Development Review* 1 (1983); "Women, Technology and Sexual Divisions," *Trade and Development* 6 (1985); "Missing Women," *British Medical Journal* 304 (March 1992); "Gender and Cooperative Conflict," *Persistent Inequalities: Women and World Development*, edited by Irene Tinker (New York: Oxford University Press, 1990); "Gender Inequality and Theories of Justice," *Women, Culture and Development: A Study of Human Capabilities*, edited by Martha Nussbaum and Jonathan Glover (Oxford: Clarendon Press, 1995); (jointly with Jean Drèze) *India: Economic Development and Social Opportunity* (Delhi: Oxford University Press, 1995); "Agency and Well-Being: The Development Agenda," in *A Commitment to the Women*, edited by Noeleen Heyzer (New York: UNIFEM, 1996).

2. My paper "Well-Being, Agency and Freedom: The Dewey Lectures 1984," *Journal of Philosophy* 82 (April 1985), investigates the philosophical distinction between the "agency aspect" and the "well-being aspect" of a person, and attempts to identify the far-reaching practical implications of this distinction, applied to many different fields.

3. Alternative statistical estimates of the extent of "extra mortality" of women in many countries in Asia and North Africa also are discussed in my *Resources, Values and Development* (Cambridge, Mass.: Harvard University Press, 1984); (jointly with Jean Drèze) *Hunger and Public Action* (Oxford: Clarendon Press, 1989). See also Stephen Klasen, "'Missing Women' Reconsidered," *World Development* 22 (1994).

4. There is a vast literature on this; my own attempts at analyzing and using the available evidence can be found in "Gender and Cooperative Conflict" (1990), and "More Than a Hundred Million Women Are Missing," *New York Review of Books*, (Christmas number, December 20, 1990).

5. These issues have been discussed in my *Resources, Values and Development* (1984), "Gender and Cooperative Conflict" (1990), and "More Than a Hundred Million Women Are Missing" (1990). A pioneering study of this general field was presented in Ester Boserup's

classic work, *Women's Role in Economic Development* (London: Allen & Unwin, 1971). The
recent literature on gender inequality in developing countries include a number of
interesting and important studies of different types of determining variables. See, for
example, Hanna Papanek, "Family Status and Production: The 'Work' and 'Non-Work' of
Women," *Signs* 4 (1979). Martha Loutfi, ed., *Rural Work: Unequal Partners in Development*
(Geneva: ILO, 1980); Mark R. Rosenzweig and T. Paul Schultz, "Market Opportunities,
Genetic Endowment and Intrafamily Resource Distribution," *American Economic Review* 72
(1982); Myra Buvinic, M. Lycette and W.P. McGreevy, eds., *Women and Poverty in the
Third World* (Baltimore: Johns Hopkins University Press, 1983); Pranab Bardhan, *Land,
Labor and Rural Poverty* (New York: Columbia University Press, 1984); Devaki Jain and
Nirmala Banerjee, eds., *Tyranny of the Household: Investigative Essays in Women's Work* (New
Delhi: Vikas, 1985); Gita Sen and C. Sen, "Women's Domestic Work and Economic
Activity," *Economic and Political Weekly* 20 (1985); Martha Alter Chen, *A Quiet Revolution:
Women in Transition in Rural Bangladesh* (Dhaka: BRAC, 1986); Jere Behrman and B. L.
Wolfe, "How Does Mother's Schooling Affect Family Health, Nutrition, Medical Care
Usage and Household Sanitation?" *Journal of Econometrics* 36 (1987); Monica Das Gupta,
"Selective Discrimination against Female Children in India," *Population and Development
Review* 13 (1987); Gita Sen and Caren Grown, *Development, Crises and Alternative Visions:
Third World Women's Perspectives* (London: Earthscan, 1987); Alaka Basu, *Culture, the Status of
Women and Demographic Behaviour* (Oxford: Clarendon Press, 1992); Nancy Folbre, Barbara
Bergmann, Bina Agarwal and Maria Flore, eds., *Women's Work in the World Economy*
(London: Macmillan, 1992); United Nations ESCAP, *Integration of Women's Concerns into
Development Planning in Asia and the Pacific* (New York: United Nations, 1992); Bina
Agarwal, *A Field of One's Own* (Cambridge: Cambridge University Press, 1995); Edith
Kuiper and Jolande Sap, with Susan Feiner, Notburga Ott and Zafiris Tzannatos, *Out of
Margin: Feminist Perspectives on Economics* (New York: Routledge, 1995); among other
contributions.

6. Gender divisions within the family are sometimes studied as "bargaining problems"; the
literature includes, among many other contributions, Marilyn Manser and Murray Brown,
"Marriage and Household Decision Making: A Bargaining Analysis," *International Economic
Review* 21 (1980); M. B. McElroy and M. J. Horney, "Nash Bargained Household
Decisions: Toward a Generalization of Theory of Demand," *International Economic Review*
22 (1981); Shelley Lundberg and Robert Pollak, "Noncooperative Bargaining Models of
Marriage," *American Economic Review* 84 (1994). For approaches different from that of
"bargaining models," see Sen, "Women, Technology and Sexual Divisions" (1985); Nancy
Folbre, "Hearts and Spades: Paradigms of Household Economics," *World Development* 14
(1986); J. Brannen and G. Wilson, eds., *Give and Take in Families* (London: Allen & Unwin,
1987); Susan Moller Okin, *Justice, Gender, and the Family* (New York: Basic Books, 1989);
Sen, "Gender and Cooperative Conflict" (1990); Marianne A. Ferber and Julie A. Nelson,
eds., *Beyond Economic Man: Feminist Theory and Economics* (Chicago: Chicago University
Press, 1993); among other contributions. Useful collections of papers on these issues can
also be found in Jane Humphries, ed., *Gender and Economics* (Cheltenham, U.K.: Edward
Elgar, 1995), and Nancy Folbre, ed., *The Economics of the Family* (Cheltenham, U.K.:
Edward Elgar, 1996).

7. On this see Okin, *Justice, Gender, and the Family* (1989); Drèze and Sen, *Hunger and Public
Action* (1989); Sen, "Gender and Cooperative Conflict" (1990); Nussbaum and Glover,
Woman, Culture and Development (1995). See also the papers of Julie Nelson, Shelley

Lundberg, Robert Pollak, Diana Strassman, Myra Strober and Vivians Zelizer in the 1994 Papers and Proceedings in *American Economic Review* 84 (1994).

8. This issue has started receiving considerable attention in India. See Asoke Mitra, *Implications of Declining Sex Ratios in India's Population* (Bombay: Allied Publishers, 1980); Jocelyn Kynch and Amartya Sen, "Indian Women: Well-Being and Survival," *Cambridge Journal of Economics* 7 (1983); Bardhan, *Land, Labor and Rural Poverty* (1984); Jain and Banerjee, eds., *Tyranny of the Household* (1985). The "survival problem" relates to the broader issue of neglect, on which see also the studies presented in Swapna Mukhopadhyay, ed., *Women's Health, Public Policy and Community Action* (Delhi: Manohar, 1998), and Swapna Mukhopadhyay and R. Savithri, *Poverty, Gender and Reproductive Choice* (Delhi: Manohar, 1998).

9. On this see Tinker, *Persistent Inequalities* (1990). My own paper in this collection ("Gender and Cooperative Conflict") goes into the economic and social influences that affect the divisions within the family, and discusses why the divisions vary so much between regions (for example, antifemale bias being much stronger in South Asia, West Asia, North Africa and China than in sub-Saharan Africa or Southeast Asia), and also within different areas inside the same country (for example, gender bias at this level being very strong in some Indian states, such as Punjab and Uttar Pradesh, and effectively absent in Kerala). There are also close linkages between different influences on women's relative position, such as those connecting legal rights and basic education (since the use of legal provisions relates to the ability to read and write); see Salma Sobhan, *Legal Status of Women in Bangladesh* (Dhaka: Bangladesh Institute of Legal and International Affairs, 1978).

10. The role of gender divisions in the sharing of hunger has been illuminatingly studied by Megan Vaughan, *The Story of an African Famine: Hunger, Gender and Politics is Malawi* (Cambridge: Cambridge University Press, 1987); Barbara Harriss, "The Intrafamily Distribution of Hunger in South Asia," in *The Political Economy of Hunger*, edited by Jean Drèze and Amartya Sen (Oxford: Clarendon Press 1990), among others.

11. Some of these issues have been discussed in the specific context of India, with comparisons *within* and *outside* India in Drèze and Sen, *India: Economic Development and Social Opportunity* (1995); see also Alaka Basu, *Culture, the Status of Women and Demographic Behaviour* (1992), and Agarwal, *A Field of One's Own*, (1995). The different sources of disadvantage are particularly important to study in analyzing the special deprivation of groups with little economic or social leverage – for example, widows, especially from poorer families. On that, see Martha Alter Chen, ed., *Widows in India* (New Delhi: Sage, 1998), and her forthcoming book, *Perpetual Mourning: Widowhood in Rural India* (Delhi: Oxford University Press, 1999; Philadelphia, Pa.: University of Pennsylvania Press, 1999).

12. On the issues involved, see my "Gender and Cooperative Conflict," in Tinker, *Persistent Inequalities* (1990), and the literature cited there.

13. See L. Beneria, ed., *Women and Development: The Sexual Division of Labor in Rural Societies* (New York: Praeger, 1982). See also Jain and Banerjee, *Tyranny of the Household* (1985); Gita Sen and Grown, *Development, Crises and Alternative Visions* (1987); Haleh Afshar, ed., *Women and Empowerment: Illustrations from the Third World* (London: Macmillan, 1998).

14. See Mamta Murthi, Anne-Catherine Guio and Jean Drèze, "Mortality, Fertility and Gender Bias in India: A District Level Analysis," *Population and Development Review* 21 (December 1995). See also Jean Drèze and Amartya Sen, eds., *Indian Development: Selected Regional Perspectives* (Delhi: Oxford University Press, 1996). Questions can certainly be raised about the direction of causation in the identified relations – for example, whether women's

literacy influences the status and standing of women in the family *or* whether women's higher standing inclines a family to send young girls to school. There could be, statistically, also a third factor that correlates with both. And yet recent empirical studies suggest that most families – even in socially backward areas in India – seem to have a strong preference for educating the children, including girls. One large survey indicates that the proportion of parents who think it is "important" to send girls to school even in the states with the *least* female literacy is remarkably high: 85 percent in Rajasthan, 88 percent in Bihar, 92 percent in Uttar Pradesh, and 93 percent in Madhya Pradesh. The main barrier to the education of girls appears to be the absence of convenient schools in the neighborhood – a major difference between high-literacy and low-literacy states. See the Probe Team, *Public Report on Basic Education in India* (Delhi: Oxford University Press, 1999). Public policy, therefore, has a central role to play. There have been recent public policy initiatives with good effect on literacy, especially in Himachal Pradesh, and more recently in West Bengal, Madhya Pradesh and a few other states.

15. The 1991 Indian census indicates that the death rate per thousand in the 0–4 age group was 25.6 for males and 27.5 for females at the all-India level. The female mortality rate in that age group was lower than the male mortality rate in Andhra Pradesh, Assam, Himachal Pradesh, Kerala and Tamil Nadu, but higher in all the other major Indian states. The female disadvantage was most pronounced in Bihar, Haryana, Madhya Pradesh, Punjab, Rajasthan and Uttar Pradesh.

16. Murthi, Guio and Drèze, "Mortality, Fertility and Gender Bias in India" (1995).

17. See Jean Drèze and Mamta Murthi, "Female Literacy and Fertility: Recent Census Evidence from India," mimeographed, Centre for History and Economics, King's College, Cambridge, U.K., 1999.

18. There were, apparently, not enough data with adequate interdistrict variations to examine the impact of different forms of property rights, which are relatively more uniform across India. On an isolated basis, there is, of course, the strong and much-discussed example of the Nairs in Kerala, who have had matrilineal inheritance for a long time (an association that confirms, rather than contradicts, insofar as it goes, the positive impact of female property rights on child survival in general and the survival of female children in particular).

19. There is, it appears, a positive association between female labor force participation and under-five mortality in these fits, but this association is not statistically significant.

20. See, among other important contributions, J. C. Caldwell, "Routes to Low Mortality in Poor Countries," *Population and Development Review* 12 (1986); and Behrman and Wolfe, "How Does Mother's Schooling Affect Family Health, Nutrition, Medical Care Usage and Household Sanitation?" (1987).

21. These have been extensively discussed in my joint book with Jean Drèze, *India: Economic Development and Social Opportunity* (1995).

22. The various sources of evidence on this have been subjected to critical examination, and not surprisingly, the different empirical studies emerge with rather disparate force in these critical scrutinies. See particularly the "critical perspectives" on this issue presented in Caroline H. Bledsoe, John B. Casterline, Jennifer A. Johnson-Kuhn and John G. Haaga, eds., *Critical Perspectives on Schooling and Fertility in the Developing World* (Washington, D.C.: National Academy Press, 1999). See also Susan Greenhalgh, *Situating Fertility: Anthropology and Demographic Inquiry* (Cambridge: Cambridge University Press, 1995); Robert J. Barro and Jong-Wha Lee, "International Comparisons of Educational Attainment," paper

presented at a conference on How Do National Policies Affect Long-Run Growth?, World
Bank, Washington, D.C., 1993; Robert Cassen, with contributors, *Population and
Development: Old Debates, New Conclusions* (Washington, D.C.: Transaction Books for
Overseas Development Council, 1994).

23. On these and related general issues, see my "Population: Delusion and Reality," *New York
Review of Books*, September 22, 1994; *Population Policy: Authoritarianism versus Cooperation*
(Chicago: MacArthur Foundation, 1995); and "Fertility and Coercion," *University of Chicago
Law Review* 63 (summer 1996).

24. See United Nations, ESCAP, *Integration of Women's Concerns into Development Planning in Asia
and the Pacific* (New York: United Nations, 1992), especially the paper of Rehman Sobhan
and the references cited there. The practical issues relate closely to the social conception
of women's role in society and thus touch on the central focus of feminist studies. A
wide-ranging collection of papers (including many classics) can be found in Susan Moller
Okin and Jane Mansbridge, eds., *Feminism* (Cheltenham, U.K.: Edward Elgar, 1994). See
also Catherine A. Mackinnon, *Feminism Unmodified* (Cambridge, Mass.: Harvard University
Press, 1987), and Barbara Johnson, *The Feminist Difference: Literature, Psychology, Race and
Gender* (Cambridge, Mass.: Harvard University Press, 1998).

25. See Philip Oldenberg, "Sex Ratio, Son Preference and Violence in India: A Research
Note," *Economic and Political Weekly*, December 5–12, 1998; Jean Drèze and Reetika Khera,
"Crime, Society and Gender in India: Some Clues for Homicidal Data," mimeographed,
Centre for Development Economics, Delhi School of Economics, 1999. The explanations
of this interesting finding can invoke cultural factors as well as economic and social ones.
Though the brief discussion here concentrates on the latter, there are obvious connections
with psychological and valuational questions raised by those who see a basic gender
contrast in morals and attitudes, most notably Carol Gilligan; see *In a Different Voice*
(Cambridge, Mass.: Harvard University Press, 1982). Importance may well be attached to
the fact that the most remarkable case of humane prison reform in India came from one of
that rare breed, a woman prison governor, Kiran Bedi. Her own account of the radical
change and the opposition she faced can be found in Kiran Bedi, *It's Always Possible:
Transforming One of the Largest Prisons in the World* (New Delhi: Sterling, 1998). I do not
pursue further here the important issue of distinguishing between alternative explanations
of the nature of women's leadership in social change of this type, since the analysis
presented in this work does not require that we try to resolve this complex issue.

26. Oldenberg argues for the former hypothesis; but see also Arup Mitra, "Sex Ratio and
Violence: Spurious Results," *Economic and Political Weekly*, January 2–9, 1993. Drèze and
Khera argue for an explanation with the opposite direction of causation. See also the
literature cited there, including older studies, such as Baldev Raj Nayar, *Violence and Crime
in India: A Quantitative Study* (Delhi: Macmillan, 1975); S. M. Edwards, *Crime in India*
(Jaipur: Printwell Publishers, 1988); S. Venugopal Rao, ed., *Perspectives in Criminology*
(Delhi: Vikas, 1988).

27. Another factor has been the use of group responsibility in seeking a high rate of repayment.
On this see Muhammad Yunus with Alan Jolis, *Banker to the Poor: Micro-Lending and the
Battle Against World Poverty* (London: Aurum Press, 1998). See also Lutfun N. Khan
Osmani, "Credit and Women's Relative Well-Being: A Case Study of the Grameen Bank,
Bangladesh" (Ph.D. thesis, Queen's University of Belfast, 1998). See also Kaushik
Basu, *Analytical Development Economics* (Cambridge, Mass.: MIT Press, 1997), chapters 13

and 14; Debraj Ray, *Development Economics* (Princeton: Princeton University Press, 1998), chapter 14.

28. See Catherine H. Lovell, *Breaking the Cycle of Poverty: The BRAC Strategy* (Hartford, Conn.: Kumarian Press, 1992).

29. See John C. Caldwell, Barkat-e-Khuda, Bruce Caldwell, Indrani Pieries and Pat Caldwell, "The Bangladesh Fertility Decline: An Interpretation," *Population and Development Review* 25 (1999). See also John Cleland, James F. Phillips, Sajeda Amin and G. M. Kamal, *The Determinants of Reproductive Change in Bangladesh: Success in a Challenging Environment* (Washington, D.C.: World Bank, 1996), and John Bongaarts, "The Role of Family Planning Programmes in Contemporary Fertility Transition," in *The Continuing Demographic Transition*, edited by G.W. Jones et al. (New York: Oxford University Press, 1997).

30. See Agarwal, *A Field of One's Own* (1995).

31. See Henrietta Moore and Megan Vaughan, *Cutting Down Trees: Gender, Nutrition and Agricultural Change in the Northern Province of Zambia, 1890–1990* (Portsmouth, N.H.: Heinemann, 1994).

32. The difficulties to be overcome by women in the labor market and in economic relations in society have been plentiful even in advanced market economies. See Barbara Bergmann, *The Economic Emergence of Women* (New York: Basic Books, 1986); Francine D. Blau and Marianne A. Ferber, *The Economics of Women, Men and Work* (Englewood Cliffs, N.J.: Prentice-Hall, 1986); Victor R. Fuchs, *Women's Quest for Economic Equality* (Cambridge, Mass.: Harvard University Press, 1988); Claudia Goldin, *Understanding the Gender Gap: An Economic History of American Women* (New York: Oxford University Press, 1990). See also the collection of papers in Marianne A. Ferber, *Women in the Labor Market* (Cheltenham, U.K.: Edward Elgar, 1998).

33. There is a danger of oversimplification in seeing the issue of women's "agency" or "autonomy" in too formulaic terms, focusing on simple statistical connections with variables such as female literacy or employment. On this see the insightful anthropological analysis of Alaka M. Basu, *Culture, Status of Women, and Demographic Behavior* (Oxford: Clarendon Press, 1992). See also the studies presented in Roger Jeffery and Alaka M. Basu, eds., *Girls' Schooling, Women's Autonomy and Fertility Change in South Asia* (London: Sage, 1996).

34. See Naila Kabeer, "The Power to Choose: Bangladeshi Women and Labour Market Decisions in London and Dhaka," mimeographed, Institute of Development Studies, University of Sussex, 1998.

35. The changing role of women (and its far-reaching effects) in India since independence is discussed in an interesting collection of papers edited by Bharati Ray and Aparna Basu, *From Independence towards Freedom* (Delhi: Oxford University Press, 1999).

36. UNDP's *Human Development Report 1995* (New York: Oxford University Press, 1995) presents an intercountry investigation of gender differences in social, political and business leadership, in addition to reporting on gender inequality in terms of more conventional indicators. See also the literature cited there.

REVIEW AND DISCUSSION QUESTIONS

1   Explain how, according to Sen, promoting women's agency is more important for economic development than just promoting women's well-being (start by explaining what Sen means by "women's agency").

2   In what ways is greater empowerment of women likely to affect gender inequality within the family according to Sen?

3   What does evidence from India show about the relation between women's employment outside the household and child mortality? What does it show about the relation between women's literacy and child mortality? Why is there a difference between these two relations according to Sen?

4   Sen states that "the agency role of women is also particularly important for the reduction of fertility rates." Explain why this is the case.

5   What other economic and social effects can result from an increase in women's agency?

6   What specific government policies would you propose to increase women's agency? Explain.

Suggestions for further reading

Banerjee, A. V., Bénabou, R., and Mookherjee, D. (eds.) (2006) *Understanding Poverty*, New York: Oxford University Press.

In this wonderful collection of essays, some of the best-known development economists discuss poverty from a wide variety of angles, incorporating the results of the most recent research in the field. The book is divided in three parts: the first examines the causes of poverty, the second discusses a variety of policy interventions aimed at reducing it, and the third presents some innovative ways to think about poverty that show, according to the editors, "willingness to take the social and psychological environment of the poor seriously."

Goldberg, P. K. and Pavcnik, N. (2007) "Distributional Effects of Globalization in Developing Countries," *Journal of Economic Literature*, 45: 39-82.

In this essay, the authors discuss the extent to which globalization in developing countries has led to increased inequality within each country. They examine in detail the various channels through which globalization may affect inequality and conclude that the effects depend crucially on a variety of factors that tend to differ from one country to another – no simple, consistent pattern emerges.

Narayan, D., with Patel, R., Schafft, K., Rademacher, A., and Koch-Schule, S. (2000) *Voices of the Poor: Can Anyone Hear Us?*, New York: Oxford University Press.

This book is the result of a World Bank study that involved interviewing over 40,000 poor people from 50 developing countries to learn about various aspects of poverty that may be hard to measure or quantify but that the poor point to as affecting their lives. Quotations from the interviewees are interspersed throughout the book. This volume is the first of three in the World Bank's *Voices of the Poor* project.

Sen, A. (1983) *Poverty and Famines: An Essay on Entitlement and Deprivation*, Oxford: Oxford University Press.

In this book the Nobel Laureate examines closely several historic famines, from the Bengal famine of 1943 to more recent episodes in Africa, and uses the concept of "entitlements" to explain the causes of such disasters. He emphasizes that famines often take place even though food is not in short supply; rather, a variety of economic, political, and legal constraints prevent certain groups of people from gaining access to food. While Sen occasionally uses mathematical concepts and notation, the vast majority of the book is non-technical and accessible to the general reader.

Winters, A. L., McCulloch, N., and McKay, A. (2004) "Trade Liberalization and Poverty: The Evidence So Far," *Journal of Economic Literature*, 42: 72-115.

The authors review in this paper the empirical evidence on whether trade liberalization increases or reduces poverty. They discuss the various channels through which trade liberalization may affect the poor, including the impact on economic growth, macroeconomic stability, wages, and unemployment. They conclude that trade liberalization is likely to reduce poverty in the long run and on average, but also note that negative effects on the poor are possible under a variety of circumstances.

PART FOUR

People in development

Population growth, health, education,
and child labor

INTRODUCTION

\\ T HE BATTLE TO FEED ALL OF HUMANITY IS OVER. In the 1970s
and 1980s hundreds of millions of people will starve to death in spite of any crash
programs embarked upon now" (Ehrlich 1975: xi). These menacing words open a famous
1968 book by Paul Ehrlich appropriately titled *The Population Bomb*. Ehrlich, a renowned
Stanford biologist, was one of many scientists who in the 1960s and 1970s believed fast
population growth to be the key obstacle to economic development in low-income countries.
The fact that in the 1960s global population growth reached the highest level ever recorded
in the history of humanity – over 2 percent a year – helps explain the mindset of the times.
But times have changed. Global population growth has since declined steadily, and is now
at little more than 1 percent a year (US Census Bureau 2006). The large-scale famines
that Ehrlich predicted never took place. And economists, who were always skeptical about
doomsday predictions of the effects of population growth, have continued to accumulate
evidence on the links between population growth and standards of living, developing an
increasingly sophisticated view of the issue.

In Robert Solow's model of economic growth – discussed in Part One – the effect of
population growth on standards of living is unambiguously negative. While having more
people means having more workers and, therefore, increasing the total output produced,
economic growth measures changes in output *per person*. Solow noted that if the number
of workers increases but the amount of capital stays the same, capital per worker decreases.
In other words, the economy's capital is spread over a greater number of workers, a
phenomenon sometimes referred to as "capital shallowing." If workers have less capital
to work with, they will be less productive. In neoclassical growth models such as Solow's,
therefore, the inverse correlation between population growth and standards of living is
clear: other things being equal, population growth reduces the amount of capital per

worker, causing output per worker and income per worker to fall (Solow 1956). As a consequence, a policy-maker intent on raising standards of living would be well advised to put in place policies to reduce population growth.

Since the development of the Solow model, the so-called "population pessimists" – those who believe population growth has adverse effects on economic development – have advanced several other arguments to support their views. They have pointed out, for instance, that fast population growth may reduce both national saving and educational levels. If we think of population growth at the level of the family, fast population growth implies large families. In large families, parents must spend more resources on providing for the basic needs of their children, and this may reduce their ability to save and to invest in the children's education. There are also concerns that countries with high population growth rates may have worse health conditions – evidence shows that the health of both mother and children is negatively affected when a woman bears many children (see, e.g., Menken et al. 2003; Todaro and Smith 2006: 293). The impact of fast population growth on natural resources and on the environment is often an additional concern of population pessimists. In particular, the fear that it may be impossible for global food supply to keep up with a rapidly growing global population – an issue famously discussed by British economist Thomas Malthus at the end of the eighteenth century – often recurs in the literature. Those who see fast population growth as a source of increasing inequality raise additional concerns. Research shows that fertility is higher among the poor than among the rich (Perkins et al. 2001: 264). If so, and if larger families are worse off than smaller ones, high fertility makes poor families poorer and widens the gap between low-income and high-income households. Additionally, as more and more relatively uneducated and unskilled people join the labor force, their wages fall relative to the wages of the few educated ones. The incomes of unskilled workers also fall relative to the incomes of those who make their living by renting land or running firms – relatively wealthy people. The gap between rich and poor, therefore, widens (Birdsall 1989: 37).

Economists have always shown skepticism toward the views of population pessimists. It is not that economists reject the possibility of fast population growth hindering economic development; rather, they point to the existence of both positive and negative effects. They also emphasize the many indirect effects of population growth that may alleviate or eliminate altogether some of the concerns that population pessimists raise. Because many of these indirect effects only manifest themselves in the long run, economists warn that looking only at short-run effects of fast population growth is likely to lead to incomplete conclusions – a longer time horizon is needed for a thorough assessment (Kelley 2001: 24–25). This less alarmist view of the effects of population growth has been referred to as "revisionist" (ibid.).

Large families, for example, may actually save more, as parents with many children may decide to consume less or work more instead of saving less. In fact, having children may provide an incentive to increase saving in order to provide for the future needs of the children, such as paying for their education. Economists also argue that governments may increase saving to offset the decrease caused by a high birth rate. They also note that most of the saving in poor countries is done by the rich. Since the fertility of richer people is likely to be low even when population growth is fast for the country as a whole, national saving need not decline as a result of fast population growth (Birdsall 1989: 32–3).

In similar fashion, economists are skeptical of Malthusian concerns about global population growth outstripping growth in global food production. While resources like land and water used to produce food are indeed limited, it is the *productivity* of resources – not their quantity – that matters. Improvements in agricultural technologies, for example, allow a certain plot of land to produce a greater amount of food. The family whose livelihood depends on that plot of land, therefore, can become larger without experiencing a reduction in food output per person. In fact, data show that while global population doubled in the second half of the twentieth century, global food supply nearly *tripled* over the same period – largely thanks to technological improvements in agriculture (see, e.g., Kates and Parris 2003: 8063). Of course, there is no certainty that the rate of productivity growth will forever allow food production to rise more rapidly than population. But economists emphasize that people respond to incentives. If increased population puts pressure on limited resources, there is an increasing incentive to deal with the problem – by using resources more effectively, discovering new resources, developing alternatives to the resources in short supply, and so on. It is important to realize that taking into account possible long-run responses is not a way to deny the immediate problem or to ignore the possibility that fast population growth may hinder development. Instead, the goal is to provide a more accurate long-run analysis that helps to qualify the consequences of the problem and, often, show that doomsday scenarios are not nearly as likely as the population pessimists suggest (Kelley 2001).

Revisionists are less alarmed by fast population growth also because of the potential positive effects of a growing population. In his case study of population growth in a Kenyan village (reprinted in Chapter 18), John Tierney brings up some of these effects. For example, an increase in the size of the population may allow firms to experience economies of scale: as production takes place on a larger scale, costs per unit decrease. Population growth also increases population density, putting pressure on limited resources such as land; but the increasing relative scarcity of land is precisely what may provide an incentive to develop new and better technologies – an argument developed by Danish economist Ester Boserup (see Crook 1997: 11). And while pessimists worry that a larger population of consumers will exhaust limited resources, economists remind us that a large consumer market is also an incentive for firms to invest and expand. The risk inherent in such investments is reduced when the pool of potential consumers gets larger; and more investment, of course, can lead to increased standards of living.

Julian L. Simon is probably the best known of the economists who have challenged population pessimists. In the selection from his book *The Ultimate Resource 2* (reprinted in Chapter 19), Simon argues that people are, indeed, the ultimate resource. Human capital – emphasized in recent economic growth theories as key to achieve economic development – is embodied in people. Similarly, technological progress has been widely recognized as a major source of economic growth. But generating technological progress means generating new ideas. Simon emphasizes that new ideas come from people – the same people whose numbers population pessimists are keen to reduce. In his words, "the most important benefit of population size and growth is the increase it brings to the stock of useful knowledge. Minds matter economically as much as, or more than, hands or mouths. Progress is limited largely by the availability of trained workers."

Testing empirically the arguments of pessimists and revisionists is challenging. It is tempting to look at countries around the world and simply determine whether countries with faster population growth experience faster or slower economic growth than countries with slower population growth. A look at the data typically reveals that countries with fast population growth tend to have lower standards of living than countries with slow population growth (see, e.g., Mankiw 2007: 210). This correlation seems to support the pessimists' arguments – if population grows faster, standards of living will be lower. By itself, however, the negative correlation does not prove much – economists like to say that "correlation is not causation." The reason is that population growth may be both a cause and a result of economic growth. While faster population growth may well reduce standards of living, it may also be the case that countries where standards of living are low (for whatever reason) experience faster population growth as a result. In poor countries, for example, infant mortality tends to be higher (because of worse health conditions); couples, therefore, tend to have more children, so as to increase the chances that at least one of their children will survive to adulthood. If this is the case, fast population growth will be a *result* – not necessarily a cause – of low standards of living, and we will observe a negative correlation between the rate of population growth and standards of living. Similarly, there is clear evidence that less educated women have more children, on average, than better educated women. Lack of education, of course, is also associated with lower incomes and standards of living. Fast population growth and low standards of living, therefore, can be expected to go hand in hand even when one is not the cause of the other – lack of education may be the cause of both phenomena. In short, there is not a simple empirical test that makes it possible to determine clearly the effects of population growth on standards of living. More sophisticated tests are certainly possible and have been conducted, but even with these tests drawing firm conclusions remains difficult (Kelley 2001: 47).

While the debate goes on – as do the studies of the empirical evidence – most development economists continue to subscribe to a revisionist view and, therefore, to avoid overemphasizing the role of population growth in their explanations of economic development. Population size and population growth are just two of the many factors that help us understand the constraints to economic development in a certain country or area. Alarmist views or broad generalizations about the need to control (or encourage) population growth are unlikely to help us formulate effective development policies.

If the issue of population growth commands less attention today among development economists than it used to, the same cannot be said of the related issues of health and education. I mentioned that Simon refers to people as the "ultimate resource"; health conditions and educational levels have a dramatic impact on the productivity of this resource. More importantly, Amartya Sen reminds us that living a healthy life and having access to education are two of the most widely shared goals of people everywhere; even if more health and education were not instrumental for economic growth, they would be valuable goals for development policy in and of themselves (1995: 8–9). Development economists, therefore, have investigated thoroughly the causes and consequences of improvements in health and education, and they have tried to devise effective policies to help countries make progress in these areas.

As far as health is concerned, most developing countries have experienced dramatic improvements over the last few decades. We saw in Part One, for example, that life expectancy at birth rose significantly in a variety of developing countries. Other indicators of health such as infant mortality have seen similar improvements. In the 1950s, for example, more than 160 infants born in Uganda died on average for every 1,000 live births; fifty years later, the number of infant deaths has fallen to 84 per 1,000. Infant mortality during the same period of time has fallen even more rapidly in other LDCs – from 121 to just 21 per thousand in Mexico, 118 to 12 per thousand in Thailand, and 66 to 3 per thousand in Singapore (United Nations 2007). While advances in medicine and biology have contributed much to improving health conditions in developing countries, economic factors often dictate people's ability to take advantage of these scientific advances. This is because most improvements in health are the result of investments – in such areas as new medical technologies, development of vaccines and pharmaceuticals, construction of clinics and hospitals, and training of doctors and nurses. All these investments are costly and often force governments of LDCs to face difficult trade-offs. As tempting as it may be to recommend investing in health "as much as possible," limited budgets force difficult choices. Money spent on building a hospital is money taken away from building a road; money spent training nurses is money that will not be available to train teachers; and so on. Development economists try to estimate the costs and benefits of different health investments and the effectiveness of alternative policies to promote better health.

While there is no doubt that people value improvements in their longevity and health conditions, one may wonder exactly *how valuable* such improvements are. Imagine, for example, two developing countries where average per-capita incomes are exactly the same – say, $8,000 a year. Also suppose, however, that in the first country life expectancy is 50, whereas in the second country life expectancy is 70. Other things being equal, people in the second country are better off. But can the benefits of an extra 20 years of life be quantified and expressed in dollar terms? You may think that they cannot and should not – life does not have a price. But now imagine that incomes in the first country, where life expectancy is 50, are $12,000. The second country has only incomes of $8,000, but life expectancy of 70. Which country would you rather live in? Your answer gives us an idea of the monetary value that you attach to an extra 20 years of life. The reading by Harvard economists David E. Bloom and David Canning and UCSF economist Dean T. Jamison (reprinted in Chapter 20) explains the concept of "full income" and "value of a statistical life." Economists have developed these concepts to try to assess the monetary value of improvements in health. Doing so is important because of the costs of health improvements discussed earlier. In order to decide whether building a new clinic is a better use of our money than building a new road, we need some way of quantifying the benefits of each project. As one might expect, the evidence suggests that people place great value on improvements in health conditions. In fact, if the value of these improvements were included in national accounts, the economic progress of many developing countries would appear much more substantial than their rate of income growth suggests. The 21-year increase in life expectancy experienced in Sri Lanka over the past five decades, for example, adds very significant benefits to the growth in monetary incomes that also took place.

While better health is, in and of itself, a sign of economic development, improvements in health conditions also have positive effects on several other indicators of development, including per-capita incomes. The reading by Bloom, Canning, and Jamison addresses the main channels through which better health can help raise incomes. Labor productivity is probably the most obvious of the channels: healthier workers are more productive workers, i.e., they can produce more output per hour of labor. Less obvious is the fact that saving tends to be higher when health conditions improve. This is because the expectation to live a longer life provides an incentive to save for retirement. Fifty years ago a Vietnamese person expecting to live to age 40 did not have to worry about saving for old age; this person's grandchild, who can expect to live to age 70, is much more likely to put some money aside to provide for retirement. More saving, as discussed in Part One, can lead to more investment and faster growth in incomes.

Another major health issue discussed by Bloom and his co-authors (as well as in some of the other selections) is the spread of HIV/AIDS over the past 25 years or so. The effects of the pandemic have been especially devastating in sub-Saharan Africa, where the disease quickly reversed gains in life expectancy experienced since the 1950s. In Uganda, for example, life expectancy rose from 40 in the early 1950s to 52 in the late 1980s, but fell to less than 45 in the following ten years or so largely because of HIV/AIDS (United Nations 2007; see also United Nations 2005). And just as health improvements raise incomes while independently improving quality of life, HIV/AIDS works in the opposite direction, delivering a double blow to economic development. In addition to causing loss of life and a deterioration in the lives of those affected by the disease, HIV/AIDS lowers the productivity of workers, decreases incentives for saving (because it reduces longevity), and discourages investment from abroad (multinationals are reluctant to invest in countries where life-threatening diseases are common). The authors estimate that in 2000 the full cost of HIV/AIDS was equal to about 15 percent of Africa's GDP (see also UNDP 2005: 22).

Prevention and treatment can both be used to fight disease and improve health conditions in developing countries. The reading by Harvard economist Michael Kremer (reprinted in Chapter 21) provides a thorough discussion of the economics of pharmaceuticals in LDCs. Kremer explains the reasons why pharmaceutical companies are often reluctant to conduct research on diseases that affect primarily the developing world, and he warns against programs of foreign assistance for health expenditures that, while politically popular, may ignore the economic realities of the market for pharma-ceuticals. He suggests, for example, that foreign financing of antiretroviral drugs to treat HIV/AIDS in developing countries is unlikely to be an effective use of funds, since "many more lives could be saved with alternative interventions." Kremer offers specific recommendations for the kind of interventions that the governments of more developed countries should focus on.

Because of its dramatic impact, HIV/AIDS has been at the forefront of recent discussions of health policies in developing countries; it is important to realize, however, that many other diseases that have either disappeared or are easily treated in rich countries still cause a large number of deaths and much suffering in poor countries. The World Health Organization, for example, estimates that in 2002 over 1.6 million people in low-income countries died of diarrheal diseases, over 1 million died of childhood diseases such as measles and pertussis, another million died of tuberculosis, and nearly 900,000 died of malaria (World Health Organization 2004). The article by Economics Nobel Laureate Kenneth J. Arrow (reprinted in Chapter 22) looks at the challenges of introducing new drugs to fight malaria. Once again, the problems are economic more than medical. New treatments have been developed to replace old drugs to which the malaria parasite had developed resistance. But the new drugs are much more expensive, and effective distribution of such drugs faces several obstacles. Arrow suggests "a possible new direction" to tackle the disease effectively (see also Laxminarayan et al. 2006).

If health improvements can both improve quality of life directly and raise labor productivity, increased provision and improved quality of education can have very similar effects. Much like investments in health, investments in education have the power to deliver increases in incomes while also enhancing people's ability to live satisfying lives. We saw in Part One that recent economic growth theories give educational investments a major role in promoting economic development. In fact, there is hardly any controversy among development economists about the significant positive role that investments in education can play. Much debate continues, however, about the *kind* of educational investments that are most likely to be helpful and cost-effective in developing countries. "Investing in education" can mean many different things – building more schools, improving existing schools, training more teachers, enhancing the curriculum, providing incentives for parents to send children to school, and so on. As is always the case, policy-makers need to make difficult choices. Should they invest more in primary education or in higher education? Should they focus on rural schools or on urban schools? Recent research provides us with important information on the relative benefits and costs of different kinds of investment (what economists refer to as "rates of return") and on the kind of educational policies that make the greatest difference in helping developing countries.

The article titled "The Learning Deficit" (reprinted in Chapter 23) reports the results of a study by Harvard and World Bank economist Lant Pritchett. The article explains that quality of education in developing countries is often poor, so that focusing only on getting more children to go to school is unlikely to have a significant effect on educational achievement. Pritchett emphasizes instead the need to raise the quality of schooling through reforms that increase the ability of local communities – the ones with the highest stake in educational quality – to provide careful oversight of the effectiveness of the educational system. The issue of educational quality is also addressed by Clive Crook in the article reprinted in Chapter 24. Crook reports the results of research by education policy professor James Tooley, who has studied a common yet little known response of the poor in developing countries to low-quality education: the use of private schools. While it may seem counterintuitive that children of poor families would be able to attend private schools, Tooley has found that in places where public schools are ineffective, as is often the case in developing countries, small black-market private schools often spring up and serve large shares of the school-age population. These schools are typically simple operations, but they appear to be more effective than public schools, a fact recognized by poor parents who will often choose to pay a fee – even when they can barely afford it – to provide their children with higher-quality education.

The issue of higher education in developing countries is taken up in the article reprinted in Chapter 25. In the past, investments in higher education often seemed misguided in that they were costly and tended to benefit an extremely small share of the population; but as more and more students attend secondary school in countries such as China and India, demand for higher education rises, spreading the benefits of investments in higher education across a larger section of the population. The article details some recent promising changes in the structure of university education, but also points out that countries such as China still have much work to do if they want to reap more fully the benefits of investments in higher education.

Both health and education are issues closely linked with a phenomenon pervasive in many developing countries: child labor. The concerns about the impact of work on the health and education of children and, even more fundamentally, the belief that basic human rights are being violated when parents force their children to work make child labor a widely debated issue. Concerns about multinational corporations employing children in their offshore plants has further inflamed the debate and generated protests and boycotts in developed countries. Development economists have tried to understand the causes of child labor in developing countries, assess the impact of child labor on the well-being of children and families, and evaluate policies for dealing with this issue.

The reading by Martha Nichols (reprinted in Chapter 26) presents a hypothetical but very realistic case study of a U.S. executive traveling to Pakistan and discovering that child labor is taking place in one of the company's plants – against company policy. The case study helps bring to light some of the reasons why child labor takes place and the pros and cons of different approaches to dealing with it. The reading does not provide simple answers – it simply offers a starting point for discussion. The article by Cornell University economist Kaushik Basu (reprinted in Chapter 27) offers a critique of international labor standards, or specific regulations intended to reduce child labor in all countries. Basu argues that such standards are generally ineffective and may, in fact, have a negative impact on both children and families. He notes that "parents who send their children to work do not do so out of sloth and meanness, but to escape extreme poverty and hunger for the household, which includes the child." Basu is especially skeptical of developed countries banning the imports of goods produced by developing countries that allow child labor. Basu warns that while such policies may reduce the incidence of child labor in export sectors, the result will probably be to push children into other sectors – such as construction or, even worse, prostitution – where they will be much worse off. He recommends an alternative to bans that, he believes, is more likely to help developing countries "achieve what they want to achieve."

The final selection (reprinted in Chapter 28) is an article by Dartmouth economists Eric V. Edmonds and Nina Pavcnik. It provides a thorough treatment of the economics of child labor in developing countries, and it reviews much of the recent empirical evidence about the causes and effects of child labor. It stresses that while child labor in manufacturing plants often captures the headlines, most of the work children do is actually in agriculture and within the household. While most of the children who work also attend school, the evidence suggests that work may well have a negative impact on educational attainment. Regarding the causes of child labor, Edmonds and Pavcnik find evidence suggesting that poverty is the fundamental cause of child labor. Indeed, in cases when wages rise for both adults and children, so that parents could earn more by making their children work, data show that parents choose instead to reduce child labor – the improvement in family incomes that higher wages for the parents bring about is strongly associated with a decrease in child labor. The authors conclude their article by reviewing policy options for dealing with child labor; like Basu, they are skeptical of outright bans and emphasize instead the need for reforms in the area of access to credit and education.

Investments in health and education are likely to be two of the most productive uses of the scarce resources of governments in developing countries. Yet, there is a long history of health and educational investments that failed to promote development. The research development economists have done helps us understand the costs and benefits of alternative policies and ensure that investments are directed into the most productive projects.

REFERENCES

Birdsall, N. (1989) "Economic Analyses of Rapid Population Growth," *World Bank Research Observer*, 4: 23–50.

Crook, N. (1997) *Principles of Population and Development with Illustrations from Asia and Africa*, Oxford: Oxford University Press.

Ehrlich, P. R. (1975) *The Population Bomb*, Revised edn, Rivercity, MA: Rivercity Press.

Kates, R. W. and Parris, T. M. (2003) "Long-term Trends and a Sustainability Transition," *Proceedings of the National Academy of Sciences of the United States of America*, 100: 8062–7.

Kelley, A. C. (2001) "The Population Debate in Historical Perspective: Revisionism Revised," in N. Birdsall, A. C. Kelley, and S. W. Sinding (eds) *Population Matters: Demographic Change, Economic Growth, and Poverty in the Developing World*, New York: Oxford University Press.

Laxminarayan, R., Over, M., and Smith, D. L. (2006) "Will a Global Subsidy of New Antimalarials Delay the Emergence of Resistance and Save Lives?" *Health Affairs*, 25: 325–36.

Mankiw, N. G. (2007) *Macroeconomics*, 6th edn, New York: Worth Publishers.

Menken, J., Duffy, L., and Kuhn, R. (2003) "Childbearing and Women's Survival: New Evidence from Rural Bangladesh," *Population and Development Review*, 29: 405–26.

Perkins, D. H., Radelet, S., Snodgrass, D. R., Gillis, M., and Roemer, M. (2001) *Economics of Development*, 5th edn, New York: W. W. Norton.

Sen, A. (1995) "Economic Development and Social Change: India and China in Comparative Perspectives," Development Economics Research Programme Working Paper No. 67, STICERD, London School of Economics and Political Science.

Solow, R. M. (1956) "A Contribution to the Theory of Economic Growth," *Quarterly Journal of Economics*, 70: 65–94.

Todaro, M. P. and Smith, S. C. (2006) *Economic Development*, 9th edn, Boston, MA: Pearson Addison Wesley.

UNDP (2005) *Human Development Report 2005*, New York: United Nations Development Programme.

United Nations (2005) *Progress towards the Millennium Development Goals, 1990–2005*. Online. Available HTTP: <http://unstats.un.org/unsd/mi/mi_coverfinal.htm> (accessed 2 September 2007).

—— (2007) *World Population Prospects: The 2006 Revision Population Database*. Online. Available HTTP: <http://esa.un.org/unpp/> (accessed 2 September 2007).

US Census Bureau (2006) *Total Midyear Population for the World: 1950–2050*. Online. Available HTTP: <http://www.census.gov/ipc/www/idb/worldpop.html> (accessed 2 September 2007).

World Health Organization (2004) *Global Burden of Disease Estimates*. Online. Available HTTP: <http://www.who.int/healthinfo/bodestimates/en/index.html> (accessed 2 September 2007).

Chapter 18

John Tierney

FANISI'S CHOICE

How many children should a woman have in the fastest growing country in the world?

NO **MATTER HOW BORED** you were by the population explosion, the scene inside the hut was startling. It was early 1976, and a high-cheekboned black woman in a pink dress was leaning against the mud wall. She looked at the camera in amusement as she listened to the African anthropologist. He was making a documentary about her village, Maragoli, eight miles above the equator in western Kenya. The United Nations, the World Bank, and private donors had paid for him to come to this village, here in the middle of the most crowded farmland of the fastest growing nation in the history of the world, to ask her how many children she wanted.

"Oh, even up to 20!" she said, giggling with delight, practically oblivious as the anthropologist pestered her with questions about how she expected to care for her family. "Mother-in-law will cook for me," she said, and the camera panned to an old woman sitting on the cowdung floor with two children. Then the camera went back to the young woman in pink, and you saw her bulging belly.

"Where will you deliver?" asked the anthropologist.

"In this house."

"Who will help you deliver?"

"God himself."

And there in one room you had the population explosion: a smiling Madonna and Child for our age. The documentary, titled *Maragoli*, became something of a classic among the globally minded. It was one thing to hear Robert McNamara, then president of the World Bank, warn that "rampant population growth" left humanity "more certainly threatened than it has been by any catastrophe the world has yet endured." But here you could see one of the world's poorest women, barely surviving on her tiny patch of land, living in a village whose population was projected to double within 20 years, and she not only shunned contraceptives, she *wanted* 20 mouths to feed. At the end of the film, a freeze-frame of her appeared above a subtitle: "On May 26, 1976, Fanisi Kalusa gave birth to twins."

Congratulations did not seem in order. That they were twins only made Thomas Malthus's famous warning of 1798 all the more depressingly apt: "Population, when unchecked, increases in a geometrical ratio. Subsistence increases only in an arithmetical ratio." Ecologist Paul Ehrlich put it more directly in his 1968 best seller, *The Population Bomb*. It began. "The battle to feed all humanity is over. In the 1970s the world will undergo famines – hundreds of millions of people are going to starve to death. . . ." This did not in fact occur, but the problem didn't go away either. It seemed as urgent as ever when *Time* magazine put it on the cover in 1984 under a new metaphor, "The Population Curse."

There were a few dissenters – the Vatican, most prominently, but also some academics, the most outspoken of whom was a business professor at the University of Maryland named Julian Simon. I had heard about his theories, but I wasn't quite ready for the response I got when I called him. This was shortly after the Live Aid concert for Africa, and I explained that I was planning to write about the impact of population growth on the food crisis in Africa. I was going to Kenya because it seemed to have the potential for future disaster. In Africa, the fastest growing continent in history, Kenya was the fastest growing nation. The average Kenyan woman was bearing eight children during her lifetime. The growth rate had accelerated to 4.1 percent per year, enough to double Kenya's population every 17 years –

"Yes," Simon interrupted, "isn't it wonderful that so many people can be alive in that country today?" He proceeded to explain why he thought that population growth was good in the long run, that the world's poor were becoming better fed in India, in China, in the rest of Asia, in Latin America.

Everywhere, that is, except Africa. The average person there had less food than he had had a decade ago. Across Kenya's northern border last year people were starving on worldwide television. Not even ardent Malthusians blamed the Ethiopian famine primarily on population growth; the more obvious culprits were drought, civil war, and a horrendously inept government. But the country's 2.8 percent annual growth did seem a factor. As Malthus had written, "Famine seems to be the last, the most dreadful resource of nature." Ehrlich and McNamara updated their pleas for population control.

And I found myself in the hut of the Maragoli deputy assistant chief asking directions to the woman in the pink dress. On the drive up from Lake Victoria I had been surprised to see a secretarial school and a photocopying store, but here in the village, a half-mile from the paved road, things looked relatively unchanged from the movie: a gorgeous green valley with thatched roofs and tiny farm fields jammed next to one another. There were still no electric lights or indoor plumbing. The only immediate sign of Westernization – and it was a disheartening one – came when the deputy assistant chief, Jotham Mudiri, introduced me to his 30-year-old son.

"It has been my dream to become a journalist," said the son.

His name was Cubic. It had been inspired by his father's job as a clerk at a construction company. "My father liked mathematics very much, and he wanted to keep remembrance of his skill for calculating the cubic yardage of the bricks."

Cubic said he would take me to Fanisi Kalusa's hut and act as interpreter. She, like most villagers, preferred the Maragoli tribal language to Swahili or English, Kenya's national languages. I told Cubic that I wanted to use her family as a retrospective experiment, a look at what 10 years of population growth had wrought. I wanted to know how many children she had, whether she now used contraceptives, whether she had any regrets. It would be a case study of two of the most controversial and mysterious questions in social science: How do a man and woman decide to have a child? And what happens to them and their neighbors after the child arrives?

I had a feeling that Cubic was pondering another question. Why had this American traveled 8,000 miles to talk to Fanisi Kalusa about her sex life? This was harder to explain. My only excuse was that her sex life – well, it seemed to be on everyone's agenda. A 65-year-old celibate man from Rome had just been through Kenya lecturing married couples on the proper purpose of intercourse. Shortly after Pope John Paul II's anticontraceptive sermon, Kenyan President Daniel Moi, father of seven, was on Radio Kenya offering contradictory advice more in line with the thinking of McNamara and Ehrlich. Back in Manhattan and Washington, two of the more densely populated places on Earth, thousands of experts at the U.N. and organizations like the Population Crisis Committee were debating how to stop the Maragolis of the world from becoming overcrowded. About the only thing that everyone agreed on was that Fanisi Kalusa badly needed outside advice.

It was nice of them all to care. But what exactly did they know about childbearing that she didn't?

Two sad stories

In 1968 the ecologist Garrett Hardin published a remarkably influential and oddly flawed essay called "The Tragedy of the Commons." It was one of the few parables ever to appear in the professional journal *Science*, and it has probably been more widely quoted than any other research published in that magazine over the past century. The essay was primarily an attempt to prove that "freedom to breed is intolerable," but the parable was applicable to more than the population issue. It became the philosophical underpinning of the environmentalist and conservationist establishment.

Hardin's Malthusian parable involves a large grazing pasture open to all herdsmen and their cattle – a commons, as it was called in English and colonial American villages. At first, with just a few cattle, everyone thrives. The cattle nibble at the grass in one area, then move elsewhere until it grows back. But the herds grow larger and fill the commons, and their overgrazing starts killing the grass and threatening to ruin the entire commons.

Obviously, it would be in everyone's interest to preserve the commons by limiting the number of cattle. But why should any single herdsman make a sacrifice? He personally benefits by adding a cow to his own herd. Not adding the cow would merely leave some grass to be eaten by the expanding herd of another, less altruistic herdsman. So each herdsman, acting out of rational self-interest, goes on adding cattle until the commons is destroyed and the herds die.

The parable gives a fresh insight into a marvelously broad range of public problems. Congress as a whole deplores the budget deficit, but each member goes on increasing it with pork-barrel projects benefiting his district. A community wants to keep its lake clean, but no cost-conscious homeowner or factory manager has any personal incentive to stop dumping his own pollutants into the water. Each whaler contributes to the extinction of his livelihood.

The only solutions are to regulate the commons — pass a law requiring sewage treatment, for instance — or convert it from common property into private property. During Africa's drought in the 1970s, a satellite photograph of the Sahel region revealed a green pentagon amidst the devastated brown expanse. A puzzled American agronomist went to the spot and found a 250,000-acre private cattle ranch with a very restricted herd. Fenced outside this enormous plot, nomads' cattle grazed the surrounding grassland to destruction.

Hardin's conclusion from the parable was that humans must abandon "the commons in breeding." Relying only on voluntary birth control was a "tragic ideal" that would not "rescue us from the misery of overpopulation."

"Freedom to breed will bring ruin to all," he warned. It sounded sensible unless you paused to consider one difference between breeding humans and breeding cattle: children do not eat grass.

The distinction is crucial. While a herdsman on the commons can feed his cattle for free, a parent must pay to feed a child. The tragedy of the commons is caused by individuals seeking private profit at the cost of the entire community's welfare; there is no reason to suppose that childbearing fits this description. The rest of the community does pay some costs when a child is born — it may provide schooling, for instance, and endure added pollution from the household (such as noise). But the village may also benefit when the child becomes an adult who not only supports his aged parents but pays taxes as well. There's no universal answer to the question of who pays and who benefits from the child. You can imagine a village in which parents pay most of the costs and the community gets most of the benefits, so that it would not be in anyone's economic self-interest to have a child — a situation that in fact seems to exist in the United States and most developed countries today.

So why was Hardin quick to assume that population would grow out of control? Why were he and so many intellectuals sure that a population disaster was looming?

Perhaps the answer is in another parable. Call it "The Melodrama of the Commons."

This time suppose that the commons is vast and the number of cattle small, so there is no danger of overgrazing for at least a century. And suppose that two well-meaning intellectuals arrive on the scene. One is an optimist. She realizes that the cattle could ultimately ruin the commons, but before that day arrives a lot could happen. Maybe by then the commons will have an indestructible grass that grows back overnight. Maybe the villagers won't want cattle. This intellectual may devote her research to replacing beef with her dream of the future — tofu. Or she may decide to become an astronomer, because the commons just doesn't interest her.

The other intellectual is a pessimist who feels duty-bound to warn the villagers. He draws graphs forecasting the rate of cattle reproduction with certain dates highlighted. "Doomsday for the Commons," reads one. Further along the graph is the date on which the village's cattle will have eaten all the grass on Earth.

"These projections could be wrong," he tells the audience at his increasingly popular lectures, but somehow the caveat tends to be forgotten by the time he finishes. He likes to close by reminding everyone of the calf that died in the drought several years earlier. "Think of the commons completely covered with dying calves," he says. "Can we sit by and do nothing if there is a chance this will happen?" Soon the better-educated villagers speak knowingly of the "commons crisis." A retired herdsman donates money so the intellectual can refine his graphs.

Meanwhile, the village's other intellectual is too busy with her work to argue about the commons. (If she needs research money for her tofu project, she may secretly welcome the doomsday predictions for beef.) And even if she wanted to dispute these graphs, who would pay attention? The pessimist would dismiss her as a novice, and she couldn't very well ask a philanthropist to give her money to study something she thinks is not a problem.

Thus the melodrama of the commons is inevitable, and for the same basic reason as the tragedy: although it may be in the community's interest to avoid worrying about a nonexistent problem, it is not in anyone's self-interest to refute the village pessimist.

Which is not to say that the village pessimist is always wrong. Humans have turned grasslands into deserts and starved to death. Until now most villages have avoided tragedy, but then up until now most villages haven't grown as fast as Maragoli.

The Curse of the aunt

Before we reached Fanisi Kalusa's, Cubic and I ran into the prominent figure of the assistant chief, Wilfred Bwasu. He was strolling down the village's one dirt road wearing a green army jacket and carrying a Masai sword sheathed in a red leather walking stick. He had the most ample belly that I saw in Maragoli – a source of some envy, as I later discovered when I happened to tell some villagers about the American longing for a flat stomach. They explained that a stomach like the assistant chief's was a status symbol.

He was in an expansive mood. Yes, the village had grown during the past decade – the number of people in his jurisdiction had reached 10,000, an increase of some 40 percent – and yes, only 25 percent of the men had full-time jobs, but no, growth was not really a problem. At least not from his perspective.

"Living is a bit hard because of the small plots, but we have more food now from our neighbors in other villages. In days to come we will have electricity," he said, pointing his sword at the power line over the road. Hundreds of households had applied for electric service. Even more were waiting for telephones, which were already in a few homes. "We have now plenty of piped water," he said, pointing at the spigots in nearby yards. "People are very happy. Our living today is very good."

An uneasy grin came over the assistant chief when I asked about family planning programs. He looked at the other men gathered around us. They had the same grin. "Many people are now trying to use family planning," he said, but he wasn't one of them. Nor were the other men.

"The pills cause side effects," said Timothy Osayo, a 30-year-old veterinarian. He and everyone else I met in Kenya had a horror story about the Pill or the IUD or the Depo-Provera injection – or almost anything. A rumor had just swept the country concerning a new premium beer. Because it came in a green bottle instead of the traditional brown – and apparently thus seemed part of a foreign plot – it was said to contain a chemical that caused sterility. Cubic's father told me that when the British arrived in Maragoli at the turn of the century, the natives had refused to drink tea for fear of sterility.

"Many men prefer another family planning method," Osayo said. "A man will go to the sister of his father and ask her to come and curse his wife so that she has no more children. The aunt will come and hold the wife's hand and say, 'I curse you by your grandfather's grave.'"

Osayo laughed, and I tried to imagine the incongruities of village life for this educated veterinarian. He was holding a plastic briefcase from the Fifth International Farm Management Congress in Nairobi. How strange for him to come home to his neighbors' superstitions.

"Well, does the Curse work?" I joked.

"It depends how tough the aunt's language is," said Osayo, perfectly seriously.

He and Cubic discussed the intricacies of this contraceptive – it seemed to be more effective if the aunt really was mad at the wife for some reason – and then he said it would probably be his choice someday. Ever the nitpicker, I wondered if it was a reversible method.

"Suppose you later decide to have more children?"

"Then you ask the aunt to remove the curse."

"What if the aunt has died?"

"Then you find another aunt or relative and you go to your grandfather's grave and say the words, and everything is all right."

We were near the health clinic, so I stopped in for a second opinion. The nurse in charge, Lizzy Opanda, estimated that only five percent of the local women used the contraceptives – the Pill, the coil IUD, condoms – available free at the clinic. "Most of the mothers here realize the problem and want to stop having children," she said. "It's the men who don't want family planning. Africans believe that to call yourself a man you have to have lots of children. They want 15 or more. They also say that if we give a woman the Pill, she will become a prostitute."

"Incidentally," I said, "I understand many people practice family planning by having an aunt give a curse."

"Yes, but it doesn't work," said Nurse Opanda.

"Yes it does," said another nurse working nearby. "It works. The aunt comes and you can't deliver."

The question was unresolved when I left to visit Fanisi Kalusa.

"She has rejected that proposal"

We were filing down the hillside between maize fields and banana trees when a skinny girl in a blue school uniform met us. She was one of the twins. Her mother had named her after Sandra Nichols, the American producer of the documentary. Young Sandra still hadn't seen her prenatal appearance on film, nor had the other villagers. The Kenyan government, for reasons known only to some civil servant, had not allowed *Maragoli* to be shown outside Nairobi.

Sandra led us down to the family's farm at the bottom of the valley. This was the "down by the stream" neighborhood, the poor side of the village because it was a quarter-mile walk down from the road. Pieces of scrap metal covered holes in the thatched roof of the family's 20-foot-square hut. In the yard several children were playing next to a tethered cow.

Fanisi was inside. She was wearing a different pink dress, and she looked much older. Her face wasn't wrinkled, but it was leaner, tougher. She wasn't pregnant now, which partly explained why she had lost some of that fullness, but it also had obviously been a hard 10 years. You could see that from the muscles in her forearms.

For her every day began at dawn. Her bed, which she shared with five daughters, was a few scraps of matting on the floor of a room seven feet wide. The six of them shared a blanket. Her sons, as well as two cows and a goat, slept in the kitchen; her husband, Isaac, had his own room with a lock on the door and a wooden bed with a thin foam mattress. It was Fanisi's job to make breakfast (which was usually just tea), get the children ready for school, sweep the house, and then go off with her three-gallon pail to fetch water. Each morning Fanisi made a half-dozen trips to the spring, 200 yards down the steep slope behind her house.

Then she tended the farm, which in Maragoli is considered woman's work. From eight until noon she dug and weeded her three-quarter-acre plot of maize, beans, and bananas. The children came home for a lunch of porridge made from the maize, after which she washed the dishes and left them out in the sun to dry. Then it was time to fetch water again and make a few more trips down the hill to gather firewood from the family's small stand of trees. The midafternoon was reserved for picking vegetables for dinner or walking up to the market a mile away. By four the children were home, and it was time to wash them and start cooking dinner, which she was about to do when we arrived.

Standing in the front room, next to the wall where she had been filmed 10 years earlier, she ticked off the children: five daughters, two sons; aged four to 16. She had been pregnant again in 1983, but the child died at birth. Fanisi was now 36 years old.

"In the movie you said that you wanted to have 20 children," I said. "Do you still feel that way?" Cubic translated it for her, and Fanisi slumped against the wall, bowed her head, clapped her hands, and went into an even wilder fit of laughter than that in the movie. She was still giggling as she dashed behind the mud partition to see if her cauldron of water was boiling. From the kitchen she shouted something in Maragoli.

"She has rejected that proposal," Cubic translated, "because there is not enough food to meet the demand."

We went into the kitchen, where she was dumping maize flour into the boiling water and stirring it with a two-foot-long wooden spoon. "You don't want more children?" I repeated, and she answered in English, "No. I have gone in the family planning."

"Which method?" I asked. She conferred with Cubic.

"Condoms," he said.

Fanisi explained her decision with a list of arguments similar to those of the Population Crisis Committee. The days when a father in Maragoli could divide 20 acres among his sons were gone. Her husband's plot couldn't feed his own family. So the children would have to get outside jobs, which required an education, and that meant paying school fees. The government provided teachers free in elementary schools, but it still cost $10 per child – more than two weeks' wages at an unskilled job in Maragoli – to buy a uniform and cover incidental fees (such as the continuing expense of building classrooms for the Maragoli baby boom). Fanisi and her husband had paid these fees, but they hadn't been able to afford the $175 tuition for secondary school. Their oldest child, 16-year-old Beatrice, had been forced to drop out after elementary school two years earlier, and Fanisi was still upset about it.

"How many children would you advise Beatrice to have?" I asked.

"Six."

"Two," came a voice from the doorway. It was Fanisi's husband, Isaac, a lanky man in a pair of pants with holes in both knees and a shirt with both sleeves in the process of ripping off. He was an unemployed mason. The traditional male full-time work, keeping cattle, had disappeared when the open pasture at the bottom of the valley had been turned into farmland. Nowadays the women coming from the market with sacks of maize on their heads walked past clusters of unemployed men loitering along the road. Isaac still did some work around the *shamba* – taking care of the few cows that grazed on the family's land, repairing the hut, and occasionally helping Fanisi with the farm. But it had been six months since his last job as a mason.

"Have your many children caused financial problems for you?" I asked. Isaac looked puzzled as he conferred with Cubic. I think he was trying to decide whether I was being facetious or was merely an idiot.

'He says that if you were a typical Maragoli, he would ask you for the shirt off your back," Cubic explained.

Fanisi insisted we stay for dinner. She cooked it, served it, cleaned up afterward – and did not get to join the men at the table in the front room. She would eat later with the children. She came out with a pitcher of water to wash our hands and then served the Kenyan national dish, *ugali*, which is maize flour boiled in water until it attains the consistency of day-old Play-doh. Fanisi also served up one of the family's chickens – an especially valued treat in Maragoli, I suspected, and my suspicions were confirmed by a loud crunch across the table. It was Cubic eating the bones.

But as hard as life here was, there seemed to be good news: the population bomb in this room had fizzled out. Fanisi and Isaac had used contraceptives to stop at seven children instead of 20. Their daughter Beatrice, with the benefit of their hindsight, could be expected to have an even smaller family. By the end of dinner I was sure I'd found the model African family for Planned Parenthood.

As it turned out, this was hardly the case. But before ruining a perfectly good theory with the messy facts, before prying any further into this family's affairs, let me give you the historical perspective as neatly as it appeared to me that evening.

Malthus's first mistake

It's possible that the very first population crisis took place not far from Fanisi's hut. Hominids were roaming these hills when the first stone tools were invented about two million years ago, a discovery that increased the ability to collect food and presumably enabled more people to survive. Before long somebody must have complained about overcrowding.

But there was a whole planet open to those first humans, and not until 10,000 years ago did their descendants occupy the six major continents. At this point the Earth's population was about eight million – astoundingly small when you consider that humans had existed for one or two million years. The average growth rate works out to less than 0.0007 percent per year, or just seven people added to a population of one million. What restrained their numbers?

Early death, according to the standard Malthusian explanation. But recent research among surviving hunter-gatherers such as the !Kung bushmen has challenged this assumption. They turn out to be surprisingly healthy and long-lived. What keeps their population stable is their unexpectedly low fertility rate, apparently due to the women's low level of body fat (a result of their lean diet and constant exercise) and to their habit of breastfeeding a child for three or four years.

The development of agriculture 10,000 years ago may well have increased the death rate among humans. People living close together in settlements spread more diseases and created more pollution. But more food was available and women weaned their children earlier, so any increase in the death rate was offset by rising birth rates. The annual growth rate soared, relatively speaking, but the average remained well under 0.1 percent. In virtually all agricultural societies, some cultural practices developed that limited births. In some medieval European nations, younger siblings were expected not to marry; in Maragoli, sex was taboo after a woman became a grandmother. But constantly high mortality from disease and hardship was apparently the main force that stabilized population.

With the Industrial Revolution came another population crisis: better health and longer life. In Europe the growth rate shot up three centuries ago and kept rising until early in this century. Then it fell, as couples made the "demographic transition" from high to low fertility. Families were smaller because people married at a later age or never married at all. Growth rates dropped further when modern contraceptives and legal abortion became available. Today a dozen European countries have nearly steady or falling population levels, and the fertility rate for the entire developed world has dropped below the replacement level.

So Malthus's first assumption was wrong. Population does not grow geometrically. Humans have effectively limited their numbers in modern societies, and also in some primitive ones. Population has shot up occasionally to a new plateau after a technological advance, but for most of history, from hunter-gatherers to yuppies, it has remained quite stable. The latest explosion, in which the population rose from 800 million in 1750 to over 4.5 billion today, already seems to be abating. Since 1973 the world's growth rate has once again slowed (from two percent to 1.7 percent) as fertility rates have dropped sharply in Asia and Latin America. It seems inevitable that Africa's fertility will decline too, but demographers are loath to predict when. They point out that fertility rates in Asia and Latin America soared abruptly before dropping, but they still have a hard time fathoming Africa's fecundity. In Kenya half the population is under the age of 15, a result of two decades of growth at nearly four percent per year – double what any European country ever experienced.

One explanation, maybe even the most important one, is – well, basically it's the Curse of the Aunt, although John Caldwell doesn't use that precise term.

Caldwell, an Australian demographer, is the author of one of the leading current theories explaining fertility decline. During the 1960s, when many Westerners assumed that peasants had large families because they were too backward to know better or to get contraceptives, Caldwell argued that the peasants were making rational economic decisions. In these societies a child costs the parents relatively little and benefits them by working on the farm and later supporting them in their old age. The "intergenerational flow of wealth" goes from the young to the old, and in particular to the patriarch, so a rational man wants to have many wives, children, and grandchildren to do his work and shower him with gifts. A common saying in these societies is, "Each extra mouth comes attached to two extra hands."

Children become a burden only when the society is Westernized. Then the patriarch's power wanes: the nuclear family replaces the extended family as the basic economic unit, and the wife acquires more status. A man has new obligations to her and especially to his children, who must now be educated. Schooling costs the parents money and prevents the child from working full-time on the farm, and the Westernized child feels less obligation to support the parents. So the flow of wealth has been reversed. It goes from parent to child, and the rational parent wants fewer children.

This model gives a useful but incomplete accounting of Maragoli's baby boom. As you may have gathered from Fanisi's and Isaac's eating and sleeping habits, the Western ideal of marriage has not permeated the village. Some of the neighbors still practice polygamy. Children are still expected to support their aged parents. Yet the village is slowly becoming educated and Westernized, and Caldwell himself recently concluded that socioeconomic factors alone aren't enough to explain why fertility in Africa is so much higher than in Asia or Latin America. Something irrational is going on.

"The central fact of African high fertility," Caldwell writes, "is a culture, molded by religion, that encourages repeated child-bearing and abhors sterility at any stage." Throughout Africa children are regarded as God's greatest gift, a sign of divine approval. Every adult is expected to honor his ancestors by having children. In some cultures, when a woman prematurely stops having children, it is often considered a sign that her evilness has displeased God or her ancestors. These beliefs perpetuate the older generation's power – thus helping to preserve the extended family – and cause infertility to be regarded as the ultimate curse. Some peoples punish the childless after death by tossing their bodies to wild animals or sexually mutilating them.

These traditional beliefs are so strong that they persist even among converts to Christianity or Islam. Many Maragolis (including Fanisi's family) are Quakers, but they're happy to talk about the Curse of the Aunt on their way home from Sunday services. In some ways they have the worst of both worlds. Traditionally, a Maragoli man was forbidden to have sex with a wife during the two or three years she was breastfeeding for fear that his semen would poison her milk. Missionaries disapproved of this taboo because it supported polygamy by encouraging a man to turn to other women for sex, and today most couples no longer abide by it. But most haven't replaced this traditional spacing technique with anything. They talk knowledgeably about modern contraceptives one moment and then, upon being asked how many children they plan to have, shrug and say, "This is up to God."

And yet Fanisi and Isaac were using contraceptives. They had somehow transcended the traditional beliefs and superstitions about fertility. It was comforting, that evening at dinner, to think that the demographic transition was proceeding so rationally. The next afternoon, however, I heard Isaac's side of the story.

"Maybe he doesn't know"

Up the hill in his mother's hut, where he had retreated for privacy, Isaac first explained the rational economic reasons that had caused him to stop having children. In Cubic's translation: "The world today is full of inflation, joblessness, landlessness, clotheslessness." Then Isaac said that he would never let Fanisi use the Pill or any other contraceptive. So, I asked as casually as possible, which method do you use now?

"I have no need for any of them," he said. "My wife has stopped giving birth."

I tried not to look surprised. "How has she stopped?"

"After the infant died at birth two years ago, my mother cursed us not to give any more births."

"Oh. I thought it was to be done by an aunt."

"I believe that the mother can give the same curse as the aunt."

"In America we do not believe the Curse is effective."

Isaac considered this with an open mind. "Maybe the Curse doesn't work in America. But here in Africa it is a good means of family planning."

As Isaac went off to bring the cows in out of the rain, Cubic and I walked down to see Fanisi. "What's going on?" I asked. "She says they use condoms."

"Maybe he doesn't know about it."

I stopped to take a good look at Cubic as I explained why I doubted this possibility. He tugged at his corduroy cap in apparent confusion for a moment, then nodded.

"Oh yes," said Cubic. "You know, men in the village think these condoms will cause damage to a man."

"Of course."

Down at the hut, Fanisi's mother-in-law was happy to explain her role. She herself did not believe in family planning, but in this case it was necessary. It seems that Fanisi's growing family was making some neighbors jealous. Mother-in-law feared the neighbors were casting a spell on Fanisi's children, and this fear intensified after the stillbirth. So, to end the neighbors' jealousy, Fanisi's mother-in-law cast the Curse.

Fanisi nodded in confirmation as she listened to her mother-in-law's chronology. When she went back into the kitchen by herself, Cubic and I followed.

"But you said yesterday you were using condoms," I whispered. She and Cubic conferred.

"I made a mistake in translation," Cubic said. "She uses the coil."

"But your husband is against it."

Fanisi giggled as she poked wood in the fire. "He doesn't know."

Fanisi said the coil had been recommended to her by members of the local women's cooperative, which she had joined in 1982. The next year, after the stillbirth, she had gone to the local clinic and gotten a coil without telling Isaac. I thought it strange that she would talk about this in front of Cubic (and later in front of other men), but Fanisi didn't seem worried. "No one will tell him," she said.

"So you let your mother-in-law give the Curse?"

"Yes."

"But you didn't think it would work?"

"No, the Curse works, of course, but it brings complications. It may only work for five or six years, and then you get pregnant, and then you have a miscarriage because of the Curse."

"So you chose the coil because it has fewer side effects?"

"Yes."

"Which do you think your daughter Beatrice will choose when she marries, the coil or the Curse? Or will she even use family planning? Will she want 20 children the way you did?"

"You must ask Beatrice."

This would have to wait three days, though, because Beatrice was off visiting her aunt. Not, I was assured, for the Curse.

The telltale roof

If you imagine a family in a suburb like Scarsdale, New York, trying to survive on a corn crop in the backyard, you get a rough idea of what it was like to live in Fanisi's village 10 years ago. The population density was about 2,000 persons per square mile. Since then, village officials estimate that the density has grown closer to 3,000. They recently banned drumbeating at night. Farmland has been cleared to build huts and classrooms for the new children. Logically, there should be less corn and more hunger. The evidence, however, is not so logical.

"When I started here eight years ago," Nurse Opanda told me at the clinic, "we used to see a lot of malnourished children. Sometimes there were 10 a week. Now it's one case a week, or none." The elementary school's headmaster said he has noticed a similar decline in the number of malnourished students – and during the past 10 years the proportion of children attending elementary school had risen to virtually 100 percent.

It was hard to account for this trend. Kenya had recently done several nationwide studies determining the number of young children who are "stunted" – those who are 10 percent shorter than the average height for their age. Being short, of course, isn't harmful in itself, but it can be a sign of poor nutrition. The percentage of stunted children had remained fairly constant nationwide, but it had increased sharply in the province that includes Maragoli. So how could malnutrition be declining in Maragoli, which was the most densely populated part of the province?

I went to see Richard Walukano, the province's public health officer. He attributed Maragoli's improvement partly to general health measures – measles vaccinations, for instance – that eliminated some serious diseases leading to malnutrition. He also attributed the improvement to the parents of Maragoli.

"You go in some of the less crowded parts of the province and see a family with four children, and two or three of them are malnourished," said Walukano. "But the Maragolis know how to farm better than many of the others. They work hard to feed their children. They keep cows to have milk, and they plant beans along with the maize so the children get a balanced diet. You go in a home there and find 10 or 12 children, and all of them are healthy."

Still, wouldn't they have been even healthier if the family were smaller? Fanisi's seven children were not malnourished, but their high-starch diet could have been more balanced if their mother had more money for meat and vegetables. The youngest, four-year-old Mathias, who was being treated for worms, might have avoided this common ailment if he'd owned shoes. Fewer children might have meant tuition for Beatrice, a new shirt for Isaac, no more trips to the well for Fanisi.

Yet when I looked around at the neighbors who did enjoy these benefits, the families were as large or even larger. Up the hill a family with eight children (and no more land than Isaac) could afford piped water because the husband was in the army. Another couple had sent 12 children through school, some through college, and were now the richest people in the village, thanks to the money from their children's jobs. And a couple of cornfields away from Fanisi was the baffling case of Rose Vuguza.

Rose was another woman who had appeared in the documentary, but in a different role – someone who wished she'd had fewer children. She was then pregnant with her 16th. "Looking after them is defeating me," she said. After the documentary she did use contraceptives. Then, in 1977, her husband died. She was left with no income, less than an acre, and 16 children. When I visited, she was 48 and her children ranged from 9 to 30.

"I am struggling," she told me. "Children are not beneficial. The land is not enough." An older daughter, who had been forced by finances to drop out of elementary school, was now unmarried and working in a bar, a highly disreputable job for a woman. Her 18-year-old son had left secondary school because of fees, the next son remained only because of a scholarship, and the 16-year-old daughter might have to drop out this year. The only respite in her litany of gloom was the oldest son, 22-year-old Simon, who had used a scholarship to go two years beyond secondary school. Now a part-time schoolteacher, he was helping to support the family, but it wasn't enough.

"I have no food in the house," Rose said. "I must borrow maize. Some days I lack breakfast and lunch."

I was sure then, and I still am, that she was telling the truth about her hardships. But I was puzzled midway through our conversation when I glanced up and noticed that the roof was not thatched grass. It was iron, the kind that Fanisi and Isaac wanted but couldn't afford.

"When did you install the roof?" I asked.

"When we built the hut. In 1981."

"Where did you live before?"

Rose took me out the back door and pointed to her old home a few feet away, a slightly larger hut with a thatched roof, where four children still slept. She and seven children had moved into the new four-room hut. It had cost $400, which would take an unskilled worker nearly two years to earn. Most of the money had come from an uncle of Rose's who was a doctor in a nearby town.

At the time Rose struck me as an anomaly – a widow with 16 children, living in less crowded conditions than she was 10 years ago. But I kept finding equivalents of Rose's uncle in other Maragoli households. Isaac, for instance, got help from his brother. Later, back at the University of Nairobi, I looked up Joseph Ssennyonga, the anthropologist who had interviewed Fanisi and Rose 10 years earlier. He had lived in Maragoli for 20 months while making the documentary and researching his doctoral thesis on population growth and rural poverty. He was not surprised to hear about Rose's new house.

"You'll never understand anything in Maragoli if you just look at the amount of land and the number of children in a family," Ssennyonga said. "If anything, you'll find that the bigger families are better off. There's so much outside income from relatives working in other parts of the country. If you just look at the household, you can't understand how they stay alive for a week, let alone put up a new building. The old theories of ecological determinism don't apply in an ecosystem with so many links to the outside world."

In some ways, then, villages like Maragoli are simply exporting their growth problems to the rest of Kenya. But so far the national results don't appear disastrous. Since 1975 a Kenyan's life expectancy has increased five years, and infant mortality has declined 20 percent. The country's total economic output has grown faster than the population. So has agricultural production, thanks to the doubling of the coffee and tea crops. Food production has lagged behind population growth in some years, and it plummeted in 1984, when the drought forced Kenya to import maize temporarily. But analysts expect the 1985 statistics to show that Kenya's food output per person is back up to its level of a decade ago.

To keep up with the six million people born since 1975, Kenya's farmers improved their techniques and put more land into cultivation. Environmentalists argue that some of this land is too fragile to be farmed or grazed, that forests and pastures are being turned into deserts. Some even suggest that recent overuse of land is drying up Africa's weather by setting off a chain of events that prevents water vapor from accumulating in clouds. But most meteorologists doubt that humans had anything to do with the recent African drought, because similarly severe droughts have occurred before.

The rains returned last year, and there wasn't much environmental degradation evident in Maragoli. Previous generations had avoided the tragedy of the commons by converting the village's public pasture into private farms, and now the farmers were planting trees and digging trenches to prevent erosion of their land. But 100 miles to the southeast, in a place Fanisi had never heard of, was a problem attracting international attention. It was in the Masai Mara, a vast plain that may be the most spectacular commons left on Earth.

Malthus's second mistake

When Robert Redford and Meryl Streep filmed *Out of Africa* last year in Kenya, they had to compensate for population growth. Baroness Karen Blixen's memoir of the 1920s concludes with a dramatic scene of two lions resting on a grave high in the Ngong Hills. Today those hills overlook the suburbs of Nairobi. For the unspoiled vista in Blixen's book, the filmmakers placed the grave and the lions in the Masai Mara preserve.

There you still see lions, zebras, giraffes, gazelles, and the world's largest group of migrating land mammals: 1.5 million wildebeests. These antelopes, also called gnus, follow the seasonal rains across a 10,000-square-mile plain stretching far south into Tanzania. They have been rumbling back and forth for at least a million years, but many wonder whether the enormous herds will survive another hundred. "The modern world is closing in," the New York Zoological Society warned in a 1984 report on the Mara titled, "Paradise Lost?" The intruders include tourists in Land Rovers, native poachers, and cattle herders driven by land scarcity to invade the Masai Mara game preserve.

Just northeast of the Masai Mara, pastureland has been turned into huge, commercial wheat farms to help feed Kenya's 20 million people. How many more farms will another 50 million people need? That's one projection of the increase in Kenya's population by 2020, and it's hard to contemplate the statistic and not agree with Paul Ehrlich. "The conservation battle is presently being lost," he wrote. "Nothing 'undeveloped' can long stand in the face of the population explosion." I saw the wildebeests blackening the savanna all the way to the horizon, and I thought of the Great Plains – before the buffalo felt the effects of population growth.

Back in civilization, I later contemplated some other statistics and succumbed to that longstanding hazard of population research: the irresistible urge to draw a graph.

[. . .]

Despite the obvious correlation, most historians would doubt that each birth in Maragoli adds several wildebeests to the Mara. They attribute last century's decline in the herd not to infertility in Maragoli but to the rinderpest virus, which came to Kenya in cattle brought by German and British settlers. Europeans also spread human diseases (smallpox, measles, sleeping sickness) that devastated villages. In the 1950s, the rinderpest virus was checked by a campaign to vaccinate cattle. The virus disappeared among wildebeests, and the herds were further protected by the establishment of game preserves.

The point, of course, is not that humans are always good for animals. You could show the opposite with a graph of the black rhino population decimated by poachers. The point is that unpredictable things happen on the commons when humans arrive – a trivially obvious point, you might think, but it's consistently forgotten. "The Tragedy of the Commons" and *The Population Bomb* both urge researchers to determine the world's "optimum" population, which will be a "stable" size based on the planet's "carrying capacity." The terminology is borrowed from studies of animal populations in isolated, stable ecosystems. But unlike wildebeests, humans have a habit of altering an ecosystem before anyone can figure out what the carrying capacity is. They discover how to make tools for hunting, they introduce and then eliminate viruses, they turn the commons into a game preserve or farms, they build a new house with money from an uncle.

Most important, they learn new ways to grow food. Malthus's second assumption was an even bigger mistake than his first. Food production has increased geometrically. The real price of food has been failing fairly steadily since the time of Malthus.

This long-term trend was obvious in the 1960s, but many scientists believed it was finally reversing. America's "vast agricultural surpluses are gone," said Ehrlich, who pointed to India as the prime example of "population outstripping food production." Congress held a series of hearings on the population crisis that produced 17 volumes filled with reputable scientists warning that mankind was "hitting the ceiling" and that even the United States was bound for a crash "on the Malthusian reefs." Lester Brown, then an economist at the U.S. Department of Agriculture, reported in 1965 that "the food problem emerging in the less-developed regions may be one of the most nearly insoluble problems facing man over the next few decades." He noted that food output per person had declined during the early 1960s in Asia and Latin America. "Only in Africa," he wrote, ". . . has a downward trend been avoided." India's growing reliance on imported wheat especially worried him. "One thing is evident," Brown concluded. "The less-developed world is losing the capacity to feed itself."

Since then the less developed world has increased its food output per person by about 10 percent. American farmers are worried by huge global surpluses of most foods, and India no longer relies on grain imports. In fact, it currently exports grain and recently donated 100,000 tons of wheat to Africa. India's turnaround was due to new high-yield seeds and a government that offered farmers technical help as well as attractive prices – and Brown deserves credit for being one of the foreign advisers who helped shape these policies. But India's success doesn't seem to have changed Brown's attitude about population growth, or at least not his prose. Now the president of the Worldwatch Institute, he recently surveyed the one less developed continent that was not headed downhill in 1965. Noting the "desperation inherent in existing population trends," Brown concluded in 1985 that Africa "is losing the capacity to feed itself."

Brown illustrated this problem with a graph comparing Africa's recent decline in per-capita grain production with China's increase. Most observers credit China's dramatic improvement largely to its shift from communal farms to private plots. Brown, however, focused on the recent slowdown in China's population growth. "China appears to be breaking out" of the trap of rapid growth, Brown wrote, "and Africa, having failed to do so, appears to be breaking down."

But suppose you compared China to a country with a similar cultural heritage and farming system – Taiwan. It was more densely populated than China in 1950, and it has grown more rapidly since. Today Taiwan has five times as many people per square mile as China. Yet its standard of living is far above China's by any measure: life expectancy, infant mortality, per-capita income and food production.

This happens to be a graph that Julian Simon likes to show. Facts like these helped convert him in the mid-1960s. Like any village pessimist, he began studying population because he was worried. Like Robert McNamara, he thought nuclear war and population growth were the two great threats to humanity. Simon published papers that discussed giving poor women large bonuses at the end of every year they didn't have a child. But his faith was shaken by other findings. Economists Simon Kuznets and Richard Easterlin compared economic growth records over the past century and found that countries have something in common with the families of Maragoli: there is no consistent link between population growth and economic growth. And when Simon looked at the overall picture, he couldn't understand all the gloom.

"Perhaps the two greatest miracles in all of human history have occurred in the past three centuries," he laid recently. "One miracle was the rise in life expectancy in rich countries such as France, from a life expectancy at birth of less than 30 years for a woman in the middle of the 17th century to well into the mid-70s at present. The second miracle is that in the three decades since World War II, life expectancy in the poor countries of the world has risen perhaps 15 years. Those are unequivocal facts, and they happened in the presence of the fastest population growth rates that humanity has ever known." But does population growth *cause* longer life? Isn't it vice versa? Simon believes it works both ways. In his economic model, an additional child causes a short-term economic loss, mainly for the parents who have to provide food and care. But the child eventually more than makes up for the loss – although the benefits to society may not show up for many decades. A larger population permits economies of scale and capital improvements such as communication, transportation, and irrigation systems. (The low population density in the Ethiopian highlands actually hindered relief efforts, because there were so few good roads for the trucks carrying food.) Most important, a larger population means that more people are making innovations that benefit the entire society.

People constitute *The Ultimate Resource*, as Simon's anti-Malthusian manifesto is titled. Its graphs show that natural resources – fuel, timber, grains, metals – are becoming *less* scarce. By this Simon means that the real price of resources has been dropping over the past century. An hour's pay in the United States today buys more than three times more coal or copper than an hour's pay did in 1886. Malthus's "law of diminishing returns" may be theoretically true – as we use coal, less remains in the ground – but in practice the law is irrelevant with respect to natural resources. Humans have consistently found new ways to extract coal, and new and better materials to substitute for it, so it's become cheaper. And the more people there are to make problems and find solutions, Simon argues, the better off everyone is.

Simon has gradually been winning respect for his views, but his happy vision is hardly the norm. His critics say that he overestimates the long-term benefits and underestimates the short-term costs of population growth, and that a larger population is not necessarily going to produce more innovations – especially if the society is growing so fast that it can't afford to feed or educate its children properly. The experience in Europe may not be relevant when growth rates are as high as Kenya's.

But even some of the critics are glad that Simon is presenting the public with a different perspective – an economist's instead of an ecologist's. Economists deal not with fixed resources or "overpopulated" environments but with supplies and demands that adjust to changing conditions. The current oil glut is dramatic proof of how quickly humans can adapt, and other evidence has been accumulating in the past 20 years. Studies have found that faster population growth seems to neither lower a country's rate of school enrollment nor increase the national level of unemployment. In the 1960s it was commonly assumed that population growth in developing countries hurt the economy because each extra child prevented a family from saving money, thereby reducing investment capital. But a recent influential study done in Kenya found that parents of large families don't save any less than other parents. One possible explanation is that parents simply work harder and spend less on themselves after a child is born.

If there's a consensus in academia today, it's probably in a forthcoming study by the National Academy of Sciences. The report is expected to conclude that poor countries would in general raise their standard of living faster if their population growth slowed. But according to sources familiar with the study, it also cautions that the evidence is too weak and contradictory to justify governments imposing drastic financial or legal restrictions on childbearing. One of the report's authors, Samuel Preston, director of the Population Study Center at the University of Pennsylvania, offered his personal interpretation of the evidence a year ago: "Population growth in most times and places is a relatively minor factor in reducing per-capita income and other measures of welfare."

Preston takes a clever middle position in the argument about resource scarcity. To paraphrase it: Suppose that there is only enough fossil fuel left for 10 billion people. A pessimist can argue that humanity is doomed to freeze to death because the fuel is irreplaceable. An optimist can argue that the next 10 billion people will include someone who will find a substitute for fossil fuel – and someone else who will extend life expectancy to 100. But either way, does it really matter how fast population grows? The 10 billionth person is due sooner or later. Why should we worry what year that freezing or that long-lived person happens to arrive?

The situation is different with renewable resources, and there's no doubt that rapid population growth can exacerbate food shortages and environmental problems on commons like the Mara. But what really matters is how people respond to the problems. I think population growth is merely the most convenient excuse for failure – one that doesn't put the blame on socialists, capitalists, African politicians, or foreign aid donors. It obviously doesn't explain why Kenyans are healthier and better off economically than the slower-growing populations in neighboring Ethiopia, Tanzania, and Uganda. Africa's real problems go deeper: chaotic political regimes, misguided foreign aid projects, primitive technologies and infrastructures, unskilled workers, and large bureaucracies more adept at stifling innovation (and banning documentaries) than giving farmers technical assistance. Most African countries actually discourage farm production by keeping food prices artificially low to placate city dwellers. Kenya's government is one of the few that pays its farmers close to the full world-market price, a policy that probably does more to combat hunger than any population program.

Preston worries that the neo-Malthusians not only distract from the crucial issues, they also endanger the international effort to help parents in poor countries plan their families. This is one cause that almost everyone from Ehrlich to Simon agrees on. Simon believes in making contraceptives and abortion available on the simple grounds that they make life better for each individual. Preston goes further – he thinks there are probably societal benefits from voluntary birth control – but he warns advocates of family planning to dissociate themselves from "doomsday rhetoric" and "the catalogue of horrors that many attribute to rapid population growth."

"So much of the rhetoric is simple-minded and incorrect," he says, "casually attributing any human problem to there being too many humans. If and when the balloon bursts, I think it would be a pity if family planning programs were an automatic victim."

Beatrice's choice

Back from her aunt's, Beatrice was waiting for me in the front yard, near the spot under the guava tree where her grandparents had sat down to negotiate the marriage of 18-year-old Fanisi. (Fanisi's parents had demanded to be compensated with a bridewealth of seven cows; Isaac's family eventually gave them three.) Beatrice was born in 1969, two years after Kenya established a national family planning program, making her a member of the first generation to grow up hearing official pronouncements against fertility. She was presumably more Westernized than her parents, thanks to her education (neither Fanisi nor Isaac had finished elementary school), and she had spent all her life watching them struggle to feed a large family from a small plot of land.

At 16, as she shyly introduced herself in English, she seemed an excellent candidate for the demographic transition except for one detail. Beatrice was quite pregnant.

"I met the boy in Nairobi," she explained as she sat down on the grass. "I went there to be a house girl when I could not continue my education here." The father, who was from a village less than a mile away, had a factory job in Nairobi. The child was due in December of 1985, and Beatrice said that she and the father were planning to marry sometime in 1986. She expected to move to his father's plot of land, which was smaller than three acres and would be divided among four sons. He would continue living and working nearly 200 miles away in Nairobi, a common practice of husbands from Maragoli

This pregnancy did not seem a rational decision. The stigma of premarital pregnancy is probably greater in Maragoli than in America. Fanisi seemed embarrassed by the situation, and Beatrice sounded regretful when she talked about her failure to use contraceptives. "I didn't know how to use family planning," she said. The idea of going to a clinic for contraceptives seemed not to have occurred to her.

"How many children do you plan to have?" I asked.

"I'll give four children only, if possible. There is lack of money, food, school fees, and so on. I'll stop."

"How will you stop?"

"I'll use the Curse."

"You'll ask your aunt to curse you?"

"I prefer my grandmother."

"Does the Curse have side effects?"

"Yes, but I can use it."

"What if the Curse doesn't work?"

"Then I'll go into family planning for some medicine."

"What if your husband doesn't want you to practice family planning?"

"I'll just go and do it myself."

So, the final results of our little fertility survey: the average preferred family size, which was 20.0 in the previous generation, has dropped to 4.0 in this generation. But this sharp decline in desired fertility has been accompanied by an increase of 1.0 in actual fertility at the age of 16.

How to explain the contradiction? Purists might quibble about the size of the sample population or certain translation difficulties in data gathering, but it actually does reflect an important national trend. Surveys show that the average young woman in Kenya today says she wants a smaller family than her mother, but meanwhile she's starting her family at an earlier age than her mother did. The great question is whether Beatrice and her peers will actually stop when they reach the desired size. Family planning advocates are discouraged because fewer than 15 percent of the married women of childbearing age use modern contraceptives. Yet in some more developed areas of Kenya the use of contraceptives has shot up in just a few years to 30 percent, and the more optimistic demographers think that the national figure could rise to 40 percent before long. If Beatrice's generation really does turn from the Curse to the Pill, during the next decade Kenya may become one of the first African countries to proceed with the demographic transition.

However many children Beatrice has, some of them will probably be forced to leave the village and find their food elsewhere, either by working in city jobs or moving to less densely populated farmland in Kenya. It's possible that they or their children will move to other parts of Africa that have much more open land available for cultivation. The Food and Agriculture Organization of the United Nations estimates that sub-Saharan Africa has the potential to feed twice its current population without even resorting to fertilizer. With fertilizer and pesticides – techniques already common in Maragoli – the continent has the potential to feed eight times its current population. When the U.N. projections allow for more intensive techniques – again, ones based on technology that already exists – then even a country as densely populated as Kenya can feed more than twice its current population.

So I suspect that Beatrice's grandchildren will be better fed than she and her children. They should enjoy the capital improvements made by the expanding workforce in previous generations. They probably won't walk to the well or burn kerosene lamps. They may still put some credence in the Curse, but they will probably augment it with contraceptives before the fifth child arrives. They will be more Westernized. They may be *in* the West. America's baby boomers, having made the "rational" decision that children are no longer necessary for financial security in old age, should be anxious for Social Security contributions from young immigrant laborers. Sociologists will talk of the West being "Africanized."

I also suspect that Beatrice's great-great-grandchildren will live in a world whose population is growing very slowly, if at all. They may hear dire warnings about an incipient population decline. They will read about today's "population crisis" as a quaint, short-lived episode in intellectual history. They may be amused by the hysteria and simultaneously impressed by the generous foreign aid that enabled women in poor countries to plan their families.

But certain moments may look very ugly from their historical perspective – moments when intellectuals went beyond drawing graphs and offering warnings. In the 1960s articles in scientific journals debated the technical possibility of putting a "fertility control agent" in public drinking water. The physicist William Shockley recommended that the government use compulsory sterilization to enforce a national limit on the number of births. In 1974 Garrett Hardin proposed that the United States adopt a "lifeboat ethic" and refuse to give food aid, even during emergencies, to countries with fast-growing populations. In 1984 Robert McNamara urged countries to set "fertility targets" to achieve "optimal" population size; he didn't endorse mandatory limits, but neither did he offer any criticism when discussing the "compulsion and coercion" of China's one-child-per-family policy. This policy, while officially voluntary, subjects recalcitrant parents to financial penalties and personal visits from disapproving officials, and it has reportedly led to infanticide and forced abortion. Paul Ehrlich recently praised China for being "far ahead" of the United States in "understanding population problems." In a revised edition of *The Population Bomb*, printed in 1983, Ehrlich also criticizes America for not offering encouragement when an official in the Indian government proposed mandatory sterilization for all Indian men with three or more children.

"We should have volunteered logistic support in the form of helicopters, vehicles, and surgical instruments. We should have sent doctors . . ." Ehrlich writes. "Coercion? Perhaps, but coercion in a good cause."

What will Beatrice's descendants make of these incidents? I tend to think they will be mentioned in history-of-science courses along with the eugenics movement. I may be wrong, of course. The day may come when Hardin and Ehrlich and McNamara are revered as prophets before their time. In the meantime, I suggest that the village pessimists acknowledge that their unsolicited advice is based not on any expert consensus but on an ideology that is not really any more scientific than the Vatican's. They have as much right as the Pope to tell Beatrice how to conduct the most private aspect of her life. But I like to think she has inherited the good sense to do what she thinks best.

"What do you think life will be like for you and your family 10 years from now?" I asked at the end of our talk. The question held no interest for her. She seemed mildly surprised and bemused at the notion that she might be thinking these days about something as abstract as long-range forecasts. Toying with a twig on the grass, she smiled indulgently.

"I don't know what God will do. But I'll thank Him if I get a child."

REVIEW AND DISCUSSION QUESTIONS

1   According to the evidence collected by the author in the Kenyan village of Maragoli, what kind of obstacles do family planning programs in LDCs seem to run against?

2   Did the author find any evidence that parents take into account economic factors when deciding how many children to have?

3   According to the author, what was Thomas Malthus's "first mistake"?

4   How did Australian demographer John Caldwell explain why families in poor countries have many children? Did the author find any support for Caldwell's hypothesis in the village of Maragoli?

5   Did the author find any evidence supporting the argument that faster population growth and increased population density lead to technological innovations that may help economic development?

6   What was Malthus's "second mistake" according to the author?

7   What do you think is the main point of this article?

Chapter 19

Julian L. Simon

THE ULTIMATE RESOURCE 2
Preface

THIS BOOK ORIGINATED IN MY interest in the economics of population. When (starting about 1969) my studies showed that population growth does *not* hinder economic development or reduce the standard of living, critics asserted that adding more people to the planet causes natural resource scarcities and environmental decay. Hence, I was forced to broaden my inquiries. That's how the first edition of this book came to be written.

Ironically, when I began to work on population studies, I assumed that the accepted view was sound. I aimed to help the world contain its "exploding" population, which I believed to be one of the two main threats to humankind (war being the other). But my reading and research led me into confusion. Though the then-standard economic theory of population (which had hardly changed since Malthus) asserted that a higher population growth implies a lower standard of living, the available empirical data did not support that theory. My technical 1977 book, which is the predecessor of this volume, is an attempt to reconcile that contradiction. It arrived at a theory implying that population growth has positive economic effects in the long run, although there are costs in the short run.

The all-important point in this personal history: It was the facts that changed my mind about population growth away from the conventional belief. It was not some wider, preexisting set of beliefs that brought me to the point my work is now at. Indeed, the facts and my new conclusions about population economics altered my wider set of beliefs, rather than the converse.

About this author and his values

One spring day about 1969, I visited the U.S. AID office on the outskirts of Washington, D.C., to discuss a project intended to lower fertility in less-developed countries. I arrived early for my appointment, so I strolled outside in the warm sunshine. Below the building's plaza I noticed a road sign that said "Iwo Jima Memorial." There came to me the memory of reading a eulogy delivered by a Jewish chaplain over the dead on the battlefield at Iwo Jima, saying something like, How many who would have been a Mozart or a Michelangelo or an Einstein have we buried here?[1] And then I thought: Have I gone crazy? What business do I have trying to help arrange it that fewer human beings will be born, each one of whom might be a Mozart or a Michelangelo or an Einstein – or simply a joy to his or her family and community, and a person who will enjoy life?

I still believe that helping people fulfill their desires for the number of children they want is a wonderful human service. But to persuade them or coerce them to have fewer children than they would like to have – that is something entirely different.

The longer I have read the literature about population, the more baffled and distressed I have become that one idea is omitted: Enabling a potential human being to come into life and to enjoy life is a good thing, just as protecting a living person's life from being ended is a good thing. Of course a death is not the same as an averted life, in large part because others feel differently about the two. Yet I find no logic implicit in the thinking of those who are horrified at the starvation of a comparatively few people in a faraway country (and apparently more horrified than at the deaths by political murder in that same faraway country, or at the deaths by accidents in their own country) but who are positively gleeful with the thought that a million or ten million times that many lives will never be lived that might be lived.

Economics alone cannot explain this attitude, for though the economic consequences of death differ from those of non-life, they are not so different as to explain this difference in attitude. So what is it? Why does Kingsley Davis (one of the world's great demographers) respond to U.S. population growth during the 1960s, "I have never been able to get anyone to tell me why we needed those [additional] 23 million"?[2] And why does Paul Ehrlich say, "I can't think of any reason for having more than one hundred fifty million people [in the U.S.], and no one has ever raised one to me."[3] By 1991 he and Anne Ehrlich had even lowered the ceiling: "No sensible reason has ever been given for having more than 135 million people."[4]

I can suggest to Davis and Ehrlich more than one reason for having more children and taking in more immigrants. Least important is that the larger population will probably mean a higher standard of living for our grandchildren and great-grandchildren. (My technical 1977 and 1992 books and a good many chapters in this book substantiate that assertion.) A more interesting reason is that we need another person for exactly the same reason we need Davis and Ehrlich. That is, just as the Davises and Ehrlichs of this world are of value to the rest of us, so will the average additional person be of value.

The most interesting reason for having additional people, however, is this: If the Davises and Ehrlichs say that their lives are of value to themselves, and if the rest of us honor that claim and say that our lives are of value to us, then in the same manner the lives of additional people will be of value to those people themselves. Why should we not honor their claims, too?

If Davis or Ehrlich were to ask those twenty-three million Americans born between 1960 and 1970 whether it was a good thing that they were born, many of them would be able to think of a good reason or two. Some of them might also be so unkind as to add, "Yes, it's true that you gentlemen do not *personally* need any of us for your own welfare. But then, do you think that we have greater need of you?"

What is most astonishing is that these simple ideas, which would immediately spring to the minds of many who cannot read or write, have never come into the heads of famous scientists such as Davis and Ehrlich – by their own admission. And by repeating the assertion in 1991, Ehrlich makes it clear that he does not consider the above ideas, which I suggested to him earlier, to be "sensible."

The absence of this basic value for human life also is at the bottom of Ehrlich's well-known restatement of Pascal's wager. "If I'm right, we will save the world [by curbing population growth]. If I'm wrong, people will still be better fed, better housed, and happier, thanks to our efforts. [All the evidence suggests that he is wrong.] Will anything be lost if it turns out later that we can support a much larger population than seems possible today?"[5]

Please note how different is Pascal's wager: Live as if there is God, because even if there is no God you have lost nothing. Pascal's wager applies entirely to one person. No one else loses if she or he is wrong. But Ehrlich bets what he thinks will be the economic gains that we and our descendants might enjoy against the unborn's very lives. Would he make the same sort of wager if his own life rather than others' lives were the stake?

I do not say that society should never trade off human life for animals or even for nonliving things. Indeed, society explicitly makes exactly this trade-off when a firefighter's life is lost protecting a building or a forest or a zoo, and neither I nor hardly anyone else says it should not be so. And I have no objection in principle to the community taxing its members for the cost of parks or wilderness or wildlife protection (although a private arrangement may be better) any more than I object to taxes for the support of the poor. But according to my values, we should (1) have a clear quantitative idea of the trade-offs we seek to make, rather than make them on some unquantified principle such as "the loss of a single human being [or of a single nonhuman species or animal] is obscene," implying that the costs of saving that entity should not be reckoned; (2) recognize that economic science does not show that a greater number of human beings implies slower economic development or a lower standard of living in the long run; and (3) understand that foregoing the births of additional human beings is costly according to the value systems of some other human beings.

[. . .]

Notes

1. Donald Bishop, with the help of the Marine historian, was kind enough to exhume the oration in 1993. It was Chaplain Roland B. Gittlesohn, a Navy lieutenant, who said,

    > This is perhaps the grimmest, and surely the holiest task we have faced since D-Day. Here before us lie the bodies of comrades and friends. Men who until yesterday or last week laughed with us, joked with us, trained with us. Men who were on the same ships with us, and went over the sides with us, as we prepared to hit the beaches of this island. Men who fought with us and feared with us. Somewhere in this plot of ground there may lie the man who could have discovered the cure for cancer. . . .

2. *Newsweek*, March 30, 1970, p. 87.
3. *Saturday Review*, March 11, 1972, p. 49.
4. *Washington Post*, "From a Report for Negative Population Growth," May 1991.
5. Ehrlich, Paul R. 1968, *The Population Bomb*. New York: Ballantine, p. 198.

THE BIG PICTURE II: LDCs

> If population be connected with national wealth, liberty and personal security is the great
> foundation of both. . . . The statesman in this, as in the case of population itself, can do
> little more than avoid doing mischief.
>
> *(Ferguson 1995)*

In time, the countries we now refer to as less-developed will fall into the category of more-developed countries. But for now, their situations are still sufficiently different to warrant separate discussion, though it should be noted that the basic economic principles apply equally in all cases.[1]

During several decades starting in the 1960s, economic models of the effect of population growth upon the standard of living in less-developed countries (LDCs) have had great influence on governmental policies, as well as on the thinking of social scientists and the public. Phyllis Piotrow's historical account attributes enormous impact to Ansley J. Coale and Edgar M. Hoover's book of 1958 which concluded that population growth hampers LDC economic growth: "The Coale-Hoover thesis eventually provided the justification for birth control as a part of U.S. foreign aid policy."[2] The highest-ranking State Department official involved in population matters, immediately after his appointment in 1966, prepared an extensive position paper:

> Adopting completely the Coale-Hoover thesis . . . [Philander] Claxton [Jr.] argued that the U.S. government must move from reaction and response to initiation and persuasion. . . . By the time the paper reached the Secretary of State's desk, it had already achieved part of its purpose. All the appropriate State Department and Aid bureaus had reviewed, revised, commented, added to, and finally cleared the document. The rest of its purpose was accomplished when [Secretary of State Dean] Rusk agreed to every single one of Claxton's ten recommendations.[3]

This U.S. policy, based on a now-falsified model, continues to the time of writing. The foreign activities that are part of it expend more funds than ever in activities as shady as ever that may again draw other countries' hostility to the United States, as happened in India and elsewhere. More about these political aspects was said in the first edition, but the subject is now so extensive that it must be left for part of a subsequent book.

Since the first edition, U.S. policy has become more complex, however. At the 1984 UN World Population Conference, the United States declared that the effect of population growth is "neutral." The material presented in this book, and in its 1977 technical predecessor, played some role in this turn-about — to what extent it would be hard to say, given that I played no role in person, contrary to what population "activists" have flattered me with. But the politics of the matter since then have been turbulent, with the population-control movement still being exceedingly dominant in the Congress, and U.S. AID continuing its foreign activities much as before.

This history makes clear the importance of having a sound economic-demographic model for LDCs, which in turn requires sound empirical research and sound theory. Progress has been aided by the landmark 1986 Report of the National Research Council of the National Academy of Sciences, which repudiated the Coale-Hoover view, and arrived at a point not far from what is discussed here, as mentioned in the Introduction.

The conventional theoretical models

The long-accepted population model of Coale and Hoover has two main elements: (1) an increase in the number of consumers, and (2) a decrease in saving due to population growth (a proposition whose validity was discussed in chapter 25, with ambiguous results). Their well-known conclusion is that, whereas in India with continued high fertility, income per consumer during 1956–1986 could be expected to rise from an index of 100 to 138, with declining fertility it could be expected to rise from 100 to 195 – that is, India could expect some two and a half times as fast economic growth with low fertility as with high fertility.

It is crucial to notice that the main Coale-Hoover model simply *assumed* that the total national product in an LDC would not be increased by population growth for the first thirty years, either by a larger labor force or by additional productive efforts. Therefore, their model boils down to the ratio of output divided by consumers; an increase in the number of consumers decreases the per capita consumption, by simple arithmetic. In their words, "The inauspicious showing of the high-fertility case in terms of improvement in levels of living is traceable entirely to the accelerated growth in the number of consumers that high fertility produce."[4] To repeat: The main mechanism producing the Coale-Hoover result is simply an increase in the denominator of the output/consumer ratio, where output is the same *by assumption* for the first thirty years for all rates of population growth.

Subsequent LDC models (including a variant by Coale and Hoover) took into account that a faster-growing population produces a larger labor force, which in turn implies a larger total output. But this modification still implies Malthusian capital dilution, and while slightly altering the main Coale-Hoover result, such a model still necessarily indicates that a faster-growing population leads to a lower output per worker and lower per capita income.

In sum, the conventional theory suggests that a larger population retards the growth of output per worker in LDCs. The overwhelming element in the conventional theory is the Malthusian concept of diminishing returns to labor, operating with the assumption that the stock of capital (including land) does not increase in the same proportion as labor.

Another important theoretical element is the dependency effect, which suggests that saving is more difficult for households where there are more children, and that higher fertility causes social investment funds to be diverted away from industrial production. Combined in simulation models, these conventional elements imply that relatively high fertility and population growth diminish the output per worker (and even more the income per consumer, because the proportion of consumers to workers is higher when the birthrate is higher).

Again – the data contradict the popular models

But the empirical studies data do not support this a priori reasoning. The data do not show that a higher rate of population growth decreases the rate of economic growth, for either LDCs or MDCs. These data include the long-run historical data. Also relevant are cross-sectional studies that relate the rate of population growth to the growth rate of per capita income in various LDCs; no correlation between the two variables is found.[5]

Another sort of study plots the growth rate of per capita income as a function of population *density*. Roy Gobin and I found that density has a *positive* effect on the rate of economic growth.[6] And a study by J. Dirck Stryker found that among the French-speaking African countries, lower population density is associated with lower economic growth – that is, higher population density implies a higher standard of living.[7] And Kelley and Schmidt (1994) have massively confirmed the Simon-Gobin finding.

Check for yourself: Fly over Hong Kong – just a few decades ago a place seemingly without prospects because of insoluble resource problems – and you will marvel at the astounding collection of modern high-rise apartments and office buildings. Take a ride on its excellent smooth-flowing highways for an hour or two, and you will realize that a very dense concentration of human beings does not prevent comfortable existence and exciting economic expansion – as long as the economic system gives individuals the freedom to exercise their talents and to take advantage of opportunities. And the experience of Singapore demonstrates that Hong Kong is not unique. Two such examples do not prove the case, of course. But these dramatic illustrations are backed by the evidence from the aggregate sample of countries, and hence do not mislead us.

Hong Kong is a special thrill for me because I first saw it in 1955 when I went ashore from a U.S. Navy destroyer. At the time I felt great pity for the thousands who slept every night on the sidewalks or on small boats. It then seemed clear to me, as it must have to almost any observer, that it would be impossible for Hong Kong to surmount its problems – huge masses of impoverished people without jobs, total lack of exploitable natural resources, more refugees pouring across the border each day. But upon returning in 1983, I saw bustling crowds of healthy, vital people full of hope and energy. No cause for pity now.

The most important benefit of population size and growth is the increase it brings to the stock of useful knowledge. Minds matter economically as much as, or more than, hands or mouths. Progress is limited largely by the availability of trained workers.

The role of the political-economic system

A crucial element in the economics of resources and population is the extent to which the political-social-economic system provides personal freedom from government coercion. For an economy to grow, individuals require a social and economic framework that provides incentives for working hard and taking risks, enabling their talents to flower and come to fruition. The key elements of such a framework are economic liberty, respect for property, and fair and sensible rules of the market that are enforced equally for all.

To illuminate the importance of the system as a crucial condition for whether additional people quickly become a benefit, it is useful to mention two extreme situations when additional people have been a negative force – sometimes reducing the standard of living all the way to misery and subsistence – rather than a force for growth, simply because of a lack of economic freedom:

1. A shipful of illiterate African slaves coming toward the United States. Additional slaves on the ship would only contribute toward faster death aboard, because freedom was totally absent.

2. A German prisoner-of-war camp for British soldiers in World War II. Despite the large stock of technology among the inmates in such a situation, and despite modern values and free-enterprise culture, the outside authority structure was strong enough to prevent any real growth. Additional inmates would not produce faster growth, only more crowding. If conditions got bad enough, the additional misery might lead to an explosion, and conceivably toward the "growth" of an escape. But chances of the latter were small.

Technology is not enough to distinguish the above two cases from that of, say, Hong Kong, where the addition of so many people after World War II almost surely did have a positive effect upon growth, as in Singapore. Values and culture also are not enough to distinguish. Only the social system, including the low taxation of Hong Kong, can distinguish the cases. China is much more like a prison than is Hong Kong because it suppresses mobility and opportunity. And if one takes the political-economic structure of China as given, the Chinese may be right that slower population growth means a higher standard of living in the present generation.[8]

Powerful evidence that the world's problem is not too many people, but lack of political and economic freedom, comes from pairs of countries that have the same culture and history, and had much the same standard of living when they split apart after World War II – East and West Germany, North and South Korea, Taiwan and China. In each case the centrally planned economy began with less population "pressure," as measured by density per square kilometer, than did the market-directed economy. And the Communist and non-communist countries also started with much the same birthrates. But the market-directed economies have performed much better economically than the centrally planned economies. This powerful explanation of economic development cuts the ground from under population growth as a likely explanation.

A bus trip across the Karelian peninsula – seeing first the part now in Finland, and then the part that was in Finland until 1940 but afterwards was in the Soviet Union and now is in Russia – reveals differences like night and day at the border. And there were dramatically different 1990s living standards in two towns on opposite sides of the (then) Czechoslovakia-Austria border, and in East and West Germany, which had similar standards of living before World War II, but vastly different situations now.

Or consider Mauritius. In the 1960s, James Meade, the Nobel-prize-winning British economist – but also a believer in eugenics, who embodied in his work the idea that a human life could be so poor materially that it was better not lived – offered Mauritius as his example of a densely crowded country whose rapid birthrate was ruining its chances of economic development. He foresaw terrible unemployment, and Mauritius did suffer this blight for many years. But in the early 1980s Mauritius radically changed its economic-political framework, allowing free enterprise a chance to flourish. By 1988 one could read that "Offshore Jobs Dynamo Offers Model for Africa. . . . The government here says that unemployment, which ran at 23 percent six years ago, no longer exists."[9] This is as close to an economic miracle as this world is likely to see. The change over those few years had nothing to do with changes in Mauritius' birthrate, nor was there a reduction in the high population density. Economic freedom was the only new element.

Some readers (though fewer than at the time of the first edition) may not know how well the poorer countries have been progressing. Contrary to common belief, per capita income in LDCs has been growing as fast as or faster than in the MDCs, despite the fact that population growth in LDCs has been much faster than in MDCs. This is prima facie evidence that population growth does not have a negative effect on economic growth. Indeed, the fact that countries with high densities have higher income *levels* on average implies that they must on average have had higher *growth* throughout the past than countries with lower population densities.

Aggregate statistics sometimes lack conviction because they are abstract. To give the data more realism, let us consider the change in a typical Indonesian village between 1953 and 1985 when Nathan Keyfitz studied it:

> [In 1985 the villagers] typically wear shoes, have houses of brick and plaster, and send their children to the elementary school in the village. Some have electric lights and a television set, own a motorcycle, and hope their children will go to the secondary school a few kilometers away. Thirty-one years earlier shoes were rare, houses were almost all of thatch and bamboo with earth floors; lighting was at best with kerosene, and even that was something of a luxury; there was no primary school.[10]

Keyfitz calculated that per person income rose about 3 percent per year, a very respectable rate by any measure. People's diets had improved. The poorest class improved itself considerably – the daily wage in terms of kilos of rice doubling.[11]

The poor also improved in dignity and independence, Keyfitz reports. Concerning the responsibility of each citizen to "spend one night per week on guard duty. . . . In our earlier visit we found that the landowner could order one of his gedok [subservient client-dependents] to take his place; today that is more difficult. The patron cannot even send one of his gedok on a daytime errand in the matter-of-fact way that was once acceptable. At one time the village headman's land was cultivated for him by village laborers acting without pay; now the headman has to pay them the going wage." One cause may be that "much easier travel, by which nearly everyone has a chance to observe the freedom of nearby towns, not to mention larger cities . . . makes them intolerant of unnecessary bondage at home."[12]

One of the most arduous and omnipresent tasks of women in 1953 was pounding rice to hull it. In 1985 the job was done with mechanical rice dryers and hullers, operated as businesses.

Population grew substantially, from 2,400 to 3,894,[13] so income grew despite population growth (or because of it), the opposite of what Malthusian Coale-Hoover type theory would expect.

Keyfitz and his colleagues assumed in advance that in 1985 "unemployment would be the great problem of the village," because of population growth. But they found that this was not so. Better-off people were using their additional income to hire others, who had now become specialized workmen, to build houses professionally instead of do-it-yourself productions; schools and mosques were being built, too. The researchers also found, contrary to their expectations, that the proportion of the crop going to labor had risen and the proportion going to the landowner had fallen,[14] the opposite of what simple Ricardian theory of increased population would predict; increased productivity of the land is the explanation,

Keyfitz's systematic account of the East Javanese village squares with the vivid anecdotal descriptions by Richard Critchfield, who over a quarter century visited villages in poor countries, and then revisited some (1981). The universal improvement that he found came as a surprise to him.

My personal experiences agree. In almost all the non-European countries I visited from the beginning of the 1970s to the present – Israel, India, Iran, China, the Soviet Union, Thailand, Hong Kong (yes, there is agriculture in Hong Kong), Philippines, Colombia, Costa Rica, Chile, and others – I have made it my business to visit agricultural villages, and to ask (through translators, of course) villagers about their farming practices at present and in the past, about their possessions and consumption present and past, and about the number and the education of their children. (Only in the Soviet Union was it not possible for me to find out what was what, despite the bluntest possible inquiries.) Improvement could be seen everywhere, in all respects – tractors, roads to the market, motorbikes, electric pumps for wells, schools where there were none before, and children gone on to university in the city.

A model that reconciles theory and evidence for LDCs

When the theory and the data do not jibe, either (or both) may be at fault. The available raw data have been re-examined several times, always with the same anti-Malthusian result. Let us therefore turn to a re-examination of the theory.

The model whose results are presented below includes the standard economic elements of the well-known earlier models, plus the main additional effects discussed in earlier chapters but left out of earlier models. These newly added elements include, among others: (1) the positive effect of increased demand (due to a larger population) upon business and agricultural investment; (2) the propensity of people to devote more hours to work and fewer hours to leisure when family size increases; (3) the shift in labor from agriculture to industry as economic development proceeds; and (4) economies of scale in the use of social infrastructure and other sources. All of these elements are well documented.

Further, if we are to understand the effect of population growth upon income and the standard of living, we must know the effect of income on population size and growth. All else being equal, income raises fertility and reduces mortality. But other factors do not remain the same while income changes, except in the very short run. In the long run, an increase in income in a poor country with a high fertility rate reduces the fertility rate. (This is the demographic transition, which results from income-induced changes in mortality, urbanization, the higher costs of rearing children, and so on.) And after some point, mortality no longer falls significantly with additional income. Hence the long-run effect of an increase in income is a decrease in the rate of population growth. These effects also must be added to a realistic simulation.

When these important economic elements are included, rather than excluded as they are from earlier economic-demographic models of LDCs of the Coale-Hoover variety, and when reasonable assumptions are made about the various dimensions of the LDC economy, the results are very different than those from past models. The simulation indicates that moderate population growth produces considerably better economic performance in the long run (120 to 180 years) than does slower-growing population, though in the shorter run (up to sixty years) the slower-growing population performs slightly better. A declining population does very badly in the long run. And in the experiments with the "best" estimates of the parameters for a representative Asian LDC (the "base run"), moderate population growth has better long-run performance than either fast population growth (doubling over thirty-five years or less) or slow population growth.

Experiments with one variable at a time reveal that the difference between these results and the opposite results generated by previous models is produced, not by any single variable, but by the combination of the novel elements – the leisure-versus-work decision with extra children in the family, economies of scale, the investment function, and depreciation; no single factor is predominant. And over the range of positive population growth, different parameters lead to different positive rates of population growth as "optimum." This means that no simple qualitative theory of population growth of the classical Malthusian sort can be very helpful, and a more complex, quantitatively based theory such as this one is necessary.

For the interested technical readers, a fuller statement of the findings follows. Others may skip ahead.[15]

1. Using those parameters that seem most descriptive of LDCs today, the model suggests that very high birthrates and very low birthrates both result in lower long-run per-worker outputs (hereafter referred to as "economic performance") than do birthrates in between. It will surprise few that very high birthrates are not best. But the outcome that moderate birthrates produce higher income in the long run than do low birthrates runs very much against the conventional wisdom. The same result appears with quite different levels of the various parameters. The moderate-fertility populations also enjoy more leisure in the long run than do the low-fertility and high-fertility populations.

2. In a variety of conditions, over quite a wide range of moderate to high birthrates, the effect of fertility upon income is not spectacularly large – seldom as much as 25 percent, even after 180 years (though the difference in results produced by low and moderate birthrates is great). This is quite surprising at first thought. But it is what Kuznets anticipated:

> [G]iven the political and social contest, it does not follow that the high birth rates in the underdeveloped countries, per se, are a major cause of the low per capita income; nor does it follow that a reduction of these birth rates, without a change in the political and social context (if this is possible), will raise per capita product or accelerate its rate of growth. We stress the point that *the source of the association between demographic patterns and per capita product is a common set of political and social institutions and other factors behind both* to indicate that any direct causal relations between the demographic movements and economic growth may be quite limited; and that we cannot easily interpret the association for policy purposes as assurance that a modification of one of the variables would necessarily change the other and in the directions indicated by the association.[16]

The results of my model suggest a population "trap" – but a benevolent one very different from the Malthusian trap: If population growth declines too fast as a result of increasing income, total output fails to rise enough to stimulate investment; depreciation is then greater than investment, and income falls. In the model, this results in a return to higher fertility and then another cycle. Hence the ill results follow from population decline in this model, rather than from population increase as in the Malthusian trap.

3. The advantage of moderate birthrates over low birthrates generally appears only after quite a while – say, seventy-five to one hundred years. This is another reason why the results found here differ from those of the Coale-Hoover and similar models in which the time horizon is only twenty-five to thirty years (fifty-five years in the Coale-Hoover minor extension), whereas the time horizon here is 180 years (or longer in some cases). This points up the grave danger of using short-horizon models in the study of population growth. Population effects take a long time to begin and a much longer time to accumulate.

4. Perhaps the most important result of this simulation is that it shows that there are some reasonable sets of conditions under which fairly high fertility has better economic performance at some times than does low fertility, but there are also other reasonable sets of conditions under which the opposite is true. There are even sets of conditions well within the bounds of possibility under which extremely high fertility offers the highest income per capita and output per worker in the long run. That is, the results depend upon the choice of parameters within ranges that seem quite acceptable. This implies that any model of population that concludes that any one fertility structure is unconditionally better or worse than another must be wrong, either because that model's construction is too simple or for some other reasons. The sole exception to this generalization is fertility below replacement. Such a low-fertility structure does poorly under every set of conditions simulated here, largely because a reasonable increase in total demand is necessary to produce enough investment to overcome the drag of depreciation.

In sum, the differences between the results produced by this method and the results obtained by Coale and Hoover are due to the inclusion in this model of several factors omitted from the Coale-Hoover model: (a) the capacity of people to vary their work input in response to their varying income aspirations and family-size needs; (b) an economies-of-scale social-capital factor; (c) an industrial investment function (and an industrial technology function) that is responsive to differences in demand (output); and (d) an agricultural savings function that is responsive to the agricultural capital/output ratio. These factors together, at reasonable parameter settings, are enough to offset the capital-dilution diminishing-returns effect as well as the effect of dependency on saving found in the Coale-Hoover model. The difference in overall conclusions between this model and others, however, is also due to the much longer time horizon used in this model.

One's judgment about the overall effect of an additional child depends upon the discount rate chosen for weighing the costs and benefits in immediate periods together with periods further into the future, as was discussed in the context of the MDC model. If we give little or no weight to society's welfare in the far future, but rather pay attention only to the present and the near future, then additional children clearly are a burden. But if we weigh the welfare of future generations almost as heavily as the welfare of present generations, then additional children now are on balance a positive economic force. In between, there is some discount rate that, depending upon the circumstances of each country, marks the point at which additional children now are at the borderline of having a negative or positive effect. The choice of that discount rate is ultimately a matter of personal values.

In brief, whether we assess the effect of additional children now as being negative or positive depends largely upon our time perspective. And given the economic analysis developed here, anyone who takes a long-range view – that is, gives considerable weight to the welfare of future generations – should prefer a growing population to a stationary or declining population.

Some objections considered

This chapter has reached conclusions contrary to prevailing popular opinion as well as to most of the professional literature since before Malthus (though professional opinion has shifted in the 1980s). Therefore, it may be useful to consider some of the objections to these conclusions. Of course, the full text of this book and my 1977, 1987, and 1992 books, including both the analysis and the empirical data, constitute the basic rebuttal to these objections. The following paragraphs take up the objections in a lighter and more casual fashion.

Objection 1. But population growth must stop at *some* point. There is *some* population size at which the world's resources must run out, *some* moment at which there will be "standing room only."

When someone questions the need to immediately check population growth in the United States or in the world, the standard response ever since Malthus has been a series of calculations showing how, after population doubles a number of times, there will be standing room only – a solid mass of human bodies on the Earth or in the United States This apparently shows that population growth ought to stop sometime – well before "standing room only," of course. But even if we stipulate that population growth must *sometime* stop, by what reasoning do people get from "sometime" to "now"? At least two aspects of such reasoning can be identified.

First, the stop-now argument assumes that if humans behave in a certain way now they will inevitably continue to behave the same way in the future. But one need not assume that if people decide to have more children now, their descendants will continue to have them at the same rate indefinitely. By analogy, because you decide to have another beer today, you must automatically drink yourself to death. But if you are like most people, you will stop after you recognize a reasonable limit. Yet many seem to have a "drunkard" model of fertility and society: if you take one drink, you're down the road to hell.

Another line of reasoning that leads people away from the reasonable conclusion that humankind will respond adaptively to population growth derives from the mathematics of exponential growth, the "geometric increase" of Malthus. The usual argument that population will "explode" to a doomsday point is based on the crudest sort of curve fitting, a kind of hypnotism by mathematics. Starkly, the argument is that population will grow exponentially in the future because it has always grown so in the past. This proposition is not even true historically; population has remained stationary or gotten smaller in large parts of the world for long periods of time (for example, in Europe after the Roman Empire, and among aborigine tribes in Australia). And many other sorts of trends have been reversed in the past before being forced to stop by physical limits (the length of women's skirts, and the spread of Christianity and Islam).

If you are attracted to the sort of curve fitting that underlies most arguments about the need to control population growth, you might do well to consider other long trends that we have discussed earlier. For example, the proportion of people who die each year from famine from natural causes has surely been decreasing for at least a century since the beginning of mankind, and even the *absolute* number of people who die of famine has been decreasing despite the large increases in total population. An even more reliable and important statistical trend is the steady increase in life expectancy over recorded history. Why not focus on these documented trends rather than on the hypothetical total-population trend?

An absurd counterspeculation is instructive. The exponential increase of university buildings in the past decades, and perhaps in the past one hundred years, has been much faster than the rate of population growth. Simple-minded curve fitting will show that the space occupied by university buildings will overtake and pass the amount of space in which people stand long before there is "standing room only." This apparently makes university growth the juggernaut to worry about, not population growth!

Some will reply that the analogy is not relevant because universities are built by reasonable people who will stop when there are enough buildings, whereas children are produced by people who are acting only out of passion and are not subject to the control of reason. This latter assertion is, however, empirically false. Every tribe known to anthropologists, no matter how "primitive," has some effective social scheme for controlling the birthrate. Children are born for the most part because people choose to have them.

Even the proposition that population growth must stop *sometime* may not be very meaningful. The length of time required to reach any absolute physical limits of space or energy is far into the future (if ever), and many unforeseeable things could happen between now and then that could change those apparent limits.

Objection 2. But do we have a right to live high on the hog – consume all we want, have as large families as we want – and let later generations suffer?

The facts suggest that the opposite assumption is the more appropriate: If population growth is higher in a given generation, later generations benefit rather than suffer. During the industrial revolution in England the standard of living might (or might not) have been higher for a while if population had not grown so quickly. But we today clearly benefit from that high population growth rate and the consequent high economic growth of that period, just as the LDC model suggests.

Objection 3. Your models emphasize the long-run positive effects of population growth. But as Keynes said, in the long run we're all dead.

I've addressed Keynes's clever-but-silly wisecrack earlier. It's true that you and I will die. But in the long run others will be alive, and those people matter – just as the future of the "planet" properly matters to ecologists and others. And as emphasized earlier, one's overall judgment about population growth depends upon one's discount rate – how you weigh the immediate and the future effects against each other.

Summary

History since the industrial revolution does not support the simple Malthusian model or the Coale-Hoover extension. No negative relationship between population growth and economic growth is revealed in anecdotal history, in time-series studies over the past 100 years, or in contemporary cross-sections. Rather, the data suggest that there is no simple relationship at all, for either less-developed-countries (LDCs) or for more-developed-countries (MDCs) (as discussed in the previous chapter).

For MDCs, the most general and most appealing explanation of this discrepancy between theory and evidence is the nexus of economies of scale, the creation and adaptation of new knowledge by additional people, and the creation of new resources from new knowledge. Therefore the MDC model incorporates this fundamental influence on economic progress that has previously been left out of population models. And that model – more complete than Malthusian and neo-Malthusian models such as *The Limits to*

Growth – indicates that, after a few years during which a representative additional child has a net negative effect, the net effect upon per capita income comes to be positive. And these positive long-run effects are large compared with the added costs to the community until the child reaches full productivity. A present-value weighing of the short and long run at reasonable costs of capital reveals that the on-balance effect of additional persons is positive, an attractive "investment" compared to other social investments.

In LDCs the explanation is somewhat different, but the outcome is similar. Additional children influence the LDC economy by inducing people to work longer hours and invest more, as well as by causing an improvement in the social infrastructure, such as better roads and communication systems. Additional population also induces economies of scale in other ways. The upshot is that, although additional children cause additional costs in the short run, a moderate rate of population growth in LDCs is more likely to lead to a higher standard of living in the long run than either zero population growth or a high rate of population growth.

Notes

1. Some members of the economics profession for decades after World War II thought that different economic principles applied to economic development, but that view is now happily passé.
2. Piotrow 1973, p. 15.
3. Ibid., p. 124.
4. Coale and Hoover 1958, p. 275.
5. Kuznets 1967; Easterlin 1967; Chesnais and Sauvy 1973; Simon and Gobin 1979. See also Simon 1977, chapter 3; 1989; Chesnais 1985; Lee 1983; Kelley 1988; Ahlburg 1987.
6. Simon and Gobin 1979.
7. Stryker 1977.
8. Of course exceptional individual events can occur in unpromising circumstances. A little town in Illinois can produce several gold medalists in speed skating because of one person's vision. Occasional great minds may come out of backward villages in Serbia (Michael Pupin) and Lebanon (Philip Hitti), simply because of inexplicable accidents such as a broken arm that keeps a child from returning to his/her village (see their autobiographies).
9. *Washington Post*, October 9, 1988, pp. A29, A36; by Blaine Harden.
10. Keyfitz 1985.
11. Ibid., p. 699
12. Ibid., p. 697.
13. Ibid., p. 696.
14. Ibid., p. 701.
15. Full details are in Simon 1992, chapter 8.
16. Kuznets 1965, p. 29 (italics added).

References

Ahlburg, Dennis A. 1987. "The Impact of Population Growth on Economic Growth in Developing Nations: The Evidence from Macroeconomic-Demographic Models." In

D. Gale Johnson, and Ronald D. Lee. *Population Growth and Economic Development: Issues and Evidence*. Madison, Wis.: University of Wisconsin Press, pp. 479–522.

Chesnais, Jean-Claude. 1985. "Progres Economique et Transition Demographique dans les Pays Pauvres: Trente Ans D'Experience (1950–1980)." *Population* 40: 11–28.

Chesnais, Jean-Claude, and Alfred Sauvy. 1973. "Progrès économique et accroissement de la population; une expérience commentée." *Population* 28: 843–57.

Coale, Ansley, and Edgar M. Hoover. 1958. *Population Growth and Economic Development in Low-Income Countries*. Princeton, N.J.: Princeton University Press.

Easterlin, Richard. 1967. "Effects of Population Growth in the Economic Development of Developing Countries." *Annals of the American Academy of Political and Social Science* 369: 98–108.

Kelley, Allen C. 1988. "Economic Consequences of Population Change in the Third World." *Journal of Economic Literature* (December): 1685–1728.

Keyfitz, Nathan. 1985. "An East Javanese Village in 1953 and 1985: Observation on Development." *Population and Development Review* 11, no. 4 (December): 695–719.

Kuznets, Simon. 1965. "Demographic Aspects of Modern Economic Growth." Paper presented at World Population Conference, Belgrade, September.

———. 1967. "Population and Economic Growth." *Proceedings of the American Philosophical Society* 11: 170–93.

Lee, Ronald. 1983. "Economic Consequences of Population Size, Structure and Growth." International Union for the Scientific Study of Population, *Newsletter* no. 17 (January–April): 43–59.

Piotrow, Phyllis Tilson. 1973. *World Population Crisis: The United States' Response*. New York: Praeger.

Simon, Julian L. 1977. *The Economics of Population Growth*. Princeton, N.J.: Princeton University Press.

———. 1989. "On Aggregate Empirical Studies Relating Population Variables to Economic Development." *Population and Development Review* 15, no. 2 (June): 323–32.

———. 1992. *Population and Development in Poor Countries*. Princeton, N.J.: Princeton University Press.

Simon, Julian L., and Roy Gobin. 1979. "The Relationship between Population and Economic Growth in LDCs." In *Research in Population Economics*, vol. 2 edited by Julian L. Simon and Julie deVanzo. Greenwich, Conn.: JAI Press.

Stryker, J. Dirck. 1977. "Optimum Population in Rural Areas: Empirical Evidence from the Franc Zone. *Quarterly Journal of Economics* 91: 177–93.

REVIEW AND DISCUSSION QUESTIONS

1   Why did Julian L. Simon change his views about the effects of population growth?

2   How does Simon object to Coale and Hoover's thesis, according to which population growth hinders economic growth?

3   According to Simon, what are some key reasons why population growth may have a positive effect on standards of living?

4   Is it Simon's belief that faster population growth always raises standards of living? Why or why not?

5   How does Simon object to the belief that eventually the earth's resources will run out if global population continues to grow indefinitely?

6   Do you find Simon's arguments about the positive effects of population growth persuasive? Why or why not? Explain.

Chapter 20

David E. Bloom, David Canning, and Dean T. Jamison

HEALTH, WEALTH, AND WELFARE

THE LAST 150 YEARS HAS witnessed a global transformation in human health that has led to people living longer, healthier, more productive lives. While having profound consequences for population size and structure, better health has also boosted rates of economic growth worldwide. Between the 16th century and the mid-19th century, average life expectancy around the world fluctuated but averaged under 40 years, with no upward trend. Life spans slowly but steadily increased in the second half of the 19th century and then jumped markedly in the 20th century, initially in Europe and then in the rest of the world (see Table 20.1). Economic historians and demographers still debate the genesis of these changes, but they increasingly point to rising incomes (and resulting improvements in sanitation and food availability) as the major cause of declines in 19th-century mortality rates. For the 20th century, however, they believe technical improvements were the catalysts – particularly the discovery of the germ theory of disease, a better understanding of hygiene, and the development of antibiotics and vaccines.

Chile provides a well-documented example of dramatic mortality decline. A Chilean female born in 1910 had a life span of 33 years. Today, her life expectancy exceeds 78 (only 2 years shorter than that in the United States). In 1910, the odds were more than one in three that she would die before age 5; today, they are less than one in fifty. Moreover, for middle-aged people, death rates are also now far lower: today's Chilean female is far less likely to die as a young adult from tuberculosis or childbearing or in middle age from cancer. Mirroring these mortality changes are marked changes in her quality of life. She can choose to have fewer pregnancies and spend less time raising children: from an average of 5.3 children in 1950, Chilean women's fertility has dropped to 2.3 (barely above replacement). She suffers fewer infections and has greater strength and stature and a quicker mind. Her life is not only much longer, it is much healthier as well.

What has this improvement in population health since the mid-19th century meant for economies as a whole? And what does the recent fall in life expectancy in Africa and elsewhere as a result of the HIV/AIDS epidemic portend? This article tries to answer these

Table 20.1   Living longer: Life expectancy rose sharply around the world in the second half of the 20th century, but AIDS is undermining progress in Africa and elsewhere.

Region	Lifeexpectancy, years			Rate of change in years per decade	
	1960	*1990*	*2001*	*1960–90*	*1990–2001*
Low and middle income	**44**	**63**	**64**	**6.3**	**0.9**
East Asia and Pacific	39	67	69	9.3	1.8
Europe and Central Asia	n/a	69	69	n/a	0.0
Latin America and Caribbean	56	68	71	4.0	2.7
Middle East and North Africa	47	64	68	5.7	3.6
South Asia	44	58	63	4.7	4.5
sub-Saharan Africa	40	50	46	3.3	−3.6
High income	**69**	**76**	**78**	**2.3**	**1.8**
World	**50**	**65**	**67**	**5.0**	**1.8**

Source: *World Development Indicators 2003* (Washington: World Bank, 2003).

Note: Entries are the average of male and female life expectancies. Assignment of countries to regions uses the World Bank convention for 2003 that is listed on the inside back cover of *WDI 2003*.

questions by exploring the increasingly strong body of evidence showing that better health contributes to the more rapid growth of GDP per capita. The article also delves into recent studies that argue that past estimates of economic progress have been understated and that recent economic losses caused by HIV/AIDS are likewise being understated if economists rely on GDP per capita as a yardstick. A better indicator would be "full income," a concept that captures the value of changes in life expectancy by including them in an assessment of economic welfare. For Africa, this new yardstick sharply illuminates the economic consequences of AIDS in the past 15 years and signals catastrophe ahead.

How health affects GDP per capita

How does health influence GDP per capita? To begin with, healthy workers are more productive than workers who are otherwise comparable but for their health. One strand of supporting evidence comes from studies on individuals that link investments in health and nutrition of the young to adult wages.

Better health also raises per capita income through a number of other channels (see Figure 20.1). One way is by altering decisions about expenditures and savings over the life cycle. The idea of planning for retirement occurs only when mortality rates become low enough for retirement to be a realistic prospect. Rising longevity in developing countries has opened a new incentive for the current generation to save – an incentive that can have dramatic effects on national saving rates. While this saving boom lasts for only one generation and is offset by the needs of the elderly once population aging occurs, it can substantially boost investment and economic growth rates while it lasts.

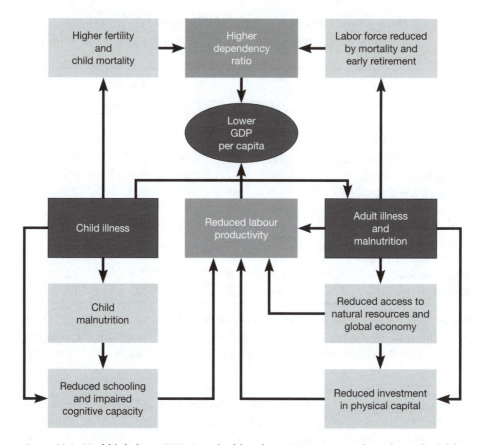

Figure 20.1 Health's links to GDP. Poor health reduces GDP per capita by reducing both labor productivity and the relative size of the labor force.

Source: Ruger, Jennifer Prah, Dean T. Jamison, and David E. Bloom, 2001, "Health and the Economy," page 619 in *International Public Health*, edited by Michael H. Merson, Robert E. Black, and Anne J. Mills (Sudbury, Massachusetts: Jones and Barlett).

Another channel is by encouraging foreign direct investment: investors shun environments where the labor force suffers a heavy disease burden. Endemic diseases can also deny humans access to land or other natural resources, as occurred in much of West Africa prior to the successful control of river blindness. Yet another channel is through boosting education. Healthier children have higher rates of school attendance and improved cognitive development, and a longer life span can make investment in education more attractive.

The initial beneficiaries of health improvements are often the most vulnerable group: children. Lower infant mortality initially creates a "baby boom" cohort and often leads to a subsequent reduction in the birth rate as families choose to have fewer children in the new low-mortality regime. A baby-boom cohort is thus unique and affects the economy profoundly as it enters education, then finds jobs, saves for retirement, and, finally, leaves the labor market. The cohorts before and after a baby boom are much smaller.

If better health improves an economy's productive potential, we would expect good health to go hand in hand with higher steady-state output. However, there may be a lag such that economies adjust gradually to their steady-state output level over time. In this case, we expect countries that have high levels of health but low levels of income to experience relatively faster economic growth as their income adjusts. How big an overall contribution does better health make to economic growth? Evidence from cross-country growth regressions suggests the contribution is large. Indeed, the initial health of a population has been identified as one of the most robust and potent drivers of economic growth – among such well-established influences as the initial level of income per capita (once countries reach their steady-state level of income, growth slows), geographic location, institutional environment, economic policy, initial level of education, and investments in education. For example, Bloom, Canning, and Sevilla (Harvard University) found that one extra year of life expectancy raises steady-state GDP per capita by about 4 percent.

But not all countries benefit equally from this link. Alok Bhargava (University of Houston) and colleagues found that better health matters more for wages in low-income countries than in high-income ones. Studies also show that better health matters more for countries with good economic policies, such as openness to trade and good governance. Work undertaken by Bloom, Canning, and Malaney (Harvard University) concluded that the East Asian growth miracle was actually no miracle at all: rather, it represents compelling evidence for a process in which health improvements played a leading role in the context of generally favorable economic policies (Box 20.1).

BOX 20.1   THE EAST ASIAN "MIRACLE"

There is a growing body of evidence that the East Asian countries that sustained high rates of economic growth in the second half of the 20th century did so largely thanks to high rates of growth of factor inputs – labor, physical capital, and human capital – rather than increases in total factor productivity. One reason for the rapid increase in labor supply per capita in East Asia has been the effect of better health. Improvements in health, feasible at modest cost, preceded and helped catalyze the so-called miracle. Life expectancy increased from 39 years in 1960 to 67 years in 1990, with a concomitant decline in fertility. Declining mortality and fertility rates meant that between 1960 and 2000 the ratio of working-age people (15–64) to the dependent population (0–14 and 65 plus) rose from about 1.3 to over 2, which facilitate a much higher input of workers per capita into production and a higher GDP per capita.

Another key element in East Asia's economic success stories was the region's exceptionally high rates of capital accumulation, driven by saving levels that often exceeded 30 percent of income. Increases in longevity led to an increase in the need for saving to secure retirement income, as studies have suggested. Savings by individuals peak when they are between 40 and 65 and are preparing for retirement, resulting in a savings boom when the baby-boom cohort enters this age range. Not only did East Asia have a large fraction of its population in this peak savings age range, but also this cohort was the first in the region to be living in a low-mortality environment and to be saving for retirement on a larger scale.

Virtuous and vicious circles

Health improvements can spur economic performance, but causality also runs in the reverse direction. This reverse causality makes estimating the causal effect of health on economic performance difficult, but work in the area usually identifies the effect through timing; using childhood health and nutrition inputs as a determinant of adult wages or taking population health in, say, 1960 as a factor influencing economic growth during 1960–95. More important, this two-way causality can give rise to cumulative causality, with health improvements leading to economic growth, which can facilitate further health improvements, and so on. While this virtuous circle of improvements in health and income can continue for a time, it will eventually come to an end as returns to health improvements diminish and demographic change leads to an aging population.

There is also scope, however, for vicious circles, with health declines setting off impoverishment and further ill health. This pattern has been particularly evident in the former Soviet Union, where male life expectancy declined sharply during the transition from communism, and in sub-Saharan Africa, where HIV infection rates are high and AIDS is already dramatically increasing adult mortality rates.

The effect of HIV/AIDS on GDP per capita could eventually prove devastating. There is an enormous waste of human capital as prime-age workers die. A high-mortality environment deters the next generation from investing in education and creating human capital that may have little payoff. The creation of a generation of orphans means that children may be forced to work to survive and may not get the education they need. High mortality rates may reduce investment. Saving rates are thus likely to fall, as the prospect of retirement becomes less likely. And foreign companies are less likely to invest in a country with a high HIV prevalence rate because of the threat to their own workers, the prospect of high labor turnover, and the likely loss of workers who have gained specific skills by working for the firm.

How health influences "full income"

Judging countries' economic performance by GDP per capita, however, fails to differentiate between situations where health differs: a country whose citizens enjoy long and healthy lives clearly outperforms another with the same GDP per capita but whose citizens suffer much illness and die sooner. Individual willingness to forgo income to work in safer environments and social willingness to pay for health-enhancing safety and environmental regulations provide measures, albeit approximate, of the value of differences in mortality rates. Many such willingness-to-pay studies have been undertaken in recent decades, and their results are typically summarized as the "value of a statistical life" or VSL (Box 20.2).

Although the National Income and Product Accounts (NIPA) include the value of inputs into health care (such as drugs and physician time), standard procedures do not incorporate information on the value of changes in mortality rates. In a pathbreaking (but long-neglected) paper, Dan Usher of Queen's University, Canada, first brought the value of mortality reduction into the economic analysis of national income accounting. He did this by generating estimates of the growth in "full income" – a concept that captures the value of changes in life expectancy by including them in an assessment of economic welfare

BOX 20.2   THE "VALUE OF A STATISTICAL LIFE"

How should governments evaluate the consequences of public sector health, safety, and environmental interventions that reduce mortality risks? Over several decades, a substantial body of research has addressed this question by using information from individuals' choices about willingness to take risks. W. Kip Viscusi of Harvard University has closely tracked this literature, and, in a recent overview, he and colleague Joseph Aldy provide a clear statement of the approach:

> Individuals make decisions everyday that reflect how they value health and mortality risks, such as driving an automobile, smoking a cigarette and eating a medium rare hamburger. Many of these choices involve market decisions, such as the purchase of a hazardous product or working on a risky job. Because increases in health risks are undesirable, there must be some other aspect of that activity that makes it attractive. Using evidence on market choices that involve implicit tradeoffs between risk and money, economists have developed estimates of the value of a statistical life (VSL).

> (Viscusi and Aldy, 2003)

If, for example, a worker requires (and is paid) $500 a year of additional pay to accept a more risky but otherwise similar job, where the increase in the mortality rate is 1 in 10,000 a year, the value placed on reducing risk by this magnitude is simply $500. The value of a statistical life is defined as the observed amount required to accept a risk divided by the level of the risk – that is, in the example we have chosen, the VSL would be $500/(1/10,000) = $5,000,000, a number in the range of estimates for the United States today. Viscusi and Aldy provide a comprehensive overview of the methods used in this research and summarize results of 60 studies from 10 countries.

Willingness to pay to avoid risks rises, not surprisingly, with income. A reasonable range of values for a country's VSL appears to be 100–200 times GDP per capita, with values estimated in richer countries more likely to occur toward the high end of the range.

– for six countries and territories (Canada, Chile, France, Japan, Sri Lanka, and Taiwan Province of China) during the middle decades of the 20th century. For the upper-income countries in this group, perhaps 30 percent of the growth of full income resulted from declines in mortality. In the developing countries, where this was a period of particularly rapid mortality decline, full income was influenced even more by mortality changes. Estimates of changes in full income are typically generated by adding the value of changes in annual mortality rates (calculated using VSL figures) to changes in annual GDP per capita. Even these estimates of full income are conservative in that they incorporate only the value of mortality changes and do not account for the total value of changes in health status.

For almost 15 years, little further work was done on the effects of mortality change on full income (although the number of carefully constructed estimates of VSLs increased enormously). Two papers then appeared that kindled substantial new interest.

Newly appointed World Bank Chief Economist François Bourguignon and Christian Morrisson (University of Paris) addressed the long-term evolution of inequality among world citizens starting from the premise that a "comprehensive definition of economic well-being would consider individuals over their lifetime."Their conclusion was that rapid increases in life expectancy in poorer countries had resulted in declines in inequality, broadly defined, beginning sometime after 1950, even though income inequality had continued to rise. (Table 20.1 shows life expectancy increasing between 1960 and 1990 in developing countries at a rate of 6.3 years a decade, whereas in the high-income countries, the rate was "only" 2.3 years a decade.) In another important paper, Yale University's William Nordhaus assessed the growth of full income per capita in the United States in the 20th century. He concluded that somewhat over half of the growth in full income in the first half of the century had resulted from mortality decline, and somewhat less than half in the second half of the century. This was a period when real income in the United States increased sixfold, and life expectancy increased by a little over 25 years. Nordhaus's paper also provides a valuable summary of the theory and methods of estimation of full income.

Three lines of more recent work extend these methods to the interpretation of the economic performance of developing countries in recent decades, and all reach conclusions that differ substantially from analyses based on GDP alone. Two of these studies – one undertaken for the World Health Organization's Commission on Macroeconomics and Health (CMH) and the other at the IMF – assessed the impact of the AIDS epidemic on full income. Both concluded that the AIDS epidemic in the 1990s had far more adverse economic consequences than its effects on per capita GDP would suggest (see Box 20.3). Gary Becker and colleagues at the University of Chicago extended the earlier work of Bourguignon and Morrisson in finding strong absolute convergence in full income across countries over time, in contrast to the standard finding of continued divergence of GDP per capita. Finally, Jeffrey Sachs (Columbia University) and colleagues have extended the earlier CMH work by using standard cross-country growth regressions to model determinants of full income (rather than GDP per capita). They also conclude that economies have been converging in terms of full income, and, tentatively, they find the determinants of growth in full income to be similar to those of growth in GDP.

Conclusion

The dramatic mortality declines of the past one and a half centuries – and their reversal by AIDS in Africa and elsewhere subsequent to 1990 – have had major economic consequences. The impact of health on GDP is substantial – an extra year of life expectancy is estimated to raise a country's per capita GDP by about 4 percent, for example. The intrinsic value of mortality changes – measured in terms of the value of a statistical life or VSL – is even more substantial.

What are the implications of these findings for development strategy and for benefit-cost analyses of public sector investment options? Using full income in benefit-cost analyses of investments in health (and in health-related sectors such as education, water supply and sanitation, and targeted food transfers) would markedly increase our estimates of net benefits or rates of return. Currently, only about 10 percent of official development assistance (ODA) is committed directly to health. Given the highly efficacious and

BOX 20.3   THE DEVASTATING ECONOMIC IMPACT OF AIDS IN SUB-SAHARAN AFRICA

Life expectancy in Africa increased from 40 years in 1960 to 50 years in 1990, but the AIDS epidemic is reversing these gains. By 1990, infection with HIV had penetrated deeply into Africa, although the number of deaths remained fairly small (218,000 out of an estimated 7,940,000 deaths in 1990, or 2.7 percent of the total). But by 2001, the number of AIDS deaths had climbed to an estimated 2,197,000, or 20.6 percent of total deaths, with projections for continued increases. As a result, life expectancy has declined to 46 years.

Despite this fall in life expectancy, however, many investigators have so far found little, if any, impact of the AIDS epidemic on GDP per capita in the region – pointing to the shortcomings of GDP per capita as a measure of national economic well-being. While GDP per capita may suffer in the long run as education rates and savings fall because of high mortality rates, AIDS has certainly created a human disaster in many countries in sub-Saharan Africa. The measures of full income now entering the literature – a concept that captures the value of changes in life expectancy by including them in an assessment of economic welfare – provide a quantitative indicator of this disaster and convey a more accurate picture of the economic effect of AIDS. They suggest that AIDS is already having a devastating economic effect on Africa.

How is the change in full income resulting from the AIDS epidemic assessed? It consists of two components: the change in GDP per capita and the value of changes in mortality rates as estimated in the VSL literature. To obtain the latter component, the first step is to calculate the impact of AIDS on mortality rates. By 2000, the epidemic had, on average, progressed to the point that mortality rates (in middle ages) were beginning to increase substantially. In 1990, a 15-year-old male had a 51 percent chance of dying before his 60th birthday, and this had increased to 57 percent by 2000. For females, the increase was from 45 to 53 percent. (By comparison, in Japan, the comparable probability for females in 1999 was only 4.8 percent.) Taking the average of the change in annual mortality probabilities gives 0.35 percent a year from 1990 to 2000.

The next step is to calculate the economic cost of these mortality increases. Conservatively, using 100 times GDP per capita as the VSL, Africa's mortality changes imply an economic cost of the epidemic approximately equal to 15 percent of Africa's GDP in 2000 (assuming that about 50 percent of the population is aged 15–60 and that 90 percent of AIDS deaths are in this age group). This corresponds to a decline in income of 1.7 percent a year from 1990 to 2000, far higher than existing estimates of the effect of AIDS on GDP.

Before 1990, in contrast, improvements in adult health led to large economic benefits relative to changes in GDP per capita. The estimated effect adds several percentage points a year to the GDP growth rate in many African countries during 1960–90. This changes the overall perception of performance. Malawi, for example, in the 1980s had a slightly negative growth rate of GDP per capita, but a rather larger positive growth rate of full income that turned sharply negative in the 1990s. To the extent that full-income is a better indicator of overall economic performance than GDP per capita, Kenya's economic performance before 1990 has been significantly underestimated and, after 1990, dramatically overestimated.

low-cost technologies that exist for improving health (particularly in high-mortality settings), a careful, quantitative reassessment of competing investment priorities for improving living standards will likely conclude that existing ODA and budgetary allocations to health are richly deserving of a substantial boost.

References

Becker, Gary S., Tomas J. Philipson, and Rodrigo R. Soares, 2003, "The Quantity and Quality of Life and the Evolution of World Inequality," NBER Working Paper No. 9765 (Cambridge, Massachusetts: National Bureau of Economic Research).

Bhargava, Alok, Dean T. Jamison, Lawrence J. Lau, and Christopher J. L. Murray, 2001, "Modeling the Effects of Health on Economic Growth," *Journal of Health Economics*, Vol. 20 (May), pp. 423–40.

Bloom, David E., David Canning, and Bryan Graham, 2003, "Longevity and Life-cycle Savings," *Scandinavian Journal of Economics*, Vol. 105 (September), pp. 319–38.

Bloom, David E., David Canning, and Pia Malaney, 2000, "Demographic Change and Economic Growth in Asia," *Supplement to Population and Development Review*, Vol. 26, pp. 257–90.

Bloom, David E., David Canning, and J. Sevilla, 2004, "The Effect of Health on Economic Growth: A Production Function Approach," *World Development*, Vol. 32 (January), pp. 1–13.

Bourguignon, François and Christian Morrisson, 2002, "Inequality Among World Citizens: 1820–1992," *American Economic Review*, Vol. 92 (September), pp. 727–44.

Crafts, Nicholas, and Markus Haacker, 2003, "Welfare Implications of HIV/AIDS," IMF Working Paper No. 03/118 (Washington: International Monetary Fund).

Jamison, Dean T., Eliot Jamison, and Jeffrey Sachs, 2003, "Assessing the Determinants of Growth When Health Is Explicitly Included in the Measure of Economic Welfare," presented at the 4th World Congress of the International Health Economics Association, San Francisco, June.

Jamison, Dean T., Jeffrey Sachs, and Jia Wang, 2001, "The Effect of the AIDS Epidemic on Economic Welfare in sub-Saharan Africa," Paper No. WGI:13, CMH Working Paper Series (World Health Organization Commission on Macroeconomics and Health).

Nordhaus, William, 2003, "The Health of Nations: The Contribution of Improved Health to Living Standards," in *Measuring the Gains from Medical Research: An Economic Approach*, edited by Kevin H. Murphy and Robert H. Topel (Chicago: University of Chicago Press).

Usher, Dan, 1973, "An Imputation to the Measure of Economic Growth for Changes in Life Expectancy," in *The Measurement of Economic and Social Performance*, edited by Milton Moss (New York: Columbia University Press for National Bureau of Economic Research).

Viscusi, W. Kip, and J. E. Aldy, 2003, "The Value of a Statistical Life: A Critical Review of Market Estimates from Around the World," *The Journal of Risk and Uncertainty*, Vol. 27 (August), pp. 5–76.

World Health Organization, Commission on Macroeconomics and Health, 2001, *Macroeconomics and Health: Investing in Health for Economic Development* (Geneva: WHO).

REVIEW AND DISCUSSION QUESTIONS

1   Through what channels does poor health reduce GDP per capita?
2   Explain what the value of a statistical life (VSL) is and why this concept is useful in development economics.
3   Why might HIV/AIDS reduce GDP per capita even more than other diseases with similar mortality rates?
4   How is "full income" different from GDP and why does it provide a better indicator of the economic impact of diseases?
5   Several recent studies have examined the links between changes in health conditions and changes in full income. What are the implications for development policy of such studies?

Chapter 21

Michael Kremer

PHARMACEUTICALS AND THE DEVELOPING WORLD

PHARMACEUTICALS HAVE BROUGHT tremendous health benefits to developing countries, but existing pharmaceuticals are often underused or misused, and pharmaceutical R&D on health problems specific to poor countries is woefully inadequate.

The role of pharmaceuticals and medical technology in improving health in developing countries stands in contrast to the historical experience of the developed countries. Historically, health in currently developed countries improved largely due to higher incomes and consequent improvements in nutrition, sanitation and water supplies. Fogel (1986) finds that half of the decline in standardized British death rates and 70 percent of the decline in standardized American death rates between 1700 and 1980 occurred before 1911, in an era with few effective medicines. However, modern medical technologies allow tremendous improvements in health even at low income levels. The outward shift of the technological frontier is illustrated by Vietnam, which has a life expectancy of 69 years despite a per capita income that according to official statistics is less than one-tenth that of the United States in 1900, which had a 47-year life expectancy.[1] To take another example, per capita GDP in low-income sub-Saharan African nations decreased 13 percent from 1972 through 1992, but life expectancy increased by 10 percent, from 45 to 49 years, and infant mortality fell 30 percent, from 133 per thousand births to 93 per thousand births (World Bank, 2001b). (Unfortunately, since then, life expectancy in sub-Saharan Africa has fallen due to the AIDS pandemic.) Indeed, analysis of worldwide health trends in the twentieth century has found that most improvements resulted from technological advances rather than from income growth. Using the cross-sectional relationship between income and life expectancy, Preston (1975) estimated that income growth accounted for only 10 to 25 percent of the growth in world life expectancy between the 1930s and 1960s and suggested that the diffusion of technological advances was a major factor for the increase in life expectancy at any given income level. Jamison et al. (2001) attribute 74 percent of the decline in infant mortality rates over the period from 1962 to 1987 to technical progress, 21 percent to greater education and only about 5 percent to income growth.

While other technological improvements – such as the development of oral rehydration therapy against diarrhea and the use of radios in public health campaigns – may have played a role in improving health, the development and dissemination of pharmaceuticals has played a key role. To take one example, about three-quarters of the world's children receive a standard package of cheap, off-patent vaccines through the World Health Organization's (WHO) Expanded Program on Immunization, and these vaccines are estimated to save 3 million lives per year (Kim-Farley, 1992). Though vaccination rates are uneven around the world, the World Bank (2001b) estimates that 70 percent of infants in low-income countries received the three-dose DTP (diphtheria, tetanus and pertussis) vaccine over the period from 1995 through 1999.

Yet many people in developing countries who could benefit from pharmaceuticals do not receive them. The failure of antiretroviral therapy to reach more than a tiny fraction of people with AIDS in developing countries has attracted widespread publicity, but even medicines that are far cheaper and easier to deliver are not reaching many of the people who need them. More than a quarter of children worldwide and over half of children in some countries do not receive the vaccines that are part of WHO's Expanded Program on Immunization, although these cost only pennies per dose and require no diagnosis. Three million lives are lost annually as a result (World Bank, 2001a). Only a small fraction of children in poor countries receive the newer hepatitis B and Haemophilus influenzae b (Hib) vaccines, which cost a dollar or two per dose. One in four people worldwide suffer from intestinal worms, although treatments only need to be taken once or twice per year, have virtually no side effects, and cost less than a dollar per year. These examples suggest that while intellectual property rights undoubtedly prevent some from obtaining needed pharmaceuticals, eliminating these rights would not help the majority of those without access to drugs.

While developing countries have obtained substantial benefits from pharmaceuticals originally developed for rich country markets, little research is conducted on diseases that primarily affect poor countries, such as malaria or tuberculosis. Pecoul et al. (1999) report that of the 1,233 drugs licensed worldwide between 1975 and 1997, only 13 were for tropical diseases. Of these, five came from veterinary research, two were modifications of existing medicines, and two were produced for the U.S. military. Only four were developed by commercial pharmaceutical firms specifically for tropical diseases of humans. According to WHO (1996), 50 percent of global health research and development in 1992 was undertaken by private industry, but less than 5 percent of that was spent on diseases specific to less developed countries. Even for diseases that affect both rich and poor countries, research tends to focus on products that are best suited for use in rich countries. For example, much research is conducted on sophisticated AIDS drugs that are useful in developed countries, but are too expensive and difficult to deliver to the majority of the population in the poorest countries. Much less research is conducted on vaccines, which are typically much more feasible to deliver than drugs in developing countries, since they often require only a few doses to deliver and can be delivered by personnel with limited medical training.

The controversy over intellectual property rights for pharmaceuticals and access to antiretroviral therapies in developing countries has been the subject of much public debate recently. This article provides a broader context for the debate. It first reviews characteristics of the developing country market for pharmaceuticals, including small markets, distinct disease environments and weak health care and regulatory systems. It then outlines key market and government failures. Existing products are underused to the extent that patients do not take into account positive externalities from reducing the spread of communicable disease and that monopoly/oligopoly pricing of pharmaceuticals leads to prices greater than marginal cost; overused to the extent that patients do not take into account negative externalities from encouraging the development of drug-resistant strains; and underused, overused and misused due to asymmetric information between patients and providers and inefficient government health care delivery. R&D on new pharmaceuticals is undersupplied because competitive markets do not reward R&D expenditures and because governments face free-rider problems in supplying the global public good of R&D and have time-inconsistent preferences regarding rewarding firms for doing so.

Drawing on this background, the article then explores policy options for broadening access to pharmaceuticals and encouraging R&D on products needed in developing countries. In particular, it explores differential pricing; priorities for foreign assistance in health; the prospects for addressing pharmaceutical misuse by improving health care delivery systems; drug regulation; and the potential for rich countries or international organizations to encourage research and development on products needed by developing countries by committing to buy the products, once they are developed, and make them available to those who need them.

Characteristics of the pharmaceutical market in developing countries

The market for pharmaceuticals in developing countries differs in several ways from that in the developed world.

Small markets

The market for pharmaceuticals in the poorest countries is tiny. Connecticut spends more on health than the 38 low-income countries of sub-Saharan Africa combined (World Bank, 2001b; U.S. Census, 2000). In 1998, U.S. public and private health spending constituted 13 percent of its almost $32,000 per capita income, for a total of more than $4,000 per person. In contrast, low-income sub-Saharan African nations spent only 6 percent of their average $300 per capita GDP on health, or around $18 per person (World Bank, 2001b), though developing countries spend a higher percentage of their health budgets on pharmaceuticals than do developed countries. Drug developers often do not even bother to take out patents in small, poor countries (Attaran and Gillespie-White, 2001).

Middle-income country markets are small, but comprise a significant and growing source of revenue for pharmaceutical firms. The Pharmaceutical Research and Manufacturers of America (PhRMA) estimate that while only 1 percent of their market is in Africa, including middle-income countries such as South Africa, 7 percent is in Southeast Asia and China, and 7.5 percent is in Latin America (PhRMA, 2000), as shown in Table 21.1.

Table 21.1   World pharmaceutical market, sales by region, 1998

Region	Percentage of Market
United States	39.6
Europe	26.1
Japan	15.4
Latin America	7.5
Southeast Asia & China	7.0
Canada	1.9
Africa	1.0
Middle East	0.9
Australasia	0.6

Source: PhRMA (2000, adapted from Figure 7.2).

Different disease environment

Developing countries face a significantly different disease environment than developed countries due to both their poverty and their geography. The burden of different diseases can be compared across countries using the concept of Disability Adjusted Life Years (Murray and Lopez, 1996). DALYs take into account not only the lives lost through disease, but also the number of years of disability caused. World Health Organization (2001) estimates imply that infectious and parasitic diseases account for one-third of the disease burden in low-income countries (in fact, for nearly half of Africa's disease burden), but only 3 percent of the burden in high-income countries, as seen in Table 21.2 (WHO, 2001). In contrast, the disease burden in high-income countries mainly consists of noncommunicable conditions like cancer and cardiovascular disease. Table 12.3 lists specific diseases for which more than 99 percent of the burden falls in low- and middle-income countries, which include malaria, schistosomiasis and leprosy (Lanjouw and Cockburn, 2001).

Table 21.2   Percentage of disease burden

Cause	World	Low-income countries	Middle-income countries	High-income countries
Infectious and parasitic diseases	23.1%	33.3%	13.9%	3.0%
Tuberculosis	2.4%	2.9%	2.2%	0.3%
HIV/AIDS	6.1%	9.7%	2.6%	0.7%
Malaria	2.7%	4.5%	1.0%	0.0%
Noncommunicable conditions	46.1%	33.2%	55.5%	82.7%
Malignant neoplasms (cancers)	5.3%	2.9%	6.7%	14.4%
Cardiovascular diseases	10.3%	7.7%	12.3%	16.4%

Sources: World Health Report (2001), World Bank (2001b).

Table 21.3   Diseases for which 99 percent or more of the global burden fell on low- and middle-income countries in 1990

Disease	Disability adjusted life years (thousands, 2000)	Deaths per year (2000)
Chagas disease	680	21,299
Dengue	433	12,037
Ancylostomiasis and necatoriasis (hookworm)	1,829	5,650
Japanese encephalitis	426	3,502
Lymphatic filariasis	5,549	404
Malaria	40,213	1,079,877
Onchocerciasis (river blindness)	951	—
Schistosomiasis	1,713	11,473
Tetanus	9,766	308,662
Trachoma	1,181	14
Trichuriasis	1,640	2,123
Trypanosomiasis	1,585	49,668
Leishmaniasis	1,810	40,913
Measles	27,549	776,626
Poliomyelitis	184	675
Syphilis	5,574	196,533
Diphtheria	114	3,394
Leprosy	141	2,268
Pertussis	12,768	296,099
Diarrhoeal diseases	62,227	2,124,032

Sources: Global Burden from WHO (1996), quoted in Lanjouw and Cockburn (2001, Table 1). Figures updated from Lanjouw and Cockburn (2001), using WHO (2001).

However, many diseases affect both developed and developing countries. For instance, cancer and heart disease account for 15 percent of the total disease burden even in low- and middle-income countries (Lanjouw, 2001). Moreover, the disease environment in developing countries is projected to become substantially more like that in developed countries over the next 20 years (WHO, 2000).

Weak health care systems and misuse of pharmaceuticals

Misuse of pharmaceuticals is a significant problem in developed countries, but it is a much greater problem in many developing countries, where health care systems are often weak and qualified medical personnel are scarce. Whereas the United States has 2.7 trained physicians per thousand people and Europe has 3.9, sub-Saharan Africa has only 0.1 physicians per thousand people (World Bank, 2001b). In some low-income countries, medical personnel assigned to public clinics often do not show up, particularly in rural areas. Moreover, clinics in developing countries often lack drugs because salaries of health care workers take priority in budget allocations and because drug procurement and distribution is inefficient or corrupt.[2]

Many patients therefore rely on the private health care system, but private practitioners are often untrained (Das, 2000). Medical personnel often prescribe inappropriate pharmaceuticals, in part to demonstrate effort to the patient. For instance, in Africa, injections are often given rather than pills, as many patients see these as more powerful. In a detailed study of medication in India, Phadke (1998) categorized more than 50 percent of all drugs prescribed as "unnecessary" or "contra-indicated," although some of these judgments are subjective.

Moreover, while self-prescription is not uncommon in the west, it is extremely common in the poorest countries, where rules requiring prescriptions for pharmaceutical are typically not enforced, perhaps in part because of the shortage of trained physicians (Kamat and Nichter, 1998). Many patients purchase and consume only an incomplete course of medication, especially when symptoms subside after a partial course (Nichter and Nichter, 1996). Drug overuse and misuse speeds the development of drug-resistant forms of diseases because the most resistant parasites are not eliminated, and these resistant parasites are then transmitted to others. For example, chloroquine was once highly effective for preventing and treating malaria, but strains of chloroquine-resistant malaria have emerged in most parts of the world (NIH, 2000). Strains of multidrug-resistant tuberculosis have also emerged over the last decade (NIH, 2000), and the development of resistance to the remaining tuberculosis drugs would pose a severe threat not only to developing countries but also to developed ones.

Pharmaceutical regulation

Developing countries often simply follow the approval decisions of developed countries rather than conducting their own risk-benefit calculations. While this practice may be appropriate in some cases, it may also block the adoption of needed drugs and vaccines. For example, rotavirus kills three-quarters of a million children each year in developing countries, but it is a minor health nuisance in the United States, causing more than three million cases of childhood diarrhea each year, but few deaths (CVI, 1999; Murphy et al., 2001a). An oral rotavirus vaccine received regulatory approval in the United States and was introduced into the U.S. market in 1998. A few months later, it was withdrawn following evidence that it can cause intususception, a form of intestinal obstruction. Because children in developing countries would have had much greater exposure to disease prior to inoculation, it is not clear that the risk of intususception would be as significant in developing countries. Moreover, even if the risk of intususception were similar, the risk-benefit calculation in countries with high rotavirus mortality would likely overwhelmingly favor vaccine use. The investigators who recommended removing the vaccine from the U.S. market therefore advocated conducting a risk-benefit analysis for the rotavirus vaccine in the developing world (Murphy et al., 2001b).

Yet no such testing and analysis is taking place. There is little hope for profit from selling rotavirus vaccine in the poorest countries, and neither the vaccine developer nor health authorities in developing countries have much incentive to take on the risk of being attacked by activists for conducting trials of a vaccine that is not deemed safe for use in more developed countries. Top-level political leadership from the World Health Organization (WHO) or UNICEF potentially could have provided industry and national authorities with political cover against this risk, perhaps making it feasible for the vaccine developer to give the rights to a nonprofit organization that could conduct testing, but this leadership was not forthcoming.

While following drug approval decisions in the developed countries may sometimes prevent approval of useful drugs, developing countries that depart from this practice can encounter other problems. For instance, the South African government has discouraged the widespread use of Nevirapine, which prevents mother-to-child transmission of AIDS and is an extremely cost-effective intervention, in part because President Mbeki gave credence to discredited scientific theories that HIV does not cause AIDS and that Nevirapine is toxic. (The South African government recently lost a lawsuit that may force the government to allow Nevirapine to be distributed widely, and as of this writing, it appears that the government has conceded and will eventually support the widespread use of Nevirapine.) Kenya and South Africa also each backed several domestically developed but ineffective AIDS drugs. None of these quack remedies provided a cure for AIDS, but they were promoted in part for nationalistic reasons.

Industry factors

Some of the characteristics of the pharmaceutical industry that differentiate it from other industries are particularly relevant for developing countries. First, the pharmaceutical industry has high fixed R&D costs and low marginal costs of production. Second, the industry is exceptional in that patents rather than first-mover advantages or other sources of monopoly power provide the key protection for innovators. Third, pharmaceutical regulation and prescription requirements in developed countries facilitate price discrimination across countries by making resale across national borders easier to block. As a result, price differentials between countries are often large.

The chief constraint on further price discrimination is the potential for a political backlash in higher-price markets. Selling pharmaceuticals cheaply in developing countries reveals an upper bound on the marginal cost of production, and developed country politicians and activists may be able to use this information to strengthen their appeals for lower prices. For example, when President Clinton announced his childhood immunization initiative in 1993, he said, "I cannot believe that anyone seriously believes that America should manufacture vaccines for the world, sell them cheaper in foreign countries, and immunize fewer kids as a percentage of the population than any nation in this hemisphere but Bolivia and Haiti" (Mitchell et al., 1993). After a 1982 Congressional hearing in which U.S. Senator Paula Hawkins asked a major vaccine manufacturer how it could justify charging nearly three times as much to the U.S. government for vaccines as to foreign countries, U.S. manufacturers stopped submitting bids to UNICEF to supply vaccines (Mitchell et al., 1993).

Limited intellectual property rights

Many developing countries have historically provided little or no intellectual property rights protection for pharmaceuticals. India, for example, offers patents on pharmaceutical processes but not on products and has developed a large industry that reverse engineers existing drugs. Developed countries, the United States in particular, have pressed developing countries to strengthen protection of intellectual property rights by linking the issue to trade negotiations. The 1994 Agreement on Trade-Related Aspects of Intellectual Property Rights (TRIPS) required the least developed countries to join the rest of WTO member countries in providing 20-year patent protection for pharmaceuticals by 2006 (WTO, 2001a).

However, it is unclear what impact TRIPS will ultimately have on intellectual property rights in developing countries. Several provisions of the agreement provide potential escape hatches. For instance, countries can impose compulsory licensing in national emergencies, the definition of which is deliberately not set out (WTO, 2001a). Countries are still free to impose price controls as well (though firms, of course, are not required to sell to countries with price controls). Moreover, the public storm over pricing of AIDS drugs led WTO negotiators to extend the transition period for instituting patent protection for pharmaceuticals in the least developed countries to 2016 (WTO, 2001b), and it seems possible the deadline could be extended further. Finally, enforcement of WTO provisions relies on countries bringing suits, but as a result of the public outcry, the United States dropped its dispute with South Africa over the country's imports of pharmaceutical products from countries with weaker patent laws and abandoned its dispute with Brazil over generic manufacturing of drugs that are still under patent. It is not clear whether the WTO will lead to effective intellectual property rights enforcement in developing countries.

Market failures, government failures and policy implications

Clearly, the pharmaceutical market in developing countries is rife with market and government failures. Pharmaceutical use is sometimes suboptimal due to pricing above marginal cost and positive treatment externalities for infectious diseases; sometimes too great due to the failure of consumers to take into account externalities from drug resistance; and sometimes simply inappropriate due to information asymmetries between health care providers and their patients. Drug procurement is often inefficient and corrupt, and inappropriate regulation can hinder access. In addition, health care workers are politically powerful relative to patients.

However, the most severe distortions in developing country pharmaceutical markets probably involve dynamic issues. Pharmaceutical firms are reluctant to invest in R&D on the diseases that primarily affect developing countries not only because the poverty of the potential users reduces their willingness to pay, but also because the potential revenue from product sales is far smaller than the sum of customers' potential willingness to pay due to the lack of intellectual property protection and the tendency for governments to force prices down after firms have sunk their research and development costs. The underprovision of R&D on problems facing the poor, even relative to their incomes, implies that a redirection of foreign assistance from private goods, such as food, or even public goods, such as roads, to the international public good of R&D on health problems of the poor could make the poor better-off.

One reason why governments provide suboptimal R&D incentives is that pharmaceutical research and development is a global public good, so each country has an incentive to free ride on research financed by the governments of other countries or induced by their intellectual property rights protection. This is a general problem faced by all countries, not just developing ones. Indeed, the mystery is not why developing countries have historically offered little protection for intellectual property rights, but why small developed countries offer so much. A second reason for suboptimal R&D incentives is that the high fixed costs of R&D and low marginal costs of production for pharmaceuticals create a time-inconsistency problem for governments. Once products have been developed, governments have an incentive to set prices at or near marginal cost. Products are then consumed at the efficient level, and surplus is transferred from (typically foreign) producers to consumers. Governments are in a strong bargaining position because they are major pharmaceutical purchasers, they regulate products and often prices, and they are arbiters of intellectual property rights. However, if pharmaceutical firms anticipate low prices, they will be reluctant to invest. In a repeated game between nations and pharmaceutical producers, this time-inconsistency problem could potentially be overcome through reputation formation. Indeed, one reason why developed countries are developed may be that these countries were able to establish good reputational equilibria in a variety of areas, including research incentives. Developed countries typically have more stable governments that are more likely to invest in reputation formation for the long run.

Whatever the underlying causes, intellectual property rights for pharmaceuticals in developing countries are weak, and hence the private returns for developing products to fight diseases of developing countries are likely to be a tiny fraction of the social returns to these products. For example, consider a hypothetical future malaria vaccine. A standard way to assess the cost-effectiveness of a health intervention is the cost per Disability Adjusted Life Year saved. A common cost-effectiveness threshold for health interventions in the poorest countries is $100 per DALY. For comparison, health interventions are considered cost-effective in the United States at up to 500 to 1000 times this amount: $50,000–$100,000 per year of life saved (Neumann et al., 2000). At a threshold of $100 per DALY, a malaria vaccine would be cost-effective even at a price of $40 per immunized person (Glennerster and Kremer, 2001), but based on the historical record of vaccine prices, the developer of a malaria vaccine would be lucky to receive payments of one-tenth or one-twentieth of that amount. Of course, a full comparison of the social and private values of a vaccine would also take into account the positive and negative externalities that vaccine development would create for other researchers.

The rest of this article considers a number of public policy issues regarding the availability and use of pharmaceuticals in developing countries from the standpoint of these market and government failures: differential pricing, foreign assistance for health, misuse of pharmaceuticals, drug regulation and procurement and ways of encouraging R&D on products needed by developing countries.

Differential pricing

Noneconomists often resent price discrimination, but it can improve both access and R&D incentives. Price discrimination allows those who value the product at more than the marginal cost of production to obtain it, so the product reaches more people than under a single worldwide monopoly price. It also allows firms to capture closer to the full social surplus of their products, thus providing them with a greater incentive for product development.

Since the chief constraint on further price discrimination is the fear of undermining prices in developed and middle-income countries, public acknowledgements by politicians in developed countries that different prices are appropriate for different countries could potentially make pharmaceutical firms more willing to risk lowering prices in developing countries. Rich country governments could also facilitate price discrimination by prohibiting imports of pharmaceutical products from countries with weaker patent laws. Individual rich countries can gain by taking advantage of lower-priced imports, but the developed world as a whole is unlikely to benefit, because if developed countries began importing drugs from developing countries on a wider scale, pharmaceutical firms would simply charge higher prices in developing countries, and their incentives to conduct R&D would be curbed by the smaller total market available to them with lower sales. There is therefore a justification for international agreements to limit such imports since they create negative externalities for other countries. Poor country governments can facilitate price discrimination by taking steps to prevent re-export of pharmaceuticals to rich countries.

However, given that markets in the poorest countries are so small, profit-maximizing prices in poor countries are likely to be substantially above marginal cost if selling at a lower price in these countries has any appreciable effect on prices in rich or even middle-income country markets. Indeed, prices in at least some markets will remain substantially above marginal cost even if governments adopt policies to encourage price discrimination further. Hence, many have called not just for differential pricing in poor countries, but also for using compulsory licensing of patents and/or the threat of compulsory licensing to lower prices closer to marginal cost in poor countries. One potential objection to compulsory licensing is that it could reduce R&D incentives. If restrictions on intellectual property rights were limited to the poorest countries, the impact on research incentives would be minimal for most diseases, but for diseases that primarily affect poor countries, R&D incentives may be affected. Indeed, Lanjouw and Cockburn (2001) find some evidence of a limited reallocation of funds toward malaria research with the introduction of intellectual property concerns into the GATT in the 1990s and the consequent move toward strengthening intellectual property rights protection for pharmaceuticals in developing countries.

Lanjouw (2001) proposes limiting the extension of patent protection in poor countries for pharmaceuticals for global diseases, while allowing patent protection in these countries to increase, as envisaged by the 1994 Agreement on Trade-Related Aspects of Intellectual Property Rights (TRIPS), on products for diseases that predominately affect the poor. Under her proposal, pharmaceutical developers would effectively have to choose patent protection in either rich or poor countries for a designated list of global diseases, such as cancer. Because developing countries contribute little to the profits firms can realize from pharmaceuticals for global diseases, patent applicants would choose protection in developed countries. Differential patent protection would facilitate beneficial differential pricing. If a firm sold a product for a global disease in a developing country at a high price, other firms could enter the market. (This is essentially equivalent to allowing compulsory licensing for global diseases.)

Lanjouw's (2001) proposal would be fairly close to returning to a pre-TRIPS patent regime for global diseases, but would preserve the limited existing incentives to develop products primarily needed in developing countries, such as a malaria vaccine, because it preserves intellectual property protections in those cases. Moreover, the proposal is robust to errors in the list of global diseases. For example, if all forms of cancer were designated as global diseases, but a form of cancer specific to Africa was later identified, the developer of a drug against this form of cancer could choose patent protection in developing countries. However, since incentives for R&D on diseases of developing countries are inadequate, new ways of providing incentives for R&D on these products would still be needed.

A potentially difficult problem with limiting intellectual property rights in the poorest countries is the political effects on prices in the middle- and high-income countries. If sanctioning weak or no intellectual property rights in the poorest countries weakened political support for intellectual property rights in richer countries or put pressure on prices there, it could have a significant impact on research incentives for global diseases. If India has limited intellectual property rights, Brazil may not be inclined to provide intellectual property rights either; and if antiretroviral drugs cost $500 per year in Brazil, European governments may lower the prices they pay for the drugs, and U.S. AIDS activists may object to paying $10,000 per year. Moreover, the existence of different intellectual property rights rules in different countries may undermine attempts to cast intellectual property rights protection as a natural, self-evident right rather than as an institution justified by its instrumental value. Of course, it is difficult to predict the political links between pricing in low-, middle- and high-income countries, but the fact that pharmaceutical firms pressed for the TRIPS agreement suggests that they think these links could be significant. If this channel is indeed important, weak intellectual property rights in poor countries could limit R&D incentives.

It may therefore be worth considering an alternative approach in which firms simply donate products to the poorest countries rather than charging the manufacturing cost. This could bolster firms' reputations, rather than posing a public relations challenge in maintaining prices in developed countries. In fact, in the fight over pricing AIDS drugs, antiretroviral producers sought to donate their AIDS drugs in Africa, but activists insisted on countries paying for the drugs at low prices, believing that firms would not continue the donations once the political heat was off.

To give firms an incentive to continue donating their products, developed country governments could provide enhanced tax deductions to pharmaceutical firms that make approved donations of drugs or vaccines for use in developing countries. The U.S. government currently provides a tax deduction for donations, but it is based on the product's manufacturing cost, which is often very low. An enhanced tax deduction or credit could be based on some fraction of a product's U.S. price or on an estimate of the social benefit of the product, perhaps measured in dollars per Disability Adjusted Life Years saved. Such a provision would have to be limited to appropriate donations, requested by approved organizations and shown to be reaching those who need them, or else firms could profit by donating unneeded products with low production costs. This approach would provide the benefits of price discrimination without jeopardizing either research incentives or the principle of intellectual property rights.

Priorities for foreign assistance in health

The World Health Organization's Commission on Macroeconomics and Health (CMH), chaired by economist Jeffrey Sachs, has called for developed countries to increase assistance for health in the developing world by $27 billion annually by 2007 and $38 billion annually by 2015 (CMH, 2001). A significant share of this would be for pharmaceuticals, including antiretroviral treatments for AIDS.

The Commission report argues that these investments in health will pay for themselves six times over through higher productivity and increased earnings (CMH,

2001). However, evidence on the magnitude of the economic impact of health gains is patchy. Extravagant claims based on cross-country regressions should be taken with a grain of salt in light of the poor economic performance of Africa from the 1960s through the 1990s, despite the substantial technology-driven improvements in health over the period, and by the more recent stellar growth performance of Uganda, one of the countries earliest and hardest hit by AIDS morbidity and mortality. In my view, a stronger case for health spending rests on its effect on welfare rather than measured GDP. Indeed, the 13 percent decline in official GDP in the low-income countries of sub-Saharan Africa from 1972 to 1992 while life expectancy increased by nearly 10 percent and infant mortality fell 30 percent suggests that measured GDP can in some cases be a poor guide to welfare. A version of GDP that was corrected to measure improvements in the productivity of health services over this period would probably not have declined over the period.

Economists have advocated two main approaches for determining priorities for the limited foreign assistance that is likely to be forthcoming for health from the developed world. Some argue that the interventions that save the greatest number of lives at the least cost should be prioritized, using cost per Disability Adjusted Life Years saved as a guideline. Others argue that outside assistance should concentrate on addressing market failures, for example by funding public goods. However, the debate between advocates of the cost-effectiveness and market failure approaches may be overblown. To the extent that analysts estimate DALYs correctly and consumers value DALYs incurred by different diseases equally (rather than being willing to pay more to avoid deaths from airplane crashes than automobile accidents, for example), the two approaches should yield broadly similar results. Indeed, they do point to similar health priorities. For example, the WHO Expanded Program on Immunization is extremely cost-effective, at only around $20 to $40 per DALY saved, in part because vaccination creates positive externalities by preventing the spread of disease. Treatments for some infectious diseases would likely be another priority under both approaches. For example, school-based mass treatment of intestinal worm infections would cost as little as $7 per DALY saved, and the externality benefits of such treatments can account for over 70 percent of the reduction in disease burden (Miguel and Kremer, 2002). Some AIDS interventions are also very cost-effective. Nevirapine is extremely cost-effective in preventing mother-to-child transmission of AIDS, at $5 to $20 per DALY saved (Marseille et al., 1999), and a targeted AIDS prevention program in Tanzania costs an estimated $10 to $12 per DALY saved (World Bank, 1999).

Given a fixed budget, helping extend the programs above to reach more people is likely to be a much higher priority than using antiretroviral drugs to treat HIV/AIDS. The well-known call by 133 Harvard faculty members for antiretroviral treatment in developing countries estimates that, even given the recent dramatic reductions in prices by pharmaceutical firms, purchasing and delivering antiretrovirals will cost $1,100 per person per year (Adams et al., 2001). This is in large part because the drugs are so difficult to deliver safely and effectively. Because the drugs cause significant side effects and must be taken according to a rigid schedule if they are to be effective and not lead to the spread of drug resistance, they require monitoring by medical personnel. Adherence to drug regimes is highly imperfect even in rich countries with good medical care (Ammassari et al. 2001; Brook et al., 2001; Nieuwkerk et al., 2001). The statement by the 133 Harvard faculty members therefore advocates "directly observed therapy," wherein a community health worker visits each patient and observes him or her taking the antiretroviral medication. It is worth noting, however, that recent randomized controlled trials find that direct observation is no more effective than self-administered treatment for tuberculosis (Walley et al., 2001). But even setting this issue aside, many more lives could be saved with alternative interventions given the $1,100 per patient per year estimated cost of antiretroviral therapy. For instance, for every person treated for a year with antiretroviral therapy, 25 to 110 Disability Adjusted Life Years could be saved through targeted AIDS prevention efforts or vaccination against easily preventable diseases.

Advocates of antiretroviral drugs for HIV/AIDS often argue that treatment encourages prevention and slows transmission, since people do not have incentives to be tested unless treatment is available. However, the impact of antiretrovirals on the spread of the AIDS epidemic is unclear. Even if the availability of treatment encourages testing, knowledge of HIV status may not prevent the spread of the disease, since people who are infected may decide they have nothing left to lose. Moreover, while treatment with antiretroviral therapy may lower viral loads and reduce transmission, it may also help HIV-infected people stay sexually active longer, contributing to the spread of the disease. Finally, the expectation of treatment could reduce incentives to adopt safer behaviors. While there is no clear theoretical presumption about the effect of subsidizing antiretroviral therapies on the rate of transmission of HIV in low-income countries, there is at least some empirical evidence that the availability of treatment has led to a resurgence of risky behavior in the United States (Lehman et al., 2000). There is also anecdotal evidence that risky sexual behavior increased in Kenya following fraudulent announcements of an AIDS cure (McGreal, 1996).

Some advocates of antiretroviral treatment argue that public campaigns to extend antiretroviral treatment will generate enough new aid that both antiretrovirals and other interventions can be funded. It is worth bearing in mind, however, that even if 90 percent of funds for antiretroviral therapy were "new" foreign aid, and only 10 percent were diverted from vaccination efforts, more lives would be lost from reductions in vaccinations than would be gained through antiretroviral therapy. Calls for foreign assistance to provide antiretroviral therapy might thus stipulate that any available funds should be used in the way that saves the most lives, so that if only a small amount was provided, it would be used to cover low-cost interventions such as vaccinations, but that if a larger amount was made available, it could be used to cover antiretroviral therapy.

Since individual countries can potentially correct market failures within their borders, it may make sense to focus foreign assistance on the provision of global public goods. Key global public goods include slowing the development of drug resistance, creating knowledge on drug efficacy and safety, and, most important, R&D on new pharmaceuticals. Since the spread of a disease once it crosses national borders is determined primarily by conditions within the host nation, cross-border externalities from improved disease control are likely to be small, with the exception of diseases near eradication, such as smallpox in the 1970s and polio now.

Addressing misuse of pharmaceuticals

Since misuse of pharmaceuticals that facilitates the development of drug resistance creates negative externalities for the rest of the world, discouraging drug misuse is a global public good. However, the impact of pharmaceutical prices on externalities from drug resistance is ambiguous. Higher prices could reduce the number of people taking drugs and thus reduce the spread of drug resistance, but higher prices could also lead those people who do take the drug to take incomplete doses, promoting the spread of drug resistance. The latter effect may be particularly likely in developing countries, where pharmaceuticals are often taken with weak medical supervision. Conceivably, governments could require medicines to be packaged for sale only in complete courses and could penalize stores selling fractions of a course. However, shopkeepers in developing countries routinely sell individual units from packages, and monitoring this would be difficult. Another possibility would be to subsidize combination therapies that are less likely to induce drug resistance.[3]

Improving the overall quality of medical care would also reduce the spread of drug resistance by helping to ensure that pharmaceuticals are used appropriately and that patients are encouraged to complete the course of treatment. Branding and franchising of medical practices and care facilities could potentially help address the problems of asymmetric information between patients and providers. Mission hospitals in Africa have managed to develop reputations for providing quality care, for example (Leonard, 2002). Managing such branding efforts could be difficult, however, and the effectiveness of such efforts is uncertain. In some countries, the Internet might potentially play a role in facilitating the standardization of medical care. Clinic workers with only moderate levels of training could enter patient information, and programs on the Internet could offer possible diagnoses for them to consider as well as advice on when referrals are needed. Such a system could complement the services currently provided by health care workers and help to monitor whether local health care workers were showing up to work or were likely to be routinely mistreating patients. Efforts to experiment with such approaches deserve international support since they could potentially lead to innovations in health care delivery that would be beneficial across much of the developing world.

R&D on needed products

As discussed earlier, current incentives for the development of products needed primarily by developing countries are inadequate. Vaccines for malaria, tuberculosis and the strains of AIDS prevalent in Africa are a prime example. Programs to encourage R&D can take two broad forms. "Push" programs subsidize research inputs – for example, through grants to researchers or R&D tax credits. "Pull" programs reward research outputs, for example, by committing in advance to purchase a specified amount of a desired product at a specified price. Both approaches have important roles, but current policy underutilizes pull programs.

Push programs are subject to asymmetric information between researchers and program administrators and between these groups and politicians and the public, giving rise to both moral hazard and adverse selection. Moral hazard arises because funders cannot perfectly monitor the actions of grant recipients, and grant recipients may have incentives to devote effort to pursuing general scientific research or preparing their next grant application rather than focusing on development of the desired product. In contrast, under a pull program, researchers will not receive payment unless a useable product is delivered, so researchers have incentives to focus on developing the desired product.

Adverse selection arises because researchers have more information than do funders about the probability that their research will lead to successful products. Research administrators and their ultimate employers – elected officials and the general public – may not be able to determine which research projects in response to certain diseases are worth pursuing, nor which diseases and products should be targeted. Decision makers may therefore wind up financing ideas with only a minute probability of success, or worse, failing to fund promising research because they do not have confidence that its backers are presenting objective information on its prospects. In contrast, under a pull program in which developers are rewarded only if they successfully produce the desired product, there is a strong incentive for firms considering research investments to assess the prospects for success realistically.

The moral hazard and adverse selection problems that plague push programs are illustrated by the U.S. Agency for International Development's (USAID) 1980s program to develop a malaria vaccine. During the USAID program, external evaluators suggested that additional funding should not be provided to two of the three research teams. However, as a result of information provided by the project director, USAID provided substantial new resources to all three teams and was sufficiently confident that vaccines would be developed that it even arranged to purchase monkeys for testing a vaccine. Two of three researchers diverted grant funds into their private accounts and were later indicted for theft and criminal conspiracy. The project director received kickbacks from the contract to purchase monkeys and eventually pleaded guilty to accepting an illegal gratuity, filing false tax returns and making false statements. In 1984, before the indictments, the agency claimed that there had been a "major breakthrough in the development of a vaccine against the most deadly form of malaria in human beings. The vaccine should be ready for use around the world, especially in developing countries, within five years" (Desowitz, 1991). By the end of the project, USAID had spent $60 million on its malaria vaccine effort with few results. While the example is extreme, it vividly illustrates the problems with push programs.

As an alternative to direct government financing of research, some have proposed R&D tax credits targeted to private research on drugs and vaccines needed by developing countries. However, such tax credits are subject to similar problems. Firms would have an incentive to relabel as much of their R&D as possible as eligible for the targeted credit. For example, if there were an R&D tax credit for a malaria vaccine, researchers might focus on a vaccine that would likely only provide temporary protection and would be suitable for travelers and military personnel spending only short times in developing countries, but not for residents of these areas. To take another example, modern vaccines typically include both antigens specific to a particular organism and adjuvants that potentially boost the effectiveness of several different vaccines. Firms would have every incentive to claim that an adjuvant intended for an ineligible vaccine was actually for a malaria vaccine, so as to claim a tax credit. Finally, R&D tax credits will not improve access to products once they are developed.

In contrast, under pull programs, the public pays nothing unless a viable product is developed. Pull programs give researchers incentives to self-select projects with a reasonable chance of yielding a viable product and to focus on developing a marketable product. Under pull programs, governments do not need to "pick winners" among R&D proposals – they simply need to decide what success would be worth to society and offer a corresponding reward. Moreover, appropriately designed pull programs can help ensure that if new products are developed, they will reach those who need them. One kind of pull program is a purchase commitment in which sponsors would commit to purchase a specified number of doses at a specified price if a vaccine meeting certain specifications were developed. Purchase commitment programs are discussed in Kremer (2001a, b), World Bank (1999) and Batson and Ainsworth (2001), while shorter treatments of the idea in the popular press appear in Kremer and Sachs (1999) and Sachs (1999).[4] An example of a purchase commitment would be for developed countries or private foundations to commit to purchase malaria vaccine at $5 per immunized person and to make it available to developing countries either free or for a modest copayment.

A key limitation of pull programs is that they require specifying the output in advance. A pull program could not have been used to encourage the development of the Post-It Note® or the graphical user interface, because these products could not have been adequately described before they were invented. Similarly, pull programs may not work well to encourage basic research, because it is typically difficult to specify the desired results of basic research in advance. (Of course, some basic research outputs, such as proving Format's last theorem, can be defined in advance.) Simply rewarding the development of applied products is not a good way to stimulate basic research, since a program that tied rewards to the development of a specific product would encourage researchers to keep their results private as long as possible to have an advantage in the next stage of research. Indeed, a key objective of basic research is to provide information to other researchers, rather than to develop products, and grant-funded academics and scientists in government laboratories have career incentives to publish their results quickly. In contrast to unanticipated inventions, like the Post-It Note®, or to basic research, it is comparatively easier to define what is meant by a safe and efficacious vaccine, especially as existing institutions, such as the U.S. Food and Drug Administration (FDA), are already charged with making these determinations.

Nonetheless, if donor governments, international organizations or private foundations commit to purchase a future vaccine, the eligibility rules they set will be key. Eligibility conditions for candidate products would likely include some minimal technical requirements. These technical requirements could include clearance by a regulatory agency, such as the U.S. FDA, or a waiver of regulatory approval in developed countries for products that would pass a risk-benefit analysis for use in developing, but not developed, countries. Products that pass these requirements might then be subject to a market test: nations wishing to purchase products might be required to provide a modest copayment tied to their per capita income, so that countries would have an incentive to investigate carefully whether candidate products are appropriate for their local conditions. This provision would also help to assure that limited donor funds are allocated well and would increase incentives for developers by increasing the payment offered to the successful developer. On the other hand, it could reduce the confidence of potential vaccine developers in the program. A purchase commitment could also include a system of bonus payments for products that exceed the minimum requirements. Eligibility conditions should also specify who will have authority to judge whether the eligibility conditions have been fulfilled. Ideally, these adjudicators should be insulated from political pressure through long terms of service.

A well-written contract should also be credible to potential vaccine developers. Courts have held that similar public commitments to reward contest winners or to purchase specified goods constitute legally binding contracts and that the decisions of independent parties appointed in advance to adjudicate such programs are binding. For example, in the 1960s, the U.S. government pledged to purchase, at a minimum price, domestically produced manganese. After the world price of the commodity fell, the General Services Administration (GSA), the U.S. agency in charge of administering the program, attempted to renege, but U.S. courts forced the GSA to honor the commitment (Morantz and Sloane, 2001).

The total market promised by a purchase commitment should be large enough to induce substantial effort by vaccine developers, but less than the social value of the vaccine. The larger the market for a product, the more firms will enter the field, the more research leads each firm will pursue, and the faster a product will be developed. Given the enormous burden of diseases such as malaria, tuberculosis, and HIV/AIDS, it is important to provide sufficient incentive for many researchers to enter the field and to induce major pharmaceutical firms to pursue several potential leads simultaneously so that products can be developed quickly. There is little risk that payments made as a result of a purchase commitment could exceed the cost of saving the equivalent number of lives using today's treatments.

Prior work by the author and others suggests that an annual market of $250 million to $500 million is needed to motivate substantial research (Kettler, 1999; Kremer, 2001b; Mercer Management Consulting, 1998). A commitment at this level to purchase vaccines for malaria, tuberculosis and HIV/AIDS would be extremely cost effective, costing nothing if a useable product was not developed and as little as $4 per year of life saved if a vaccine were developed.

Purchase commitments could potentially be implemented by national governments, international organizations, or private foundations. A number of policymakers have indicated interest in this approach. As U.S. Treasury Secretary, Lawrence Summers advocated a closely related tax credit for sales of vaccines, where every dollar of qualifying vaccine sales to nonprofit and international organizations serving developing countries would be matched by a dollar of tax credit, effectively doubling the incentive to develop vaccines for neglected diseases. This proposal was part of the Clinton administration's FY 2001 budget, but did not become law. Senators William Frist (R-TN) and John Kerry (D-MA) and Representatives Nancy Pelosi (D-CA) and Jennifer Dunn (R-WA) have proposed both the tax measure and a purchase commitment in the Vaccines for the New Millennium Act.

The purchase commitment approach has also attracted interest from policymakers internationally, including the United Kingdom's Chancellor of the Exchequer, the United Kingdom Cabinet Office, the German foreign minister, and the Dutch development minister (Brown, 2001; Elliott and Atkinson, 2001; PIU, 2001). The World Bank president, James Wolfensohn, has said that the institution plans to create a $1 billion fund to help countries purchase specified vaccines if and when they are developed ("Discovering Medicines for the Poor," 2000). However, the World Bank has yet to act on this commitment. The Gates Foundation, with $22 billion in assets and a focus on children's health in developing countries and vaccines in particular, is also well-placed to forward a vaccine purchase commitment. While continuing to fund its other priorities, such a foundation could simply pledge that if a product were actually developed, the foundation would purchase and distribute it in developing countries.

Drug regulation and procurement

The case of rotavirus vaccine suggests that if developing countries simply rely on regulatory institutions in developed countries, decisions will not always be appropriate given the different benefit-cost ratios for particular pharmaceuticals in developing countries. On the other hand, the Kenyan and South African governments' endorsement of ineffective but domestically developed AIDS "cures" suggests that if individual developing countries without adequate domestic institutions make regulatory decisions, decisions may reflect politics and nationalism as much as health concerns. Since gathering information on drug safety and efficacy is an international public good, there may be a role for an international body to review developed country pharmaceutical approval decisions for relevance to developing country conditions and, where appropriate, to sponsor additional trials or issue alternative certification. The organization could make a recommendation on the appropriateness of the product for use in different circumstances, and each country could then decide whether to follow that recommendation. However, the World Health Organization has historically eschewed such a role, and it is not clear that it is equipped to act as a regulatory body. Like many other international organizations, the quality of WHO'S work sometimes suffers as member countries invest resources in seeking funding, contracts, or leadership positions rather than in trying to improve the organization as a whole.[5]

Milton Friedman (Friedman and Friedman, 1980) has suggested replacing pharmaceutical regulation and prescription requirements with a system of mandatory labeling and letting consumers make their own decisions on pharmaceutical use. While proponents of strict drug regulation point to disasters of premature approval, such as thalidomide, opponents argue that the health burden of regulatory delays in approving new drugs far exceeds the health costs of these well-publicized disasters. It seems possible, for example, that the failure to proceed with the rotavirus vaccine in developing countries will cost millions of lives.

In my view, the justification for pharmaceutical regulation needs to be reconceptualized. Were the declared purpose of pharmaceutical regulation – to protect current consumers from unsafe and ineffective drugs – the main reason for regulation, Friedman's (Friedman and Friedman, 1980) proposal would be appealing. I would argue, however, that the primary advantage of drug regulation is that it creates incentives for firms to conduct the randomized trials that provide information on product effectiveness for future consumers. The current regulatory system, in which products that have not undergone clinical trials cannot be sold legally, gives pharmaceutical firms an incentive to conduct these trials and to do so in a rigorous enough manner to pass muster with regulators. If new pharmaceuticals were available during trials, it may be difficult to preserve the integrity of the comparison group necessary for conducting randomized trials. Seen in this light, drug regulation denies current consumers the option of taking unproven drugs, but it provides future consumers with information about the drugs.

Since incentives from large rich country markets are sufficient to encourage testing, small poor countries may want to consider requiring labels that tell customers whether the product received regulatory approval, but not prohibiting sales of products for which approval had not been granted. On the other hand, the traditional justification for drug regulation may better apply in environments where consumers are often illiterate, deceptive advertising is difficult to regulate and tort law is weak. In such environments, replacing prohibition with labeling could potentially exacerbate misuse of pharmaceuticals. The best case for replacing drug regulation with labeling requirements could therefore be made in small developed countries, such as Australia or New Zealand.

Some have proposed posting information on all public pharmaceutical purchases on the Internet as a way to improve pharmaceutical procurement by developing country governments, and such a system has been tried in Brazil. This system has been advocated as a way to provide information to ill-informed public purchasers and strengthen their bargaining power, but posting prices could also facilitate collusion among suppliers to keep prices high. A better rationale for the system is that publicly posting prices could help reduce corruption in drug procurement, which is likely a bigger problem than collusion by sellers.

Conclusions

Pharmaceuticals have brought tremendous health improvements to developing countries. The international community could greatly increase these benefits by implementing systems to provide better access to existing pharmaceuticals and to manage their use, as well as by investing in the global public good of R&D on diseases that disproportionately affect the poor. Developing countries could redirect their health budgets away from salaries and toward cost-effective public health measures, such as vaccination and school-based control of intestinal worms, and could explore institutional reforms for health care delivery. Developed countries and international organizations could encourage differential pricing, allow more favorable tax treatment of appropriate drug donations, and encourage R&D and facilitate access to new products by committing in advance to purchase products needed in developing countries if and when they are developed.

Notes

I am grateful to Jessica Leino for outstanding research assistance and to Ernst Berndt, Jishnu Das, Brad De Long, Varun Gauri, Dean Jamison, Lynn Johnson, Jenny Lanjouw, Mead Over, Timothy Taylor, Michael Waldman and David Webber for suggestions.

1   Data are from Balke and Gordon (1989), Johnston and Williamson (2002), Kurian (1994) and World Bank (2001b). Even if GDP growth in the United States were underestimated by two percentage points annually, 1990 U.S. per capita GDP exceeds Vietnam's current per capita GDP.
2   See Di Tella and Schargrodsky (2001) on purchases by public hospitals in Argentina.
3   For example, Mead Over has suggested that subsidizing combination therapies for AIDS might reduce the risk of drug resistance developing since while this practice would encourage greater use of multidrug therapy, it might discourage the use of monotherapies that are more prone to drug resistance.
4   An alternative push program design that has been proposed is to reward developers with extensions of patents on other pharmaceuticals. This would inefficiently and inequitably place the entire burden of financing development on patients who need these other pharmaceuticals. For example, giving a patent extension on Prozac for developing an HIV vaccine could prevent some people from getting needed treatment for depression.
5   For instance, in 1993, Hiroshi Nakajima was re-elected to head WHO amid allegations that Japan bribed developing nations to vote for the Japanese Director General (Crossette, 1998).

References

Adams, Gregor et al. 2001. "Consensus Statement on Antiretroviral Treatment for AIDS in Poor Countries." Available at <http://www.hsph.harvard.edu/organizations/hai/overview/news_events/events/consensus.html>.

Ammassari, Adriana et al. 2001. "Self-Reported Symptoms and Medication Side Effects Influence Adherence to Highly Active Antiretroviral Therapy in Persons with HIV Infection." *Journal of Acquired Immune Deficiency Syndromes*. December 15, 28:5, pp. 445–49.

Attaran, Amir and Lee Gillespie-White. 2001. "Do Patents for Antiretroviral Drugs Constrain Access to AIDS Treatment in Africa?" *Journal of the American Medical Association*, October 17, 286: 15, pp. 1886–892.

Balke, Nathan S. and Robert J. Gordon. 1989. "The Estimation of Prewar Gross National Product: Methodology and New Evidence." *Journal of Political Economy*. February, 97, pp. 38–92.

Batson, Amie and Martha Ainsworth. 2001. "Private Investment in AIDS Vaccine Development: Obstacles and Solutions." *Bulletin of the World Health Organization*. 79:8, pp. 721–27.

Brook, M.G. et al. 2001. "Adherence to Highly Active Antiretroviral Therapy in the Real World: Experience of Twelve English HIV Units." *AIDS Patient Care STDS*. September, 15:9, pp. 491–94.

Brown, Gordon. 2001. Speech given by Gordon Brown, Chancellor of the Exchequer, at the International Conference Against Child Poverty, London, February 26. Available at <http://www.hm-treasury.gov.uk/docs/2001/child_poverty/chxspeech.htm).

CMH (Commission on Macroeconomics and Health). 2001. "Macroeconomics and Health: Investing for Health." Available at <http://www.cid.harvard.edu/cidcmh/CMHReport.pdf>.

Costa, Dora. 2001. "Estimating Real Income in the United States from 1988 to 1994: Correcting CPI Bias Using Engel CURVES." *Journal of Political Economy*. December, 109:6, pp. 1288–310.

Crossette, Barbara. 1998. "At W.H.O., 2 Physicians Lead the Race for Top Job." *New York Times*. January 11, Section 1, p. 4.

CVI (Children's Vaccine Initiative). 1999. CVI Forum No. 16. Geneva.

Das, Jishnu. 2000. "Do Patients Learn About Doctor Quality?: Theory and an Application to India." Manuscript, Harvard.

Desowitz, Robert S. 1991. *The Malaria Capers: Tales of Parasites and People*. New York: W. W. Norton.

Di Tella, Rafael and Ernesto Schargrodsky. 2001. "The Role of Wages and Auditing during a Crackdown on Corruption in the City of Buenos Aires." Manuscript, Harvard.

Elliott, Larry and Mark Atkinson. 2001. "Fund to Beat Third World Disease." *Guardian*. February 23. Available at <http://www.guardian.co.uk/international/story/0,3604,441835,00.html>.

"Discovering Medicines for the Poor." 2000. *Financial Times*. February 2, p. 7.

Fogel, Robert W. 1986. "Nutrition and the Decline in Mortality Since 1700: Some Preliminary Findings," in *Long-Term Factors in American Economic Growth*. Stanley L. Engerman and Robert E. Gallman, eds. Chicago: University of Chicago Press, pp. 439–527.

Friedman, Milton and Rose Friedman. 1980. *Free to Choose*. New York: Harcourt Brace Jovanovich.

Glennerster, Rachel and Michael Kremer. 2001. "A Vaccine Purchase Commitment: Cost-Effectiveness Estimates and Pricing Guidelines." Unpublished Manuscript.

Jamison, Dean T. et al. 2001. "Cross-Country Variation in Mortality Decline, 1962–87: The Role of Country-Specific Technical Progress." CMH Working Paper No. WG1:4, April.

Johnston, Louis and Samuel H. Williamson. 2002. "The Annual Real and Nominal GDP for the United States, 1789–Present." Economic History Services, April, available at <http://www.eh.net/hmit/gdp/>.

Kamat, Vinay R. and Mark Nichter. 1998. "Pharmacies, Self-Medication and Pharmaceutical Marketing in Bombay, India." Social Science and Medicine. 47:6, pp. 779–94.

Kettler, Hannah E. 1999. "Updating the Cost of a New Chemical Entity." London, Office of Health Economics.

Kim-Farley, R. and the Expanded Programme on Immunization Team. 1992. "Global Immunization." Annual Review of Public Health. 13, pp. 223–37.

Kremer, Michael. 2001a. "Creating Markets for New Vaccines: Part I: Rationale," in Innovation Policy and the Economy. Adam B. Jaffe, Josh Lerner, and Scott Stern, eds. Cambridge: MIT Press, pp. 35–72.

Kremer, Michael. 2001b. "Creating Markets for New Vaccines: Part II: Design Issues," in Innovation Policy and the Economy. Adam B. Jaffe, Josh Lerner, and Scott Stern, eds. Cambridge: MIT Press, pp. 73–118.

Kremer, Michael and Jeffrey Sachs. 1999. "A Cure for Indifference." Financial Times. May 5, available at <http://www.brook.edu/views/oped/kremer/19990505.htm>.

Kurian, George Thomas. 1994. Datapedia of the United States 1790–2000. Lanham, Md.: Bernan Press.

Lanjouw, Jean O. 2001. "A Patent Policy Proposal for Global Diseases." Brookings Policy Brief, June.

Lanjouw, Jean O. and Iain M. Cockburn. 2001. "New Pills for Poor People? Empirical Evidence after GATT." World Development. 29:2, pp. 265–89.

Lehman, Stan et al. 2000. "Are At-Risk Populations Less Concerned about HIV Infection in the HAART Era?" San Francisco, CDC Seventh Conference on Retroviruses and Opportunistic Infections, January 30–February 2.

Leonard, Kenneth L. 2002. "When Both States and Markets Fail: Asymmetric Information and the Role of NGOs in African Health Care." International Review of Law and Economics. July, 22:1, pp. 61–81.

Marseille, E. et al. 1999. "Cost-Effectiveness of Single-Dose Nevirapine Regimen for Mothers and Babies to Decrease Vertical HIV-1 Transmission in sub-Saharan Africa," Lancet, September 4, 354:9181, pp. 803–09.

McGreal, Chris. 1996. "Horror Greets AIDS 'Miracle Cure.'" Guardian. May 25, p. 11.

Mercer Management Consulting. 1998. "HIV Vaccine Industry Study October-December 1998." World Bank Task Force on Accelerating the Development of an HIV/AIDS Vaccine for Developing Countries.

Miguel, Edward and Michael Kremer. 2002. "Worms: Education and Health Externalities in Kenya." Manuscript, Harvard.

Mitchell, Violaine S. et al. 1993. The Children's Vaccine Initiative: Achieving the Vision. Washington, D.C.: National Academy Press.

Morantz, Alison and Robert Sloane. 2001. ''Vaccine Purchase Commitment Contract: Legal Strategies for Ensuring Enforceability," Mimeo, Harvard University.

Murphy, Trudy V. et al. 2001a. "Intussusception Among Infants Given an Oral Rotavirus Vaccine." *New England Journal of Medicine*, February 22, 344:8, pp. 564–72.

Murphy, Trudy V. et al. 2001b. "Intussusception and an Oral Rotavirus Vaccine." *New England Journal of Medicine*. June 14, 344:24, pp. 1866–867.

Murray, Christopher J. L. and Alan D. Lopez. 1996. *The Global Burden of Disease: a Comprehensive Assessment of Mortality and Disability from Diseases, Injuries, and Risk Factors in 1990 and Projected to 2020. Global Burden of Disease and Injury Series, Volume 1.* Cambridge, Mass.: Published by the Harvard School of Public Health on behalf of the World Health Organization and the World Bank, Distributed by Harvard University Press.

Neumann, Peter J. et al. 2000. "Are Pharmaceuticals Cost-Effective? A Review of the Evidence." *Health Affairs*. March/April. 19:2, pp. 92–109.

Nichter, Mark and Mimi Nichter. 1996. *Anthropology and International Health: Asian Case Studies.* Amsterdam: Gordon and Breach.

Nieuwkerk, P.T. et al. 2001. "Limited Patient Adherence to Highly Active Antiretroviral Therapy for HIV-1 Infection in an Observational Cohort Study." *Archives of Internal Medicine.* September 10, 161:16, pp. 1962–968.

NIH (National Institutes of Health). 2000. "Fact Sheet: Antimicrobial Resistance." Available at <http://www.niaid.nih.gov/factsheets/antimicro.htm/>, June.

Pecoul, Bernard et al. 1999. "Access to Essential Drugs in Poor Countries: A Lost Battle?" *Journal of the American Medical Association.* January 27, 281:4, pp. 361–67.

Phadke, Anant. 1998. *Drug Supply and Use: Towards a Rational Policy in India.* New Delhi: Sage Publications.

PhRMA. 2000. *PhRMA Industry Profile 2000.* Available at <http://www.phrma.org/publications/publications/profile00/>.

PIU (Performance and Innovation Unit, Cabinet Office). 2001. "Tackling the Disease of Poverty: Meeting the Okinawa/Millenium Targets for HIV/AIDS, Tuberculosis, and Malaria." London, May 8. Available at <http://www.cabinet-office.gov.uk/innovation/healthreport/default.htm>.

Preston, Samuel H. 1975. "The Changing Relation between Mortality and Level of Economic Development." *Population Studies.* July, 29:2, pp. 231–48.

Sachs, Jeffrey. 1999. "Helping the World's Poorest." *Economist.* August 14, 352:8132, pp. 17–20.

United States Census. 2000. Available at <http://www.census.gov/dmd/www/2k home.htm>.

Walley, John D. et al. 2001. "Effectiveness of the Direct Observation Component of DOTS for Tuberculosis: A Randomised Controlled Trial in Pakistan." *Lancet.* March 3, 357, pp. 664–69.

WHO (World Health Organization). 1996. *Investing in Health Research and Development: Report of the Ad Hoc Committee on Health Research Relating to Future Intervention Options.* Geneva: WHO.

WHO (World Health Organization). 2000. *World Heath Report 2000.* Geneva: WHO.

WHO (World Health Organization). 2001. *World Health Report 2001.* Geneva: WHO.

World Bank. 1999. *Confronting AIDS: Public Priorities in a Global Epidemic.* Washington, D.C.: Oxford University Press.

World Bank. 2001a. *Immunization at a Glance.* Washington, D.C.: World Bank, November.

World Bank. 2001b. *World Development Indicators.* Washington, D.C.: Oxford University Press.

WTO. 2001a. ''Fact Sheet: TRIPS and Pharmaceutical Patents.'' April.

WTO. 2001b. "Declaration on the TRIPS Agreement and Public Health." Available at <http://www-chil.wto-ministerial.org/english/thewto_e/minist_e/min01_e/min01_l4nov_e.htm>.

REVIEW AND DISCUSSION QUESTIONS

1   What are the major differences between the market for pharmaceuticals in developing countries and the market for pharmaceuticals in high-income countries?

2   Pharmaceutical companies have few economic incentives to invest in developing drugs to treat diseases that affect mostly developing countries. Why don't governments in such countries make a greater effort to provide companies with greater incentives (e.g., subsidies for such research)?

3   Explain what price discrimination is and why pharmaceutical companies are reluctant to engage in it; also discuss possible alternatives to it.

4   Explain why Kremer does not consider the provision of antiretroviral treatment in developing countries to be a priority in the fight against HIV/AIDS.

5   Explain the difference between "push" and "pull" programs to encourage research and development of new drugs. What are the advantages and disadvantages of each approach?

Chapter 22

Kenneth J. Arrow

NEW ANTIMALARIAL DRUGS
Biology and economics meet

MALARIA HAS BEEN AND REMAINS one of the greatest scourges of humanity. Its geographical range is wide, even today. It is a particularly devastating health problem in Africa, especially between the Sahara Desert and South Africa. At one time, malaria was a major illness in the southern United States and southern Europe and was much more widespread in Latin America. Although figures are far from reliable, malaria deaths are estimated at over one million children a year – about 9 percent of all childhood deaths. However, with malaria more than many other killer diseases, mortality is a small fraction of morbidity. In the highly epidemic regions of Africa, the approximately 650,000,000 inhabitants are infected, on average, more than once a year.

The economic implications of a frequently sick population are evident. To some observers, the economic retardation of sub-Saharan Africa can be substantially explained by the prevalence of malaria. In addition to its direct effects on productivity, the presence of this devastating disease scares off foreign investors and traders.

There are several strategies other than drugs for controlling and reducing the incidence of malaria: draining standing water, spraying pesticides on potential breeding grounds for mosquitoes and on houses, and using netting to protect people from mosquito bites at night. Vaccine development continues but offers no medium-term prospects. These strategies are all important, but none is likely to eliminate malaria, especially in sub-Saharan Africa. Drugs remain our best hope. In this article, I focus on the use of drugs to combat malaria and the need for those currently in use in Africa to be replaced by new and much more expensive ones – the subject of a study by a committee, which I chair, of the Institute of Medicine of the U.S. National Academy of Sciences.

Alternative drugs

A synthetic variation of quinine, called chloroquine, was introduced into general usage around 1950. It was effective and, at about 10 cents a treatment, remarkably cheap. Cost was no obstacle to its use, even in the poorest countries. Chloroquine was and still is widely used in Africa, Southeast Asia, and India, where it has contributed greatly to the control of malaria. But as a result of mutation, the malaria parasite has become resistant to chloroquine in Southeast Asia and most parts of East Africa. The resistant strains will soon undoubtedly take over elsewhere, such as in West Africa. An alternative inexpensive drug, sulfadoxine-pyremethamine, which replaced chloroquine in some places, has also been effective. But resistance to it developed even more rapidly than to chloroquine.

Faced with malaria in its southern areas, Chinese researchers reexamined traditional herbal medicine – specifically the claim that *Artemisia annua* (sweet wormwood) was useful against fevers and particularly periodic fevers (presumably malaria). Researchers were able to verify that claim and identify the active antimalarial elements in *Artemisia*. These derivatives, artemisinins, are the standard and highly effective treatment in Vietnam and Thailand and are increasingly being used in India. So far, despite intense use of artemisinins in Southeast Asia, the malaria parasite does not appear to have developed resistance. Their only immediate drawback is cost – about $2 a treatment. In moderate- and high-income countries, this amount would be of no consequence. But in low-income countries, which have the greatest malaria incidence and where individuals may be infected a few times a year, the cost would be prohibitive – even though costs per death averted are remarkably low.

One other consideration is the knowledge that resistance to artemisinins will develop. For this reason, it is widely agreed that artemisinins should be given in combination with some other medication (artemisinin combination therapy, or ACT). The emergence of resistance would thus require two simultaneous mutations, a most unlikely event. And the combination conveys therapeutic advantages while raising the cost only slightly, if at all, over artemisinin monotherapy.

Drug production and distribution

What are the critical economic aspects of antimalarials? First, because malaria affects only poor nations – those with highly restricted purchasing power – biology collides with economics. The creation of new pharmaceuticals involves high fixed expenses for research, development, and testing. These expenses are recovered, and profits made, in the markup of the price charged for a drug over the costs of producing it. Government imposition of temporary monopolies – patents – allows this markup in what would otherwise be competitive markets. But poor countries cannot afford the markup.

When the demand for a drug is worldwide, it is possible to charge more in richer countries than in poor countries. Such price discrimination is clearly emerging for antiretroviral drugs to treat AIDS and the drugs needed for tuberculosis, and it has characterized other drugs. But, with malaria, there is no scope to recover the fixed costs in the countries most affected. Development of new antimalarials has consequently been confined to a dwindling number of private companies, the U.S. military, and public-private partnerships.

Second, the distribution of antimalarials in Africa is, for the most part, private. Governments, of course, set standards and impose tariffs, but drugs are largely imported, distributed, and sold at retail through purely market transactions. Although there are exceptions, public health systems are geographically less dense than retail stores, drugs in these facilities are frequently out of stock, and their operation is unpredictable. There seems no reason to expect their operation to improve enough to handle the proposed ACTs. Hence, it is important to ensure that private distribution continues for the time being.

Third, the costs of producing artemisinins and ACTs should, according to all precedents, decline because of larger scales of production, experience, and innovation (for example, artemisinins and chemically related drugs will probably be produced through synthesis instead of extraction from plants). But increasing supplies in the near future will take time – it takes about 18 months to plant and bring *Artemisia* to maturity – as will increasing productive capacity. Moreover, there must be ways to encourage competition, particularly through modifications of the drugs or of their manufacturing processes.

A possible new direction

For a large and expanding part of the world, avoiding deaths from malaria will require much greater use of artemisinins. Protecting artemisinins from resistance will require combination therapy. How can the international public sector create financial and other incentives for countries and individuals to use artemisinins and to use them in combinations? Suppose, for the moment, we assume that ACTs must be subsidized because of their cost relative to African incomes. The case for doing so is strong. How is this best accomplished? Policymakers will need to find a way to provide a reliable and predictable demand for ACTS to encourage planting of *Artemisia* and a building up of capacity. They must not interfere with the functioning of the existing private distribution system and must prevent the diversion of funds to other purposes by governments or other agencies. Policymakers will also need to implement mechanisms for maintaining quality control over the manufacturers – internationally subsidized centralized-purchasing and quality-control mechanisms are one possible approach, particularly if allowed to supply private sector distribution systems.

What is the justification for subsidizing a particular good (antimalarial drugs or ACTS, in particular) rather than making general income transfers to poor countries? A standard economic argument says that imposing constraints on an individual's spending is bound to reduce his or her welfare. Therefore, it is usually concluded, income transfers should take the form of purchasing power and not of specific goods. For this reason, most advanced countries have largely abandoned housing subsidies. The counterarguments take three forms: the recipient does not know his or her welfare as well as the giver; the direct recipient is the local government, whose interests may conflict with those of the people; and spending has spillover effects (externalities). There is also the idea that antimalarials are an international public good. If a country does not use ACT – in particular if it uses artemisinins as monotherapy – resistance is more likely to develop. With international travel, the spread of resistance is inevitable, and currently no other effective drug is available for widespread use. Another kind of externality is that donor nations are clearly more willing to give to overcome disease than for other reasons.

Finally, how can we, in the longer run, encourage the further development of antimalarial drugs and related strategies? Even better therapies are clearly possible, such as a single-dose drug that is as effective as artemisinins. Malaria vaccines have been researched but still need extensive exploration. Given the lack of research by major pharmaceutical companies (because there is no profitable market), there must be a lot of unexplored potential. What incentives can be created to encourage private and public research of these issues? Something beyond ordinary intellectual property rights seems to be necessary: public sector investment in research and development.

Note

This paper draws on the author's experience as Chair of the Committee on the Economics of Anti-Malarial Drugs of the Institute of Medicine. The opinions expressed are strictly his and are not to be attributed to the institute or the committee. The committee will publish its report in the spring of 2004.

REVIEW AND DISCUSSION QUESTIONS

1   Why does Arrow believe that the traditional drugs used to treat malaria (such as chloroquine) will need to be replaced?
2   What are the economic obstacles to greater production and more widespread distribution of effective antimalarial drugs?
3   What "new direction" does Arrow propose to improve treatment of malaria? Do you agree with his recommendations? Why or why not?

Chapter 23

THE ECONOMIST

THE LEARNING DEFICIT

Lack of education holds much of the world back. Would more money help?

PEOPLE IN RICH COUNTRIES OFTEN have little sense of how poor the quality of education is in many developing countries. Where schools exist, there may be no teachers; and where teachers are employed, often they might as well not be, either because they fail to turn up or because, even if they do appear, they do not know how to teach. Schools may be shacks, lacking basic equipment such as desks or chairs, with few if any teaching materials such as books, paper and pencils. Up to now, much stress has been laid on raising the proportion of children who enrol in schools (and, to a lesser extent, on ensuring that they keep going once they have enrolled). But what is the point of "universal enrolment" if schools and teachers are unable to provide a decent education?

This is one of the points emphasised by Lant Pritchett of Harvard University, in a new paper for the Copenhagen Consensus project.* It is important, he argues, to concentrate on educational achievement, rather than on simpler but potentially misleading measures of success. Only in that way will it be possible to know in what way extra resources can best be deployed in improving education in poor countries, and what sort of value for money might then be expected.

There is no question that education in many third-world countries is failing. Some of the findings reviewed by Mr Pritchett are positively startling. With the exception of eastern Europe, the former Soviet Union and the East Asian tigers, the developing countries lag far behind the rich OECD countries on measures of learning achievement – and most such comparisons, remember, underestimate the gap because test results are available only for children who actually attend school, which many children in poor countries do not. Even on this basis, results show that most developing countries have levels of educational attainment that are not merely at the lower end of the range for OECD countries, but far worse than even the worst-performing rich country (which is Greece, by the way).

In the most recent assessment, only 3% of students in Indonesia had a reading competence better than the average of French students; the average Brazilian student had maths skills at the level of the lowest 2% of Danish students. Americans worry from time to time about the undeniably impressive lead that Japanese students have over students in the United States – but the gap between American students and students in Peru is fully three times bigger.

There can be no doubt that an educational deficit as wide as this is holding poor countries back, thwarting the opportunities that they might otherwise be able to exploit in a rapidly globalising world economy. What, then, can be done?

Money changes everything?

Supposing that more resources were made available – the premise of the Copenhagen Consensus project – Mr Pritchett considers four broad ways of using them. First, build more schools. Second, improve the quality of existing school systems, either by expanding budgets across the board or by increasing spending in specific target areas. These first two ideas aim to increase the supply of education. Third, raise the demand for education, either through interventions that raise living standards generally, or by fostering new opportunities for the better educated. Fourth, raise the demand for education by reducing its cost to consumers.

Mr Pritchett weighs the pros and cons of each approach. He sees some scope for making progress by targeting additional resources to particular supply-side bottlenecks. These may be important in some countries. Raising the demand for education would help even more. Economic growth is pro-education, because higher living standards do raise the demand for schooling – but, obviously, policies to raise the growth rate need not be educational policies at all in the usual sense.

In any event, all four of the "policy-action opportunities" take the overall structure of existing education systems and methods for granted. And for that reason, Mr Pritchett argues, all four are neglecting the main issue: "the problem in many countries is the way in which the production of schooling is organised." Systemic reform – involving clear objectives for the school system, adequate financing, autonomy for schools in "managing for results", and proper accountability of schools to their users – may be necessary before higher spending on any of the four policy-action opportunities can be expected to succeed.

There are many ways to press forward this kind of systemic reform, Mr Pritchett argues. Vouchers and a "market" for education might work well in some circumstances, but other approaches could achieve good results too in some cases: school autonomy (as granted to "charter schools" in the United States, for instance), decentralisation of control, community management, and the use of non-government providers, could all, Mr Pritchett argues, serve the goal of structural reform that he regards as necessary if the application of extra resources is to succeed.

One striking indication of how easy it is to spend money fruitlessly in education comes from the rich countries. According to one study cited by Mr Pritchett, Britain increased its real spending per pupil by 77% between 1970 and 1994; over the same period, the assessment score for learning in maths and science fell by 8%. Australia increased its real spending per pupil by 270%; its pupils' scores fell by 2%. Extra spending by itself is likely to be no more successful in the poor countries than it has been in the rich.

Overall expansion of education systems – the first policy-action opportunity – is likely to work well only in countries where demand exceeds supply (which would be indicated by large class sizes and children travelling great distances to school) and where new schools of good quality can be readily provided. These conditions are rarely satisfied, Mr Pritchett finds. In practice, lack of appropriate incentives for the efficient supply of education frustrates most spending initiatives, even those that try hard to spend money only where it is most needed. The most promising way forward is to embark on reforms that provide for greater autonomy and local accountability for schools. In many cases, Mr Pritchett notes, some extra financing may indeed help to facilitate those changes. But in improving education in the developing countries, additional resources are not usually the crux of the matter.

Note

* The Copenhagen Consensus project, organised by Denmark's Environmental Assessment Institute with the cooperation of *The Economist*, aims to consider, and to establish priorities among, a series of proposals for advancing global welfare. The initiative was described in our Economics focus of March 6th. That article can be read along with other material, including an Economics Focus on armed conflicts, published this week in our print edition. A book, "Global Crises, Global Solutions", containing the full set of papers written for the project is forthcoming from Cambridge University Press.

REVIEW AND DISCUSSION QUESTIONS

1 Why might building more schools or sending more children to school have a limited impact on economic development in poor countries?
2 What kind of reforms does Pritchett suggest to increase the effectiveness of educational investments?
3 Do you agree with Pritchett's recommendations? Why or why not? Explain.

Chapter 24

Clive Crook

THE TEN-CENT SOLUTION

First principles

Cheap private schools are educating poor children across the developing world – but without much encouragement from the international aid establishment.

IF GOOD IDEAS WERE ALL THAT MATTERED, everybody who has heard of Jeffrey Sachs would have heard of James Tooley as well – but they aren't, and you almost certainly haven't. In fact, even if you are keenly interested in education, aid, or Third World development, which are Tooley's areas of research, you still probably haven't heard of him.

This is not because his work is dull or unimportant. His findings are surprising, and they bear directly and profoundly on the relief of extreme poverty all over the world. (Name me a more important issue than that.) The reason you haven't heard of James Tooley is that his work is something of an embarrassment to the official aid and development industry. He has demonstrated something that many development professionals would rather not know – and would prefer that you not know, either.

Tooley is a professor of education policy at England's University of Newcastle upon Tyne. Several years ago he was working as a consultant in Hyderabad, India, for the International Finance Corporation, an arm of the World Bank. One afternoon, while wandering around the alleys beside the Charminar (a sixteenth-century monument and Hyderabad's best-known tourist attraction), he came across a school for the children of slum dwellers. To his surprise, he found that this was not a state school but a private one – providing education to the extremely poor and collecting fees (of a few rupees a day, or less than a dime) for its services. Intrigued, he kept looking, and found other, similar schools. They were typically small and shabby operations, sometimes occupying a single classroom, staffed in some cases by just the teacher-proprietor and an assistant. Yet they were busy – crowded with eager pupils – and the teacher was actually teaching. (This, Tooley knew, was not something you could take for granted in the classrooms of Indian public schools.)

For years education officials in most developing countries (and workers in international aid agencies, too) have talked as though private education for the very poor barely existed. The only hope for equipping these unfortunate people with basic literacy and numeracy, they've said, was to improve the reach and quality of free, compulsory, state-provided schooling.

But that hope appears dim at the moment. Public schools in most poor countries, where they operate at all, have long been recognized to be ineffective. Teachers are frequently unqualified for their work. Perhaps worse, they are often uninterested in it: In many poor countries, teaching jobs are viewed as sinecures, and many teachers are disinclined to show up for work at all. They do tend to organize, however. Their salaries add up, and public schools in most developing countries make heavy demands on the public purse. The whole issue has therefore been seen as a daunting question of resources: Vast sums will be required to provide free universal education of tolerable quality in Africa and South Asia; there is no cheap alternative; and the help of foreign donors will be essential.

The many fee-based slum schools that Tooley saw within a few minutes' walk of the Charminar made him wonder about all this. So he began researching the reach and performance of private schools for the extremely poor in India and elsewhere, supported not by an official agency but by the private Templeton Foundation. What he found was startling.

In Hyderabad, a city of more than 6 million people, Tooley and his team – confining their search to poor areas lacking amenities such as running water, electricity, and paved roads – counted 918 schools. Only about 40 percent were run or financed by the government; 60 percent were private. Of those, some were "recognized" by the government, but most were officially unknown to the authorities. These black-market private schools were smaller on average than the other kinds – but they still accounted for about a quarter of all the children in any sort of school. Remarkably, some of the slots in these private slum schools were offered free or at reduced rates: The parents of full-fee students, desperately poor themselves, willingly subsidized those in direst need.

This flourishing educational enterprise is all the more surprising once you understand that India has deliberately discriminated against private education – forbidding for-profit schools, for instance, and requiring schools to be run as trusts rather than proprietorships, and limiting their ability to borrow. Despite these handicaps, private education for the very poor has evidently thrived.

What Tooley stumbled onto in Hyderabad turns out to be typical not just of India but of all the other places he subsequently researched – including parts of China, Ghana, Kenya, and Nigeria In every case, private education is a principal lifeline for the abjectly poor. In the areas of Ghana and Nigeria that Tooley's team has canvassed, an outright majority of poor children are attending private schools run without support from the government. Often, the schools are run by just a few teachers. They put out shingles in the way that physicians do in the United States, and are paid directly by their charges.

As Tooley relates it, the response of the international development community to his research has been less than enthusiastic. Even if private schools are much more prevalent than we had previously thought, he's been told, they are obviously no good. Standards in such schools are bound to be low.

But the development community seems to be wrong about that, too. On the whole, dime-a-day for-profit schools are doing a better job of teaching the poorest children than the far more expensive state schools. In many localities, private schools operate alongside a free, government-run alternative. Many parents, poor as they may be, have chosen to reject it and to pay perhaps a tenth of their meager incomes to educate their children privately. They would hardly do that unless they expected better results.

Better results are what they get. After comparing test scores for literacy and basic math, Tooley has shown that pupils in private schools do better than their state-school equivalents – at between a half and a quarter of the per-pupil teacher cost. In some places, such as Gansu, China, the researchers found that private schools serving the poor had worse facilities than comparable state schools; in Hyderabad, they were better equipped (with blackboards, desks, toilets, drinking water, and so on). Regardless, the tests so far show that private-school students do better across the board.

Why have these findings been so reluctantly received? The answer is politics. The consensus on economic development – specifically, on the role of the state in promoting growth – cycles to and fro. At the moment, orthodox thinking embraces a leading role for the market in most areas of economic life. But in most developing countries, as in many rich ones (including the United States), schooling is widely regarded as quite another matter. Children's education is higher than commerce. These realms must not be allowed to mix. Many development and education officials wish to enshrine free education as a universal human right. Education, in other words, is too important to be left to the market.

In this view, if state schools are failing, which nobody denies, they need to be fixed, whatever the cost. And this is how the challenge of education in developing countries is currently framed: Governments need to spend more on their schools. One could more easily sympathize with that view if the state systems were easily fixable. In many developing countries, certainly in India, it would be unrealistic to think so, even if one could say, "Hang the expense." The problems seem systemic, not fiscal.

Most of those who campaign for greatly increased aid to poor countries would wish to see governments spend much of that money on state-run schools. The goal is admirable, but the method may be counterproductive. Tooley's research suggests that small-scale support for private slum schools – through scholarship programs, backing for school-voucher schemes, or subsidized microfinance – might do far more good than a big aid push directed at government-run education.

Tooley has been publishing his research in education journals but has also written for libertarian and conservative think tanks. Unfortunately, these associations have pushed him further outside the development mainstream. Perhaps most alienating, his findings (as he notes) conform very well to the views of the late Milton Friedman, who spent the last years of his life arguing that publicly funded vouchers and a market of privately run competing schools were the way to fix another education system in urgent need of repair: America's. All the more reason why, so far as some development officials are concerned, Tooley's obscurity is welcome.

As for Tooley himself, he is now moving beyond research alone, preparing to embark on a new project: the management of a new $100 million fund to invest in private schools for the very poor in developing countries. Development professionals need not be concerned, however. The money is from a private foundation. It won't waste any country's aid budget.

REVIEW AND DISCUSSION QUESTIONS

1   Why does black-market private education appear to be so common in developing countries?
2   Why does the author believe that the "official aid and development industry" prefers that the results of Tooley's research not be known?
3   Do you agree with Crook's suggestion that supporting small private schools in developing countries may be a better idea than strengthening public education? Why or why not? Explain.

Chapter 25

THE ECONOMIST

A WORLD OF OPPORTUNITY

Developing countries see the point of higher education.

A CROSS THE DEVELOPING WORLD, higher education is coming in from the cold. Gone are the days when it was purely a luxury for the elite. Governments are rapidly expanding their higher-education systems, with China probably witnessing the biggest expansion of student numbers in history. They are trying to create centres of excellence and throwing open the sector to private entrepreneurs.

The main reason for this flurry of activity is the dramatic growth in the supply of potential students. Secondary school enrolment rates have grown rapidly across the developing world. But there has also been a revolution in economic thinking. Not so long ago the World Bank pooh-poohed spending on higher education as both economically inefficient and socially regressive. Now many development economists are warming to higher education, pointing to the demand for graduates – as demonstrated by their wage premium – and to the positive effect of university-based research on the economy.

Nobody doubts the difficulty of building decent universities in the developing world. In most countries the legacy of colonialism has been compounded by the legacy of anti-colonialism. Colonialism meant that universities concentrated on producing a tiny group of elite administrators, and anti-colonialism tightened their bonds with government.

Public spending on universities in developing countries is highly regressive. In Latin America the professional classes, who account for 15% of the population, take up nearly half of all university places. In Rwanda, 15% of the total education budget is spent on the 0.2% of students who attend universities. Most universities in the developing world are also hopelessly badly managed.

But there are a few bright spots on the horizon. Some universities in poorer countries have been doing world-class research. The botany department of the University of São Paulo, for example, was first to crack the genetic code of a bacterium called *Xylella fastidiosa*, which has been laying waste to vineyards in southern California. This work attracted global funding as well as attention from, among others, America's Department of Agriculture and the American Vineyard Foundation.

A second bright spot is that good management can produce striking improvements. Uganda's Makerere University, which in the late 1980s was on the verge of bankruptcy, has increased its student numbers fivefold and is investing in its infrastructure. It has introduced fees for 80% of its students, and now generates a third of its revenue from a variety of commercial ventures such as a bakery and an in-house consultancy.

A third cause for cheer is the proliferation of different kinds of universities. A few years ago most universities in the developing world were much the same: designed for the elite and dominated by the state. Now there is more variety. The biggest change is the emergence of a for-profit sector that concentrates on subjects such as accounting and computer skills, and often pioneers educational innovation.

What are the prospects that the good news will outweigh the bad? To answer this question, it is worth looking more closely at the two countries that are currently conducting the world's biggest experiments in the "massification" of higher education: India and China.

India's higher-education system has plenty of inherited handicaps. Some of them are left over from colonialism and some from anti-colonialism; some arise from poor management and political confusion. B.S. Baswan, the country's secretary for secondary and higher education, notes that his sector lacks a clear political constituency. Yet the problem is deeper than that: the government does not have the resources to fund the expansion it wants, but cannot summon up the political courage to start charging students realistic fees. The result is that India often seems to take one step back for every two steps forward.

Undoubtedly, though, it is making advances. The number of people attending universities almost doubled in the 1990s, from 4.9m to 9.4m. The price of this has been a decline in overall quality. That said, India has two valuable things going for it. One is its collection of elite institutions. For decades, India has been pouring resources into the All India Institute of Medical Sciences, the Indian Institute of Science in Bangalore and, above all, the Indian Institutes of Technology. These institutions take their pick from an army of candidates every year, with 180,000 hopefuls taking the screening test for around 3,500 places in the seven IITs. They provide a highly intensive education, with all students and often professors too living on campus. And they produce a stream of highly educated people who help to set professional standards. "They are a class apart, like Oxford and Cambridge," says P.V. Indiresan, an expert on universities.

These elite institutions help to keep India plugged into the global knowledge economy. R.S. Sirohi, the former director of IIT Delhi, explains that he used to give his staff long sabbaticals in western universities, and that about a third of them spend time in America every summer. His institute receives sponsorship for research from multinationals such as Sun Microsystems, Cisco, Volvo and Ford. Granted, the elite institutions produce many people who get brain-drained away, but they also keep many bright people from emigrating, and may even attract émigrés back if India's economy keeps booming. It is accepted wisdom in India that the brightest students go to the IITs and the second-best to American universities.

India's other big advantage is a more recent development: a booming private sector. This being India, the sector is plagued by scandal. In February, India's Supreme Court ordered the closure of nearly 100 private universities because of quality concerns. Still, the best private colleges are doing admirable work, responding to unmet demand for technical and managerial education, often in highly creative ways, correcting India's bias towards theoretical education, and encouraging entrepreneurs to pour millions into a sector that has traditionally been starved of funds.

Vinay Rai, a telecoms and steel magnate, is just such an entrepreneur. Rai University bills itself as "India's best private university", with 16 campuses across the country. Mr Rai wants the university to fill a gap in the market, and sees huge demand for education in practical subjects such as management, media, accounting and tourism. But he is interested in more than just tapping a booming market, pointing out that half his students are on scholarships. He wants to shift from training obedient clerks towards training self-starting entrepreneurs. He waxes lyrical about the "beautiful model" of higher education he encountered in America at the Massachusetts Institute of Technology.

The contrast between Rai University's main campus in Delhi and that of Jawaharlal Nehru University, one of India's most distinguished public universities, is striking. Rai University is spick and span whereas JNU is sprawling and untidy. Rai is full of computers, whereas JNU is resolutely low-tech. Rai's students are determined to take part in the global economy, whereas JNU is plastered with signs protesting against the evils of capitalism.

A growing band of successful private companies are pioneering the democratisation of technical education. NIIT, a computer-training company, has 40 wholly owned centres and more than 1,000 franchised operations, and is expanding to America and Britain. It has also established a research-and-development department to discover the most effective teaching methods. One of its cleverest ideas was to give illiterate children free access to computers in order to see how easily they could master them. It has also established links with Citibank to enable students to take out loans to pay fees. The company has become such a brand name that some advertisements in the matrimonial pages of the *Times of India* specify graduates of NIIT.

China enrols the market

In higher education, as in so much else, China is visibly pulling ahead of India. The Chinese are engaged in the biggest university expansion in history. In the 1980s, only 2–3% of school-leavers went to university. In 2003, the figure was 17%. The watershed year was 1999, when the number of students enrolled jumped by almost half. The expansion at the doctoral level is even faster than for undergraduates: in 1999–2003, nearly 12 times as many doctorates were awarded as in 1982–89. And there is more to come: the number of new doctoral students jumped from 14,500 in 1998 to 48,700 in 2003.

The Chinese are determined to create a super-league of universities to rival the best in the world. The central government is investing heavily in chosen universities, such as Peking, Tsinghua and Fudan, offering higher salaries and more research funding. The state governments are doing likewise. It is no accident that the most widely used annual ranking of the world's research universities, the Shanghai index, is produced by a Chinese university.

What lies behind all this is a gigantic exercise in technology transfer. The Chinese are trying to recreate the best western universities at home in order to compete in more sophisticated industries. They have stocked up with foreign PhDs: in some departments of the University of Peking, a third of the faculty members have American doctorates. They are using joint ventures with foreign universities in much the same way as Chinese companies use joint ventures with foreign companies.

The Chinese have no qualms about using market mechanisms to achieve this technology transfer. Tuition charges now make up 26% of the earnings of public universities, nearly twice the level in 1998; many professors are paid according to the number of students they attract; and China is creating a parallel system of private universities alongside the public ones. For example, the University of Peking has more applicants than places, so it has created a parallel university that charges higher fees and accepts slightly less able students. Links between universities and industry are commonplace. The majority of doctorates earned in China between 1992 and 2003 were in practical subjects, which attract the brightest students: engineering (38% of the total), natural sciences (22%) and medicine (15%).

But will China achieve its academic ambitions? The trouble is that investment will not do the trick without broader cultural changes. Rui Yang, a professor at Australia's Monash University, points out that academic corruption is rife. The powerful academies that distribute much of the research funding are prey to both political favouritism and lobbying. Plagiarism is commonplace. Many academics use a good part of their research funding for personal rather than academic ends.

The country's authoritarianism will also prove a limiting factor, affecting not only the humanities but the sciences as well. For example, Chinese scientists suppressed information on SARS because it contradicted the official line. A world-class university without freedom of thought is still a contradiction in terms.

REVIEW AND DISCUSSION QUESTIONS

1   What recent changes in the higher educational systems of developing countries make investments in higher education increasingly attractive?

2   In what ways has higher education in India improved recently? What problems still remain?

3   What problems does the higher educational system in China still face?

4   Do you agree that "broader cultural changes" are needed for China to achieve its goal of creating world-class universities? Why or why not?

Chapter 26

Martha Nichols

THIRD-WORLD FAMILIES AT WORK
Child labor or child care?

JONATHAN STEIN, the new vice president of international contracts for Timothy & Thomas North America, shifted restlessly in his plane seat. During his two-month swing through Asia, he'd been on more planes than he could remember, many of them far more uncomfortable than this flight back to Boston. But he couldn't forget the Pakistani girls who had looked no older than ten years old, sweeping the floor between the rows of sewing machines the women worked on.

In that plant in Lahore, the women and girls had been hard at work assembling T&T shorts – currently the hottest item in Timothy & Thomas's 40-year-old line of casual clothes. Like the rest of the company's products, the shorts had that wholesome American "feel good-look good" image.

But that image didn't fit the image of those girls at work, and the contradiction left Stein with a quandary. In keeping with Timothy & Thomas's reputation for social responsibility, the company's new Global Guidelines for Business Partners prohibited the use of child labor – with "child" defined as anyone under 14 or the compulsory school age. Until his trip to Asia, Stein had felt good about working for a company that valued employee empowerment and diversity. Yet when it came to Pakistan and other developing countries, he'd found the company's policies no help at all.

In Lahore, Stein had enjoyed the city itself, which was a thriving textile and market center. Its colorful bazaar, wedged between the opulently wealthy and extremely poor districts of the city, was full of silks and the hand-embroidered clothing Lahore was famous for. He had liked the desert landscape and bright white walls, all backed by a cold blue sky. When Stein first met Timothy & Thomas's Pakistani sourcing manager, on a taxi ride to one of the local plants, he was still distracted by so many new sights.

"I should warn you," said Yusuf Ahmed, the sourcing manager, just minutes after shaking Stein's hand. "There's some confusion about the guidelines."

Stein stopped admiring the scenery. "What do you mean?"

"All the good contractors use kids. The little girls come to the plant with their mothers, and I know there are others on the machines who are younger than 14. That's just how it's done here."

"Haven't you told them they have to do it differently?" Stein's hands tensed on his knees. The taxi jounced through the narrow streets, no longer surrounded by the picturesque overflow from the bazaar.

"I'm not a cop," Ahmed said. "Besides, I'm not sure you'd really want me to do that. The situation is more complicated than you think."

"What's complicated? You say contractors aren't in compliance, so we threaten to cut off the contracts until they are."

Ahmed leaned forward impatiently. "Do you realize how committed we are? We've got the Lahore contractors alone assembling half a million T&T products a year – at competitive prices, I can assure you."

"I know the numbers," Stein said. "But that doesn't change the guidelines. We can't have kids in the plants, right?"

Ahmed wiped his brow. He looked more than hot under his neatly pressed collar and dark tie. Although he had gone to the University of Pennsylvania and worked in the United States, Yusuf Ahmed had been back in Pakistan as Timothy & Thomas's sourcing manager for the past two years.

"We're lucky to have these guys, if you want the truth," Ahmed said. "Our contractors produce on time and with good quality, which is no small feat. They could set up somewhere else, but in their heart of hearts, many of these guys want to stay in Pakistan, to improve the quality of life a little bit, if they can, by bringing in jobs. Then here we come, the big company from the United States, saying we won't buy what they produce unless it comes incredibly cheap, but of course they have to follow our company guidelines, even if it means that their costs go up –"

"Hold on," Stein broke in. "We have contractors in other countries who are complying with the guidelines, and they seem to be producing just fine."

Now the sourcing manager looked more tired than angry. "Sure. If we ask them to, the contractors here will fire any kids who are under 14. But that will affect at least 60 families, all of them very poor in the first place, do you realize that? And the contractors will still want assurances from us. These guys will want to know that we'll pay our share, even if the price goes up and we have to renegotiate the contracts."

"How much are we talking about?" Stein asked.

"The young kids who come with their mothers do more than you think. They are paid nothing, of course." Ahmed said. "Even the older ones on the machines get paid subminimum wages as trainees, so labor will go up by at least a third to pay adults minimum wage – or more for skilled work. Or if our contractors stick with the kids, they'll have to document that they're really 14. In Pakistan, you can't count on birth registrations, and I'm sure you've seen enough in Asia to know that most kids look younger than their real age."

"So how could you tell they were too young?"

"You can tell." Ahmed shrugged. "With some it's hard, and maybe the only way to be certain is to have a doctor examine them. The children themselves will lie. They'll say they're 14, because they need the work. What are their alternatives, really? They can hire themselves out as maids for almost nothing, or spend hours on embroidery at home, work that is not regulated at all. Or they can go to a carpet factory, would you like that any better?"

Stein shook his head. "I don't feel good about any of this."

The sourcing manager turned away. "I can't help you there. I don't agree with the guidelines, you know, but since I work for the company, I'll do what I'm told." Ahmed lit a cigarette and stared out the taxi's dirty window. "Forgive me for being blunt, but sometimes I don't know what you managers in Boston are thinking about, I really don't. As far as I'm concerned, imposing American values on the Third World just creates more problems. You have no idea what it's like to live in Pakistan, do you?"

"That's why I'm here."

"For one week. Fine. Then let me tell you about the reality. You don't know what those kids want." Ahmed unrolled the window. He raised his voice above the raucous street sounds outside. "We're not just talking about Pakistan. You can go to Bangladesh, Sri Lanka, Brazil, Mexico, the Azores – you're a Timothy & Thomas man, so you know what I mean. You can go all over the world and find street kids hustling and trying to make some money. Don't you think any of them would rather be working for one of our contractors? I'd say we're doing everyone here a favor."

Stein didn't answer, since by then the taxi had screeched to a halt. However, at the first plant they visited, he still felt uneasy. All of the workers on the floor were girls or women, because working side by side with men was considered improper. Ahmed had explained that this plant owner provided separate buses to bring the women to work. Farhan Hanafi, who led them on a tour of the plant, also made clear to Stein that he provided meals for his workers and wages of 5,000 rupees a month, or about $200, for the skilled women – much more than the minimum wage of 1,200 rupees, Hanafi insisted.

The plant floor wasn't dirty or overcrowded, but there was no heat. The women wore layers of long blouses over thin flowing pants, and many of their heads were covered with brightly woven shawls. Their bare hands, reddened in the cold room, still moved deftly around the mechanical needles, pushing the pre-cut pieces of cloth forward. He saw small girls winding thread on sewing-machine spools for their mothers. Some older girls squatted near piles of patterns and cast-off cloth, stacking and sorting, talking as they worked. They only became silent when Stein and the other men moved closer.

Yusuf Ahmed asked one of the girls some questions in Punjabi. The girl kept her head bowed down and answered in a low voice, shrugging her thin shoulders as she spoke. The girl was about the same height as Stein's eight-year-old daughter, and he had always considered Jessica small for her age.

"She says she likes to work here." Ahmed glanced at the plant owner. "Mr. Hanafi is very kind to them and pays them very well. They have a roof over their heads, and they can keep their hands clean. She's old enough, she claims, because all her friends are here, and they are all the same age. They are all very good workers, she wants Mr. Hanafi to know this."

"But why aren't they in school?" Stein asked.

"The families need them to work," Ahmed said. "I think at least half of the kids in Pakistan don't make it to primary school, and it's more important for boys to get an education, if the families can afford it."

Ahmed's answer depressed Stein even more. Based on the rest of his Asian trip, he knew conditions in this particular Pakistani plant weren't bad. He told himself that the workers were probably grateful for walls that kept out the grit and dry wind outside, for decent lighting and a clean concrete floor. Lahore wasn't Calcutta, of course, but Stein remembered the crowds of people in the poor district outside the plant, many sleeping or begging in the dirt. They had rolled to the side just in time when their taxi honked through. The women were probably glad to have their young daughters inside with them, where the girls could also be useful.

But Stein imagined *60 Minutes* sinking its teeth into this story – a real exposé of how those popular T&T shorts, brought to you by lovable, reliable Timothy & Thomas, were stitched together by poor Pakistani kids. It wouldn't play well in Poughkeepsie.

Now, on the plane back to Boston and company headquarters, Stein twisted around in his seat, trying to get comfortable. If he didn't renew the Lahore contracts, the girls and their families would lose a major source of income. Or was that just a convenient rationale for looking the other way? After all, adhering to the company guidelines would send production costs for the T&T line, at least temporarily, through the roof. Timothy & Thomas's clothing empire was now scrambling to keep its edge in the North American and European markets. There were U.S. warehouses and stores depending on shipments of T&T products, Stein thought. A high volume of shorts and blouses that, to date, had been produced quickly and cheaply by the contractors in Lahore.

The Pakistani girls posed the first test of the Global Guidelines for Business Partners. Yet being on the cutting edge of company policy just made his decision more difficult. Jonathan Stein realized that he was now responsible for the outcome. Unfortunately, all the talk of values and social responsibility in the world didn't erase the bottom line.

Note

HBR's cases are derived from the experiences of real people and real companies. As written, they are hypothetical, and the names used are fictitious.

REVIEW AND DISCUSSION QUESTIONS

1 Who is Jonathan Stein, and what problem does he run into during his trip to Lahore, Pakistan?

2 What reasons does Yusuf Ahmed give to explain his reluctance to enforce T&T's guidelines on child labor?

3 If Jonathan Stein and T&T are serious about being "socially responsible," what should they do about the Lahore plant? Suggest a specific course of action and discuss the implications for Pakistan's economic and human development.

4 What can the governments of developing countries do to eliminate child labor? How can the governments of rich countries help? Suggest specific policies and indicate any pros and cons.

Chapter 27

Kaushik Basu

INTERNATIONAL LABOR STANDARDS AND CHILD LABOR

INTERNATIONAL LABOR STANDARDS ARE meant to be policy measures aimed at helping poor nations achieve certain minimal living standards. What is remarkable about these measures is that the most consistent opposition to them has come from the alleged beneficiaries. The fear of the poor nations is that labor standards are a facade for hiding the true agenda of developed nations, to wit, protectionism. The fear is partly justified. The demand for labor standards, as it stands today, comes overwhelmingly from protectionist lobbies in industrialized nations.

While labor standards as they are currently conceived ought to be rejected, there is nevertheless scope for a minimal and differently conceived set of international labor standards (ILS). I call this the "third" formulation, not only to distinguish it from the two viewpoints most often heard – that labor standards as currently recommended are a must, or that labor standards ought to be shunned altogether – but because this approach argues that labor standards should be devised so as to give voice to certain muted demands in the *third* world. As such, the third formulation consists of a package that helps poor countries collude to maintain better standards for their workers. It is a construct meant to counter the problem of free-riding *among developing nations*. This approach envisages that the industrialized nations themselves, ironically, will help the poor countries collude.

A notable feature of this third approach is that it does not consist of deontic rules – for example, that child labor must never be used. Whether children are allowed to work or not will depend on the welfare consequences of such a decision. It is also compatible with the view – which I maintain – that, in general, the best way to help poor nations is to open the doors of industrialized nations so there can be greater demand for goods and services (and therefore, indirectly, labor) from the third world. Such openness would cause wages to rise in the developing countries, thereby increasing the bargaining power of the workers, which would then result in higher living standards.

The subject of international labor standards has been debated extensively by policymakers, especially before the Uruguay Round of the General Agreement on Tariffs and Trade (GATT), and in the seminar rooms of the World Trade Organization (WTO) and the International Labor Organization (ILO). There is also a substantial academic literature on this, with contributions by Jagdish Bhagwati, Dani Rodrik, T.N. Srinivasan, and Keith Maskus touching on some of the same issues that I am concerned with here.

The United States had campaigned for labor standards and a "social clause" in the Uruguay Round. And from some recent statements of President Clinton – for instance, his address to the Economic Club of Detroit on January 8, 1999 – it is evident that the United States will continue to push for international labor standards. But ILS is not a unique set of prescriptions, and the portents are that the kind of ILS policy being debated by the industrialized nations, if adopted, will be detrimental to the poorest nations.

The problem stems from the fact that the idea of minimal labor standards is a Trojan horse that not only encompasses those who are genuinely concerned about workers' well-being but also is a convenient hiding place for those with a much more selfish, protectionist agenda. Regrettably, the initiative for ILS has moved into the hands of the protectionist lobbies, which has driven a wedge between the interests of the industrialized nations and the developing countries. Yet it will be sad if this backlash against the *current conception* of ILS results in rejecting the very idea of minimal labor standards.

North vs. South or South vs. South?

A myth that has fueled support for protectionism among the uninitiated of the North is that the low work standard in developing countries is robbing the jobs of adults in developed countries. First, many people seem unaware that most of the so-called powerhouses among the developing nations import more from the industrialized nations than they export to them. In 1995 Korea's exports to the industrialized nations constituted 12.3 percent of its gross domestic product (GDP), while its imports from the industrialized nations were 13.9 percent of its GDP.[1] In brief, relative to industrialized nations, Korea ran a trade deficit of 1.6 percent. Indonesia in the same year also ran a deficit, 2.2 percent; Malaysia ran a deficit of 11.8 percent; Thailand a deficit of 9.1 percent; Brazil a deficit of 1.4 percent. With a trade surplus of 1 percent, China is more the exception than the rule. Moreover, the Chinese surplus is a relatively recent phenomenon. What all this means is that, if the exports of these countries are cut off, in all likelihood their imports from industrialized nations will shrink as well, making the net effect on the industrialized nations negative instead of positive, though of course some specific sectors may gain. So the fear that the developing countries with their cheap labor are swamping industrialized-country markets is a myth. By and large, they continue to buy more than they sell.

Second, the products manufactured in the worst conditions, often using child labor, are not the sectors in which there is any serious competition between the industrialized nations and the developing countries. Consider the celebrated soccer ball industry. High-quality soccer balls entail hand-stitching leather panels into geometric patterns. Such labor intensity implies that the bulk of soccer balls are produced in developing countries. In 1996 the United States imported $34.2 million worth of soccer balls. The top five suppliers were Pakistan, China, Indonesia, India, and Thailand, which together supplied 96.9 percent of soccer balls imported by the United States. It is also worth keeping in mind that the United States does not produce any soccer balls. If any of these countries is banned from exporting to the United States, it is highly unlikely that the demand will shift to another industrialized nation. It will be some other developing country that picks up the slack. It is therefore a completely erroneous view that there is competition between the child laborers of the third world and the adult workers of the industrialized nations.

One natural experiment demonstrating this proposition actually occurred in the carpet industry. Hand-knotted carpets are another classic example of labor-intensive production. Indeed it is widely believed that children have a relative advantage in this because of their "nimble fingers," though a recent ILO study of the carpet industry contests this belief as yet another myth (see Deborah Levison et al. 1998). For historical reasons, Iran was the largest exporter of hand-knotted carpets to the United States. Then in the late 1980s the United States placed an embargo on imports from Iran. Did that boost production in industrialized nations? The answer is an unsurprising no. India, China, Nepal, and other poor nations stepped in. India, which used to be a small exporter of carpets, suddenly became a big player. In 1996, the United States, which does not make any hand-knotted carpets, imported $316 million worth of this product. The five biggest sellers were India (45 percent), China (25 percent), Pakistan (16 percent), Turkey (6.5 percent), and Nepal (2.9 percent). The competition is clearly much more acute among developing countries than between developing and developed countries.

A natural consequence of this, often overlooked by the North, is that labor standards are a great concern *within* the developing countries. This concern is combined with a fear that any action on this front by any one country will cause a shift in production to some other developing country.[2] Indians point out that China's lack of democracy enables it to use forms of forced labor, such as prison labor, that would not be feasible in India. China, on the other hand, worries about India's greater poverty pushing wages down and sending larger numbers of children into the labor force. And in today's world of mobile capital, each of these countries is aware that capital can easily leave its territory and go to another if its cost of labor goes up.

What ILS can do is address this fear among the *developing* nations, a fear that makes it difficult for each of them to act on its own in raising labor standards. However, this would require us to think of international labor standards in a very different way from how we are used to. ILS, according to this "third approach," has to be viewed as an instrument of collusion among the southern countries for raising labor standards, which none of these nations can do alone, without driving out capital. Before spelling out this approach, let us take a look at some of the policies currently being espoused.

Child labor, legal action, and product labeling

The existing international efforts are of two kinds, which I have elsewhere (Basu 1999) called "extranational" and "supranational." An extranational effort is an action taken within the boundaries of an industrial nation that creates incentives in the third world to raise labor standards. A classic example of this is the Child Labor Deterrence Bill in the United States, which, by stopping the import of products made with child labor, tries to create incentives in the exporting nations to change their method of production. A supranational effort, on the other hand, is a multicountry effort, executed through an international organization such as the WTO or the ILO, to discourage whatever it is that we want to discourage.

Given the difficulty of mobilizing the opinions of several nations, it is not surprising that most of the actions thus far have been the result of extranational effort. Despite rhetoric to the contrary, these have frequently and increasingly been used as weapons of protection. Nevertheless, being weapons of protection does not preclude them from having concomitant beneficial effects elsewhere. So irrespective of what they are used for, we need to evaluate their worth in terms of their impact on the third world. But even by this measure they fail.

These instruments, especially in the context of child labor, suffer from two weaknesses. First, they fail to take into account that parents who send their children to work do not do so out of sloth and meanness, but to escape extreme poverty and hunger for the household, which includes the child (Basu and Van 1998).[3] When child labor occurs as a mass phenomenon, it must be distinguished from child abuse. Second, these instruments are very sector-specific; they penalize a nation for using child labor in export industries. Put these two arguments together and it is evident why these policies are likely to fail. If implemented properly, they are likely to drive children from the carpet industry or garment industry or soccer ball industry to other sectors, some of which are more dismal, such as prostitution or welding. Indeed there is some evidence from Bangladesh that, in anticipation of such laws, children have been removed from some of these export sectors, resulting in a rise in child prostitution. Similarly, a UNICEF study found that between 5,000 and 7,000 young girls moved from the carpet industry to prostitution as a result of these policies.

Fortunately, there is increasing realization among academics and activists in the North that, if our real aim is to help the children, then extranational action has to be much more nuanced than just banning the import of any product that has been tainted by child labor.[4] Some recent legislation, such as the Sanders Amendment to the Tariff Act of 1930, which prohibits the import of products that use *forced* or *indentured* child labor, is a move in the right direction. As an aside, it is worth noting that one of the first uses of this amended law illustrates the overwhelming tendency to use such social legislation for self-interest. This law was recently cited to criticize Brazil's largest juice exporter, Sucocitrico Cutrale Ltd., for using forced child labor to pick oranges. However, what brought the charge was not new evidence of forced child labor but the fact that Cutrale bought up a Minute Maid processing plant in Florida and then cut back its workforce. The law was plainly being used as an instrument.

One policy that has found increasing favor among activists is product labeling, that is, pasting labels on products with messages such as "Guarantee: Manufactured without child labor." This is, in fact, the exact label used by Reebok on soccer balls manufactured in Pakistan and sold in the United States. The reason this has found favor is that the choice is laid at the doorstep of the consumer. She can decide, according to her own morals, whether or not to boycott imported goods that do not have such a label. This additional information and additional choice has a democratic flavor, so to argue against it is that much more difficult.

Product labeling is not the right way to battle child labor for several reasons. The authenticity of these labels is highly questionable. In many of the sectors where child labor flourishes, production takes place in thousands of little sheds and homes. To avoid this situation, Reebok has centralized its manufacture of soccer balls in Pakistan by setting up a large facility in Sialkot, despite the increased cost of doing so. However, decentralized production is pervasive in a range of industries, including carpets and shoe uppers. The joke used to be that stitching product labels could be another industry for employing children.

Even if we can get around the authenticity problem with a reasonable degree of accuracy, product labeling is still a bad idea. First, it shares with the Child Labor Deterrence Bill the problem that it attacks child labor in a few export-goods sectors and is therefore likely to push children into indigenous productive activities, some of which are much more harmful to them. Second, as suggested earlier, in some of the poorest economies, if we try to eradicate child labor suddenly (whether by law or by a consumer boycott of such products), we may push poor households into even greater poverty and possible starvation. In some countries, such as Ethiopia, where 42.3 percent of all children in the ten-to-fourteen age group work, and per capita income is a precarious $110 per annum, a sudden cessation of child labor will have a devastating effect on many households. In countries such as India and China (and certainly Thailand, Malaysia, and other more prosperous Asian countries), where industrialization has proceeded further and the incidence of child labor has fallen – it is 14.4 percent in India and 11.6 percent in China – a sudden ban will be difficult but will not derail the economies. So a refusal to import products that use *any* child labor will put the poorest economies of the world at a disadvantage because they may not be in a position to overhaul their production structure in the short run. More specifically, this policy is likely to shift advantage away from the African economies in favor of those in Asia and Latin America. Herein lies another lesson for designing a good ILS policy. It must make allowances for variations across countries, and not create advantages for those that are stronger.

Finally, even in nations like China and India, it is not a good idea to try to eradicate child labor in one fell swoop. Field workers in India have reported that some areas are so poor that perhaps the best policy is to allow children to combine schooling with some work. Indeed, doing some work and earning some money may be the only way that children can afford to attend school. Recent research in Peru tends to confirm this view. It is also sobering to recall that one of the first laws in the United States to curb child labor, passed by the state of Massachusetts in 1837, prohibited firms from employing children below the age of fifteen *who had not attended school for at least three months in the previous year*. Likewise in Britain, during the first half of the nineteenth century, until 1861, the incidence of both child labor *and* of schooling continued to rise. In other words, we need to limit the amount a child may work and be prepared to vary this according to the country's general economic condition. Such variations are difficult to capture on product labels (the labels would have to be too long and complicated), but an international organization can work out detailed outlines and at least try to enforce these. So ILS has to be mediated through international organizations as a collective effort.

The third approach

The third approach views ILS as an instrument for *third world* countries to achieve what they want to achieve, but cannot, because of the lack of coordination among themselves and the consequent fear that they will drive capital out of their country. The three essential ingredients of the third approach to international labor standards are as follows.

First, it must be recognized that to look for a single set of standards for all countries is to have virtually no standards. ILS must be flexible enough to take account of the different stages of development of different nations. Second, we should abandon the idea of banning child labor (as implicit in the product-labeling program or the Child Labor Deterrence Bill). Instead, restrictions should be placed on the number of hours that a child is allowed to work and on the conditions of work. Finally, if a certain product is manufactured in a certain country in violation of the agreed-upon international labor standards, punitive action should not take the form of boycotting that product alone, but be more generalized. This is to prevent driving children from one sector into another.

To elaborate on these proposals, the first requirement says that we will have to decide whether there is a minimal set of labor standards to which all countries should be required to adhere, and then be prepared to face the answer that this set may be empty. We may, for instance, decide that nations with per capita income below a certain level are exempt from all the ILS strictures. In the past, ILS discussions have run aground in international forums – first, because they were motivated by the interests of the developed nations, and, second, because of the insistence that there had to be a program common to all countries, irrespective of their level of economic development. It is being suggested here that each item discussed in the many previous GATT and ILO meetings will have to be considered explicitly from the point of view of the developing nations' interests. We may reach the conclusion that forced labor should not be allowed anywhere, but that legal minimum wages are not desirable for poor nations. In that case, we must not have minimum wages as a part of international labor standards. Protectionists in industrialized nations will not be happy about this, but if we are to have an ILS that does what it is supposed to do, then we must resist the forces of protection.

A central element in most ILS discussion pertains to child labor. It is hard for people in developed nations to realize that child labor is a fact of life that cannot be wished away. There is enough evidence now to suggest that with very poor countries we cannot use the law to banish it, unless we are insensitive to the well-being of the children. The second ingredient of the third approach is a plea to recognize this and to work for steps that seek to curb child labor, leaving the idea of eliminating it to the long run. Steps should be taken to make it possible for children to work flexible hours so they can, if they want, combine some child work with schooling. Of course, "collaborative" measures, such as school meals and subsidies for going to school, can be used to make it attractive for parents to pull their children out of the labor force of their own accord. Industrialized nations can contribute to such an effort, and one possibility is to make such a commitment by industrialized nations a part of ILS.

If we do decide to back up the standards with punitive action for their violation, these actions ideally should not be product-specific. It is not clear that trade sanctions are a good way to deal with labor-standards violation, but if we *do* decide to use them, the final condition suggests that these sanctions should be imposed regardless of which sector the violation occurs in. A country must not be exempt from punishment because the violation occurs in a nonexportable sector. The present method of not buying a product, the manufacture of which violates an agreed-upon labor standard, drives some of the worst practices into sectors that have no connection with exports.

Let us now turn to the subject of enforcement. A question that has been discussed on occasion is who should be the enforcer of ILS. In particular, as Jagdish Bhagwati has discussed at some length, should it be the WTO or the ILO? At an abstract level, it does not matter, as long as we agree on what the standards are and what the punishments are. In reality, institutions come with baggage of history – their own structures and modes of operation. So the same set of rules may be perceived differently depending on whether the WTO or the ILO carries them out, and in this area perception matters. Moreover, even if we start from one set of rules, the evolution of these over time may be very different, depending on who is entrusted with them.

There are two factors that weigh against the WTO as an agency for carrying out this task. Given the history of GATT, in the WTO the battle lines have historically been drawn between the developed nations and the developing nations, with the ILS viewed as what the North wants to impose on an unwilling South. Since the third approach to ILS is an attempt to reverse this, with the initiative being shifted to the countries supposed to be helped by the standards, it is doubtful whether our perceptions, rooted in history, can be changed adequately for old suspicions not to reappear. Second, it is not clear to me that trade sanctions (the domain of the WTO) are the right way to deal with labor standards enforcement. The risk is that protectionism will again work its way back and thwart trade, once the door is opened to blocking trade for a limited class of actions.

On balance, ILS is better left to the ILO. Conventions, which nations are encouraged to sign and then are expected to adhere to, are the standard method used to orchestrate various kinds of labor rights. This is not a powerless instrument. In today's interconnected world with its easy information flow, the violation of a convention that a nation has signed can have plenty of consequences without anyone having to orchestrate it. The mere "news" of Nike's having possibly violated some standards was like a negative advertisement and was enough to change manufacturing practices in a large number of multinationals. Moreover, the voluntary nature of conventions can be backed up with some incentives and punitive ammunition. One possibility is linking the ILO and the WTO in enforcing labor standards, wherein the ILO drafts the standards and monitors them and the WTO is empowered to take action only after it gets the go-ahead from the ILO.

The policy of international labor standards is a dangerous one, where a desirable end can easily become a conduit for protectionism, which is likely to harm not only the developing nations but also the population at large in the developed countries. Hence, even if a particular action seems desirable today, one has to be aware that one act can lead to another and, somewhere along the line, cross over into policies that hurt the very people they were supposed to help. This article outlines a minimal, pragmatic program, as well as the agency for implementing it, keeping in mind that this is an area where policy designers have to consider not just economic desirability but also the risk of future misuse.

Notes

1   The statistics cited in this paragraph are from Stephen Golub (1997).
2   This point has been made by several commentators, including Bjorne Grimsrud and Liv Jorunn Stokke (1997), Pharis J. Harvey, Terry Collingsworth, and Bama Athreya (1998), and Thomas I. Palley (1999).
3   A recent paper (Basu, Genicot, and Stiglitz 1999) analyzes the more general proposition that in altruistic households the mere risk of unemployment for the primary wage earner may cause secondary earners (typically, women and children) to look for work.
4   For a lucid statement of the need for a multipronged approach to policy, see Peter Fallon and Zafiris Tzannatos (1998).

For further reading

Basu, Kaushik. 1999. "Child Labor: Cause, Consequence, and Cure with Remarks on International Labor Standards." *Journal of Economic Literature* (September), forthcoming.

Basu, Kaushik; Garance Genicot; and Joseph Stiglitz. 1999. "Household Labor Supply, Unemployment and Minimum Wage Legislation." Policy Research Working Paper no. 2049. Washington, DC: World Bank.

Basu, Kaushik, and Pham Hoang Van. 1998. "The Economics of Child Labor." *American Economic Review* 88.

Bhagwati, Jagdish. 1995. "Trade Liberalization and 'Fair Trade' Demands: Addressing Environmental and Labor Standards Issues." *World Economy* 18.

Fallon, Peter, and Zafiris Tzannatos. 1998. "Child Labor: Issues and Directions for the World Bank." Human Development Network. Washington: World Bank.

Golub, Stephen. 1997. "Are International Labor Standards Needed to Prevent Social Dumping?" *Finance & Development* (December).

Grimsrud, Bjorne, and Liv Jorunn Stokke. 1997. "Child Labor in Africa: Poverty or Institutional Failures." *FAFO Report* 223.

Harvey, Pharis J.; Terry Collingsworth; and Bama Athreya. 1998. "Developing Effective Mechanisms for Implementing Labor Rights in the Global Economy." Washington: International Labor Rights Fund (http://www.laborights.org/ilrf.html).

Levison, Deborah, et al. 1998. "Is Child Labor Really Necessary in India's Carpet Industry?" In *Economics of Child Labor in Selected Industries of India*, ed. Richard Anker et al. New Delhi: Hindustan Publishers, forthcoming.

Maskus, Keith. 1997. "Should Core Labor Standards Be Imposed Through International Trade Policy?" Policy Research Working Paper no. 1817. Washington: World Bank.

Palley, Thomas I. 1999. "The Economic Case for International Labor Standards." Paper no. E025, Public Policy Department, AFL-CIO.

Rodrik, Dani. 1996. "Labor Standards in International Trade: Do They Matter and What Do We Do About Them?" Policy Essay no. 20. Washington: Overseas Development Council.

Srinivasan, T.N. 1996. "International Trade and Labor Standards from an Economic Perspective." In *Challenges to the New World Trade Organization*, ed. P. van Dyck and G. Faber. Amsterdam: Kluwer.

REVIEW AND DISCUSSION QUESTIONS

1 One way of tackling the problem of child labor in developing countries is to put in place laws that prevent rich countries from importing products made with child labor. Why does Basu believe that this is not an effective approach? Do you agree?

2 Explain what "product labeling" is and why Basu does not see it as a promising way to fight child labor.

3 Basu suggests a "third approach" to dealing with child labor. Explain the key characteristics of this approach and assess its strengths and weaknesses.

Chapter 28

Eric V. Edmonds and Nina Pavcnik

CHILD LABOR IN THE GLOBAL ECONOMY

POPULAR OPINION IN HIGH-INCOME countries often seems to hold that child labor in developing countries is nearly always a form of child abuse, in which children work in hazardous conditions in run-down factories for callous businesses. There have been recent attempts to combat child labor by lowering employment opportunities for children through harmonized international child labor standards and by consumer boycotts of products produced by child laborers. The U.S. Congress has repeatedly considered legislation that would prohibit imports into the United States of all products made with child labor. Under threat of such sanctions, export oriented garment factories in Bangladesh released more that 10,000 child workers under the age of 14 in the mid-1990s. More recently, the U.S. House of Representatives has deliberated the "Child Labor Elimination Act," which would impose general trade sanctions, deny all financial assistance, and mandate U.S. opposition to multilateral credits to 62 developing countries with a high incidence of child labor. This threat is implicit in a 2002 act of the U.S. Congress that mandated a study by the Department of Labor's Bureau of International Labor Affairs about the relationship between military and education spending in countries with a high incidence of child labor.

But in fact, the broad term "child labor" covers a considerable diversity between and within countries in the types of activities in which children participate. Fortunately, abhorrent images of children chained in factories or forced into prostitution stand out for their relative rarity. Most working children are at home, helping their family by assisting in the family business or farm and with domestic work. This paper begins by quantifying the extent and main characteristics of child labor. It then considers the evidence on a range of issues about child labor. Fundamentally, child labor is a symptom of poverty. Low income and poor institutions are driving forces behind the prevalence of child labor worldwide. As a result, some economic events or policies can have ambiguous effects on child labor; for example, a country that experiences an increase in labor demand, perhaps because of globalization, may experience greater demand for both adult and child labor.

However, the greater demand for adult labor can raise family incomes in a way that tends to reduce child labor. The final section assesses the policy options to reduce worldwide child labor. While some children do work in circumstances so hideous as to command immediate attention, development is the best overall cure for child labor. However, historical growth rates suggest that reducing child labor through improvements in living standards alone will take time. If a more rapid reduction in the general incidence of child labor is a policy goal, improving educational systems and providing financial incentives to poor families to send children to school may be more useful solutions to the child labor problem than punitive measures designed to prevent children from earning income.

What is child labor?

Estimating the number of children working around the world is a difficult task. Most working children live in low-income countries. These countries often lack reliable data on many aspects of their labor market. Even more difficult, some policymakers have until recently defined "child labor" as economic activities that are deleterious to the well-being of children. There are some situations where it is hard to imagine how an activity could not be harmful to the child – forced prostitution, child soldiers – but as we will discuss, these activities are very rare. Most working children participate in activities that can be harmful or beneficial for the child, depending on the circumstances of the activity, and ultimately, the impact of child labor on the well-being of the child depends on the counterfactual of what the child would be doing in the absence of work.

   Thus, rather than assuming that all child labor is by definition harmful to children, it is more useful to define child labor as including *all aspects* of child work and then study the effects of that work. Recent policy documents have taken this broad approach, often identifying certain occupations such as prostitution, stone quarrying and rag picking as "hazardous" or "exploitive" and monitoring them separately.[1] Article 4 of International Labor Convention 182 on the worst forms of child labor establishes this precedent by encouraging countries to decide for themselves what specific activities need to be tracked and targeted independently for policy while allowing for a more general definition of child labor.

Survey evidence on child labor

The ILO's Statistical Information and Monitoring Program on Child Labor (SIMPOC) most recently estimated that 211 million children, or 18 percent of children 5–14, are economically active worldwide (ILO, 2002). A child is defined as economically active if he or she works for wages (cash or in-kind); works in the family farm in the production and processing of primary products; works in family enterprises that are making primary products for the market, barter or own consumption; or is unemployed and looking for these types of work. The academic literature also uses the phrase "market work" to refer to these activities (with the exception of unemployment).[2] The estimated 211 million economically active children correspond to 18 percent of the world's population of 5–14 year olds. Sixty percent of these working children are in Asia, and 52 percent are boys. While 23 percent of economically active children are believed to be in sub-Saharan Africa, participation rates are highest there with an estimated 30 percent of children 5–14 working. Most economically active children are in low-income countries, but SIMPOC estimates that 4 percent of children are working in transition economies and 2 percent work in what it terms "developed" economies.

These SIMPOC counts are based wherever possible on existing household based survey data. These data are typically collected in three different types of surveys. Labor force surveys, especially child labor force surveys often assisted by SIMPOC, collect detailed information on the different types of work in which children participate. However, they usually do not provide information about time in school and studying, nor other aspects of the household. Multipurpose household surveys often offer greater details about the child's family environment at the expense of sample size and detail about the activities performed by children. Population censuses typically offer little detail about the activities of children and the activities of the family, but their large sample sizes are useful for identifying smaller population groups.

These data sources are increasingly becoming available to researchers and hold considerable promise for improving our understanding of why and how children work.[3] However, the data are in general frustratingly incomplete. Information on the domestic activities of children is unusual, and detailed data on time in school and time studying is generally not available. Moreover, a high fraction of children report neither attending school nor working in market or domestic work, and these so-called "idle" children are not well understood. Thus, in the available data, it is very hard to establish what children would do in the absence of participation in a particular type of work and therefore very difficult to evaluate the consequences of work for children.

Who employs children?

Contrary to popular perception in high-income countries, most working children are employed by their parents rather than in manufacturing establishments or other forms of wage employment. In 2000 and 2001, UNICEF coordinated detailed household surveys with virtually identical questionnaires in 36 low-income countries as a part of UNICEF's End of Decade Assessment. Table 28.1 tabulates participation rates in market work and domestic work for 124 million children from these 36 countries. Of the 25 percent of children ages 5–14 that participate in market work, few work outside of their own household. Less than 3 percent of children age 5–14 work outside of their household for pay, and this work for pay is actually more common in rural settings than in urban centers where manufacturing is generally located. In addition, 6 percent of children participate in unpaid work for someone outside of the child's household. We suspect that most of these children are involved in unpaid labor exchanges where neighboring families help one another in their business or farm, but these unpaid workers may also be children who are paid in-kind with meals or food (the questionnaire is unclear), or the work relationship may involve apprenticeships, children fostered out (that is, receiving food and board with another family in exchange for work), children held in bondage (that is, where the child's family has received a cash payment or bond that the child must work off) and children who work in their schools. The minimal incidence of wage employment in these UNICEF surveys concords with other datasets from countries as diverse as India, Nepal, South Africa and Vietnam, where it is unusual to find more than 3 percent of children 5–14 working outside of the household for pay. Even in urban Bangladesh, where much attention has been paid to child labor in the garment industry, a 2002 child labor survey found only

Table 28.1   Participation rates in various activities for 124 million children 5–14 from 36 countries in 2000

	All children	Age		Gender		Location	
	5–14	5–9	10–14	Male	Female	Urban	Rural
Market work (MAR)	25.0	15.3	35.2	26.6	23.3	18.9	30.5
Paid	2.4	1.0	4.0	2.8	2.0	2.2	2.5
Unpaid	5.8	4.4	7.3	5.6	5.9	4.0	7.3
Family	20.8	12.4	29.7	22.4	19.1	14.8	26.2
Domestic work (DOM)	64.6	50.8	79.2	59.3	69.9	60.7	67.4
Any work (MAR + DOM)	68.4	53.5	84.3	64.8	72.1	64.1	71.7
20 or more hours per week	20.7	10.3	31.8	19.4	22.1	14.1	26.4
40 or more hours per week	6.4	2.7	10.3	6.1	6.7	3.6	8.8

Notes: Each cell contains participation rates in indicated activity in the last week. Children may participate in multiple activities. *Paid* refers to children who worked outside of their household for wages in the last week. *Unpaid* refers to children who worked outside of their household in the last week without pay. *Family* refers to children that worked in their family business or farm in the last week. *Market work* indicates that the child participated in paid, unpaid or family work. *Domestic work* indicates that the child participated in household chores in her own household in the last week. *Any work* indicates that the child participated in market work or domestic work in the last week. UNICEF's summary statistics available at <http://www.childinfo.org> report a higher incidence of unpaid work outside of the child's household. The discrepancy may owe to a missed change in coding in the Angolan and Kenyan data and shows up as a slightly higher incidence of working children in UNICEF summary statistics than those presented.

Source: Authors' calculations from UNICEF Multiple Indicator Cluster Survey End of Decade Assessment microdata: <http://www.childinfo.org/MICS2/MICSDataSet.htm>. Countries included are Albania, Angola, Azerbaijan, Bolivia, Bosnia and Herzegovina, Burundi, Cameroon, Central African Republic, Chad, Comoros, Côte d'Ivoire, Democratic Republic of Congo, Dominican Republic, Gambia, Guinea Bissau, Guyana, Kenya, Lao People's Democratic Republic, Lesotho, Madagascar, Moldova, Mongolia, Niger, Philippines, Rwanda, São Tome and Principe, Senegal, Sierra Leone, Sudan, Swaziland, Tajikistan, Togo, Trinidad and Tobago, Uzbekistan, Venezuela and Vietnam. Individual country means are weighted to reflect survey design and are weighted by 5–14 population totals in computing cross-country means. Population 5–14 estimates are from <http://esa.un.org/unpp/index.asp?panel=2>, medium variant, 2000.

1.2 percent of children 5–14 working as paid employees. In contrast, 20.8 percent of children 5–14 in countries surveyed by UNICEF work in their family business or farm. Participation rates in this category are highest in rural areas, but 14.8 percent of urban children 5–14 work in a family business or farm.

Most economically active adults in low-income countries work in agriculture (Food and Agricultural Organization (FAO), 2004). Most children work side by side with their parents. Thus, most economically active children are employed in agriculture. Consider the findings of a particularly well regarded and detailed labor force survey conducted in

Nepal in 1999 (Central Bureau of Statistics, 2000). In Nepal, 85 percent of economically active children are in agriculture. The domestic service industry is the next largest employer, with roughly 10 percent of economically active children, while manufacturing accounts for only about 1 percent of economically active children. Although we are not aware of any global estimates of the distribution of working children by industry, agriculture is the dominant sector of employment in nearly every example that the authors have encountered. For example: in Cambodia, 73 percent of economically active children are in agriculture in 2001; Ethiopia, 89 percent in 2001; Guatemala, 63 percent in 2000; Kenya, 77 percent in 1998; Morocco, 84 percent in 2000; Pakistan, 67 percent in 1996; Vietnam, 92 percent in 1998; and Yemen, 92 percent in 1998.[4] Children perform a variety of tasks in agriculture. At young ages, they can be effective in caring for animals and in tasks such as weeding that do not require a developed physical stature.

The help children offer their families is not limited to market work – a majority of children also perform domestic duties within their own household. Table 28.1 suggests that almost 65 percent of children age 5–14 report participation in domestic work. Altogether, then, 68 percent of children 5–14 report working in either market work or domestic work. The participation rates are especially high among older children age 10–14, girls and children in rural areas. Children, particularly older ones, devote substantial time to work. Thirty-two percent of children 10–14 report working 20 or more hours per week; over 10 percent working more than 40 hours per week. Girls are more likely to work long hours than are boys (largely because of the additional domestic work performed by girls in most cultures), and the prevalence of all types of work, including over 40 hours per week, is higher in rural areas than in urban areas.

It has been sometimes argued that for a child to work outside of the household is fundamentally different and likely to be more hazardous than when a child works inside the household – especially when the work is domestic in nature. This conclusion is not obvious, as work outside of the household is typically more visible. Moreover, a number of researchers have emphasized that a decision to exclude domestic duties in the analysis of child labor can be misleading. Consider the example of the average 14-year-old girl living in rural Nepal. She works about 35 hours per week. She spends 19 hours of that time in market work, largely in agriculture for her family, and nine hours helping her family with domestic work, including cooking, cleaning, caretaking, shopping and minor repairs on home items. She does not work for pay. Her remaining work time is divided among an array of activities, but gathering firewood and collecting water are two of her more time- and physically-intensive obligations. Her domestic duties create time tradeoffs that are very similar to her time spent working in agriculture for her family.

Indeed, there is often a substitution pattern between market and domestic work; for example, if a parent leaves the household to work for a local employer, a child may take over many household roles, like collecting wood and water, tending to animals, preparing foods and meals, or caring for family members. This substitution pattern between hours worked in market and domestic work is, for example, evident in the data in Vietnam and Nepal for children working extreme hours in either category of work (Edmonds, 2003). In addition, for most children who do not work extreme hours in either market or domestic work, hours in each type of work are positively correlated (the correlation coefficient is 0.2 in both the Nepal and Vietnam data). Moreover, domestic work is at least as likely as market work to trade off with schooling, as shown by evidence from Egypt (Assaad, Levison and Zibani, 2003), Mexico (Levison, Moe and Knaul, 2001) and Peru

(Levison and Moe, 1998) and as discussed in the next section. Thus, any analysis of child labor should consider work outside of the child's household, work inside of the child's household in market work and domestic work. Unfortunately, few surveys collect data on domestic work, so in practice it is often neglected by official statistics and econometric studies.

Allocating time between work and school

Many working children attend school, and the average hours worked by a typical child worker are not necessarily incompatible with schooling. Table 28.2 shows how total hours of work are related to different types of work and to school attendance using the same UNICEF data as Table 28.1. Children are grouped into rows based on whether they participate in indicated activities. Thus, the first row contains average total hours worked in the last week for children that participate in market work. Children that participate in market work devote on average 26 hours per week to work. Children that work in the family farm/business or work outside the household in unpaid market work tend to work similar hours (27 hours per week on average). Working outside the household for wages is associated with slightly more total hours worked for older children. Children working in domestic work also spend considerable time working, at 16 hours per week. The fact that total hours worked for children active in domestic work is lower than for children active in market work should not lead one to conclude that domestic work is insignificant. On average, a majority of the total hours worked by children active in market work is

Table 28.2   Total hours worked in last week, conditional on activity, for 124 million children 5–14 from 36 countries in 2000

	All children	Age		Gender		Location	
	5–14	*5–9*	*10–14*	*Male*	*Female*	*Urban*	*Rural*
Market work (MAR)	26.1	21.1	28.5	25.3	27.1	21.7	28.3
Paid	30.9	21.0	33.5	30.0	32.2	27.3	33.6
Unpaid	26.9	20.9	30.6	26.3	27.4	20.6	29.6
Family	27.2	22.6	29.2	26.3	28.3	22.3	29.2
Domestic work (DOM)	15.8	11.6	18.6	15.4	16.1	12.4	18.5
Any work (MAR + DOM)	16.1	11.9	18.9	15.9	16.2	12.8	18.6
Schooling status							
Not attend school	11.6	6.3	23.7	10.3	12.9	8.0	13.4
Attends school	10.7	6.4	14.1	10.3	11.1	8.2	13.3

Notes: Each cell contains total hours worked (in both market and domestic work) in the last week for individuals that report participating in the indicated (row) activity. Children may participate in multiple activities. See Table 1 for row descriptions. *Attends school* indicates that the child attended school during the last year.

Source: Authors' calculations from UNICEF Multiple Indicator Cluster Survey End of Decade Assessment microdata. See Table 28.1 for description.

actually time spent in domestic work. Overall, a working child devotes on average 16
hours per week to working, but working children that are older, female or live in rural
areas work on average longer hours.

Though time devoted to work is considerable, it is not necessarily incompatible
with schooling attendance. Reported school attendance rates in these UNICEF data only
drop below 50 percent on average for children working more than 40 hours per week.
However, children who attend school spend less time working than children who do not
attend school. Seventy-three percent of children who attend school also work. The bottom
two rows show that children who attend school work 10.7 hours per week on average,
below the average 11.6 hours worked by children 5–14 that do not attend school.
Differences in hours worked are especially pronounced among older children ages 10–14,
with older children who do not attend school working almost 10 hours more than those
in school.

In fact, most children that work attend school. The top part of Table 28.3 reports
school attendance for children 5–14 in the UNICEF surveys. Overall, almost 70 percent
of children ages 5–14 attend school, and attendance rates are particularly high for older
children, boys and children in urban areas. School attendance varies by work status. The
middle part of Table 28.3 reports school attendance conditional on work status. Almost
74 percent of working children 5–14 attend school. Children that do not work are actually

Table 28.3   Work and schooling status for 124 million children 5–14 from 36 countries
in 2000

	All children	Age		Gender		Location	
	5–14	5–9	10–14	Male	Female	Urban	Rural
Attend school	69.5	58.9	80.8	70.7	68.3	75.1	63.9
Attendance rates conditional on							
Any work	73.9	64.1	80.6	75.7	72.3	80.1	68.3
Not work	60.0	52.9	82.2	61.6	57.8	64.9	52.8
Conditional on nonattendance							
Domestic only	32.0	30.8	34.9	27.1	36.6	31.8	32.0
Market only	4.5	2.8	8.3	6.3	2.7	4.9	4.3
Both market and domestic	22.0	13.1	42.2	20.3	23.5	12.8	26.6
Not work	41.5	53.3	14.6	46.2	37.1	50.6	37.1

Notes: The first row contains school attendance rates by column group. All rows listed under
"Attendance Rates Conditional on:" restrict the population to children whose labor status is in the
indicated category (works in any type of work, does not work). The rows listed under "conditional
on non attendance" restrict the sample to children that do not attend school. These non-attenders
are then divided into four categories: works only in domestic work, works only in market work,
works in domestic and market work, and does not work. Thus all four rows under the "conditional
on non-attendance" row sum to 100 (with some rounding error).

Source: Authors' calculations from UNICEF Multiple Indicator Cluster Survey End of Decade
Assessment microdata. See Table 28.1 for description.

about 14 percentage points less likely to attend school, but this mostly reflects lower school attendance among younger nonworking children. Among older children 10–14, school attendance is slightly lower for the group that works.

What do the 30 percent of children 5–14 that do not attend school do? The bottom part of Table 28.3 summarizes participation rates of children that do not attend school in various activities. Less than 5 percent of these children participate in market work alone. Participation in domestic work without schooling or market work is much more common – 32 percent of children 5–14 that do not attend school participate in domestic work alone. Thus, ignoring domestic work within the child's own household will cause researchers to miss one of the largest segments of children that do not attend school. Interestingly, almost 42 percent of the children that do not attend school also do not work. These so called "idle" children are predominately younger. They may largely be children too young to start school or work, but little is known about how their apparent idle status should be considered.

Even though most working children attend school, there may still be substantive consequences of work for schooling attainment. Time spent working takes away from study, play and sleep and might undermine the effectiveness of the classroom for child workers that attend school. That said, it is at least possible that some working children may also be learning valuable skills, accumulating experience, bringing in resources, establishing independence, supporting their family, paying for their schooling, developing a sense of effectiveness and enhancing their self-confidence – even if such effects are potentially difficult to capture in the data. Overall, deciphering how work impacts schooling attendance, performance or attainment depends on knowing what children would do if they were not working, and this is a major challenge for research.

Several studies have documented a negative correlation between working and grade advancement, years of completed education and test scores (Orazem and Gunnarsson, 2004; Psacharopoulos, 1997). For example, with data from 12 Latin American countries, Orazem and Gunnarsson (2004) find that third and fourth graders who attend school but never work in market or domestic work perform 28 percent better on mathematics tests and 19 percent better on language tests than children who attend school and work. However, the negative correlations might reflect that low-performing students tend to engage in work rather than that work creates low-performing students. Studies such as Boozer and Sari (2001) and Beegle, Dehejia and Gatti (2004) that try to address the endogeneity of child labor also find a negative association between child labor and educational attainment. For example, Beegle, Dehejia and Gatti examine the status of young adults in Vietnam five years after they are observed working and attending school. They find that a one standard deviation increase in hours worked for children attending school is associated with a 35 percent decrease in educational attainment five years later. Hence, even though most working children attend school, work may still have substantive consequences for schooling attainment.

Hazardous forms of child labor

The patterns of child labor described above come from large-scale household surveys. The advantage of these surveys is that they are randomized, so that it is possible to use them for inference about the scope of child labor in a country. However, some relatively rare forms of child labor are difficult to identify in household surveys. For these difficult-to-monitor forms of child labor, the ILO and interested organizations conduct specialized surveys that interview only those individuals engaged in the activity. It is a challenge to use these surveys to understand why children are engaged in relatively rare activities, but they are useful for estimating the incidence of some of the most hazardous forms of child labor.

The ILO's SIMPOC estimates that a total of 8.4 million children are involved in child trafficking, in forced or bonded labor, are soldiers, are prostitutes or involved in pornography or participate in illicit activities (ILO, 2002). Of these children, 68 percent are in bonded or forced labor. The reasons why children participate in hazardous forms of child labor have been given ample theoretical consideration, but systematic empirical evidence is scarce. An open research question is whether the determinants of participation in these hazardous activities that are universally condemned differ from the forces that drive young children to work on their family farm or in domestic duties.

It is also important to remember that children can face hazards in the most common kinds of labor, too. Especially as children get older, they become active in all aspects of agriculture, and it is not unusual to see reports of injuries in operating farm machinery in child labor surveys. The self-reported injury rate from child labor surveys of children working in agriculture is actually higher, at 12 percent, than the 9 percent level reported in manufacturing (Ashagrie, 1997). Agriculture can also be hazardous for children because of exposure to dangerous chemicals such as chemical herbicides or pesticides, exposure to heat or weather, repetitive work injuries and threats posed by animals, reptiles, insects, parasites and some plants. Recent research has emphasized not only the physical threats of child labor (O'Donnell, Doorslaer and Rosati, 2004), but also the psychosocial consequences for children of especially hard work (Woodhead, 2004).

Obviously, there is considerable scope for improvement in the basic data on the extent and circumstances of child labor. What is clear is that most working children are at home, helping their family in the family business or farm and with domestic work. The question of when child labor merits separate policy attention is still largely unresolved. However, one fundamental fact about child labor that emerges from the research discussed in the next section is that when families improve their economic status so that they no longer need children to work, they are quick to move children out of work. This observation, more than anything else, emphasizes the general undesirability of the high levels of child labor around the world today and the need to consider child labor in the formulation of development policy.

Economic conditions and policies that affect child labor

Since the seminal work of T.W. Schultz (1960), economists generally consider child labor in the context of the family's welfare optimization problem. Families take into account their valuation of child time in its various possible uses and allocate it accordingly. Thus, factors that raise the relative return to schooling may discourage child labor while increases in the child's wages or the family's valuation of the child's wages may encour-age it. While one often sees assertions that child labor is determined by cultural norms, the vast literature on how child labor responds to changes in the child's economic environment suggests that economic incentives matter, too. For example, decisions about how to allocate child time are often made by a parent. This gives rise to an agency problem, because the parent may not fully internalize all of the returns or benefits of how child time is allocated. Norms will influence the extent of the agency problem. For instance, in cultures where girls depart the family but boys stay and support the parents, the parent perceives a greater return to investing in the boy. This norm in turn makes investment in boys more profitable for the immediate family, and girls accordingly may work more. However, even with these norms, a vast body of research suggests that various aspects of poverty are of primary importance in understanding why children work.

Evidence on three facets of poverty is particularly compelling. First, child labor seems to decline dramatically with improvements in household living standards. Some of the evidence from household responses to trade liberalization is particularly interesting here. Despite rising employment opportunities for children, we observe declines in child labor as family incomes rise with trade. Second, child labor seems to be highly responsive to unexpected changes in the family's economic environment. Difficulty in transferring income over time (through saving or borrowing) is a common correlate of poverty, and research from several countries suggests that credit constraints and financial market imperfections increase the number of children who have to work. Third, poor local institutions such as ineffective or expensive schools associated with poverty may leave children with few sensible options other than work. We describe the evidence on how these three facets of poverty affect child labor in this section.

The role of living standards

Improvements in family incomes may affect child labor in four ways. First, child labor itself may be a bad in the family's welfare function. Thus, as incomes improve, the family chooses to have children work less. This idea is central in Basu and Van's (1998) seminal paper where children only work when the family cannot meet its subsistence needs. Second, with diminishing marginal utility of income, the value of the marginal contribution of the child's income decreases. Third, higher family incomes may facilitate the purchase of substitutes for child labor that may potentially lower the return to child labor within the household. For example, a washboard, fertilizer spreader or a combine harvester may replace child labor within the home. Fourth, the child's productivity in other activities such as schooling might improve because the family might be able to afford better inputs to schooling such as school fees, textbooks and uniforms.

The cross-country data on living standards and child labor suggests a strong connection between the two. Figure 28.1 plots the ILO's LABORSTA estimates of economic activity rates for children 10–14 against estimates of real GDP per capita (using purchasing power parity exchange rates) from the Penn World Tables 6.1. Each country observation is pictured as a circle where the size of the circle represents the size of the country's population between ages 10 and 14. While child labor is pervasive in poor economies such as Ethiopia and Nepal, child labor is unusual in a country wealthier than Gabon with a GDP per capita of $8,400. The curve in Figure 28.1 is from the regression of a country's economic activity rate for children on a third-order polynomial in GDP per capita (to allow a nonlinear relationship). The regression curve shown here is weighted by the population of children aged 10–14 in each country, but the unweighted regression curve is nearly identical. With this specification, variation in GDP per capita explains 73 percent of the variation in the economic activity rates of children.

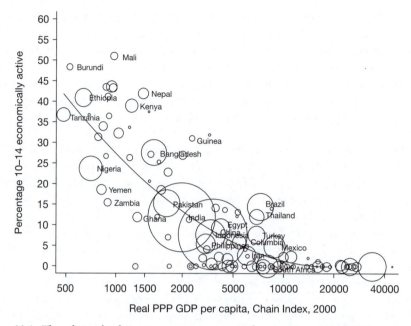

Figure 28.1   The relationship between economic status and economic activity, 2000

Source: Economic activity for 2000 from LABORSTA at <http://laborsta.ilo.org>, GDP per capita from Penn World Tables 6.1, and population aged 10–14 weights from UNStat.

Countries differ in many ways that may be associated with child labor and GDP per capita. Hence, the relationship in Figure 28.1 cannot be interpreted as causal. There are two types of within-country studies on the link between poverty and child labor that try to answer the question of what happens to child labor as income improves: those that look across different households at a point in time and those that look at the same households in two different time periods. In general, researchers that compare poor households to rich households at a single point in time in a country find mixed evidence of a link between poverty and child labor. Poor households differ from rich households in many ways that might be associated with child labor, and disentangling these omitted factors from the underlying causal relationship is difficult. For example, poorer households may live in areas with few employment opportunities, or poor households may lack capital, like tools or livestock, that make work more productive. In this case, at a single point in time, researchers could observe more child labor in wealthier families. This seems especially likely if researchers only focus on the types of work that are strongly correlated with living in a relatively well-off location (like wage work).

Studies tracking families over time almost universally find large declines in child labor with substantive changes in family incomes. For example, in tracking children over a three-year period in rural Tanzania, Beegle, Dehejia and Gatti (2003) find that children tend to work when households experience an unexpectedly poor harvest and that children stop working when households recover from the bad harvest. Yang (2004) examines how Philippine households with overseas workers responded to the 1997 Asian financial crisis. Remittance income increased in households whose overseas worker experienced more favorable exchange rate movements. Consequently, children in households with increased remittance income from abroad devoted less time to work and increased school attendance.

Let us consider in more detail the evidence on the relationship between poverty and child labor based on data from an elaborate survey project that tracked child labor and living standards in over 3,000 Vietnamese households between 1993 and 1998. Figure 28.2 plots participation rates in market work (defined as participation in wage work, work on the family farm or work in a household business) for children 6–15 against household per capita expenditure. The top line in Figure 28.2, which compares households at different levels of per capita expenditure in 1993, suggests a strong negative correlation between household living standards and child labor. For households below the 1993 poverty line, participation of children in market work exceeds 30 percent. From 1993 to 1998, real expenditure per capita increased by more than 50 percent for the poorest 10 percent of the population. For Vietnam overall, the incidence of poverty declined 36 percent.

The bottom curve in Figure 28.2 pictures the relationship between participation in market work in 1998 and household's per capita expenditure in 1993. Thus, for each point on the per capita expenditure distribution in 1993, child labor participation rates are pictured for the same households in 1993 and 1998. Participation rates drop substantially, with the largest declines in child labor occurring in households in the neighborhood of the poverty line in 1993. Indeed, over 80 percent of the decline in child labor occurring in households that exit poverty between 1993 and 1998 can be explained by improvements in household living standards (Edmonds, 2005).

Some of the most compelling evidence on the relationship between child labor and improvements in family living standards comes from how child labor responds to changes

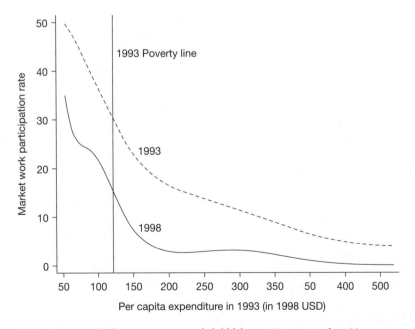

Figure 28.2 Living standard improvements and child labor in Vietnam in the 199s

Source: General Statistic Office (1994, 1999): Vietnam Living Standards Survey, Rural Panel, 1993 and 1998.

in trade policy. A common argument in the child labor literature is that foreign trade (and globalization in general) increases child labor by increasing the demand for goods produced by children. Consequently, many advocate trade sanctions by high-income countries on exports of goods from poor countries produced by child labor as a way to reduce child labor. A similar idea is implicit in consumer boycotts of products produced by child labor. Consumers who do not wish to consume goods produced by child labor can do so by purchasing products labeled as "child labor free" at a premium. Visible examples of such policies include RUGMARK-approved hand knotted rugs and "FIFA approved" soccer balls. However, economic theory suggests that the connection from expanded trade to child labor is ambiguous. After all, if expanded trade increases the incomes of parents, households may use the greater wealth to reduce child labor. In fact, Edmonds and Pavcnik (2004b) consider the cross-country data on child labor and openness to trade. They find that countries that trade more have less child labor, rather than more, and that this association is driven entirely by the strong association between trade and income.

Individual-level data that directly compare the effects of rising employment opportunities associated with increasing trade to the effects of changes in family income is relatively rare. Edmonds and Pavcnik (2004a) find declines in child labor during an episode of liberalization of rice markets in Vietnam. Between 1993 and 1998, Vietnam phased out quotas that restricted the export of rice and eliminated constraints on the trade of rice within the country. During this period, the average real price of ordinary rice increased by almost 30 percent. In Vietnam, 70 percent of households produce rice, and rice production is the largest employer of both children and adults. In fact, 26 percent of children 6–15 worked in agriculture (likely largely in rice production), and many more helped in the processing of rice or helped with household tasks that enabled parents to work in rice production. Moreover, rice accounts on average for 29 percent of the household budget.

The study uses the intertemporal and spatial variation in rice prices within Vietnam to consider potential effects of trade-induced price changes on child labor. Liberalization of rice markets appears to be associated with higher wages paid to both children and to adults. However, despite increased earning opportunities, Edmonds and Pavcnik (2004a) find that rice price increases can account for 45 percent of the decline in child labor that occurs in rural Vietnam in the 1990s. Children in households that are large net rice producers experience the largest declines in child labor, while child labor actually increases with rice price increases in households that are large consumers of rice. Land and labor are the two primary inputs into rice production, and overall, both are sufficiently equally distributed in Vietnam that most households were well positioned to enjoy the additional income stemming from this trade liberalization.

Of course, it is possible that a growth in trade could have opposite effects when the income gains are not distributed to those whose employment opportunities are rising. For example, Kruger (2004) observes that during the coffee boom of the mid-1990s in Nicaragua, there is an overall increase in child labor that is especially large in poor households in coffee producing areas. One explanation for her findings is that because of the concentration of land in coffee (and the resulting market power in local labor markets), poor laborers have received increases in income that are minor compared to the growth in labor demand, and, hence, child labor has increased. Thus, it is not inevitable that a growth in trade and employment opportunities will increase child labor, nor is it inevitable that such growth will decrease child labor either. The data, however, are clear on one point:

significant increases in family income are ceteris paribus strongly associated with reductions in child labor.

Credit market imperfections

Impoverished families may choose to have their children work either because they need the child's economic contribution to the household income or because that is the most sensible use of the child's time given the opportunities available to the child. Child labor seems particularly tragic when a child is compelled to work because of family need when the family would rather not have the child work given its environment. Several theoretical studies emphasize that if credit markets allowed households to borrow against future earnings, child labor could be much reduced (Baland and Robinson, 2000; Ranjan, 2001). (Note that there is a somewhat distinct literature considering whether educational decisions in high-income countries are influenced by an inability to borrow against the returns to a college education.) The main focus of attention in the developing country-child labor context is whether families can manage resources to in effect borrow against the next crop cycle (or pay period).

Three recent studies with individual-level data suggest that financial market imperfections that limit a household's ability to borrow may cause a greater number of children to work. In rural Tanzania, households increase child labor to mitigate the consequences of large crop losses (Beegle, Dehejia and Gatti, 2003). In urban Brazil, when male household heads enter unemployment, their children are more likely to work and less likely to advance in school (Duryea, Lam and Levison, 2003). These studies are consistent with credit market imperfection coupled with insurance failures, but it is difficult to exclude permanent income effects and changes in the value of child time as explanations for their findings. To isolate the credit channel, Edmonds (2004) compares child labor and schooling in black South African households that are about to receive a large anticipated cash transfer to child labor and schooling in households already receiving the cash. These two types of households have similar permanent income, but differ in cash on hand. He finds that child labor declines and schooling increases substantially when households begin receiving the anticipated income, which suggests that household access to credit is weak. These findings suggest that the credit and financial market imperfections associated with poverty are an important contributor to child labor.

In fact, problems with access to credit may be one of the most important reasons we observe children in bondage. The United Nations (1998) estimates that some 20 million people around the world are held in debt-bondage, and the ILO (2002) argues that nearly 30 percent of these bonded laborers are children. A child enters bondage when the child or the parents take out a debt from an employer against the child's future earnings. The bonded serves the creditor-master until the debt is repaid. However, because the bonded laborer is not free to negotiate the terms of employment after initial contracting, it can be very difficult for the worker to repay the debt and exit bondage. Often debts are inheritable. Edmonds and Sharma (2004) examine one debt-bondage system in the plains of Nepal and argue that the inheritability of the debt, coupled with a general insecurity in property rights over the indentured, makes debt-bondage particularly pernicious. With more developed credit markets, there would be little reason for children or their parents ever to consent to bondage in the first place.

Education reform

The family's external environment also influences whether and how much a child works. While we have already discussed the importance of the return to work for child labor, the return to other uses of the child's time, especially schooling, can also play a role in the child labor decision. Poverty often coexists with inadequate local institutions such as schools. When the alternatives to working are expensive or of poor quality, work may be the best use of a child's time. Although child labor might be compatible with school attendance, this does not preclude the family's schooling environment from influencing child labor.

One reason why families might choose not to send children to school is low perceived returns to attending school, and there is some evidence that child labor can be reduced by improving the incentive for households to send children to school. For example, Foster and Rosenzweig (2004) argue that school construction accompanying the green revolution in India facilitated increased schooling and decreased child labor. A number of countries have adopted policies designed to discourage child labor and increase schooling by lowering the cost of schooling via educational subsidies.[5] Examples of such programs include PETI and Bolsa Escola in Brazil, the Mid-day meals program in India and the Progresa program in Mexico. The Progresa program is particularly important because many countries are emulating it. The most relevant aspect of Progresa in the present context is that the transfers to poor households contain additional cash incentives for schooling. These incentives increase with age of the child, to compensate the household for the older child's greater opportunity cost of schooling. These programs can influence child labor through lowering the costs of schooling and raising family income. The evaluation data on Progresa is extremely encouraging. Schultz (2004) finds a significant reduction in wage and market work associated with eligibility for Progresa. He also projects a two-thirds of a year rise in schooling attainment (over a baseline level of 6.8 years) associated with the program. Of course, these schooling incentives might have larger effects on schooling than on child labor, depending on the program and the economic context, as Ravallion and Wodon (2000) found in their evaluation of Bangladesh's Food for Education program, which pays students in rice for attending school. But overall, these studies suggest a strong connection between child labor decisions and the return to sending the child to school.

Thus, improving the quality of education in a way that raises the return to education might also provide an incentive to reduce the quantity of child labor. When schools are bad, there is likely little return to education and households will not choose to educate their children. Formal studies of the link between child labor and school quality are conspicuously absent, but there is ample evidence of a strong link between school quality and school attendance. For example, Case and Yogo (1999) use variation in school quality for blacks in apartheid South Africa to study the link between the pupil-teacher ratio, the returns to schooling and school attendance. A decline in the pupil-teacher ratio by 10 students is associated with a 2 percent increase in the return to education and an additional 0.6 years of completed schooling. Foster and Rozensweig (1996) examine how the schooling of children responds to changes in the returns to education in Green Revolution India. With economic growth and advances in technology, the economic return to education appears to have increased dramatically, and households are more likely to give up present consumption to capture the benefit of education for their children.

A variety of evidence suggests that making education more attractive can be used as a policy tool to reduce child labor or at least to mitigate the schooling consequences of child labor. Thus, policies that seek to reduce the costs of schooling, increase school quality or improve the market return to education all have the power to reduce child labor.

Policy implications

Child labor is pervasive across low-income countries, as children help their parents on the family farm or business and in domestic work. Images of children forced into prostitution, fighting as soldiers or enslaved capture the popular imagination, but these hideous working conditions are rare. Of course, their rarity does not diminish the case for immediate, carefully targeted policy against these worst forms of child labor. But what should be done about the general incidence of child labor? Perhaps the strongest case for the need for direct attention to the types of child labor that pervade the low-income world is made by poor families themselves. By their behavior, these families reveal that they do not want their children to be working: child labor declines very rapidly as families become richer and their dependence on the income of children decreases.

Economic development that raises the incomes of the poor is the best way to reduce child labor around the world. But this process may take a long time. If we were to take the cross-country relationship between per capital income and child labor presented earlier in Figure 28.1 seriously as a forecast of what will happen to economic activity rates as countries grow richer – which it clearly is not – we could compute how economic growth will reduce child labor in the future. Based on the relationship in Figure 28.1 and historically average rates of growth of GDP per capita of 1.7 percent (Besley and Burgess, 2003), the economic activity rates of children should decline by 20 percent by 2015 and almost 50 percent by 2050. If economic development is to be accompanied by policies aimed directly at child labor, what types of national and international policies might be most effective?

Direct policy tools like bans on child labor or requirements that children attend school, however politically appealing, are of doubtful effect. First, enforcement is difficult. Developing countries often lack resources to enforce child labor bans, especially when most children work for their parents on family farms. Non-compliance with compulsory schooling laws continues to be a large problem in today's developing world (Krueger, 1997; Brown 2001).

Second, there is no guarantee that such policies will alter local labor markets in a way that increases family income, and thus an economic incentive for children to work will remain. The case for prohibitions on child labor is often framed as a multiple equilibrium problem. For example, in Basu and Van (1998) child labor persists because child labor depresses adult wages, making child labor necessary. However, punitive measures may actually increase child labor. For example, Basu (2003) shows that fining firms in violation of the child labor laws might actually increase child labor. The fines raise the expected cost of employing children, so that firms only find it profitable to employ children at lower wages, and more children are required to work to cover a family's subsistence needs. Moreover, bans on child labor in the real world typically apply only to certain relatively small kinds of child labor, like working for pay in a factory, rather than large categories like child laborers employed by their parents or children in unpaid domestic work. It is difficult to imagine that real-world labor market regulation can affect enough of the child labor market to have general equilibrium effects on wages as required in Basu and Van (1998). For example, the high-profile ban on child labor in Bangladesh involved mainly children working for pay in the garment industry. This ban allegedly affected the employment of 10,000 children, which corresponds to a tenth of one percent of economically active children in Bangladesh. Thus, although a legal ban *might* reduce child labor, this outcome is not guaranteed, especially when labor can easily substitute inside the household and thereby outside of the reach of labor laws. Without large general equilibrium effects on wages, the loss of a child's income, however small, might hurt the working child as well as her siblings.

Third, policies that keep children from working in one type of job might push children into nonexporting sectors or even into worse forms of child labor (in the Bangladesh case, anecdotes abound about children leaving garment factories for prostitution or work in stone quarries). That said, scientific evidence on what happens to children displaced from formal work is essentially nonexistent even in the most publicized prohibitions on the employment of children owing to the threat of sanctions, like the Bangladeshi garment industry and Pakistani soccer balls (Elliott and Freeman, 2003, pp. 112–115).

Empirical evidence on the effectiveness of child labor bans is scarce and draws mainly on the historical experiences of developed countries. Several careful empirical studies exploit variation in the implementation of the child labor and compulsory schooling laws across the United States to examine whether these legislative measures were the driving force behind the drastic declines in child labor at the turn of the twentieth century and increases in secondary school enrollment and educational attainment between 1910 and 1940. Moehling (1999), for example, finds little evidence that minimum age laws for manufacturing employment implemented between 1880 and 1910 contributed to the decline in child labor during this period. Several other U.S. studies suggest that some later child labor and compulsory schooling laws affected high school enrollment rates and subsequent educational attainment, but these legislative measures can explain at most 5 percent of the increase in high school enrollment and subsequent educational attainment between 1910 and 1939 (Goldin and Katz, 2003).

Might trade-related pressure help to reduce child labor? The U.S. government has repeatedly considered restricting trade or trade preferences for countries where child labor is endemic.[6] At the international level, some advocate for the World Trade Organization or the International Labor Organization to oversee harmonized child labor standards, with violators to be punished via trade sanctions.[7] At the consumer level, boycotts of products produced by child labor and more generally antisweatshop activism have become popular. Such campaigns seek to pressure multinational producers of high-profile brand name products to improve their labor practices.

Although these trade policies have highlighted the issue of child labor on the political agenda, there are several problems in using them in practice. First, if these policies lead to trade sanctions that reduce average family income, they could potentially increase the incidence of child labor. On the other hand, if the sanctions are only implemented very rarely, then they will not be a credible threat. Second, the recent history of trade sanctions aimed to promote broader political change does not suggest much optimism about their efficacy (Elliott and Freeman, 2003). Third, it's not clear what specific action the trade pressures should be seeking to create. For example, preventing children from working in one high-profile job may do nothing more than force children to change employers –

perhaps for the worse. Attempts to require either bans on child labor or compulsory school attendance are subject to the problems above. Fourth, it is difficult to distinguish whether these measures reflect genuine interest in the well-being of children in poor countries or whether they are just a palatable excuse for protectionism. Overall, it is difficult to make a strong case for trade policy or consumer boycotts as an effective tool to combat child labor. Consumer activism has brought the problem of child labor into the spotlight, but we are not aware of any systematic empirical evidence of the effectiveness of consumer activism in reducing child labor. It seems a blunt tool that is unlikely to reach the typical child laborer who helps parents on the family farm and in domestic chores.

Policies targeted at improving school infrastructure and reducing the cost of schooling provide the most promising targeted ways to reduce child labor. These initiatives might work best when combined with conditional cash transfers programs for households that send children to school, such as Food for Education in Bangladesh and Progresa in Mexico. Such programs have been successful in increasing school attendance, which ameliorates one of the concerns about child labor, and there is some evidence that these policies have, to a lesser extent, also reduced child labor. One great advantage of this type of positive program to discourage child labor through increasing schooling is that it addresses the agency problems and difficulty in monitoring that plague many other methods of attempting to reduce child labor. For example, though bans on child labor or laws for compulsory schooling can be difficult to enforce in, say, rural areas of low-income countries, linking a cash payment to the family to school attendance is much more practical.

International donors have been active in supporting similar positive initiatives that recognize the interconnection of poverty and child labor. While these programs appear promising, formal and independent evaluation of programs designed to help ameliorate child labor remains unusual. This unfortunate absence of evaluation work significantly limits our knowledge about the effectiveness of interventions aimed at child labor and prevents any learning from these experiences to design more effective policies concerning child labor. Whether anything other than economic development is an effective, long-term solution to the widespread incidence of child labor is an open question.

Notes

We are grateful for the research assistance of John Bellows, Evgeniya Petrova, Smita Reddy, and Savina Rizova and to Patty Anderson, Kaushik Basu, Drusilla Brown, James Hines, Deborah Levison, Doug Miller, Carol Rogers, Jay Shambaugh, Andrei Shleifer, Ken Swinnerton, Timothy Taylor, Michael Waldman and Dartmouth Junior Lunch participants for comments and suggestions.

1   One exception to this standard is the ILO's (International Labour Organization, 2002) global counts estimates, which define an economically active child as a child laborer if she is under 12 and economically active for one or more hours per week, 12–14 and working more than 14 hours per week or one or more hours per week in activities that are "hazardous by nature or circumstance," and if she is 15–17 and works in "unconditional work forms of child labor" (trafficked children, children in bondage or forced labor, armed conflict, prostitution, pornography, illicit activities).

2   Cross-country estimates of economic activity rates are also available from the International Labor Organization's LABORSTA database at <http://laborsta.ilo.org/>. In theory, the labor force in these data includes all wage workers, employers, own-account workers, members of producer cooperatives, unpaid family workers, apprentices, members of the armed forces and the unemployed. These LABORSTA estimates of economic activity rates are generally believed to understate the extent of economic activity, because data on work inside the household (even market work) are often not collected. Moreover, although the LABORSTA data are available over time, very few low-income countries have multiple data sources on child labor over time. Much of the intertemporal variation in child labor in the LABORSTA data is thus driven by the imputations and adjustments done for LABORSTA rather than independent observations on child labor. As a result, we do not view the LABORSTA data as useful for analyzing changes in child labor over time.

3   The Understanding Children's Work Project at <http://www.ucw-project.org> maintains a searchable database of datasets with basic child labor information. Many datasets with detailed child labor questions are publicly available. Several SIMPOC child labor surveys are available in English at <http://www.ilo.org/public/english/standards/ ipec/simpoc/microdata/index.htm>. Multipurpose household surveys conducted under the Living Standards Measurement Surveys of the World Bank are available at <http://www.worldbank.org/lsms/>. Other household survey projects with child labor information such as the most recent Indonesian Family Life Survey available at <http://www.rand.org/labor/FLS/IFLS/> and UNICEF's Multiple Indicator Cluster Surveys (MICS) available at <http://www.childinfo.org/MICS2/MICSDataSet.htm> are freely available.

4   The only exception that we are aware of is that a 2000 Department of Labor study claims that only 39 percent of economically active children 10–14 in Indonesia work in agriculture in 1993.

5   A related set of empirical studies, not directly linked to child labor, suggest, a direct link between schooling costs and school attendance. For example, there are recent reports of dramatic increases in school enrollment with initiatives to eliminate school fees (Kremer, 2003). In Kenya, Kremer, Moulin, Myatt and Namunyu (1997) evaluate a randomized intervention providing uniforms to students who would otherwise need to pay for uniforms. After five years, students with the free uniforms had completed 15 percent more schooling. Indirect schooling costs, such as the costs associated with accessing schooling, may also be important. For example, Duflo (2001) finds a large increase in schooling attainment accompanying a school construction program in Indonesia that would have lowered the commuting costs of schooling dramatically.

6   The U.S. government, for example, passed a 1997 amendment to the 1930 Tariff Act that prohibits imports of goods produced by forced or indentured child labor. Although the bill has yet to pass, the proposed Child Labor Deterrence Act aims to go further and to prohibit all imports of products into the United States that are manufactured by child labor. Also, under the Generalized System of Preferences (GSP), the United States can withdraw a poor country's eligibility for trade preferences based on the country's poor record in child labor practices (and other worker's rights). Finally, the 2000 Trade and Development Act restricts eligibility for trade benefits to countries that the Secretary of Labor certifies as showing progress towards eliminating the worst forms of child labor.

7   Abolition of child labor is one of the ILO's four core labor standards that some view should

be respected by all nations regardless of their level of economic development. Discussion of international labor standards is beyond the scope of this paper and is covered in Basu (1999), Brown (2001) and Elliott and Freeman (2003).

References

Ashagrie, Kebebew. 1997. *Statistics on Working Children and Hazardous Child Labour in Brief*. Geneva: International Labor Office.

Assaad, Ragui, Deborah Levison and Nadia Zibani. 2003. "The Effect of Child Work on Schooling in Egypt." Manuscript, University of Minnesota.

Baland, Jean-Marie and James A. Robinson. 2000. "Is Child Labor Inefficient?" *Journal of Political Economy*. August, 108:4, pp. 663–79.

Basu, Kaushik. 1999. "Child Labor: Cause, Consequence, and Cure, with Remarks on International Labor Standards." *Journal of Economic Literature*. 37:3, pp. 1083–119.

Basu, Kaushik. 2003. "Policy Dilemmas for Controlling Child Labor." CAE Working Paper No. 03–17, Cornell University.

Basu, Kaushik and Pham Hoang Van. 1998. "The Economics of Child Labor." *American Economic Review*. 88:3, pp. 412–27.

Beegle, Kathleen, Rajeev H. Dehejia and Roberta Gatti. 2003. "Child Labor, Crop Shocks, and Credit Constraints." NBER Working Paper No. 10088.

Beegle, Kathleen, Rajeev H. Dehejia and Roberta Gatti. 2004. "The Education, Labor Market, and Health Consequences of Child Labor." Manuscript, Columbia University.

Besley, Timothy and Robin Burgess. 2003. "Halving Global Poverty." *Journal of Economic Perspectives*. 17:3, pp. 3–22.

Boozer, Micheal and Tanveet Suri. 2001. "Child Labor and Schooling Decisions in Ghana." Manuscript, Yale University.

Brown, Drusilla. 2001. "Labor Standards: Where Do They Belong on the International Trade Agenda?" *Journal of Economic Perspectives*. 15:3, pp. 89–112.

Case, Anne and Motohiro Yogo. 1999. "Does School Quality Matter? Returns to Education and the Characteristics of Schools in South Africa." NBER Working Paper No. 7399.

Central Bureau of Statistics. 2000. *Report On The Nepal Labour Force Survey 1998/99*. Kathmandu: National Planning Commission Secretariat of His Majesty's Government.

Duflo, Esther. 2001. "Schooling and Labor Market Consequences of School Construction in Indonesia: Evidence from an Unusual Policy Experiment." *American Economic Review*. 91:4, pp. 795–813.

Duryea, Suzanne, David Lam and Deborah Levison. 2003. "Effects of Economic Shocks on Children's Employment and Schooling in Brazil." Population Studies Center Research Report 03–541, December, University of Michigan.

Edmonds, Eric. 2003. "Child Labor in South Asia." OECD Social, Employment and Migration Working Papers No. 5, Paris.

Edmonds, Eric. 2004. "Does Illiquidity Alter Child Labor and Schooling Decisions? Evidence from Household Responses to Anticipated Cash Transfers in South Africa." NBER Working Paper No. 10265, February.

Edmonds, Eric. 2005. "Does Child Labor Decline with Improving Economic Status?" *Journal of Human Resources*. Forthcoming.

Edmonds, Eric and Nina Pavcnik. 2004a. "The Effect of Trade Liberalization on Child Labor." *Journal of International Economics.* Forthcoming.

Edmonds, Eric and Nina Pavcnik. 2004b. "International Trade and Child Labor: Cross-Country Evidence." NBER Working Paper No. 10317.

Edmonds, Eric and Salil Sharma. 2004. "Investments in Children Vulnerable to Bondage." Manuscript, Dartmouth College.

Elliot, Kimberly Ann and Richard B. Freeman. 2003. *Can Labor Standards Improve Under Globalization?* Washington, DC: Institute for International Economics.

Food and Agricultural Organization (FAO). 2004. "Population and Labour Force Indicators," in *The State of Food and Agriculture 2003–2004.* Food and Agricultural Organization of the United Nations: Rome, part 3, Table A4.

Foster, Andrew and Mark Rosenzweig. 1996. "Technical Change and Human Capital Returns and Investments: Evidence from the Green Revolution." *American Economic Review.* September, 86:4, pp. 931–53.

Foster, Andrew and Mark Rosenzweig. 2004. 'Technological Change and the Distribution of Schooling: Evidence from Green Revolution India." *Journal of Development Economics.* 74:1, pp. 87–112.

General Statistical Office. 1994. *Vietnam Living Standards Survey 1992–93.* Ha Noi, Vietnam: Vietnamese General Statistical Office.

General Statistical Office. 1999. Vietnam Living Standards Survey, 1998. Ha Noi, Vietnam: Vietnamese General Statistical Office.

Goldin, Claudia and Larry Katz. 2003. "Mass Secondary Schooling and the State: The Role of State Compulsion in the High School Movement." NBER Working Paper No. 10075.

International Labour Organization (ILO). 2002. *Every Child Counts: New Global Estimates on Child Labour.* Geneva: ILO.

Kremer, Micheal. 2003. "Randomized Evaluations of Educational Programs in Developing Countries: Some Lessons." *American Economic Review.* 93:2, pp. 102–15.

Kremer, Micheal, Sylvie Moulin, David Myatt and Robert Namunyu. 1997. "The Quality-Quantity Tradeoff in Education: Evidence from a Prospective Evaluation in Kenya." Manuscript, Harvard University.

Krueger, Alan. 1997. "International Labor Standards and Trade," in *Annual World Bank Conference on Development Economics, 1996.* Michael Bruno and Boris Pleskovic, eds. Washington, D.C.: World Bank, pp. 281–302.

Kruger, Diana. 2004. "Child Labor and Schooling during a Coffee Sector Boom: Nicaragua 1993–1998," in *Trabjo Infantil: Teoría y Evidencia desde Latinoamerica.* Luis F. Lopez Calva, ed. Mexico, D.F.: Fondo de Cultura Económica de México, forthcoming.

Levison, Deborah and Karine Moe. 1998. "Household Work as a Deterrent to Schooling: An Analysis of Adolescent Girls in Peru." *Journal of Developing Areas.* Spring, 32, pp. 339–56.

Levison, Deborah, Karine Moe and Felicia Knaul. 2001. "Youth Education and Work in Mexico." *World Development.* 29:1, pp. 167–88. Moehling, Carolyn. 1999. "State Child Labor Laws and the Decline of Child Labor." *Explorations in Economic History.* 36:1, pp. 72–106.

O'Donnell, Owen, Eddy van Doorslaer and Furio Rosati. 2004. "Health Effects of Child Work: Evidence from Rural Vietnam." *Journal of Population Economics.* Forthcoming.

Orazem, Peter and L. Victoria Gunnarsson. 2004. "Child Labour, School Attendance, and Performance: A Review." Iowa State Department of Economics Working Paper No. 04001.

Psacharopoulos, George. 1997. "Child Labor versus Educational Attainment: Some Evidence from Latin America." *Journal of Population Economics*. 10:4, pp. 377–86.

Ranjan, Priya. 2001. "Credit Constraints and the Phenomenon of Child Labor." *Journal of Development Economics*. 64:1, pp. 81–102.

Ravallion, Martin and Quentin Wodon. 2000. "Does Child Labor Displace Schooling? Evidence on Behavioural Responses to an Enrollment Subsidy." *Economic Journal*. March, 110, pp. C158–C175.

Schultz, T. Paul. 2004. "School Subsidies for the Poor: Evaluating the Mexican Progresa Poverty Program." *Journal of Development Economics*. 74:1, pp. 199–250.

Schultz, Theodore W. 1960. "Capital Formation by Education." *Journal of Political Economy*. December, 68, pp. 571–83.

United Nations Working Group on Contemporary Forms of Slavery. 1998. *Debt Bondage*. Geneva: United Nations Economic and Social Council, Commission on Human Rights, Subcommission on Prevention of Discrimination and protection of Minorities, Working Group on Contemporary Forms of Slavery, 23rd Session.

Woodhead, Martin. 2004. *Psychosocial Impacts of Child Work: A Framework for Research, Monitoring, and Intervention*. Florence: Understanding Children's Work.

Yang, Dean. 2004. "Remittances and Human Capital Investments: Child Schooling and Child Labor in the Origin Households of Oversees Filipino Workers." Manuscript, University of Michigan.

REVIEW AND DISCUSSION QUESTIONS

1 What kind of work do most working children in developing countries do? Who employs them?
2 The authors point out that the relation between child labor and school attendance and performance is more complicated than one might expect. Explain why this is the case.
3 Increases in family income may affect child labor in a number of ways. Explain why.
4 Explain what the evidence shows regarding the relation between child labor and foreign trade (or, more broadly, globalization).
5 In what ways is the pervasiveness of child labor linked to the level of development of a country's financial markets?
6 According to the authors, what kind of policies should developing countries pursue to address child labor? Do you agree with the authors' recommendations?

Suggestions for further reading

Caldwell, John C. (2005) "On Net Intergenerational Wealth Flows: An Update," *Population and Development Review*, 31: 721-40.

The Australian demographer updates his famous theory, according to which the high benefits and low costs of additional children in developing countries help explain high fertility. He uses data accumulated over the past thirty years to show that the benefits of additional children may have been overestimated.

Crook, N. (1997) *Principles of Population and Development with Illustrations from Asia and Africa*, Oxford: Oxford University Press.

This is a very readable book that starts with a critical examination of Malthus and goes on to discuss the environmental impact of population growth, famines and disease control, changes in fertility, urbanization and migration, and several other issues that connect demographic changes to economic development.

Kelley, A. C. (2001) "The Population Debate in Historical Perspective: Revisionism Revised," in N. Birdsall, A. C. Kelley, and S. W. Sinding (eds) *Population Matters: Demographic Change, Economic Growth, and Poverty in the Developing World*, New York: Oxford University Press.

Kelley provides a detailed summary of the economic research on the impact of population growth on economic development. He reviews the debate about the effects of population growth and the evolution of the debate since the 1950s, and he explains the meaning of the "revisionist" position that most economists espouse. Such a position rejects doomsday scenarios with little empirical support and emphasizes instead the need to look at long-run effects and take into account both positive and negative effects of population growth.

Malthus, T. (1798) *An Essay on the Principle of Population*, reissued as Malthus, T. and Gilbert, G. (ed.) (1999) *An Essay on the Principle of Population* (Oxford World's Classics), New York: Oxford University Press.

The famous essay by Thomas Malthus introduces the idea that population grows geometrically while "subsistence" (food supply) only grows arithmetically. Controversial even at the time, Malthus's dire prediction that famines and starvation would result if couples did not voluntarily reduce their fertility has resurfaced regularly in the literature on population and development.

World Health Organization, *The World Health Report* (published annually).

Published since 1995, the report includes up-to-date information on the state of global health as well as a focus on a specific topic which changes every year (recent topics have included global public health security, mortality of mothers and children, HIV/AIDS, and reducing risks to human health).

PART FIVE

Agriculture, the environment, and sustainable development

INTRODUCTION

IN 2005, 0.7 PERCENT OF THE LABOR FORCE IN THE U.S. was employed in agriculture. Over 75 percent was employed in services – from banking and insurance to entertainment and retail sales (Central Intelligence Agency 2007). In most high-income countries employment numbers are similar. No more than 5 percent of the labor force is still in agriculture, while services employ by far the largest share of the population (ibid.). The employment pattern is very different in developing countries. Agriculture still employs the majority of the labor force in countries such as Bangladesh, Cambodia, Vietnam, Ghana, Madagascar, Tanzania, and Uganda (World Bank 2007: 48–50). In addition, most LDCs have much more poverty in rural than in urban areas (ibid: 60–62). Those who derive their living from agriculture, in other words, are significantly more likely to be among the poor. The implication is that understanding the economies of poor countries and the nature of poverty and poverty reduction in such countries requires understanding the workings of the agricultural sector.

Agriculture is dependent on land, and land is a relatively fixed resource. Agriculture also depends on labor, and because rural–urban migration is a nearly universal phenomenon, agricultural labor is a resource that often decreases over time. Development economists, therefore, are especially interested in studying how agricultural productivity can be raised, i.e., how to increase agricultural output when the amount of resources needed to produce it is fixed or declining. The concern is especially pressing because, as we have seen in Part Four, populations in many developing countries are still growing quickly, and a growing population requires a growing food supply. In turn, a growing food supply requires finding ways of increasing agricultural output.[1]

The two most common approaches to increasing agricultural productivity involve changing the system of land ownership and changing agricultural technology. Because land is such a crucial input in agriculture, the land ownership system can have a substantial impact on the productivity of the land, i.e., on the amount of output obtained from each acre of land. Farmers who own a plot of land, for example, have strong incentives to be productive and make long-term investments in the land because they will fully benefit from any increase in output resulting from their efforts. On the other hand, farmers who lease a plot of land for a short period of time have no incentive to make long-term investments in the land. Another important issue is the size of the plots, which has an effect on farming methods. For example, agricultural machines may be helpful and cost-effective on very large tracts of land, but are unlikely to be used productively on small plots. Changing the system of land ownership, therefore, is likely to affect agricultural productivity through a number of channels (see Perkins et al. 2006: Ch. 16 and Ray 1998: Ch. 12 for a discussion of land ownership and land reform).

Agricultural technology also has a significant effect on productivity. The article by University of Minnesota economist Vernon W. Ruttan (reprinted in Chapter 29) discusses whether we can expect technological improvements to continue to raise agricultural productivity in the decades to come. Ruttan explains the key distinction between improvements in mechanical technology and improvements in biological technology. Improvements in mechanical technology are those that make workers more productive, such as the introduction of agricultural machines. These improvements are especially important in countries where land is abundant and labor relatively scarce, so enabling workers to produce increasing quantities of output is the key to raising productivity. Improvements in biological technology, on the other hand, make land more productive. Pesticides, fertilizers, and irrigation, for example, all help farmers obtain more output from a given amount of land. These improvements are especially important in countries where land is scarce and labor abundant, i.e., where the priority is generating as much output as possible from each acre of land.

In the second half of the twentieth century, increases in agricultural productivity worldwide were so dramatic that global food production increased very rapidly – as mentioned in Part Four, it increased much faster than global population. Much of this increase in productivity was due to a specific advance in biological technology: the introduction of new crop varieties especially suited to the climatic conditions of developing countries. The so-called "Green Revolution," which took place in the 1960s and 1970s, involved the development of new crops and led to dramatic increases in yields, especially in a number of Asian countries (see, e.g., Cypher and Dietz 2004: 328–30). But this technological revolution was not successful everywhere. Norman E. Borlaug, an agricultural scientist, received the Nobel Peace Prize in 1970 for his contributions to the Green Revolution. In the article reprinted in Chapter 30, he discusses the obstacles to improvements in agricultural productivity on the African continent. He emphasizes the very limited use of fertilizer, the lack of irrigation, and the many ways in which lack of adequate transportation infrastructure prevents improvements in productivity. Borlaug believes that the provision of aid and technical assistance by developed countries is essential to help Africa improve farming techniques.

The introduction of genetically modified (GM) crops in recent years represents an additional step toward improvements in agricultural technology; it has also generated enormous controversy. In the article reprinted in Chapter 31, Wellesley College political scientist Robert Paarlberg discusses a report on GM crops by the Food and Agriculture Organization (an arm of the United Nations) and sheds light on the controversy. Supporters of GM crops have emphasized that the new varieties lead to higher yields, are more resistant to pests, and are better able to survive in dry climates. Opponents worry about the safety of these genetically engineered crops and warn that the new crops may change entire ecosystems, with unpredictable effects on other crops and animal species. They also point out that private corporations developed GM seeds, whereas research sponsored by government and international organizations was largely responsible for the high-yield varieties of the original Green Revolution. The fact that corporate interests are behind the development of GM crops makes some worry that the interests of the poor will be neglected. Paarlberg believes that "the ideological divide between those who accept and those who reject science-enhanced farming practices (versus traditional ones) will thus remain as wide as ever."

The debate over agricultural technologies is part of a broader debate on the most effective use of natural resources and on the potential trade-offs between short-run economic growth and the long-run effects of growth strategies. The concept of sustainable development, which has received increasing attention in the past couple of decades, addresses the relation between development and the environment as well as the tensions that developing countries face between satisfying present economic needs and looking after the interests of future generations. In the article reprinted in Chapter 32, scientists Robert W. Kates, Thomas M. Parris, and Anthony A. Leiserowitz review the history of sustainable development and discuss the many facets of this complex idea. They note that there is not much agreement about what sustainable development is supposed to "sustain" or what it is supposed to "develop." The "sustainable" part sometimes refers simply to the need to protect natural resources, but it has also been used to argue for protection of biodiversity and even cultural diversity, "including livelihoods, groups, and places that constitute distinctive and threatened communities." Similarly, the "development" part of sustainable development encompasses the wide range of indicators of standards of living discussed in Part One – from narrow measures of output or output per capita to broad measures of human development. Another area of disagreement in the discussion of what sustainable development is and what it should be involves the time horizon of sustainability: if short-run gains must be balanced against future costs of current policies, how far into the future should we look? And, of course, there is a variety of points of view on what may be the most important question in sustainable development, i.e., how exactly we should balance the interests of current and future generations. For instance, if cutting down the rain forest helps development in the short run and hinders it in the long run, exactly how much cutting should we be doing? The authors explore sustainable development from several other points of view as well, including its goals, the indicators used to measure it, the values that represent it, and the activities of the actual groups and organizations that have been promoting it. They summarize their inquiry by referring to sustainable development as "a concept that, in the end, represents diverse local to global efforts to imagine and enact a positive vision of a world in which basic human needs are met without destroying or irrevocably degrading the natural systems on which we all depend."

Putting a country's natural resources to work for the well-being of its people is a crucial step in the process of economic development, but it is also a step fraught with challenges and risks. As we have seen in the case of population growth, economists are skeptical of doomsday scenarios suggesting that agricultural technologies cannot continue to advance or that pursuing economic growth will inevitably lead to resource exhaustion or environmental catastrophes. Nonetheless, there are certainly examples of failed agricultural policies (such as Zimbabwe's land reform) and costly misuse of natural resources (such as the mismanagement of the Amazon in Brazil). As is often the case in development economics, governments can play a constructive role by devising policies that protect the interests of the poor and incorporate the insights of economics into what drives incentives – to farm productively, to develop new agricultural technologies, to adopt such technologies, and to manage natural resources effectively.

NOTE

1   Of course, a country may also be able to import food from abroad; that, however, requires having enough foreign currency to purchase food produced by other countries, i.e., it requires the ability to export other goods. See Eswaran and Kotwal (2006: 115–17); see also Perkins et al. (2006: 610–12) for a discussion of food self-sufficiency.

REFERENCES

Central Intelligence Agency (2007) *The World Factbook*. Online. Available HTTP: <https://www.cia.gov/library/publications/the-world-factbook> (accessed 2 September 2007).

Cypher, M. C. and Dietz, J. L. (2004) *The Process of Economic Development*, 2nd edn, London: Routledge.

Eswaran, M. and Kotwal, A. (2006) "The Role of Agriculture in Development," in A. V. Banerjee, R. Bénabou, and D. Mookherjee (eds), *Understanding Poverty*, New York: Oxford University Press.

Perkins, D. H., Radelet, S. and Lindauer, D. (2006) *Economics of Development*, 6th edn, New York: W. W. Norton.

Ray, D. (1998) *Development Economics*, Princeton, NJ: Princeton University Press.

World Bank (2007) *World Development Indicators 2007*. Washington, DC: World Bank.

Chapter 29

Vernon W. Ruttan

PRODUCTIVITY GROWTH IN WORLD AGRICULTURE
Sources and constraints

PRIOR TO THE BEGINNING OF THE twentieth century, almost all increases in crop and animal production occurred as a result of increases in the area cultivated. By the end of the century, almost all increases were coming from increases in land productivity – in output per acre or per hectare. This was an exceedingly short period in which to make a transition from a natural resource-based to a science-based system of agricultural production. In the presently developed countries, the beginning of this transition began in the latter half of the nineteenth century. In most developing countries, the transition did not begin until well into the second half of the twentieth century. For some of the poorest countries in the world, the transition has not yet begun.

During the second half of the twentieth century, world population more than doubled – from approximately 2.5 billion in 1950 to 6.0 billion in 2000. The demands placed on global agricultural production arising out of population and income growth almost tripled. By 2050, world population is projected to grow to between 9 and 10 billion people. Most of the growth is expected to occur in poor countries, where the income elasticity of demand for food remains high. Even moderately high income growth, combined with projected population growth, could result in close to doubling the demands placed on the world's farmers by 2050 (Johnson, 2000; United Nations, 2001).

The most difficult challenges will occur during the next two or three decades as both population and income in many of the world's poorest countries continue to grow rapidly. But rapid decline in the rate of population growth in such populous countries as India and China lends credence to the United Nations projections that by midcentury, the global rate of population growth will slow substantially. The demand for food arising out of income growth is also expected to slow as incomes rise and the income elasticity of demand for food declines. In the interim, very substantial increases in scientific and technical effort will be required, particularly in the world's poorest countries, if growth in food production is to keep pace with growth in demand.

Agriculture in development thought

Economic understanding of the process of agricultural development has made substantial advances over the last half-century. In the early post-World War II literature, agriculture, along with other natural resource-based industries, was viewed as a sector from which resources could be extracted to fund development in the industrial sector (Lewis, 1954, p. 139; Rostow, 1956; Ranis and Fei, 1961). Growth in agricultural production was viewed as an essential condition, or even a precondition, for growth in the rest of the economy. But the process by which agricultural growth was generated remained outside the concern of most development economists.

By the early 1960s, a new perspective, more fully informed by both agricultural science and economics, was beginning to emerge. It had become increasingly clear that much of agricultural technology was "location specific." Techniques developed in advanced countries were not generally directly transferable to less developed countries with different climates and resource endowments. Evidence had also accumulated that only limited productivity gains were to be had by the reallocation of resources within traditional peasant agriculture.

In an iconoclastic book, *Transforming Traditional Agriculture*, Theodore W. Schultz (1964) insisted that peasants in traditional agrarian societies are rational allocators of available resources and that they remained poor because most poor countries provided them with only limited technical and economic opportunities to which they could respond – that is, they were "poor but efficient." Schultz (1964, pp. 145–147) wrote:

> The principle sources of high productivity in modern agriculture are reproducible sources. They consist of particular material inputs and of skills and other capabilities required to use such inputs successfully. . . . But these modern inputs are seldom ready made. . . . In general what is available is a body of knowledge, which has made it possible for the advanced countries to produce for their own use factors that are technically superior to those employed elsewhere. This body of knowledge can be used to develop similar, and as a rule superior, new factors appropriate to the biological and other conditions that are specific to the agriculture of poor countries.

This thesis implies three types of relatively high payoff investments for agricultural development: 1) the capacity of agricultural research institutions to generate new location-specific technical knowledge; 2) the capacity of the technology supply industries to develop, produce and market new technical inputs; and 3) the schooling and nonformal (extension) education of rural people to enable them to use the new knowledge and technology effectively. The enthusiasm with which this high-payoff input model was accepted and transformed into doctrine was due at least as much to the success of plant breeders and agronomists in developing fertilizer and management responsive "green revolution" crop varieties for the tropics as to the power of Schultz's ideas.[1]

The Schultz "high-payoff input model" remained incomplete, however, even as a model of technical change in agriculture. It did not attempt, to explain how economic conditions induce an efficient path of technical change for the agricultural sector of a particular society. Nor does the high-payoff input model attempt to explain how economic conditions induce the development of new institutions, such as public sector agricultural experiment stations, that become the suppliers of location-specific new knowledge and technology.

Beginning in the early 1970s, Hayami and Ruttan (1971, 1985) and Binswanger and Ruttan (1978) formulated a model of induced technical change in which the development and application of new technology is endogenous to the economic system. Building on the Hicksian model of factor-saving technical change, and their own experience in southeast Asia, they proposed a model in which the direction of technical change in agriculture was induced by changes (or differences) in relative resource endowments and factor prices. In this model, alternative agricultural technologies are developed to facilitate the substitution of relatively abundant (hence, cheap) factors for relatively scarce (hence, expensive) factors. Two kinds of technology generally correspond to this taxonomy. Mechanical technology is "labor saving," designed to substitute power and machinery for labor. Biological and chemical technology is "land saving," designed to substitute labor-intensive production practices and industrial inputs such as fertilizer and plant and animal protection chemicals for land. Both the technical conditions of production and historical experience suggest that changes in land productivity and labor productivity are relatively independent (Griliches, 1968).

The process of induced technical change can be illustrated from the historical experience of Japan and the United States from 1880 to 1980. As the price of fertilizer declined relative to the price of land, fertilizer use per hectare rose in both countries. Similarly, as the price of draft power declined relative to the price of labor, the use of power per worker rose in both countries.

Throughout the period 1880–1980, Japanese farmers used more fertilizer per hectare than U.S. farmers, and U.S. farmers used more power per worker than did Japanese farmers. These differences in use of fertilizer per unit of land and of draft power per worker between the two countries, and the changes in each country between 1880 and 1980, were not the result of simple factor substitution in response to relative price changes. The large changes in factor ratios were made possible only by the very substantial advances in biological and mechanical technology that facilitated the substitution of fertilizer for land and draft power for labor. These technical changes were induced by the differences and changes in relative factor price ratios (Hayami and Ruttan, 1985, pp. 176–197).[2] Over time, particularly since World War II, there has been some convergence in relative factor prices and in relative intensity of factor use in the two countries.

Advances in mechanical technology in agriculture have been intimately associated with the industrial revolution. But the mechanization of agriculture cannot be treated as simply the adaptation of industrial methods of production to agriculture. The spatial dimension of crop production requires that the machines suitable for agricultural mechanization must be mobile – they must move across or through materials that are immobile (Brewster, 1950). The seasonal characteristic of agricultural production requires a series of specialized machines – for land preparation, planting, pest and pathogen control and harvesting – designed for sequential operations, each of which is carried out for only a few days or weeks in each season. One result is that a fully mechanized agriculture is typically very capital intensive. Advances in biological technology in crop production involve one or more of the following three elements: land and water resource development to provide a more favorable environment for plant growth; the addition of organic and inorganic sources of plant nutrition to the soil to stimulate plant growth and the use of biological and chemical means to protect plants from pests and pathogens; and selection and breeding of new biologically efficient crop varieties specifically adapted to respond to those elements in the environment that are subject to management.

Advances in mechanical technology are a primary source of growth in labor productivity; advances in biological technology are a primary source of growth in land productivity. There are, of course, exceptions to this analytical distinction. For example, in Japan, horse plowing was developed as a technology to cultivate more deeply to enhance yield (Hayami and Ruttan, 1985, p. 75). In the United States, the replacement of horses by tractors released land from animal feed to food production (White, 2000; Olmstead and Rhode, 2001). At the most sophisticated level, technical change often involves complementary advances in both mechanical and biological technology. For most countries, the research resource allocation issue is the relative emphasis that should be given to advancing biological and mechanical technology.

The model of induced technical change has important implications for resource allocation in agricultural research. In labor abundant and land constrained developing countries, like China and India, research resources are most productively directed to advancing yield-enhancing biological technology. In contrast, land abundant Brazil has realized very high returns from research directed to releasing the productivity constraints on its problem soils. Discovery of the yield-enhancing effects of heavy lime application on acidic aluminum containing soils has opened its *Campos Cerrado* (great plains) region to extensive mechanized production of maize and soybeans.

Measuring the rate and direction of productivity growth

Comparative research on the rate and direction of productivity growth in agriculture has gone through three stages. Initially, efforts were directed to the measurement of partial productivity ratios and indexes, such as output per worker and per hectare. Intercountry cross-section and time series comparisons of output per unit of land and labor were first assembled by Colin Clark in his pioneering study, the *Conditions of Economic Progress* (1940). In the late 1960s, Clark's inter-country comparisons were revived and updated by Yujiro Hayami and associates (Hayami, 1969; Hayami and Inagi, 1969; Hayami, Miller, Wade and Yamashita, 1971). These early partial productivity studies identified exceedingly wide differences in land and labor productivity, both among countries and major world regions. Recent trends in land and labor productivity indicate that these wide differences have persisted. In Figure 29.1, labor productivity (output per worker) is measured on the horizontal axis. Land productivity (output per hectare) is measured on the vertical axis. The dashed diagonal lines, with the units appearing across the top and down the right-hand side of the figure, trace the land-labor factor ratios (hectares of agricultural land per worker). The country and regional lines indicate land-labor trajectories for specific countries or regions. The partial productivity growth patterns of Figure 29.1 are displayed in much greater detail in the work of Hayami and Ruttan (1985, pp. 117–129). The several country and regional growth paths fall broadly into three groups: a) a land constrained path in which output per hectare has risen faster than output per worker; b) a land abundant path in which output per worker has risen more rapidly than output per hectare; and c) an intermediate growth path in which output per worker and per hectare have grown at somewhat comparable rates. During the later stages of development, as the price of labor begins to rise relative to the price of land, the growth path tends to shift in a labor

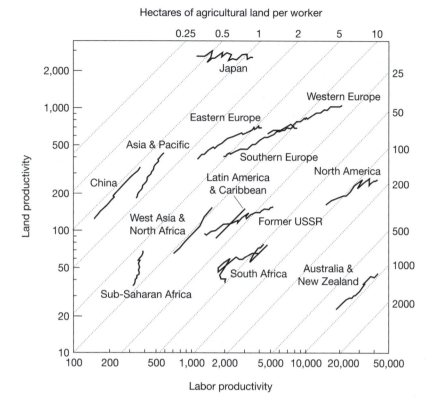

Figure 29.1   International comparison of land and labor productivities by region: 1961 to 1990

Notes: AgGDP in nominal local currency units was first deflated to base year 1980 using country-specific AgGDP deflators and then converted to U.S. dollars using Purchasing Power Parity exchange rates for agricultural output. The number of countries on which the regional (weighted averages) area is based is as follows: sub-Saharan Africa (17), Asia and the Pacific (11), Latin America and the Caribbean (18), West Asia and North Africa (9), Europe (13) and North America (2). Hectares of agricultural land per economically active member of the agricultural population includes arable plus permanently cropped and permanently pastured land. "Agricultural workers" is here defined as economically active in agricultural production.

Source: Craig, Pardey and Roseboom (1997).

saving direction. Partial productivity ratios such as those plotted in Figure 29.1 were employed by Hayami and Ruttan (1970, 1971, pp. 163–205) in their initial tests of the induced technical change hypothesis.

A second stage of the research on technical change in agriculture involved the estimation of cross-country production functions and the construction of multifactor productivity estimates. In these studies, factor inputs-typically land, labor, livestock, capital equipment (machinery) and current inputs (fertilizer) – were aggregated using either factor shares or statistical estimates as the weights for factor aggregation in multifactor productivity estimates or as elasticity coefficients in Cobb-Douglas type production functions.[3] Over time, improvements in data availability and estimation methods have contributed to greater reliability in the estimates.

The Hayami and Ruttan (1970) and the Kawagoe, Hayami and Ruttan (1985) cross-country metaproduction functions (Lau and Youtopoulos, 1989) have been used in growth accounting exercises to partition the sources of differences in agricultural labor and land productivity between developed and developing countries and among individual countries. The results indicated that internal resource endowments (land and livestock), modern technical inputs (machinery and fertilizer) and human capital (general and technical education) each accounted for approximately one-fourth of the differences in labor productivity between developed countries and less developed countries as groups. Scale economies, present in developed countries but not in less developed countries, accounted for about 15 percent of the difference.[4]

The implications of these results for potential growth of labor productivity in the agricultural production of less developed countries were encouraging. The pressure of population against land resources was not a binding constraint on agricultural production. Scale diseconomies were not an immediate constraint on labor productivity. Labor productivity could be increased by several multiples – to levels approximating the levels in western Europe in the early 1960s – by investment in human capital, in agricultural research and by more intensive use of technical inputs. The historical experience of Japan, and the more recent experience of Korea and Taiwan, did suggest, however, that as demand for labor, associated with rapid urban-industrial development, draws substantial labor from agriculture, small farm size could become a more serious constraint. As the agricultural labor force declines, farm consolidation results in a rise in the land/labor ratio and a rise in labor productivity.

A third stage in agricultural productivity analysis has involved efforts to test for the convergence of growth rates and levels of multifactor productivity between and among developing and less developed countries. Most of these studies have employed the Malmquist or frontier productivity approach. The basic idea of the Malmquist approach is to construct the *best practice*, or *frontier*, production function and to measure the distance of each country in the sample from the frontier by applying a linear programming method known as data envelopment analysis. The combination of inputs is allowed to vary along an efficient frontier, rather than the fixed coefficient production functions employed in the second-stage studies, to partition changes in multifactor productivity into technical change and efficiency change components.[5] Technical change measures the shift in the best practice or frontier production functions; efficiency change measures change in the difference between average practice and the "best practice" productivity frontier.

These studies generally indicate a widening of the agricultural productivity gap between developed and developing countries between the early 1960s and the early 1990s. Within the group of developed countries, except for continuing divergence between northern and southern Europe, productivity levels have converged modestly. Developing countries as a group experienced declining total factor productivity relative to the frontier countries. There is, however, some evidence of convergence toward the still relatively low frontier productivity levels within African agriculture (Thirtle, Hadley and Townsend, 1995; Fulginiti and Perrin, 1997, 1998; Ball et al., 2001; Chavas, 2001; Suhariyanto, Lusigi and Thirtle, 2001; Trueblood and Coggins, 2001).

The partitioning of total factor productivity into technical efficiency and technical change in Asian agriculture shows that during the period 1965/66–1995/96, the gap between average practice, as measured by technical *efficiency change*, and best practice, as measured by *technical change*, widened. As a result, average *total factor productivity change* (TFP) advanced more slowly than the rate of technical change in the countries on the efficiency frontier. Another way of making the same point is that technical efficiency has lagged relative to technical change associated with the rapid adoption of green revolution seed-fertilizer technology in the frontier countries (Rosegrant and Hazel, 2000, pp. 123–160). The results are not inconsistent with a technical trajectory implied by the induced technical change hypothesis. Technical change in Asia has been strongly biased in a land saving direction, in response to the relatively severe constraints on land resources. This bias is reflected in both a land saving shift in the production function and the substitution of technical inputs, particularly fertilizer and pest and pathogen control chemicals, for land (Murgai, Ali and Byerlee, 2001; Murgai, 2001). Similar trends have taken place in some of the more land constrained labor intensive agricultural systems in Africa and Latin America.

Transition to sustainability

Growth in total factor productivity in agriculture, arising out of technical change and improvements in efficiency, has made an exceedingly important contribution to economic growth. Within rural areas, growth of land and labor productivity has led to substantial poverty reduction. Productivity growth has also released substantial resources to the rest of the economy and contributed to reductions in the price of food in both rural and urban areas (Shane, Roe and Gopinath, 1998; Irz et al., 2001). The decline in the price of food, which in many parts of the world is the single most important factor determining the buying power of wages, has been particularly important in reducing the cost of industrial development in a number of important emerging economies. These price declines have also meant that, in countries or regions that have not experienced such gains in agricultural productivity, farmers have lost competitive advantage in world markets and consumers have failed to share fully in the gains from economic growth. But what about the future? In the next two sections, I will first address the environmental and resource constraints and then the scientific and the technical constraints that will confront the world's farmers as they attempt to respond to demands that will be placed on them.[6]

Resource and environmental constraints

The leading resource and environmental constraints faced by the world's farmers include soil loss and degradation; water logging and salinity; the coevolution of pests, pathogens and hosts; and the impact of climate change. Part of my concern is with the feedback of the environmental impacts of agricultural intensification on agricultural production itself (Tilman et al., 2001).

Soil. Soil degradation and erosion have been widely regarded as major threats to sustainable growth in agricultural production in both developed and developing countries. It has been suggested, for example, that by 2050, it may be necessary to feed "twice as many people with half as much topsoil" (Harris, 1990, p. 115). However, attempts to assess the implications of soil erosion and degradation confront serious difficulties. Water and wind erosion estimates are measures of the amount of soil moved from one place to another rather than the soil actually lost. Relatively few studies provide the information necessary to estimate yield loss from erosion and degradation. Studies in the United States by the Natural Resources Conservation Service have been interpreted to indicate that if 1992 erosion rates continued for 100 years, the yield loss at the end of the period would amount to only 2 to 3 percent (Crosson, 1995a). An exceedingly careful review of the long-term relationship among soil erosion, degradation and crop productivity in China and Indonesia concludes that there has been little loss of organic matter or mineral nutrients and that use of fertilizer has been able to compensate for loss of nitrogen (Lindent, 2000). A careful review of the international literature suggests that yield losses at the global level might be roughly double the rates estimated for the United States (Crosson, 1995b).

At the global level, soil loss and degradation are not likely to represent a serious constraint on agricultural production over the next half-century. But soil loss and degradation could become a serious constraint at the local or regional level in some fragile resource areas. For example, yield constraints due to soil erosion and degradation seem especially severe in the arid and semiarid regions of sub-saharan Africa. A slowing of agricultural productivity growth in robust resource areas could also lead to intensification or expansion of crop and animal production that would put pressure on soil in fragile resource areas – like tropical rain forests, arid and semiarid regions and high mountain areas. In some such areas, the possibility of sustainable growth in production can be enhanced by irrigation, terracing, careful soil management and changes in commodity mix and farming systems (Lal, 1995; Smil, 2000; Niemeijer and Mazzucato, 2000).

Water. During the last half-century, water has become a resource of high and increasing value in many countries. In the arid and semiarid areas of the world, water scarcity is becoming an increasingly serious constraint on growth of agricultural production (Seckler, Molden and Barker, 1999; Raskin et al., 1998; Gleick, 2000). During the last half-century, irrigated area in developing countries more than doubled, from less than 100 million hectares to more than 200 million hectares. About half of developing country grain production is grown on irrigated land. The International Water Management Institute had projected that by 2025, most regions or countries in a broad sweep from north China across east Asia to north Africa and northern sub-saharan Africa will experience either absolute or severe water scarcity.[7]

Irrigation systems can be a double-edged answer to water scarcity, since they may have substantial spillover effects or externalities that affect agricultural production directly. Common problems of surface water irrigation systems include water logging and salinity resulting from excessive water use and poorly designed drainage systems (Murgai, Ali and Byerlee, 2001). In the Aral Sea basin in central Asia, the effects of excessive water withdrawal for cotton and rice production, combined with inadequate drainage facilities, has resulted in such extensive water logging and salinity, as well as contraction of the Aral Sea, that the economic viability of the entire region is threatened (Glazovsky, 1995). Another common externality results from the extraction of water from underground aquifers in excess of the rate at which the aquifers are naturally recharged, resulting in a falling groundwater level and rising pumping costs. In some countries, like Pakistan and India, these spillover effects have in some cases been sufficient to offset the contribution of expansion of irrigated area to agricultural production.

However, the lack of water resources is unlikely to become a severe constraint on global agricultural production in the next half-century. The scientific and technical efforts devoted to improvement in water productivity have been much more limited than efforts to enhance land productivity (Molden, Amarasinghe and Hussain, 2001), so significant productivity improvements in water use are surely possible. Institutional innovations will be required to create incentives to enhance water productivity (Saleth and Dinar, 2000).

But in 50 to 60 of the world's most arid countries, plus major regions in several other countries, competition from household, industrial and environmental demands will reallocate water away from agricultural irrigation. In many of these countries, increases in water productivity and changes in farming systems will permit continued increases in agricultural production. In other countries, the reduction in irrigated area will cause a significant constraint on agricultural production. Since these countries are among the world's poorest, some will have great difficulty in meeting food security needs from either domestic production or food imports.

Pests. Pest control has become an increasingly serious constraint on agricultural production in spite of dramatic advances in pest control technology. In the United States, pesticides have been the most rapidly growing input in agricultural production over the last half-century. Major pests include pathogens, insects and weeds. For much of the post-World War II era, pest control has meant application of chemicals. Pesticidal activity of Dichlorodiphenyl-trichloroethane (DDT) was discovered in the late 1930s. It was used in World War II to protect American troops against typhus and malaria. Early tests found DDT to be effective against almost all insect species and relatively harmless to humans, animals and plants. It was relatively inexpensive and effective at low application levels. Chemical companies rapidly introduced a series of other synthetic organic pesticides in the 1950s (Ruttan, 1982; Palladino, 1996). The initial effectiveness of DDT and other synthetic organic chemicals for crop and animal pest control after World War II led to the neglect of other pest control strategies.

By the early 1960s, an increasing body of evidence suggested that the benefits of the synthetic organic chemical pesticides introduced in the 1940s and 1950s were obtained at substantial cost. One set of costs included the direct and indirect effects on wildlife populations and on human health (Carson, 1962; Pingali and Roger, 1995). A second set of costs involved the destruction of beneficial insects and the emergence of pesticide resistance in target populations. A fundamental problem in efforts to develop methods of control for pests and pathogens is that the control results in evolutionary selection pressure for the emergence of organisms that are resistant to the control technology (Palumbi, 2001). When DDT was introduced in California to control the cottony cushions scale, its predator, the vedelia beetle, turned out to be more susceptible to DDT than the scale. In 1947, just one year after the introduction of DDT, citrus growers were confronted with a resurgence of the scale population. In Peru, the cotton bollworm quickly built up resistance to DDT and to the even more effective – and more toxic to humans – organophospate insecticides that were adopted to replace DDT (Palladino, 1996, pp. 36–41).

The solution to the pesticide crisis offered by the entomological community was Integrated Pest Management (IPM). IPM involved the integrated use of an array of pest control strategies: making hosts more resistant to pests, finding biological controls for pests, cultivation practices and also chemical control, if needed. At the time Integrated Pest Management began to be promoted in the 1960s, it represented little more than a rhetorical device. But by the 1970s, a number of important Integrated Pest Management programs had been designed and implemented. However, exaggerated expectations that dramatic reductions in chemical pesticide use could be achieved without significant decline in crop yields as a result of Integrated Pest Management have yet only been partially realized (Gianessi, 1991; Lewis et al., 1977).

My own judgment is that the problem of pest and pathogen control will represent a more serious constraint on sustainable growth in agricultural production at a global level than either land or water constraints.[8] In part, this is because the development of pest and pathogen resistant crop varieties and chemical methods of control both tend to induce the evolution of more resistant pests or pathogen. In addition, international travel and trade are spreading the newly resistant pests and pathogens to new environments. As a result, pest control technologies must constantly be replaced and updated. The coevolution of pathogens, insect pests and weeds in response to control efforts will continue to represent a major factor in directing the allocation of agricultural research resources to assuring that agricultural output can be maintained at present levels or continue to grow.[9]

Climate. Measurements taken in Hawaii in the late 1950s indicated that carbon dioxide (CO_2) was increasing in the atmosphere. Beginning in the late 1960s, computer model simulations indicated possible changes in temperature and precipitation that could occur due to human-induced emission of CO_2 and other "greenhouse gases" into the atmosphere. By the early 1980s, a fairly broad consensus had emerged in the climate change research community that energy production and consumption from fossil fuels could, by 2050, result in a doubling of the atmospheric concentration of CO_2, a rise in global average temperature by 2.5 to 4.5°C (2.7 to 8.0°F) and a complex pattern of worldwide climate change (Ruttan, 2001, pp. 515–520).

Since the mid-1980s, a succession of studies has attempted to assess how an increase in the atmospheric concentration of greenhouse gases could affect agricultural production through three channels: a) higher CO_2 concentrations in the atmosphere may have a positive "fertilizer effect" on some crop plants (and weeds); b) higher temperatures could result in a rise in the sea level, resulting in inundation of coastal areas and intrusion of saltwater into groundwater aquifers; and c) changes in temperature, rainfall and sunlight may also alter agricultural production, although the effects will vary greatly across regions. Early assessments of the impact of climate change on global agricultural suggested a negative annual impact in the 2 to 4 percent range by the third decade of this century (Parry, 1990). More recent projections are more optimistic (Mendelsohn, Nordhaus and Shaw, 1994; Rosenzweig and Hillel, 1998). The early models have been criticized for a "dumb farmer" assumption – they did not incorporate how farmers would respond to climate change with different crops and growing methods. Efforts to incorporate how public and private suppliers of knowledge and technology might adjust to climate change are just beginning (Evenson, 1998). But even the more sophisticated models have been unable to incorporate the synergistic interactions among climate change, soil loss and degradation, ground and surface water storage and the incidence of pests and pathogens. These interactive effects could combine into a significantly larger burden on growth in agricultural production than the effects of each constraint considered separately. One thing that is certain is that a country or region that has not acquired substantial agricultural research capacity will have great difficulty in responding to anticipated climate change impacts.

Scientific and technical constraints

The achievement of sustained growth in agricultural production over the next half-century represents at least as difficult a challenge to science and technology development as the transition to a science-based system of agricultural production during the twentieth century. In assessing the role of advances in science and technology to release the several constraints on growth of agricultural production and productivity, the induced technical change hypothesis is useful. To the extent that technical change in agriculture is endogenous, scientific and technical resources will be directed to sustaining or enhancing the productivity of those factors that are relatively scarce and expensive. Farmers in those countries who have not yet acquired the capacity to invent or adapt technology specific to their resource endowments will continue to find it difficult to respond to the growth of domestic or international demand.

In the 1950s and 1960s, it was not difficult to anticipate the likely sources of increase in agricultural production over the next several decades (Ruttan, 1956; Schultz, 1964; Millikan and Hapgood, 1967). Advances in crop production would come from expansion in area irrigated, from more intensive application of improved fertilizer and crop protection chemicals and from the development of crop varieties that would be more responsive to technical inputs and management. Advances in animal production would come from genetic improvements and advances in animal nutrition. At a more fundamental level, increases in crop yields would come from genetic advances that would change plant architecture to make possible higher plant populations per hectare and would increase the ratio of grain to straw in individual plants. Increases in production of animals and animal products would come about by genetic and management changes that would decrease the proportion of feed devoted to animal maintenance and increase the proportion used to produce usable animal products.

I find it much more difficult to tell a convincing story about the likely sources of increase in crop and animal production over the next half-century than I did a half-century ago. The ratio of grain to straw is already high in many crops, and severe physiological constraints arise in trying to increase it further. There are also physiological limits to increasing the efficiency with which animal feed produces animal products. These constraints will impinge most severely in areas that have already achieved the highest levels of output per hectare or per animal unit – in western Europe, north America and east Asia. Indeed, the constraints are already evident. The yield increases from incremental fertilizer application are falling. The reductions in labor input from the use of larger and more powerful mechanical equipment are declining as well. As average grain yields have risen from the 1 to 2 metric tons per hectare range to the 6 to 8 metric tons per hectare range in the most favored areas, the share of research budgets devoted to maintenance research – the research needed to maintain existing crop and animal productivity levels – has risen relative to total research budgets (Plucknet and Smith, 1986). Cost per scientist year has been rising faster than the general price level (Pardey, Craig and Hallaway, 1989; Huffman and Evenson, 1993). I find it difficult to escape a conclusion that both public and private sector agricultural research, in those countries that have achieved the highest levels of agricultural productivity, has begun to experience diminishing returns.

Perhaps advances in molecular biology and genetic engineering will relieve the scientific and technical constraints on the growth of agricultural production. In the past, advances in fundamental knowledge have often initiated new cycles of research productivity (Evenson and Kislev, 1975). Transgenetically modified crops, particularly maize, soybeans and cotton, have diffused rapidly since they were first introduced in the mid-1990s. Four countries – United States, Argentina, Canada and China – accounted for 99 percent of the 109 million acres of transgenic crop area in 2000 (James, 2000). The applications that are presently available in the field are primarily in the area of plant protection and animal health. Among the more dramatic examples is the development of cotton varieties that incorporate resistance to the cotton bollworm. The effect has been to reduce the application of chemical control from 8 to 10 to 1 to 2 spray applications per season (Falck-Zepeda et al., 2000). These advances are enabling producers to push crop and animal yields closer to their genetically determined biological potential. But they have not yet raised biological yield ceilings above the levels that that have been achieved by researchers employing the older methods based on Mendelian genetics (Ruttan, 1999).

Advances in agricultural applications of genetic engineering in developed countries will almost certainly be slowed by developed country concerns about the possible environmental and health impacts of transgenetically modified plants and foods.

One effect of these concerns has been to shift the attention of biotechnology research effort away from agricultural applications in favor of industrial and pharmaceutical applications (Committee on Environmental Impact Associated with Commercialization of Transgenic Plants, 2002, pp. 221–229). This shift will delay the development of productivity-enhancing biotechnology applications and agricultural development in less developed economies.

I find it somewhat surprising that it is difficult for me to share the current optimism about the dramatic gains to be realized from the application of molecular genetics and genetic engineering. One of my first professional papers was devoted to refuting the pessimistic projections of agricultural productivity and production that were common in the early 1950s (Ruttan, 1956). Other students of this subject have presented more optimistic perspectives (Waggoner, 1997; Alston et al. 2000, p. 77; Runge et al., 2001). But I am skeptical that the new genetics technologies, although undoubtedly powerful, will or can overcome the long-term prospect of diminishing returns to research on agricultural productivity.

Agricultural research systems

I have given major attention to this point, to the role of agricultural research as a source of technical change and productivity growth. In this section, I sketch the evolution and structure of national and international agricultural research systems.[10] The institutional arrangements for the support of agricultural research began in the middle of the nineteenth century. In 1843, Sir John Bennett Laws established, and later endowed, an agricultural experiment station on his ancestral estate at Rothamsted (England). The introduction by Justus von Liebig of the laboratory method of training in organic chemistry at Giessen led directly to the establishment of the first publicly supported agricultural experiment station at Mockern, Saxony, in 1852. The German model of public sector agricultural research became the model for agricultural research in the United States. A number of American students who studied with Liebig were responsible for establishing the research program of the U.S. Department of Agriculture and the agricultural experiment stations at the new land grant public universities in the late 1800s (Ruttan, 1982). The basic structure of the U.S. agricultural research system has become increasingly complex, with the federal government, individual states and the private sector each playing an important role.

Substantial progress was made in the first several decades of the twentieth century in initiating public sector agricultural research capacity in Latin America and in the colonial economies of Asia and Africa. Research efforts were focused primarily on tropical export crops such as sugar, rubber, cotton, banana, coffee and tea. The disruption of international trade during the Great Depression of the 1930s and during World War II, followed by the breakup of colonial empires, aborted or severely weakened many of these efforts.

By the early 1960s, the U.S. development assistance agency and the assistance agencies of the former colonial powers were beginning to channel substantial resources into strengthening agricultural education and research institutions with a stronger focus on domestic food crops in developing countries. The Ford and Rockefeller Foundations collaborated in the establishment of four international agricultural research institutes: the International Rice Research Institute (IRRI) in the Philippines; the International Center for the Improvement of Maize and Wheat (CIMMYT) in Mexico; the International Institute of Tropical Agriculture (IITA) in Nigeria; and the International Center for Tropical Agriculture (CIAT) in Columbia. In 1971, the two foundations, joined by the World Bank, the United Nations Food and Agricultural Organization (FAO), the United Nations Development Program (UNDP) and a number of bilateral donor agencies, formed a Consultative Group on International Agricultural Research (CGIAR). By the early 1990s, the CGIAR systems had expanded to 18 centers or institutes.

From the 1950s through the 1980s, the resources available to the new national and international research institutions from national and international sources expanded rapidly. Both the national and international systems achieved dramatic success in the development of higher yielding "green revolution" wheat, rice and maize varieties (Alston et al., 2000; Ruttan, 2001, pp. 203–223). Several developing countries – India, China, Brazil, Argentina and South Africa – achieved world class agricultural research capacity. During the 1990s, however, growth of public sector support for both national and international agricultural research slowed substantially. Support for private sector agricultural research, which remains concentrated primarily in developed countries, has continued to grow rapidly.[11]

An active and vibrant global agricultural research system will be needed to sustain growth in agricultural productivity into the twenty-first century. But the system itself is still incomplete. When it is completed, it will include strong public national research institutions, linked to higher education, that can work effectively with the international system and other national systems. This network will be complemented by a scientifically sophisticated technology supply industry, composed of both national and multinational firms. The research systems in most developing countries have yet to establish sufficient capacity to make effective use of the existing advances in knowledge and technology. The private sector agricultural technology supply industry, although growing rapidly, still remains poorly represented in most developing countries.

Perspective

What are the implications of the resource and environmental constraints, the scientific and technical constraints, and the institutional constraints on agricultural productivity growth over the next half-century? In those countries and regions in which land and labor productivity are already at or approaching scientific and technical frontiers, it will be difficult to achieve growth in agricultural productivity comparable to the rates achieved over the last half-century (Pingali, Moya and Velasco, 1990; Reilly and Fuglie, 1998; Pingali and Heisey, 2001). But in most of these countries at the technological frontier, the demand for food will rise only slowly. As a result, these countries, except perhaps those that are most land constrained, will have little difficulty in achieving rates of growth in agricultural production that will keep up with the slowly rising demand for food. Several of the countries near the technological frontier, particularly in east Asia, will find it economically advantageous to continue to import substantial quantities of animal feed and food grains (Rosegrant and Hazel, 2000).

For those countries in which land and labor productivity levels are furthest from frontier levels, particularly those in sub-saharan Africa, opportunities exist to enhance agricultural productivity substantially. Countries that are land constrained, such as India, can be expected to follow a productivity growth path that places primary emphasis on biological technology. In contrast, Brazil, which is still involved in expanding its agricultural land frontier while confronting crop yield constraints in its older agricultural regions, can be expected to follow a more balanced productivity growth path. Most of the poor countries or regions that find it advantageous to follow a biological technology path will have to invest substantially more than in the past to acquire a capacity for agricultural research and technology transfer. These investments will include general and technical education, rural physical infrastructure and building appropriate research and technology transfer institutions. Moreover, gains in labor productivity will depend on the rate of growth in demand for labor in the nonfarm sectors of the economy, which in turn create the incentives for substituting of mechanical technology for labor in agricultural production. If relatively land abundant countries, in sub-saharan Africa, for example, fail to develop a strong intersector labor market in which workers can move from rural agricultural jobs to urban manufacturing and service jobs, they will end up following an east Asian land saving biological technology path.

I find it more difficult to anticipate the productivity paths that will be followed by several other regions. The countries of the former USSR have in the past followed a trajectory somewhat similar to North America (as shown in Figure 29.1). If they recover from recent stagnation, these countries may resume their historical trajectory.[12] The trajectories that will be followed by west Asia, north Africa and other arid regions are highly uncertain. Very substantial gains in water productivity will be required to realize gains in land productivity in these areas, and very substantial growth in nonagricultural demand for labor will be required to realize the substantial gains in labor productivity that would enable them to continue along the intermediate technology trajectory that has characterized the countries of southern Europe. The major oil-producing countries will continue to expand their imports of food and feed grains. If the world should move toward more open trading arrangements, a number of tropical or semitropical developing countries would find it advantageous to expand their exports of commodities in which their climate and other resources give them a comparative advantage and import larger quantities of food and feed grains.

While many of the constraints on agricultural productivity discussed in this paper are unlikely to represent a threat to global food security over the next half-century, they will, either individually or collectively, become a threat to growth of agricultural production at the regional and local level in a number of the world's poorest countries. A primary defense against the uncertainty about resource and environmental constraints is agricultural research capacity. The erosion of capacity of the international research system will have to be reversed; capacity in the presently developed countries will have to be at least maintained; and capacity in the developing countries will have to be substantially strengthened. Smaller countries will need, at the very least, to strengthen their capacity to borrow, adapt and diffuse technology from countries in comparable agroclimatic regions. It also means that more secure bridges must be built between the research systems of what have been termed the "island empires" of the agricultural, environmental and health sciences (Mayer and Mayer, 1974).

If the world fails to meet its food demands in the next half-century, the failure will be at least as much in the area of institutional innovation as in the area of technical change. This conclusion is not an optimistic one. The design of institutions capable of achieving compatibility between individual, organizational and social objectives remains an art rather than a science. At our present stage of knowledge, institutional design is analogous to driving down a four-lane highway looking out the rear-view mirror. We are better at making course corrections when we start to run off the highway than at using foresight to navigate the transition to sustainable growth in agricultural output and productivity.

Notes

I am indebted to Jay Coggins, Charles Muscoplat, Glenn Pederson, Munisamy Gopinath, David Norse, Philip Pardey, Philip Raup, Timothy Taylor, Colin Thirtle, Michael Trueblood and Michael Waldman for comments and suggestions on an earlier draft of this paper. I have also benefited from access to a draft manuscript of a forthcoming book on food security by Runge, Senauer, Pardey, Rosegrant and Kuchinsky (October 2001).

1   The Schultz "poor but efficient" hypothesis was received skeptically by development economists who had posited a "backward bending" labor supply curve in developing countries' agriculture. See, for example, Lipton (1968). For a particularly vicious review of *Transforming Traditional Agriculture*, see Balogh (1964). Schultz was the recipient of the 1979 Nobel Award in economics, along with W. Arthur Lewis, for his contribution to development economics.

2   The Hayami and Ruttan (1985) induced innovation interpretation of technical change has been criticized on both theoretical and empirical grounds. See, for example, Olmstead and Rhode (1993) and Koppel (1995). For a response to these criticisms, see Ruttan and Hayami (1995).

3   Multifactor productivity estimates for agriculture in the United States were first constructed in the late 1940s and early 1950s (Barton and Cooper, 1948; Schultz, 1953; Ruttan, 1956). For a comparative review and analysis of the sources of differences in the several aggregate agricultural production functions that have been estimated for U.S. agriculture, see Trueblood and Ruttan (1995). Note that from the beginning, agricultural economists were using what, in the recent literature, have been termed "augmented" neoclassical production functions rather the Solow-type two-factor production functions. For a review of total factor productivity estimates in developing countries, see Pingali and Heisey (2001).

4   In cross-country growth accounting, it has not been possible to account directly for improvement in the quality of inputs. Attempts are made to capture improvements in the quality of labor input by including education and for improvements in the quality of capital and intermediate inputs by including investment in technical education or research and development in the cross-country production functions. Jorgenson and Gollop (1995) have

estimated that during 1947–1985, when total factor productivity in U.S. agriculture grew at an annual rate of 1.58 percent, input quality change accounted for about one-third of the total factor productivity growth. Using a somewhat different approach, Shane, Roe and Gopinath (1998) estimated that private research and development embodied in factor input quality, accounting for about 25 percent of total factor productivity between 1949 and 1991.

5   The advantages of the Malmquist, or frontier, productivity index, in addition to the decomposition of total factor productivity into efficiency change and technical change, are that: a) it is nonparametric and does not require a specification of the functional form of the production technology; and b) it does not require an economic behavior assumption such as cost minimization or revenue maximization (Färe, Grosskopf and Knox Lovell, 1994; Färe et al., 1994). The contemporaneous Malmquist approach employed by Trueblood and Coggins (2001) identifies the "best practice" countries in each period and measures the change in each country's performance relative to the change in the frontier. A country that shows a positive growth in total factor productivity may show negative Malmquist productivity change because it may lag relative to the best practice frontier. The sequential Malmquist approach that has been employed by Suhariyante, Lusigi and Thirtle (2001) does not permit negative technology shifts.

6   The issues discussed in this section are addressed in greater detail in Ruttan (1999).

7   Countries characterized by "absolute water scarcity" do not have sufficient water resources to maintain 1990 levels of per capita food production from irrigated agriculture, even at high levels of irrigation efficiency, and also meet reasonable water demands for domestic, environmental and industrial purposes. Countries characterized by "severe water scarcity" are in regions in which the potential water resources are sufficient to meet reasonable water needs by 2025, but only if they make very substantial improvements in water use efficiency and water development (Seckler, Molden and Barker, 1999).

8   Estimates of losses in crop and animal production due to pests vary greatly by commodity, location and year. However, estimates by reputable investigators run upwards of 33 percent of global food crop production. Losses represent a higher percentage of output in less developed countries than in developed countries. Among major commodities, the highest losses are experienced by rice (Yudelman, Ratta and Nygaard, 1998).

9   I have not in this paper discussed the potential impacts of health constraints on agricultural production. The increase in use of insecticides and herbicides associated with agricultural intensification have had important negative health effects on agricultural workers. The health effects, which include the incidence of new diseases, such as AIDS, and of the resurgence of older diseases, such as malaria and tuberculosis, are greatest in rural communities in developing countries. It is not too difficult to visualize situations in particular villages in which the coincidence of several of these health factors could result in serious constraints on agricultural production (Pingali and Roger, 1995; Bell, Clark and Ruttan, 1994; Haddad and Gillespie, 2001).

10   For a more detailed discussion of the evolution and structure of national and international agricultural research, see Ruttan (1982) and Huffman and Evenson (1993).

11   In 1995, it was estimated that global agricultural research expenditures amounted to $33 billion (in 1993 dollars). Of this amount, public sector expenditures amounted to $12.2 billion in developed countries and $11.5 billion in developing countries. Private sector expenditures for agricultural research amounted to $10.8 billion in developed and $0.7 billion in developing countries. Support for the CGIAR system declined from $334 million in 1990 to $305 million (1993 prices) in 2000 (Pardey and Beintema, 2001).

12   Between 1962 and 1990, crop yields in the former Soviet Union experienced modest gains relative to the world's leaders. Since the early 1990s, however, yield growth rates became negative, and by 1997, the yield gap between the countries of the former Soviet Union and the world leaders exceeded the levels of 1962 (Trueblood and Arnade, 2001).

References

Alston, Julian M. et al. 2000. *A Meta-Analysis of Rates of Return to Agricultural R&D: Ex Pede Herculem*. Washington, D.C.: International Food Policy Research Institute.

Arnade, Carlos. 1998. "Using a Programming Approach to Measure International Agricultural Efficiency and Productivity." *Journal of Agricultural Economics*. 49:1, pp. 67–84

Ball, V. Eldon et al. 2001. "Levels of Farm Sector Productivity: An International Comparison." *Journal of Productivity Analysis*. January, 15:1, pp. 5–29.

Balogh, Thomas. 1964. "Review of *Transforming Traditional Agriculture*." *Economic Journal*. 74: 296, pp. 996–99.

Barton, Glenn T. and Martin R. Cooper. 1948. "Relation of Agricultural Production to Inputs." *Review of Economics and Statistics*. 30:1, pp. 117–26.

Bell, David E., William C. Clark and Vernon W. Ruttan. 1994. "Global Research Systems for Sustainable Development: Agriculture, Health and Environment," in *Agriculture, Environment, and Health: Sustainable Development in the 21st Century*. Vernon W. Ruttan, ed. Minneapolis, Minn.: University of Minnesota Press, pp. 358–79.

Binswanger, Hans P. and Vernon W. Ruttan, eds. 1978. *Induced Innovation: Technology, Institutions and Development*. Baltimore, Md.: Johns Hopkins University Press.

Brewster, John M. 1950. "The Machine Process in Agriculture and Industry." *Journal of Farm Economics*. February, 32, pp. 69–81.

Carson, Rachel. 1962. *Silent Spring*. New York: Fawcett.

Chavas, Jean-Paul. 2001. "An International Analysis of Agricultural Productivity," in *Agricultural Investment and Productivity in Developing Countries*. Lydia Zepeda, ed. Rome, Italy: Food and Agricultural Organization of the United Nations, pp. 21–37.

Clark, Collin. 1940. *The Conditions of Economic Progress, First Edition*. London: Macmillan, Third Edition, 1957.

Committee on Environmental Impacts Associated with Commercialization of Transgenic Plants. 2002. *Environmental Effects of Transgenic Plants: The Scope and Adequacy of Regulation*. Washington, D.C.: National Academy Press.

Conway, Gordon R. 1998. *The Doubly Green Revolution: Food for All in the Twenty-First Century*. Ithaca, N.Y.: Cornell University Press.

Craig, Barbara J., Philip G. Pardey and Johannes Roseboom. 1997. "International Productivity Patterns: Accounting for Input Quality, Infrastructure and Research." *American Journal of Agricultural Economics*. November, 79:4, pp. 1064–076.

Crosson, Pierre. 1995a. "Soil Erosion Estimates and Costs." *Science*. 269:5223, pp. 461–63.

Crosson, Pierre. 1995b. "Soil Erosion and its On-Farm Productivity Consequences: What Do We Know?" Washington, D.C., Resources for the Future Discussion Paper 95–29.

Evenson, Robert E. 1998. "Technology, Climate Change, Productivity and Land Use in Brazilian Agriculture." Yale University Economic Growth Center Staff Paper.

Evenson, Robert E. and Yoav Kislev. 1975. *Agricultural Research and Productivity*. New Haven, Conn.: Yale University Press.

Falck-Zepeda, José B. et al. 2000. "Surplus Distribution from the Introduction of a Biotechnology Innovation." *American Journal of Agricultural Economics*. May, 82, pp. 360–69.

Färe, Rolf, Shawna Grosskopf and C. A. Kox Lovell. 1994. *Production Frontiers*. Cambridge, U.K.: Cambridge University Press.

Färe, Rolf et al. 1994. "Productivity Growth, Technical Progress, and Efficiency Changes in Industrialized Countries." *American Economic Review*. 84:1, pp. 66–83.

Fuglie, Keith, et al. 1996. "Agricultural Research and Development: Public and Private Investment Under Alternative Markets and Institutions." Washington, D.C., USDA Economic Research Service Report AE 35.

Fulginiti, Lilyan E. and Richard K. Perrin. 1997. "LDC Agriculture: Nonparametric Malmquist Productivity Indexes." *Journal of Development Economics*. 53:2, pp. 373–90.

Fulginiti, Lilyan E. and Richard K. Perrin. 1998. "Agricultural Productivity in Developing Countries." *Agricultural Economics*. 19:1–2, pp. 45–51.

Gianessi, L. P. 1991. "Reducing Pesticide Use with No Cost in Yields? A Critique of a Recent Cornell Report." Washington, D.C., Resources for the Future Discussion Paper 0E91–16.

Glazovsky, N. F. 1995. "The Aral Sea Basin," in *Regions at Risk: Comparisons of Threatened Environments*. J. X. Kasperson, R. E. Kasperson and B. L. Turner, eds. New York: United Nations University Press, pp. 92–140.

Gleick, Peter H. 2000. "The Changing Water Paradigm: A Look at Twenty-first Century Water Resource Development." *Water International*. 25:1, pp. 127–38.

Griliches, Zvi. 1968. "Agriculture: Productivity and Technology," in *International Encyclopedia of the Social Sciences, Volume 1*. David L. Sills, ed. New York: Macmillan Press, pp. 241–45.

Haddad, Lawrence and Stuart Gillespie. 2001. "Effective Food and Nutrition Responses to HIV/AIDS: What We Know and What We Need to Know." Washington, D.C., International Food Policy Research Institute/FCN Discussion Paper, March 13.

Harris, J. M. 1990. *World Agriculture and the Environment*. Garland: New York.

Hayami, Yujiro. 1969. "Industrialization and Agricultural Productivity: An International, and Comparative Study." *Developing Economies*. 7, pp. 3–21.

Hayami, Yujiro and Kinuyo Inagi. 1969. "International Comparisons of Agricultural Productivity." *Farm Economist*. 11, pp. 407–19.

Hayami, Yujiro and Vernon W. Ruttan. 1970. "Agricultural Productivity: Differences Among Countries." *American Economic Review*. December, 60:5, pp. 895–911.

Hayami, Yujiro and Vernon W. Ruttan. 1971. *Agricultural Development: An International Perspective, First Edition*. Second Edition, 1985. Baltimore, M.D.: Johns Hopkins University Press.

Hayami, Yujiro et al. 1971. *An International Comparison of Agricultural Production and Productivities*. St. Paul, Minn.: University of Minnesota Agricultural Experiment Station Technical Bulletin 277.

Huffman, Wallace E. and Robert Evenson. 1993. *Science for Agriculture: A Long-Term Perspective*. Ames, Iowa: Iowa State University Press.

Irz, Xavier et al. 2001. "Agricultural Productivity Growth and Poverty Alleviation." *Development Policy Review*. 19: 4, pp. 449–66.

James, Clive. 2000. *Global Review of Commercialized Transgenic Crops: 2000*. Ithaca, N.Y.: International Service for the Acquisition of Agri-biotech Applications.

Johnson, D. Gale. 2000. "Population Food and Knowledge." *American Economic Review*. 90:1, pp. 1–14.

Jorgenson, Dale W. and Frank M. Gollop. 1995. "Productivity Growth in U.S. Agriculture: A Postwar Perspective," in *Productivity, Volume 1: Postwar U.S. Economic Growth*. Dale W. Jorgenson, ed. Cambridge, Mass.: MIT Press, pp. 389–400.

Kawagoe, T., Yujiro Hayami and Vernon W. Ruttan. 1985. "The Intercountry Agricultural Production Function and Productivity Differences Among Countries." *Journal of Development Economics*. September/October, 19, pp. 113–32.

Koppel, Bruce M., ed. 1995. *Induced Innovation Theory and International Agricultural Development: A Reassessment*. Baltimore, M.D.: Johns Hopkins University Press.

Lal, Rattan. 1995. "Erosion-Crop Productivity Relationships for Soils in Africa." *Soil Science Society of America Journal*. 59:3, pp. 661–67.

Lau, Lawrence and Pan Yotopoulos. 1989. "The Meta-Production Function Approach to Technological Change in World Agriculture." *Journal of Development Economics*. October, 31:2, pp. 241–69.

Lewis, W. Arthur. 1954. "Economic Development With Unlimited Supply of Labor." *Manchester School of Economic and Social Studies*. 22, pp. 139–91.

Lewis, W. J. et al. 1997. "A Total System Approach to Sustainable Pest Management." *Proceedings of the National Academy of Sciences*. 94:23, pp. 12243–2249.

Lindent, Peter H. 2000. *Shifting Ground: The Changing Agricultural Soils of China and Indonesia*. Cambridge, Mass.: MIT Press.

Lipton, Michael. 1968. "The Theory of the Optimizing Peasant." *Journal of Development Studies*. 4:3, pp. 327–51.

Mayer, André and Jean Mayer. 1974. "Agriculture, the Island Empire." *Daedalus*. Summer, 103, pp. 83–95.

Mendelsohn, Robert, William D. Nordhaus and D. Shaw. 1994. "The Impact of Global Warming on Agriculture: A Ricardian Analysis." *American Economic Review*. 84:4, pp. 753–71.

Millikan, Max F. and David Hapgood. 1967. *No Easy Harvest: The Dilemma of Agriculture in Underdeveloped Countries*. Boston, Mass.: Little, Brown.

Molden, David, Upali Amarasinghe and Intizar Hussain. 2001. "Water for Development: Background Paper in Water for Rural Development Prepared for the World Bank." Colombo, Sri Lanka, International Water Management Institute Working Paper 32.

Murgai, Rinku. 2001. "The Green Revolution and the Productivity Paradox: Evidence from the Indian Punjab." *Agricultural Economics*. September, 25:2–3, pp. 199–209.

Murgai, Rinku, Mubarik Ali and Derek Byerlee. 2001. "Productivity Growth and Sustainability in Post-Green Revolution Agriculture: The Case of the Indian and Pakistan Punjabs." *World Bank Research Observer*. Fall, 16:2, pp. 199–218.

Niemeijer, David and Valintina Mazzucato. 2000. "Soil Degradation in the West African Sahel: How Serious Is It?" *Environment*. March, 41:2, pp. 20–31.

Olmstead, Alan L. and Paul Rhode. 1993. "Induced Innovation in American Agriculture: A Reconsideration." *Journal of Political Economy*. February, 101:1, pp. 100–18.

Olmstead, Alan L. and Paul Rhode. 2001. "Reshaping the Landscape: The Impact and Diffusion of the Tractor in American Agriculture, 1910–1960." *Journal of Economic History*. September, 61:3, pp. 663–68.

Palladino, Paulo. 1996. *Entomology, Ecology and Agriculture: The Making of Scientific Careers in North America, 1885–1995*. Amsterdam, Netherlands: Harwood Academic Publishers.

Parry, Martin L. 1990. *Climate Change and World Agriculture*. London, U.K.: Earthscan Publications.

Palumbi, Stephen R. 1986. "Humans as the World's Greatest Evolutionary Force." *Science*. 293:5536, pp. 1786–790.

Pardey, Philip G. and Nienke M. Beintema. 2001. *Slow Magic: Agricultural R&D a Century After Mendel.* Washington, D.C.: International Food Policy Research Institute.

Pardey, Philip J., Barbara J. Craig and Michelle J. Hallaway. 1989. "U.S. Agricultural Research Deflators: 1890–1985." *Research Policy.* October, 18, pp. 289–96.

Pingali, Prabhu L. and Paul W. Heisey. 2001. "Cereal Crop Productivity in Developing Countries: Past Trends and Future Prospects," in Julian M. Alston, Philip G. Pardey and M. J. Taylor, eds. *Agricultural Science Policy, Changing Global Agendas.* Baltimore, M.D.: Johns Hopkins University Press, pp. 56–82.

Pingali, Prabhu L. and Pierre A. Roger, eds. 1995. *Impact of Pesticides on Farmer Health and the Rice Environment.* Boston, Mass.: Kluwer Academic Publishers.

Pingali, Prabhu L., F. Moya and L. E. Velasco. 1990. "The Post-Green Revolution Blues in Asian Rice Production: The Diminished Gap Between Experiment Station and Farmer Yields." Los Baños, Laguna, Philippines, International Rice Research Institute Social Science Division Paper No. 90–01.

Plucknett, Donald L. and Nigel J. H. Smith. 1986. "Sustaining Agricultural Yields." *Bioscience.* 36:1, pp. 40–45.

Qi, Shunrong, Lan Xu and Jay Coggins. 2001. "Integrated Environmental-Economic Accounting." *American Journal of Agricultural Economics.* Forthcoming.

Ranis, Gustav and John C. H. Fei. 1961. "A Theory of Economic Development." *American Economic Review.* September, 51:4, pp. 533–65.

Raskin, Paul et al. 1998. *Comprehensive Assessment of the Freshwater Resources of the World.* Stockholm, Sweden: Stockholm Environment Institute.

Reilly, John M. and Keith O. Fuglie. 1998. "Future Yield Growth in Field Crops: What Evidence Exists?" *Soil and Tillage Research.* July, 47: 3–4, pp. 283–98.

Rosegrant, Mark W. and Peter B. Hazel. 2000. *Transforming the Rural Asian Economy: The Unfinished Revolution.* Hong Kong: Oxford University Press.

Rosenzweig, Cynthia and D. Hillel. 1998. *Climate Change and the Global Harvest.* New York: Oxford University Press.

Rostow, Walt W. 1956. "The Take-off Into Self-Sustained Growth." *Economic Journal.* March, 66, pp. 25–48.

Runge, C. Ford et al. 2001. *Ending Hunger in Our Lifetime: Food Security and Globalization.* Washington, D.C.: International Food Policy Research Institute.

Ruttan, Vernon W. 1956. "The Contribution of Technological Progress to Farm Output: 1950–1975." *Review of Economics and Statistics.* February, 38, pp. 61–69.

Ruttan, Vernon W. 1982. *Agricultural Research Policy.* Minneapolis, Minn.: University of Minnesota Press.

Ruttan, Vernon W. 1999. "The Transition to Agricultural Sustainability." *Proceedings of the National Academy of Sciences.* May, 96, pp. 5960–967.

Ruttan, Vernon W. 2001. *Technology, Growth and Development: An Induced Innovation Perspective.* Oxford, U.K.: Oxford University Press.

Ruttan, Vernon W. and Yujiro Hayami. 1995. "Induced Innovation Theory and Agricultural Development: A Personal Account," in *Induced Innovation Theory and International Agricultural Development: A Reassessment.* Bruce M. Koppel, ed. Baltimore: Johns Hopkins University Press, pp. 22–36.

Saleth, R. Maria and Ariel Dinar. 2000. "Institutional Changes in Global Water Sector: Trends, Patterns and Implications." *Water Policy.* 2:3, pp. 175–99.

Seckler, David, D. Molden and Randolph Barker. 1999. "Water Scarcity in the Twenty-First Century." *International Journal of Water Resources Management.* 15:1–2, pp. 29–42.

Schultz, Theodore W. 1953. *The Economic Organization of Agriculture*. New York: McGraw Hill.

Schultz, Theodore W. 1964. *Transforming Traditional Agriculture*. New Haven, Conn.: Yale University Press.

Shane, Mathew, Terry Roe and Munisamy Gopinath. 1998. "U.S. Agricultural Growth and Productivity: An Economy Wide Perspective." Washington, D.C., United States Department of Agriculture, Economic Research Service, Agricultural Economic Report 758.

Smil, Vaclav. 2000. *Feeding the World: A Challenge for the Twenty-First Century*. Cambridge, Mass.: MIT Press.

Suhariyanto, K., A Lusigi and Colin Thirtle. 2001. "Productivity Growth and Convergence in Asian and African Agriculture," in *Asia and Africa in Comparative Economic Perspective*. P. Lawrence and Colin Thirtle, eds. London: Palgrave, pp. 258–74.

Thirtle, Colin G., David Hadley and Robert Townsend. 1995. "A Multilateral Malmquist Productivity Index Approach to Explaining Agricultural Growth in sub-Saharan Africa." *Development Policy Review*. 13:4, pp. 323–48.

Tilman, David et al. 2001. "Forecasting Agriculturally Driven Global Environmental Change." *Science*. April 13, 292, pp. 281–84.

Trueblood, Michael A. and Carlos Arnade. 2001. "Crop Yield Convergence: How Russia's Yield Performance has Compared to Global Yield Leaders." *Comparative Economic Studies*. 43:2, pp. 59–81.

Trueblood, Michael A. and Jay Coggins. 2001. "Intercountry Agricultural Efficiency and Productivity: A Malmquist Index Approach." Washington, D.C., U.S. Department of Agriculture, Economic Research Service, June.

Trueblood, Michael A. and Vernon W. Ruttan. 1995. "A Comparison of Multifactor Productivity Calculation of the U.S. Agricultural Sector." *Journal of Productivity Analysis*. December, 6:9, pp. 321–32.

United Nations. 2001. "World Population Prospects: The 2000 Revision." United Nations Department of Economic and Social Affairs, ESA/P/WP 165. Available at <http://www.un.org/esa/population/wpp2000.htm>.

Waggoner, Paul E. 1997. "How Much Land Can Ten Billion People Spare for Nature?" in *Technology Trajectories and the Human Environment*. Jesse H. Ausubel and H. D. Langford, eds. Washington, D.C.: National Academy Press, pp. 57–73.

White, William J. III. 2000. "An Unsung Hero: The Farm Tractor's Contribution to Twentieth-Century United States Economic Growth." Ohio State University, Ph.D. Thesis.

Yudelman, Montague, Anna Ratta and David Nygaard. 1998. "Pest Management and Food Production." Washington, D.C., International Food Policy Research Institute, Food, Agriculture and the Environment Discussion Paper 25.

REVIEW AND DISCUSSION QUESTIONS

1 Brazil has abundant land and low population density. China, on the other hand, has a relatively limited amount of land and very high population density. What kind of agricultural technologies is Brazil likely to develop? How about China? Explain.

2 Data reported by Ruttan show that in Australia agricultural labor productivity is very high, but land productivity is low – about as low as in sub-Saharan Africa. How can we explain this dramatic difference between labor and land productivity in Australia?

3 Explain the difference between technical change and efficiency change.
4 According to Ruttan, what are the major resource and environmental constraints to continued productivity growth in agriculture? Which of these constraints does Ruttan consider most serious at a global level? Why?
5 What is Ruttan's assessment of the likelihood of continued growth in agricultural productivity over the next half-century and of the risks that we may face threats to global food security? Do you agree with his assessment?

Chapter 30

Norman E. Borlaug

THE NEXT GREEN REVOLUTION

THE KEY TO ECONOMIC DEVELOPMENT in Africa is agriculture. As President Bush concludes his trip to the continent, and Americans ponder ways to help it emerge from decades of poverty and turmoil, we would do well to remember that crucial point. Fortunately, we have the economic and technological means to bring about an agricultural revolution.

Using proven agricultural techniques, Africa could easily double or triple the yields of most of its crops. It has the potential not only to feed itself but even to become a dynamic agricultural exporter within a few decades.

African farmers face three main problems: depleted soil, a scarcity of water and distorted economics caused in large part by primitive transportation systems. None of these problems is beyond our capacity to solve.

Low soil fertility is one of the greatest biological obstacles to increasing food production and improving land productivity. (Because of overfarming and insufficient crop rotation, Africa's soil is actually less rich than it was 30 years ago.) Yet there is a man-made solution to the sub-Saharan soil's lack of nutrients – namely, fertilizer, either chemical or organic. Unfortunately, economic forces keep fertilizer out of many African farmers' hands.

Because of transportation costs, fertilizer costs two to three times more in rural sub-Saharan Africa than it does in rural Asia. As a result, fertilizer consumption in Africa is about 10 percent what it is in Asia. That's a market failure, and it could be remedied by a mix of public and private programs. Aid organizations might buy fertilizer at its point of entry into Africa and distribute it at reduced cost to wholesalers. Alternatively, poor farmers might be given fertilizer vouchers.

Chronic water shortages are another challenge. Nearly half of Africa's farmland suffers from periodic and often catastrophic drought. But here, too, the problem isn't beyond our control. About 4 percent of farmland south of the Sahara is irrigated, compared with 17 percent of farmland worldwide.

Large-scale irrigation projects are prohibitively expensive and can ruin villages and ecosystems. But clever, small-scale technologies – including subterranean pools for capturing rainfall, pumps on river banks, and cisterns under drain spouts – can make parched land bloom.

Because of the dismal state of roads in Africa, farmers there face the highest marketing costs in the world. A study by the World Bank, completed in the late 1990s, found that it cost roughly $50 to ship a metric ton of corn from Iowa to Mombasa, Kenya, more than 8,500 miles away. In contrast, it cost $100 or so to move the same amount of corn from Mombasa inland to Kampala, Uganda – about 550 miles. And not much has changed in recent years.

The challenge is that African produce is conveyed to buyers via a vast network of footpaths, tracks and dirt roads, where the most common mode of transport is walking. American- and European-financed road projects would connect farmers with consumers while improving life in countless other ways.

As agriculture takes off, agricultural-improvement and food-aid programs should dovetail. School lunch programs, for example, can provide a significant stimulus to the expansion of commercial food markets if the produce involved is locally grown.

Biotechnology absolutely should be part of African agricultural reform; African leaders will be making a grievous error if they turn their backs on it. (Zambia's president notoriously barred shipments of food aid from America last year that included genetically modified corn.) Genetic technology can help produce plants with greater tolerance of insects and diseases, improve the nutritional quality of food staples and help farmers to expand the areas they cultivate. Rather than looking to European leaders, who have demonized biotechnology, African leaders ought to work to manage and regulate this technology for the benefit of their farmers and citizens.

Africa's warm temperatures, abundant sunlight and wide open spaces and diverse climates make it a place where agriculture can thrive. Countries with tropical climates, like Nigeria, Liberia and Sierra Leone, should be exporting, not importing, rice. Drier places – including Burkina Faso, Mali and Chad – have the potential to be major producers of sorghum and millet. But you can't eat potential.

Nothing will happen without an infusion of money and technical help from the industrialized world. President Bush is right to emphasize a new emphasis on standards of evaluation. sub-Saharan countries that make significant progress in producing food and diminishing poverty should be rewarded with additional financial support.

Lest we forget, helping African agriculture to prosper is not merely a humanitarian issue – it's a matter of enlightened self-interest. Smallholder African farmers, after all, are stewards of one of the earth's major land masses. And as the Kenyan paleontologist Richard Leakey once said, "You have to have at least one square meal a day to be a conservationist." Aiding African farmers will not only save lives, it will also, in a uniquely literal sense, help to save the earth.

REVIEW AND DISCUSSION QUESTIONS

1   Borlaug points out that "Africa's soil is actually less rich than it was 30 years ago." What are the causes of this decrease in soil fertility, and how can the problem be fixed according to the author?

2   Why is it that "fertilizer consumption in Africa is about 10 percent what it is in Asia"? How could this situation be changed?

3   Borlaug worries about the fact that only 4 percent of farmland in sub-Saharan Africa is irrigated. What does he suggest to address this problem?

4   According to Borlaug, what is the appropriate role for rich countries in helping Africa increase food production? Do you agree with his recommendations? Why or why not?

Robert Paarlberg

FROM THE GREEN REVOLUTION TO THE GENE REVOLUTION
Review of Agricultural Biotechnology: Meeting the Needs of the Poor?

SINCE 1995, GENETICALLY ENGINEERED AGRICULTURAL crops, including multiple varieties of soybeans, maize, and cotton, have been approved by regulators and grown widely in the United States, Argentina, Canada, China, South Africa, and elsewhere. These genetically modified (GM) agricultural crops were initially approved by regulators in Europe and Japan as well. However, in 1996, when an unrelated but traumatic mad cow disease crisis undermined the credibility of European food safety regulators, some consumer, environmental, and antiglobalization activist groups began a determined campaign against GM crops, and the new technology fell under a cloud. Many developing countries, upon hearing mixed messages about GM crops from the United States and Europe, decided for the moment to try to remain GM-free.

After several years of sitting on the fence, the Food and Agricultural Organization (FAO) of the United Nations has now come down on the pro-GM side of this global policy debate, with a new report entitled *Agricultural Biotechnology: Meeting the Needs of the Poor?*[1] This 106-page report is embedded within FAO's latest (2003–2004) annual State of Food and Agriculture report, published in May 2004. FAO has been publishing annual statistical reports on the global state of food and agriculture since 1947, presenting official production and trade data gathered systematically from member governments around the world. These reports have always been useful to technicians and scholars working in the agricultural field but otherwise have seldom drawn much attention. When FAO began making its worldwide FAOSTAT database continuously available online (http://apps.fao.org/default.jsp), the annual publication of these State of Food and Agriculture reports fell to an even lower profile.

No longer. In its 2003–2004 report, FAO initiated a practice of adding an in-depth analysis of an "important theme" in agricultural and economic development, beginning with the most controversial theme it could have chosen: GM crops. By concluding that GM crops can provide significant benefits to poor farmers in the developing world, FAO has invited criticism from globally mobilized GM crop opponents and skeptics.

GM crops in developing countries

The biotechnology portion of the State of Food and Agriculture report was written by FAO's own Agricultural and Development Economics Division, working with a team of international consultants (most of whom were agricultural economists). The report draws many of its technical conclusions from reviews of previously published scholarly studies in the economics and crop science literature. As its title suggests, the analysis is framed to address the production problems of poor farmers, particularly those in Africa who missed out on the productivity gains provided by the earlier Green Revolution of the 1960s and 1970s, a technology upgrade based on conventional plant breeding that introduced high-yielding varieties of wheat and rice (accompanied by expanded irrigation and increased chemical fertilizer applications) into the developing countries of Asia.[2] New GM crop varieties now can help Africans, the reports' authors say, by providing better systems for containing insect damage: GM varieties of cotton and maize have now been engineered to contain genes from Bt (*Bacillus thuringiensis*), naturally occurring soil bacteria that cannot be digested by certain insects. (These same bacteria are widely used by organic farmers to control insects.) In the years ahead, genetic engineering may also be able to give poor farmers new varieties of crops that are drought tolerant or, like legumes, are capable of capturing and adding atmospheric nitrogen nutrients to the soil. The FAO report takes considerable time at the outset to provide the scientific and economic background that nonspecialists may need to appreciate the large stake that poor farmers have in crop improvements of these kinds.

Chapter 3 of the report considers why so few farmers in poor countries are currently growing GM crops. One reason is that many poor farmers in the tropics grow crops such as cassava, millet, or cowpea that are not yet available in a genetically modified form. The private seed companies that have led the world's research investments in GM have little incentive to invest in these "orphan crops," because the farmers that grow them seldom can afford expensive seeds. The solution to this problem is larger government investments in GM crop research. Such investments, the report says, could be carried out by public-sector research institutes in the developing world or by the 15 international agricultural research centers of the Consultative Group on International Agricultural Research (CGIAR). The FAO report stresses the important role that such public-sector researchers originally played in developing and extending Green Revolution high-yielding wheat and rice varieties, and they lament the reluctance of the public sector to invest as much today in the "Gene Revolution."

One of the most important findings of the report, however, is that in the one case where a suitable GM crop variety (Bt cotton) is widely available for planting by poor farmers in tropical countries, the technology has performed well. Chapter 4 summarizes results from various field-level studies in Argentina, China, India, Mexico, and South Africa – all of which show that insect-resistant GM varieties of cotton plants have worked well even for small-scale farmers, bringing about "higher average yields, lower pesticide use, and higher net return than their conventional counterparts." Yet few developing-country governments have been moving beyond this GM cotton success. They fear that if they start planting GM varieties of food or feed crops (such as maize or soybean) they will run commercial risks of losing export sales to markets such as the European Union, where consumers continue to harbor anxieties regarding the healthfulness and environmental safety of GM crops. In 2004, the European Union implemented strict new regulations regarding the labeling and tracing of GM food and feed products that will further discourage the planting of GM crops in countries that export to Europe.

Food safety and biosafety

In this report, FAO attempts to address the food safety and biosafety issues surrounding GM crops by summarizing the best scientific evidence available. On food safety, Chapter 5 reviews the published scientific evidence and concludes, "To date, no verifiable untoward toxic or nutritionally deleterious effects resulting from the consumption of foods derived from genetically modified foods have been discovered anywhere in the world." The key foundation for reaching this important finding is a 2003 report from the International Council for Science (ICSU) that in turn drew upon 50 independent scientific assessments carried out by authoritative groups in the European Union, Brazil, China, and India, as well as the United States.[3] No evidence of added food safety risk following 10 years of widespread GM food consumption deserves to be seen as a strong finding, yet this is unlikely to satisfy those committed to a hard version of the "precautionary principle," which permits withholding regulatory approval so long as any uncertainties remain. The FAO report does not address the precautionary principle directly, but it does implicitly challenge the need for tighter food safety regulations by pointing to the absence of any scientific evidence of harm to date.

Chapter 5 of the report also addresses the question of GM crop biosafety, a more complex problem because ecosystems around the world are more diverse than human biology. Here another finding from the ICSU report is summarized, a finding that the environmental effects of the GM crops approved so far – including effects such as gene transfer to other crops and wild relatives, weediness, and unintended adverse effects on nontarget species – have been similar to those that already existed for conventional agricultural crops. It must be remembered that GM varieties of agricultural crops are still domesticated species and thus less likely than wild exotic species to become damaging bioinvaders. Regarding hypothetical threats to monarch butterflies from GM maize, FAO recounts that six independent teams of researchers were unable in 2001 to find more than a negligible new risk to monarch butterflies from GM maize pollen under field conditions, despite worrying inferences drawn earlier from laboratory studies that did not replicate field conditions. Once again, FAO emphasizes actual test results on GM crop plants that are currently being grown rather than hypothetical risks associated with crops still in the laboratory. The one serious biosafety concern that is raised by FAO – the possible environmental release of GM animal species, particularly transgenic fish – goes beyond the world of agricultural crops.

Taking a clear position

FAO is not the first organization to have attempted a summary of what the scientific and economic literature can now tell us regarding the possible use of GM crops by farmers in developing countries. In 2003, the U.K. Nuffield Council on Bioethics produced a revised discussion paper on the use of genetically modified crops in reduce developing countries[4] that was similar in many ways to the new FAO report. What makes the FAO report noteworthy is that it comes from a United Nations agency that had previously taken a politically cautious approach toward GM technologies. Caught between the United States government, which promotes GM crops, and so many European green party leaders, organic-farming movements, and antiglobalization activist groups opposed to GM, most intergovernmental organizations have until now tried to avoid taking a clear position. Prior to 2004, FAO's own Director-General, Jacques Diouf, had asserted that GM crops would not be needed at least in the short run to meet the World Food Summit goal of reducing by half the number of hungry persons in the world by 2015. In his endorsement of this new 2004 State of Food and Agriculture report, Diouf explains FAO's switch to a more positive tone on GM crops by pointing to a more distant and challenging time horizon: the anticipated need to feed an additional two billion people by 2030. In the important case of Africa, FAO does not have to look this far into the future to find unmet food production requirements. As UN Secretary-General Kofi Annan pointed out at an international food conference prior to the 2004 African Union summit meeting in Ethiopia, roughly one-third of all adults in sub-Saharan Africa are currently undernourished, and food output has actually been declining in 31 out of 53 African countries.[5]

FAO knew it would be criticized for taking this more positive view toward GM crops. Soon after the report was issued, Diouf received an open letter signed by 670 separate non-governmental organizations (NGOs) and 816 individuals expressing their outrage and complete disagreement and calling the FAO report a "stab in the back" to the farmers and rural poor.[6] This widely publicized NGO letter did not attempt to refute FAO's summary of the scientific evidence regarding GM crops; instead it raised concerns about private corporate control of GM seeds (while at the same time not accepting FAO's solution to this problem: larger public-sector investments in GM crop research). More fundamentally, the letter challenged the pursuit of any "technological fix" as a response to food problems in poor countries. In a public reply to this NGO letter, Diouf defended the report, emphasized that FAO's vision for reducing hunger had always stressed much more than just new technologies, and reminded the NGOs of the need by 2050 (now using an even more distant time horizon) to feed an additional three billion people on Earth.[7]

FAO's new report will probably do little to reduce the acute skepticism toward GM crops felt widely within the NGO community, where many have never been able to accept even the original Green Revolution (which the NGO letter calls a "tragedy"[8]), let alone a new Gene Revolution. Many NGOs continue to reject evidence that Green Revolution seed varieties brought valuable productivity gains to poor as well as rich farmers; reduced hunger by lowering food prices and increasing rural income; and saved vast areas of forest, grazing land, and wildlife habitat from a further expansion of low-yield farming. The ideological divide between those who accept and those who reject science-enhanced farming practices (versus traditional ones) will thus remain as wide as ever. This new report nonetheless stands at least some chance of moving the debate forward, by presenting — this time on behalf of a UN agency — yet another summary of the accumulating economic and scientific evidence that GM crops have so far been healthy to eat, safe for the environment, and profitable to grow even for the poor.

Notes

1   Food and Agriculture Organization of the United Nations (FAO), *The State of Food and Agriculture 2003–2004: Agricultural Biotechnology: Meeting the Needs of the Poor?* (Rome: FAO, 2004, http://www.fao.org/documents/show_cdr.asp?url_file=/docrep/006/Y5160E/Y5160E00.HTM.

2   For a comparison of GM crops to these earlier Green Revolution varieties, see F. Wu and W. Butz, *The Future of Genetically Modified Crops: Lessons from the Green Revolution*, RAND report MG-161-RC (Santa Monica, CA: RAND Corporation, 2004).

3   International Council for Science (ICSU), *New Genetics, Food and Agriculture: Scientific Discoveries – Societal Dilemmas* (Paris: ICSU, 2003), http://www.icsu.org/1_icsuinscience/INIT_GMOrep_1.html.

4   Nuffield Council on Bioethics, "The Use of GM Crops in Developing Countries," discussion paper (London: Nuffield Council on Bioethics, 2003), http://www.nuffieldbioethics.org/go/print/ourwork/gmcrops/publication_313.html.

5   Text of remarks available at http://www.un.org/News/Press/docs/2004/sgsm9405.doc.htm

6   "FAO Declares War on Farmers Not On Hunger," http://www.grain.org/front_files/fao-open-letter-june-2004-final-en.pdf.

7   "Biotechnology: FAO Response to Open Letter from NGOs," http://www.fao.org/newsroom/en/news/2004/46429.

8   "FAO Declares War on Farmers Not On Hunger," note 6 above.

REVIEW AND DISCUSSION QUESTIONS

1   According to the FAO report reviewed by the author, in what ways can genetically modified (GM) crops be especially helpful to African farmers?

2   How does the FAO explain why GM crops are not widespread in developing countries? What does it recommend to address the obstacles to greater adoption of these crops?

3   Why are governments in developing countries reluctant to promote greater adoption of GM crops?

4   What does the evidence collected so far suggest about the possible risks imposed by GM crops on consumers and on the environment?

5   Why do many non-governmental organizations oppose the use of GM crops?

6   In your opinion, what should governments in developing countries do about GM crops? Why? Explain.

Chapter 32

Robert W. Kates, Thomas M. Parris, and Anthony A. Leiserowitz

WHAT IS SUSTAINABLE DEVELOPMENT

Goals, indicators, values, and practice

Sustainable development is . . .

CONSIDERING THAT THE CONCEPT of sustainable development is now enshrined on the masthead of *Environment* magazine, featured on 8,720,000 Web pages,[1] and enmeshed in the aspirations of countless programs, places, and institutions, it should be easy to complete the sentence.[2] But the most widely accepted definition is creatively ambiguous: "Humanity has the ability to make development sustainable – to ensure that it meets the needs of the present without compromising the ability of future generations to meet their own needs."[3] This malleability allows programs of environment or development; places from local to global; and institutions of government, civil society, business, and industry to each project their interests, hopes, and aspirations onto the banner of sustainable development.

A brief history of the concept, along with the interpretive differences and the common ground in definitions, goals, indicators, values, and practice follows. Taken together, these help explain what is meant by sustainable development.

Antecedents

In the last half of the twentieth century, four key themes emerged from the collective concerns and aspirations of the world's peoples: peace, freedom, development, and environment.[4] The peace that was thought to be secured in the postwar world of 1945 was immediately threatened by the nuclear arms race. Throughout the Cold War, peace was sustained globally but fought locally, often by proxies for the superpowers. While the number of wars has diminished over the last decade,[5] peace is still sought, primarily in Africa and the Middle East.

Freedom was sought early in the post-war world in the struggle to end imperialism; to halt totalitarian oppression; and later to extend democratic governance, human rights, and the rights of women, indigenous peoples, and minorities. The success of many former colonies in attaining national independence was followed by a focus on economic development to provide basic necessities for the poorest two-thirds of the world and higher standards of living for the wealthy third. Finally, it is only in the past 40 years that the environment (local to global) became a key focus of national and international law and institutions.

Although reinterpreted over time, peace, freedom, development, and the environment remain prominent issues and aspirations. In the 1970s and 1980s, world commissions of notables[6] were created to study such international concerns, producing major documents that were often followed by global conferences. Characteristic of these international commissions was the effort to link together the aspirations of human-kind – demonstrating how the pursuit of one great value required the others. Sustainable development, with its dual emphasis on the most recent concerns – development and environment – is typical of such efforts.

The World Commission on Environment and Development was initiated by the General Assembly of the United Nations in 1982, and its report, *Our Common Future*, was published in 1987.[7] It was chaired by then-Prime Minister of Norway Gro Harlem Brundtland, thus earning the name the "Brundtland Commission." The commission's membership was split between developed and developing countries. Its roots were in the 1972 Stockholm Conference on the Human Environment – where the conflicts between environment and development were first acknowledged – and in the 1980 World Conservation Strategy of the International Union for the Conservation of Nature, which argued for conservation as a means to assist development and specifically for the sustainable development and utilization of species, ecosystems, and resources.[8] Drawing on these, the Brundtland Commission began its work committed to the unity of environment and development. As Brundtland argued:

> The environment does not exist as a sphere separate from human actions, ambitions, and needs, and attempts to defend it in isolation from human concerns have given the very word "environment" a connotation of naivety in some political circles. The word "development" has also been narrowed by some into a very limited focus, along the lines of "what poor nations should do to become richer," and thus again is automatically dismissed by many in the international arena as being a concern of specialists, of those involved in questions of "development assistance." But the "environment" is where we live: and "development" is what we all do in attempting to improve our lot within that abode. The two are inseparable.[9]

As with previous efforts, the report was followed by major international meetings. The United Nations Conference on Environment and Development (UNCED) in Rio de Janeiro in 1992 (the so-called "Earth Summit") issued a declaration of principles, a detailed Agenda 21 of desired actions, international agreements on climate change and biodiversity, and a statement of principles on forests.[10] Ten years later, in 2002, at the World Summit on Sustainable Development in Johannesburg, South Africa, the commitment to sustainable development was reaffirmed.[11] In the interim, sustainable development as a concept, as a goal, and as a movement spread rapidly and is now central to the mission of countless international organizations, national institutions, corporate enterprises, "sustainable cities," and locales.

Definitions

The Brundtland Commission's brief definition of sustainable development as the "ability to make development sustainable – to ensure that it meets the needs of the present without compromising the ability of future generations to meet their own needs"[12] is surely the standard definition when judged by its widespread use and frequency of citation. The use of this definition has led many to see sustainable development as having a major focus on intergenerational equity. Although the brief definition does not explicitly mention the environment or development, the subsequent paragraphs, while rarely quoted, are clear. On development, the report states that human needs are basic and essential; that economic growth – but also equity to share resources with the poor – is required to sustain them; and that equity is encouraged by effective citizen participation. On the environment, the text is also clear:

> The concept of sustainable development does imply limits – not absolute limits but limitations imposed by the present state of technology and social organization on environmental resources and by the ability of the biosphere to absorb the effects of human activities.[13]

In the years following the Brundtland Commission's report, the creative ambiguity of the standard definition, while allowing a range of disparate groups to assemble under the sustainable development tent, also created a veritable industry of deciphering and advocating what sustainable development really means. One important study – by the Board on Sustainable Development of the U.S. National Academy of Sciences – sought to bring some order to the broad literature its members reviewed.[14] In its report, *Our Common Journey: A Transition toward Sustainability*, the board focused on the seemingly inherent distinction between what advocates and analysts sought to sustain and what they sought to develop, the relationship between the two, and the time horizon of the future (see Figure 32.1).

Thus under the heading "what is to be sustained," the board identified three major categories – nature, life support systems, and community – as well as intermediate categories for each, such as Earth, environment, and cultures. Drawing from the surveyed literature, the board found that most commonly, emphasis was placed on life support systems, which defined nature or environment as a source of services for the utilitarian life support of humankind. The study of ecosystem services has strengthened this definition over time. In contrast, some of the sustainable development literature valued nature for its intrinsic value rather than its utility for human beings. There were also parallel demands to sustain cultural diversity, including livelihoods, groups, and places that constitute distinctive and threatened communities.

Similarly, there were three quite distinct ideas about what should be developed: people, economy, and society. Much of the early literature focused on economic development, with productive sectors providing employment, desired consumption, and

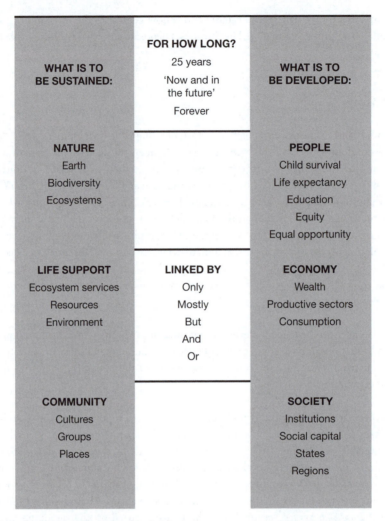

Figure 32.1 Definitions of sustainable development

Source: U.S. National Research Council, Policy Division, Board on Sustainable Development, *Our Common Journey: A Transition Toward Sustainability* (Washington, DC: National Academy Press, 1999).

wealth. More recently, attention has shifted to human development, including an emphasis on values and goals, such as increased life expectancy, education, equity, and opportunity. Finally, the Board on Sustainable Development also identified calls to develop society that emphasized the values of security and well-being of national states, regions, and institutions as well as the social capital of relationships and community ties.

There was ready agreement in the literature that sustainable development implies linking what is to be sustained with what is to be developed, but here, too, the emphasis has often differed from extremes of "sustain only" to "develop mostly" to various forms of "and/or." Similarly, the time period of concern, ambiguously described in the standard definition as "now and in the future," has differed widely. It has been defined from as little as a generation – when almost everything is sustainable – to forever – when surely nothing is sustainable.

The 2002 World Summit on Sustainable Development marked a further expansion of the standard definition with the widely used three pillars of sustainable development: economic, social, and environmental. The Johannesburg Declaration created "a collective responsibility to advance and strengthen the interdependent and mutually reinforcing pillars of sustainable development – economic development, social development and environmental protection – at local, national, regional and global levels."[15] In so doing, the World Summit addressed a running concern over the limits of the framework of environment and development, wherein development was widely viewed solely as economic development. For many under the common tent of sustainable development, such a narrow definition obscured their concerns for human development, equity, and social justice.

Thus while the three pillars were rapidly adopted, there was no universal agreement as to their details. A Web search of the phrase "three pillars of sustainable development" finds a wide variety of environmental, economic, and social pillars with differences most pronounced in characterizing the social pillar. Three major variants of social development are found, each of which seeks to compensate for elements missing in the narrow focus on economic development. The first is simply a generic noneconomic social designation that uses terms such as "social," "social development," and "social progress." The second emphasizes human development as opposed to economic development: "human development," "human, well-being," or just "people." The third variant focuses on issues of justice and equity: "social justice," "equity," and "poverty alleviation."

Goals

Another way to define sustainable development is in what it specifically seeks to achieve. To illustrate, it is helpful to examine three sets of goals that use different time-horizons: the short-term (2015) goals of the Millennium Declaration of the United Nations; the two-generation goals (2050) of the Sustainability Transition of the Board on Sustainable Development; and the long-term (beyond 2050) goals of the Great Transition of the Global Scenario Group.

UN Millennium Declaration

To mark the millennium, heads of state gathered in New York at the United Nations in September 2000. There, the UN General Assembly adopted some 60 goals regarding peace; development; environment; human rights; the vulnerable, hungry, and poor; Africa; and the United Nations.[16] Many of these contained specific targets, such as cutting poverty in half or insuring universal primary school education by 2015. For eight of the major goals, progress is monitored by international agencies.[17] In 2004, these agencies concluded that at existing rates of progress, many countries will fall short of these goals, particularly in Africa. Yet the goals still seemed attainable by collective action by the world community and national governments. To do so, the Millennium Project, commissioned by the UN secretary-general, recently estimated that the additional financial resources that would be required to meet the Millennium Development Goals are $135 billion in 2006, rising to $195 billion in 2015. This roughly represents a doubling of official aid flows over current levels and is still below the UN goal of aid flows from industrialized to developing countries of 0.7 percent of the gross national product for industrialized countries.[18]

Sustainability Transition of the Board on Sustainable Development

In 1995, the Board on Sustainable Development of the U.S. National Academy of Sciences sought to make sustainable development more meaningful to scientific analysis and contributions.[19] To do so, the board decided to focus on a two-generation time horizon and to address the needs of a global population with half as many more people as there are today – needs that, if met successfully, are not likely to be repeated within the next century or two because of the demographic transition. In that time period, the board suggested that a minimal sustainability transition would be one in which the world provides the energy, materials, and information to feed, nurture, house, educate, and employ the many more people of 2050 – while reducing hunger and poverty and preserving the basic life support systems of the planet. To identify more specific goals, of meeting human needs, reducing hunger and poverty, and preserving the basic life support systems of the planet, the board searched the text and statements from recent global conferences, world summits, international environmental treaties, and assessments. In so doing, the board in 1995 anticipated the 2000 Millennium Declaration goals, many of which were incorporated into its analysis and targets. Less sanguine than the UN, the board determined it would take a generation to reach the 2015 goals of the Millennium Declaration and another generation to achieve the board's goals of meeting human needs for a 2050 population.

Great Transition of the Global Scenario Group

With the assistance of the Global Scenario Group,[20] the Board on Sustainable Development conducted a scenario analysis of a proposed "Sustainability Transition," focusing specifically on hunger and the emission of greenhouse gasses. This initial analysis served as the subsequent basis of the Policy Reform Scenario of the Global Scenario Group[21] and concluded that a sustainability transition is possible without positing either a social revolution or a technological miracle. But it is "just" possible, and the technological and social requirements to move from business as usual – without changing lifestyles, values, or economic system – is daunting. Most daunting of all is the governmental commitment required to achieve it and the political will to do so.

Finally, the Global Scenario Group also prepared a more idealistic Great Transition Scenario that not only achieved the goals of the sustainability transition outlined by the Board on Sustainable Development but went further to achieve for all humankind "a rich quality of life, strong human ties and a resonant connection to nature."[22] In such a world, it would be the quality of human knowledge, creativity, and self-realization that represents development, not the quantity of goods and services. A key to such a future is the rejection of material consumption beyond what is needed for fulfillment or for a "good life." Beyond these goals, however, the details of this good life are poorly described.

Indicators

Still another way to define sustainable development is in how it is measured. Indeed, despite sustainable development's creative ambiguity, the most serious efforts to define it, albeit implicit in many cases, come in the form of indicators. Combining global, national, and local initiatives, there are literally hundreds of efforts to define appropriate indicators and to measure them. Recently, a dozen such efforts were reviewed.[23] Half were global in coverage, using country or regional data (the UN Commission on Sustainable Development, Consultative Group on Sustainable Development Indicators, Wellbeing Index, Environmental Sustainability Index, Global Scenario Group, and the Ecological Footprint). Of the remaining efforts, three were country studies (in the United States, the Genuine Progress Indicator and the Interagency Working Group on Sustainable Development Indicators, and in Costa Rica, the System of Indicators for Sustainable Development); one was a city study (the Boston Indicators Project); one was global in scope but focused on indicators of unsustainability (State Failure Task Force); and one focused on corporate and non-governmental entities (Global Reporting Initiative). Table 32.1 lists each study with its source, the number of indicators used, and the implicit or explicit definitions used to describe what is to be sustained, what is to be developed, and for how long.

Two major observations emerge. The first is the extraordinarily broad list of items to be sustained and to be developed. These reflect the inherent malleability of "sustainable development" as well as the internal politics of the measurement efforts. In many of the cases, the initiative is undertaken by a diverse set of stakeholders, and the resulting lists reflect their varied aspirations. For example, in the UN Commission on Sustainable Development, the stakeholders are nations negotiating how to measure their relative progress or lack of progress toward sustainable development. In the Boston Indicators Project, the stakeholders are community members with varied opinions about desirable goals, policies, and investment priorities for the future. In the Global Reporting Initiative, the stakeholders are corporations, investors, regulatory agencies, and civil society groups discussing how to account for corporate actions affecting sustainable development. With many stakeholders, each with different definitions, achieving consensus often takes the form of long "laundry lists" of indicators, and definitional differences are downplayed in favor of reaching a common set of indicators. Thus, to be inclusive, the range of indicators becomes very broad. Half the examined initiatives, however, represent less-inclusive research or advocacy groups who share a more narrow and homogenous view of sustainable development. While also assembling large numbers of indicators, these groups tend to aggregate them to reflect their distinctive vision of sustainability.

A second observation is that few of the efforts are explicit about the time period in which sustainable development should be considered. Despite the emphasis in the standard definition on intergenerational equity, there seems in most indicator efforts a focus on the present or the very short term. Three exceptions, however, are worth noting: The UN Commission on Sustainable Development uses some human development indicators defined in terms of a single generation (15–25 years),[24] the Global Scenario Group quantifies its scenarios through 2050 (approximately two generations), and the Ecological Footprint argues that in the long run an environmental footprint larger than one Earth cannot be sustained. Overall, these diverse indicator efforts reflect the ambiguous time horizon of the standard definition – "now and in the future."

Table 32.1 Definitions of sustainable development implicitly or explicitly adopted by selected indicator initiatives

Indicator initiative	Number of indicators	Implicit or explicit definition?	What is to be sustained?	What is to be developed?	For how long?
Commission on Sustainable Development[a]	58	Implicit, but informed by Agenda 21	Climate, clear air, land productivity, ocean productivity, fresh water, and biodiversity	Equity, health, education, housing, security, stabilized population	Sporadic references to 2015
Consultative Group on Sustainable Development Indicators[b]	46	Same as above	Same as above	Same as above	Not stated; uses data for 1990 and 2000
Wellbeing Index[c]	88	Explicit	"A condition in which the ecosystem maintains its diversity and quality – and thus its capacity to support people and the rest of life – and its potential to adapt to change and provide a wide change of choices and opportunities for the future"	"A condition in which all members of society are able to determine and meet their needs and have a large range of choices to meet their potential"	Not stated; uses most recent data as of 2001 and includes some indicators of recent change (such as inflation and deforestation)
Environmental Sustainability Index[d]	68	Explicit	"Vital environmental systems are maintained at healthy levels, and to the extent to which	Resilience to environmental disturbances ("People and social systems are not vulnerable (in the	Not stated; uses most recent data as

			levels are improving rather than deteriorating" [and] "levels of anthropogenic stress are low enough to engender no demonstrable harm to its environmental systems."	way of basic needs such as health and nutrition) to environmental disturbances; becoming less vulnerable is a sign that a society is on a track to greater sustainability"); "institutions and underlying social patterns of skills, attitudes, and networks that foster effective responses to environmental challenges"; and cooperation among countries "to manage common environmental problems"	of 2002 and includes some indicators of recent change (such as deforestation) or predicted change (such as population in 2025)
Genuine Progress Indicator[e]	26	Explicit	Clean air, land, and water	Economic performance, families, and security	Not stated; computed annually from 1950–2000
Global Scenario Group[f]	65	Explicit	"Preserving the essential health, services, and beauties of the earth requires stabilizing the climate at safe levels, sustaining energy, materials, and water resources, reducing toxic emissions, and maintaining the world's ecosystems and habitats."	Institutions to "meet human needs for food, water, and health, and provide opportunities for education, employment and participation"	Through 2050

Table 32.1 Continued

Indicator initiative	Number of indicators	Implicit or explicit definition?	What is to be sustained?	What is to be developed?	For how long?
Ecological Footprint[g]	6	Explicit	"The area of biologically productive land and water required to produce the resources consumed and to assimilate the wastes produced by humanity"		Not explicitly stated; computed annually from 1961–1999
U.S. Interagency Working Group on Sustainable Development Indicators[h]	40	Explicit	Environment, natural resources, and ecosystem services	Dignity, peace, equity, economy, employment, safety, health, and quality of life	Current and future generations
Costa Rica[i]	255	Implicit	Ecosystem services, natural resources, and biodiversity	Economic and social development	Not stated: includes some time series dating back to 1950
Boston Indicator Project[j]	159	Implicit	Open/green space, clean air, clean water, clean land, valued ecosystems, biodiversity, and aesthetics	Civil society, culture, economy, education, housing, health, safety, technology, and transportation	Not stated; uses most recent data as of 2000 and some indicators of recent change (such as change in poverty rates)
State Failure Task Force[k]	75	Explicit		Intrastate peace/security	Two years

			Reduced consumption of raw materials and reduced emissions of environmental contaminants from production or product use	Profitability, employment, diversity of workforce, dignity of workforce, health/safety of workforce, and health/safety/privacy of customers	Current reporting year
Global Reporting Initiative[l]	97	Implicit			

Source: Adapted from T. M. Parris and R. W. Kates, "Characterizing and Measuring Sustainable Development," *Annual Review of Environment and Resources* 28 (2003): 559–86.

[a] United Nations Division of Sustainable Development, *Indicators of Sustainable Development: Guidelines and Methodologies* (2001), http://www.un.org/esa/sustdev/natlinfo/indicators/indisd/indisd-mg2001.pdf.

[b] Consultative Group on Sustainable Development Indicators, http://www.iisd.org/cgsdi/.

[c] R. Prescott-Allen, *The Wellbeing of Nations: A Country-by-Country Index of Quality of Life and Environment* (Washington DC: Island Press, 2001).

[d] World Economic Forum, *2002 Environmental Sustainability Index* (Davos, Switzerland: World Economic Forum, 2002), http://www.ciesin.org/indicators/ESI/downloads.html; and D. C. Esty and P. K. Cornelius, *Environmental Performance Measurement: The Global Report 2001–2002* (Oxford, UK: Oxford University Press, 2002).

[e] C. Cobb, M. Glickman, and C. Cheslog, *The Genuine Progress Indicator: 2000 Update* (Oakland, CA: Redefining Progress, 2000).

[f] P. Raskin et al., *The Great Transition: The Promise and Lure of the Times Ahead* (Boston, MA: Stockholm Environmental Institute, 2002), http://www.tellus.org/seib/publications/Great_Transitions.pdf; and P. Raskin, G. Gallopin, P. Gutman, A. Hammond, and R. Swart, *Bending the Curve: Toward Global Sustainability*, Polestar Report 8 (Boston, MA: Stockholm Environmental Institute, 1998), http://www.tellus.org/seib/publications/bendingthecurve.pdf.

[g] M. Wackernagel et al., "Tracking the Ecological Overshoot of the Human Economy," *Proceedings of the National Academy Science* 99, no. 14 (2002): 9266–71; and M. Wackernagel, C. Monfreda, and D. Deumling, *Ecological Footprint of Nations: November 2002 Update* (Oakland, CA: Redefining Progress, 2002).

[h] U.S. Interagency Working Group on Sustainable Development Indicators (WGSDI), *Sustainable Development in the United States: An Experimental Set of Indicators*, IWGSDI Report PR42.8:SU 8/EX 7 (Washington, DC, 1998).

[i] Sistema de Indicadores sobre Desarrollo Sostenible (System of Indicators for Sustainable Development), *Principales Indicadores de Costa Rica* (Principal Indicators of Costa Rica) (San José, Costa Rica: Ministerio de Planificación Nacional y Política Económica (Ministry of National Planning and Political Economy), 1998), http://www.mideplan.go.cr/sides/.

[j] The Boston Indicator Project, *The Wisdom of Our Choices: Boston's Indicators of Progress, Change and Sustainability 2000* (Boston, MA: Boston Foundation, 2002), http://www.tbf.org/indicators/shared/news.asp?id=1542.

[k] D. C. Esty et al., 1998. "The State Failure Project: Early Warning Research for US Foreign Policy Planning," in J. L. Davies and T. R. Gurr, eds., *Preventive Measures: Building Risk Assessment and Crisis Early Warning Systems* (Boulder, CO: Rowman & Littlefield), 27–38; and D. C. Esty, J. A. Goldstone, T. R. Gurr, P. T. Surko, and A. N. Unger, *Working Paper: State Failure Task Force Report* (McLean, VA: Science Applications International Corporation, 1995); State Failure Task Force, "State Failure Task Force Report, Phase II Findings," *Environmental Change and Security Project Report* 5 (1999): 49–72.

[l] Global Reporting Initiative, http://www.globalreporting.org/.

> ## BOX 32.1   VALUES UNDERLYING THE MILLENNIUM DECLARATION
>
> The Millennium Declaration – which outlines 60 goals for peace; development; the environment; human rights; the vulnerable, hungry, and poor; Africa, and the United Nations – is founded on a core set of values described as follows.
>
> "We consider certain fundamental values to be essential to international relations in the twenty-first century. These include:
>
> - **Freedom**. Men and women have the right to live their lives and raise their children in dignity, free from hunger and from the fear of violence, oppression or injustice. Democratic and participatory governance based on the will of the people best assures these rights.
> - **Equality**. No individual and no nation must be denied the opportunity to benefit from development. The equal rights and opportunities of women and men must be assured.
> - **Solidarity**. Global challenges must be managed in a way that distributes the costs and burdens fairly in accordance with basic principles of equity and social justice. Those who suffer or who benefit least deserve help from those who benefit most.
> - **Tolerance**. Human beings must respect one other, in all their diversity of belief, culture and language. Differences within and between societies should be neither feared nor repressed, but cherished as a precious asset of humanity. A culture of peace and dialogue among all civilizations should be actively promoted.
> - **Respect for nature**. Prudence must be shown in the management of all living species and natural resources, in accordance with the precepts of sustainable development. Only in this way can the immeasurable riches provided to us by nature be preserved and passed on to our descendants. The current unsustainable patterns of production and consumption must be changed in the interest of our future welfare and that of our descendants.
> - **Shared responsibility**. Responsibility for managing worldwide economic and social development, as well as threats to international peace and security, must be shared among the nations of the world and should be exercised multi-laterally. As the most universal and most representative organization in the world, the United Nations must play the central role."[1]
>
> 1. United Nations General Assembly, "United Nations Millennium Declaration." Resolution 55/2. United Nations A/RES/55/2, 18 September 2000, page x.

Values

Still another mode of defining sustainable development is through the values that represent or support sustainable development.[25] But values, like sustainable development, have many meanings. In general, values are expressions of, or beliefs in, the worth of objects, qualities, or behaviors. They are typically expressed in terms of goodness or desirability or, conversely, in terms of badness or avoidance. They often invoke feelings, define or direct us to goals, frame our attitudes, and provide standards against which the behaviors of individuals and societies can be judged. As such, they often overlap with sustainability goals and indicators. Indeed, the three pillars of sustainable development; the benchmark goals of the Millennium Declaration, the Sustainability Transition, and the Great Transition; and the many indicator initiatives are all expressions of values.

But these values, as described in the previous sections, do not encompass the full range of values supporting sustainable development. One explicit statement of supporting values is found in the Millennium Declaration. Underlying the 60 specific goals of the Millennium Declaration are an articulated set of fundamental values seen as essential to international relations: freedom, equality, solidarity, tolerance, respect for nature, and shared responsibility (see Box 32.1).

The Millennium Declaration was adopted by the UN General Assembly, but the origins of the declaration's set of fundamental values are unclear. In contrast, the origins of the Earth Charter Initiative – which defines the Earth Charter as a "declaration of fundamental principles for building a just, sustainable, and peaceful global society in the 21st century"[26] – is well documented. The initiative answers the call of the World Commission on Environment and Development for creation of "a universal declaration" that would "consolidate and extend relevant legal principles," create "new norms . . . needed to maintain livelihoods and life on our shared planet," and "guide state behavior in the transition to sustainable development."[27] An effort to draft a charter at the 1992 Earth Summit was unsuccessful. In 1994 a new Earth Charter Initiative was launched that involved "the most open and participatory consultation process ever conducted in connection with an international document. Thousands of individuals and hundreds of organizations from all regions of the world, different cultures, and diverse sectors of society . . . participated."[28] Released in the year 2000, the Earth Charter has been endorsed by more than 14,000 individuals and organizations worldwide representing millions of members, yet it has failed to attain its desired endorsement or adoption by the 2002 World Summit on Sustainable Development or the UN General Assembly.

The values of the Earth Charter are derived from "contemporary science, international law, the teachings of indigenous peoples, the wisdom of the world's great religions and philosophical traditions, the declarations and reports of the seven UN summit conferences held during the 1990s, the global ethics movement, numerous non-governmental declarations and people's treaties issued over the past thirty years, and best practices for building sustainable communities."[29] For example, in 1996, more than 50 international law instruments were surveyed and summarized in *Principles of Environmental Conservation and Sustainable Development: Summary and Survey*.[30] Four first-order principles were identified and expressed in the Earth Charter as the community of life, ecological integrity, social and economic justice, and democracy, nonviolence, and peace. Sixteen second-order principles expand on these four, and 61 third-order principles elaborate on the 16. For example, the core principal of social and economic justice is elaborated by principles of equitable economy, eradication of poverty, and the securing of gender equality and the rights of indigenous peoples. In turn, each of these principles is further explicated with three or four specific actions or intentions.[31]

Practice

Finally – and in many ways, most importantly – sustainable development is defined in practice. The practice includes the many efforts at defining the concept, establishing goals, creating indicators, and asserting values. But additionally, it includes developing social movements, organizing institutions, crafting sustainability science and technology, and negotiating the grand compromise among those who are principally concerned with nature and environment, those who value economic development, and those who are dedicated to improving the human condition.

A social movement

Sustainable development can be viewed as a social movement – "a group of people with a common ideology who try together to achieve certain general goals."[32] In an effort to encourage the creation of a broadly based social movement in support of sustainable development, UNCED was the first international, intergovernmental conference to provide full access to a wide range of nongovernmental organizations (NGOs) and to encourage an independent Earth Summit at a nearby venue. More than 1,400 NGOs and 8,000 journalists participated.[33] One social movement launched from UNCED was the effort described above to create an Earth Charter, to ratify it, and to act upon its principles.

In 2002, 737 new NGOs[34] and more than 8,046 representatives of major groups (business, farmers, indigenous peoples, local authorities, NGOs, the scientific and technological communities, trade unions, and women) attended the World Summit on Sustainable Development in Johannesburg. These groups organized themselves into approximately 40 geographical and issue-based caucuses.[35]

But underlying this participation in the formal international sustainable development events are a host of social movements struggling to identify what sustainable development means in the context of specific places and peoples. One such movement is the effort of many communities, states, provinces, or regions to engage in community exercises to define a desirable sustainable future and the actions needed to attain it. Examples include Sustainable Seattle,[36] Durban's Local Agenda 21 Programme,[37] the Lancashire County Council Local Agenda 21 Strategy,[38] and the Minnesota Sustainable Development Initiative.[39]

Three related efforts are the sustainable livelihoods movement, the global solidarity movement, and the corporate responsibility movement.[40] The movement for sustainable livelihoods consists of local initiatives that seek to create opportunities for work and sustenance that offer sustainable and credible alternatives to current processes of development and modernization. Consisting primarily of initiatives in developing countries, the movement has counterparts in the developed world, as seen, for example, in local efforts in the United States to mandate payment of a "living wage" rather than a minimum wage.

The global solidarity movement seeks to support poor people in developing countries in ways that go beyond the altruistic support for development funding. Their campaigns are expressed as antiglobalization or "globalization from below"[41] in critical appraisals of major international institutions, in the movement for the cancellation of debt,[42] and in critiques of developed-world policies – such as agricultural subsidies – that significantly impact developing countries and especially poor people.[43]

The corporate responsibility movement has three dimensions: various campaigns by NGOs to change corporate environmental and social behavior;[44] efforts by corporations to contribute to sustainable development goals and to reduce their negative environmental and social impacts;[45] and international initiatives such as the UN Global Compact[46] or the

World Business Council for Sustainable Development[47] that seek to harness the knowledge, energies, and activities of corporations to better serve nature and society. For instance, in the just-selected Global 100, the most sustainable corporations in the world, the top three corporations were Toyota, selected for its leadership in introducing hybrid vehicles; Alcoa, for management of materials and energy efficiency; and British Petroleum, for leadership in greenhouse gas emissions reduction, energy efficiency, renewables, and waste treatment and handling.[48]

A related social movement focuses on excessive material consumption and its impacts on the environment and society and seeks to foster voluntary simplicity of one form or another. These advocates argue that beyond certain thresholds, ever-increasing consumption does not increase subjective levels of happiness, satisfaction, or health.[49] Rather, it often has precisely the opposite effect. Thus, these efforts present a vision of "the good life" in which people work and consume less than is prevalent in today's consumer-driven affluent societies.

As with any social movement, sustainable development encounters opposition. The opponents of sustainable development attack from two very different perspectives: At one end of the spectrum are those that view sustainable development as a top-down attempt by the United Nations to dictate how the people of the world should live their lives – and thus as a threat to individual freedoms and property rights.[50] At the other end are those who view sustainable development as capitulation that implies development as usual, driven by the interests of big business and multilateral institutions and that pays only lip service to social justice and the protection of nature.[51]

Institutions

The goals of sustainable development have been firmly embedded in a large number of national, international, and nongovernmental institutions. At the intergovernmental level, sustainable development is now found as a central theme throughout the United Nations and its specialized agencies. Evidence of this shift can be seen in the creation of the Division of Sustainable Development within the United Nations Department of Economic and Social Affairs, the establishment of a vice president for environmentally and socially sustainable development at the World Bank, and the declaration of the United Nations Decade of Education for Sustainable Development. Similarly, numerous national and local governmental entities have been established to create and monitor sustainable development strategies.[52] According to a recent survey by the International Council for Local Environment Initiatives, "6,416 local authorities in 113 countries have either made a formal commitment to Local Agenda 21 or are actively undertaking the process," and the number of such processes has been growing dramatically.[53] In addition to these governmental efforts, sustainable development has emerged in the organization charts of businesses (such as Lafarge[54]), consultancies (including CH2M Hill[55]), and investment indices (such as the Dow Jones Sustainability Index).

Sustainability science and technology

Sustainable development is also becoming a scientific and technological endeavor that, according to the Initiative on Science and Technology for Sustainable Development, "seeks to enhance the contribution of knowledge to environmentally sustainable human development around the world."[56] This emerging enterprise is focused on deepening our understanding of socio-ecological systems in particular places while exploring innovative mechanisms for producing knowledge so that it is relevant, credible, and legitimate to local decisionmakers.[57]

The efforts of the science and technology community to contribute to sustainable development is exemplified in the actions of the major Academies of Science[58] and International Disciplinary Unions,[59] in collaborative networks of individual scientists and technologists,[60] in emerging programs of interdisciplinary education,[61] and in many efforts to supply scientific support to communities.[62]

A grand compromise

One of the successes of sustainable development has been its ability to serve as a grand compromise between those who are principally concerned with nature and environment, those who value economic development, and those who are dedicated to improving the human condition. At the core of this compromise is the inseparability of environment and development described by the World Commission on Environment and Development. Thus, much of what is described as sustainable development in practice are negotiations in which workable compromises are found that address the environmental, economic, and human development objectives of competing interest groups. Indeed, this is why so many definitions of sustainable development include statements about open and democratic decisionmaking.

At the global scale, this compromise has engaged the wealthy and poor countries of the world in a common endeavor. Before this compromise was formally adopted by UNCED, the poorer countries of the world often viewed demands for greater environmental protection as a threat to their ability to develop, while the rich countries viewed some of the development in poor countries as a threat to valued environmental resources. The concept of sustainable development attempts to couple development aspirations with the need to preserve the basic life support systems of the planet.

So, what is sustainable development?

Since the Brundtland Commission first defined sustainable development, dozens, if not hundreds, of scholars and practitioners have articulated and promoted their own alternative definition; yet a clear, fixed, and immutable meaning remains elusive. This has led some observers to call sustainable development an oxymoron: fundamentally contradictory and irreconcilable. Further, if anyone can redefine and reapply the term to fit their purposes, it becomes meaningless in practice, or worse, can be used to disguise or greenwash socially or environmentally destructive activities.

Yet, despite these critiques, each definitional attempt is an important part of an ongoing dialogue. In fact, sustainable development draws much of its resonance, power, and creativity from its very ambiguity. The concrete challenges of sustainable development are at least as heterogeneous and complex as the diversity of human societies and natural ecosystems around the world. As a concept, its malleability allows it to remain an open, dynamic, and evolving idea that can be adapted to fit these very different situations and contexts across space and time. Likewise, its openness to interpretation enables participants at multiple levels, from local to global, within and across activity sectors, and in institutions of governance, business, and civil society to redefine and reinterpret its meaning to fit their own situation. Thus, the concept of sustainability has been adapted to address very different challenges, ranging from the planning of sustainable cities to sustainable livelihoods, sustainable agriculture to sustainable fishing, and the efforts to develop common corporate standards in the UN Global Compact and in the World Business Council for Sustainable Development.

Despite this creative ambiguity and openness to interpretation, sustainable development has evolved a core set of guiding principles and values, based on the Brundtland Commission's standard definition to meet the needs, now and in the future, for human, economic, and social development within the restraints of the life support systems of the planet. Further, the connotations of both of the phrase's root words, "sustainable" and "development" are generally quite positive for most people, and their combination imbues this concept with inherent and near-universal agreement that sustainability is a worthwhile value and goal – a powerful feature in diverse and conflicted social contexts.

Importantly, however, these underlying principles are not fixed and immutable but the evolving product of a global dialogue, now several decades old, about what sustainability should mean. The original emphasis on economic development and environmental protection has been broadened and deepened to include alternative notions of development (human and social) and alternative views of nature (anthropocentric versus ecocentric). Thus, the concept maintains a creative tension between a few core principles and an openness to reinterpretation and adaptation to different social and ecological contexts.

Sustainable development thus requires the participation of diverse stakeholders and perspectives, with the ideal of reconciling different and sometimes opposing values and goals toward a new synthesis and subsequent coordination of mutual action to achieve multiple values simultaneously and even synergistically. As real-world experience has shown, however, achieving agreement on sustainability values, goals, and actions is often difficult and painful work, as different stakeholder values are forced to the surface, compared and contrasted, criticized and debated. Sometimes individual stakeholders find the process too difficult or too threatening to their own values and either reject the process entirely to pursue their own narrow goals or critique it ideologically, without engaging in the hard work of negotiation and compromise. Critique is nonetheless a vital part of the conscious evolution of sustainable development – a concept that, in the end, represents diverse local to global efforts to imagine and enact a positive vision of a world in which basic human needs are met without destroying or irrevocably degrading the natural systems on which we all depend.

Notes

1   http://www.google.com/search?q=%22sustainable+development%22&start=0& start=0&ie=utf-8&oe=utf-8&client=firefox-a&rls=org.mozillaten-US:official (accessed 31 January 2005).

2   For an example of an economics answer, see G. Chichilinisky, "What is Sustainable Development?" *Land Economics* 73. no. 4 (1997): 467–91.

3   World Commission on Environment and Development (WCED), *Our Common Future* (New York: Oxford University Press, 1987), 8.

4   National Research Council, Policy Division, Board on Sustainable Development, *Our Common Journey: A Transition toward Sustainability* (Washington, DC: National Academy Press, 1999), 22.

5   M. G. Marshall and T. R. Gurr, *Peace and Conflict 2003*, (College Park, MD: Center for International Development and Conflict Management, University of Maryland, 2003), http://www.cidem.umd.edu/paper.asp?id=2.

6   Independent Commission on Disarmament and Security Issues, *Common Security: A Blueprint for Survival* (Palme Report) (New York: Simon & Schuster, 1982); and Independent Commission on International Development Issues. *North-South: A Program for Survival* (Brandt Report) (Cambridge, MA: MIT Press, 1980).

7   WCED, note 3 above.

8   W. M. Adams, *Green Development: Environment and Sustainability in the Third World* (London: Routledge, 1990).

9   WCED, note 3 above, page xi.

10   The United Nations Conference on Environment and Development (UNCED), http://www.un.org/geninfo/bp/enviro.html; and E. A. Parson and P. M. Haas, "A Summary of the Major Documents Signed at the Earth Summit and the Global Forum," *Environment*, October 1992, 12–18.

11   *The Johannesburg Declaration on Sustainable Development*, 4 September 2002, http://www.housing.gov.za/content/legislation_policies/johannesburg.htm.

12   WCED, note 3 above, page 8.

13   WCED, note 3 above, page 8.

14   National Research Council, note 4 above, pages 22–26.

15   *The Johannesburg Declaration on Sustainable Development*, note 11 above, page 1.

16   United Nations General Assembly, "United Nations Millennium Declaration," Resolution 55/2, United Nations A/RES/55/2, 18 September 2000.

17   Careful monitoring is under way for 8 goals with 18 targets and 48 indicators to measure progress by experts from the United Nations Secretariat, International Money Fund, Organisation for Economic Co-operation and Development and the World Bank (ST/ESA/STAT/MILLENNIUMINDICATORS2003/WWW (unofficial working paper)), 23 March 2004, http://millenniumindicators.un.org/unsd/mi/mi_goals.asp; http://www.developmentgoals.org/).

18   UN Millennium Project, *Investing in Development: A Practical Plan to Achieve the Millennium Development Goals, Overview* (New York: United Nations Development Program, 2005).

19   National Research Council, note 4 above.

20   The Global Scenario Group was convened in 1995 by the Stockholm Environment Institute to engage a diverse international group in an examination of the prospects for world development in the twenty-first century. Numerous studies at global, regional, and national levels have relied on the group's scenario framework and quantitative analysis. For more information see http://gsg.org/.

21   P. Raskin et al., *Great Transition: The Promise and Lure of the Times Ahead* (Boston: Stockholm Environment Institute, 2002).

22   Ibid., page 43. A Great Transition Initiative has been launched to help crystallize a global citizens movement to advance the vision of the scenario. For more information, see http://www.gtinitiative.org/.

23   T. M. Parris and R. W. Kates, "Characterizing and Measuring Sustainable Development,"
     Annual Reviews of Environment and Resources 28 (2003): 559–86.

24   For a thorough review of internationally negotiated targets related to sustainable
     development, see T. M. Parris, "Toward a Sustainability Transition: The International
     Consensus," *Environment*, January/February 2003, 12.

25   A. Leiserowitz, R. W. Kates, and T. M. Parris, "Sustainability Values, Attitudes and
     Behaviors: A Review of Multi-National and Global Trends." CID Working Paper No. 112
     (Cambridge, MA: Science, Environment and Development Group, Center for
     International Development, Harvard University, 2004).

26   Earth Charter International Secretariat, *The Earth Charter: Values and Principles for a
     Sustainable Future*, http://www.earthcharter.org/files/resources/Earth%20Charter%
     20-%20Brochure%20ENG.pdf, page 1.

27   WCED, note 3 above, page 332.

28   Earth Charter International Secretariat, *The Earth Charter Handbook*,
     http://www.earthcharter.org/files/resources/Handbook.pdf, page 4.

29   Earth Charter International Secretariat, note 26 above.

30   S. C. Rockefeller, "Principles of Environmental Conservation and Sustainable
     Development: Summary and Survey," unpublished paper prepared for the Earth Charter
     Project, April 1996.

31   *The Earth Charter*, 2000, from http://www.earthcharter.org/

32   *WordNet 2.0* (Princeton University, 2003), http://www.cogsci.princeton.edu/~wn/.

33   P. Haas, M. Levy, and T. Parson, "Appraising the Earth Summit: How Should We Judge
     UNCED's Success?" *Environment*, October 1992, 6–11, 26–33.

34   In addition, 2,500 organizations accredited with the Economic and Social Council and on
     the Commission on Sustainable Development list attended.

35   Report of the World Summit Sustainable Development, A/CONF.199/20*

36   *Sustainable Seattle*, http://www.sustainableseattle.org/.

37   *Ethekwini Online*, http://www.durban.gov.za/eThekwini/Services/environment/
     about_la21/index_html.

38   *Lancashire County Council Environmental Directorate*,
     http://www.lancashire.gov.uk/environment/beyondla21/County21.asp.

39   *Minnesota Environmental Quality Board: Sustainable Development Initiative*,
     http://www.eqb.state.mn.us/SDI/.

40   F. Amalric, "The Relevance of Selected Social Movements for the Great Transition
     Initiative," October 2004, University of Zurich (mimeo), and forthcoming as a Great
     Transition Initiative report, http://www.gtinitiative.org.

41   J. Brecher, T. Costello, and B. Smith, *Globalization from Below: The Power of Solidarity*
     (Boston: South End Press, 2000).

42   See, for example, the Jubilee Debt Campaign,
     http://www.jubileedebtcampaign.org.uk/?ce=1.

43   See, for example, C. Godfrey, "Stop the Dumping: How EU Agricultural Subsidies
     are Damaging Livelihoods in the Developing World," Oxfam International briefing
     paper 31, http://www.oxfam.org.uk/what_we_do/issues/trade/bp31_dumping.
     htm.

44   See, for example, the Interfaith Center for Corporate Responsibility,
     http://www.iccr.org; or CorpWatch, http://www.corpwatch.org/.

45   One measure of the extent of this activity is the 625 corporations or other entities

referring to or using sustainability-reporting guidelines in their corporate reports as part of the Global Reporting Initiative, http://www.globalreporting.org/.

46   The Global Compact seeks to bring companies together with UN agencies and labor and civil society to support 10 principles in the areas of human rights, labor, the environment, and anticorruption (http://www.unglobalcompact.org/).

47   The World Business Council for Sustainable Development (WBCSD) is a coalition of 170 international companies that share a commitment to sustainable development via the three pillars of economic growth, ecological balance, and social progress. See http://www. wbcsd.ch/.

48   *The Global 100: Most Sustainable Corporations in the World*, http://www.global100.org/what.asp.

49   R. Inglehart, "Globalization and Postmodern Values," *Washington Quarterly* 23, no. 1 (1990): 215–28; H. Nearing and S. Nearing, *The Good Life* (New York: Schocken, 1990); and D. Elgin, *Voluntary Simplicity* (New York: William Morrow, 1993).

50   Freedom 21 Santa Cruz, *Understanding Sustainable Development (Agenda 21): A Guide for Public Officials*, http://www.freedom21santacruz.net/guide.pdf.

51   J. G. Clark, "Economic Development vs. Sustainable Societies: Reflections on the Players in a Crucial Contest," *Annual Review of Ecology and Systematics* 26 (1995): 225–48.

52   B. Dalal-Clayton and S. Bass, *Sustainable Development Strategies: A Resource Book* (London, UK, and Sterling, VA: Earthscan Publications Ltd., 2002), http://www.nssd.net/res_ book.html.

53   The International Council for Local Environmental Initiatives, "Second Local Agenda 21 Survey," UN Department of Economic and Social Affairs Background Paper No. 15 (2001), http://www.iclei.org/rioplusten/final_document.pdf.

54   *Lafarge: Sustainable Development*, http://www.lafarge.com/cgi-bin/lafcom/jsp/ content.do?function=responsables&lang=en.

55   *CH2M Hill: Sustainable Development*, http://www.ch2m.com/corporate_2004/Services/ Capabilities/Sustainable_Development/sd.asp.

56   Initiative on Science and Technology for Sustainable Development, http://sustsci.harvard.edu/ists/; also see R. W. Kates et al., "Sustainability Science." *Science*, 27 April 2001, 641–42.

57   International Council for Science, Initiative on Science and Technology for Sustainability, and Third World Academy of Sciences, *Science and Technology for Sustainable Development*, ICSU Series on Science for Sustainable Development, no. 9 (Paris: ICSU, 2002), http:// www.icsu.org/Gestion/img/ICSU_DOC_DOWNLOAD/70_DD_FILE_Vol9.pdf.

58   See statement of the World Academy of Sciences, http://www.4.nationalacademies.org/iap/iaphome.nsf/weblinks/SAIN-4XVLCT?OpenDocument; and R. W. Kates, "Sustainability Science," in Transition to *Sustainability in the 21st Century: The Contribution of Science and Technology* (Washington, DC: National Academies Press, 2003), 140–45.

59   International Council for Science, Initiative on Science and Technology for Sustainability, and Third World Academy of Sciences, note 57 above.

60   See the Forum on Science and Technology for Sustainability, http://sustsci.harvard.edu/index.html, for reports of many activities by scientific organizations and individual scientists.

61   See programs listed on http://sustsci.harvard.edu/education.htm.

62   See for example, A. L. Mabogunje and R. W. Kates, "Sustainable Development in Ijebu-Ode, Nigeria: The Role of Social Capital, Participation, and Science and Technology," CID

Working Paper No. 102 (Cambridge, MA: Sustainable Development Program. Center for International Development, Harvard University, 2004).

REVIEW AND DISCUSSION QUESTIONS

1 According to the authors, what is the "standard definition" of sustainable development?
2 In the narrowest sense, what does pursuing sustainable development involve? How about in the broadest sense?
3 How did the Board on Sustainable Development refine the time horizon and goals of sustainable development in 1995?
4 What are some of the fundamental values that the idea of sustainable development is based on?
5 Come up with a definition of sustainable development that makes sense to you and discuss the advantages and limitations of your definition.

Suggestions for further reading

Binswanger, H. P. and Deininger, K. (1997) "Explaining Agricultural and Agrarian Policies in Developing Countries," *Journal of Economic Literature*, 25: 1958-2005.

In this comprehensive article the authors discuss the peculiarities of the agricultural sectors of developing countries, the effects of such peculiarities on agricultural productivity, and the political reasons why agricultural policies differ across countries. They also investigate what it takes for policies to change, concluding with some policy advice for developing countries.

Esty, D. C. (2001) "Bridging the Trade–Environment Divide," *Journal of Economic Perspectives*, 15: 113-130.

This is a thorough examination of the clashes between environmentalists and free-trade advocates. The author reviews the many issues that have generated controversy and argues that environmental protection and trade liberalization in developing countries need not be in opposition.

Food and Agriculture Organization of the United Nations, *The State of Food and Agriculture* (published annually).

In this annual report, the arm of the United Nations that deals with agriculture and food security provides a summary and data on the global agricultural situation; in addition, every year the report focuses on a different topic (e.g., bioenergy, food aid, agricultural trade and poverty, etc.).

Margolis, M. (2002) "A Plot of Their Own," *Newsweek*, 21 January.

This is a case study of land reform in Brazil. Margolis explains the many practical obstacles that the program ran against, emphasizing that the success of a land reform program depends crucially on the existence of many other complementary reforms and Government interventions.

Masood, E. (2003) "A Continent Divided," *Nature*, 6964: 224-226.

Masood discusses the controversy surrounding the adoption of genetically modified crops in Africa. He emphasizes the political dimensions of the debate and the role of U.S. companies, European governments, and NGOs.

Financial markets and microcredit

INTRODUCTION

I N 2005, CHINA'S GROSS SAVING was a remarkable 51 percent of its GDP. This number indicates that the share of China's national income that was not spent on consumption goods was over half of China's GDP. Saving rates that year were high in a few other developing countries as well – 46 percent in Botswana, 36 percent in Malaysia, and 32 percent in India. Yet, they were much lower in many other developing countries – 7 percent in Sierra Leone, 4 percent in Mozambique, and 3 percent in Zimbabwe. In fact, saving rates were negative in a few countries (e.g., Malawi), indicating that domestic consumption exceeded national income and was financed in part by foreign aid (all data are from World Bank 2007: 218–20; the definition of "gross savings" used by the World Bank includes net transfers from abroad). Economists agree that domestic saving can play a crucial role in promoting economic development. A country cannot develop without substantial investment – in new factories, roads, schools, hospitals, and so on – and the money to pay for these projects must either come from abroad or from domestic saving. When a worker deposits a share of her daily wage in the bank instead of spending it on consumption goods, the money she saved can be lent out and used to pay for investment projects. And when the government decides to spend a share of its tax revenue on building a new road or a new school, rather than on embellishing the presidential palace, it is saving and investing this money.

Saving can be difficult when incomes are low, as is the case in developing countries. Households may find that they have barely enough money to pay for their basic consumption expenditures and have very little left over to save. If saving is low, paying for investment is more difficult, and economic development becomes harder to achieve. For this reason, it is especially crucial that whatever saving a developing country does have is invested in a productive way. If the worker we mentioned above deposits a share of her daily wage in her cookie jar rather than in a bank, the money cannot be lent out and be used to finance investment projects. Saving helps development only when it is turned into investment; it is the job of financial markets to ensure that saving does indeed finance productive investment projects. Banks are important players in these markets: they collect deposits (saving) from people and lend the money to private firms, which may use it to build new factories (private investment), or to the government, which may use it for such projects as building new schools (public investment). Firms may also raise money to pay for investment by issuing stocks or bonds, and the government may borrow money by issuing bonds. A country's financial system encompasses any instruments (such as stocks and bonds) and institutions (such as banks) that help facilitate the transformation of money saved into money invested.

In many developing countries, financial markets are relatively primitive and do not do a very effective job at turning saving into productive investment. The article reprinted in Chapter 33 discusses the case of India, a country where financial markets are in clear need of reform. Authors Diana Farrell and Susan Lund, of the McKinsey Global Institute, explain that India's financial markets fail to attract a large share of saving and tend to allocate whatever saving they do attract in unproductive ways. Data collected by the authors show that households place no more than half of their saving in bank deposits and other financial instruments; much of the rest is invested in houses and gold – assets that do little to spur economic growth. A large share of household saving is also invested in small-scale family businesses. While this is indeed investment, the authors worry that these businesses tend to be very inefficient, so that saving is not used in the most productive way. According to Farrell and Lund, government regulations are mostly to blame for the inability of the financial system to work effectively. These regulations require banks to distribute a significant share of their deposits to the government itself and to specific industries chosen according to political criteria. The government also owns the vast majority of banks, limiting the extent of competition from private (including foreign) banks. Lack of competition tends to result in higher interest rates on loans (which discourage investment) and lower interest rates on deposits (which may discourage saving). Farrell and Lund recommend relaxing government constraints and allowing banks and other financial intermediaries to respond to market incentives.

While relatively undeveloped financial markets can make it hard and expensive for firms to obtain loans, in developing countries certain entrepreneurs tend to be shut out of the formal financial system altogether. These are people who often live in rural areas, far from major financial centers, and who run informal and very small businesses – creating small crafts, selling home-made food products to fellow villagers, or growing crops on tiny plots of land. While credit is often crucial for these businesses to thrive, urban banks are rarely interested in providing loans to these borrowers. The size of the loan is often too small to justify the cost of providing it, and since borrowers typically lack assets to put up as collateral, banks consider these loans too risky. Small rural borrowers, therefore, are forced to borrow from relatives and friends, and often from moneylenders – local informal lenders who are able to exploit the relative lack of competition and charge very high interest rates.

In 1976, a Bangladeshi economics professor named Muhammad Yunus noticed how serious the consequences of this lack of credit could be for the livelihood of small entrepreneurs and resolved to find a solution. In the selection from his autobiographical book reprinted in Chapter 34 Yunus describes his experience visiting with stool maker Sufiya Begum in the village adjacent to his university: Begum borrowed 22 cents every day from a middleman to buy bamboo, worked all day to turn the bamboo into stools, and sold the stools to the middleman for a profit of just 2 cents. Her inability to borrow at reasonable rates a very small amount of money and use it to buy bamboo forced her into an agreement that doomed her to a life of poverty. Yunus soon found out that other entrepreneurs in the village were in the same situation, and he started thinking about how much access to credit could improve the lives of these very poor, very small-scale entrepreneurs. He began a number of projects aimed at serving these customers and in 1983 founded the Grameen Bank, designing it specifically to provide small loans, or "microcredit," to the poor.

The idea of microcredit has since become increasingly popular and has had an enormous impact on the activities of international development institutions and non-governmental organizations. Instead of requiring collateral before giving out loans, Yunus's bank *excluded* borrowers who had assets to put up as collateral, as traditional banks already served these borrowers. Instead, it lent specifically to poor people without assets, betting that the prospect of earning a higher income and moving out of poverty would be enough to motivate borrowers to pay back their loans. It also adopted a variety of other unconventional practices, such as the gradual repayment of loans, the requirement that borrowers take out loans in groups, and the focus on serving female entrepreneurs. Today the Grameen Bank "has 7.06 million borrowers, 97 percent of whom are women. With 2,399 branches, GB provides services in 76,848 villages, covering more than 91 percent of the total villages in Bangladesh" (Grameen Bank 2007). The bank also reports a remarkable 98 percent repayment rate (ibid.). Since the early 1980s, microcredit has become a "movement" that has spread throughout the developing world. Today, Yunus estimates that there are over 3,000 microcredit institutions reaching nearly 100 million borrowers worldwide (Yunus 2006). In 2006, Yunus and the Grameen Bank shared the Nobel Peace Prize "for their efforts to create economic and social development from below" (Nobelprize.org 2006).

The success and popularity of microcredit have not escaped criticism. In an article published in the *Wall Street Journal* and reprinted in Chapter 35, Daniel Pearl and Michael M. Phillips report that repayment rates for Grameen loans have been declining in certain areas of Bangladesh, and that Grameen may be overstating these rates. Grameen "isn't under any formal supervision," and it has been argued that its definition of overdue loans is out of line with the standards used in the banking industry. One concern is that loans are not always used for what they were intended. Borrowers may apply for a loan to finance a business but end up spending much of the money on consumption. In a response to the *Wall Street Journal* article, Yunus wrote that the repayment snag was temporary, and he pointed out that "whatever accounting system, procedures and definitions we have today, we had them with us for the last twenty-five years" (Grameen Bank 2007).

In the years since the founding of Grameen, the ability of the poor in developing countries to gain access to credit and other financial services has increased but remains limited. In the article from *The Economist* reprinted in Chapter 36, Tom Easton explains why many people in developing countries still struggle to obtain credit, open savings accounts, or buy insurance. The author blames mostly the inability of governments to create the conditions that allow the financial industry to develop. Inadequate supervision of banks, for example, encourages risky loans and downright fraud, decreasing people's willingness to deposit their money in the banking system; widespread corruption raises the cost of getting loans; and unreliable power supply makes it impossible to run modern financial institutions that rely on computer networks. But new technologies are helping overcome some of these problems, and private firms are showing increasing interest in serving a market where demand for financial services is very strong, although profit opportunities were seen as limited until recently.

There is wide agreement among development economists – and increasing evidence – that the role of the financial system in promoting economic development is extremely important. Just as well-functioning financial systems can stimulate productive investment, economic growth, and poverty reduction, inefficient and poorly regulated financial systems can make it nearly impossible for a country to achieve economic progress. The spread of microcredit has shown the tremendous impact that financial services can have in helping the poor raise their standards of living. Access to these services cannot be expected to eradicate poverty by itself – we have seen that development is a complex process with many components. But anything that helps channel scarce financial resources to people with entrepreneurial ideas has the potential to promote economic development. And to the extent that taking out small loans or insuring against risk makes it easier for the poor in developing countries to achieve their personal goals, financial services promote human development directly.

REFERENCES

Grameen Bank (2007) *Grameen Bank*. Online. Available HTTP: <http://www.grameen-info.org/bank/index.html> (accessed 6 June 2007).

Nobelprize.org (2006) *The Nobel Peace Prize for 2006*. Online. Available HTTP: <http://nobelprize.org/nobel_prizes/peace/laureates/2006/press.html> (accessed 6 June 2007).

World Bank (2007) *World Development Indicators 2007*, Washington, DC: World Bank.

Yunus, M. (2006) "A Hand Up Doesn't Always Require a Handout," *Wall Street Journal*, 14 October.

Chapter 33

Diana Farrell and Susan Lund

UNLEASHING INDIA'S POTENTIAL
The key is to modernize the financial system

A CASUAL OBSERVER MIGHT INFER from India's flourishing stock markets, fast-growing mutual funds, and capable private banks that the country's financial system is one of its strengths. But closer inspection reveals that tight government control over almost every other part is undermining the overall performance and curbing India's economic resurgence. If India is to sustain rapid GDP growth and spread its benefits more broadly, it needs a financial system that is comprehensively market-oriented and efficient.

The financial system's shortcomings largely fall into three areas. First, India's formal financial institutions attract only half of Indian households' savings, and none of the $200 billion they keep tied up in gold. Second, India's financial institutions allocate more than half of the capital they do attract to the least productive areas of the economy: state-owned enterprises, agriculture, and the unorganized sector (mostly made up of tiny businesses). The more productive corporations in India's dynamic private sector receive only 43 percent of all commercial credit. Third, India's financial system is inefficient in both of its main tasks of mobilizing savings and allocating capital. That means Indian borrowers pay more for their capital and depositors receive less than in comparable economies.

These failings place a heavy burden on India's economy, and fixing them would give it an immense boost. Research by the McKinsey Global Institute (MGI) calculates that an integrated program of financial system reforms could add $48 billion to GDP each year. This would raise India's real GDP growth rate to 9.4 percent per year, from the current three-year average of roughly 7 percent. India's growth would be roughly on par with China's and just shy of the government's 10 percent target, and household incomes would be 30 percent above current projections by 2014, lifting millions more households than expected out of poverty.

Where they are saving

Not long into our study we discovered that, despite India's 130-year-old stock market, long history of private banks, and generally well-developed public institutions, the nation's financial system intermediates a surprisingly small amount of the economy's total capital. This is demonstrated by the relative shallowness of India's financial system, measured by the value of all financial assets in the country relative to GDP. At 160 percent, India's financial depth is significantly lower than that of other fast-growing Asian economies, notably China (Figure 33.1).

Closer examination revealed just how much of the savings and investment fueling India's economic growth occurs outside India's formal financial system. Indian households save 28 percent of their disposable income, but invest only half of these savings in bank deposits and other financial assets. Of the other half, they invest 30 percent in housing, and put the remainder – which amounted to $24 billion last year – into machinery and equipment for the 44 million tiny household enterprises that make up the economy's unorganized sector. This is despite the fact that, with a few exceptions, household businesses are below efficient scale, lack technology and business know-how, and have low levels of productivity. In 2005, Indian households also bought more than $10 billion worth of gold, arguably another form of non-financial savings, and are now the world's largest gold consumers.

India's economy would grow faster if the financial system could attract more of the nation's savings and channel them into larger-scale, more productive enterprises. We calculate that a program of reforms that helped India's financial system to capture and invest more productively just half of the household savings now used for gold purchases and investments in subscale household enterprises could add $7 billion each year to GDP.

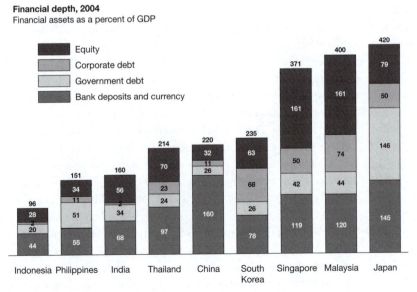

Financial depth, 2004
Financial assets as a percent of GDP

Figure 33.1 India's financial depth remains low compared to other nations

Note: Numbers may not add due to rounding.

Source: McKinsey Global Institute Global Financial Stock Database; team analysis.

Financing the least-productive investments

On the face of it, India's financial system is better at allocating capital than those in many other emerging markets. It has some high-performing private and foreign banks, and its stock of non-performing loans, at about 5 percent of all loan balances, is manageable. It has a well-run equity market that lists mostly private companies.

But a closer look reveals significant room for improvement. India's financial system in fact channels only a minority of the savings it does manage to capture to entrepreneurs in the private sector. The majority of funding goes to the government, and to those investments that the government designates as priorities. India's private corporations receive just 43 percent of total commercial credit – a level that has not changed much since 1999.

The rest goes to state-owned enterprises, agriculture, and the tiny businesses in the unorganized sector. This pattern of capital allocation impedes growth because state-owned enterprises are, on average, only half as productive as India's private firms, and require twice as much investment to achieve the same additional output. Productivity in agriculture and the micro-businesses of the unorganized sector is only one-tenth as high as in India's modern private firms, and investment efficiency is commensurately low.

India's equity market, as we have noted, does a somewhat better job of funding the private sector – private company shares represent 70 percent of market capitalization. But new equity issues account for little of the funding raised by companies in any country, and in India, they amount to just 2 percent of the gross funds they raise. Not surprisingly, Indian companies rely heavily on retained earnings to fund their operations and investments – these account for nearly 80 percent of the funds they raise, a far higher level than in other Asian economies (Figure 33.2).

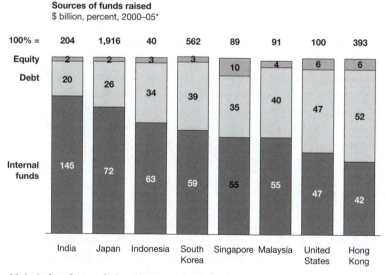

Figure 33.2 Indian firms rely heavily on retained earnings
*Based on sample of 160 companies per country outside of United States. Companies were ranked by gross sales, and 40 companies from each quartile were taken as the sample. U.S. sample includes all listed companies with revenues exceeding $500 million, 1995 to 2004.
Source: Bloomberg; McKinsey Global Institute analysis.

Reforms that enabled the financial system to channel a larger portion of credit to private companies would raise the economy's productivity. State-owned firms and household enterprises would need to improve their operations to compete successfully for finance. Accompanied by complementary reforms to India's labor and product markets, India would be able to get more output for each rupee invested with a resulting boost to GDP we calculate at up to $19 billion a year.

In the government's grip

The government's tight control of India's financial system explains its poor allocation of capital. Regulations oblige banks and other intermediaries to direct a high proportion of their funding to the government, and to its priority investments. Banks have to hold 25 percent of their assets in government bonds – and in practice, the state-owned banks that dominate the banking sector choose to hold even more. Government policies then require banks to direct 36 percent of their loans to agriculture, household businesses, and the state's other priority sectors. However, loans directed in this way have higher default rates than others and are more costly to administer because of their small size. As well as diverting credit from the more productive private sector, this policy also lowers lending overall, since banks' unprofitable directed lending has to expand in proportion with their discretionary lending. Not surprisingly, Indian banks lend just 60 percent of deposits, compared to 83 percent for Thai banks, 90 percent for South Korean banks, and 130 percent for Chinese banks.

Similar policies require that 90 percent of the assets of provident funds (essentially pension funds) and 50 percent of life insurance assets are held in government bonds and related securities. Without these rules, pension funds, mutual funds, and insurance companies would be an important source of demand for corporate bonds and equities in India, as they are in other countries.

These policies have allowed India's government and state-owned enterprises to absorb an astonishing 70 percent of the savings funneled into the financial system since 2000. Some of this funding flows to rural areas and to public sector enterprises to ensure that employment remains robust. But the government also maintains these policies to finance a persistently large budget deficit that, together with state deficits, has consistently averaged around 9 percent of GDP over the past 25 years, despite large variations in the macroeconomic environment over that time.

A costly intermediary

The government's influence on India's financial system also lowers its efficiency and raises the cost of financial intermediation. India has the highest level of state ownership of banks of any major economy today, apart from China – and even China is now seeking foreign investment in most of its major commercial banks. India's new private banks have a combined market share of only 9 percent. Foreign banks account for another 5 percent of deposits, but cannot expand because of limits on foreign investment in banking.

The prevalence of state-owned banks means that there is little competitive pressure to improve operations. These banks meet their costs by maintaining high margins between lending and deposit rates: bank margins are 6.3 percent in India, compared with an average of 3.1 percent in the case of South Korea, Malaysia, Singapore, and the United States.

Banks also face negligible competition from India's tiny corporate bond market, whose value amounts to just 2 percent of GDP. The reason the market has remained so small is a mass of regulations that unnecessarily raise the cost of issuing bonds, lengthen listing procedures, and increase disclosure requirements. To avoid these hassles, most Indian companies look for funding elsewhere. Some turn to private placements of debt, which total $44 billion – more than ten times the amount of publicly traded bonds. The largest companies also issue international bonds, despite the currency risk involved.

However, most sizable companies are forced to seek funding from banks, and this in turn crowds out bank lending to smaller companies and consumers, the banks' natural customers. If India were to develop a vibrant corporate bond market and the financial system were to offer the mix of bonds and bank loans seen in other emerging economies, India's companies – large and small – would enjoy substantially lower funding costs.

Even India's equity market is constrained by heavy regulation elsewhere in the financial sector. The market would function even better if domestic financial intermediaries, with their long-term mindset, held more shares – but they are currently required to invest in government bonds. Instead, corporate insiders own half of all shares, and this not only weakens the degree of market oversight but also potentially lowers the quality of governance. Retail investors own only 17 percent of shares, but account for 85 percent of trading – suggesting that they view the market as a gambling opportunity rather than a source of steady, long-term returns.

Reform will spur growth

The necessary reforms will primarily affect the banking sector, the corporate bond market, and India's domestic institutional investors. But the set of reforms must be carefully integrated, since many problems in India's financial system cut across its various markets. To achieve their full potential, reforms in one area will require complementary changes in others – for instance, changes in capital account and foreign investment policies.

Still, a single principle should guide the whole reform program. The government must loosen its grip on the financial system and allow financial institutions and intermediaries to respond to market signals. This means lifting directed lending policies and restrictions on the asset holdings of banks and other intermediaries, in order to release more capital for more productive investment in the Indian economy. It also requires reducing state ownership in the banking sector, developing a corporate bond market, and easing the many regulations holding back the development of pensions, mutual funds, and insurance companies. In addition to raising efficiency and returns, so doing will also enable intermediaries to create more attractive consumer financial products, draw a larger share of household savings into the financial system, and increase total investment in the economy.

Financial sector reforms are also needed to allow reforms of the rest of the Indian economy to succeed. To achieve higher rates of growth, both corporate and infrastructure investments must increase, and this will require a robust bond market to provide long-term funding, as well as more investment by foreign companies in many sectors. Faster growth will, in turn, necessitate a large increase in construction of both residential housing and commercial properties – and that will be impossible without similarly rapid growth in mortgage financing, which currently comprises only 3 percent of GDP.

Some of India's regulators are understandably resistant to financial system reform because they perceive it to involve risks and political trade-offs. They fear, for instance, that abandoning directed lending would stifle growth in the rural economy, potentially increasing rural unemployment. However, India's rural poor, as well as its entrepreneurs, would be better served if the financial system was free to allocate all its available capital to more productive businesses that can create waged jobs. If total liberation of the financial system seems a step too far, the government could, as a transitional measure, provide market-based incentives – such as tax breaks or subsidies – for banks to go on lending to priority areas rather than direct their lending by fiat.

Expanding the most productive parts of the Indian economy is, over time, not only the best way to increase the number of well-paid jobs and lift more people out of poverty, but also to fill the public purse. The last fifteen years of liberalization of the real economy have allowed India's economy to surge ahead. It is now time that the Indian government allowed its financial system to do the same.

REVIEW AND DISCUSSION QUESTIONS

1   According to Farrell and Lund, what are the main problems with India's financial system?
2   Indian households invest a substantial amount of money in small, family-run businesses. Why do the authors believe that this kind of investment is not the best way to promote economic growth?
3   What are the major differences between how firms in India and firms in other Asian countries pay for their investment?
4   In what ways does the Indian Government intervene in the financial system?
5   Do you agree with the authors' recommendations for improving Indian financial markets? Why or why not?

Chapter 34

Muhammad Yunus

BANKER TO THE POOR
Micro-lending and the battle against world poverty

THE STOOL MAKERS OF JOBRA VILLAGE

IN 1976, I BEGAN VISITING the poorest households in Jobra to see if I could help them directly in any way. There were three parts to the village: a Muslim, a Hindu, and a Buddhist section. When I visited the Buddhist section, I would often take one of my students, Dipal Chandra Barua, a native of the Buddhist section, along with me. Otherwise, a colleague, Professor H. I. Latifee, would usually accompany me. He knew most of the families and had a natural talent for making villagers feel at ease.

One day as Latifee and I were making our rounds in Jobra, we stopped at a rundown house with crumbling mud walls and a low thatched roof pocked with holes. We made our way through a crowd of scavenging chickens and beds of vegetables to the front of the house. A woman squatted on the dirt floor of the verandah, a half-finished bamboo stool gripped between her knees. Her fingers moved quickly, plaiting the stubborn strands of cane. She was totally absorbed in her work.

On hearing Latifee's call of greeting, she dropped her bamboo, sprang to her feet, and scurried into the house.

"Don't be frightened," Latifee called out. "We are not strangers. We teach up at the university. We are neighbors. We want to ask you a few questions, that is all."

Reassured by Latifee's gentle manner, she answered in a low voice, "There is nobody home."

She meant there was no male at home. In Bangladesh, women are not supposed to talk to men who are not close relatives.

Children were running around naked in the yard. Neighbors peered out at us from their windows, wondering what we were doing.

In the Muslim sections of Jobra, we often had to talk to women through bamboo walls or curtains. The custom of *purdah* (literally, "curtain" or "veil") kept married Muslim women in a state of virtual seclusion from the outside world. It was strictly observed in Chittagong District.

As I am a native Chittagonian and speak the local dialect, I would try to gain the confidence of Muslim women by chatting. Complimenting a mother on her baby was a natural way to put her at ease. I now picked up one of the naked children beside me, but he started to cry and rushed over to his mother. She let him climb into her arms.

"How many children do you have?" Latifee asked her.

"Three."

"He is very beautiful, this one," I said.

Slightly reassured, the mother came to the doorway, holding her baby. She was in her early twenties, thin, with dark skin and black eyes. She wore a red sari and had the tired eyes of a woman who labored every day from morning to night.

"What is your name?" I asked.

"Sufiya Begum."

"How old are you?"

"Twenty-one."

I did not use a pen and notepad, for that would have scared her off. Later, I only allowed my students to take notes on return visits.

"Do you own this bamboo?" I asked.

"Yes."

"How do you get it?"

"I buy it."

"How much does the bamboo cost you?"

"Five taka." At the time, this was about twenty-two cents.

"Do you have five taka?"

"No, I borrow it from the *paikars*."

"The middlemen? What is your arrangement with them?"

"I must sell my bamboo stools back to them at the end of the day as repayment for my loan."

"How much do you sell a stool for?"

"Five taka and fifty poysha."

"So you make fifty poysha profit?"

She nodded. That came to a profit of just two cents.

"And could you borrow the cash from the moneylender and buy your own raw material?"

"Yes, but the moneylender would demand a lot. People who deal with them only get poorer."

"How much does the moneylender charge?"

"It depends. Sometimes he charges 10 percent per week. But I have one neighbor who is paying 10 percent per day."

"And that is all you earn from making these beautiful bamboo stools, fifty poysha?"

"Yes."

Sufiya did not want to waste any more time talking. I watched as she set to work again, her small brown hands plaiting the strands of bamboo as they had every day for months and years on end. This was her livelihood. She squatted barefoot on the hard mud. Her fingers were callused, her nails black with grime.

How would her children break the cycle of poverty she had started? How could they go to school when the income Sufiya earned was barely enough to feed her, let alone shelter her family and clothe them properly? It seemed hopeless to imagine that her babies would one day escape this misery.

Sufiya Begum earned two cents a day. It was this knowledge that shocked me. In my university courses, I theorized about sums in the millions of dollars, but here before my eyes the problems of life and death were posed in terms of pennies. Something was wrong. Why did my university courses not reflect the reality of Sufiya's life? I was angry, angry at myself, angry at my economics department and the thousands of intelligent professors who had not tried to address this problem and solve it. It seemed to me the existing economic system made it absolutely certain that Sufiya's income would be kept perpetually at such a low level that she would never save a penny and would never invest in expanding her economic base. Her children were condemned to live a life of penury, of hand-to-mouth survival, just as she had lived it before them, and as her parents did before her. I had never heard of anyone suffering for the lack of *twenty-two cents*. It seemed impossible to me, preposterous. Should I reach into my pocket and hand Sufiya the pittance she needed for capital? That would be so simple, so easy. I resisted the urge to give Sufiya the money she needed. She was not asking for charity. And giving one person twenty-two cents was not addressing the problem on any permanent basis.

Latifee and I drove back up the hill to my house. We took a stroll around my garden in the late-afternoon heat. I was trying to see Sufiya's problem from her point of view. She suffered because the cost of the bamboo was five taka. She did not have the cash necessary to buy her raw materials. As a result, she could survive only in a tight cycle – borrowing from the trader and selling back to him. Her life was a form of bonded labor, or slavery. The trader made certain that he paid Sufiya a price that barely covered the cost of the materials and was just enough to keep her alive. She could not break free of her exploitative relationship with him. To survive, she needed to keep working through the trader.

Usurious rates have become so standardized and socially acceptable in Third World countries that the borrower rarely realizes how oppressive a contract is. Exploitation comes in many guises. In rural Bangladesh, one *maund* (approximately 37 kilograms) of husked rice borrowed at the beginning of the planting season has to be repaid with two *maunds* at harvest time. When land is used as security, it is placed at the disposal of the creditor, who enjoys ownership rights over it until the total amount is repaid. In many cases, a formal document such as a *bawnanama* establishes the right of the creditor. According to the *bawnanama*, the creditor usually refuses to accept any partial payment of the loan. After the expiration of a certain period, it also allows the creditor to "buy" the land at a predetermined "price." Another form of security is the *dadan* system, in which traders advance loans against standing crops for purchase of the crops at predetermined prices that are below the market rate. Sufiya Begum was producing her bamboo stools under a *dadan* arrangement with a *paikar*.

In Bangladesh, the borrowing is sometimes made for specific and temporary purposes (to marry off a daughter, to bribe an official, to fight a court case), but sometimes it is necessary for physical survival – to purchase food or medication or to meet some emergency situation. In such cases, it is extremely difficult for the borrower to extricate himself or herself from the burden of the loan. Usually the borrower will have to borrow again just to repay the prior loan and will ultimately wind up in a cycle of poverty like Sufiya. It seemed to me that Sufiya's status as a bonded slave would only change if she could find that five taka for her bamboo. Credit could bring her that money. She could then sell her products in a free market and charge the full retail price to the consumer. She just needed twenty-two cents.

The next day I called in Maimuna Begum, a university student who collected data for me, and asked her to help me make a list of people in Jobra, like Sufiya, who were dependent on traders. Within one week, we had a list prepared. It named forty-two people, who borrowed a total of 856 taka – less than 27 dollars.

"My God, my God. All this misery in all these families all for of the lack of twenty-seven dollars!" I exclaimed.

Maimuna stood there without saying a word. We were both sickened by the reality of it all.

My mind would not let this problem lie. I wanted to help these forty-two able-bodied, hard-working people. I kept going around and around the problem, like a dog worrying a bone. People like Sufiya were poor not because they were stupid or lazy. They worked all day long, doing complex physical tasks. They were poor because the financial institutions in the country did not help them widen their economic base. No formal financial structure was available to cater to the credit needs of the poor. This credit market, by default of the formal institutions, had been taken over by the local moneylenders. It was an efficient vehicle; it created a heavy rush of one-way traffic on the road to poverty. But if I could just lend the Jobra villagers the twenty-seven dollars, they could sell their products to anyone. They would then get the highest possible return for their labor and would not be limited by the usurious practices of the traders and moneylenders.

It was all so easy. I handed Maimuna the twenty-seven dollars and told her, "Here, lend this money to the forty-two villagers on our list. They can repay the traders what they owe them and sell their products at a good price."

"When should they repay you?" she asked.

"Whenever they can," I said. "Whenever it is advantageous for them to sell their products. They don't have to pay any interest. I am not in the money business."

Maimuna left, puzzled by this turn of events.

Usually when my head touches the pillow, I fall asleep within seconds, but that night sleep would not come. I lay in bed feeling ashamed that I was part of a society that could not provide twenty-seven dollars to forty-two skilled persons to make a living for themselves. It struck me that what I had done was drastically insufficient. If others needed capital, they could hardly chase down the head of an economics department. My response had been ad hoc and emotional. Now I needed to create an institutional answer that these people could rely on. What was required was an institution that would lend to those who had nothing. I decided to approach the local bank manager and request that his bank lend money to the poor. It seemed so simple, so straightforward. I fell asleep.

The next morning I climbed into my white Volkswagen beetle and drove to my local branch of the Janata Bank, a government bank and one of the largest in the country. Janata's university branch is located just beyond the gates of the campus on a stretch of road lined with tiny stores, stalls, and restaurants where local villagers sell students everything from betel nuts to warm meals, notebooks, and pens. It is here that the rickshaw drivers congregate when they are not ferrying students from their dormitories to their classrooms. The bank itself is housed in a single square room. Its two front windows are covered with bars and the walls are painted a dingy dark green. The room is filled with wooden tables and chairs. The manager, sitting in the back to the left, waved me over.

"What can I do for you, sir?"

The office boy brought us tea and cookies. I explained why I had come. "The last time I borrowed from you was to finance the Three Share Program in Jobra village. Now I have a new proposal. I want you to lend money to the poor people in Jobra. The amount involved is very small. I have already done it myself. I have lent twenty-seven dollars to forty-two people. There will be many more poor people who will need money. They need this money to carry on their work, to buy raw materials and supplies."

"What kind of materials?" The bank officer looked puzzled, as if this were some sort of new game whose rules he was not familiar with. He let me speak out of common respect for a university head, but he was clearly confused.

"Well, some make bamboo stools. Others weave mats or drive rickshaws. If they borrow money from a bank at commercial rates, they will be able to sell their products on the open market and make a decent profit that would allow them to live better lives. As it is now, they work as slaves and will never manage to get themselves out from under the heel of the wholesalers who lend them capital at usurious rates."

"Yes, I know about *mahajons* [moneylenders]," the manager replied.

"So I have come here today because I would like to ask you to lend money to these villagers."

The bank manager's jaw fell open, and he started to laugh. "I can't do that!"

"Why not?" I asked.

"Well," he sputtered, not knowing where to begin with his list of objections. "For one thing, the small amounts you say these villagers need to borrow will not even cover the cost of all the loan documents they would have to fill out. The bank is not going to waste its time on such a pittance."

"Why not?" I said. "To the poor this money is crucial for survival."

"These people are illiterate," he replied. "They cannot even fill out our loan forms."

"In Bangladesh, where 75 percent of the people do not read and write, filling out a form is a ridiculous requirement."

"Every single bank in the country has that rule."

"Well, that says something about our banks then, doesn't it?"

"Even when a person brings money and wants to put it in the bank, we ask him or her to write down how much she or he is putting in."

"Why?"

"What do you mean, 'Why?'"

"Well, why can't a bank just take money and issue a receipt saying, 'Received such and such amount of money from such and such a person?' Why can't the banker do it? Why must the depositors do it?"

"Well, how would you run a bank without people reading and writing?"

"Simple, the bank just issues a receipt for the amount of cash that the bank receives."

"What if the person wants to withdraw money?"

"I don't know . . . there must be a simple way. The borrower comes back with his or her deposit receipt, presents it to the cashier, and the cashier gives back the money. Whatever accounting the bank does is the bank's business."

The manager shook his head but did not answer this, as if he did not know where to begin.

"It seems to me your banking system is designed to be anti-illiterate," I countered.

Now the branch manager seemed irritated. "Professor, banking is not as simple as you think," he said.

"Maybe so, but I am also sure that banking is not as complicated as you make it out to be."

"Look, the simple truth is that a borrower at any other bank in any place in the world would have to fill out forms."

"Okay," I said, bowing to the obvious. "If I can get some of my student volunteers to fill out the forms for the villagers, that should not be a problem."

"But you don't understand, we simply cannot lend to the destitute," said the branch manager.

"Why not?" I was trying to be polite. Our conversation had something surreal about it. The branch manager had a smile on his face as if to say he understood that I was pulling his leg. This whole interview was humorous, absurd really.

They don't have any collateral," said the branch manager, expecting that this would put an end to our discussion.

"Why do you need collateral as long as you get the money back? That is what you really want, isn't it?"

"Yes, we want our money back," explained the manager. "But at the same time we need collateral. That is our guarantee."

"To me, it doesn't make sense. The poorest of the poor work twelve hours a day. They need to sell and earn income to eat. They have every reason to pay you back, just to take another loan and live another day! That is the best security you can have – their life."

The manager shook his head. "You are an idealist, Professor. You live with books and theories."

"But if you are certain that the money will be repaid, why do you need collateral?"

"That is our bank rule."

"So only those who have collateral can borrow?"

"Yes."

"It's a silly rule. It means only the rich can borrow."

"I don't make the rules, the bank does."

"Well, I think the rules should be changed."

"Anyway, we do not lend out money here."

"You don't?"

"No, we only take deposits from the faculty members and from the university."

"But don't banks make money by extending loans?"

"Only the head office makes loans. We are here to collect deposits from the university and its employees. Our loan to your Three Share Farm was an exception approved by our head office."

"You mean to say that if I came here and asked to borrow money, you would not lend it to me?"

"That is right." He laughed. It was evident the manager had not had such an entertaining afternoon in a long time.

"So when we teach in our classes that banks make loans to borrowers, that is a lie?"

"Well, you would have to go through the head office for a loan, and I don't know what they would do."

"Sounds like I need to talk to officials higher up."

"Yes, that would be a good idea."

As I finished my tea and got ready to leave, the branch manager said, "I know you'll not give up. But from what I know about banking, I can tell you for sure that this plan of yours will never take off."

A couple of days later, I arranged a meeting with Mr. R. A. Howladar, the regional manager of the Janata Bank, in his office in Chittagong. We had very much a repeat of the conversation I had with the Jobra branch manager, but Howladar did bring up the idea of a guarantor, a well-to-do person in the village who would be willing to act on behalf of the borrower. With the backing of a guarantor, the bank might consider granting a loan without collateral.

I considered the idea. It had obvious merit, but the drawbacks seemed insurmountable.

"I can't do that," I explained to Howladar. "What would prevent the guarantor from taking advantage of the person whose loan he was guaranteeing? He could end up a tyrant. He could end up treating that borrower as a slave."

There was a silence. It had become clear from my discussions with bankers in the past few days that I was not up against the Janata Bank per se but against the banking system in general.

"Why don't I become guarantor?" I asked.

"You?"

"Yes, can you accept me as guarantor for all the loans?"

The regional manager smiled. "How much money are you talking about?"

To give myself a margin of error and room to expand, I answered, "Altogether probably 10,000 taka ($300), not more than that."

"Well," he fingered the papers on his desk. Behind him I could see a dusty stack of folders in old bindings. Lining the walls were piles of similar pale blue binders, rising in teetering stacks to the windows. The overhead fan created a breeze that played with the files. On his desk, the papers were in a state of permanent fluttering, awaiting his decision.

"Well," he said. "I would say we would be willing to accept you as guarantor up to that amount, but don't ask for more money."

"It's a deal."

We shook hands. Then something occurred to me. "But if one of the borrowers does not repay, I will not step in to honor the defaulted loan."

The regional manager looked up at me uneasily, not certain why I was being so difficult.

"As guarantor, we could force you to pay."

"What would you do?"

"We could start legal proceedings against you."

"Fine. I would like that."

He looked at me as if I were crazy. That was just what I wanted. I felt angry. I wanted to cause some panic in this unjust, archaic system. I wanted to be the stick in the wheels that would finally stop this infernal machine. I was a guarantor, maybe, but I would not guarantee.

"Professor Yunus, you know very well we would never sue a department head who has personally guaranteed the loan of a beggar. The bad publicity alone would offset any money we might recover from you. Anyway, the loan is such a pittance it would not even pay for the legal fees, much less our administrative costs of recovering the money."

"Well, you are a bank, you must do your own cost-benefit analysis. But I will not pay if there is any default."

"You are making things difficult for me, Professor Yunus."

"I am sorry, but the bank is making things difficult for a lot of people – especially those who have nothing."

"I am trying to help. Professor."

"I understand. It is not you but banking rules I have a quarrel with."

After more such back and forth, Howladar concluded, "I will recommend your loan to the head office in Dhaka, and we will see what they say."

"But I thought you as regional officer had the authority to conclude this matter?"

"Yes, but this is far too unorthodox for me to approve. Authorization will have to come from the top."

It took six months of writing back and forth to get the loan formalized. Finally, in December 1976, I succeeded in taking out a loan from the Janata Bank and giving it to the poor of Jobra. All through 1977, I had to sign each and every loan request. Even when I was on a trip in Europe or the United States, the bank would cable or write to me for a signature rather than deal with any of the real borrowers in the village. I was the guarantor and as far as the bank officials were concerned I was the only one that counted. They did not want to deal with the poor who used their capital. And I made sure that the real borrowers, the ones I call the "banking untouchables," never had to suffer the indignity and demeaning harassment of actually going to a bank.

That was the beginning of it all. I never intended to become a moneylender. I had no intention of lending money to anyone. All I really wanted was to solve an immediate problem. Out of sheer frustration, I had questioned the most basic banking premise of collateral. I did not know if I was right. I had no idea what I was getting myself into. I was walking blind and learning as I went along. My work became a struggle to show that the financial untouchables are actually touchable, even huggable. To my great surprise, the repayment of loans by people who borrow without collateral has proven to be much better than those whose borrowings are secured by assets. Indeed, more than 98 percent of our loans are repaid. The poor know that this credit is their only opportunity to break out of poverty. They do not have any cushion whatsoever to fall back on. If they fall afoul of this one loan, they will have lost their one and only chance to get out of the rut.

A PILOT PROJECT IS BORN

I did not know anything about how to run a bank for the poor, so I had to learn from scratch. In January 1977, when Grameen started, I studied how others ran their loan operations and I learned from their mistakes. Conventional banks and credit cooperatives usually demand lump sum payments. Parting with a large amount of cash at the end of a loan period is often psychologically trying for borrowers. They try to delay the repayment as long as they can and in the process they make the loan grow bigger and bigger. In the end, they decide not to pay back the loan at all. Such long-term lump sum payments also prompt both borrowers and lenders to ignore difficulties that come up early on; rather than tackle problems as they appear, they hope that the problems will go away by the time the loan is due.

In structuring our credit program, I decided to do exactly the opposite of traditional banks. To overcome the psychological barrier of parting with large sums, I decided to institute a daily payment program. I made the loan payments so small that borrowers would barely miss the money. And for ease in accounting, I decided to ask that the loans be paid back fully in one year. Thus, a 365 taka loan could be paid at the rate of 1 taka a day over the course of one year.

To most of those who will read this book, a taka a day may seem like a laughable sum, but it does produce steady incremental gains. The power of the daily taka reminds me of the clever prisoner who was condemned to death. Brought before the king on his execution day, the prisoner was granted one last wish. He pointed to the chessboard at the right of the king's throne and said, "I wish only for a single grain of rice on one square of the chessboard and that that grain be doubled for each succeeding square."

"Granted," said the king, who could not fathom the power of geometrical progression. Soon the prisoner reigned over the entire kingdom.

Slowly my colleagues and I developed our own delivery-recovery mechanism and, of course, we made many mistakes along the way. We adapted our ideas and changed our procedures as we grew. For example, when we discovered that support groups were crucial to the success of our operations, we required that each applicant join a group of like-minded people living in similar economic and social conditions. Convinced that solidarity would be stronger if the groups came into being by themselves, we refrained from managing them, but we did create incentives that encouraged the borrowers to help one another succeed in their businesses. Group membership not only creates support and protection but also smoothes out the erratic behavior patterns of individual members, making each borrower more reliable in the process. Subtle and at times not-so-subtle peer pressure keeps each group member in line with the broader objectives of the credit program. A sense of intergroup and intragroup competition also encourages each member to be an achiever. Shifting the task of initial supervision to the group not only reduces the work of the bank but also increases the self-reliance of the individual borrowers. Because the group approves the loan request of each member, the group assumes moral responsibility for the loan. If any member of the group gets into trouble, the group usually comes forward to help.

In Jobra, we discovered that it is not always easy for borrowers to organize themselves into groups. A prospective borrower first has to take the initiative and explain how the bank works to a second person. This can be particularly difficult for a village woman. She often has a difficult time convincing her friends – who are likely to be terrified, skeptical, or forbidden by their husbands to deal with money – but eventually a second person, impressed by what Grameen has done for another household, will take the leap of joining the group. Then the two will go out and seek out a third member, then a fourth, and a fifth. Once the group of five is formed, we extend loans to two members of the group. If these two repay regularly for the next six weeks, two more members may request loans. The chairperson of the group is normally the last borrower of the five. But often, just when the group is ready, one of the five members changes her mind, saying, "No, my husband won't agree. He doesn't want me to join the bank." So the group falls back to four, or three, or sometimes back to one. And that one has to start all over again.

It can take anywhere from a few days to several months for a group to be recognized or certified by Grameen Bank. To gain recognition, all the members of a group of five prospective borrowers have to present themselves to the bank, undergo at least seven days of training on our policies, and demonstrate their understanding of those policies in an oral examination administered by a senior bank official. Each of the members must be individually tested. The night before her test, a borrower often gets so nervous that she lights a candle in a saint's shrine and prays to Allah for help. She knows that if she fails she will let down not only herself but also the others in her group. Though she has studied, she worries that she will not be able to answer the questions about the duties and responsibilities of a Grameen Bank member. What if she forgets? The bank worker will send the group away, telling all the members to study some more, and the others in the group will chastise her, saying, "For God's sake, even this you can't do right! You have ruined not only yourself but us as well."

Some critics argue that our rural clients are too submissive and that we can intimidate them into joining Grameen. Perhaps this is why we make our initiation process so challenging. The pressure provided by the group and the exam helps ensure that only those who are truly needy and serious about joining Grameen will actually become members. Those who are better off usually do not find it worthwhile. And even if they do, they will fail our means test and be forced to leave the group anyway. We want only courageous, ambitious pioneers in our micro-credit program. Those are the ones who will succeed.

Once all members pass the exam, the day finally comes when one of them asks for a first loan, usually about twenty-five dollars. How does she feel? Terrified. She cannot sleep at night. She struggles with the fear of failure, the fear of the unknown. The morning she is to receive her loan, she almost quits. Twenty-five dollars is simply too much responsibility for her. How will she ever be able to repay it? No woman in her extended family has ever had so much money. Her friends come around to reassure her, saying, "Look, we all have to go through it. We will support you. We are here for just that. Don't be scared. We will all be with you."

When she finally receives the twenty-five dollars, she is trembling. The money burns her fingers. Tears roll down her face. She has never seen so much money in her life. She never imagined it in her hands. She carries the bills as she would a delicate bird or a rabbit, until someone advises her to put the money away in a safe place lest it be stolen.

This is the beginning for almost every Grameen borrower. All her life she has been told that she is no good, that she brings only misery to her family, and that they cannot afford to pay her dowry. Many times she hears her mother or her father tell her she should have been killed at birth, aborted, or starved. To her family she has been nothing but another mouth to feed, another dowry to pay. But today, for the first time in her life, an institution has trusted her with a great sum of money. She promises that she will never let down the institution or herself. She will struggle to make sure that every penny is paid back.

[. . .]

REVIEW AND DISCUSSION QUESTIONS

1 Where did Jobra's stool maker borrow the funds to run her small business? Why didn't she borrow from moneylenders?

2 What reasons did the manager of the government-owned Janata Bank give to explain why he was not interested in lending money to Jobra's craftspeople?

3 Why was Yunus opposed to the idea of having a well-to-do guarantor to back the loans?

4 According to Yunus, how has the Grameen Bank achieved an amazing 98 percent repayment rate for its loans? Why hasn't the absence of collateral resulted in more frequent defaults?

5 How is the repayment of Grameen Bank loans structured? What is the logic behind this structure?

6 Why must Grameen borrowers be part of a group of five borrowers to obtain a loan?

7 Do you see any limitations to the Grameen Bank "model"? Can institutions like the Grameen Bank make a significant contribution to economic development in poor countries? Why or why not?

Chapter 35

Daniel Pearl and Michael M. Phillips

SMALL CHANGE
Bank that pioneered loans for the poor hits repayment snag

MICROCREDIT IS A GREAT IDEA with a problem: the bank that made it famous.

Grameen Bank, launched in Bangladesh in 1976 by an economics professor named Muhammad Yunus, popularized the idea of giving poor people tiny loans to launch businesses. The bank has helped inspire an estimated 7,000 so-called microlenders with 25 million poor clients worldwide.

To many, Grameen proves that capitalism can work for the poor as well as the rich. It has become an icon for the drive to give needy entrepreneurs a share in economic development. And that iconic status owes a lot to an almost miraculous loan-repayment rate of "over 95 percent," as the bank's Web site says.

But Grameen's performance in recent years hasn't lived up to the bank's own hype. In two northern districts of Bangladesh that have been used to highlight Grameen's success, half the loan portfolio is overdue by at least a year, according to monthly figures supplied by Grameen. For the whole bank, 19 percent of loans are one year overdue. Grameen itself defines a loan as delinquent if it still isn't paid off two years after its due date. Under those terms, 10 percent of all the bank's loans are overdue, giving it a delinquency rate more than twice the often-cited level of less than 5 percent.

Some of Grameen's troubles stem from a 1998 flood, and others from the bank's own success. Imitators have brought more competition, making it harder for Grameen to control its borrowers. The bank's loan portfolio grew rapidly in the early 1990s, but it has now shrunk to 1996 levels, at $190 million. Profits have declined about 85 percent, to the equivalent of $189,950 last year from $1.3 million in 1999. The bank, with 1,170 branches, all in Bangladesh, has high operating costs. Grameen would be showing steep losses if the bank followed the accounting practices recommended by institutions that help finance microlenders through low-interest loans and private investments. And the situation may be worse than it appears; the bank is converting many overdue loans into new "flexible" loans that Grameen reports as up-to-date.

Microlenders have been reluctant to call attention to Grameen's troubles. "Grameen's repayment rates have never been as good as they've claimed," says Jonathan J. Morduch, associate professor of economics and public policy at New York University. "Because Grameen has been so well-known, nobody has wanted to risk undermining the reputation of the idea."

Microcredit is getting renewed attention as other poverty-fighting tools come under attack. Left-wing protesters accuse the World Bank of selling out the poor to corporate interests. Right-wing U.S. politicians argue that aid to the Third World has been wasted. U.S. lobbies often try to quash efforts to open American markets to imports from poor countries.

But microcredit is an idea everyone can agree on: It uses private enterprise, can be profitable and gets money straight to the poor. Bridging the gap between rich and poor "will help eliminate conditions of despair and hopelessness that breed violence and extremism," declares an electronic-mail message circulated after Sept. 11 by Bill Clapp, the chairman of Global Partnerships, a microcredit support organization based in Seattle.

The microcredit industry knows its reputation rides largely on Grameen's. Damian von Stauffenberg, chairman of a Washington-based microcredit rating agency called Microrate, was alarmed by recent rumors of financial weakness at Grameen, even though the agency doesn't rate the bank. "If it's true, it would be a blow to the rest of us, because of the symbol Grameen is," Mr. von Stauffenberg says. He says he repeatedly asked a Grameen affiliate, Grameen Foundation USA, this summer for detailed information on the bank's loan portfolio, but got only a brochure and a 1998 annual report.

"I didn't hear back from him after that, so I assumed he had the information he wanted," says Alex Counts, president of the foundation, which promotes Grameen in the U.S.

Mr. Yunus, a congenial man of 61, acknowledges that Grameen has had some repayment difficulties in the past five years. He blames political upheavals, the 1998 flood and management errors. Told that the Web site still claimed a 95 percent recovery rate, Mr. Yunus said it was through "inefficiency" that Grameen hadn't updated some information. Grameen has added a footnote to the Web site saying the information was true as of 1996. But more recent figures still aren't listed.

The repayment troubles are temporary, according to Mr. Yunus. "There is no problem," he said in an August interview in his modest office, which has no air conditioning despite Bangladesh's steamy climate. He says three-fourths of borrowers repay on time every week, and Grameen assumes that the poor will repay even long-delinquent loans. The bank, he says, is stronger than ever.

Mr. Yunus says borrowers have surprised him with their ability to take on new challenges. Borrowers who reach a certain level of savings can buy one share in Grameen, and collectively they own 93 percent. Mr. Yunus is setting up a mutual fund allowing borrowers to invest in other ventures under the Grameen umbrella: mobile phones, textiles and high-tech office space for rent on the top floors of the Grameen Bank tower.

"We have proved beyond a reasonable doubt that poor people are bankable," Mr. Yunus says. "We are not looking for charity."

Grameen, which means "village" in Bengali, got started after Mr. Yunus visited a village in southern Bangladesh. He met a woman who wove bamboo stools but had to sell them for meager profits to the man providing the materials. As an experiment, Mr. Yunus lent a total of $27 to 42 women in the village. All of them repaid.

When Mr. Yunus approached the Bangladesh government for funds in 1979 to expand his experiment, government bankers were skeptical that poor, landless women would repay. So Mr. Yunus conducted an experiment in Tangail, a fertile district north of Dhaka. His staffers showed up unannounced in villages and recruited groups of women to take loans. Again, all of them repaid.

The new bank was a kind of small-business lender, with some unusual policies. It took no deposits at first. It lent only to poor women who had no collateral. Borrowers formed groups of five, each member getting loans only as long as everybody made payments. Borrowers recited Mr. Yunus's "16 decisions" – including enforcing loan "discipline" within the group, keeping families small and not giving a dowry for a daughter's wedding – a difficult "decision" to follow in this culture.

Grameen, which has provided millions of poor Bangladeshi women with access to credit, became the industry's symbol mostly through Mr. Yunus's personality and proselytizing. He set up the Grameen Trust, which gives loans and holds workshops for start-up lenders who have adopted the Grameen model from Arkansas to Zimbabwe, with mixed results.

Mr. Yunus is also the guiding force behind the industry's main public-relations vehicle, the Microcredit Summit. At the first summit, in Washington in 1997, Mr. Yunus sat at the head table at a private lunch with Queen Sofia of Spain and World Bank President James D. Wolfensohn, who ended the meal by giving Mr. Yunus a big hug. At a regional summit last month, he gave an opening address beside Mexican President Vicente Fox. Friends tout Mr. Yunus for a Nobel Peace Prize.

Mr. Yunus's 1997 autobiography, "Banker to the Poor," gave no hint of doubt in Grameen's future. "All the strength of Grameen comes from its near-perfect recovery performance," he wrote. "It is not merely the money which is reflected through the recovery rate, it is the discipline."

Even then, however, Grameen's recovery rate was slipping. In 1997, 4.6 percent of Grameen's loans were more than two years overdue, up from 0.7 percent a couple of years earlier. And Tangail has now become Grameen's worst region, with 32.1 percent of loans two-years overdue as of August.

One reason is that microlending has lost its novelty. In Tangail, signboards for rival microlenders dot a landscape of gravel roads, jute fields and ponds with simple fishing nets. Shopkeepers playing cards in the village of Bagil Bazar can cite from memory the terms being offered by seven competing microlenders – a typical repayment plan for a 1,000-taka ($17) loan is 25 taka a week for 46 weeks. At an annualized rate, that works out to 30 percent in interest. Surveys have estimated that 23 percent to 40 percent of families borrowing from microlenders in Tangail borrow from more than one.

Borrowers have also become more rebellious. "The experience was good in the beginning," says Munjurani Sharkan, who became leader of a Grameen group in Tangail's Khatuajugnie village in 1986. To put pressure on "lazy" group members who were slow making payments, she says she used to start removing the tin roofs of their homes. But one day, the whole group decided to stop making payments.

They were protesting Grameen's handling of a fund it created for each group, using 5 percent of each loan and additional mandatory deposits. The "group fund" was meant for emergencies, but many borrowers wanted to withdraw money from the group fund. After a protest movement, complete with placards and amplified speeches, Grameen finally agreed to give borrowers easier access to the fund.

Borrower groups had become lobbying groups, and Mr. Yunus hadn't noticed the change, says Muhammad Yahiyeh, former director of Grameen Trust. "An entire group would say, 'Unless you pay this person 5,000 taka, we will all stop paying,'" says Mr. Yahiyeh, who now runs a small microlender. Mr. Yunus says he still thinks groups are good for loan discipline. Grameen just didn't explain the group fund properly, he says, and politicians stirred up the borrowers.

The typical Grameen success story features a woman who turns a small loan into a successful shop or craft business. But Grameen also has customers such as Belatun Begum, a borrower in Khatuajugnie since the late 1980s. She took one loan in three installments, totaling 30,000 taka (about $525). She says the original loan was to buy a cow, but she actually gave some money to her husband, a well-digger, and used the rest to improve her house. She confesses to borrowing a neighbor's cow to show Grameen at meetings. One recent study found one-fourth of microcredit loan money in Bangladesh is used for household consumption.

Mr. Yunus says that doesn't bother him as long as borrowers repay. Grameen tells women to think of a loan as a mango tree and to eat only the fruits, he says, not the tree itself.

But Grameen introduced so many loan options in the early 1990s – housing loans, student loans, seasonal loans – that borrowers were often paying off one with another, says Aminur Rahman, an anthropologist based in Ottawa, Canada, who studied Grameen borrowers in a Tangail village six years ago. Returning earlier this year, he found only six of 120 borrowers were getting income from Grameen-funded investments.

Massive floods in 1998 hit Grameen's borrowers hard. The bank let borrowers skip several payments. Grameen borrowed $80 million from Bangladesh's government banks, with a sovereign guarantee, and used the money to make new loans to borrowers. Informally, it forgave the old loans.

Grameen also bailed out borrowers whose problems had nothing to do with the flood. Ms. Begum, for instance, stopped paying when she had to provide dowries for two daughters. She skipped group meetings, but Grameen workers came to her door asking for her 200-taka weekly payment, she says. "Let us make some income and we'll pay you," she told them.

Earlier this year, Grameen came up with a proposal: pay just 50 taka a week for six months, and then take a new Grameen loan for twice the amount she repaid. Ms. Begum accepted. Grameen calls the program a "flexible loan," and treats the old, delinquent loans as back on schedule, as long as some regular payment is being made.

At a Grameen branch near Khatuajugnie, manager Mohammed Imam Modem shows his computer-printed ledger, full of cross marks to indicate missed payments. The rescheduling program and Grameen's personal visits to husbands as well as wives are improving the picture: The branch had 1,510 defaulters before; now it has 846. Attendance at weekly meetings is up to 66 percent, from 47 percent before.

"Grameen Bank's philosophy is not to abandon but to rehabilitate," says Muzzamal Huq, a Grameen general manager.

But Grameen may simply be delaying inevitable defaults and hiding problem loans. One paper produced by the Consultative Group to Assist the Poorest, or CGAP, a donor group that sets industry standards, warns that heavy use of refinancing "can cloud the ability to judge its loan-loss rate." CGAP is a collective of 27 public and private donors, including the World Bank, the U.S. Agency for International Development and several

U.N. agencies, that account for the vast majority of aid to microcredit institutions around the world.

CGAP says refinanced loans should at least be listed separately. Grameen doesn't do so. It says refinanced loans are one-fifth of its portfolio.

CGAP recommends that microlenders report as at risk the entire remaining balance of any loan with a payment more than 90 days overdue. The Palli Karma-Sahayak Foundation (PKSF), which Mr. Yunus helped set up in 1991 to distribute foreign funds to other Bangladesh microlenders, requires its microlenders to report as overdue any loan that is one week late. The average overdue rate among the foundation's lenders is 2 percent. It's impossible to know Grameen's overdue rate by that standard, since it reports only loans that are one year and two years overdue.

PKSF also says it requires borrowers to make a 50 percent provision against potential loan losses for any loan overdue by a year. Grameen made a 15 percent provision for such loans in 1999, and none last year. Following PKSF guidelines would have produced a loss of more than $7.5 million for 2000 instead of Grameen's reported profit of less than $200,000.

In early 1998, Grameen approached the International Finance Corp., the business-finance arm of the World Bank, about turning some of Grameen's portfolio into securities. The IFC declined to proceed, in part because Grameen "didn't provide all the account information the IFC requested," an IFC official said. The official requested anonymity because the IFC is reticent about discussing its negotiations with clients.

Mr. Yunus denied the IFC official's claims. He said Grameen is "generously covered" against loan defaults.

Other microlenders have become much more stringent. Accion International, a U.S.-based network of microfinance institutions, requires its affiliates in Africa and Latin America to list as "at risk" any loan overdue by 30 days or more. Asked about Grameen's two-years standard, Accion Chief Executive Maria Otero says, "I don't think any [bank] superintendency in a million years would agree to something like that."

Grameen Bank isn't under any formal supervision. "They are regulated, but they are regulated by themselves," says Akhtaruz Zaman, director of the Financial Institution Department for the Bangladesh Bank, the country's central bank. He means the board of directors, which is led by borrowers. Mr. Zaman says Grameen's deposits are "well-protected" and the bank is "doing fine."

Harder-headed microlenders are stealing the spotlight, though. One rising star is the Association for Social Advancement (ASA), a Bangladesh charity, which boasts 1.5 million borrowers and just 0.7 percent of loans overdue, even by a week. Dispensing with borrower groups, ASA leans on borrowers' husbands and relatives if payments are missed, says the managing director, Shafiqual Haque Choudhury. To him, Grameen's approach is an ingenious idea that didn't stand the test of time.

"If we manage our operation in the Grameen way," says Mr. Choudhury, "we'll never be able to cover our costs."

REVIEW AND DISCUSSION QUESTIONS

1   According to Pearl and Phillips, what are the major problems that the Grameen Bank has run into?

2   Why does Grameen founder Muhammad Yunus feel that these problems are just temporary?

3   According to the authors, what possible weaknesses does the microcredit system exhibit?

4   What are some of the differences between how Grameen operates and how other microcredit lenders do?

5   If you were in charge of a microcredit organization, would you organize it along the Grameen model or use a different approach? Why? Explain.

Chapter 36

THE ECONOMIST

THE HIDDEN WEALTH OF THE POOR

Financial services are at last spreading from the rich to the developing world – and even making money [. . .]

IN RICH COUNTRIES, FINANCIAL services on the whole work remarkably well, despite the exotic salaries, the crackpot deals and the occasional bust. The vast majority of people have access to interest-bearing savings accounts, mortgages at reasonable rates, abundant consumer credit, insurance at premiums that reflect the risk of losses, cheap ways of transferring money, and innumerable sources of capital for funding a business.

By contrast, financial services for poor people in developing countries – a business known as "microfinance" – have mostly been awful or absent. With no safe place to store whatever money they have, the poor bury it, or buy livestock that may die, or invest in jewellery that may be stolen and can be hard to sell. Basic life and property insurance is rarely available. Home loans are costly, if indeed they can be found at all. For many people, the only source of credit is a pawnshop or a moneylender who may charge staggeringly high interest and beat up clients who fail to pay on time. In the Philippines, lenders who zip from town to town on motorcycles expect six pesos back for every five they lend. That translates into an annual interest rate of over 1,000 percent on a loan for a month.

For workers from poor countries who venture abroad to earn a better living, sending money home to relatives can be hugely expensive. Such remittances have become an important source of income in many developing countries, dwarfing other inflows of capital from overseas such as foreign direct investment and multilateral aid. But if the money is being sent, say, from America to Venezuela, charges can amount to as much as 34 percent of the sum involved, according to Dilip Ratha of the World Bank.

Why are the poor so badly served? The easy answer, that people who have little money do not make suitable clients for sophisticated financial services, is at most a half-truth. A better explanation, this survey will argue, is that the poor have been hurt by massive market and regulatory failure. Fortunately that failure can be, and increasingly is being, remedied.

In most developing countries, the barriers to providing financial services for the masses are all too clear. Inflation tends to be high and volatile; government is often incompetent; and the necessary legal framework for financial services is often missing. Property laws can make it impossible for poor borrowers to use assets such as their home as collateral for loans.

In the past, many countries have outlawed "usury", and today many Islamic countries prohibit the charging of interest. Governments in developing countries often impose caps on the interest rates charged on loans for the poor. Despite their popular appeal, such caps undermine the profitability of lending and thus reduce the supply of loans.

Incomplete and erratic regulation of financial institutions has also undermined the confidence of the poor in the financial services that are available. When they can find an institution that will accept their tiny deposits, it often lacks the sort of government deposit insurance that is routine in rich countries, so when a bank goes under, savers suffer. For example, Indonesia's PT Bank Dagang Ball, once known for its work with poor clients, was closed by regulators last year after it was discovered to be insolvent and riddled with fraud. Many savers did not get their money back.

Corruption is also commonplace in many developing countries. A recent study by the World Bank found that in two poor states in India where the financial system is largely controlled by the government, borrowers paid bribes to officials amounting to between 8 percent and 42 percent of the value of their loans. Corruption raises the cost of every financial transaction, allows undesirable transactions to take place and undermines consumer confidence in the financial system. This, and the related curse of cronyism, explains why access to financial services in countries where the state has control over the financial sector is poorer than where it does not.

Inadequate basic public services add to the burden on financial firms. SKS, a fast-growing microfinance institution in India, has had to build back-office systems that can work on two hours of power a day; it closely monitors voltage when its computers are running and keeps a diesel generator on hand. Many others simply give up on the idea of modern technology and continue to use paper instead. This makes them vulnerable. The tsunami in December 2004 wiped out financial records at many small Indonesian banks.

But not all the blame goes to poor-country governments. Financial-services firms too have failed to do enough to deal with the lack of the sort of data (for example, about a client's financial history) that are taken for granted in rich-country financial systems, and to find ways of reaping economies of scale. Many have simply dismissed the possibility that serving the poor might be a viable business.

The start of something big

In recent years, at least in some parts of the world, this bleak picture has begun to change, first in credit, then in savings and more recently in remittances. Even insurance – not only the basic life sort but also more sophisticated forms for things like cattle and weather risk – is gradually being introduced.

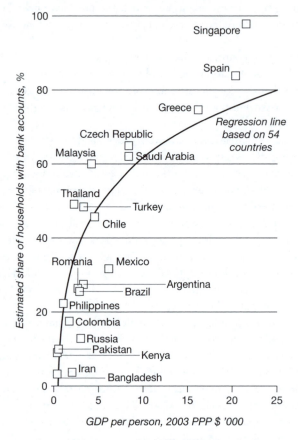

prevalence of bank accounts at different income levels

Figure 36.1 You don't have to be rich, but it helps:

Source: World Bank

These changes have recently received a lot of attention in policymaking circles. Grand claims have been made that credit can end poverty. A World Bank report by Thorsten Beck, Asli Demirguc-Kunt and Soledad Martinez published last month shows a strong correlation between lack of financial access and low incomes (see Figure 36.1). Earlier research by the first two authors and Ross Levine concluded that a sound financial system boosts economic growth and particularly benefits people at the bottom end of the income league. A long-term study in Thailand by Robert Townsend of the University of Chicago and Joe Kaboski of Ohio State University showed that families with access to credit invested more, consumed more and saved less than those without such access.

What makes microfinance such an appealing idea is that it offers "hope to many poor people of improving their own situations through their own efforts," says Stanley Fischer, former chief economist of the World Bank and now governor of the Bank of Israel. That marks it out from other anti-poverty policies, such as international aid and debt forgiveness, which are essentially top-down rather than bottom-up and have a decidedly mixed record.

Studies by Stuart Rutherford, who runs an experimental bank that provides loans and takes deposits in the slums of Bangladesh, show that the poor attach great value to having a safe place to keep money and some means of providing for life's risks, either through savings or, better still, through insurance. When financial services are available to them, the poor, just like the rich, snap them up.

In one sense, microfinance has been around for a long time. What is now generating so much hope and excitement is less the discovery of some entirely new way to deliver financial services to the poor than the effect of the rapid innovation that has taken place in the past three decades.

From pawnshop to Citigroup

The oldest financial institution in the Americas is a pawnshop on Mexico City's central square. Set up in 1775 under an edict by the Spanish crown to assist people in financial trouble, it is called Monte de Piedad, variously translated as the mountain of mercy or the mountain of pity. Pity or mercy come in the form of cash in return for valuables. Unclaimed items end up for sale in a series of glittering rooms near the main banking hall.

By transforming trinkets into capital, pawnshops perform an important (if under-appreciated) service, but they have three limitations. They advance cash only to people with assets. Their loans are based on the value of collateral, not of a business venture. And the valuables held as collateral cannot be used to fund businesses, as banks' cash deposits can.

There have been two notable attempts to find alternatives. One has been the creation by developing-country governments of state banks, particularly to finance the rural poor. These have mostly been a disaster. The other, much more successful one involved a number of organisations extending uncollateralised loans to very poor borrowers. In 1971, Opportunity International, a not-for-profit organisation with Christian roots, began lending in Colombia. ACCION International, also not-for-profit, made the first of what it called "micro" loans in 1973. Grameen Bank started in 1976 and soon became extraordinarily famous for offering "microcredit" to women in small groups.

To qualify, Grameen's customers had to be extremely poor, probably earning less than a dollar a day. To overcome the lack of collateral or data about creditworthiness, group members were required to monitor each other at weekly meetings, applying varying degrees of pressure to ensure repayment. As loans were repaid, people were allowed to borrow more. The group replaced the security that pawnshops gained from collateral. The model is not perfect, but it does have real virtues and has since spread around the world.

Why did these organisations start with providing credit? They assumed that poor people were unable to save, and that their sole need for capital. But that was not the whole story. When BRI, a failing state-controlled rural lender in Indonesia, was transformed into a bank for the poor in 1984, it offered not only the usual loan products but also a government-guaranteed savings account with no minimum deposit. This has been an extraordinary success: BRI now has 30m savings accounts.

Nobody knows how many institutions are providing microfinance in some form, but the number is certainly huge. They are growing fast and serving a vast number of people in absolute terms, although still only a small proportion of the billions who earn only a few cents a day. Local banking giants that used to ignore the poor, such as Ecuador's Bank Pichincha and India's ICICI, are now entering the market. Even more strikingly, some of the world's biggest and wealthiest banks, including Citigroup, Deutsche Bank, Commerzbank, HSBC, ING and ABN Amro, are dipping their toes into the water.

The downsides

Not everyone has been pleased with the prospect of better financial services for the poor. Islamic fundamentalists have bombed branches of Grameen in Bangladesh and attacked loan officers of other institutions in India. Maoists have looted microfinance offices in Nepal. The head of a microfinance effort in Afghanistan was murdered, possibly by drug traders.

To drug lords in Afghanistan, the availability of credit is unwelcome because it gives a choice to farmers who were previously forced to grow poppies for want of other ways to finance their crops. For the elites in closed markets running inefficient monopolies, credit raises the prospect of future challenges from entrepreneurs. For radical Muslims, it means that women (who in many countries make up the bulk of microfinance borrowers) are able to run viable businesses and become independent. And for everyone in poor countries, credit can mean social upheaval as merit and enterprise replace inheritance, family ties and position.

Nor does microlending always have a happy outcome. The clients of K-Rep, an excellent Kenyan microfinance bank in a small town on the fringes of Nairobi, are a pretty resourceful lot, but when the government stopped repairing roads, picking up rubbish and spraying for malaria, some were at their wits' end. Drainage in the marketplace was plugged by uncollected garbage and customers stopped coming. Maria Njambi, a single mother with a ten-year-old child, used to have a viable business selling fruit and vegetables she bought with credit from K-Rep, but she had to watch her inventory rot and has stopped repaying her loan. She is not alone in her misfortune. A report in 2002 by CARD, a microfinance organisation in the Philippines, offers the following explanation for borrower attrition: "It is a tragic fact that over time, husbands will fall sick, *sari-sari* [variety] stores will be robbed, harvests will be poor and children will die."

Yet microfinance institutions typically claim extraordinarily low loan losses of 1–3 percent, a bit better than the rate for big banks in rich countries and much better than for the big credit-card companies. Given the difficulties facing businesses in poor areas, some critics question the accuracy of these figures. Many of the banks lending to the poor are not-for-profit organisations whose accounts are rarely scrutinised by outsiders. Much of their capital has been provided by governments or philanthropists, and often does not have to be repaid, so perhaps microfinance institutions are being quietly lenient with their customers. Indeed, large-scale defaults in microfinance may go unreported. The Townsend-Kaboski research project in Thailand informally tracked hundreds of microfinance institutions and found that in the five years before the Asian financial crises, 10 percent failed and a quarter stopped lending.

So there is room for scepticism, but also plenty of reason for hope. The biggest of these is just how much progress the industry has made in the past 30 years.

REVIEW AND DISCUSSION QUESTIONS

1 Explain why, according to the author, the poor in developing countries have such limited access to financial services.

2 Why does the author doubt the wisdom of interest rate ceilings, or laws that cap the interest rate that can be charged on loans? Don't these ceilings prevent lenders from exploiting borrowers and, therefore, protect the poor? Explain.

3 According to the author, what are some of the obstacles that limit the potential of microfinance to help the poor?

4 What kind of government policies would you recommend to help make financial services more accessible to the poor? Explain.

Suggestions for further reading

Armendáriz de Aghion, B. and Morduch, J. (2005) *The Economics of Microfinance*, Cambridge, MA: MIT Press.

The authors of this book combine their knowledge of economic theory with their experience in the field to provide a thorough overview of the economics of microfinance. They discuss not only microcredit but also other financial services such as saving organizations and microinsurance. Most chapters make use of math and assume familiarity with economic theory, but many of the key points and conclusions are accessible to the general reader.

Bruck, C. (2006) "Millions for Millions," *The New Yorker*, 35: 62–73.

Bruck provides a thorough review of how microcredit has gradually evolved into a more profit-driven industry. She addresses the tensions between people like Muhammad Yunus, who see microcredit simply as a tool to fight poverty, and entrepreneurs who are interested in making microfinance a profitable sector that will attract private investors.

Gulde, A. and Pattillo, C. (2006) "Adding Depth," *Finance & Development*, 43.

The authors review the weaknesses in Africa's financial sector, such as the lack of access to savings accounts and the scarcity of credit. They discuss the obstacles to improvement in the financial system and provide suggestions for reform.

Prahalad, C. K. (2005) *The Fortune at the Bottom of the Pyramid: Eradicating Poverty Through Profits*, Upper Saddle River, NJ: Pearson Education.

Written by a business professor largely for a business audience, this book argues that private firms can help remove poverty in developing countries by realizing that the poor constitute a profitable market with enormous potential. Prahalad tries to dispel myths about the poor and suggest ways in which private firms can take advantage of this opportunity in ways that will earn them a profit while helping the poor raise their standards of living. The book includes several case studies and a CD with short videos about the case studies.

Yunus, M. (1999) *Banker to the Poor: Micro-Lending and the Battle Against World Poverty*, New York: Public Affairs.

In this autobiography, the Bangladeshi economist who won the 2006 Nobel Peace Prize explains how he went from being a college professor to founding the Grameen Bank, one of the first and most successful microcredit institutions. Yunus also discusses the many directions in which the Grameen Bank has expanded and his views of the future of microcredit.

Globalization and financial crises

INTRODUCTION

I N 1990 THE VALUE OF EXPORTS AND IMPORTS of the average low-income country was 23.6 percent of its GDP (this is the *sum* of merchandise exports and imports as a percentage of GDP). By 2005, this percentage had almost doubled to 41.1 percent (World Bank 2007: 316–18). For some developing countries, the increase in international trade during these fifteen years was much faster than average: trade as a percentage of GDP rose from 27.2 percent to 70.1 percent in Chad, from 11.4 percent to 44.8 percent in Ethiopia, and from 7.5 percent to 42.0 percent in Sudan (ibid.). Few words today elicit stronger reactions and greater controversy than "globalization." While international development institutions like the World Bank portray globalization as a key tool to eliminate poverty and policy-makers in many developing countries work hard to increase their economies' integration with the global economy, grassroots organizations have protested against globalization vehemently. Through alternative media outlets, such groups have argued that "the intent of globalization is to make the poverty of the so-called 'developing sector' permanent" (Baker 2007) and that "globalization amount[s] to plundering of resources and creation of worse forms of poverty everyday" (Mehrotra 2007).

Development economists also have their disagreements in regard to the effects of globalization on economic development; by and large, however, they believe that international trade has the potential to increase standards of living and reduce poverty in developing countries. In the article reprinted in Chapter 37, Anne O. Krueger, a Johns Hopkins economist and former first deputy managing director at the International Monetary Fund, presents several arguments supporting the view that countries increasing their involvement in the global economy are likely to experience faster economic growth. Krueger starts by reminding us that many developing countries in the postwar period adopted so-called "import-substitution" development strategies. The idea behind this approach is to help domestic industry develop by protecting it from foreign competition (through tools such as tariffs and quotas). A developing country intending to develop the domestic shoe industry, for example, might restrict imports of foreign shoes, so as to "force" consumers to buy domestic shoes and allow a new domestic shoe industry (sometimes referred to as "infant industry") to grow without being pushed out of the market by well-established and more competitive foreign industries. According to Krueger, there is ample evidence showing that developing countries moving away from import substitution and toward free trade experience faster economic growth.

Krueger reviews the many possible reasons why abandoning import substitution tends to speed up economic growth. For example, the country that protects the domestic shoe industry will see increasing investment in this industry (which produces shoes for the domestic market) and less investment in export industries (e.g., agricultural sectors that produce food for export). This will create a problem: the shoe industry most likely needs to import from abroad the machines and raw materials needed to produce shoes. But a fall in exports reduces the availability of foreign currency needed to import these goods and stunts the growth of the shoe industry. Another problem is that the size of the domestic market will constrain the expansion of the shoe industry. If the number of consumers is relatively small, as is often the case, the number of firms in this industry will be small, leading to less competition; alternatively, the size of the firms in this industry will be small, and firms will not be able to exploit economies of scale. It is straightforward to see how liberalizing trade can fix many of these problems. If the bias toward production for local markets is removed, firms will produce more for export, and foreign currency will be in greater supply; if domestic producers can sell to foreign consumers, their market is much larger, making room for more firms (more competition) and larger firms (which produce at lower cost); and so on.

Krueger emphasizes that the problems with import-substitution strategies tend to become worse over time, so that countries that have placed restrictions on trade for long periods are especially likely to see an increase in economic growth when they start engaging in trade liberalization. The author also points out that trade liberalization only helps when it goes along with "supporting policies" such as the removal of constraints on the determination of exchange rates.

If there is a positive relation between trade liberalization and economic growth, as Krueger claims, can the same be said for the relation between trade liberalization and poverty reduction? More broadly, might the gains from globalization only benefit a small number of people in developing countries, possibly at the expense of the poor? Or does globalization make the poor better off as well? Columbia economist Jagdish Bhagwati addresses this issue in a chapter from one of his books (the selection is reprinted in Chapter 38). According to Bhagwati, both theory and evidence point to a positive correlation between globalization and poverty reduction. His main argument is simply that international trade promotes economic growth and economic growth promotes poverty reduction. Like Krueger, however, Bhagwati notes that these correlations are found only under certain circumstances, and he emphasizes the role of government policies, making an analogy with the Green Revolution (discussed in Part Five). He explains that the introduction of new seeds risked raising growth but making poverty worse. As production of food increased, the price of food fell; if only richer farmers could afford to adopt the new crops, poor farmers would have found themselves producing at the same cost as before but getting a lower price for their crop. Bhagwati believes that this did not occur because governments intervened and established support systems to extend the benefits of the Green Revolution to the poor. In a similar vein, Bhagwati observes that microcredit, by extending loans to the poor, makes it more likely that poor entrepreneurs will be able to benefit from the opportunities that globalization provides. If the poor are unable to borrow and invest, their ability to take advantage of globalization will be greatly reduced.

Bhagwati also argues that the growth generated by globalization can help reduce poverty to the extent that it allows the poor to take advantage of "social legislation aimed at helping the poor and peripheral groups." He believes, for example, that legislation granting rights to women has less impact when the economy is stagnant and women do not have the economic independence to take advantage of such legislation. Bhagwati concludes with a discussion of China and India, noting that both countries have experienced fast growth and dramatic poverty reduction in recent years as they engaged increasingly in international trade and received growing amounts of foreign direct investment.

Krueger and Bhagwati are just two of many economists who see globalization as a key ingredient for economic growth and poverty reduction. Harvard economist Dani Rodrik, on the other hand, has expressed doubts about free-trade enthusiasm for years, emphasizing instead the dangers of promoting globalization as an economic development panacea. In the article reprinted in Chapter 39, Rodrik acknowledges that integration with the global economy can yield benefits for developing countries, but he also remarks that opening up to free trade has not always delivered the rewards that free-trade proponents had promised. He notes, for example, that some countries in Latin America and Africa have been growing more slowly after liberalizing their trade regimes than they did when they restricted trade through import substitution. In fact, Rodrik challenges much of the evidence suggesting a positive correlation between trade and growth and argues that the causation may go the other way around: as countries grow richer, they get rid of trade barriers and become more involved in trade. Rodrik also warns that trade liberalization nowadays can have significant costs. In order to join the World Trade Organization (WTO) and participate fully in the global economy, developing countries are required to change many of their laws, regulations, and practices. While these changes may well help development, they also require significant expenditures, and Rodrik wonders whether developing countries would not be better off investing their scarce resources in other areas with a more direct impact on poverty reduction.

Whereas Bhagwati was keen to emphasize that the East Asian countries experienced dramatic growth after increasing their integration with the global economy, Rodrik reminds us that these countries followed "unorthodox policies" that today are often prohibited by WTO rules. South Korea and Taiwan, for example, imposed tariffs on foreign imports, subsidized exports, and restricted the flow of capital across borders. The author believes that the success of many of these countries is more likely to be a cause than a consequence of globalization insofar as it is easier for countries with sound economies and established domestic development strategies to integrate with the global economy. Rodrik's key points are that the benefits of globalization can easily be exaggerated and that openness to trade, while generally helpful, cannot replace a development strategy that focuses on domestic strengths.

Another strong critique of trade liberalization as a key ingredient of a successful development strategy comes from Economics Nobel Laureate Joseph Stiglitz. In the article reprinted in Chapter 40, Stiglitz argues that while trade liberalization can indeed promote growth and poverty reduction, the details of such liberalization are tremendously important: if the right circumstances are not in place, liberalization may well hurt the poor. Like Rodrik, Stiglitz believes that the success of East Asian countries such as South Korea is best explained by their gradual and unconventional strategy of integration with the global economy, which initially involved substantial trade barriers and export subsidies. Stiglitz also emphasizes that politics, rather than economics, tend to drive trade liberalization; he laments U.S. demands that developing countries lower trade barriers while U.S. cotton farmers benefit from billions of dollars of government subsidies per year. In short, Stiglitz sees trade liberalization as an "asymmetric" process that benefits richer countries at the expense of poorer ones. He recommends changes to the trade liberalization approach intended to ensure that poor countries are able to share in the benefits that globalization can deliver.

While international trade is a major aspect of globalization, it is not the only one. Economists make a clear distinction between trade and private capital flows. While trade involves an exchange of goods and services, private capital flows involve the movement of money across borders to finance investments of various kinds. Mexico, for example, experiences "capital inflows" when an American investor buys Mexican government bonds, when a German pension fund buys stocks of a Mexican corporation, when a Japanese firm buys an auto plant in Mexico, or when a Swiss bank makes a loan to a Mexican firm. In all cases foreign entities are investing in the Mexican economy and hoping to earn a return on their investment. This kind of flow can certainly help economic development. In fact, since rich countries have substantial wealth that they want to earn a return on and poor countries have little wealth but many investment opportunities, a flow of capital from rich to poor countries would seem mutually beneficial. The scarcity of saving in many developing countries makes it especially attractive to tap foreign sources of saving to pay for investment expenditures.

Private capital flows have increased dramatically over the past several decades. Between 1990 and 2005, total private flows to low-income countries (as defined by the World Bank) increased from a little over $4 billion to $35 billion (World Bank 2007: 342; these amounts include foreign direct investment, portfolio investment in stocks and bonds, and bank lending). Especially rapid was the increase in purchases of stocks from developing countries, which went from $7 million in 1990 to over $12 billion in 2005 (ibid.). The inflow of these resources has definitely helped some countries, but it has also exposed them to serious risks. A number of developing countries have experienced devastating economic crises after borrowing funds from abroad and running into repayment problems. In the article reprinted in Chapter 41, Harvard economist Martin Feldstein discusses one of the most severe recent crises linked to capital flows, the one that Argentina experienced in 2001–02. Feldstein explains that Argentina borrowed increasingly from abroad in the 1990s, with its central government and provincial governments doing much of this borrowing. To repay the foreign loans, Argentina needed to earn foreign currency, which it did by exporting goods to other countries. Toward the end of the 1990s, however, Argentina's exports started to decline, partly because the country had a fixed exchange rate with the U.S. dollar and the dollar rose in value against most other currencies. Feldstein notes that Argentina's foreign debt "eventually reached 50 percent of GDP," making it impossible for the country to repay these loans on schedule. The government, therefore, was forced to default (i.e., declare that it was unable to meet its debt obligations) and, in January 2002, to devalue the currency.

The devaluation of the currency had a devastating effect on the economy. Since many firms had borrowed dollars from abroad, the devalued peso made it much more expensive to repay the debts in dollars, causing a great number of bankruptcies. As firms went bankrupt, people lost their jobs and the economy experienced a dramatic recession. Argentina's GDP decreased by 10.9 percent between 2001 and 2002 (World Bank 2004: 14), the rate of unemployment rose above 20 percent, and poverty increased from 38.3 percent of the population in October 2001 to 53 percent in May 2002 (Fiszbein 2004). While several factors played a role in causing Argentina's economic crisis, there is no doubt that large foreign borrowing was a major contributor (see Blustein 2005 for an extended discussion of the crisis).

In his article, Feldstein also discusses briefly the role of the International Monetary Fund (IMF) during the crisis. Like the World Bank, the IMF is an international organization and was created in 1944 by representatives from 45 governments. The main goal of the governments involved was to establish economic institutions that would help avoid another Great Depression (International Monetary Fund 2006). Unlike the World Bank, however, the IMF is not a development institution, in the sense that its major goal is not helping poor countries reduce poverty. Rather, the IMF was created explicitly "to ensure the stability of the international monetary system" (ibid.). In practice, the IMF's major role is lending money to countries that are unable to repay their foreign debt and helping them reform their economies in ways that will prevent similar problems from occurring in the future.

In recent years, the IMF has come under heavy criticism for the role it has played in major economic crises such as Argentina's. Feldstein believes that the IMF made two major mistakes in the way it dealt with Argentina: first, it encouraged the government to maintain a fixed exchange rate that, eventually, proved impossible to sustain; second, it provided large loans that allowed Argentina to "postpone dealing with its fundamental problems."

A scathing critique of the IMF comes from Jeffrey Sachs in the article reprinted in Chapter 42. On the occasion of the appointment of Rodrigo Rato as new IMF managing director, Sachs writes him a memo that outlines his views of the problems with the structure of the IMF and puts forward a number of suggestions for reform. Sachs starts by reviewing the peculiar governing structure of the IMF: countries contribute funds to the IMF in proportion to the size of their economy, and their voting power is proportional to their contribution to the IMF's funds. As a result, the U.S. and Europe hold over 50 percent of the votes. According to Sachs, this creates a situation in which "the institution prioritizes the interests of rich countries, and especially those of the United States, at every turn." Sachs believes that IMF loans are given out more on the basis of a country's ideological ties to the U.S. than on the basis of economic need. A second concern of Sachs's is that too often the IMF pursues the achievement of macroeconomic stability in member countries above all else, ignoring the impact on the poor of the policies it requires. He recommends a different focus that gives priority to poverty reduction in poor countries over other economic indicators such as price stability or a balanced budget.

Development economists do not always share the enthusiasm for free trade and globalization that other economists who work mostly on rich countries often display. All economists know that globalization has the potential to raise standards of living everywhere and need not benefit only some countries at the expense of others; but they also know that globalization involves benefits and costs and creates winners and losers within each country. Development economists worry that the costs may be exceedingly hard to bear, even if temporary, when they affect the poor in developing countries. Yet, even free-trade skeptics like Dani Rodrik or Abhijit V. Banerjee believe that rejecting globalization (or engaging in systematic trade restrictions) is not a good strategy for developing countries. Rather, they caution that developing countries need to put in place the appropriate domestic policies if they are to reap the rewards of globalization without letting its side effects take too much of a toll on the poor (see Banerjee 2006).

REFERENCES

Baker, M. M. (2007), "Globalization Is the New Imperialism: Don't Try To 'Improve' It, Bury It!" Online. Available HTTP: <http://www.larouchepub.com/other/govt_docs/2007/3406_eir_testimony.html> (accessed 12 June 2007).

Banerjee, A. V. (2006) "Globalization and All That," in A. V. Banerjee, R. Bénabou, and D. Mookherjee (eds) *Understanding Poverty*, New York: Oxford University Press.

Blustein, P. (2005) *And the Money Kept Rolling In (and Out): Wall Street, the IMF, and the Bankrupting of Argentina*, New York: PublicAffairs.

Fiszbein, A. (2004) *Argentina: Safety Nets in Times of Crisis*. Online. Available HTTP: <http://info.worldbank.org/etools/docs/library/111334/Fiszbein_Argentina percent20+ percent20Colombia_12-04.pdf> (accessed 12 June 2007).

International Monetary Fund (2006) *What is the IMF?* Online. Available HTTP: <http://www.imf.org/external/pubs/ft/exrp/what.htm> (accessed 12 June 2007).

Mehrotra, D. P. (2007) "Voices Against Globalization." Online. Available HTTP: <http://www.boloji.com/wfs5/wfs740.htm> (accessed 12 June 2007).

World Bank (2004) *World Development Indicators 2004*, Washington, DC: World Bank.

—— (2007) *World Development Indicators 2007*, Washington, DC: World Bank.

Chapter 37

Anne O. Krueger

WHY TRADE LIBERALISATION IS GOOD FOR GROWTH*

THERE ARE THREE TITLES that might have been assigned for this paper: 1) Why Is Growth so Rapid with Outer-Oriented Trade Strategies?; 2) Do Countries with Outer-Oriented Trade Strategies Grow Faster? and 3) the one actually assigned. They are not the same. Of the three, the first is probably the most difficult to answer. The second is a factual question, and the empirical demonstration is straightforward (Sachs and Warner, 1995). The third, by focusing on trade liberalisation, implies that developing countries have highly restrictive trade regimes and thus asks if a move away from those regimes is good for growth. It is far easier to show why, especially over time, liberalising a restrictive trade regime is conducive to more rapid growth than it is to show why outer oriented trade strategies have been so highly successful.

Trade strategies and development strategies are closely related, and it is useful to start by defining a few terms. An import-substitution (IS) industrialisation strategy was adopted by most developing countries in the years following the Second World War. In most cases those countries were then predominantly agricultural and exporters of primary commodities.

The belief then was that rapid industrialisation was the essential (if not the sole) feature of economic growth and that only by domestically producing goods then imported could developing countries industrialise.[1] Under IS, it was intended to provide protection to new industries during their developmental period until they could compete with their counterparts in industrialised countries. In practice, the IS strategy pulled most new resources into import-competing activities (with a number of negative consequences discussed later) and one result was that export earnings grew less rapidly than the demand for foreign exchange and usually less rapidly even than real GDP.

An almost universal policy response was then to impose restrictive import licensing in response to 'foreign exchange shortage'. The stated reasons for this were the need to 'conserve scarce foreign exchange' for 'essential' developmental needs. The outcome was, of course, a restrictive trade regime. For reasons to be discussed below, as IS strategies continued, trade regimes increased in restrictiveness and growth slowed.

Hence, to discuss trade liberalisation is to address the removal (or at least reduction) of incentives for IS industrialisation. And, because – again to be discussed below – growth spurred under an IS industrialisation strategy slows down over time, trade liberalisation is therefore associated with more rapid growth than the final phases of IS which precede it. It was and is in response to this phenomenon that trade liberalisation offers the only known way to escape from the ever-slowing growth rates of developing countries. Many liberalisation episodes in fact take place in response to economic crisis.[2]

By contrast, by the early 1960s a few then-developing countries[3] – most notably Korea, Taiwan, Hong Kong and Singapore – had abandoned import substitution and adopted outer-oriented trade strategies. The results were spectacularly rapid growth.

By outer-oriented is meant a trade strategy that is *not* biassing incentives in favour of import-competing industries and that provides roughly equal incentives to all exporting activities. Thus, an exporter shipping goods for $1 million of foreign exchange can expect to receive approximately the same amount of local currency regardless of the nature of the goods actually shipped.

It is important, in this regard, to note that outer-oriented does *not* mean more incentives for producing for export than for the domestic market. It does, however, imply relatively uniform across-the-board incentives for exports, and that the growth and industrialisation strategy relies on rapid growth of exports.

It should now be evident why the three questions differ. There is no doubt that the countries following outer-oriented strategies grew faster. Moreover, even among larger samples of countries, there is no question that more rapid growth of exports is associated with a more rapid rate of growth of real GDP.

There are, however, questions about why the East Asian economies grew more rapidly. These focus on issues such as whether productivity growth was more rapid in East Asia,[4] how much the government intervened in the market,[5] and other policies that were complementary to the outer-oriented trade strategy. It is for that reason that an article on why an outer-oriented trade strategy is so successful would be more difficult than one on why trade liberalisation is desirable. We know an outer-oriented trade strategy has led to more rapid growth, but there are arguments as to exactly why.

1. Trade strategies and development

Trade policy is integrally tied up with overall development strategy. Although we have learned through painful experience that productivity and output growth in agriculture, services, and manufacturing are all essential for growth, and that overemphasis on any subset of economic activities is almost certain to result in retarding the development process, the linkages between trade policy and development-cum-industrialisation strategy are crucial.

First, development does entail more rapid changes in economic structure (from agriculture to industry, from household production to market production, and so on) than does continuing growth in developed countries. Moreover, developing countries typically depend on imports for the preponderance of manufactured goods used domestically and are, at least in initial stages of development, highly specialised.[6] Consequently, there is even greater sensitivity to trade policy than in developed countries: protection of some industries, and especially high protection, will pull resources, and especially new resources, into those industries and out of disprotected industries. Thus, whereas an increase or decrease in protection in developed countries normally results in changes at the margin in the composition of output, in developing, countries the structure of protection (or lack thereof) virtually determines the direction in which new resources are allocated and, in the context of low income countries, therefore the entire pattern of production, especially in manufacturing.

Second, developing countries have production patterns which are skewed toward labour-intensive services, agriculture, and manufacturing. In accordance with comparative advantage, they import most capital-intensive goods and services. Since the latter category includes many investment and intermediate goods, developing countries' growth is contingent upon their ability to import those goods and services. When, instead, they confront relatively slow growth of foreign exchange earnings, they substitute domestically produced goods at higher cost for these capital-intensive items. Not only does this substitution process pull resources out of labour-intensive areas (such as textiles and clothing) where comparative advantage resides, but it implies slower growth because a given fraction of national income saved implies a lower level of real investment as the prices of capital goods are higher.

Third, because people have such low per capita incomes, most developing countries' markets are relatively small, outside of food and housing. Protection of production activities in these small markets results in a dilemma: either the number of firms producing a given good must be very small, or the size of individual plants may well be below minimum efficient size. If the number of firms is very small, the absence of competition results in low-quality high-cost production over and above that resulting from comparative disadvantage as producers have monopoly or quasi-monopoly positions. If the number of firms is large, each one is producing on a very small scale with consequent higher costs. By contrast, a liberalised trade regime permits low-cost producers to expand their output well beyond that demanded in the domestic market. Whereas industrialisation based on protection of domestic industries thus results in ever-higher capital intensity of production (as the 'easy import substitution' phase is exhausted), the open trade regime permits enjoyment of constant returns to scale over a much wider range.[7]

Fourth, because import substitution policies pull new resources (and even existing resources from agriculture) into import-substitution industries, export growth lags, if exports do not decline absolutely. Import substitution itself is import intensive, both because rising rates of investment in 'modern industries' have a high component of imported goods and because many IS industries rely on imports of intermediate goods and raw materials. Hence, the demand for foreign exchange for imports grows at a rate normally well in excess of GDP while the supply of foreign exchange from exports grows more slowly. The authorities have typically been reluctant to increase the price of foreign exchange, believing that doing so would make goods 'essential for development' more expensive. The result has been an ever-widening gap between the demand and the supply of foreign exchange at the prevailing official exchange rate. The authorities' response has been to move to ever more restrictive import licensing and exchange controls (the latter so that exporters will not be able to keep their earnings abroad) along with increasing black market activity and smuggling.[8] At some point, the negative effects were sufficiently undesirable that policy makers adopted a stabilisation programme. This resulted in a stop-go pattern of economic activity, itself with negative effects on the overall growth rate.[9]

Fifth, because of its centrality, decisions with respect to trade policy almost force a number of other policies. Import substitution regimes normally give bureaucrats considerable discretion either in determining which industries should be encouraged or in allocating scarce foreign exchange in a regime of quantitative restrictions. Open trade regimes force much greater reliance on the market, if for no other reason than that bureaucrats cannot very effectively force foreigners to accede to their edicts.

That, under import-substitution regimes, bureaucrats have control over import licensing implies great power over all producers, not only producers of tradables. It typically makes all foreign exchange scarce, thus inducing the imposition of additional regulations (to 'conserve scarce foreign exchange'). One consequence is a major temptation to corruption. Another is a belief that all producers are cheating (which may be true), which in turn leads to additional scrutiny of import licensing applications, delays in receiving needed imports, and other production inefficiencies.

Sixth, as import substitution continues, most regimes become increasingly complex. The costs of the regime, and the likely costs and benefits of alternative choices, become increasingly less transparent to decision-makers. Additional governmental resources become engaged in attempting to make the licensing system work, almost always to the detriment of other essential government functions, including the development of infrastructure.[10]

2. Static inefficiencies of import substitution

Even if all that IS did was to misallocate resources and result in static inefficiency, the gains from liberalising might be sufficient so that the growth rate accelerated for a period of years. If, for example, the resource cost of static misallocations were 20 percent of GDP and it required 5 years after liberalisation to reallocate resources appropriately, the realised growth rate would be between 3 and 4 percentage points higher during the transition to the more efficient growth path because of gains in economic efficiency.

If, in fact, growth is at a standstill prior to the liberalisation effort, the apparent gain can be even greater.[11] Static sources of loss include the production cost of trade distortions, the losses associated with rent-seeking for import licenses and corruption, the losses associated with delays and other costs imposed by quantitative restrictions, and the losses associated with producers' monopoly positions in the domestic market.[12] The total far exceeds the production cost,[13] the trade theoretic measure defined as the difference in the international value added under existing incentives and that which could be achieved under a regime that more accurately reflected international marginal rates of substitution between goods.

3. Dynamic costs of IS

However, it would appear that the dynamic losses under IS far outweigh the static losses. That is ironic, because the early arguments for IS always were based on the assertion that, while comparative advantage showed that free trade was superior from a 'static resource allocation' viewpoint, dynamic considerations (presumably derived from the infant industry notion) outweighed the static, and tilted the balance in favour of IS.

In practice, the outer-oriented trade strategies win the dynamic gains argument easily because IS strategies were and are associated with increasing costs and slowing growth over time.

There are a number of reasons for this, many of them emanating from phenomena already described. First of all, if a country embarks on an IS strategy, the 'easy' IS opportunities will likely be largely exploited first. These opportunities may lie relatively close to the country's comparative advantage.[14] As the IS proceeds and the 'easy' opportunities are already exploited, the new activities induced by protection would lie further away from comparative advantage. For developing countries with relative abundances of relatively unskilled labour, lying further away from comparative advantage means more human- and physical-capital using activities. This, in turn, means rising incremental capital-labour ratios. For a given savings and investment rate, that implies a declining rate of economic growth.

In addition to rising capital-labour ratios because new activities are more capital-using, the fact that the domestic market for many industrial commodities can be small further intensifies the problem. Once such relatively widely-consumed (at low income levels) items as shoes, clothing, and radios are produced, the size of the market for other manufactured goods can dwindle rapidly. Underutilised pieces of capital equipment (because either of indivisibilities or because of multiple products) also contribute to increasing incremental capital-output ratios and hence reduced growth rates.[15]

Other factors also contribute. The stop-go pattern, described above, clearly reduced growth rates. So, too, did increasing corruption and greater smuggling in response to larger black market premiums. One can even argue that the tension between the private sector and government officials rose over time.

In recent years, the focus on endogenous growth has pointed to another source of reduced growth rates under IS. It focuses on the opportunities for growth through use of ideas, and knowledge capital. Here, the argument is that imports provide domestic producers and consumers with new ideas (which are an externality) and that the restriction of imports (in response to lower export earnings) reduces the growth rate by reducing the rate at which people accumulate and use knowledge capital.[16]

To be sure, *anything* that is a property of trade that leads to an endogenous growth mechanism could equally well account for differences in growth rates between alternative trade strategies. It might be that exporters acquire more knowledge by their interaction with foreign buyers than do producers for the domestic market. Or learning by doing might take place more rapidly in export industries. But that countries whose economics are relatively more insulated from international trade do seem to fall behind in production techniques, quality, and other attributes of production associated with knowledge and new goods seems evident. It remains to determine how this source of growth might be quantified.

Finally, feedback mechanisms to policy makers under IS seem weaker than those under outer oriented regimes. The obvious point is that the tariff equivalent of import quotas or prohibitions is not known. But there are others. With import licensing, policy makers are less sensitive to the degree of overvaluation of the exchange rate than they are under outer-oriented trade regimes, where diminishing rates of export growth serve as a signal that things are not going well, and pressures rise from export interests (which relatively are more important and more influential than under IS) to adjust the exchange rate. The high costs of poor infrastructure are less evident than under a more open trade regime, and those costs spill over far beyond the tradable goods activities in an economy.

4. Need for supporting policies

While most countries liberalise from an initial situation that is sufficiently extreme so that gains are almost inevitable, trade policy does not operate in a vacuum. Other policies supporting trade liberalisation may be necessary and in any event can greatly increase the benefits.

The most obvious such policy pertains to exchange rate determination. The move from a regime in which quantitative restrictions have restrained foreign exchange expenditures to foreign exchange availability to one in which producers and consumers are to be free to choose at prevailing prices requires an adjustment of the nominal exchange rate. In fact, even if one moved from a regime in which there had been a uniform tariff of x percent to one in which the tariff was $0.5x$, an alteration in the nominal exchange rate would be called for.[17]

There have been a number of instances where trade liberalisation was not accompanied by a change, or at least a meaningful change, in the nominal exchange rate. In such circumstances, excess demand for foreign exchange has once again emerged and the authorities must either adjust the exchange rate or reimpose quantitative restrictions. Until they do so, however, incentives for domestic production of import substitutes have fallen while there has been no increased incentive for production of exportables (whose price remains unchanged in domestic currency as long as the nominal exchange rate is unaltered) or for production of home goods. The result is often a period during which the level of economic activity declines. Such a period not only leads to output losses, but also to political pressures to reverse the liberalisation.

Often, too, other regulations are built into the system which buttress quantitative restrictions. If they are not removed when an attempt at import liberalisation is made, the entire effort can be thwarted.[18]

Beyond the policy mistakes which prevent accelerated growth from starting or persisting after liberalisation, there are a number of policies whose alteration can greatly enhance the gains. It was already mentioned that infrastructure inadequacies become glaringly apparent with an open trade regime. Often, the evidence has been sufficient to convince leaders that improvements must be made.

Other growth-inhibiting policies can also usefully be altered. These include but are by no means limited to labour market regulations, policies favouring procurement by public sector enterprises, reform of tax laws and/or administration, and changes in agricultural pricing policies.

In most instances, failure to address these issues results in smaller gains from trade liberalisation than would otherwise have occurred. But in extreme cases, policies may be so restrictive that little can happen before they, too, are altered.

5. What differences are there between trade liberalisation and outer-oriented trade strategy?

As stated at the outset, explaining why outer-oriented economies have achieved such high rates of economic growth is subject to considerable debate. Answers range all the way from high productivity growth (which might result from endogenous growth theoretic bases), to getting *all* the policies (not only prices) right, clever government intervention, to laissez-faire policies, to good luck.

That argument cannot be resolved here. But one can, at least, address the difference between simply liberalising the trade regime and moving to an outer-oriented trade policy. Liberalisation is, by definition, the action of making a trade regime less restrictive.

There are always benefits to liberalisation, although their size may depend on many things. But clearly one could not expect to achieve an outer oriented trade regime simply by replacing quotas with tariffs[19] or increasing the size of quotas.

An outer-oriented trade strategy is one in which the development strategy itself is based on the growth of domestic economic activity in response to producer incentives that closely mirror international prices. As such, it is expected that rapid growth of industry will occur (as agricultural productivity rises) as producers find their best alternatives in the global economy. That means that policy makers must focus on delivering adequate transport and communications, permitting imports for exporters at world prices, and going well beyond simply the easing or removal of restrictions on imports. If one ignores the variance across commodities, one can define the bias of a trade regime as the extent to which the ratio of domestic prices of import competing goods to their international prices relative to the ratio of the domestic prices of exportables relative to their international prices deviates from unity. An outer oriented trade regime is one where the deviation is small, while an IS regime is one in which it is larger.

Trade liberalisation clearly implies a reduction in the bias of the regime. Moving to an outer-oriented trade strategy implies moving to a very small, or even zero, deviation. Turkey liberalised the trade regime in 1958–60 and again in 1970. Turkey then moved to an outer-oriented trade strategy in 1980–3.

6. Conclusion

There is much still to be learned about trade liberalisation, the best means of achieving an outer-oriented trade regime, and the reasons for the very rapid growth that the outer-oriented economies have achieved. But the reason why trade liberalisation delivers more rapid growth is that IS, over time, becomes a failed strategy. As such, any significant degree of relaxation of restrictiveness can result in gains, unless there are other policies in effect in the economy that thwart their impact.

Trade liberalisation undertaken from a period of declining growth rates or even falling real GDP can normally lead to a period of growth above the rates previously realised. It cannot, however, lead to sustained growth at the sorts of high rates achieved by the truly outer-oriented economies unless policy makers adopt far reaching measures that effectively provide incentives within the tradables sector at world prices and thus an outer oriented trade regime.

Notes

*   I am indebted to Philip Levy for helpful comments on an earlier draft of this paper.

1   See Krueger (1997) and the references therein for a fuller statement of the logic behind the IS policies.

2   See Little *et al.* (1993) and Michaely *et al.* (1991) and the individual studies on which they are based.

3   These all have very low per capita incomes in the 1950s. Korea was estimated to have one of the lowest per capita incomes in Asia. Korea and Taiwan both followed policies of import substitution in the 1950s, and then changed to outer oriented trade policies in the 1960s. Singapore's history with regard to early trade strategy is somewhat more murky because it did not separate from Malaya until 1965. Hong Kong, of course, followed a laissez-faire policy continuously. The World Bank now classifies Korea, Hong Kong and Singapore as high-income countries. See World Bank (1997), pp. 214–5. Taiwan is not included in the Bank's *World Tables*, but has a higher per capita income than Korea.

4   See Young, (1992) and (1994).

5   See World Bank (1993) for one view.

6   This is both because of their factor endowment which typically lies well away from the world mean and also because of the small size of their domestic markets (discussed further below).

7   See Ventura (1997) on this.

8   The nominal exchange rate typically is altered at times of 'foreign exchange crisis', which happened to most countries periodically under import substitution. Those alterations were typically 'too little, too late', and, while providing for some liberalisation of trade regimes in the short run, did nothing to alter the underlying policy stance toward IS. Over the longer run, the restrictiveness of the trade regime increased. See Krueger (1978) for a discussion.

9   See Diaz Alejandro (1978) for the argument.

10   The inadequacy of transport and communications facilities in developing countries that have followed import-substitution policies is well known. The precise mechanisms that result in their inadequacy are not clear. It is evident, however, that – almost by definition – a liberalised trade regime cannot persist unless ports, loads, and communications are adequate to service a large and rapidly growing volume of trade. Bottlenecks become visible very quickly.

11   A large number of countries have reversed slow growth for a period of years after liberalisation. For example, the Turkish rate of economic growth in the 1956–58 period was about 2–3 percent annually. After liberalisation in 1958–60, growth averaged around 7 percent for the next 7 years. The same pattern was observed after the 1980 Turkish liberalisation. In Ghana, real GDP was declining at 1–2 percent annually prior to the 1984 structural adjustment programme began. It averaged around 5 percent a year for the next half decade or more.

12   One frequently encounters the argument that countries cannot liberalise their trade regimes because they depend upon tariff revenues for support of their fiscal programmes. In fact, when quantitative restrictions and import prohibitions are the mechanisms by which excess demand is suppressed, there is scope for trade liberalisation accompanied by *increased* government revenue at lower rates of protection through tariffs or their QR-equivalents.

13   See Johnson (1960) for a rigorous definition of the production costs of a tariff.

14   This appears empirically to have been roughly the pattern actually followed. However, in theory, a would-be producer, deciding upon which activity to undertake, would consider not only his costs relative to prices of imports, but also the degree of monopoly power he would attain. This latter would not necessarily be correlated with the excess of domestic production costs over world prices.

15   In fact, developing countries' savings rates rose dramatically from the 1950s to the 1980s, while growth rates on average did not. See World Bank (1983).

16   See Grossman and Helpman (1991).

17   Of course, as an alternative, one could always subject the domestic economy to deflation, but in most instances that would require a period of domestic recession until expectations as to the price level adjusted. It should be noted that removal of quantitative restrictions is in itself deflationary, but the additional imports accompanying the liberalisation would have to be financed by additional foreign exchange earnings, which must be induced by the exchange rate adjustment (or by an absolute drop in the price of nontradable goods as well as the domestic price of imports).

18   An example will illustrate. In India in the mid-1980s, an effort was made to liberalise imports by removing licensing requirements under certain circumstances. But producers sometimes found that when they wanted, e.g. state government licenses to operate, they had to show their documents from national investment licensing officials, which in turn were contingent upon approval by the import authorities.

19   The empirical evidence, however, is that efforts to replace quotas with tariff equivalents seems nonetheless to reduce protection. This was found in several of the countries reported upon in Krueger (1978), including Egypt and the Philippines.

References

Diaz-Alejandro, Carlos, (1978). *Foreign Trade Regimes and Economic Development: Colombia.* New York: Columbia University Press.

Grossman, Gene and Helpman, Elhanan (1991). Innovation and Growth in the World Economy. Cambridge, MA: MIT Press.

Johnson, Harry G., (1960). 'The cost of protection and the scientific tariff', *Journal of Political Economy*, vol 68, no. 4. August, pp. 327–45.

Krueger, Anne O., (1978). *Foreign Trade Regimes and Economic Development: Liberalisation Attempts and Consequences*, Lexington, MA: Ballinger Press.

Krueger, Anne O., (1997). 'Trade policy and economic development: how we learn', *American Economic Review*, vol. 87, no. 1, March, pp. 1–22.

Little, I. M. D., Cooper, Richard N., Corden, W. Max and Rajapatirana, Sarath., (1996). *Boom, Crisis, and Adjustment. The Macroeconomic Experience of Developing Countries.* Oxford and New York: Oxford University Press.

Michaely, Michael, Papageorgiou, Demetris and Choksi, Armeane M. (1993). *Lessons of Experience in the Developing World*, Volume 7 of Michaely *et al*, editors, *Liberalizing Foreign Trade*, Oxford: Basil Blackwell.

Sachs, Jeffrey and Warner, Andrew (1995). 'Economic Reform and the Process of Global Integration', Brookings Papers on Economic Activity, no. 1, pp. 1–118.

Ventura, Jaume, (1997). 'Growth and interdependence', *Quarterly Journal of Economics*, vol. 112(1), February, pp. 57–84.

World Bank, (1983). *World Development Report*, Oxford and New York: Oxford University Press.

World Bank, (1993). *The East Asian Miracle*, Oxford and New York: Oxford University Press.

World Bank, (1997). *World Development Report*, Oxford and New York: Oxford University Press.

Young, Alwyn, (1992). 'A tale of two cities: factor accumulation and technical change in Hong Kong and Singapore', in (Olivier Blanchard and Stanley Fischer, eds), *NBER Macroeconomics Annual*, Cambridge MA: MIT Press, pp. 13–54.

Young, Alwyn, (1994). 'Lessons from East Asian NICs: a contrarian view', *European Economic Review*, vol. 38, no. 3–4. (April) pp. 964–73.

REVIEW AND DISCUSSION QUESTIONS

1   What are the basic features of import-substitution industrialization?

2   How is an "outer-oriented" development strategy different from import substitution?

3   According to Krueger, what are the key reasons why trade liberalization has given a boost to economic development in countries that used to pursue import-substitution policies?

4   Does the author agree with the view that import substitution has short-run costs but long-term benefits? Why or why not?

5   According to Krueger, what does it take for trade liberalization to be successful?

6   While the author emphasizes the benefits of trade liberalization, this policy is likely to involve costs as well. What do you think are some of these costs?

Chapter 38

Jagdish Bhagwati

POVERTY
Enhanced or diminished?

I N ACT III, SCENE 4 of *King Lear*, the proud old king, transported profoundly by the tragedy that relentlessly unfolds and engulfs him, kneels to pray as a storm rages around him, to regret his neglect of the wretched of the earth:

> Poor naked wretches, whereso'er you are,
> That bide the pelting of this pitiless storm,
> How shall your houseless heads and unfed sides,
> Your looped and windowed raggedness, defend you
> From seasons such as these? O, I have ta'en
> Too little care of this!

and then to cry for empathy and justice:

> Take physic, pomp;
> Expose thyself to feel what wretches feel,
> That thou mayst shake the superflux to them,
> And show the heavens more just.

How well Shakespeare's Lear seems to capture our present situation! Echoing Lear's sentiments half a millennium later, nearly 150 prime ministers and presidents of the world's nations converged in September 2000 for the UN'S Millennium Summit, embracing poverty removal as their goal. They resolved to "halve, by the year 2015, the proportion of the world's people whose income is less than one dollar a day and the proportion of people who suffer from hunger."[1]

They were joined at the time by countless NGOs that had congregated for parallel events, by the bureaucrats that head the international institutions (such as the World Bank and the UN Development Programme) charged with developmental objectives, and by the liberal media.

Of course, the acute sensitivity to poverty and the moral commitment to reduce it are nothing new. It would be strange indeed if the many enlightened leaders and intellectuals of these nations had not already resolved to wage a war on poverty half a century ago. That, in fact, was the very focus of the leaders in the many independence movements that resulted in extensive decolonization at the end of the Second World War. Let me just cite India's first prime minister, Pandit Jawaharlal Nehru, a Fabian by temperament and training from his student days in Cambridge. Writing in 1946, he recalled the resolve of the prewar National Planning Committee of Mahatma Gandhi's Indian National Congress to

> insure an adequate standard of living for the masses; in other words, to get rid of the appalling poverty of the people . . . [to] insure an irreducible minimum standard for everybody.[2]

Writing some decades earlier, even the conservative Winston Churchill, who had observed acutely a shift in public opinion in the decade of the 1880s, had remarked:

> The great victories had been won. All sorts of lumbering tyrannies had been toppled over. Authority was everywhere broken. Slaves were free. Conscience was free. Trade was free. But hunger and squalor were also free and the people demanded something more than liberty.[3]

Indeed, few in the twentieth century have not had poverty on their minds and a passion to remove it in their hearts.

It's the policy, stupid

So, the compelling question is altogether different as we consider the issue of poverty as the new century, and even the new millennium, begins: what do we know now, after five decades of experimentation, that will make our efforts even more effective? In short, drawing on former President Clinton's words, we must assert: "It's the policy, stupid." But then, which policy?

And that returns us to the central question: does globalization, in the specific form of freer trade (and inward direct foreign investment, addressed directly in Chapter 12), imply a closer integration into the world economy, part of that poverty-reducing policy, or are wisdom and knowledge on the side of those who claim the contrary? As it happens, the proponents of globalization have it right.

Two types of supporting argumentation can be produced: shrewd observation and scientific evidence. A brilliant observer such as the Swedish journalist Tomas Larsson in his new book, *The Race to the Top: The Real Story of Globalization*, has written from his firsthand experiences in Asia and described with telling stories and portraits from the ground how poverty has been licked by globalization. Let me cite one example that stayed with me long after I had read the book:

[B]etting on poultry [in cockfighting] wasn't what I had in mind when I came to Navanakorn, an industrial area in the northern outskirts of Bangkok. I'd taken the afternoon off from the UNCTAD conference to find out for myself what globalization looks like up close. The combined chicken farm and gambling den is right next door to a Lucent factory that manufactures microelectronics components – the factory floor of the broadband revolution and the knowledge economy.

The work is done in large square buildings that look like giant sugar cubes. At the entrance stands a shrine honoring Brahma with yellow garlands and small wooden elephants. . . . Inside are thousands of Thai laborers.

"When they started, the workers came on foot. Then they got motorbikes. Now they drive cars," says the rooster guardian. "Everyone wants to work there, but it is hard to get in."

. . . On my way back into town I amble through the industrial estate in search of a ride. A shift is ending. Thousands of women (for it is mostly women who work in the foreign-owned electronics factories) pour through the factory gates. I pass restaurants, drugstores, supermarkets, jewelers, tailors, film shops, vendors of automatic washing machines.[4]

The scientific analysis of the effect of trade on poverty is even more compelling. It has centered on a two-step argument: that trade enhances growth, and that growth reduces poverty.

These propositions have been supported by many economists and policy makers of very different persuasions over the years. Thus as long ago as 1940 the famous Cambridge economist Sir Dennis Robertson characterized trade as an "engine of growth," a colorful phrase that has caught on in the scholarly literature on trade and growth.

But the argument that growth would reduce poverty can be found in Adam Smith himself, as when he wrote that when society is "advancing to further acquisition . . . the condition of the laboring poor, of the great body of the people, seems to be the happiest."[5] And in modern times, Jawaharlal Nehru wrote just as India was about to become independent and all minds were turning to the enormous task of reducing India's massive poverty through planning:

[To] insure an irreducible minimum standard for everybody, the national income had to be greatly increased. . . . We calculated that a really progressive standard of living would necessitate the increase of wealth by 500 or 600 per cent. That was however too big a jump for us, and we aimed at a 200 or 300 per cent increase within ten years.[6]

Indeed, this connection between growth and poverty reduction was built into the earliest five-year plans, starting from 1951: they tried to accelerate the growth of the Indian economy while remaining focused on poverty reduction as a general target. But it was made yet sharper by the leading Indian planners in the early 1960s when they zeroed in on the target of raising the income of the bottom 30 percent of India's population to a minimum level within a specified period.

It fell to me to work on this problem since I had just returned from Oxford and was the economist assigned to assist the proponents in the Indian Planning Commission of this plan to raise the minimum incomes of the poor. I assembled the income distribution data that were available at the time; their quality was pretty awful because of inadequate statistical expertise in most countries, nor were they standardized for international comparability. But a quick scan seemed to suggest that there was no magic bullet: countries seemed to have somewhat similar income distributions regardless of their political and economic cast. So the primary inference I made was that if there was no way to significantly affect the share of the pie going to the bottom 30 percent, the most important thing was to grow the pie. In short, my advice – what I might call with some immodesty the Bhagwati hypothesis and prescription – was that growth had to be the *principal* (but, as I argue below, not the only) strategy for raising the incomes, and hence consumption and living standards, of the poor.

In this view, growth was not a passive, trickle-down strategy for helping the poor. It was an active, pull-up strategy instead. It required a government that would energetically take steps to accelerate growth, through a variety of policies, including building infrastructure such as roads and ports and attracting foreign funds. By supplementing meager domestic savings, the foreign funds would increase capital formation and hence jobs. Those of us who were present at the creation therefore dismiss as nothing but ignorance and self-serving nonsense the popular and populist propositions that, first, growth was regarded as an end in itself and poverty removal was forgotten until a new, socially conscious generation of economists who worried about poverty arrived on the scene, and second, that the strategy of growth in order to reduce poverty was a laissez-faire, hands-off, passive strategy.

Growth and poverty

We were also aware that growth had to be differentiated. Some types of growth would help the poor more than others. For instance, as argued more fully below, an outward trade orientation helped the Far Eastern economies in the postwar years to export labor-intensive goods; this added to employment and reduced poverty rapidly. In India, the emphasis on autarky and on capital-intensive projects reduced both growth rates and increase in the demand for labor, so the impact on poverty was minimal.

Then again, growth can paradoxically immiserize a country and hence its poor as well (unless corrective policies are undertaken simultaneously). In 1958, I published a paper on what I called "immiserizing growth," where I demonstrated that an economy could become worse off even though it had grown through accumulating capital or improving productivity.[7] The argument was straightforward. Consider Bangladesh, which exports a lot of jute. Growth in the shape of more jute production, resulting in greater exports, would depress the international price of jute. Suppose then that one hundred additional bales of jute have been produced. If the world price of jute remains the same at $50 a bale, Bangladesh's export earnings go up by $5,000. But if the world price falls such that Bangladesh's total export earnings fall drastically as the additional hundred bales are exported, the total earnings of Bangladeshi jute exports could fall by as much as $6,000. This loss of $6,000 (from what economists call, in jargon, the fall in the Bangladeshi terms of trade) then outweighs the $5,000 gain from growth. Immiseration is the result.

This paradox earned me a lot of attention, partly because economists love paradoxes; whoever got attention for saying the obvious?[8] But partly it was also because many developing countries feared that international markets were tight in exactly the way I had hypothesized in arriving at the paradox of immiserizing growth. This was either because of economic reasons such as market saturation or because of protectionism that would choke off markets as soon as more exports materialized. My theory of immiserizing growth showed exactly how crippling that could be to a developing country's growth prospects.[9] The way to avoid this adverse outcome, of course, is to diversify away from jute production and exports.[10] So when you can depress your export prices by selling more because you are a major supplier, restrain yourself; push in other directions. A suitable policy can always nip the immiserizing growth paradox in the bud, ensuring that growth does amount to an increase in the size of the pie.

But then consider simpler and more obvious, but no less compelling, examples of immiseration that follows from *others'*, as against one's own, growth. Think of the green revolution, the evocative phrase used to describe the arrival and use of new and vastly more productive varieties of wheat and rice that had been invented with support from the Ford and Rockefeller Foundations and for which Dr. Norman Borlaug got the Nobel prize for peace in 1970.[11] When the new seeds arrived, the farmers who benefited were naturally either those who had access to credit because they had assets and hence adequate collateral, or those who could afford to be risk takers with new technology because they had a cushion of wealth to fall back on in case things did not work out. So there you have the divide that attends every transition to a major new technology: rarely do all march in step like a Roman legion. But then imagine what happens when some innovate and increase their production so that the price falls, while others have not innovated and their stagnant output now is sold at a lower price. Those who lag behind do not merely fall behind; they fall by the wayside, struck by a blow not of their making. Thus many feared that the green revolution would usher in the red revolution! But this did not come to pass. Why?

For one thing, policies were devised to ensure that immiseration of the laggards generally did not occur. Agricultural prices did not fall because of increasing demand, which resulted from investments that added new jobs and incomes. The government in India also actively used price support schemes, providing a floor to possible declines in prices. And as for the different fear that landless labor would be replaced by the higher yields, the reality turned out to be far more agreeable. The joint use of new seeds and irrigation led to multiple cropping; this resulted in an increased demand for labor on farms, prompting improvement in wages. Yet another possible source of immiseration with new seeds is the emergence of new pests and diseases that can be destructive of yields and of farming more generally. In the Indian case again, the government was careful to establish a substantial scientific support system that contained these dangerous possibilities.

So appropriate policies will always enable us to profit from growth and to moderate, even prevent, unpleasant outcomes for the poor. While some governments have not been careful, other governments have not been blind to these problems. Other interesting issues, however, must be addressed.

First, recall that different types of growth (e.g., growth paths resulting from reliance on heavy industry as against light industry, or those favoring capital-intensive as against labor-intensive investments) affect the poor differentially. Many economists in the early years of development planning favored a growth strategy that relied on massive import substitution in heavy industry (such as steel and electrical machinery) rather than on the exports of light manufactures (such as toys and garments), on the choice of high capital intensity in production techniques, and on the proliferation of public enterprises (beyond utilities) that turned out to be white elephants making gargantuan losses. Such a development strategy undermined the cause of the poor by reducing growth and by delinking it from increased demand for the low-grade labor that constitutes the bulk of the poor.[12] If growth had been outward-oriented, with labor-intensive goods and light manufactures being exported in far greater quantities, it would have increased the demand for labor and helped the poor far more.[13] So freer trade would have promoted growth that was even more effective in reducing poverty through the salutary effects of increased demand for unskilled labor.

Second, what can we do to improve the access of the poor to expanding opportunities in a growing economy? It is not always true that growth will pull up the poor into gainful employment. Even though growth opens the doors, the traction in the legs of the poor may not be enough to carry them through these doors. For example, tribal areas in India where poverty is acute may not be connected sufficiently to the mainstream economy where growth occurs. And we know from inner-city problems in the United States that the supply response of its youth to jobs downtown may be minimal unless we also address structural problems such as the allure of drugs, transportation bottlenecks, and the lack of role models in broken and single-parent families struggling against terrible odds. I should add that those who grow up in the inner city also need to acquire the carriage and demeanor that are critical for service sector jobs downtown – though you need them less in the kitchen, where you flip hamburgers, than in the front, where you face the customers. This reminds me of the economist Alan Blinder's sophisticated spoof of the tendency by us economists to reduce everything to economic terms: he produced an economic analysis of why chefs have bad teeth and waiters have good teeth!

But if you know the history of developmental economics, then you also know that the earliest development-policy makers tried hard to improve the access of the poor to growing incomes by making it easier for them to borrow to invest. This was done in India by forcing banks to open branches in rural areas and by asking them to lower collateral requirements. The problem with this policy was that it often resulted in bad debts. A breakthrough, however, came with the invention of microcredit programs, which go down to the very poor. The problem was solved by lending very small sums to a number of poor clients for tiny investments that improved their ability to earn a livelihood, and by letting each borrower (or "agent," as economists call her) effectively monitor other borrowers. This, as against the lender (or "principal") trying to monitor the borrower, works wonders: it reduces bad debts dramatically.[14]

But an alternative innovative idea for improving the poor's access to investment has come from the economist Hernando de Soto in his book *The Mystery of Capital*.[15] Essentially, de Soto argues not that we ought to forgo collateral from the poor, but that we must recognize that they often have a huge amount of capital in the form of land and other property. The problem, de Soto says, is that these assets do not enjoy property rights and the associated rule of law that protects and enforces those rights. This prevents the poor from being able to collateralize these assets in order to borrow and invest. De Soto has made this case beautifully and convincingly, citing the nineteenth-century American experience. There is no doubt that his prescription must be tried.

We must also improve the poor's access to investment by making sure that bureaucrats are replaced by markets wherever possible. As I remarked earlier, the anti-market protesters do not adequately appreciate that, as has been documented by numerous development economists who have studied both the working of controls and the rise of corruption in developing countries, far too many bureaucrats impose senseless restrictions just to collect bribes or to exercise power.[16] Letting markets function is therefore often an egalitarian allocation mechanism. I can do no better if I am to persuade skeptics than to tell here the bon mot that Sir Arthur Lewis, the Nobel laureate in development economics from St. Lucia (which has the distinction of having produced two Nobel laureates, the other being the poet Walcott) shared with me.[17] Lewis was adviser to the centrist, intellectually inclined Hugh Gaitskell in the British Labor Party. When he met Thomas Balogh, a radical economic adviser to British prime minister Harold Wilson, he told him: "Tommy, the difference between your socialism and mine is that when you think of yourself as a socialist, you think of yourself as behind the counter; when I think of myself as a socialist, I think of myself as being in front of it."[18]

But the ability of the poor to access the growth process and to share in the prosperity depends at least as much on their ability to get their voices heard in the political process. Without a voice, it is highly unlikely that they will get appropriate and effective legislation.[19] Democracy gives the poor precisely that voice, but it obviously works well only when there are political alternatives instead of a single-party state. NGOs provide yet another support mechanism for the poor; and the Indian supreme court took great strides in the 1980s and 1990s by giving legal standing to social action groups (as the Indian NGOs are called) to bring action before the courts on behalf of the poor.[20]

Let me add that growth is also a powerful mechanism that brings to life social legislation aimed at helping the poor and peripheral groups. Thus, rights and benefits for women may be guaranteed by legislation that prohibits dowry, proscribes polygamy, mandates primary school enrollment for all children (including girls), and much else. But it will often amount to a hill of beans unless a growing economy gives women the economic independence to walk out and even to sue at the risk of being discarded. A battered wife who cannot find a new job is less likely to take advantage of legislation that says a husband cannot beat his wife. An impoverished parent is unlikely, no matter what the legislation says, to send a child to school if the prospect of finding a job is dismal because of a stagnant economy. In short, empowerment, as it is called today – a fancy word for what we development economists have long understood and written about – proceeds from both political democracy and economic prosperity, and it is a powerful tool for aiding the poor.

Finally, we need to go beyond just having incomes of the poor grow. Growing incomes would do little good if frittered away, for instance. So, drawing on a 1987 lecture I gave on poverty and public policy, let me say that we have a final set of problems that need to be addressed once income has been provided:

> First, as sociologists of poverty have long known, the poor may spend their incomes on frills rather than on food. As the Japanese proverb goes, to each according to his taste; some prefer nettles. Perhaps you have heard of the seamen's folklore that recounts the story of the sailor who inherited a fortune, spent a third on women, a third on gin, and "frittered away" the rest.
>
> In fact, there is now considerable econometric evidence . . . that supports the commonsense view that increases in income do not automatically result in nutritional improvement even for very poor and malnourished populations.[21] Their high income elasticities of expenditure on food reflect a strong demand for the nonnutritive attributes of food (such as taste, aroma, status and variety),

suggesting strongly that income generation will not automatically translate into better nutrition.

. . . Should we actively intervene so that the poor are seduced into better fulfillment of what we regard as their basic needs? I do [think so]. In fact, I see great virtue in quasi-paternalistic moves to induce, by supply and taste-shifting policy measures, more nutrient food intake, greater use of clean water, among other things, by the poor. In thus compromising the principle of unimpeded and uninfluenced choice, for the poor and not for the others, evidently I adopt the moral-philosophical position that I do not care if the rich are malnourished from feeding on too many cakes but do if the poor are malnourished from buying too little bread, when their incomes can buy them both proper nourishment if only they were to choose to do so. In this, I am in the ethical company of Sofya (Sonia) Marmeladova in Dostoevsky's *Crime and Punishment* who, in turning to prostitution to support her destitute mother, sacrifices virtue for a greater good.[22]

Of course, the question then also arises as to the distribution of the consumption, even when adequate and desirable, *within the household*. This obviously takes us right into the question of gender discrimination, a question whose relationship to globalization is discussed in Chapter 6. This is, of course, an active issue today, with the rise of feminism.[23]

Trade and growth

But then, was our earlier optimism about the benign relationship between trade and growth also justified despite the fact that one could readily imagine circumstances where, instead of helping growth, trade could harm or even bypass growth? Indeed, economists can, and do, readily build formal models to derive these unpleasant possibilities.[24] We need, however, to know *empirically* what happens in practice. And empirical evidence supports the optimism.

First, consider the late nineteenth century. Historians of this period have often thought that protection, not free trade, was associated with high growth. Paul Bairoch, in the *Cambridge Economic History of Europe*, has argued that "protectionism [went with] economic growth and expansion of trade; liberalism [went with] stagnation in both."[25] Recently, the economic historians Kevin O'Rourke and Jeff Williamson have reinforced this impression by deriving a statistical association, through running what statisticians call regressions, between economic growth and import tariffs from 1875 to 1914.[26]

But the later work of Douglas Irwin has refuted that proposition.[27] By adding to the regression analysis several countries that were on the periphery of the world economy but integrating into it, as one should, Irwin manages to break the positive association between tariffs and growth. Equally important, he shows that the rapidly growing countries, Canada and Argentina, had high tariffs but that these tariffs were for revenue and had few protective side effects. The two countries were in fact splendid examples of outward-oriented countries that built prosperity on their pro-trade orientation.

Second, we can also turn to analyses that take into account complexities that the many-country regressions necessarily ignore. These typically involve deeper examination of specific episodes that speak to the issue at hand or consist of sophisticated country studies in depth.

Two examples of such analyses, both supportive of the merits of freer trade, can be found in the empirical literature. Just because specific tariffs led an industry to grow, we cannot conclude that the strategy contributed to economic prosperity and hence growth. Recognizing this, Irwin has produced a fascinating case study of whether a classic "infant industry" tariff levied in the late nineteenth century in the United States on the tinplate industry really promoted that industry *and* whether that promotion was cost-effective.[28] Irwin's careful answer is that the McKinley tariff protection accelerated the establishment of the industry by a mere ten years, since the U.S. prices of iron and steel inputs were already converging with those in Britain and therefore making U.S. production of tinplate profitable in any event, but that this acceleration was economically expensive because it does not pass a cost-benefit test.

At the same time, the modern evidence against an inward-looking or import substitution trade strategy is really quite overwhelming. In the 1960s and 1970s, several full-length studies of the trade and industrialization strategies of over a dozen major developing countries, including India, Ghana, Egypt, South Korea, the Philippines, Chile, Brazil, and Mexico, were undertaken at the Organization for Economic Cooperation and Development (OECD) and the National Bureau of Economic Research, the leading research institution in the United States.[29] These studies were very substantial and examined several complexities that would be ignored in a simplistic regression analysis across a multitude of nations. Thus, for instance, in examining whether the 1966 trade liberalization in India worked, T. N. Srinivasan and I wrote a whole chapter assessing whether, after making allowance for a severe drought that blighted exports, the liberalization could be considered to have been beneficial compared to a decision to avoid it. Only after systematic examination of the actual details of these countries' experience could we judge whether trade liberalization had truly occurred and when; only then we could shift meaningfully to a limited regression analysis that stood on the shoulders of this sophisticated analysis. The result was to overturn decisively the prevailing wisdom in favor of autarkic policies.[30] Indeed, many of us had started with the presumption that inward-looking policies would be seen to be welfare-enhancing, but the results were strikingly in the opposite direction, supportive of outward orientation in trade and direct foreign investment instead. Why?[31]

- The outward-oriented economies were better able to gain from trade. The layman finds it hard to appreciate this because, as the Nobel laureate Paul Samuelson has remarked, perhaps the most counterintuitive but true proposition in economics has to be that one can specialize and do better.

- Economists today also appreciate that there are scale economies in production that can be exploited when trade expands markets. This is particularly the case for small countries. For this reason, Tanzania, Uganda, and Kenya, which had protected themselves with high tariffs against imports in the 1960s, found that the cost of their protection was excessively high, with each country producing a few units of several items. They decided in the 1970s therefore to have an East African Common Market so that they could specialize among themselves and each could produce at lower cost for the larger combined market.

- Then there are the gains from increased competition. Restriction of trade often is the chief cause of domestic monopolies. Freer trade produces enhanced competition and gains therefrom. India provides an amusing illustration. Sheltered from import competition, Indian car manufacturers produced such shoddy cars that, when they went up to India's Tariff Commission for renewal of their protection, the commissioners wryly remarked that in Indian cars, everything made a noise except the horn!

- In order to maintain outward orientation, countries must create macroeconomic stability (chiefly, low inflation). Inflation-prone economies with fixed exchange rate regimes, where countries only reluctantly adjust their exchange rates in response to inflation, would soon find that their currency had become overvalued. This overvaluation would make exporting less profitable and importing more rewarding, thus undermining the outward-oriented trade strategy. Hence countries committed to export-promoting trade strategy had to have macroeconomic stability, and they therefore earned the economic advantages that follow from good management of the economy.

  Today, some critics of the advantages of outward-oriented trade strategy argue that we proponents of such a trade strategy fail to appreciate that the gains come not from the trade strategy but from "fundamentals" such as macroeconomic stability. They are wrong. Aside from the fact that we did think of this almost a quarter of a century ago, it is wrong to suggest that macroeconomic stability – for example, an economy not plagued by high inflation – will necessarily lead to an export-promoting trade strategy. India and the Soviet-bloc countries enjoyed splendid macroeconomic stability, to the point where a wit observed that Karl Marx and Milton Friedman were strange bedfellows. But the economies were autarkic in trade; trade policy itself nullified the advantages that macroeconomic stability would bring.

- Finally, as discussed in Chapter 12, direct foreign investment would also be lower in the presence of trade restrictions. It would also be less productive. Trade barriers would mean that such investment would have to be primarily for the domestic market, which was generally limited, whereas in outward-oriented economies it would be for world markets, which were not. Then again, just as trade barriers reduce the efficiency of domestic investments and incur the loss from protection, so do they reduce the efficiency of foreign investments.

Third, consider the contrasting experience of India and the Far East. From the 1960s to the 1980s, India remained locked in relatively autarkic trade policies; the Far Eastern countries – Singapore, Hong Kong, South Korea, and Taiwan, the four Little Tigers – shifted to outward orientation dramatically. The results speak for themselves: exports and income grew at abysmal rates in India, at dramatic rates in the Far East. India missed the bus. No, it missed the Concorde!

Of course, the trade strategy has to be put into the full context of other policies that enabled it to translate into gigantic growth-enhancing outcomes for the Far East and into tragic shortfalls for India. To see this, consider the East Asian "miracle," as economists christened it: it is not surprising that the practitioners of the dismal science call a splendid economic performance a miracle! This spectacular performance was, it is widely recognized now, due to very high rates of productive investment almost unparalleled elsewhere. Sure enough, the Soviet-bloc countries had experienced similar rates of investment, but it had all turned out to be unproductive investment. The "blood, sweat, and tears" strategy of getting Soviet citizens to forgo consumption in the interest of investment and growth of income had proven to be a failure.

The high rates of investment reflected, in turn, the fact that the East Asian countries turned outward beginning in the 1960s and therefore had world markets to work with when planning their investments. By contrast, India turned inward, so its investment was constrained by the growth of the domestic market. Growth in that market in a largely agricultural country meant the growth of agricultural output and incomes. But nowhere in the world has agriculture grown, on a sustained basis, at more than 4 percent annually, making it a weak basis for a strong investment performance!

The Far East's phenomenally high investment rates also were exceptionally productive. They were based on export earnings, which therefore enabled the investment to occur with imported capital equipment embodying advanced and productive technology.[32] Besides, these countries had inherited tremendously high literacy rates that ensured the productive use of new technologies. Accommodating, even ahead-of-the-curve expansion of higher education also helped to increase the productivity of the investment. So the Far East generally was characterized by a virtuous interaction among beneficial policies: outward orientation, high literacy, and emphasis on higher education.

But the primary role must be assigned to the outward orientation that set up the system for high and productive investments.[33] Education by itself, especially higher education, is unlikely to help. Unemployed educated youth will likely burn tram cars rather than lead to greater growth. The Kevin Costner movie *Field of Dreams*, in which this gifted actor's character builds a baseball field and dreams that the superstars of baseball have come there to play (but do not in fact when the reality check is in) is probably the best corrective to those who think that education by itself was the magic bullet that created the East Asian miracle.

Fourth, what do the many multi-country cross-sectional studies of this question show today? Not all show a positive relationship between trade and growth. What one can say, however, is that such statistical evidence, by and large, is consonant with the views of the free trade proponents.

The latest set of such studies, by David Dollar and Aart Kraay of the World Bank, show that if one focuses on post-1980 globalizers such as Vietnam and Mexico, which were in the top third of developing countries in terms of the increase in the share of trade in GDP during 1977–1997, they show better growth performance. Since trade will generally grow even if trade barriers are not reduced, it is important to note that this group also cut import tariffs by three times as much as the non-globalizing two-thirds.[34] These authors also observe that while growth rates in the non-globalizing developing countries have generally slowed down in the past two decades, globalizers have shown exactly the opposite pattern, with their growth rates accelerating from the level of the 1960s and 1970s.[35] This is certainly true for China, and to a lesser but certain degree for India, two countries that together have nearly 2.5 billion people within their borders.

India, China, and elsewhere

So, with the usual caveat that in the social sciences one can rarely establish the degree of credibility for one's argument that one can aspire to in the physical sciences, one can conclude that freer trade is associated with higher growth and that higher growth is associated with reduced poverty. Hence, growth reduces poverty.

The best way to see that is to focus on the two countries, India and China, that have the largest pool of world poverty. Both shifted to outward orientation roughly two decades ago, and this contributed to their higher growth in the 1980s and 1990s. China adopted aggressively outward-oriented economic policies in 1978. India also began opening its insular economy in a limited fashion in the 1980s and more systematically and boldly in the 1990s. According to World Bank estimates, real income (gross domestic product) grew at an annual average rate of 10 percent in China and 6 percent in India during the two decades ending in 2000. No country in the world had growth as rapid as China's, and fewer than ten countries (and, except for China, none with poverty rates and population size comparable to India's) had a growth rate exceeding India's during these years. What happened to their poverty? Just what common sense suggests: it declined.

Thus, according to the Asian Development Bank, poverty declined from an estimated 28 percent in 1978 to 9 percent in 1998 in China. Official Indian estimates report that poverty fell from 51 percent in 1977–78 to 26 percent in 1999–2000. Contrast what happened in India during the quarter of a century prior to the economic reforms and the abysmally low annual growth rate of 3.5 percent. During that period, the poverty rate remained stagnant, fluctuating around 55 percent. China's track record on poverty reduction in the pre-reform period is dismal as well, but there were also major adverse effects from the huge famine during the Great Leap Forward of Chairman Mao and from the disruptive Cultural Revolution. This experience, showing how growth will in fact reduce poverty, just as I had predicted and prescribed at the Indian Planning Commission in the early 1960s, has been shown to be valid in other countries where Dollar and Kraay have examined the experience carefully, among them Vietnam and Uganda.

More recent estimates by my Columbia colleague Xavier Sala-i-Martin have underlined the same conclusion dramatically. He has estimated poverty rates worldwide, using data for ninety-seven countries between 1970 and 1998. His conclusion on the relationship of growth to poverty reduction is as strong a corroboration as I can find of my 1960s conjecture that growth must be reckoned to be the principal force in alleviating poverty:

> [T]he last three decades saw a reversal of roles between Africa and Asia: in the 1970s, 11 percent of the world's poor were in Africa and 76 percent in Asia. By 1998, Africa hosted 66 percent of the poor and Asia's share had declined to 15 percent. Clearly, this reversal was caused by the very different aggregate growth performances. Poverty reduced remarkably in Asia because Asian countries grew. Poverty increased dramatically in Africa because African countries did not grow. As a result, perhaps the most important lesson to be learned . . . is that a central question economists interested in human welfare should ask, therefore, is how to make Africa grow.[36]

So when we have moved away from the anti-globalization rhetoric and looked at the fears, even convictions, dispassionately with the available empirical evidence, we can conclude that globalization (in shape of trade and, I will argue later in Chapter 12, direct equity investment as well) helps, not harms, the cause of poverty reduction in the poor countries.

What about inequality?

Poverty, of course, is different from inequality. True, as many sociologists have reminded us, I may feel poorer if the rich consume commodities in a way that makes me feel more deprived. Equally, the same degree of inequality will often appear more intolerable if it is in the presence of acute poverty. Thus in a country such as India, where poverty is still immense, affluence and its display are particularly galling. So are they in Russia today, where the nouveaux riches, a few of whom have fortunes similar to those of Western tycoons such as George Soros and Ted Turner, and their offspring, who spend holidays in St. Moritz and drive through Moscow in BMWs and Mercedes-Benzes, coexist with substantial numbers of people immiserized during a mismanaged transition.

Whether increased inequality matters, and if so, how, depends therefore very much on the society in question. In contrast to modern Russia, a society where income and wealth are unequal may nonetheless be stable if that income is not spent ostentatiously but instead devoted to social uplift. The Jains of India and the Dutch burghers who suffered the "embarrassment of riches" referred to in the title of Simon Schama's book about them accumulated capital and amassed wealth but spent it not on self-indulgence but on doing social good.[37] That made capitalism's unequal outcomes inoffensive, softening capitalism and its inequalities. Yet another way in which inequality becomes acceptable is if those who are at the bottom of the scale feel that they can also make it: inequality is accepted because it excites not envy but aspiration and hope. Capitalism's inequalities then become tolerable, not because the rich deny themselves self-indulgence but because they make the poor fancy that these prizes may come to them someday too. Evidently this part of the American dream frustrates the inequality-conscious Americans, who see the poor not voting the way they "should."

Indeed, the consequences of increased inequality, in any event, might be paradoxically benign, rather than malign. If a thousand people become millionaires, the inequality is less than if Bill Gates gets to make a billion all by himself. But the thousand millionaires, with only a million each, will likely buy expensive vacations, BMWs, houses in the Hamptons, and toys at FAO Schwarz. In contrast, Gates will not be able to spend his billion even if he were to buy a European castle a day, and the unconscionable wealth would likely propel him, as in fact it has, to spend the bulk of the money on social good. So extreme inequality will have turned out to be better than less acute inequality!

In short, the preoccupation with inequality measures – and there are several – is somewhat ludicrous unless the economist has bothered to put them into social and political context. Cross-country comparisons, no matter what measure is deployed, are just so much irrelevant data mongering, it must be confessed, since societies are diverse on relevant dimensions and therefore inequality cannot be judged outside particular contexts.

And this lunacy – how else can one describe it? – extends to what the World Bank, with its abundance of economists and funds, has been doing in recent years, which is to put all the households of the world onto one chart to measure worldwide inequality of incomes.[38] But what sense does it make to put a household in Mongolia alongside a household in Chile, one in Bangladesh, another in the United States, and still another in Congo? These households do not belong to a "society" in which they compare themselves with the others, and so a measure that includes all of them is practically a meaningless construct.

But since some play this particular global inequality game, others must follow suit. Since the World Bank found, in a 2001 study, that a small increase in inequality had occurred between the late 1980s and the early 1990s – an astonishingly small period to work with since the measured changes are likely then to be transient, just a blip – the question has been posed in just this way by others. Thus, in the thorough study cited earlier on poverty, Sala-i-Martin calculates also the inequality à la World Bank, using nine alternative measures thereof. He concludes that according to all these measures, global inequality declined substantially during the last two decades. These findings are supported also by the recent work of Surjit Bhalla.[39] Between them, they raise a massive discordant note in the chorus singing from a libretto lamenting increasing inequality in the age of globalization.

And so globalization cannot be plausibly argued to have increased poverty in the poor nations or to have widened world inequality. The evidence points in just the opposite direction.

Notes

1 See http://www.un.org/millennium/declaration.htm, 5.

2 I owe this quote to T. N. Srinivasan and used it earlier in my convocation address at Panjab University, Chandigarh, India, when receiving an honorary degree in December 2000. The convocation address is available from my website, http://www.columbia.edu/~jb38.

3 See W. S. Churchill, *Lord Randolph Churchill* (New York, 1906), 268–69; and Jacob Viner, *Essays in the Intellectual History of Economics*, ed. Douglas Irwin (Princeton: Princeton University Press, 1991).

4 Tomas Larsson, *The Race to the Top* (Washington, D.C.: Cato Institute, 2001), 133–34.

5 Adam Smith, *The Wealth of Nations*, ed. Edwin Cannan (New York: Modern Library, 1937), 81.

6 Jawaharlal Nehru, *Discovery of India* (New York: John Day, 1946), 402–3.

7 For many years *immiseration* was not in the dictionary, and often I had difficulty convincing editors to allow me to use the word. By now it has entered the economists' usage, and no editor has bothered me in a decade or so. William Safire, if he runs out of ideas, can surely do a column in the *New York Times Magazine*.

8 My use of the phrase "immiserizing growth" also endeared me to the intellectuals in Sorbonne, where there is a soft corner for me, I am told, because of this early paper of mine.

9 See Jagdish Bhagwati, "Immiserizing Growth: A Geometric Note," *Review of Economic Studies*, June 1958.

10 Economists can demonstrate that the best way to do this is to impose an "optimal tariff," an argument that goes back to David Ricardo's contemporary Torrens, who produced this objection to Prime Minister Robert Peel's policy of repealing Britain's Corn Laws with a view to taking Britain unilaterally into a free trade policy. For a full statement of the theory of commercial policy and its application to conventional and modern objections to free trade, see my *Free Trade Today* (Princeton: Princeton University Press, 2002).

11 Norman Borlaug was responsible for the innovation in wheat.

12 I have discussed the role of influential economists in supporting and rationalizing these erroneous policies that proved costly for growth and for poverty reduction in my Radhakrishnan Lectures, published as *India in Transition* (Oxford: Clarendon Press, 1993).

Ironically, some of these economists are among those today lamenting the growth of poverty, failing to recognize that they are among those who caused it!

13 The economist Anne Krueger, currently the first deputy managing director at the International Monetary Fund, directed a substantial research project when she was vice president and chief economist at the World Bank, the findings of which broadly support what I say in the text. See Anne Krueger, *Trade and Employment in Developing Countries: Synthesis and Conclusions* (Chicago: University of Chicago Press, 1982). Also see the extended discussion in my "Export-Promoting Trade Strategy: Issues and Evidence," *World Bank Research Observer* 3, 1 (1988): 27–57.

14 The credit for this innovation has gone to the Bangladeshi economist Mohammed Yunus, who founded the Grameen Bank. But the original experiment was by the remarkable Ilabehn Bhatt, who founded SEWA, the Self-Employed Women's Association, in Ahmedabad. The general failure to recognize her pioneering role in microcredit is perhaps yet another instance of gender discrimination.

15 Hernando de Soto, *The Mystery of Capital* (New York: Basic Books, 2001).

16 Padma Desai and I documented these effects in India in *India: Planning for Industrialization* (London: Oxford University Press, 1970). Similar documentation and analysis exists for many countries by now.

17 A comparable feat belongs to Gary, Indiana, which also has produced two Nobel laureates: my teacher Paul Samuelson and Joe Stiglitz. I gather that St. Lucia and Gary are not that different in the size of their populations.

18 I and Padma Desai documented at length in *India: Planning for Industrialization* the enormous delays and corruption being spawned by the bureaucratic restriction and licensing requirements in India. Hernando de Soto has also tirelessly documented these delays in country after poor country. And, as I argue, these delays hurt the poor far more than the rich and the connected.

19 What I say about the role of democracy, NGOs, and others factors in giving empowerment to the poor and the peripheral groups has been argued by me in several writings over the last two decades.

On democracy, for example, see my 1993 Rajiv Gandhi Memorial Lecture, titled "Democracy and Development: New Thinking on an Old Question," reprinted in my collection *A Stream of Windows: Unsettling Reflections on Trade, Immigration and Democracy* (Cambridge: MIT Press, 1998).

20 As it happens, the lead in this was given by my brother, P. N. Bhagwati, a former chief justice of India, who also helped set up India's Legal Aid Program.

21 This literature has been reviewed splendidly by Jere Behrman and Anil Deolalikar, "Will Developing Country Nutrition Improve with Income? A Case Study for Rural South India," *Journal of Political Economy* 95, 3 (1987).

22 This is the Vikram Sarabhai Lecture given in Ahmedabad and has been reprinted as Chapter 25 in my *Political Economy and International Economics*, ed. Douglas Irwin (Cambridge: MIT Press, 1991); the quotes below are from 545–46.

23 I remarked at the time that "distribution within the household may be such as to deprive the weaker members such as females, of an adequate access to the consumption basket. In the 1970s I was somewhat isolated . . . as an economist in being seriously interested in the sex-bias that was visible in the statistics on educational enrollments, literacy, infant mortality, and nutritional levels, much of the evidence coming from anthropological findings and other surveys" (ibid., 546).

24   For a formal discussion of alternative theoretical models, see T. N. Srinivasan and Jagdish
      Bhagwati, "Outward Orientation and Development: Are Revisionists Right?" in Deepak
      Lal and Richard Snape, eds., *Trade, Development and Political Economy: Essays in Honour of
      Anne Krueger* (London: Palgrave, 2001); a fuller version is available at http://www.
      columbia.edu/~jb38.

25   Quoted in Douglas Irwin, "Interpreting the Tariff-Growth Correlation in the Late
      Nineteenth Century," Dartmouth College. A revision was published in *American Economic
      Review Papers and Proceedings*, May 2002, and this is the version that I use in the text.

26   See Michael Clemens and Jeffrey Williamson, "A Tariff-Growth Paradox? Protection's
      Impact the World Around," National Bureau of Economic Research Working Paper No.
      8459, Cambridge, Mass., September 2001; and Kevin O'Rourke, "Tariffs and Growth in
      the Late 19th Century," *Economic Journal* 110 (2000): 456–83.

27   Irwin, "Interpreting the Tariff-Growth Correlation."

28   Douglas Irwin, "Did Late-Nineteenth-Century U.S. Tariffs Promote Infant Industries?
      Evidence from the Tinplate Industry," *The Journal of Economic History* 60,2 (2000): 335–60.

29   The OECD project was directed by the Oxford economists Ian Little and Maurice Scott
      along with the Stanford economist Tibor Scitovsky. The National Bureau of Economic
      Research project, which followed it, was directed by me with Anne Krueger.

30   The results from these projects, including one from the World Bank by the late Bela
      Balassa, a pioneer in the field, are reviewed in Bhagwati, "Export-Promoting Trade
      Strategy."

31   These were among the conclusions that I drew in my synthesis volume on the findings of
      the National Bureau of Economic Research project, codirected with Anne Krueger. Aside
      from them, there are many that have been discussed in the recent literature, including
      the role of new products and variety when an economy opens up, the absorption of
      (disembodied) know-how that can come from diffusion of new methods as trade and direct
      foreign investment bring the new methods to one's attention, etc. Among the economists
      who have contributed to this literature creatively is Paul Romer of Stanford, an illustrious
      son of the illustrious Governor Romer, who has also gone on to argue that the cost of
      protection is likely to be far higher than has been commonly believed by many economists.

32   New computers embody more-advanced technology than old ones. Economists therefore
      talk of "new-vintage" capital equipment. This is also embodied technical change, as distinct
      from disembodied technical change, where – with, say, better organization – you get more
      productivity from the same equipment and manpower.

33   I have developed this argument at length in Bhagwati, "East Asian Growth: The Miracle
      that Did Happen," keynote address at a Cornell University conference, reprinted in my
      collected public policy essays, *The Wind of the Hundred Days: How Washington Mismanaged
      Globalization* (Cambridge: MIT Press, 2001).

34   There are several writings by these two authors. The latest is "Spreading the Wealth,"
      Foreign Affairs 81, 1 (2002): 120–33. The findings on trade and growth are discussed
      on 126.

35   Again, the higher globalization on trade and investment flows may have been the result of
      a mix of policies such as infrastructure development and not exclusively due to outward
      orientation in trade policy. But without such outward orientation, the globalizers would
      surely not have achieved the high globalization and the accompanying high growth rates.

36   Xavier Sala-i-Martin, "The World Distribution of Income Estimated from Individual Country Distributions," National Bureau of Economic Research Working Paper No. 8933, Cambridge, Mass., May 2002, 31.

37   Simon Schama, *The Embarrassment of Riches: An Interpretation of Dutch Culture in the Golden Age* (New York: Vintage, 1997).

38   See the studies of the World Bank economist Branko Milanovic.

39   See Surjit Bhalla, *Imagine There's No Country: Poverty, Inequality, and Growth in the Era of Globalization* (Washington, D.C.: Institute for International Economics, 2002). These findings are receiving huge attention, and scrutiny, since they tear at the guts of the fashionable pessimism on the subject of trends in global inequality. Also see a related exchange in *Foreign Affairs*, July-August 2002, on the subject of inequality among nations.

REVIEW AND DISCUSSION QUESTIONS

1   What main argument does Bhagwati use to show that globalization is likely to reduce poverty in developing countries?

2   According to Bhagwati, under what circumstances might economic growth make poverty worse?

3   Why does Bhagwati believe that certain kinds of legislation that benefit the poor are more likely to make a difference when the country is experiencing economic growth?

4   What policies does the author recommend to ensure that economic growth benefits the poor?

5   What evidence does Bhagwati discuss to show that international trade promotes economic growth?

6   Can you think of other ways in which globalization might affect the poor in developing countries?

Chapter 39

Dani Rodrik

TRADING IN ILLUSIONS

A SENIOR U.S. TREASURY official recently urged Mexico's government to work harder to reduce violent crime because "such high levels of crime and violence may drive away foreign investors." This admonition nicely illustrates how foreign trade and investment have become the ultimate yardstick for evaluating the social and economic policies of governments in developing countries. Forget the slum dwellers or *campesinos* who live amidst crime and poverty throughout the developing world. Just mention "investor sentiment" or "competitiveness in world markets" and policymakers will come to attention in a hurry.

Underlying this perversion of priorities is a remarkable consensus on the imperative of global economic integration. Openness to trade and investment flows is no longer viewed simply as a component of a country's development strategy; it has mutated into the most potent catalyst for economic growth known to humanity. Predictably, senior officials of the World Trade Organization (WTO), International Monetary Fund (IMF), and other international financial agencies incessantly repeat the openness mantra. In recent years, however, faith in integration has spread quickly to political leaders and policymakers around the world (see Box 39.1).

Joining the world economy is no longer a matter simply of dismantling barriers to trade and investment. Countries now must also comply with a long list of admission requirements, from new patent rules to more rigorous banking standards. The apostles of economic integration prescribe comprehensive institutional reforms that took today's advanced countries generations to accomplish, so that developing countries can, as the cliché goes, maximize the gains and minimize the risks of participation in the world economy. Global integration has become, for all practical purposes, a substitute for a development strategy.

This trend is bad news for the world's poor. The new agenda of global integration rests on shaky empirical ground and seriously distorts policymakers' priorities. By focusing on international integration, governments in poor nations divert human resources,

BOX 39.1   SPREADING THE FAITH

"[W]e have an enormous job to do to convince the sincere and well-motivated opponents of the WTO agenda that the WTO can be, indeed is, a friend of development, and that far from impoverishing the world's poorer countries, trade liberalisation is the only sure route to the kind of economic growth needed to bring their prosperity closer to that of the major developed economies."

– British Prime Minister Tony Blair
January 18, 2000

"[I]n every case where a poor nation has significantly overcome its poverty, this has been achieved while engaging in production for export markets and opening itself to the influx of foreign goods, investment and technology; that is by participating in globalization."

– Mexican President Ernesto Zedillo
January 28, 2000

"[A]ny serious reflection on the future of the world economy and therefore the living standards of the billions who inhabit our world, will show that a strategic shift towards a significantly larger world economy can only be achieved as a result of raising living standards in the countries of the South, and therefore the radical expansion of the world markets for capital, goods and services."

– South African President Thabo Mbeki
April 4, 2000

"Korea will continue to strive toward fully integrating itself into the global economy and adapting to the digital revolution for truly sustainable growth in the coming decades."

– South Korean Minister of Finance Lee Hun-Jai
May 11, 2000

"The economic case for NAFTA is strong and the moral case is just as powerful. As barriers fall and markets open, people in Mexico are finding good jobs in their own country. Thousands are able to start businesses for the first time. Standards for conducting businesses become more regular. Standards for education rise to meet the demands of the economy, and that economy demands literacy, skilled labor, expertise in accounting and engineering and technology. It's a gradual change and not always easy but it can uplift a country and uplift lives."

– U.S. presidential candidate George W. Bush
August 25, 2000

administrative capabilities, and political capital away from more urgent development priorities such as education, public health, industrial capacity, and social cohesion. This emphasis also undermines nascent democratic institutions by removing the choice of development strategy from public debate.

World markets are a source of technology and capital; it would be silly for the developing world not to exploit these opportunities. But globalization is not a shortcut to development. Successful economic growth strategies have always required a judicious blend of imported practices with domestic institutional innovations. Policymakers need to forge a domestic growth strategy by relying on domestic investors and domestic institutions. The costliest downside of the integrationist faith is that it crowds out serious thinking and efforts along such lines.

Excuses, excuses

Countries that have bought wholeheartedly into the integration orthodoxy are discovering that openness does not deliver on its promise. Despite sharply lowering their barriers to trade and investment since the 1980s, scores of countries in Latin America and Africa are stagnating or growing less rapidly than in the heyday of import substitution during the 1960s and 1970s. By contrast, the fastest growing countries are China, India, and others in East and Southeast Asia. Policymakers in these countries have also espoused trade and investment liberalization, but they have done so in an unorthodox manner – gradually, sequentially, and only after an initial period of high growth – and as part of a broader policy package with many unconventional features.

The disappointing outcomes with deep liberalization have been absorbed into the faith with remarkable aplomb. Those who view global integration as the prerequisite for economic development now simply add the caveat that opening borders is insufficient. Reaping the gains from openness, they argue, also requires a full complement of institutional reforms.

Consider trade liberalization. Asking any World Bank economist what a successful trade-liberalization program requires will likely elicit a laundry list of measures beyond the simple reduction of tariff and nontariff barriers: tax reform to make up for lost tariff revenues; social safety nets to compensate displaced workers; administrative reform to bring trade practices into compliance with WTO rules; labor market reform to enhance worker mobility across industries; technological assistance to upgrade firms hurt by import competition; and training programs to ensure that export-oriented firms and investors have access to skilled workers. As the promise of trade liberalization fails to materialize, the prerequisites keep expanding. For example, Clare Short, Great Britain's secretary of state for international development, recently added universal provision of health and education to the list.

In the financial arena, integrationists have pushed complementary reforms with even greater fanfare and urgency. The prevailing view in Washington and other Group of Seven (G-7) capitals is that weaknesses in banking systems, prudential regulation, and corporate governance were at the heart of the Asian financial crisis of the late 1990s. Hence the ambitious efforts by the G-7 to establish international codes and standards covering fiscal transparency, monetary and financial policy, banking supervision, data dissemination, corporate governance, and accounting standards. The Financial Stability Forum (FSF) – a G-7 organization with minimal representation from developing nations – has designated 12 of these standards as essential for creating sound financial systems in developing countries. The full FSF compendium includes an additional 59 standards the agency considers "relevant for sound financial systems," bringing the total number of codes to 71. To fend off speculative capital movements, the IMF and the G-7 also typically urge developing countries to accumulate foreign reserves and avoid exchange-rate regimes that differ from a "hard peg" (tying the value of one's currency to that of a more stable currency, such as the U.S. dollar) or a "pure float" (letting the market determine the appropriate exchange rate).

A cynic might wonder whether the point of all these prerequisites is merely to provide easy cover for eventual failure. Integrationists can conveniently blame disappointing growth performance or a financial crisis on "slippage" in the implementation of complementary reforms rather than on a poorly designed liberalization. So if Bangladesh's freer trade policy does not produce a large enough spurt in growth, the World Bank concludes that the problem must involve lagging reforms in public administration or continued "political uncertainty" (always a favorite). And if Argentina gets caught up in a confidence crisis despite significant trade and financial liberalization, the IMF reasons that structural reforms have been inadequate and must be deepened.

Free trade-offs

Most (but certainly not all) of the institutional reforms on the integrationist agenda are perfectly sensible, and in a world without financial, administrative, or political constraints, there would be little argument about the need to adopt them. But in the real world, governments face difficult choices over how to deploy their fiscal resources, administrative capabilities, and political capital. Setting institutional priorities to maximize integration into the global economy has real opportunity costs.

Consider some illustrative trade-offs. World Bank trade economist Michael Finger has estimated that a typical developing country must spend $150 million to implement requirements under just three WTO agreements (those on customs valuation, sanitary and phytosanitary measures, and trade-related intellectual property rights). As Finger notes, this sum equals a year's development budget for many least-developed countries. And while the budgetary burden of implementing financial codes and standards has never been fully estimated, it undoubtedly entails a substantial diversion of fiscal and human resources as well. Should governments in developing countries train more bank auditors and accountants, even if those investments mean fewer secondary-school teachers or reduced spending on primary education for girls?

In the area of legal reform, should governments focus their energies on "importing" legal codes and standards or on improving existing domestic legal institutions? In Turkey, a weak coalition government spent several months during 1999 gathering political support for a bill providing foreign investors the protection of international arbitration. But wouldn't a better long-run strategy have involved reforming the existing legal regime for the benefit of foreign and domestic investors alike?

In public health, should governments promote the reverse engineering of patented basic medicines and the importation of low-cost generic drugs from "unauthorized" suppliers, even if doing so means violating WTO rules against such practices? When South Africa passed legislation in 1997 allowing imports of patented AIDS drugs from cheaper sources, the country came under severe pressure from Western governments, which argued that the South African policy conflicted with WTO rules on intellectual property.

How much should politicians spend on social protection policies in view of the fiscal constraints imposed by market "discipline"? Peru's central bank holds foreign reserves equal to 15 months of imports as an insurance policy against the sudden capital outflows that financially open economies often experience. The opportunity cost of this policy amounts to almost 1 percent of gross domestic product annually – more than enough to fund a generous antipoverty program.

How should governments choose their exchange-rate regimes? During the last four decades, virtually every growth boom in the developing world has been accompanied by a controlled depreciation of the domestic currency. Yet financial openness makes it all but impossible to manage the exchange rate.

How should policymakers focus their anticorruption strategies? Should they target the high-level corruption that foreign investors often decry or the petty corruption that affects the poor the most? Perhaps, as the proponents of permanent normal trade relations with China argued in the recent U.S. debate, a government that is forced to protect the rights of foreign investors will become more inclined to protect the rights of its own citizens as well. But this is, at best, a trickledown strategy of institutional reform. Shouldn't reforms target the desired ends directly – whether those ends are the rule of law, improved observance of human rights, or reduced corruption?

The rules for admission into the world economy not only reflect little awareness of development priorities, they are often completely unrelated to sensible economic principles. For instance, WTO agreements on anti-dumping, subsidies and countervailing measures, agriculture, textiles, and trade-related intellectual property rights lack any economic rationale beyond the mercantilist interests of a narrow set of powerful groups in advanced industrial countries. Bilateral and regional trade agreements are typically far worse, as they impose even tighter prerequisites on developing countries in return for crumbs of enhanced "market access." For example, the African Growth and Opportunity Act signed by U.S. President Clinton in May 2000 provides increased access to the U.S. market only if African apparel manufacturers use U.S.-produced fabric and yarns. This restriction severely limits the potential economic spillovers in African countries.

There are similar questions about the appropriateness of financial codes and standards. These codes rely heavily on an Anglo-American style of corporate governance and an arm's-length model of financial development. They close off alternative paths to financial development of the sort that have been followed by many of today's rich countries (for example, Germany, Japan, or South Korea).

In each of these areas, a strategy of "globalization above all" crowds out alternatives that are potentially more development-friendly. Many of the institutional reforms needed for insertion into the world economy can be independently desirable or produce broader economic benefits. But these priorities do not necessarily coincide with the priorities of a comprehensive development agenda.

Asian myths

Even if the institutional reforms needed to join the international economic community are expensive and preclude investments in other crucial areas, pro-globalization advocates argue that the vast increases in economic growth that invariably result from insertion into the global marketplace will more than compensate for those costs. Take the East Asian tigers or China, the advocates say. Where would they be without international trade and foreign capital flows?

That these countries reaped enormous benefits from their progressive integration into the world economy is undeniable. But look closely at what policies produced those results, and you will find little that resembles today's rule book.

Countries like South Korea and Taiwan had to abide by few international constraints and pay few of the modern costs of integration during their formative growth experience in the 1960s and 1970s. At that time, global trade rules were sparse and economies faced almost none of today's common pressures to open their borders to capital flows. So these countries combined their outward orientation with unorthodox policies: high levels of tariff and non-tariff barriers, public ownership of large segments of banking and industry, export subsidies, domestic-content requirements, patent and copyright infringements, and restrictions on capital flows (including on foreign direct investment). Such policies are either precluded by today's trade rules or are highly frowned upon by organizations like the IMF and the World Bank.

China also followed a highly unorthodox two-track strategy, violating practically every rule in the guidebook (including, most notably, the requirement of private property rights). India, which significantly raised its economic growth rate in the early 1980s, remains one of the world's most highly protected economies.

All of these countries liberalized trade gradually, over a period of decades, not years. Significant import liberalization did not occur until after a transition to high economic growth had taken place. And far from wiping the institutional slate clean, all of these nations managed to eke growth out of their existing institutions, imperfect as they may have been. Indeed, when some of the more successful Asian economies gave in to Western pressure to liberalize capital flows rapidly, they were rewarded with the Asian financial crisis.

That is why these countries can hardly be considered poster children for today's global rules. South Korea, China, India, and the other Asian success cases had the freedom to do their own thing, and they used that freedom abundantly. Today's globalizers would be unable to replicate these experiences without running afoul of the IMF or the WTO.

The Asian experience highlights a deeper point: A sound overall development strategy that produces high economic growth is far more effective in achieving integration with the world economy than a purely integrationist strategy that relies on openness to work its magic. In other words, the globalizers have it exactly backwards. Integration is the result, not the cause, of economic and social development. A relatively protected economy like Vietnam is integrating with the world economy much more rapidly than an open economy like Haiti because Vietnam, unlike Haiti, has a reasonably functional economy and polity.

Integration into the global economy, unlike tariff rates or capital-account regulations, is not something that policymakers control directly. Telling finance ministers in developing nations that they should increase their "participation in world trade" is as meaningful as telling them that they need to improve technological capabilities – and just as helpful. Policymakers need to know which strategies will produce these results, and whether the specific prescriptions that the current orthodoxy offers are up to the task.

Too good to be true

Do lower trade barriers spur greater economic progress? The available studies reveal no systematic relationship between a country's average level of tariff and nontariff barriers and its subsequent economic growth rate. If anything, the evidence for the 1990s indicates a positive relationship between import tariffs and economic growth. The only clear pattern is that countries dismantle their trade restrictions as they grow richer. This finding explains why today's rich countries, with few exceptions, embarked on modern economic growth behind protective barriers but now display low trade barriers.

The absence of a strong negative relationship between trade restrictions and economic growth may seem surprising in view of the ubiquitous claim that trade liberalization promotes higher growth. Indeed, the economics literature is replete with cross-national studies concluding that growth and economic dynamism are strongly linked to more open trade policies. A particularly influential study finds that economies that are "open," by the study's own definition, grew 2.45 percentage points faster annually than closed ones – an enormous difference.

Upon closer look, however, such studies turn out to be unreliable. In a detailed review of the empirical literature, University of Maryland economist Francisco Rodríguez and I have found a major gap between the results that economists have actually obtained and the policy conclusions they have typically drawn. For example, in many cases economists blame poor growth on the government's failure to liberalize trade policies, when the true culprits are ineffective institutions, geographic determinants (such as location in a tropical region), or inappropriate macroeconomic policies (such as an overvalued exchange rate). Once these misdiagnoses are corrected, any meaningful relationship across countries between the level of trade barriers and economic growth evaporates.

The evidence on the benefits of liberalizing capital flows is even weaker. In theory, the appeal of capital mobility seems obvious: If capital is free to enter (and leave) markets based on the potential return on investment, the result will be an efficient allocation of global resources. But in reality, financial markets are inherently unstable, subject to bubbles (rational or otherwise), panics, shortsightedness, and self-fulfilling prophecies. There is plenty of evidence that financial liberalization is often followed by financial crash – just ask Mexico, Thailand, or Turkey – while there is little convincing evidence to suggest that higher rates of economic growth follow capital-account liberalization.

Perhaps the most disingenuous argument in favor of liberalizing international financial flows is that the threat of massive and sudden capital movements serves to discipline policymakers in developing nations who might otherwise manage their economies irresponsibly. In other words, governments might be less inclined to squander their societies' resources if such actions would spook foreign lenders. In practice, however, the discipline argument falls apart. Behavior in international capital markets is dominated by mood swings unrelated to fundamentals. In good times, a government with a chronic fiscal deficit has an easier time financing its spending when it can borrow funds from investors abroad; witness Russia prior to 1998 or Argentina in the 1990s. And in bad times, governments may be forced to adopt inappropriate policies in order to conform to the biases of foreign investors; witness the excessively restrictive monetary and fiscal policies in much of East Asia in the immediate aftermath of the Asian financial crisis. A key reason why Malaysia was able to recover so quickly after the imposition of capital controls in September 1998 was that Prime Minister Mahathir Mohamad resisted the high interest rates and tight fiscal policies that South Korea, Thailand, and Indonesia adopted at the behest of the International Monetary Fund.

Growth begins at home

Well-trained economists are justifiably proud of the textbook case in favor of free trade. For all the theory's simplicity, it is one of our profession's most significantly achievements. However, in their zeal to promote the virtues of trade, the most ardent proponents are peddling a cartoon version of the argument, vastly overstating the effectiveness of economic openness as a tool for fostering development. Such claims only endanger broad public acceptance of the real article because they unleash unrealistic expectations about the benefits of free trade. Neither economic theory nor empirical evidence guarantees that deep trade liberalization will deliver higher economic growth. Economic openness and all its accouterments do not deserve the priority they typically receive in the development strategies pushed by leading multilateral organizations.

Countries that have achieved long-term economic growth have usually combined the opportunities offered by world markets with a growth strategy that mobilizes the capabilities of domestic institutions and investors. Designing such a growth strategy is both harder and easier than implementing typical integration policies. It is harder because the binding constraints on growth are usually country specific and do not respond well to standardized recipes. But it is easier because once those constraints are targeted, relatively simple policy changes can yield enormous economic payoffs and start a virtuous cycle of growth and additional reform.

Unorthodox innovations that depart from the integration rule book are typically part and parcel of such strategies. Public enterprises during the Meiji restoration in Japan; township and village enterprises in China; an export processing zone in Mauritius; generous tax incentives for priority investments in Taiwan; extensive credit subsidies in South Korea; infant-industry protection in Brazil during the 1960s and 1970s – these are some of the innovations that have been instrumental in kick-starting investment and growth in the past. None came out of a Washington economist's tool kit.

Few of these experiments have worked as well when transplanted to other settings, only underscoring the decisive importance of local conditions. To be effective, development strategies need to be tailored to prevailing domestic institutional strengths. There is simply no alternative to a homegrown business plan. Policymakers who look to Washington and financial markets for the answers are condemning themselves to mimicking the conventional wisdom du jour, and to eventual disillusionment.

Further reading

Thomas L. Friedman provides the canonical celebratory account of global economic integration in *The Lexus and the Olive Tree: Understanding Globalization* (New York: Farrar, Straus & Giroux, 1999). The World Trade Organization's (WTO) Director General Mike Moore presents the global trading system as the best hope for developing countries in "The WTO Is a Friend of the Poor" (*Financial Times*, June 19, 2000). Dani Rodrik challenges Friedman's view of a seamlessly connected world economy in "How Far Will International Economic Integration Go?" (*Journal of Economic Perspectives*, Winter 2000).

Two of the better-known academic studies arguing that trade promotes economic growth are Jeffrey Sachs and Andrew Warner's "Economic Reform and the Process of

Global Integration" (*Brookings Papers on Economic Activity*, No. 1, 1995) and Jeffrey Frankel and David Romer's "Does Trade Cause Growth?" (*American Economic Review*, Vol. 89, No. 3, June 1999). Francisco Rodríguez and Dani Rodrik provide a detailed critique of these and other academic works in "Trade Policy and Economic Growth: A Skeptic's Guide to the Cross-National Evidence" in Ben Bernanke and Kenneth S. Rogoff, eds. *NBER Macroeconomics Annual 2000* (Cambridge: MIT Press, forthcoming).

On the costs of implementing WTO rules, see Michael J. Finger and Philip Schuler's "Implementation of Uruguay Round Commitments: The Development Challenge" (Washington: World Bank Policy Research Working Paper No. 2215, October 1999). Katharina Pistor discusses the difficulties of importing financial codes and standards in "The Standardization of Law and Its Effect on Developing Economies" (New York: G-24 Discussion Paper No. 4, June 2000).

For an account of the postwar development record that emphasizes the role of successful deviations from the prevailing economic orthodoxy, see Dani Rodrik's *The New Global Economy and the Developing Countries: Making Openness Work* (Washington: Overseas Development Council, 1999). José Antonio Ocampo's "Rethinking the Development Agenda" (Santiago: Economic Commission on Latin America and the Caribbean, December 2000) provides a parallel account from a Latin American perspective. Yingyi Qian summarizes China's institutional innovations in "The Institutional Foundations of China's Market Transition" (unpublished paper, Stanford University, April 1999). See also Moisés Naím's "Washington Consensus or Washington Confusion?" (*Foreign Policy*, Spring 2000).

For links to relevant Web sites, as well as a comprehensive index of related *Foreign Policy* articles, access www.foreignpolicy.com.

REVIEW AND DISCUSSION QUESTIONS

1 Why does Rodrik believe that integration with the global economy is not, by itself, a sound development strategy for poor countries?

2 According to Rodrik, what are some of the costs incurred by poor countries that pursue integration with the global economy?

3 The economic success of East Asian countries such as Taiwan and South Korea is often referred to as evidence of the benefits of free trade. Rodrik, however, has a different view of the reasons for these countries' success. Explain what his view is.

4 What is Rodrik's interpretation of the evidence regarding the link between trade liberalization and economic growth?

5 According to Rodrik, what should poor countries do to achieve economic development? Do you agree with his position? Why or why not?

Chapter 40

Joseph Stiglitz

SOCIAL JUSTICE AND GLOBAL TRADE

THE HISTORY OF RECENT trade meetings – from Seattle to Doha to Cancun to Hong Kong – shows that something is wrong with the global trading system. Behind the discontent are some facts and theories.

The facts: Current economic arrangements disadvantage the poor. Tariff levels by the advanced industrial countries against the developing countries are four times higher than against the developed countries. The last round of trade negotiations, the Uruguay Round, actually left the poorest countries worse off. While the developing countries were forced to open up their markets and eliminate subsidies, the advanced developed countries continued to subsidize agriculture and kept trade barriers against those products which are central to the economies of the developing world.

Indeed, the tariff structures are designed to make it more difficult for developing countries to move up the value-added chain – to transition, for instance, from producing raw agricultural produce to processed foods. As tariffs have come down, America has increasingly resorted to the use of nontariff barriers as the new forms of protectionism. Trade agreements do not eliminate protectionist sentiments or the willingness of governments to attempt to protect producer and worker interests.

The theories: Trade liberalization leads to economic growth, benefiting all. This is the prevalent mantra. Political leaders champion liberalization. Those who oppose it are cast as behind the times, trying to roll back history.

Yet the fact that so many seem to have been hurt so much by globalization seems to belie their claims. Or more accurately, it has shown that the process of "liberalization" – the details of the trade agreements – make a great deal of difference.

That Mexico has done so poorly under NAFTA has not helped the case for liberalization. If there ever was a free trade agreement that should have promoted growth, that was it, for it opened up to Mexico the largest market of the world. But growth in the decade since has been slower than in the decades before 1980, and the poorest in the country, the corn farmers, have been particularly hurt by subsidized American corn.

The fact of the matter is that the economics of trade liberalization are far more complicated than political leaders have portrayed them. There are some circumstances in which trade liberalization brings enormous benefits – when there are good risk markets, when there is full employment, when an economy is mature. But none of these conditions are satisfied in developing countries. With full employment, a worker who loses his job to new imports quickly finds another; and the movement from low-productivity protected sectors to high-productivity export sectors leads to growth and increased wages. But if there is high unemployment, a worker who loses his job may remain unemployed. A move from a low-productivity, protected sector to the unemployment pool does not increase growth, but it does increase poverty. Liberalization can expose countries to enormous risks, and poor countries – and especially the poor people in those countries – are ill equipped to cope with those risks.

Perhaps most importantly, successful development means going [from] stagnant traditional sectors with low productivity to more modern sectors with faster increases in productivity. But without protection, developing countries cannot compete in the modern sector. They are condemned to remain in the low growth part of the global economy. South Korea understood this. Thirty-five years ago, those who advocated free trade essentially told Korea to stick with rice farming. But Korea knew that even if it were successful in improving productivity in rice farming, it would be a poor country. It had to industrialize.

What are we to make of the oft-quoted studies that show that countries that have liberalized more have grown faster? Put aside the numerous statistical problems that plague almost all such "cross-country" studies. Most of the studies that claim that liberalization leads to growth do no such thing. They show that countries that have traded more have grown more. Studies that focus directly on liberalization – that is, what happens when countries take away trade barriers – present a less convincing picture that liberalization is good for growth.

But we know which countries around the world have grown the fastest: they are the countries of East Asia, and their growth was based on export-driven trade. They did not pursue policies of unfettered liberalization. Indeed, they actively intervened in markets to encourage exports, and only took away trade barriers as their exports grew. They avoided the pitfall described earlier of individuals moving from low-productivity sectors into zero productivity unemployment by maintaining their economies at close to full employment.

The point is that no country approaches liberalization as an abstract concept that it might or might not buy in to for the good of the world. Every country wants to know: For a country with its unemployment rate, with its characteristics, with its financial markets, will liberalization lead to faster growth?

If the economics are nuanced, the politics are simple. Trade negotiations provide a field day for special interests. Their agenda is also straightforward: Exporters want others' markets opened up; those threatened by competition do not. Trade negotiators pay little attention to principles (though they work hard to clothe their position under the guise of principle). They pay attention to campaign contributions and votes.

In the most recent trade talks, for example, enormous attention has been focused on developed countries' protection of their agricultural sectors – protections that exist because of the power of vested agricultural interests there. Such protectionism has become emblematic of the hypocrisy of the West in preaching free trade yet practicing something quite different. Some 25,000 rich American cotton farmers, reliant on government subsidies for cotton, divide among themselves some $3 billion to $4 billion a year, leading to higher production and lower prices. The damage that these subsidies wreak on some 10 million cotton farmers eking out a subsistence living in sub-Saharan Africa is enormous. Yet the United States seems willing to put the interests of 25,000 American cotton farmers above that of the global trading system and the well-being of millions in the developing world. It is understandable if those in the developing world respond with anger.

The anger is increased by America's almost cynical attitude in "marketing" its offers. For instance, at the Hong Kong meeting, U.S. trade officials reportedly offered to eliminate import restrictions on cotton but refused to do anything about subsidies. The cotton subsidies actually allow the U.S. to export cotton. When a country can export a particular commodity, it does little good to allow imports of that commodity. America, to great fanfare, has made an offer worth essentially zero to the developing countries and berated them for not taking it up on its "generous" offer.

At home, the Bush administration might be working harder to provide greater access to low-cost drugs. In trade negotiations, though, it takes the side of drug companies, arguing for stronger intellectual property protection, even if the protection of pharmaceutical-company patents means unnecessary deaths for hundreds of thousands of people who cannot afford the monopoly prices but could be treated if generic medicines were made available.

The international community has announced its commitment to helping the developing countries reduce poverty by half by 2015. There have been enormous efforts at increasing aid and debt relief. But developing countries do not want just a hand out; they want a hand up. They need and want enhanced opportunities for earning a living. That is what a true development round would provide.

In short, trade liberalization should be "asymmetric," but it needs to be asymmetric in a precisely opposite way to its present configuration. Today, liberalization discriminates against developing countries. It needs to discriminate in their favor. Europe has shown the way by opening up its economy to the poorest countries of the world in an initiative called Everything But Arms. Partly because of complicated regulations ("rules of origin"), however, the amount of increased trade that this policy has led to has been very disappointing thus far. Because agriculture is still highly subsidized and restricted, some call the policy "Everything But Farms." There is a need for this initiative to be broadened. Doing this would help the poor enormously and cost the rich little. In fact, the advanced industrial countries as a whole would be better off, and special interests in these countries would suffer.

There is, in fact, a broad agenda of trade liberalization (going well beyond agriculture) that would help the developing countries. But trade is too important to be left to trade ministers. If the global trade regime is to reflect common shared values, then negotiations over the terms of that trade regime cannot be left to ministers who, at least in most countries, are more beholden to corporate and special interests than almost any other ministry. In the last round, trade ministers negotiated over the terms of the intellectual property agreement. This is a subject of enormous concern to almost everyone in today's society. With excessively strong intellectual property rights, one can have monopolies raising prices and stifling innovation. Poor countries will not have access to life-saving medicines. That was why both the Office of Science and Technology Policy and the Council of Economic Advisers opposed the TRIPS (intellectual property) provisions of the Uruguay

Round. It reflected the interests of America's drug and entertainment industries, not the most important producers of knowledge, those in academia. And it certainly did not reflect the interests of users, either in the developed or less-developed countries. But the negotiations were conducted in secret, in Geneva. The U.S. trade representative (like most other trade ministers) was not an expert in intellectual property; he received his short course from the drug companies, and he quickly learned how to espouse their views. The agreement reflected this one-sided perspective.

Several reforms in the structure of trade talks are likely to lead to better outcomes. The first is that the basic way in which trade talks are approached should be changed. Now, it is a clear negotiation. Each country seeks to get the best deal for its firms. This stands in marked contrast to how legislation in all other arenas of public policy is approached. Typically, we ask what our objectives are, and how we can best achieve them. Around those themes, of course, there are negotiations. There are often large differences in views both about what should be the objectives and how best to achieve them. If we began trade talks from this position of debate and inquiry, we could arrive at a picture of what a true development round look like.

Thinking of the task of the WTO as creating a legal framework reflecting principles of fairness, social justice and efficiency – akin to how we think about domestic rules and regulations governing economic behavior – helps us think about what other reforms are needed. We simply need to think about how we attempt to improve the quality of domestic democratic processes and legislation by increasing, for instance, transparency and other governance reforms.

Transparency is essential so there can be more open debate about the merits of various proposals and a chance to put a check on the abuses special interests. Clearly, had there been more transparency and open debate, the excesses in intellectual property protection of the Uruguay Round might have been avoided.

As more and more countries have demanded a voice in trade negotiations, there is often nostalgia for the old system in which four partners (the U.S., EU, Canada and Japan) could hammer out a deal. There are complaints that the current system with so many members is simply unworkable. We have learned how to deal with this problem in other contexts, however, using the principles of representation. We must form a governing council with representatives of various "groups" – a group of the least developed countries, of the agricultural exporting countries, etc. Each representative makes sure that the concerns of his or her constituency are heard. Such a system would be far better than the current "green room" procedures wherein certain countries are put together (in the green room) to negotiate a whole or part of the deal.

Finally, trade talks need to have more focus. Issues like intellectual property should never even have been part of the Uruguay Round. There already was an international institution dealing with matters of intellectual property. It is not only that trade ministers are ill-equipped to understand what is at issue, and they are therefore subject to undue influence from the special interests that have long held sway over trade ministries. Broadening the agenda also puts developing countries at a particular disadvantage, because they do not have the resources to engage on a broad front of issues.

The most important changes are, however, not institutional changes, but changes in mindset. There should be an effort on the part of each of the countries to think about what kind of international rules and regulations would contribute to a global trading system that would be fair and efficient, and that would promote development.

Fifteen years ago, there was a great deal of optimism about the benefits which globalization and trade would bring to all countries. It has brought enormous benefits to some countries; but not to all. Some have even been made worse off. Development is hard enough. An unfair trade regime makes it even more difficult. Reforming the WTO would not guarantee that we would get a fair and efficient global trade regime, but it would enhance the chances that trade and globalization come closer to living up to their potential for enhancing the welfare of everyone.

REVIEW AND DISCUSSION QUESTIONS

1 Why does Stiglitz believe that the global trading system benefits the rich more than the poor?
2 Under what circumstances, according to Stiglitz, will trade liberalization hurt the poor in developing countries?
3 How does Stiglitz feel about agreements to protect intellectual property rights?
4 What changes in the way trade talks are structured does Stiglitz recommend? What is his rationale?
5 Do you agree with Stiglitz's critique of trade liberalization? Why or why not? Explain.

Chapter 41

Martin Feldstein

ARGENTINA'S FALL

Argentina's fall; lessons from the latest financial crisis

ARGENTINA'S 35 MILLION CITIZENS will not be the only ones to pay a heavy price for that country's latest economic crisis. The fallout may also radically alter economic policies and political relations both within Latin America and with the United States. It is already clear that Argentina will reverse at least some of the favorable economic reforms introduced by President Carlos Menem in the early 1990s. Although Menem's reforms are not responsible for the current chaos, they are a politically convenient scapegoat. Blaming them also provides a rationale for renationalizing Argentine firms, erecting barriers to imports and foreign investment, and increasing government spending.

The current crisis will weaken the prospects for the Mercosur trading arrangement among Argentina and its neighbors (Brazil, Paraguay, and Uruguay) and may kill any chance of a general Free Trade Area of the Americas. Many Argentines are already blaming their troubles on Washington, claiming that U.S. policies got them into this mess and that the United States then abandoned Argentina because, unlike Turkey, it is not of geopolitical significance.

If other emerging-market governments misinterpret Argentina's experience, they too might move away from the promarket policies that hold the best promise of raising future living standards. Gaining a better understanding of the real reasons for the Argentine crisis is therefore essential. Doing so might help Argentina and other emerging countries avoid making the wrong policy choices in the future and reduce the risk of further financial crises.

Pegged all wrong

An overvalued fixed exchange rate (locked at one peso per dollar since 1991) and an excessive amount of foreign debt were the two proximate causes of the Argentine crisis.

Because the exchange rate was fixed at too high a level, Argentina exported too little and imported too much. This trade imbalance made it impossible for the country to earn the foreign exchange it needed to pay the interest on its foreign debt. Instead, Argentina had to borrow to meet those interest payments, causing the debt to grow ever larger. The country's foreign debt, most of which was owed by the central and provincial governments, eventually reached 50 percent of GDP by late 2001 and included $30 billion due in 2002. Once it finally became clear that Argentina could no longer borrow to roll over those debts and pay the interest, Buenos Aires was forced to default and to devalue the peso.

Although the devalued peso will eventually raise Argentine exports, in the near term the weakening of the currency will cause widespread bankruptcies. This is because most local businesses borrowed in dollars. A company that took a loan for one million dollars expected to repay it with one million pesos. But if the peso is devalued by 50 percent, the firm will have to find two million pesos to repay its obligation. Companies unable to afford such an increase in the peso value of their debt will wind up in bankruptcy. Corporate failures will then weigh heavily on the Argentine banks and may cause them to collapse too. The country's already high unemployment rate will increase as a result.

The havoc that an overvalued exchange rate and excessive foreign debt caused in Argentina is certainly not unique. These two conditions, either singly or together, have been the cause of every currency crisis during at least the past 25 years. Similarly, the painful effect that dollar-denominated debt can have when a sharp devaluation occurs was dramatically demonstrated in several Southeast Asian countries during the late 1990s. All of this was well known to Argentine economists and policymakers. Why then did they allow the crisis to develop? Why did Argentina not end its fixed link to the dollar several years ago, allowing the peso to float down to a more competitive level that could improve the trade balance and start to shrink its foreign debts? Had Buenos Aires done so, the current crisis would probably have been avoided.

Greenbacked

The reason Argentina retained its fixed exchange rate too long is fairly simple, however: such a peg had cured hyperinflation at the end of the 1980s and brought a decade of price stability that provided the framework for strong economic growth. Policy officials feared that breaking the link to the dollar would bring back high inflation and all of the accompanying economic problems of the 1970s and 1980s.

This fear seemed justified. After all, at the beginning of the 1990s – before the currency was pegged – consumer prices in Argentina were rising at a rate of 200 percent per month, or more than 5,000 percent per year. Markets ceased to function and productivity declined. Street riots led President Raul Alfonsin to step down sooner than normal after the election of his successor, Carlos Menem. With his economy minister, Domingo Cavallo, Menem moved Argentina from an internationally isolated and state-dominated economy to one that encouraged foreign trade and investments and privatized state-owned industries.

In taking such steps, Argentina followed the lead of Chile and Mexico as well as the Southeast Asian nations, all of which had shown that such liberalization would lead to strong economic growth. Argentina's response was thus no exception. Buenos Aires' new policies caused the country's economy to grow at a real rate of more than 7 percent a year from 1991 to 1994, one of the highest growth rates anywhere during those years.

Argentina went further than any of those other countries, however, when it enacted a "convertibility law" that pegged the peso to the dollar at a one-to-one exchange rate and stipulated that everyone had the right to convert as many pesos to dollars as they wanted. To give credibility to that promise, the government provided that each peso in circulation would have to be backed by a dollar (or similar hard currency) at the central bank, the so-called currency board system.

If Menem and Cavallo's strategy had succeeded, Argentina today would be enjoying strong growth, low inflation, and financial stability. The fixed exchange rate could have succeeded, however, only if the peso became competitive enough to generate more exports than imports, so that the net foreign-exchange earnings could be used to pay interest on the outstanding international debt. Although the one-to-one exchange rate made Argentine products uncompetitively expensive, this could still have been remedied if productivity had risen faster than wages, permitting Argentine prices to decline relative to those abroad. Cavallo correctly foresaw that the combination of low inflation and market liberalization would lead to a rapid growth of productivity. Although this was sufficient at first to lead to both rising real wages and increased international competitiveness, eventually rigid labor laws and strong union pressures prevented the further reduction in production costs that Argentina needed to become competitive.

The pegged exchange rate prevented the adjustment necessary to shrink the current-account deficit, but the combination of the currency peg and the rule against creating pesos without foreign-exchange backing did achieve the price stability that was its original purpose. To the average Argentine, the convertibility law made a peso "as good as a dollar"; the two were fully interchangeable in everyday transactions.

Warning signs

Not everyone was convinced that the peso would remain fixed, however. Some worried about what would happen if investors who saw Argentina's rising current-account deficit and its increasing foreign debt became nervous and wanted to convert their pesos to dollars. (See, for instance, my skeptical comments about the currency board system in my "Self-Help Guide for Emerging Markets," Foreign Affairs, March/April 1999.) Although the government had enough dollars at the central bank to back the currency in circulation, it didn't have nearly enough to cover the total amount in checking and savings accounts that individuals might want to convert.

Still, in principle that disparity was not a problem. The currency board rules ensured that as individuals began to convert their pesos into dollars, the central bank would shrink the money supply and cause interest rates to rise sharply. Long before the central bank ran out of dollars, the interest rates on peso deposits would get so high that people would be encouraged to keep their funds in pesos. In that way, the central bank would never exhaust its supply of dollars. Moreover, the high interest rates would weaken domestic demand, causing wages and prices to fall until the peso became competitive again, eliminating the reason for the original investor nervousness.

Although this logic seemed impeccable, a problem remained. If the government was not willing to push interest rates high enough to prevent speculation because of the damage that those high rates would do to the economy, and if wages did not fall sufficiently in response to economic weakness, the current-account deficit would remain and investors would lose confidence in the exchange rate's long-term viability.

Cavallo hoped that the currency board would never be put to this test. In his view, the productivity gains that he foresaw would make Argentine goods competitive internationally. Once confidence in the peso became established, sound monetary policy would then prevent inflation – even if the peso were allowed to float. Ideally, the shift from the pegged rate system to a floating rate would occur when the peso was undervalued, causing the peso to rise when the peg was ended, thereby giving a further boost to price stability.

Pressure building

Unfortunately, these conditions never occurred. Wage increases kept the cost of production in Argentina high, depressing exports and encouraging imports. Argentina's competitiveness worsened as the dollar strengthened relative to most other currencies, pulling the peso up with it. The dollar rose sharply against the Japanese yen after 1995, against the currencies of Southeast Asia after their crises of 1997 and 1998, and against the European currencies in 1999 and 2000. The terms of trade also moved against Argentina, with world prices for its exports declining relative to the prices of its imports. But the biggest blow to Argentine competitiveness came when Brazil's currency, the real, fell sharply in 1999.

To keep the peso-dollar peg intact as the economy became less competitive, Buenos Aires tightened macroeconomic policy, raising interest rates and pushing the economy into recession. But despite unemployment rates of close to 15 percent, wages did not decline and competitiveness did not improve. The fixed exchange rate made it impossible to increase competitiveness by a traditional currency devaluation (as a variety of countries did, ranging from the United Kingdom in 1992 to South Korea in 1998 and Brazil in 1999) and the resistance of unions to lower wages prevented a fall in production costs that could have achieved the same real devaluation without a change in the exchange rate.

The inevitable result was increasing current-account deficits, which reached nearly five percent of GDP, and therefore mounting foreign debt. The growth of the foreign debt also reflected the combination of low private savings rates, which reduced the domestic pool of investment, and substantial deficits in the budgets of the central and provincial governments. These budget deficits were due to widespread tax evasion and to an inability to control government spending, particularly at the provincial level. The provincial deficits continued despite a constitutional rule requiring revenue sharing, which turned any increase in central government tax revenue into an extra source of finance for provincial spending. Even with these funds, the provinces still required financing through substantial capital inflows from abroad.

As the debt grew, the interest rate that Argentina had to pay foreign creditors also rose, further increasing the annual imbalance and accelerating the growth of the foreign debt. Default became unavoidable. When Argentina finally defaulted on $155 billion of central and provincial government debt in December 2001, it was the largest sovereign debt default ever.

Peg headed?

Sophisticated Argentines and foreign investors knew that the peso had to be devalued if future current-account deficits were to be reduced without a continued massive recession. The convertibility law allowed them to shift pesos into dollars and then to take the dollars out of the country. The result was a loss of dollar reserves at the Argentine central bank, making it all the more likely that a devaluation would be necessary. Although a loan from the International Monetary Fund (IMF) in 2001 gave a temporary boost to confidence that stemmed the run on the central bank, this lasted only a few months and the peso was devalued sharply in January 2002.

Why did Argentina not devalue sooner – in 1997, 1998, or even 1999 – so that the default could have been avoided, the devaluation smaller, and the adverse effects of devaluation on domestic firms and banks limited? There were three reasons. First was a fear that breaking the peg and devaluing the peso would bring back the high rates of inflation that had plagued the economy before the two currencies were tied. Brazil's experience in 1999 had shown that a country with a long history of high inflation could abandon a fixed exchange rate and avoid inflation by an explicit "inflation targeting" approach to monetary policy – i.e., raising interest rates whenever inflation increased above a low "target" rate. But Argentina's history and the centrality of the convertibility law understandably made officials nervous that its inflation was more sensitive to any departure from the fixed peg.

Second, because Argentine households and businesses had so much dollar-denominated debt, the government feared that a devaluation would prompt widespread bankruptcies and personal defaults by raising the peso value of outstanding debts. This problem would also affect the central and provincial governments themselves, which also had large dollar-denominated debts to foreign creditors that would become more of a burden after devaluation, since tax revenue was collected in pesos.

Finally, there was always the hope that the situation would improve over time. The large U.S. trade deficit suggested that the dollar might experience a sharp decline relative to the yen and the European currencies. If that happened, Argentine products would become much more competitive internationally. But that did not happen. The dollar (and therefore the peso) continued to strengthen in 2000 and 2001.

What was the role of the IMF in all of this? Critics of the fund charge three things: its staff did not adequately warn Argentina of the danger of its policies; it forced Argentina to adopt contractionary policies that led to three years of recession before the crisis hit; and it encouraged the continuation of bad policies by providing a series of large loans.

In reality, the Argentines understood the risk that they were taking at least as well as the IMF staff did. Theirs was a calculated risk that might have produced good results. It is true, however, that the IMF staff did encourage Argentina to continue with the fixed exchange rate and currency board. Although the IMF and virtually all outside economists believe that a floating exchange rate is preferable to a "fixed but adjustable" system, in which the government recognizes that it will have to devalue occasionally, the IMF (as well as some outside economists) came to believe that the currency board system of a firmly fixed exchange rate (a "hard peg," in the jargon of international finance) is a viable long-term policy for an economy. Argentina's experience has proved that belief wrong.

The contractionary policies that Argentina pursued during the past few years were exactly what the currency board system required. They may have been bad and painful policies, but they were inherent in the currency board approach. The real problem with the IMF "conditionality" in Argentina is that it did not achieve the changes that were really needed, especially the changes in such things as the constitutional revenue-sharing rule and the level of provincial spending that continued to contribute to the budget deficit.

The multi-billion-dollar loans that the IMF gave to Argentina, furthermore, permitted Buenos Aires to postpone dealing with its fundamental problems and abandoning the currency board. The IMF clung too long to the belief that the currency board system was viable. It also wanted to show support for Argentina because of that country's previous shift to favorable market-oriented policies. It should be possible, however, for the IMF to show support for a country's promarket reforms without pouring tens of billions of dollars into a losing battle.

Looking ahead

What lessons can be learned from the Argentine experience? First, a fixed exchange-rate system, even one based on a currency board or other "hard" fix, is a bad idea that is likely to lead to an overvalued exchange rate, a currency crisis, and widespread defaults. A market-determined floating exchange rate is the only way to avoid these problems.

Second, substantial foreign borrowing in dollars is a very risky strategy. This is particularly true of short-term debt but is also a problem with longer-term borrowing. It is a problem regardless of whether the borrower is the government or the private sector. Other forms of capital inflow, in particular portfolio equity investments and direct investments in plant and equipment, do not raise the problems associated with debt.

Third, the opening of the economy to trade, the encouragement of foreign direct investment, and the privatizing of state-owned firms are desirable policies. Those policies did not cause or contribute to Argentina's crisis, and it would be a serious mistake to reverse them now in Argentina or any other emerging market.

REVIEW AND DISCUSSION QUESTIONS

1 How did Argentina's "overvalued fixed exchange rate" contribute to triggering its economic crisis? And how did the devaluation affect Argentina's economy?
2 Why did the depreciation of Brazil's currency contribute to causing the crisis in Argentina?
3 Aside from the problems with the exchange rate, what contributed to triggering the crisis?
4 What role did the International Monetary Fund play in Argentina's crisis?
5 If you were Argentina's president, what would you do to ensure that a similar crisis does not occur again? Explain clearly.

Chapter 42

Jeffrey D. Sachs

HOW TO RUN THE INTERNATIONAL MONETARY FUND

TO: Rodrigo Rato,
         IMF Managing Director

YOU ARE TAKING OVER the International Monetary Fund (IMF) at a critical
moment. A decade ago, globalization looked like a sure winner. Expanding world
markets and global cooperation, many thought, would extend prosperity and foster peace.
But today, the world is at war. The gap between the richest and poorest people is
wider than ever. The vaunted capacity of economic integration to mitigate extreme poverty
and environmental degradation looks illusory. The world needs effective international
institutions more than ever, yet the legitimacy of the IMF is at a low ebb in many parts of
the world.

From the start, the IMF has lived with a particular tension. It is an international
organization with 184 member countries, and the IMP Articles of Agreement call on it to
represent all of its constituent members. Yet the fund is governed by rich nations, foremost
among them the United States. How you handle this tension will determine your own
success or failure as the new managing director, as well as the continued relevance of the
IMF at a time of enormous international strain. On key issues such as foreign aid, debt
relief, and exchange-rate policy, you must learn to represent the entire world, not just
the U.S. and European governments that put you into your job.

Money talks (and votes)

The way you arrived at the IMF speaks volumes about how the institution functions.
Although your record as minister of economy in the last Spanish government is impressive,
you were not an obvious candidate to lead a global financial institution with major
operational responsibilities in the poorest countries. You were not a leading figure in the

great debates of the past decade regarding the East Asian crisis, the initiative on highly indebted poor countries, capital market liberalization, African poverty, or other issues of central concern to the IMF. Indeed, you owe your job to a nontransparent process in which the richest countries dominate and most of humanity has little say. Still, given your professional skills and the respect you command among your peers, there is widespread hope and anticipation that you will rise to the occasion.

The fund's governance starts with some basic arithmetic. The IMF operates on a voting system based on each country's quota at the fund, rather than a system of one person, one vote (or one country, one vote). The United States, with 5 percent of the population of IMF member countries, controls 17 percent of the vote. Europe has a remarkable 40 percent of the IMF vote, with just 13 percent of the population. China and India comprise 38 percent of the world's population, and just 5 percent of the vote at the fund. Little surprise that the United States and Europe jealously guard their voting powers.

Nothing happens at the fund without the say-so of the United States and Europe. If decisions are by consensus, it is only because developing countries long ago learned not to lock horns with rich nations on matters of financial diplomacy. The IMF, after all, can do great financial damage to unruly countries, causing them to lose not only the resources of the fund, but also those of the World Bank, regional development banks, the Paris Club, the London Club, and private creditors, all of which are influenced by IMF judgments.

The institution prioritizes the interests of rich countries, and especially those of the United States, at every turn. When the United States wisely sought to forestall a Mexican default in early 1995, the IMF was induced to make an emergency loan of unprecedented size. When, on the other hand, the U.S. Treasury was wary of lending to Ecuador in late 1999 following that country's default to private creditors, the IMP withheld a pending loan. That decision helped topple the financially strapped government in Quito in early 2000. When ideologues in the Bush administration wanted to punish an allegedly left-wing government in Haiti, the IMF obligingly froze lending in 2001. Eventually, the Haitian economy crumbled and the elected government was ousted. Either through action or deliberate inaction, the IMF has repeatedly influenced politically charged issues of privatization, trade, and financial market policy in emerging markets at the behest of rich nations.

Countries siding with U.S. geopolitics have a much easier time getting IMF loans and debt relief. Countries labeled ideological opponents, by contrast, have had funding frozen at tremendous cost to their poor citizens. Most shocking, the IMF has asked the poorest of the poor for unconscionable belt-tightening and debt servicing since the early 1980s, because the United States, Japan, and most of the leading creditor countries in Europe showed little interest in extending debt relief or increasing development assistance. Debt relief for the poorest countries has been slow, grudging, and inadequate. The IMF has helped by dressing up fiscal austerity as a macroeconomic necessity.

The lives in your hands

Your new job grants you daily and pervasive influence over billions of people, especially the world's poorest. African governments cannot take a financial step without the blessing of the IMF. If you make mistakes regarding Africa's finances, people don't just suffer, they die. That is not hypothetical. For the last 20 years, the IMF has been the chief enforcer of inhuman austerity conditions imposed on Africa, because the United States could not rouse itself to give Africa more help. The rich countries collect debts from impoverished nations, while pandemic diseases cut life expectancies to half of those in the rich world. Yet wealthy nations have pretended that there is no alternative to this state of affairs.

In recent months, the IMF Executive Board has approved lending programs to Burkina Faso, Democratic Republic of the Congo, Madagascar, Nicaragua, Tanzania, and Sierra Leone, among others. The board knows very little about these countries. Most of the information from the IMF staff that goes to the board is about budget deficits, domestic credit expansion, exchange rates, and inflation – not about AIDS, malaria, malnutrition, deforestation, and drought. A basic disconnect exists between the work of the fund, which obsesses over financial indicators, and reality in much of the world, especially where people live in extreme poverty.

Poor countries need massive investment in the building blocks of economic growth – including physical infrastructure, health systems, and education systems. The IMF should help establish the financial and macroeconomic framework for these investments. I am arguing not for inflationary finance and macroeconomically irresponsible policies, but for sound strategies in which the rich countries contribute much more development assistance to poor and vulnerable nations. The IMF must appreciate that its policymaking is part of a larger reality and that its programs should be judged against a standard higher than whether they produce price stability or a balanced budget. They must be judged on how they support the escape from extreme poverty, the control of pandemic disease, and the positive evolution of the global economic and political system. On all of these counts, the United States and the other leading economic powers have failed, and they have used the IMF as a key instrument in that failure.

More truth, less debt

The financial interests of rich and poor countries are likely to be at odds in at least four areas during your tenure. The most urgent involves the poorest countries in the world, especially in sub-Saharan Africa. The rich countries signed international treaties – including the Millennium Declaration of 2000 and the Monterrey Consensus and Johannesburg Plan of Action in 2002 – committing more financial help to developing countries trying to cut extreme poverty and disease sharply by 2015, as embodied in the Millennium Development Goals (MDGS). Without deeper debt cancellation and much greater development aid, especially from the United States, these goals will not be met.

Under your leadership, will the IMF continue to enforce unconscionable austerity, or will it fulfill its pledge to support the MDGS by telling the truth about the need for much greater aid from the United States and other rich countries? The key step will be for the IMF, in conjunction with the World Bank, the U.N. agencies, and the governments of the poor countries, to insist that the richest nations finally move toward 0.7 percent of gross national product (GNP) in development aid and support well-governed poor countries trying to achieve the MDGS. For the dozens of impoverished states within the IMF, your support for these goals will signal the institution's willingness to confront the greatest economic challenge of our time: the dramatic reduction of extreme poverty.

The debt of emerging-market economies will be your second test. In 2002, IMF management considered a valuable proposal for a new system known as the Sovereign

Debt Restructuring Mechanism. This plan would have finally brought to cases of sovereign debt some of the worthy principles of bankruptcy settlements – including easing the collective action problems that arise when multiple creditors confront an insolvent debtor. When U.S. financial interests balked, however, the U.S. Treasury pulled the plug on the IMF's draft proposals. It behooves you to reopen this discussion and bring it to a more satisfactory conclusion.

Your third area of concern will be the IMF's position on the exchange-rate systems in developing countries. The United States has often politicized exchange-rate questions on mercantilist grounds by calling on other countries to appreciate their currencies vis-à-vis the dollar in order to reduce foreign exports to U.S. markets. For example, Washington pushed Japan away from a much-needed depreciation of the yen during the 1990s, and it is now pressuring China to appreciate the yuan. You should discount the fevered political advice you will get from Capitol Hill and focus on how exchange-rate changes will affect the country in question.

Taming the United States

Potentially the most dangerous problem you will face is the financial instability that will soon result from irresponsible U.S. macroeconomic policies. The Bush administration has nearly done the impossible, converting a budget surplus of more than 2 percent of GNP in 2000 to a budget deficit of 5 percent of GNP this year – a swing of $700 billion in just four years. This transformation occurred through the combination of irresponsible tax cuts, massive increases in military spending, and even a surprising splurge on some domestic social programs.

U.S. fiscal and monetary imbalances could eventually threaten global financial stability. To keep their currencies from appreciating against the dollar, Asian central banks have been accumulating massive foreign exchange reserves. Around $2 trillion now sits in the bulging central banks of China, Japan, Taiwan, South Korea, Hong Kong, Singapore, and India. Meanwhile, the U.S. Federal Reserve continues to run an irresponsibly loose monetary policy, seemingly politicking on behalf of the Bush administration in the run-up to the November elections. The United States is playing with fire: A sharp rise in long-term interest rates, higher inflation, or a plummeting dollar may result.

You must push the United States to quickly improve its fiscal situation. Realistically, Washington must raise taxes, since there is no public support for broad-based spending cuts. Another key step will be for the rest of the world to move progressively and smoothly to a multicurrency reserve system in which the U.S. dollar is no longer the single reserve currency or unit of account. The IMF can play an important advocacy role in this transition. The euro will come into its own as a major global reserve currency. East Asian countries as well will need to diversify their units of account into a more appropriate East Asian basket. South American countries should think more seriously about much closer monetary cooperation and perhaps eventual monetary union within Mercosur, the economic cooperation organization that includes Argentina, Brazil, Paraguay, and Uruguay.

I also urge you to take advantage of the IMF's superb professional staff by fostering internal debate, as well as more symposia, conferences, and outreach. You should support the work of the Independent Evaluation Office, a valuable recent addition to the fund's institutional design that objectively assesses IMF operations. You should also encourage your staff to forge closer relationships with the World Bank and with U.N. agencies such as the United Nations Development Programme, the World Health Organization, and the Food and Agriculture Organization. These organizations know vastly more about economic development and poverty alleviation than does the IMF staff. Finally, it is critical that you increase transparency of the organization, in part by opening board meetings to more scrutiny and public participation. The board is seen as a mysterious cabal – an image that is both unnecessary and debilitating.

The fund has urgent global fiscal and financial responsibilities at a time when globalization itself remains under extreme threat. More than 80 percent of humanity lives in the developing world, and half of the world's population lives on less than two dollars per day. The world wants to know whether globalization works for all or only for the most powerful nations. Representing global interests with professionalism and goodwill will be an enormously tall order. On this task you have my best wishes and strongest hopes for your success.

REVIEW AND DISCUSSION QUESTIONS

1   According to Sachs, what is the major problem with the governing structure of the IMF?
2   Why does Sachs believe that the criteria the IMF uses to make loans to poor countries are in need of reform?
3   According to Sachs, how do recent U.S. macroeconomic policies threaten global financial stability?
4   Do you agree with Sachs's advice on how to run the IMF? Why or why not? Explain.

Suggestions for further reading

Bhagwati, J. (2004) *In Defense of Globalization*, New York: Oxford University Press.

One of the most respected international trade specialists lays out the case in favor of globalization, addressing the many critiques popularized in recent years by the anti-globalization movement. He investigates whether globalization increases child labor in low-income countries, worsens poverty, threatens the environment, or causes financial instability.

Blustein, P. (2003) *The Chastening: Inside the Crisis that Rocked the Global Financial System and Humbled the IMF*, New York: PublicAffairs.

This is a fascinating account of the Asian financial crisis of 1997–98 by one of the best economic journalists in the U.S. The book also addresses some of the international events that followed in the wake of the crisis – namely the Russian bond default and the Long-Term Capital Management rescue in 1998. Blustein looks especially closely at the role of the IMF.

Blustein, P. (2005) *And the Money Kept Rolling In (and Out): Wall Street, the IMF, and the Bankrupting of Argentina*, New York: PublicAffairs.

In this book, Blustein does for the Argentine crisis of 2001–02 what he had done for the Asian financial crisis in his 2003 book. He reports the events leading up to the crisis on the basis of interviews with many of the policy-makers, IMF officials, and other key players in the international financial system, and he offers his own recommendations for preventing similar crises in the future.

Krugman, P. (1997) "In Praise of Cheap Labor: Bad Jobs at Bad Wages are Better than No Jobs at All," *Slate*, 21 March.

In this provocative article, Krugman takes on the critics of globalization, arguing that berating multinationals for paying low wages (by U.S. standards) in developing countries ignores the reality of poverty in such countries. He suggests that multinationals have done more to raise standards of living in poor countries than national or foreign governments.

Rodrik, D. (2007) *One Economics, Many Recipes: Globalization, Institutions, and Economic Growth*, Princeton, NJ: Princeton University Press.

In this book, the Harvard economist expands on the themes he is best known for – especially the idea that countries should not be afraid to build unorthodox development strategies that draw on their domestic strengths and address their particular needs. The book includes a section on economic growth and growth strategies; a section on the role of institutions in development; and a section on globalization.

Rogoff, K. (2002) "An Open Letter to Joseph Stiglitz, author of *Globalization and Its Discontents*." Online. Available HTTP: <http://www.imf.org/external/np/vc/2002/070202.htm> (accessed 1 September 2007).

In this letter, Harvard economist and former IMF economic counselor Kenneth Rogoff provides a vitriolic response to the book by Stiglitz – especially his critique of IMF recommendations during the East Asian crisis.

Stiglitz, J. E. (2002) *Globalization and Its Discontents*, New York: W. W. Norton.

In this controversial book, the Economics Nobel Laureate and former World Bank chief economist discusses the negative effects of globalization, reviewing the financial crises of the late 1990s and criticizing the IMF for "mishandling" these crises. He recommends major changes in international institutions that he believes will make globalization work for the poor.

PART EIGHT

Foreign aid and debt relief

INTRODUCTION

IN 2005, THE WEST AFRICAN COUNTRY OF LIBERIA received $236 million in foreign aid. This amounted to 54.1 percent of the country's gross national income (World Bank 2007: 348–350). Several other countries in sub-Saharan Africa (e.g., Burundi and Congo) received amounts of aid equal to more than one-third of their national income, whereas other, more advanced developing countries (e.g., Peru and Botswana) received less than 1 percent of their national income in aid (ibid.). Foreign aid typically includes grants, or money given to developing countries without expectation of repayment; loans on concessional terms, i.e., loans that carry low interest rates and can be repaid over long periods of time; commodities such as food; and "technical assistance" or "technical cooperation," terms that refer to volunteer or subsidized work that foreign experts and consultants perform to help developing countries. While most rich countries provide aid directly to developing countries, they also do so indirectly, by funding international organizations that specialize in the provision of aid. The World Bank is probably the best known of these organizations. It provides developing countries more than $20 billion a year in grants and loans (World Bank 2006).

On surface, foreign aid seems an ideal tool for helping developing countries reduce poverty: it provides badly needed resources and it comes at low or no cost to the developing countries. Yet, the experience of the last several decades shows that the reality is much more complex. Former World Bank staffer William Easterly has written at length about everything that can go wrong – and has gone wrong – when rich countries and international organizations provide aid to developing countries (see, e.g., Easterly 2001 and 2006). Money given to governments of poor countries may well end up in the pockets of corrupt politicians or be diverted from financing investment projects to paying for unproductive expenses (on weapons or on luxury consumption for the people in power). Aid may also fund investment projects that fail to generate economic growth. A modern factory, for example, will not help development if trained workers are scarce, the power supply is unreliable, and the road connecting the factory to the city is flooded six months a year. Even if aid does promote economic growth, it may still do little to reduce poverty (recall our discussion of growth and poverty in Part Three).

While it is generally accepted that foreign aid can sometimes be ineffective at promoting poverty reduction, some development economists go further, arguing that foreign aid provision may actually *hinder* economic growth and poverty reduction. If policy-makers are incompetent, for instance, and on the verge of being overthrown, the arrival of aid may allow them to stay in power longer than they might otherwise have been able to. Aid may also finance the expansion of ineffective government services, taking workers away from private economic activity that would have likely been more helpful for growth. And systematic aid provision may create "aid dependency," which puts developing countries at risk of economic disruptions when aid falls short. It may also dull incentives – for both recipient countries and aid providers – to put in place more self-reliant development policies (see Perkins et al. 2006: 550–51).

As always, when development economists are unsure about the impact of a certain development policy, they turn to the evidence. A landmark study by the World Bank, in which the institution examined the effectiveness of its own aid programs, seemed to confirm many of the fears of aid skeptics. According to the report, "few cross-country studies have found a robust effect of aid on growth" (World Bank 1998: 14). On average, therefore, foreign aid does not appear to have had a significant impact on the economic growth of recipient countries. The World Bank, however, is quick to emphasize that aid *has* had a significant positive impact on growth in countries with strong institutions (where the rule of law prevails, corruption is low, and public bureaucracy is effective) and sound economic policies (low inflation, low government budget deficits, and openness to international trade).

The article by Center for Global Development researchers Steven Radelet, Michael Clemens, and Rikhil Bhavnani, reprinted in Chapter 43, updates the World Bank study, examining evidence which suggests that the impact of aid cannot be assessed properly without looking at why the aid was given in the first place. The authors remark that much foreign aid is not intended to generate economic growth. Food aid, for example, is given to help consumption, and other types of humanitarian aid are given to provide relief in the case of natural disasters or other emergencies. Aid of this kind is not aimed at promoting economic growth and should not be expected to do so. Other kinds of aid may target economic growth only in the very long run. The authors argue, for example, that aid to pay for improvements in education and health will likely help promote growth, but it will take decades for the impact to be seen in the data (they refer to this as "late-impact aid"). Aid that finances infrastructure such as new roads or power plants, on the other hand, should have a relatively short-term impact on growth ("early-impact aid").

The authors, therefore, use data about different types of aid to test whether there is a differential effect on growth. As expected, they find that humanitarian and late-impact aid are not associated with faster growth over a four-year period, but early-impact aid has a strong positive effect on growth. While the authors also find that this impact tends to be more significant in countries with better institutions – as the original World Bank study had implied – they note that even without such institutions, early-impact aid promotes growth on average. For aid optimists, this result is encouraging. But the debate has hardly been settled. IMF researchers Raghuram Rajan and Arvind Subramanian, for example, repeated the analysis of Radelet, Clemens, and Bhavnani with a different statistical approach and did not find a significant effect of early-impact aid on growth; they also did not find that the quality of institutions made any difference (Rajan and Subramanian 2005; see also Easterly 2005: 44–51).

A concern raised by some economists is that decisions on aid provision are not always based on solid evidence about which programs are more or less likely to promote growth or reduce poverty. In the article reprinted in Chapter 44, MIT economist Abhijit Vinayak Banerjee gives several examples of aid programs that received financing in the absence of any concrete evidence showing that the programs were effective. He notes that observing improvements after the provision of aid is not sufficient to conclude that aid did its job, since we do not know what would have happened if the aid had not been provided. Banerjee recommends, therefore, the use of randomized trials whenever possible. Such trials resemble the ones used by drug manufacturers, who administer a new drug to a sample of patients and a placebo to another sample to find out whether the drug makes a difference. Because the two groups are chosen randomly, differences in outcomes can be safely ascribed to the one consistent difference between the groups – whether participants did or did not take the drug. In a similar vein, if aid is used to pay for a new teaching technique introduced in a random sample of schools and not introduced in a second sample, significantly better performance by the students attending schools in the first group would provide solid evidence that the new technique makes a difference.

Banerjee emphasizes that provision of aid not based on evidence obtained from randomized trials may well be extremely wasteful, as there are often several different interventions that can be used to achieve a certain goal. Randomized trials may show that a relatively cheap intervention is just as effective as a much more expensive one. And while Banerjee is critical of the many aid programs that are not based on solid evidence and often fail to deliver, he is equally critical of the pessimistic view according to which development is largely determined by domestic factors and unlikely to be influenced by aid. Banerjee believes that aid should not be cut but rather refocused toward specific, narrowly defined projects with measurable results.

In a reply to Banerjee's article (reprinted in Chapter 45), Ian Goldin, F. Halsey Rogers, and Nicholas Stern – all of whom are or have been associated with the World Bank – agree that randomized evaluation of aid programs has much potential and needs to be used more systematically. They also point out, however, that randomized trials can only work under certain circumstances. In many cases they are not feasible, ethical, or cost-effective. They also remind us that aid is fungible – once donors give the money, it is very hard for them to control how it is used. In this regard, trying to channel aid toward the narrowly defined projects that Banerjee prefers may not produce the desired results. For instance, money given to pay for a specific new program in primary education may cause the recipient country to move domestic budget funds from primary education to other areas – say, an increase in the salaries of government bureaucrats. In this case, while primary education gets an injection of foreign money but a decrease in domestic allocations – ending up more or less where it started – the provision of aid is really paying for higher government salaries. Donors, therefore, need to accept the limits on their ability to channel aid to narrowly defined projects.

The next two selections address another potential pitfall of foreign aid. After receiving aid in the form of concessional loans for decades, but failing to experience substantial growth, several developing countries have found themselves owing large amounts of money to the World Bank and other international development institutions. This situation has led some economists (as well as a variety of concerned politicians and celebrities, from Bono of the band U2 to the Pope) to argue that these countries are in need of *debt relief*, or of some intervention that will cancel or reduce their debts. The idea of debt relief has generated a significant debate that, in many ways, resembles the broader debate on foreign aid. In the article reprinted in Chapter 46, Jeffrey Sachs makes the case for large-scale debt relief, arguing that for many poor countries saddled by heavy debts, "there is no realistic answer other than 100 percent cancellation of the debts." According to Sachs, government officials in these countries are forced to negotiate short-term debt rescheduling agreements and are prevented from addressing the substantial development problems their populations are encountering, from the spread of HIV/AIDS to childhood malnutrition. Sachs refers to this situation as "bizarre" and "absurd": the poorest countries in the world, which one would imagine to be the recipients of substantial help from the West, are instead asked to pay billions of dollars *to* the West.

William Easterly, however, disagrees with this analysis and warns in the article reprinted in Chapter 47 that "debt relief is a bad deal for the world's poor." Easterly believes that it is naive to expect that poor countries, freed from their debt obligations, will proceed to spend more on education and health; it is more likely that these resources will be spent on programs that do little to reduce poverty. After all, these countries are crushed by debt because the loans they received in the past were not spent on productive endeavors; according to Easterly, there is no reason to expect that things will be any different now. But what if governments in these countries have changed, so that new, more democratic governments are now being held accountable for debt incurred by previous governments? Would it not make sense to give the new governments a fresh start and not hold them responsible for the mistakes of previous regimes? Easterly is not convinced by this argument either. He argues that it is often difficult to know how different the new governments are from the old ones, and he worries that this approach sends developing countries the wrong signal: responsible governments that use loans productively are expected to repay, whereas those that squander the money are given a break. An additional concern of Easterly's is that debt relief reduces the resources available to international development institutions, preventing them from lending money to countries such as China and India, which are not eligible for debt relief but are home to a large share of the world's poor.

The two final selections address foreign aid in a broad sense, suggesting two different approaches that developed countries may follow if they intend to help poor countries. In the article reprinted in Chapter 48, Jeffrey D. Sachs summarizes the key ideas presented in his recent book, *The End of Poverty* (2005). Sachs starts by emphasizing that the goal of eradicating poverty in developing countries is within reach: the tremendous declines in poverty experienced in India and China over the past two or three decades show that rapid improvements in standards of living are possible. In fact, Sachs goes so far as to argue that it would be possible to eliminate poverty worldwide by 2025. He stresses, however, that such a goal cannot be reached without a substantial increase in targeted government investments – investments aimed at helping poor countries overcome geographical disadvantages that doom them to a "poverty trap." According to Sachs's estimations, if rich countries committed to providing just 0.7 percent of their gross national product in foreign aid every year, there would be enough resources to carry out such investments and lift a billion people out of poverty. Addressing the skeptics who point to the rather dismal record of foreign aid, Sachs makes it clear that aid will be effective only if delivered in the right way. He recommends disbursing resources "directly to villages and towns to minimize the chances of their getting diverted by central governments."

Sachs also explains the need to start practicing "clinical economics," or a new kind of development economics not unlike modern medicine. A doctor treating a sick patient does not just throw a random handful of medicines at her hoping that she will get better; similarly, rich countries should not expect to fix poverty in developing countries by throwing aid money at them. Effective treatment starts with an accurate history of the patient and an understanding of the causes of the illness, which can lead to a precise and individualized diagnosis and treatment plan. In a similar vein, development economists need to come up with careful diagnoses of the obstacles to development that different countries are facing; this is the first step to designing aid-financed programs tailored to the needs of specific countries. In short, Sachs's view is that we should not be discouraged by foreign aid's limited past success. Past failures simply indicate that we need to do a better job at designing effective aid-financed programs – not that we should give up on them. Sachs believes that the opportunity of our generation is too extraordinary to pass up: "Our generation is heir to two and a half centuries of economic progress. We can realistically envision a world without extreme poverty by the year 2025 because technological progress enables us to meet basic human needs on a global scale and to achieve a margin above basic needs unprecedented in history" (2005: 347).

A different view of how to eliminate poverty worldwide comes from Nancy Birdsall, Dani Rodrik, and Arvind Subramanian in the article reprinted in Chapter 49. These economists challenge two of the key assumptions made by those who preach massive increases in aid: first, that rich countries can "shape development in the poor world"; and second, that the key issue is one of transferring resources from rich to poor countries (or providing poor countries with opportunities to trade). The authors believe that developed countries cannot take the destiny of developing countries in their own hands. They point to evidence showing that domestic initiative rather than external support is responsible for most success stories in economic development. China, Vietnam, and India received little aid or trade preferences, yet they experienced dramatic growth and poverty reduction "by enacting creative domestic reforms." Nicaragua and Mexico, on the other hand, benefited from substantial aid and preferential trade agreements, but were unable to make comparable progress. The authors blame the lack of domestic institutions conducive to growth in the latter countries. Not surprisingly, the debate over geography and institutions, discussed in Part Two, reemerges in these contributions: where Sachs sees geography as holding back development and requiring investments financed from abroad, Birdsall and her co-authors believe that foreign aid will not help overcome geographical obstacles if developing countries lack the institutions that allow aid to be used productively.

In emphasizing the role of domestic initiative, Birdsall, Rodrik, and Subramanian also point to the need for a less dogmatic approach to development policies (echoing Sachs's position about the need for "individualized diagnoses"). They believe that while countries with successful development policies do share a few common characteristics – e.g., macroeconomic stability and market-based incentives – there must be room for each country to come up with its own policies, and development institutions like the World Bank should not expect all countries to fit a standardized development model. The authors argue that most successful development experiences have involved "creative – and often heterodox – policy innovations." They use the example of South Korea and Taiwan, which engaged in international trade but also adopted high tariffs and export subsidies, and China, which turned its socialist planned economy into a more market-oriented economy gradually, rejecting Western advice to push through swift and comprehensive reforms.

If massive foreign aid is not the answer and domestically generated reforms are crucial for development, what role, if any, should rich countries play in helping poor countries on the path to development? The authors make three key recommendations. First, developed countries need to take a tougher stand toward corrupt governments in LDCs, so as to provide incentives for institutional improvement. Second, they need to sponsor technological advances that benefit developing countries directly (e.g., invest in the development of pharmaceuticals to treat tropical diseases and new crops that might generate a second "Green Revolution"). Third, rich countries need to make it easier for unskilled workers in developing countries to migrate to developed countries for short periods of time. Such migration can provide a tremendous boost to the incomes of workers from developing countries and allow them to return home with "experience, entrepreneurship, funds to invest, and an increased work ethic."

The debate about the role of foreign aid and the most effective approaches to end world poverty is as lively as ever. Perhaps what is different today is the greater sense that significant strides in poverty reduction are within reach. The dramatic recent economic progress that Asian countries have been experiencing and our increasing knowledge of what works and what does not in development economics make us hopeful: even developing areas such as sub-Saharan Africa, where enormous obstacles to development remain, might soon be finding their path to higher standards of living. To attempt to illuminate that path, development economists can only continue to collect and analyze evidence, think of creative ways to apply the tools of economics to the reality of poor countries, and keep in mind that few endeavors are as worthy of hard work and commitment as "the expansion of the capabilities of people to lead the kind of life they have reason to cherish" (Sen 1995: 9).

REFERENCES

Easterly, W. (2001) *The Elusive Quest for Growth: Economists' Adventures and Misadventures in the Tropics*, Cambridge, MA: MIT Press.
—— (2006) *The White Man's Burden: Why the West's Efforts to Aid the Rest Have Done So Much Ill and So Little Good*, New York: Penguin Press.
Perkins, D. H., Radelet, S., and Lindauer, D. (2006) *Economics of Development*, 6th edn, New York: W. W. Norton.

Rajan, R. G. and Subramanian, A. (2005) *Aid and Growth: What Does the Cross-Country Evidence Really Show?*, Cambridge, MA: NBER Working Paper 11513.

Sachs, J. (2005) *The End of Poverty: Economic Possibilities for Our Time*, New York: Penguin Press.

Sen, A. (1995) "Economic Development and Social Change: India and China in Comparative Perspectives," Development Economics Research Programme Working Paper No. 67, STICERD, London School of Economics and Political Science.

World Bank (1998) *Assessing Aid: What Works, What Doesn't, and Why*, New York: Oxford University Press.

—— (2006) *The World Bank Annual Report 2006*. Online. Available HTTP: <http://web.worldbank.org/WBSITE/EXTERNAL/EXTABOUTUS/EXTANNREP/EXTANNREP2K6/0,,menuPK:2838586~pagePK:64168427~piPK:64168435~theSitePK:2838572,00.html> (accessed 4 June 2007).

—— (2007) *World Development Indicators 2007*, Washington, DC: World Bank.

Chapter 43

Steven Radelet, Michael Clemens, and Rikhil Bhavnani

AID AND GROWTH

CONTROVERSIES ABOUT AID EFFECTIVENESS go back decades. Critics such as Milton Friedman, Peter Bauer, and William Easterly have leveled stinging critiques, charging that aid has enlarged government bureaucracies, perpetuated bad governments, enriched the elite in poor countries, or just been wasted. They cite widespread poverty in Africa and South Asia despite three decades of aid, and point to countries that have received substantial aid yet have had disastrous records – such as the Democratic Republic of the Congo, Haiti, Papua New Guinea, and Somalia. In their eyes, aid programs should be dramatically reformed, substantially curtailed, or eliminated altogether.

Supporters counter that these arguments, while partially correct, are overstated. Jeffrey Sachs, Joseph Stiglitz, Nicholas Stern, and others have argued that, although aid has sometimes failed, it has supported poverty reduction and growth in some countries and prevented worse performance in others. They believe that many of the weaknesses of aid have more to do with donors than recipients, especially since much aid is given to political allies rather than to support development. They point to a range of successful countries that have received significant aid such as Botswana, Indonesia, Korea, and, more recently, Tanzania and Mozambique, along with successful initiatives such as the Green Revolution, the campaign against river blindness, and the introduction of oral rehydration therapy. In the 40 years since aid became widespread, they say, poverty indicators have fallen in many countries worldwide, and health and education indicators have risen faster than during any other 40-year period in human history.

Throughout this debate, however, most analysts have missed a critical point by treating all aid as if it were alike in its impact on growth. In a recent Center for Global Development study, we try to rectify this gap by exploring the impact on growth of aid flows that actually are aimed at growth.

Three prevailing views on aid

Over the past three decades, three broad views have emerged on the relationship between aid and growth:

Aid has no effect on growth, and may actually undermine growth. There are several reasons why aid might not support growth. It can be wasted on frivolous expenses such as limousines or presidential palaces, or it can encourage corruption. It can undermine incentives for private sector production, including by causing the currency to appreciate, which weakens the profitability of tradable goods production (an effect known as "Dutch disease"). Similarly, food aid, if not managed appropriately, can reduce farm prices and hurt farmer income. Aid flows potentially can undermine incentives for both private and government saving. They can also sustain bad governments in power, helping to perpetuate poor economic policies and postpone reform.

This view has been supported by a range of empirical studies, mostly published from the early 1970s through the mid-1990s. While these studies have been influential, many are of questionable quality, especially using today's research standards. For example, most assume only a simple linear relationship between aid and growth in which each new dollar of aid has exactly the same impact on growth as the first (eliminating the possibility of diminishing returns) and ignore possible endogeneity (in which faster growth might attract higher aid, or both might be caused by something else), among other issues. A recent paper by Raghuram Rajan and Arvind Subramanian (2005), which also assumes a simple linear relationship for most of its results, stands in sharp contrast to the bulk of recent research on the issue, as discussed below.

Aid has a positive relationship with growth on average (although not in every country), but with diminishing returns. Aid could support growth by financing investment or by increasing worker productivity (for example, through investments in health or education). It can bring new technology or knowledge, either imbedded in capital goods imports or through technical assistance. Several early studies found a positive relationship between aid and growth, but this strand of the literature took a significant turn in the mid-1990s when researchers began to investigate whether aid might spur growth with diminishing returns – that is, that the impact of additional aid would decline as aid amounts grew. Oddly, since economic theory and research had recognized the importance of diminishing returns on investment since the 1950s, research on aid and growth until the mid-1990s tested only a linear relationship, a specification that (surprisingly) persists in some studies even today.

Although they have received comparatively less popular attention, most of these studies (some published in top peer-reviewed journals) have found a strong aid-growth relationship, including research by Michael Hadjimichael and colleagues at the IMF in the mid-1990s, and the work of Carl-Johan Dalgaard, Henrik Hansen, Finn Tarp, Robert Lensink, Howard White, and others between 1999 and 2005. These studies typically do not conclude that aid has always worked, but rather that, on average, higher aid flows have been associated with more rapid growth.

Aid has a conditional relationship with growth, helping to accelerate growth only under certain circumstances. The "conditional" view usually argues that aid effectiveness hinges on either recipient characteristics or donor practices.

Recipient country characteristics. World Bank researchers Jonathon Isham, Daniel Kaufmann, and Lant Pritchett opened this line of enquiry in 1995 by finding that World Bank projects had higher rates of returns in countries with stronger civil liberties. Craig Burnside and David Dollar followed with their influential study that concluded that aid stimulated growth in countries with good policies, but not otherwise. Others have proposed different characteristics that might affect the aid-growth relationship, including vulnerability to trade shocks, climate, institutional quality, political conflict, and geography. The statistical results of these studies tend to be fragile, however, and subsequent research has questioned some of the results.

Nevertheless, the view that aid works best (or in a stronger version, aid works only) in countries with good policies and institutions has become the conventional wisdom among donors, partly based on this research and partly due to development practitioners' own experiences. The appeal of this approach is that it can explain why aid seems to have supported growth in some countries but not others. This reasoning has had an enormous impact on donors, especially the multilateral development banks, and is the foundation of the U.S. Millennium Challenge Account (Radelet, 2003).

Donor practices. Multilateral aid might be more effective than bilateral aid, and untied aid is thought to have higher returns than aid tied to purchases in the donor country. Donors with large bureaucracies, heavy reporting requirements, or ineffective monitoring and evaluation systems probably undermine the effectiveness of their own programs. Two influential and overlapping views argue that aid is more effective when donors allow for greater "country ownership" or broader "participation" in setting priorities and designing programs (country ownership allows for the recipient country to have a stronger say in these decisions; broader participation allows civil society and faith-based and non-governmental organizations to have a voice alongside the government in these choices). These issues have been regularly debated and have begun to change donor practices, but have been subject to little systematic research.

The type of aid matters

New research has taken a different tack by exploring the idea that not all aid is alike in its impact on growth. This view suggests that most research on aid and growth is flawed regarding both substance and timing. On substance, almost all studies look at the relationship between total aid and growth, even though large portions of aid are not primarily directed at growth. For example, food and humanitarian aid are aimed primarily at supporting consumption, not growth, as is the provision of medicines, bed nets, and school books. And aid to support democracy or judicial reform is not primarily aimed at stimulating growth. These important aid-financed activities help improve recipient welfare by supporting basic consumption needs, developing political institutions, and strengthening health and education – but they are likely to affect growth only indirectly, if at all. By contrast, aid to build roads, bridges, or telecommunications facilities or to support agriculture and industry is more directly aimed at production and should be expected to accelerate growth. Given the range of likely impacts of different kinds of aid, it is not surprising that some research on aid and growth has shown a weak relationship.

On timing, most cross-country growth research uses panel data, with each observation (usually) corresponding to four years, but then investigates aid flows that cannot possibly affect growth in that period. Aid to support education and health, for example, may stimulate growth, but the impact is likely to take decades. One option for researchers is to use a longer time period, but there is a trade-off: the longer the time period, the harder it is to isolate the impact of aid (or other variables) on growth from other influences. Only a few studies have explored this idea, and most focus on specific countries. For example, one study found that household welfare in Zimbabwe was increased by "development aid" (such as infrastructure and agricultural extension) far more than by "humanitarian aid" (such as food aid and emergency transfers).

To remedy this weakness, our recent research focuses on the type of aid that is directed primarily at growth (Clemens, Radelet, and Bhavnani, 2004). We examined aid flows to 67 countries between 1974 and 2001 and divided aid into three categories:

(1) Aid for disasters, emergencies, and humanitarian relief efforts; including food aid. Here we find a negative simple relationship, since disasters simultaneously cause growth to fall and aid to increase. The recent tsunami undermined growth in Sri Lanka, and donors responded with more aid. In a simplistic growth regression, cases like this would show up as high aid with low or negative growth, making it appear that aid had a poor relationship with growth, an obviously misleading result.

Method matters

In conducting our empirical research, we focused on three issues: (1) ensuring the basic; model was consistent with theory and evidence; (2) controlling for the possible two-way relationship between aid and growth; and (3) testing the results with a broad yet reasonable set of robustness checks.

At the core of our model is a nonlinear relationship between "early impact" aid and growth that allows for diminishing returns: each additional dollar of aid has a smaller impact on growth than the last. This specification is consistent with both theory and extensive evidence, but it is often overlooked in the literature, giving rise to the weak relationships found in some studies. We then control for a wide variety of other factors that influence growth, including income level, institutional quality, trade policy, inflation, budget deficits, life expectancy, location in the tropics, and the incidence of civil war. Our results show that each of these variables is strongly related to growth, with the exceptions of initial income and budget deficits.

A positive relationship between aid and growth does not prove causality. More aid could cause higher growth, but faster growth could attract more aid, or both could be caused by something else (such as a change in government). To control for potential endogeneity, we estimate the relationship using instrumental variables, using as instruments geopolitical variables and past aid flows that have been used in previous peer-reviewed journal articles. But since no instrumentation strategy is perfect, we also estimate the model using ordinary least squares with aid lagged one four-year period, and find essentially the same results.

We further test the robustness of the results by examining differences rather than levels, eliminating outlier observations, estimating the model using the generalized method of moments procedure, controlling for more or fewer variables, and examining alternative definitions for key variables, among other tests. The results hold firm across this array of tests, giving us confidence in the robustness of the results.

(2) Aid that might affect growth, but indirectly and over a long period of time. No one would expect aid aimed at environmental conservation or democratic reform to affect economic growth quickly, and certainly not over a four-year period. Similarly, aid to strengthen health and education is likely to affect labor productivity over many years, but not immediately (with some exceptions). In a standard cross-country growth regression, these observations are likely to appear as high aid and zero or very little growth, again weakening the results. As expected, we detect only a weak positive association between this "late-impact" aid and growth.

(3) Aid aimed more directly to support growth relatively quickly. Aid to build infrastructure – roads, irrigation systems, electricity generators, and ports – should affect growth rates fairly quickly. So should aid to directly support productive sectors, such as agriculture, industry, trade, and services. Aid that comes as cash, such as budget or balance of payments support, could be spent on a wide variety of activities, but to be conservative we assume it is directed at growth (to the extent it is not, our assumption would only weaken our results). For this "early impact" aid (which accounts for about half of all aid), it is perfectly reasonable for policymakers to expect, and for researchers to test for, a positive relationship with growth over a four-year period.

Early impact aid boosts growth

Our research shows a strong, positive, and causal effect of early impact aid on economic growth. The results exhibit diminishing returns, with larger amounts of aid having a progressively smaller impact. The estimated impact is nearly triple the magnitude found in other studies. We test the results over a very wide set of specifications and estimation techniques that control for other influences on growth, possible endogeneity, lags, and other factors. Throughout, the results remain strong and robust. We estimate the model over a four-year period, following the standard used in many studies, but we show (using lags) that the impact carries into a subsequent four-year period. We find no evidence that the effect is a short-run phenomenon that is later reversed. The results do not imply that aid has worked everywhere – it most definitely has not – but that, on average, growth-oriented aid has had a positive and significant impact on growth. The results underscore that the impact of early impact aid differs significantly from other types of aid (see Figure 43.1).

How great is the effect of early impact aid on growth? Consider the mean observation, where early impact aid is 2.7 percent of GDP (roughly equivalent to where total aid is about 5.4 percent of GDP). Using our most conservative results, at the mean, a 1 percentage point of GDP increase in early impact aid produces an additional 0.31

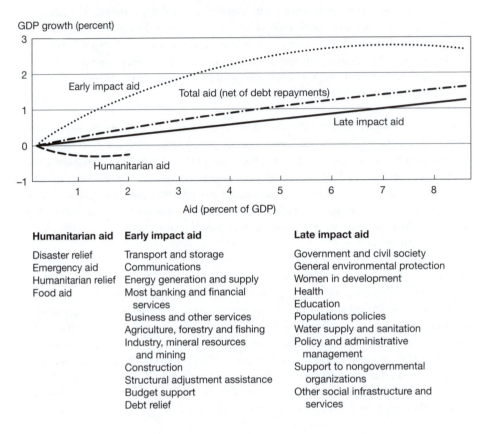

Humanitarian aid	Early impact aid	Late impact aid
Disaster relief	Transport and storage	Government and civil society
Emergency aid	Communications	General environmental protection
Humanitarian relief	Energy generation and supply	Women in development
Food aid	Most banking and financial	Health
	services	Education
	Business and other services	Populations policies
	Agriculture, forestry and fishing	Water supply and sanitation
	Industry, mineral resources	Policy and administrative
	and mining	management
	Construction	Support to nongovernmental
	Structural adjustment assistance	organizations
	Budget support	Other social infrastructure and
	Debt relief	services

Figure 43.1   Not all aid is alike

Some types of aid have a much bigger impact on growth than others – possibly why some studies examining aggregate aid find weak results.

Source: Clemens (2004).

Note: All three curves are estimated using a similar model and include a nonlinear relationship between aid and growth (which is hard to detect visually in the curve for late impact aid). The curve for humanitarian aid is cut off at 2 percent of GDP because there are no data in our sample beyond this point, and to show an upward curve would be misleading. Although only the coefficient on early impact aid is statistically significantly different from zero, the weaker relationships for late impact and humanitarian aid do not necessarily mean these flows have no impact on growth, but rather that a different modelling technique is required to explore these relationships (which we leave for future research).

percentage point of annual growth over the four-year period. With plausible assumptions about discount and depreciation rates (summing to 35 percent), we calculate that each $1 in early impact aid yields $1.64 in increased income in the recipient country in net present value terms. This country-level return roughly corresponds to a project-level rate of return of around 13 percent. For sub-Saharan Africa, we find that higher-than-average early impact aid raised per capita growth rates by about 1 percentage point over the growth that would have been achieved by average aid flows. This suggests that, while growth in sub-Saharan Africa has been disappointing, it would have been worse in the absence of this kind of aid.

What about the claim that aid works best in countries with good policies and institutions? To explore this idea, we looked at one of the most commonly used measures of institutional quality, drawn from the International Country Risk Guide. This index, which has been shown to be strongly correlated with growth, includes measures of the extent of corruption, rule of law, risk of expropriation or repudiation of contracts, and bureaucratic quality. We find some evidence that in countries with better institutions, the relationship between early impact aid and growth is stronger than otherwise. In addition, in countries with higher life expectancy (that is, better health), the aid-growth relationship is stronger than otherwise. But unlike other studies, we do not find that aid works only in countries with strong institutions or better health, and our results do not hinge on this interaction.

Are there limits on how much early impact aid typical recipients can absorb? The answer appears to be yes, but the maximum growth rate occurs on average when early impact aid represents 8–9 percent of GDP, more than three times the typical amount. As a rule of thumb, since early impact aid is slightly more than half of total aid on average, this implies that the maximum growth rate occurs when total aid reaches around 16–18 percent of GDP in the typical country. This does not mean that in any particular country, aid flows greater than this amount are necessarily a bad idea. Instead, this represents the typical pattern over the last 30 years – some countries can absorb more, and others less. Moreover, we find that absorptive capacity depends to some extent on the quality of institutions and general health of the population. In countries with stronger institutions and higher life expectancy, the impact of early impact aid is stronger throughout, and more aid can be absorbed before reaching the maximum growth rate.

The results also suggest that aid is not fully fungible, at least in the sense that all aid is interchangeable. If this were true, different subcategories would show similar relationships with growth. Instead, we find that aid flows intended for different purposes have significantly different relationships with growth. It is more likely that aid is only partially fungible, not fully so, in accordance with several recent studies.

Going forward

The intense pessimism on aid effectiveness expressed by some analysts appears to be too strong: we find a positive, causal relationship between growth-oriented aid and growth. At the same time, no one should conclude that aid has always worked or that it cannot work better. There are many countries that have received substantial aid and have stagnated or worse, and much aid has been wasted, stolen, or otherwise used to support countries with poor governance. The evidence suggests, however, that on average aid that has been aimed at growth in fact has boosted growth.

Those who argue that aid works *only* in countries with good institutions overstate their case. It would be more accurate to say that aid works *better* in countries with strong institutions, but at times can be effective in other situations. Aid has helped support growth in Mozambique and Uganda over the past decade, even though policies and institutions were far from ideal, and aid has played an important role in stabilizing Sierra Leone since its cease-fire. Aid helped to support sustained growth and poverty reduction in Indonesia during the Suharto regime – even in the 1970s and 1980s when institutions were weak, corruption was problematic, and policies were less than ideal.

We hasten to add that the weak relationship between late impact and humanitarian aid and growth over a four-year period should not be interpreted to mean that they are ineffective. Different modeling techniques are required to examine those questions, which we are exploring in subsequent research. Although (surprisingly) there is no systematic cross-country research on the relationship between health-oriented aid and health, there is evidence that at least some aid for health has been effective. For example, aid played an important role in supporting several large-scale successful health interventions, such as eradicating smallpox, significantly reducing the prevalence of polio and river blindness, and reducing the incidence of diarrheal diseases (Levine and others, 2004).

Finally, the evidence suggests that absorptive capacity constraints are real, but should not be seen as an immutable barrier to growth. Although the impact of aid on growth diminishes as aid increases, in countries with stronger institutions or better health, more aid can be absorbed effectively. This finding suggests that efforts to strengthen institutions and build human capital can increase returns to aid and help countries effectively absorb larger amounts of aid. Thus, policy discussions should not focus exclusively on determining the limits of aid on growth – but rather on how those limits can be expanded, and how aid can be made even more effective in supporting growth and development.

References

Burnside, Craig, and David Dollar, 2000, "Aid, Policies, and Growth," *American Economic Review*, Vol. 90. (September), pp. 847–68.

Clemens, Michael, Steven Radelet, and Rikhil Bhavnani, 2004, "Counting Chickens When They Hatch: the Short-Term Effect of Aid on Growth," Center for Global Development Working Paper 44 (Washington: Center for Global Development).

Isham, Jonathan, Daniel Kaufmann, and Lant Pritchett, 1995, "Governance and Returns on Investment: An Empirical Investigation," World Bank Policy Research Working Paper 1550 (Washington: World Bank).

Levine, Ruth, and the "What Works" Working Group (with Molly Kinder), 2004, *Millions Saved: Proven Success in Global Health* (Washington: Center for Global Development).

Steven Radelet, 2003, *Challenging Foreign Aid: A Policymaker's Guide to the Millennium Challenge Account* (Washington: Center for Global Development).

Rajan, Raghuram and Arvind Subramanian, 2005, "Aid and Growth: What Does the Cross-Country Evidence Really Show?" IMF Working Paper 05/127 (Washington: International Monetary Fund).

REVIEW AND DISCUSSION QUESTIONS

1 According to the "conditional view" of foreign aid, what does it take for aid to be effective at promoting economic growth?
2 How is the research on the effectiveness of aid by Radelet and his co-authors different from previous research?
3 What are the key results of the authors' research?
4 The authors note that their evidence suggests that aid is "only partially fungible." Explain what that means.
5 In light of the authors' research, how would you reform foreign aid to make it more effective at promoting economic growth and development? Explain clearly.

Chapter 44

Abhijit Vinayak Banerjee

MAKING AID WORK

BY THE FOURTH DAY after the October 2005 earthquake in northern Pakistan, the world had woken up to the fact that something very big had happened. The government was estimating that 50,000 or more people had been injured or killed, and many survivors were likely trapped somewhere without water or food.

The reaction was immediate and life-affirming. Everyone showed up to help: international and local NGOs, the United Nations, and groups of college students with rented trucks full of food and other necessities. Money flowed in from everywhere. The Indian government, reversing a policy of many years, announced that it would open the highly sensitive border between the two Kashmirs so that aid could flow more easily.

In the middle of all this excitement, a small group of economists based primarily in the United States started worrying about how the aid would get to the right people. There were thousands of villages in the area, including some that were a hike of six hours or more from the road. How would aid workers find out which ones among these were badly hit? No one seemed to know. To work efficiently, the workers would need a map of the area with the geographic coordinates of all the villages – then they would be able to figure out the distance between the villages and the epicenter of the quake. But no one in Pakistan seemed to have such a map, and no one in charge seemed to feel the need for one. So the economists, Tahir Andrabi of Pomona College; Ali Cheema of Lahore University; Jishnu Das, Piet Buys, and Tara Vishwanath of the World Bank; and Asim Khwaja of the Kennedy School of Government at Harvard, set about finding one and making it available.

Without such a map, there was an obvious danger that most of the aid would end up in the villages that were closer to the road, where the damage was more visible. There would be places that no one among the aid givers had heard of: who was going to get aid to them? To make matters worse, no one was coordinating the hundreds of aid groups. No one was keeping track of where the aid had reached and where it had yet to reach. As a result, some villages were ending up with many trucks from different donors while others were left waiting for their first consignment.

Improving coordination would not be hard, the economists realized. All that was needed was an office or Web site to which everyone could report the names and locations of the villages where they had sent aid and the amounts sent. It would then be easy to build a database with reliable information about where the next consignments should go.

So, with the help of some contacts in the IT industry and some students at Lahore University, they designed a simple form and approached donors with a simple request: whenever you send out a consignment, please fill out one of these. There were paper copies available as well as a Web-based form and a call center.

The reaction, when it was not actually hostile, tended to be derisive: "Are you mad? You want us to spend time filling out forms when people are dying? We need to go and go fast." Go where? the economists wanted to ask. But nobody seemed to care.

The Edhi Foundation, perhaps the most reputable Pakistani NGO, did not fill out a single form. The United Nations team filled out a few. The Pakistani army corps eventually agreed that the project was a good idea, but not before rejecting it completely for several days. Many smaller NGOs were eventually persuaded to join the effort, but the biggest players, for the most part, went their own way.

In many ways this episode captures very well one of the core problems with delivering aid: institutional laziness. Here many of the standard problems were not an issue: the donors and the intermediaries were both genuinely trying to help. It is true that filling out forms is less gratifying than handing out aid; but no one was trying to deprive the aid workers of that moment of satisfaction. All they had to do was to wait the extra few minutes it would take to fill out a simple form and learn about where aid had reached and where it had not. But no one could be bothered to put in the time it would have taken to think harder about what they were doing. Aid thinking is lazy thinking.

A sad and wonderful example of how deep this lazy thinking runs is a book that the World Bank brought out in 2002 with the express intention, ironically, of rationalizing the business of aid-giving. The book, called *Empowerment and Poverty Reduction: A Sourcebook*, was meant to be a catalogue of the most effective strategies for poverty reduction, brought together to give donors a sense of the current best practice. It contains a very long list of recommended initiatives, including computer kiosks for villages; cell phones for rural areas; scholarships for girls attending secondary school; school-voucher programs for poor children; joint forest-management programs; water-users groups; citizen report cards for public services; participatory poverty assessments; Internet access for tiny firms; land tiding; legal reform; micro-credit based on group lending; and many others. While many of these are surely good ideas, the authors of the book do not tell us how they know that they work.

It has been established that figuring out what works is not easy – a large body of literature documents the pitfalls of the intuitive approach to program evaluation. When we do something and things get better, it is tempting to think that it was because of what we did. But we have no way of knowing what would have happened in the absence of the intervention. For example, a study of schools in western Kenya by Paul Glewwe, Michael Kremer, Sylvie Moulin, and Eric Zitzewitz compared the performance of children in schools that used flip charts for teaching science and schools that did not and found that the former group did significantly better in the sciences even after controlling for all other measurable factors. An intuitive assessment might have readily ascribed the difference to the educational advantages of using flip charts, but these researchers wondered why some schools had flip charts when a large majority did not. Perhaps the parents of children attending these schools were particularly motivated and this motivation led independently both to the investment in the flip charts and, more significantly, to the goading of their children to do their homework. Perhaps these schools would have done better even if there were no such things as flip charts.

Glewwe and company therefore undertook a randomized experiment: 178 schools in the same area were sorted alphabetically, first by geographic district, then by geographic division, and then by school name. Then every other school on that list was assigned to be a flip-chart school. This was essentially a lottery, which guaranteed that there were no systematic differences between the two sets of schools. If we were to see a difference between the sets of schools, we could be confident that it was the effect of the flip charts. Unfortunately, the researchers found no difference between the schools that won the flip-chart lottery and the ones that lost.

Randomized trials like these – that is, trials in which the intervention is assigned randomly – are the simplest and best way of assessing the impact of a program. They mimic the procedures used in trials of new drugs, which is one situation in which, for obvious reasons, a lot of care has gone into making sure that only the interventions that really work get approved, though of course not with complete success. In many ways social programs are very much like drugs: they have the potential to transform the life prospects of people. It seems appropriate that they should be held to the same high standards.

Of course, even randomized trials are not perfect. Something that works in India may fail in Indonesia. Ideally, there should be multiple randomized trials in varying locations. There is also no substitute for thinking – there are often clear and predictable reasons why what works in Kenya will not work in Cameroon. Some other ideas are plain silly, or contrary to the logic of everything we know – there is no reason to waste time testing these. And there are times when randomized experiments are simply not feasible, such as in the case of exchange-rate policy or central-bank independence: it clearly makes no sense to assign countries exchange rates at random as you might assign them flip charts. That said, one would not want to spend a lot of money on an intervention without doing at least one successful randomized trial *if one is possible*.

When we talk of hard evidence, we will therefore have in mind evidence from a randomized experiment, or, failing that, evidence from a true *natural experiment*, in which an accident of history creates a setting that mimics a randomized trial. A wonderful natural experiment has helped us, for example, to support a classic assumption about education: that students perform better in smaller classes. This idea might seem self-evident, but it is surprisingly difficult to prove because of the way classes are usually formed: students are often assigned to smaller classes when they are performing poorly. As a result, it may look as if smaller classes are bad for students. The solution came when the economists Josh Angrist and Victor Lavy noticed that Israeli schools use what is called Maimonides' Rule, according to which classes may not contain more than 40 students. As soon as the classes get to be that size, they are broken in two, no matter how the students are performing. So if performance improves when classes are broken up, we know that the effects are due to size. Based on this observation, Angrist and Lavy found that "reducing class size induces a significant and substantial increase in test scores for fourth and fifth graders, although not for third graders."

What is striking about the list of strategies offered by the World Bank's sourcebook is the lack of distinction made between strategies founded on the hard evidence provided by randomized trials or natural experiments and the rest. To the best of my knowledge, only one of the strategies listed there – school vouchers for poor students – has been subject to a randomized evaluation (in Colombia). In this case, the evaluation happened because the Colombian government found it politically necessary to allocate the vouchers by lottery. Comparing those who won the lottery with those who did not provided the perfect experiment for studying the impact of the program, and a study by Josh Angrist and others took advantage of it. In contrast, legal reform, for example, is justified in the sourcebook thus: "The extent to which a society is law-bound affects its national income as well as its level of literacy and infant mortality." This may be true, but the available evidence, which comes from comparing the more law-abiding countries with the rest, is too tangled to warrant such a confident recommendation. One could imagine, say, that countries that have been through a long civil war may be both less law-abiding and less literate, but it would be silly to say that the country was more literate because it was more law-abiding. Yet the sourcebook shows no more enthusiasm for vouchers than it does for legal reform.

Indeed, there is reason to suspect that the authors of the sourcebook were not even looking at their own evidence. My favorite example is the description of the Gyandoot program in Madhya Pradesh, India, which provided computer kiosks in rural areas. The sourcebook acknowledged that this project was hit hard by lack of electricity and poor connectivity and that "currently only a few of the Kiosks have proved to be commercially viable." It then goes on to say, without apparent irony, "Following the success of the initiative . . ."

That this was no exception is confirmed by Lant Pritchett, a long-term World Bank employee and a lecturer at Harvard University, who writes in a 2001 article,

> Nearly all World Bank discussions of policies and project design had the character of 'ignorant armies clashing by the night' – there was heated debate amongst advocates of various activities but rarely any firm evidence presented and considered about the likely impact of the proposed actions. Certainly in my experience there was never any definitive evidence that would inform decisions of funding one broad set of activities versus another (e.g., basic education versus roads versus vaccinations versus macroeconomic reform) or even funding one instrument versus another (e.g., vaccinations versus public education about hygiene to improve health, textbook reform versus teacher training to improve educational quality).

How costly is the resistance to knowledge? One way to get at this is to compare the cost-effectiveness of plausible alternative ways of achieving the same goal. Primary education, and particularly the question of how to get more children to attend primary school, provides a fine test case because a number of the standard strategies have been subject to randomized evaluations. The cheapest strategy for getting children to spend more time in school, by some distance, turns out to be giving them deworming medicine so that they are sick less often. The cost, by this method, of getting one more child to attend primary school for a year is $3.25. The most expensive strategy among those that are frequently recommended (for example by the World Bank, which also recommends deworming) is a conditional cash-transfer program, such as Progresa in Mexico, where the mother gets extra welfare payments if her children go to school. This costs about $6,000 per additional child per year, mainly because most of the mothers who benefit from it would have sent their children to school even if there were no such incentive. This is a difference of more than 1,800 times.

One might object that this difference is somewhat exaggerated, since welfare payments would be good things even if they did not promote education. A more straightforward strategy would be to provide school uniforms in a place such as rural Kenya, where uniforms are required but expensive relative to what people earn. This costs about $100 per additional child per year, which is still a good 30 times the cost of deworming but one 60th the cost of conditional cash transfers. School meals are another option: they cost $35 per additional child per year, around a third of the cost of uniforms but more than ten times the cost of deworming.

Given the magnitude of the differences, choosing the wrong option can be very costly indeed. Yet all these strategies are either part of actual policies or part of policies that have been very seriously considered. Moreover, a priori reasoning, at least of the type that economists know how to do, is not much of a guide here – all the interventions sound quite sensible. Therefore, one can easily imagine one country choosing one of these, spending a lot, and getting the same results as another that spent very little. If both projects were aid-financed, someone comparing them would conclude that spending does not correlate with success in development projects, which is what one finds when one compares aid and growth across countries. And this lack of correlation is not just an artifact of comparing countries that received more or less aid and finding that the ones that got more aid did not grow faster. That comparison is obviously flawed, since countries often get more aid because they have bigger problems that make it harder for them to grow.

To avoid this kind of problem, in a recent paper my colleague Ruimin He and I asked the equivalent question at the project level – whether projects that are more generously funded by a particular multilateral donor do better than other projects within the same sector of the same country that it has also funded, but less generously. For the World Bank and the Asian Development Bank, the two organizations for which we have data, the answer turns out to be no; in the case of the World Bank the correlation is significantly negative, implying that projects that get more of their funding from the World Bank actually end up doing worse.

Opponents of aid see this lack of correlation as the ultimate proof of the radical impossibility of aid-driven development. In their resolutely puritanical view of the world, development is only possible when a country decides to take charge and make it happen, and aid is at best a petty player and at worst a distraction.

My sense is that this is much too pessimistic, in at least three related but distinct senses. First, while I recognize that aid will sometimes be given cynically, and that venal government officials will try to get their hands on the money, the intermediaries who actually give out the aid – the World Bank, USAID, and the rest – are not powerless. They can make government departments compete for the money by favoring the most transparent design. Indeed, one thing that must encourage corruption and misuse of funds is the fact that the donors are unclear about what they should be pushing for. Given that, it is easy to lead them to grandiose and unfocused project designs where none of the details are spelled out clearly and diverting money is a cinch. From this point of view the current fashion of channeling aid into broad budgetary support (rather than specific projects) in the name of national autonomy seems particularly disastrous. We need to go back to financing projects and insist that the results be measured.

Second, it is easy to forget that some of the greatest achievements of the last century were the eradication of diseases such as smallpox and polio and the development and widespread dissemination of high-yielding varieties of wheat, rice, corn, and many other crops. In each of these successes and in many others, international cooperation and aid played a central role.

Opponents of aid often respond to these examples by pointing out, correctly, that the development of these technologies was a global public good and therefore the one instance in which international intervention would be likely to succeed. This misses the key point that while these technologies were developed and funded internationally, they were disseminated in cooperation with national governments. In this sense, the challenges they faced were not unlike what anyone would face in trying to disseminate any kind of best practice in development – corrupt governments, lazy bureaucrats, cynical donors.

The reason they succeeded, I suspect, is that they started with a project that was narrowly defined and well founded. They were convinced it worked, they could convince others, and they could demonstrate and measure success. Contrast this with the current practice in development aid; as we have seen, what goes for best practice is often not particularly well founded. More often than not, it is also not immediately practicable: if the World Bank's flagship publication, the annual *World Development Report*, is any indication, what goes for best practice is usually some high-level concept, like decentralization or education for girls. It leaves open the key practical questions: Decentralization how – through local governments or citizens' associations? What kinds of citizens' associations – informal neighborhood groups that build solidarity and voice or formal meetings where complaints get recorded and sent up? What kind of complaint-recording mechanism – secret ballots or public discussions? Getting these details right, as we saw in the case of primary schooling, can make all the difference in the world.

But there is no reason things have to be this way. This is the third sense in which aid pessimism is misplaced. The culture of aid-giving evolved from the idea that giving is good and the more money the better (what William Easterly calls the financing-gap theory), and therefore – here comes the logical leap – one need not think too hard about how the money is spent.

We have now learned that this kind of lazy giving does not work. Perhaps it took us a while to get there, but in the scheme of things even 60 years (which is about how long aid specifically designed to promote development has been going on) is but a moment in time. Large and highly political institutions such as the World Bank tend to take a while to absorb the lessons of history, especially when they are unpleasant: I do not see why this experience teaches us that aid inevitably fails.

Indeed, the time seems ripe to launch an effort to change the way aid is given. Empirical research on best practice in development has grown apace in the last decade or so, and we now have evidence on a number of programs that work. These are programs that do something very specific – such as giving deworming drugs to schoolchildren and providing a particular kind of supplemental teaching in primary schools – that have been subjected to one or several randomized evaluations and have been shown to work.

Several years ago, Ruimin He and I put together a list of programs that meet these two criteria and calculated how much it would cost to scale them up to reach the entire population that needs them. While the calculation inevitably involved a lot of guesswork and was meant only to illustrate a point, the number we came up with, leaving out all income-transfer programs, was $11.2 billion a year. To compare, between 1996 and 2001 the World Bank's International Development Association loans (the main form of World Bank aid) totaled about $6.2 billion a year. We could clearly spend all that and more without ever funding a program that does not have a demonstrated record of success, especially given that evidence on new programs is pouring in.

Attitudes are changing. A number of the larger foundations, including the Bill and Melinda Gates Foundation and the William and Flora Hewlett Foundation, have shown a strong commitment to using evidence to inform their decisions. Even more remarkably, the U.S. government's latest aid effort, the Millennium Challenge Corporation, has expressed a strong commitment to randomized evaluations of the programs it supports. I am not naive enough to believe this effort will be easy (though enough, perhaps, to call myself an optimist). The guiltier the country, the more it will protest that it needs the independence to make its own choices and that moving away from broad budgetary support undermines its suzerainty. But we owe it to their unfortunate and oppressed citizens to hold the line.

REVIEW AND DISCUSSION QUESTIONS

1   The author believes that a major problem with the way foreign aid is currently provided is "institutional laziness." Explain what he means.
2   Explain what randomized trials are and why Banerjee believes that they can be helpful in making foreign aid effective.
3   What is the author's objection to foreign aid programs that provide cash transfers to families as an incentive to send their children to school?
4   Explain why, according to Banerjee, the view that "development is only possible when a country decides to take charge and make it happen" is "much too pessimistic."
5   According to the evidence discussed by the author, what aid programs seem to be most effective?
6   The author states that "the current fashion for channeling aid into broad budgetary support (rather than specific projects) in the name of national autonomy seems particularly disastrous. We need to go back to financing projects and insist that the results be measured." Do you agree with this position? Why or why not?

Chapter 45

Ian Goldin, F. Halsey Rogers, and Nicholas Stern

WE MUST TACKLE DEVELOPMENT PROBLEMS AT THE LEVEL OF THE ECONOMY AS A WHOLE

AS ABHIJIT BANERJEE EXPLAINS, randomized experiments solve a major problem: how to cleanly identify the effects of a given development program or project. Randomized experiments can therefore make interventions more cost-effective and bolster political support for aid. Donor institutions and governments in both wealthy and poor countries have relied too little on the powerful tool of randomization. But with better baseline data and greater attention to results, that is now changing.

This is particularly true in the areas where an experimental design can most usefully be applied – health, education, income support. Through the Development Impact Evaluation initiative (DIME), for example, the World Bank has established a far-reaching program of impact evaluations, many of them using a randomized-experiment approach. Rather than drawing policy conclusions from one-time experiments, DIME evaluates portfolios of similar programs in multiple countries to allow more robust assessments of what works. In Benin, India, Kenya, Nepal, Nicaragua, and Pakistan, for example, the Bank is supporting tests of a powerful idea: that stronger community control of schools and better community access to information (such as students' test scores) will improve school performance and learning outcomes. By carrying out the program evaluations together with the agencies running the programs, the Bank is helping to create both the demand for evidence-based policies and the developing countries' own capacity to generate that evidence.

One measure of the Bank's commitment to impact evaluations is its successful partnership with MIT's Abdul Latif Jameel Poverty Action Lab, which Banerjee co-directs. Of the 34 developing-country JPAL projects listed with funding sources, 24 have been funded partly or wholly by the Bank, and in some cases World Bank researchers are conducting the evaluations together with JPAL staff. The JPAL deserves great credit for increasing interest in and expertise on randomized evaluations. The variety of its projects – experiments with textbook provision in Kenya, nutrition for young children in India, business training for micro-entrepreneurs in Peru and the Philippines, and school vouchers in Colombia – is testament to the leadership of Banerjee and his colleagues.

But not everything can be done through randomized evaluation. First, as Banerjee notes, in some cases "randomized experiments are simply not feasible, such as in the case of exchange-rate policy or central-bank independence." The same is true in many other cases: governments are not likely to agree to randomize reductions in tariff rates, for example, or the geographical placement of power plants. Nor can broad programs of institutional, governmental, or policy reform be randomized.

Second, as with medical trials, randomization will not always be ethical. For example, where we have good reason to believe that a program works, we cannot withhold it from members of vulnerable populations simply to ensure a clean randomized evaluation.

Third, it will never be efficient to move wholly into randomized evaluation, even for well-defined projects. To evaluate earthquake preparedness, it is less costly to go to where an earthquake has just struck than to randomize interventions globally and wait for the next Big One.

Fourth, answers can depend heavily on the cultural and social context in which questions are asked. Governments understandably resist the transfer of a program evaluated in another country, or indeed another part of a country, without adaptation to local circumstances. But it will not be possible to cover all contexts by carrying out an infinite number of randomized evaluations.

Fifth, before experimentation, there must always be a prior decision on which programs to experiment with. If you want to improve education, should you run a careful randomized experiment of the effects of providing textbooks to students, or of giving them deworming medicine, or of hiring an extra teacher, or of paying for their school uniforms? The choice of interventions to test depends on the context, which is why practitioners must invest heavily in collecting baseline data and doing observational studies. Too often, we lack even the basic data needed to develop an experiment – data on the number of villages in a rural area, on health and school attendance before the trial, and so on. Getting basic statistical services up and running is often a costly precondition for effective experimentation.

Sixth, there is the crucial question of scale. If we can act only on detailed project evidence, then no action can be taken at the economy-wide level. Yet we have seen repeatedly – notably in India and China over the past two decades – that economy-wide reforms and actions are the real drivers of change.

Seventh, what about sustainability? Banerjee's analysis prioritizes cost-benefit calculations from randomized experiments above all other considerations – but those other considerations matter. Take Mexico's well-known Progresa program, which Banerjee criticizes as an expensive means of increasing primary-school enrollment. This program is successful because it achieves other goals as well, including better health outcomes, higher secondary-school enrollments, and higher investment by poor people. The resulting domestic support has cemented the program's effectiveness by sustaining it and allowing it to be expanded nationwide.

The history of development aid supports Banerjee's view that there has been too little detailed microeconomic study of program efficacy. But there is another important lesson of development aid: sustainable progress in developing countries depends on improving the overall capacity of the government to deliver services and foster growth.

Banerjee is proposing, in effect, to "ring-fence" most development aid within the confines of development interventions proven to work by randomized evaluation. However, research has shown that ring-fencing offers illusory protection. Aid is largely fungible: ill-intentioned governments can play financial shell games that undermine donor intentions by shifting their own resources from the donor-targeted sector into other areas (such as weapons purchases). Supporting accountability of public budgets and working with governments to improve the quality of overall public spending is vital, although not amenable to neat experiments. Furthermore, detailed external micromanagement at the project level can undermine local accountability and capacity-building.

Finally, it's worth taking a step back for perspective. There have been serious mistakes, particularly where aid has been politically driven, as during the Cold War. (Pouring billions into Mobutu's Zaire, for example, was tragically misguided.) Yet the development progress of the past half century has been remarkable in many ways. The number of people living in extreme poverty (subsisting on less than one dollar per day) fell by 400 million between 1981 and 2001, despite rapid population growth. In 1970 nearly two in four adults in developing countries were illiterate; now it is only one in four. And life expectancy in developing countries has increased by more than 20 years since 1950. Too many countries – especially in sub-Saharan Africa – still lag behind economically, but the last decade or so has seen improvements in governance and the return of growth across much of the continent. And even where economic growth has stagnated, there has often been major progress on some social indicators. Progress is driven primarily by domestic action, but international institutions and bilateral assistance have often promoted the kind of policies that have led to change.

Banerjee is cautiously optimistic about the future, as are we, but we should also be cautiously optimistic about the past. There are reasons to believe that the productivity of aid has risen recently. Donors and developing-country governments alike have learned from economic history and experience: developing-country policies and governance have improved, donors are giving more aid to countries that will use it well and are focusing on poverty, and donors are providing aid through less burdensome methods. This progress must continue; while microanalysis of randomized experiments has an important role to play, it alone won't get us there. Consider Mozambique, which emerged from civil war in the early 1990s. Making broad macro judgments about prospects for development, donors decided to invest heavily in Mozambique's reconstruction, and poverty there fell sharply in the 1990s. Had they insisted first on results from randomized experiments, the opportunity might have been lost.

Without the full set of tools for learning and understanding, a narrow insistence on the good science of randomized evaluation could turn into an intellectual straitjacket. We, like Banerjee, will continue to champion randomized evaluations. But policymakers and those who would support them also have to learn from a broad range of experiences and tackle the problems of governance, institutions, and policies at the level of the economy as a whole.

REVIEW AND DISCUSSION QUESTIONS

1 According to the authors, in what ways might randomized evaluation threaten the "sustainability" of aid projects?
2 The authors list seven potential drawbacks or limitations of randomized evaluation of aid. Which do you believe are the most significant drawbacks? Which are the least significant? Why? Explain.

Chapter 46

Jeffrey Sachs

UPSTAIRS, DOWNSTAIRS

THE HIGHLY-INDEBTED POOR COUNTRIES (HIPCs) command the attention of the rich world approximately in proportion to their economic weight. In other words, they command next to no attention at all. There are 700 million people living in the forty-two HIPCs (as defined by the World Bank), around 80 percent of which are in Africa. Their GDP per capita averages $350 dollars per year, or roughly one-eightieth of the per capita income of the United States. Among the world's 1000 top corporations, not one is from a HIPC country. Indeed, if the market capitalization of the thirty largest sub-Saharan companies were combined into one company, it would rank 694th in the world.

The finance ministers of the rich countries don't quite know what to do with these countries, so they send the IMF. While the IMF fiddles with value added tax reform and civil service reorganization, the AIDS epidemic sweeps through the African HIPCs. In Zambia, an estimated 19 percent of the entire population is now HIV positive, according to recent UN estimates. In Mozambique, it's 14 percent and Rwanda 12 percent. Africa now experiences more than 5,000 AIDS deaths per day, or 2 million per year. Malaria is also surging, with more than one million deaths in Africa last year, and spreading drug resistance. Life expectancy in the HIPCs is around fifty-one years and falling.

You might think that the AIDS epidemic, arguably the worst since the Black Death of the fourteenth century, would have generated an outpouring of international assistance. The dreadful reality is that the combined donor assistance on HIV/AIDS to the whole developing world is probably no more than $350 million, or about $8 per year per infected individual. Tuberculosis and malaria have been similarly neglected. More than 2 million people per year in the developing world are dying of tuberculosis. Around 30 percent of the children under five-years-old in the HIPC countries are malnourished.

In this context, the rich-country treatment of HIPC debt is nothing short of bizarre. Most of these countries need desperate help, including a long-term net infusion of resources through grant assistance. And yet they are buried in unpayable debt, even after years of public hand-wringing. Most of the HIPC debt is not actually paid – it cannot be. So HIPC finance ministers spend their days and nights rolling over the debt, postponing payments, slipping in and out of temporary defaults papered over by new rescheduling agreements and new loans from the IMF, World Bank, and bilateral creditors. The time horizon of government planning is defined as the time till the next IMF mission, usually weeks away. There is no opportunity whatsoever to address the underlying social and health calamities.

A meagre debt-relief initiative was launched in 1996, but it was derisory in ambition and outcome. Only two out of the forty-two countries (Bolivia and Uganda) have actually gotten relief under the initiative. The rest wait in line. And the relief that was on offer was pitifully small. The IMF calculated a "sustainable debt burden," arbitrarily set at 200 to 250 percent of exports. This target was analytically vacuous: exports do not measure ability to pay off indebted governments (many exports, for example, are owned by multi-nationals, and contribute little or nothing to the ability to pay), nor do these targets even attempt to recognize the social needs of the countries.

The G7 Summiteers at Cologne were shamed into an implicit recognition of the failure of the 1996 initiative. But their response was again remarkably grudging and uninventive. In their generosity, they said that they would forgive $25 to $50 billion or so of net present value of debt, perhaps one-fifth to one-fourth of the total due. (All G7 numbers remain cloudy, as the bases of the calculations have not been made public). This comes from countries whose citizens have enjoyed perhaps $5 to $10 trillion of capital gains in the past four years. The "sustainability target" was reduced to 150 percent of exports and 250 percent of government revenues. It seems that the HIPC governments could look forward to spending around one-forth of government revenues on debt servicing even after the relief package!

This absurd situation should end. Probably the most effective next step would be for each of the G7 finance ministers to spend a couple of weeks in an HIPC rural community, watching villagers fight for survival, often losing the battle for want of medicines, clean water, or access to medical assistance. The finance ministers would come back with a basic insight: When a country is struggling for survival, don't send in an accountant, send in a doctor. For half or more of the HIPCs, it is time to put the World Health Organization, the United Nations Children's Fund, and the Consultative Group for International Agricultural Research at the forefront of assistance efforts, and move the IMF, at most, to a modest supporting role.

Instead of using phony debt targets like 150 percent of exports, let's do a real social audit of each HIPC. What would be the cost of supplying the basic vaccines to 90 percent or more of the children? What would be the cost of extending vaccine coverage to include the new and more expensive vaccines such as Hib and rotavirus that would save thousands and thousands of lives but are simply not used in the poor countries because of their costs ($30–$40 per dose, in countries in which total spending per year is often $5 per person)? What would be the cost of responding to the HIV/AIDS epidemic, with massive public information campaigns, availability of condoms, AZT for pregnant mothers, other drug therapies, and increased R&D on new vaccine development? What would be the cost of guaranteeing adequate nutrition for children under five, to prevent another generation of physically, cognitively, and emotionally scarred individuals, now facing a lifetime of disability because of childhood malnutrition?

It is easy to predict the outcome of such an analysis. For a couple dozen HIPC countries in the least, there is no realistic answer other than 100 percent cancellation of the debts, combined with new and creative assistance programs to meet urgent social needs. For some other HIPCs, more limited debt relief might be sufficient. For all of the countries, a massive effort on behalf of basic human needs should be given new priority, at least as prominent as the traditional macroeconomic management tools which have dominated the international policy agenda for the past twenty years.

Can the IMF, the World Bank, and the bilateral community afford more ambitious relief? Of course, and without even blinking. Consider the case of the U.S. The $6 billion of debt owed to the U.S. by the HIPCs, a modest sum in and of itself, is already written down on U.S. books to around $600 million. Thus, for budgetary outlays equal to $600 million (about 0.000075 of U.S. GDP), the U.S. could totally eliminate its claims on the 42 HIPCs. For the IMF and World Bank, the situation is similarly straightforward. For the countries in need, both institutions could simply forgive the outstanding balances, especially IMF balances and non-concessional lending from the World Bank. Rather than worrying about replenishing the IMF's ESAF coffers – a large part of the G7 pre-occupations at Cologne – we should recognize that the most effective use of future assistance will not be through the IMF at all, but through the international agencies such as UNAIDS, the World Health Organization, and UNICEF that can really supply the technical knowledge and on-the-ground-expertise to meet the urgent social needs of the poorest countries.

REVIEW AND DISCUSSION QUESTIONS

1   Why does Sachs believe that the way rich countries treat the Heavily Indebted Poor Countries (HIPCs) is "nothing short of bizarre"?
2   What does the author think of recent debt-relief initiatives?
3   Do you agree with Sachs's views on debt relief? Why or why not?

Chapter 47

William Easterly

DEBT RELIEF

DEBT RELIEF HAS BECOME the feel-good economic policy of the new millennium, trumpeted by Irish rock star Bono, Pope John Paul II, and virtually everyone in between. But despite its overwhelming popularity among policymakers and the public, debt relief is a bad deal for the world's poor. By transferring scarce resources to corrupt governments with proven track records of misusing aid, debt forgiveness might only aggravate poverty among the world's most vulnerable populations.

"Jubilee 2000 sparked the debt relief movement"

No. Sorry, Bono, but debt relief is not new. As long ago as 1967, the U.N. Conference on Trade and Development argued that debt service payments in many poor nations had reached "critical situations." A decade later, official bilateral creditors wrote off $6 billion in debt to 45 poor countries. In 1984, a World Bank report on Africa suggested that financial support packages for countries in the region should include "multi-year debt relief and longer grace periods." Since 1987, successive G-7 summits have offered increasingly lenient terms, such as postponement of repayment deadlines, on debts owed by poor countries. (Ironically, each new batch of terms and conditions was named after the opulent site of the G-7 meeting, such as the "Venice terms," the "Toronto terms," and the "London terms.") In the late 1980s and 1990s, the World Bank and International Monetary Fund (IMF) began offering special loan programs to African nations, essentially allowing governments to pay back high-interest loans with low-interest loans – just as real a form of debt relief as partial forgiveness of the loans. The World Bank and IMF's more recent and well-publicized Highly Indebted Poor Countries (HIPC) debt relief program therefore represents but a deepening of earlier efforts to reduce the debt burdens of the world's poorest nations. Remarkably, the HIPC nations kept borrowing enough new funds in the 1980s and 1990s to more than offset the past debt relief: From 1989 to 1997, debt forgiveness for the 41 nations now designated as HIPCs reached $33 billion, while new borrowing for the same countries totaled $41 billion.

So by the time the Jubilee 2000 movement began spreading its debt relief gospel in the late 1990s, a wide constituency for alleviating poor nations' debt already existed. However, Jubilee 2000 and other pro-debt relief groups succeeded in raising the visibility and popularity of the issue to unprecedented heights. High-profile endorsements range from Irish rock star Bono to Pope John Paul II and the Dalai Lama to Harvard economist Jeffrey Sachs; even retiring U.S. Sen. Jesse Helms has climbed onto the debt relief band-wagon. In that respect, Jubilee 2000 (rechristened "Drop the Debt" before the organization's campaign officially ended on July 31, 2001) should be commended for putting the world's poor on the agenda – at a time when most people in rich nations simply don't care – even if the organization's proselytizing efforts inevitably oversimplify the problems of foreign debt.

"Third World debts are illegitimate"

Unhelpful idea. Supporters of debt relief programs have often argued that new democratic governments in poor nations should not be forced to honor the debts that were incurred and mismanaged long ago by their corrupt and dictatorial predecessors. Certainly, some justice would be served if a legitimate and reformist new government refused to repay creditors foolish enough to have lent to a rotten old autocracy. But, in reality, there are few clear-cut political breaks with a corrupt past. The political factors that make governments corrupt tend to persist over time. How "clean" must the new government be to represent a complete departure from the mis-deeds of an earlier regime? Consider President Yoweri Museveni of Uganda, about the strongest possible example of a change from the past – in his case, the notorious past of Ugandan strongman Idi Amin. Yet even Museveni's government continues to spend money on questionable military adventures in the Democratic Republic of the Congo. Would Museveni qualify for debt relief under the "good new government" principle? And suppose a long-time corrupt politician remains in power, such as Kenyan President Daniel Arap Moi. True justice would instead call for such leaders to pay back some of their loot to development agencies, who could then lend the money to a government with cleaner hands – a highly unlikely scenario.

Making debt forgiveness contingent on the supposed "illegitimacy" of the original borrower simply creates perverse incentives by directing scarce aid resources to countries that have best proved their capacity to mismanage such funds. For example, Ivory Coast built not just one but two new national capitals in the hometowns of the country's previous rulers as it was piling up debt. Then it had a military coup and a tainted election. Is that the environment in which aid will be well used? Meanwhile, poor nations that did not mismanage their aid loans so badly – such as India and Bangladesh – now do not qualify for debt relief, even though their governments would likely put fresh aid resources to much better use.

Finally, the legitimacy rationale raises serious reputation concerns in the world's financial markets. Few private lenders will wish to provide fresh financing to a country if they know that a successor government has the right to repudiate the earlier debt as illegitimate. For the legitimacy argument to be at all convincing, the countries in question must show a huge and permanent change from the corruption of past regimes. Indeed, strict application of such a standard introduces the dread specter of "conditionality," i.e., the imposition of burdensome policy requirements on developing nations in exchange for assistance from international financial institutions. Only rather than focusing solely on economic policy conditions, the international lending agencies granting debt relief would now be compelled to make increasingly subjective judgments regarding a country's politics, governance structures, and adherence to the rule of law.

"Crushing debts worsen Third World poverty"

Wrong in more ways than one. Yes, the total long-term debt of the 41 HIPC nations grew from $47 billion in 1980 to $159 billion in 1990 to $169 billion in 1999, but in reality the foreign debt of poor countries has always been partly fictional. Whenever debt service became too onerous, the poor nations simply received new loans to repay old ones. Recent studies have found that new World Bank adjustment loans to poor countries in the 1980s and 1990s increased in lock step with mounting debt service. Likewise, another study found that official lenders tend to match increases in the payment obligations of highly indebted African countries with an increase in new loans. Indeed, over the past two decades, new lending to African countries more than covered debt service payments on old loans.

Second, debt relief advocates should remember that poor people don't owe foreign debt – their governments do. Poor nations suffer poverty not because of high debt burdens but because spendthrift governments constantly seek to redistribute the existing economic pie to privileged political elites rather than try to make the pie grow larger through sound economic policies. The debt-burdened government of Kenya managed to find enough money to reward President Moi's home region with the Eldoret International Airport in 1996, a facility that almost nobody uses.

Left to themselves, bad governments are likely to engage in new borrowing to replace the forgiven loans, so the debt burden wouldn't fall in the end anyway. And even if irresponsible governments do not run up new debts, they could always finance their redistributive ways by running down government assets (like oil and minerals), leaving future generations condemned to the same overall debt burden. Ultimately, debt relief will only help reduce debt burdens if government policies make a true shift away from redistributive politics and toward a focus on economic development.

"Debt relief allows poor nations to spend more on health and education"

No. In 1999, Jubilee 2000 enthused that with debt relief "the year 2000 could signal the beginning of dramatic improvements in healthcare, education, employment and development for countries crippled by debt." Unfortunately, such statements fail to recognize some harsh realities about government spending.

First, the iron law of public finance states that money is fungible: Debt relief goes into the same government account that rains money on good and bad uses alike. Debt relief enables governments to spend more on weapons, for example. Debt relief clients such as Angola, Ethiopia, and Rwanda all have heavy military spending (although some are promising to make cuts). To assess whether debt relief increases health and education spending, one must ask what such spending would have been in the absence of debt relief – a difficult question. However, if governments didn't spend the original loans on helping the poor, it's a stretch to expect them to devote new fiscal resources toward helping the poor.

Second, such claims assume that the central government knows where its money is going. A recent IMF and World Bank study found that only two out of 25 debt relief recipients will have satisfactory capacity to track where government spending goes within a year. At the national level, an additional study found that only 13 percent of central government grants for non-salary education spending in Uganda (another recipient of debt relief) actually made it to the local schools that were the intended beneficiaries.

Finally, the very idea that the proceeds of debt relief should be spent on health and education contains a logical flaw. If debt relief proceeds are spent on social programs rather than used to pay down the debt, then the debt burden will remain just as crushing as it was before. A government can't use the same money twice – first to pay down foreign debt and second to expand health and education services for the poor. This magic could only work if health and education spending boosted economic growth and thus generated future tax revenues to service the debt. Unfortunately, there is little evidence that higher health and education spending is associated with faster economic growth.

"Debt relief will empower poor countries to make their own choices"

Not really. Pro-debt relief advocacy groups face a paradox: On one hand, they want debt relief to teach the poor; on the other, they don't want rich nations telling poor countries what to do. "For debt relief to work, let the conditions be set by civil society in our countries, not by big world institutions using it as a political tool," argued Kennedy Tumutegyereize of the Uganda Debt Network. Unfortunately, debt relief advocates can't have it both ways. Civil society remains weak in most highly indebted poor countries, so it would be hard to ensure that debt relief will truly benefit the poor unless there are conditions on the debt relief package.

Attempting to square this circle, the World Bank and IMF have made a lot of noise about consulting civil society while at the same time dictating incredibly detailed conditions on debt relief. The result is unlikely to please anyone. Debt relief under the World Bank and IMF's current HIPC initiative, for example, requires that countries prepare Poverty Reduction Strategy Papers. The World Bank's online handbook advising countries on how to prepare such documents runs well over 1,000 pages and covers such varied topics as macroeconomics, gender, the environment, water management, mining, and information technology. [See Box 47.1.] It would be hard for even the most skilled policymakers in the advanced economies to follow such complex (no matter how salutary) advice, much less a government in a poor country suffering from scarcity of qualified managers. In reality, this morass of requirements emerged as the multilateral financial institutions sought to hit on all the politically correct themes while at the same time trying hard to make the money reach the poor. If the conditions don't work – and of course they won't – the World Bank and IMF can simply fault the countries for not following their advice.

"Debt relief hurts big banks"

Wrong. During the 1970s and early 1980s, large commercial banks and official creditors based in rich nations provided substantial loans at market interest rates to countries such as Ivory Coast and Kenya. However, they pulled out of these markets in the second half of the 1980s and throughout the 1990s. In fact, from 1988 to 1997, such lenders received more in payments on old loans than they disbursed in new lending to high-debt poor countries. The multilateral development banks and bilateral lenders took their place, offering low-interest credit to poor nations. It's easy to understand why the commercial and official creditors pulled out. Not only did domestic economic mismanagement make high-debt poor countries less attractive candidates for potential loans, but with debt relief proposals in the air as early as 1979, few creditors wished to risk new lending under the threat that multilateral agencies would later decree loan forgiveness.

The IMF and World Bank announced the HIPC initiative of partial and conditional forgiveness of multilateral loans for 41 poor countries in September 1996. By the time the debt relief actually reached the HIPCs in the late 1990s, the commercial banks and high-interest official creditors were long gone and what was being forgiven were mainly "concessional" loans – i.e., loans with subsidized interest rates and long repayment periods. So really, debt relief takes money away from the international lending community that makes concessional loans to the poorest nations, potentially hurting other equally poor but not highly indebted nations if foreign aid resources are finite (as, of course, they are). Indeed, a large share of the world's poor live in India and China. Neither nation, however, is eligible for debt relief.

"Debt relief boosts foreign investment in poor nations"

A leap of faith. It is true that forgiving old debt makes the borrowers more able to service new debt, which in theory could make them attractive to lenders. Nonetheless, the commercial and official lenders who offer financing at market interest rates will not want to come back to most HIPCs any time soon. These lenders understand all too well the principle of moral hazard: Debt relief encourages borrowers to take on an excessive amount of new loans expecting that they too will be forgiven. Commercial banks obviously don't want to get caught with forgiven loans. And even the most charitable official lenders don't want to sign their own death warrants by getting stuck with forgiven debt. Both commercial and official lenders may want to redirect their resources to safer countries where debt relief is not on the table. Indeed, in 1991, the 47 least developed countries took in 5 percent of the total foreign direct investment (FDI) that flowed to the developing world; by 2000 their portion had dropped to only 2.5 percent. (Over the same period, the portion of global FDI captured by all developing nations dropped as well, from 22.3 to 15.9 percent.) Even capital flows to now lightly indebted "safe" countries might suffer from the perception that their debts also may be forgiven at some point. Ultimately, only the arms of multilateral development banks that provide soft loans – with little or no interest and very long repayment periods – are going to keep lending to HIPCs, and only then under very stringent conditions.

"Debt relief will promote economic reform"

Don't hold your breath. During the last two decades, the multilateral financial institutions granted "structural adjustment" loans to developing nations, with the understanding that governments in poor countries would cut their fiscal deficits and enact reforms – including privatization of state-owned enterprises and trade liberalization – that would promote economic growth. The World Bank and IMF made 1,055 separate adjustment loans to 119 poor countries from 1980 to 1999. Had such lending succeeded, poor countries would have experienced more rapid growth, which in turn would have permitted them to service their foreign debts more easily. Thirty-six poor countries

BOX 47.1   A FEW STRINGS ATTACHED

Nations seeking debt relief through the International Monetary Fund and World Bank's Highly Indebted Poor Countries Initiative must prepare a Poverty Reduction Strategy Paper. The World Bank's guidelines for doing so include well-meaning yet mind-numbing conditions that poor nations will be hard pressed to fulfill. Consider the following advice in the World Bank's Poverty Reduction Strategy Sourcebook:

Governments must "assess not only the appropriateness of the proposed poverty reduction spending program, but also of planned nondiscretionary, and discretionary nonpriority, spending . . . [and] the distributional and growth impact of spending in each area . . . [P]olicymakers should evaluate the extent to which government intervention in general, and the public spending in particular, can be justified on grounds of market failure and/or redistribution. . . . [P]olicymakers should consider the extent to which both technical assistance and the private sector can play a role in improving the delivery of [public] services."

If they still have time on their hands, government officials should also "analyze the main sources of risk and vulnerability of the population and . . . identify the population groups most affected by these risks. Once the groups and their characteristics are identified, the role social protection can play, alongside interventions in other sectors and at the macro level, can be investigated. . . . The second step is to determine which of the identified groups are covered by existing social protection programs and policies, and to assess the effectiveness of these instruments individually and in combination. Special attention should be paid to the compatibility of the policy context and the expenditure programs, the specific objectives of each intervention, their effectiveness at achieving these objectives, and their cost-effectiveness in delivering the observed outcomes." Moreover, policymakers in poor nations must also "integrate gender analysis into poverty diagnosis and . . . ensure that participatory consultation and planning processes are specifically designed to give voice to all sectors of society – women and men, as well as different age, ethnic, and cultural groups."

received 10 or more adjustment loans in the 1980s and 1990s, and their average percentage growth of per capita income during those two decades was a grand total of zero. Moreover, such loans failed to produce meaningful reforms, and developing countries now cite this failure as justification for debt relief. Yet why should anyone expect that conditions on debt forgiveness would be any more effective in changing government policies and behavior than conditions on the original loans?

Partial and conditional debt forgiveness is a *fait accompli*. Expanding it to full and unconditional debt forgiveness – as some groups now advocate – would simply transfer more resourcers from poor countries that have used aid effectively to those that have wasted it in the past. The challenge for civil society, the World Bank, IMF, and other agencies is to ensure that conditional debt forgiveness really does lead to government reforms that enhance the prospects of poor countries.

How can we promote economic reform in the poorest nations without repeating past failures? The lesson of structural adjustment programs is that reforms imposed from the outside don't change behavior. Indeed, they only succeed in creating an easy scapegoat: Insincere governments can simply blame their woes on the World Bank and IMF's "harsh" adjustment programs while not doing anything to fundamentally change economic incentives and ignite economic growth. It would be better for the international financial institutions to simply offer advice to governments that ask for it and wait for individual countries to come forward with homegrown reform programs, financing only the most promising ones and disengaging from the rest. This approach has worked in promoting economic reform in countries such as China, India, and Uganda. Rushing through debt forgiveness and imposing complex reforms from the outside is as doomed to failure as earlier rounds of debt relief and adjustment loans.

Further reading

This essay is based in part on William Easterly's new book *The Elusive Quest for Growth: Economists' Adventures and Misadventures in the Tropics* (Cambridge: MIT Press, 2001). For the latest news on pro-debt relief campaigns, visit the Web sites of Drop the Debt and Jubilee Plus. The Web site of the United States Conference of Catholic Bishops offers updates and statements by religious leaders on various debt relief initiatives. For a description of the World Bank and International Monetary Fund's debt relief program, visit the Debt Initiative for Highly Indebted Poor Countries (HIPC) page on the World Bank's Web site.

For critical perspectives on debt relief initiatives, see Tim Allen and Diana Weinhold's "Dropping the Debt for the New Millennium: Is It Such a Good Idea?" (London: London School of Economics Working Paper Series No. 00–09, May 2000) and David Malin Roodman's "Still Waiting for the Jubilee: Pragmatic Solutions for the Third World Debt Crisis" (Washington: Worldwatch Institute Paper No. 155, April 2001). Also see Easterly's "How Did Highly Indebted Poor Countries Become Highly Indebted? Reviewing Two Decades of Debt Relief" (Washington: World Bank Working Paper No. 2225, June 2000).

For more on the partly fictional nature of debt burdens, see "Will HIPC Matter? The Debt Game and Donor Behavior in Africa" (Washington: Carnegie ERP Discussion Paper, No. 3, March 2001) by Nancy Birdsall, Stijn Claessens, and Ishac Diwan, available on the Web site of the Carnegie Endowment for International Peace. On the impossibility of spending money simultaneously on debt relief and poverty relief, see Craig Burnside and Domenico Fanizza's "Hiccups for HIPCs" (Washington: World Bank, unpublished manuscript, 2001). Dilip Ratha examines the tendency for the World Bank to issue new loans so that countries can repay old ones in "Demand for World Bank Lending" (Washington: World Bank Working Paper No. 2652, July 2001).

For links to relevant Web sites, as well as a comprehensive index of related *Foreign Policy* articles, access www.foreignpolicy.com.

REVIEW AND DISCUSSION QUESTIONS

1   What is Easterly's objection to the view that democratic governments in poor countries should not be held responsible for debts accumulated by previous, less democratic governments?
2   Why does Easterly question the idea that debt relief would allow poor countries to spend more on education and health?
3   What is the author's view on the relation between debt relief and foreign investment?
4   Which of Easterly's objections to debt relief do you find most and least convincing? Why? Explain.

Chapter 48

Jeffrey D. Sachs

CAN EXTREME POVERTY BE ELIMINATED?

ALMOST EVERYONE WHO EVER LIVED was wretchedly poor. Famine, death from childbirth, infectious disease and countless other hazards were the norm for most of history. Humanity's sad plight started to change with the Industrial Revolution, beginning around 1750. New scientific insights and technological innovations enabled a growing proportion of the global population to break free of extreme poverty.

Two and a half centuries later more than five billion of the world's 6.5 billion people can reliably meet their basic living needs and thus can be said to have escaped from the precarious conditions that once governed everyday life. One out of six inhabitants of this planet, however, still struggles daily to meet some or all of such critical requirements as adequate nutrition, uncontaminated drinking water, safe shelter and sanitation as well as access to basic health care. These people get by on $1 a day or less and are overlooked by public services for health, education and infrastructure. Every day more than 20,000 die of dire poverty, for want of food, safe drinking water, medicine or other essential needs.

For the first time in history, global economic prosperity, brought on by continuing scientific and technological progress and the self-reinforcing accumulation of wealth, has placed the world within reach of eliminating extreme poverty altogether. This prospect will seem fanciful to some, but the dramatic economic progress made by China, India and other low-income parts of Asia over the past 25 years demonstrates that it is realistic. Moreover, the predicted stabilization of the world's population toward the middle of this century will help by easing pressures on Earth's climate, ecosystems and natural resources – pressures that might otherwise undo economic gains.

Although economic growth has shown a remarkable capacity to lift vast numbers of people out of extreme poverty, progress is neither automatic nor inevitable. Market forces and free trade are not enough. Many of the poorest regions are ensnared in a poverty trap: they lack the financial means to make the necessary investments in infrastructure, education, health care systems and other vital needs. Yet the end of such poverty is feasible if a concerted global effort is undertaken, as the nations of the world promised when they adopted the Millennium Development Goals at the United Nations Millennium Summit in 2000. A dedicated cadre of development agencies, international financial institutions, nongovernmental organizations and communities throughout the developing world already constitute a global network of expertise and goodwill to help achieve this objective.

This past January my colleagues and I on the U.N. Millennium Project published a plan to halve the rate of extreme poverty by 2015 (compared with 1990) and to achieve other quantitative targets for reducing hunger, disease and environmental degradation. In my recent book, *The End of Poverty*, I argue that a large-scale and targeted public investment effort could in fact eliminate this problem by 2025, much as smallpox was eradicated globally. This hypothesis is controversial, so I am pleased to have the opportunity to clarify its main arguments and to respond to various concerns that have been raised about it.

Beyond business as usual

Economists have learned a great deal during the past few years about how countries develop and what roadblocks can stand in their way. A new kind of development economics needs to emerge, one that is better grounded in science – a "clinical economics" akin to modern medicine. Today's medical professionals understand that disease results from a vast array of interacting factors and conditions: pathogens, nutrition, environment, aging, individual and population genetics, lifestyle. They also know that one key to proper treatment is the ability to make an individualized diagnosis of the source of illness. Likewise, development economists need better diagnostic skills to recognize that economic pathologies have a wide variety of causes, including many outside the traditional ken of economic practice.

Public opinion in affluent countries often attributes extreme poverty to faults with the poor themselves – or at least with their governments. Race was once thought the deciding factor. Then it was culture: religious divisions and taboos, caste systems, a lack of entrepreneurship, gender inequities. Such theories have waned as societies of an ever widening range of religions and cultures have achieved relative prosperity. Moreover, certain supposedly immutable aspects of culture (such as fertility choices and gender and caste roles) in fact change, often dramatically, as societies become urban and develop economically.

Most recently, commentators have zeroed in on "poor governance," often code words for corruption. They argue that extreme poverty persists because governments fail to open up their markets, provide public services and clamp down on bribe taking. It is said that if these regimes cleaned up their acts, they, too, would flourish. Development assistance efforts have become largely a series of good governance lectures.

The availability of cross-country and time-series data now allows experts to make much more systematic analyses. Although debate continues, the weight of the evidence indicates that governance makes a difference but is not the sole determinant of economic growth. According to surveys conducted by Transparency International, business leaders actually perceive many fast-growing Asian countries to be more corrupt than some slow-growing African ones.

Geography – including natural resources, climate, topography, and proximity to trade routes and major markets – is at least as important as good governance. As early as 1776, Adam Smith argued that high transport costs inhibited development in the inland areas of

Africa and Asia. Other geographic features, such as the heavy disease burden of the tropics, also interfere. One recent study by my Columbia University colleague Xavier Sala-i-Martin demonstrated once again that tropical countries saddled with malaria have experienced slower growth than those free from the disease. The good news is that geographic factors shape, but do not decide, a country's economic fate. Technology can offset them: drought can be fought with irrigation systems, isolation with roads and mobile telephones, diseases with preventive and therapeutic measures.

The other major insight is that although the most powerful mechanism for reducing extreme poverty is to encourage overall economic growth, a rising tide does not necessarily lift all boats. Average income can rise, but if the income is distributed unevenly the poor may benefit little, and pockets of extreme poverty may persist (especially in geographically disadvantaged regions). Moreover, growth is not simply a free-market phenomenon. It requires basic government services: infrastructure, health, education, and scientific and technological innovation. Thus, many of the recommendations of the past two decades emanating from Washington – that governments in low-income countries should cut back on their spending to make room for the private sector – miss the point. Government spending, directed at investment in critical areas, is itself a vital spur to growth, especially if its effects are to reach the poorest of the poor.

The poverty trap

So what do these insights tell us about the region most afflicted by poverty today, Africa? Fifty years ago tropical Africa was roughly as rich as subtropical and tropical Asia. As Asia boomed, Africa stagnated. Special geographic factors have played a crucial role.

Foremost among these is the existence of the Himalaya Mountains, which produce southern Asia's monsoon climate and vast river systems. Well-watered farmlands served as the starting points for Asia's rapid escape from extreme poverty during the past five decades. The Green Revolution of the 1960s and 1970s introduced high-yield grains, irrigation and fertilizers, which ended the cycle of famine, disease and despair.

It also freed a significant proportion of the labor force to seek manufacturing jobs in the cities. Urbanization, in turn, spurred growth, not only by providing a home for industry and innovation but also by prompting greater investment in a healthy and skilled labor force. Urban residents cut their fertility rates and thus were able to spend more for the health, nutrition and education of each child. City kids went to school at a higher rate than their rural cousins. And with the emergence of urban infrastructure and public health systems, city populations became less disease-prone than their counterparts in the countryside, where people typically lack safe drinking water, modern sanitation, professional health care and protection from vector-borne ailments such as malaria.

Africa did not experience a green revolution. Tropical Africa lacks the massive floodplains that facilitate the large-scale and low-cost irrigation found in Asia. Also, its rainfall is highly variable, and impoverished farmers have been unable to purchase fertilizer. The initial Green Revolution research featured crops, especially paddy rice and wheat, not widely grown in Africa (high-yield varieties suitable for it have been developed in recent years, but they have not yet been disseminated sufficiently). The continent's food production per person has actually been falling, and Africans' caloric intake is the lowest in the world; food insecurity is rampant. Its labor force has remained tethered to subsistence agriculture.

Compounding its agricultural woes, Africa bears an overwhelming burden of tropical diseases. Because of climate and the endemic mosquito species, malaria is more intensively transmitted in Africa than anywhere else. And high transport costs isolate Africa economically. In East Africa, for example, the rainfall is greatest in the interior of the continent, so most people live there, far from ports and international trade routes.

Much the same situation applies to other impoverished parts of the world, notably the Andean and Central American highlands and the landlocked countries of Central Asia. Being economically isolated, they are unable to attract much foreign investment (other than for the extraction of oil, gas and precious minerals). Investors tend to be dissuaded by the high transport costs associated with the interior regions. Rural areas therefore remain stuck in a vicious cycle of poverty, hunger, illness and illiteracy. Impoverished areas lack adequate internal savings to make the needed investments because most households live hand to mouth. The few high-income families, who do accumulate savings, park them overseas rather than at home. This capital flight includes not only financial capital but also the human variety, in the form of skilled workers – doctors, nurses, scientists and engineers, who frequently leave in search of improved economic opportunities abroad. The poorest countries are often, perversely, net exporters of capital.

Put money where mouths are

The technology to overcome these handicaps and jump-start economic development exists. Malaria can be controlled using bed nets, indoor pesticide spraying and improved medicines. Drought-prone countries in Africa with nutrient-depleted soils can benefit enormously from drip irrigation and greater use of fertilizers. Landlocked countries can be connected by paved highway networks, airports and fiber-optic cables. All these projects cost money, of course.

Many larger countries, such as China, have prosperous regions that can help support their own lagging areas. Coastal eastern China, for instance, is now financing massive public investments in western China. Most of today's successfully developing countries, especially smaller ones, received at least some backing from external donors at crucial times. The critical scientific innovations that formed the underpinnings of the Green Revolution were bankrolled by the Rockefeller Foundation, and the spread of these technologies in India and elsewhere in Asia was funded by the U.S. and other donor governments and international development institutions.

We in the U.N. Millennium Project have listed the investments required to help today's impoverished regions cover basic needs in health, education, water, sanitation, food production, roads and other key areas. We have put an approximate price tag on that assistance and estimated how much could be financed by poor households themselves and by domestic institutions. The remaining cost is the "financing gap" that international donors need to make up.

For tropical Africa, the total investment comes to $110 per person a year. To place this into context, the average income in this part of the world is $350 per annum, most or all of which is required just to stay alive. The full cost of the total investment is clearly beyond the funding reach of these countries. Of the $110, perhaps $40 could be financed domestically, so that $70 per capita would be required in the form of international aid.

Adding it all up, the total requirement for assistance across the globe is around $160 billion a year, double the current rich-country aid budget of $80 billion. This figure amounts to approximately 0.5 percent of the combined gross national product (GNP) of the affluent donor nations. It does not include other humanitarian projects such as postwar Iraqi reconstruction or Indian Ocean tsunami relief. To meet these needs as well, a reasonable figure would be 0.7 percent of GNP, which is what all donor countries have long promised but few have fulfilled. Other organizations, including the International Monetary Fund, the World Bank and the British government, have reached much the same conclusion.

We believe these investments would enable the poorest countries to cut poverty by half by 2015 and, if continued, to eliminate it altogether by 2025. They would not be "welfare payments" from rich to poor but instead something far more important and durable. People living above mere subsistence levels would be able to save for their futures; they could join the virtuous cycle of rising incomes, savings and technological inflows. We would be giving a billion people a hand up instead of a handout.

If rich nations fail to make these investments, they will be called on to provide emergency assistance more or less indefinitely. They will face famine, epidemics, regional conflicts and the spread of terrorist havens. And they will condemn not only the impoverished countries but themselves as well to chronic political instability, humanitarian emergencies and security risks.

The debate is now shifting from the basic diagnosis of extreme poverty and the calculations of financing needs to the practical matter of how assistance can best be delivered. Many people believe that aid efforts failed in the past and that care is needed to avoid the repetition of failure. Some of these concerns are well grounded, but others are fueled by misunderstandings.

When pollsters ask Americans how much foreign aid they think the U.S. gives, they greatly overestimate the amount – by as much as 30 times. Believing that so much money has been donated and so little has been done with it, the public concludes that these programs have "failed." The reality is rather different. U.S. official assistance to sub-Saharan Africa has been running at $2 billion to $4 billion a year, or roughly $3 to $6 for every African. Most of this aid has come in the form of "technical cooperation" (which goes into the pockets of consultants), food contributions for famine victims and the cancellation of unpaid debts. Little of this support has come in a form that can be invested in systems that improve health, nutrition, food production and transport. We should give foreign aid a fair chance before deciding whether it works or not.

A second common misunderstanding concerns the extent to which corruption is likely to eat up the donated money. Some foreign aid in the past has indeed ended up in the equivalent of Swiss bank accounts. That happened when the funds were provided for geopolitical reasons rather than development; a good example was U.S. support for the corrupt regime of Mobutu Sese Seko of Zaire (now the Democratic Republic of the Congo) during part of the cold war. When assistance has been targeted at development rather than political goals, the outcomes have been favorable, ranging from the Green Revolution to the eradication of smallpox and the recent near-eradication of polio.

The aid package we advocate would be directed toward those countries with a reasonable degree of good governance and operational transparency. In Africa, these countries include Ethiopia, Ghana, Mali, Mozambique, Senegal and Tanzania. The money would not be merely thrown at them. It would be provided according to a detailed and monitored plan, and new rounds of financing would be delivered only as the work actually got done. Much of the funds would be given directly to villages and towns to minimize the chances of their getting diverted by central governments. All these programs should be closely audited.

Western society tends to think of foreign aid as money lost. But if supplied properly, it is an investment that will one day yield huge returns, much as U.S. assistance to western Europe and East Asia after World War II did. By prospering, today's impoverished countries will wean themselves from endless charity. They will contribute to the international advance of science, technology and trade. They will escape political instability, which leaves many of them vulnerable to violence, narcotics trafficking, civil war and even terrorist takeover. Our own security will be bolstered as well. As U.N. Secretary-General Kofi Annan wrote earlier this year: "There will be no development without security, and no security without development."

Further reading

Institutions Matter, but Not for Everything. Jeffrey D. Sachs in *Finance and Development (IMF)*, Vol. 40, No. 2, pages 38–41; June 2003. www.sachs.earth.columbia.edu

Determinants of Long-Term Growth: A Bayesian Averaging of Classical Estimates (BACE) Approach. X. Sala-i-Martin, Germot Doppelhofer and Ronald I. Miller in *American Economic Review*, Vol. 94, No. 4, pages 813–835; September 2004.

Ending Africa's Poverty Trap. J. D. Sachs, J. W. McArthur, G. Schmidt-Traub, M. Kruk, C. Bahadur, M. Faye and G. McCord in *Brookings Papers on Economic Activity*, Vol. 1: 2004, pages 117–216. www.sachs.earth.columbia.edu

The Development Challenge. J. D. Sachs in *Foreign Affairs*, Vol. 84, No. 2, pages 78–90; March/April 2005. www.sachs.earth.columbia.edu

The End of Poverty: Economic Possibilities for Our Time. J. D. Sachs. Penguin Press, 2005. www.earth.columbia.edu/endofpoverty

Investing in Development: A Practical Plan to Achieve the Millennium Development Goals. United Nations Millennium Project, 2005. www.unmillenniumproject.org

REVIEW AND DISCUSSION QUESTIONS

1   Why does Sachs believe that ending poverty on a global scale is a more realistic goal today than it ever was before?

2   What does Sachs mean when he argues that development economics must be more like modern medicine?

3   According to Sachs, why have many Asian economies been able to escape poverty while many African economies have not?

4   According to the author, how should foreign aid be provided to be effective?

5   Do you agree with the idea that ending poverty requires the provision of foreign aid? Why or why not?

Chapter 49

Nancy Birdsall, Dani Rodrik, and Arvind Subramanian

HOW TO HELP POOR COUNTRIES

Getting development right

THE YEAR 2005 HAS BECOME the year of development. In September, at the UN Millennium Summit meeting of heads of state, in New York, leaders of wealthy nations will emphasize their commitment to deeper debt relief and increased aid programs for developing countries. The Millennium Development Goals, the center-piece of the conference's program, call for halving the levels of world poverty and hunger by 2015.

The summit will focus on increasing international aid to 0.7 percent of donors' gross national product to finance a doubling of aid transfers to especially needy areas, particularly in Africa. With respect to global trade, efforts will center on the Doha Round of multilateral trade negotiations and opening markets to important exports (such as cotton) from developing countries. The discussions will thus proceed based on two implicit but critical underlying assumptions: that wealthy nations can materially shape development in the poor world and that their efforts to do so should consist largely of providing resources to and trading opportunities for poor countries.

These assumptions ignore key lessons of the last four decades – and of economic history more generally. Development is something largely determined by poor countries themselves, and outsiders can play only a limited role. Developing countries themselves emphasize this point, but in the rich world it is often forgotten. So too is the fact that financial aid and the further opening of wealthy countries' markets are tools with only a limited ability to trigger growth, especially in the poorest countries. The tremendous amount of energy and political capital expended on these efforts in official circles threatens to crowd out attention to other ways in which rich countries could do less harm and more good. A singular focus on aid and market access at the September 2005 Millennium Summit should not leave other potentially rewarding measures on the back burner.

Bootstraps

Consider Nicaragua and Vietnam. Both are poor countries with primarily agricultural economies. Both have suffered from long periods of conflict. And both have benefited from substantial foreign aid. But only Vietnam has reduced poverty dramatically and enjoyed steady economic growth (five percent per capita since 1988). Nicaragua has floundered economically, with per capita growth too modest to make a real dent in the number of poor people.

Vietnam faced a U.S. embargo until 1994, and it is still not a member of the World Trade Organization (WTO). Despite these obstacles, it has found markets for its growing exports of coffee and other agricultural products and has successfully begun diversifying into manufacturing as well, especially of textiles. Nicaragua, on the other hand, benefits from preferential access to the lucrative U.S. market and had several billion dollars of its official debt written off in the 1990s. Yet its coffee and clothing export industries have not been able to compete with Vietnam's.

Why has Vietnam outpaced Nicaragua? The answers are internal: history and economic and political institutions have trumped other factors in determining economic success. Access to the U.S. market and the largesse of Western donors have not been powerful enough to overcome Nicaragua's history of social and economic inequality: land and power there have long been concentrated in the hands of a few elites, and the government has failed to invest enough in infrastructure and public welfare.

The experiences of many other developing countries confirm the importance of specific internal factors. Like Vietnam, neither China nor India – the two emerging superstars of the last quarter century – has benefited from trade preferences. And neither has received much foreign aid compared to countries in Africa and Central America. But by enacting creative domestic reforms, China and India have prospered, and in both countries poverty has plunged.

On the flip side, many African countries have been unable to match Vietnam's success, despite being no poorer or more agrarian. True, education and health indicators have improved markedly in Africa, and some of its countries have achieved macroeconomic stability. But even in the best-performing countries, growth and productivity remain modest, and investment depends completely on foreign aid infusions. It may be tempting to ascribe the rare African successes – Botswana and Mauritius, for example – to high foreign demand for their exports (diamonds and garments, respectively), but that explanation goes only so far. Obviously, both countries would be considerably poorer without access to markets abroad. But what distinguishes them is not the external advantages they enjoy, but their ability to exploit these advantages. Natural resource endowments have often hurt many developing countries: the word "diamond" hardly conjures images of peace and prosperity in the context of Sierra Leone, and oil has been more curse than blessing for Angola, Equatorial Guinea, Nigeria, and many others.

Witness the case of Mexico. It has the advantage of sharing a 2,000-mile border with the world's greatest economic power. Since the North American Free Trade Agreement went into effect in 1994, the United States has given Mexican goods duty-free access to its markets, has made huge investments in the Mexican economy, and has continued to absorb millions of Mexican laborers. During the 1994–95 peso crisis, the U.S. Treasury even underwrote Mexico's financial stability. Outside economic help does not get much better. But since 1992, Mexico's economy has grown at an annual average rate of barely more than one percent per capita. This figure is far less than the rates of the Asian growth superstars. It is also a fraction of Mexico's own growth of 3.6 percent per year in the two decades that preceded its 1982 debt crisis. Access to external markets and resources has not been able to make up for Mexico's internal problems.

A notable exception to the limitations of outside assistance is European Union membership. By offering its poorer eastern and southern neighbors not just aid transfers and market access but the prospect of joining the union, the EU has stimulated deep policy and institutional changes and impressive growth in about 20 countries. But the exception proves the rule: the EU is not just an economic arrangement; it is also a political system in which member states transfer extensive legal powers to the central authority. In return, the center shoulders significant responsibilities for the economic well-being of each member.

Unfortunately, accession to the EU or to any other major power is not an option for most of the poorest parts of the world – and increasing the financial resources and trading opportunities for the poorest countries is not a sufficient substitute.

Easy access

To start, there is the question of market access. Currently, the international trade system is full of inequities. Rich countries place their highest tariffs on imports important to developing countries – garments and agriculture, for example. The tariffs escalate as the level of processing increases, discouraging industrialization in the poor countries. In addition, multilateral trade negotiations lack transparency and often exclude developing countries from the real action. Using WTO procedures to settle trade disputes requires money and technical expertise, both of which poor countries lack.

But to say that these flaws seriously hamper development in struggling economies would be to overlook the remarkable success in the last two decades of Vietnam and China in exporting manufactured goods, of Chile in exporting wine and salmon, and most recently of India in exporting services. These countries have achieved success in exporting, despite the impediments. And barriers on manufactured exports from developing countries were even higher when the Asian "tigers" first arrived on the scene in the 1960s and 1970s.

Many argue that agricultural tariffs in particular represent an impediment to poor countries' economic growth. The World Bank and organizations such as Oxfam argue that doing away with agricultural subsidies and protectionism in industrialized nations would significantly reduce poverty in the developing world. European cows, the famous example goes, are richer – receiving $2.50 a day each in subsidies – than one-third of the world's people.

Yet the reality is that liberalizing agricultural trade would largely benefit the consumers and taxpayers of the wealthy nations. Why? Because agricultural subsidies serve first and foremost to transfer resources from consumers and taxpayers to farmers within the same country. Thus, citizens of developed countries would derive the most benefit from having those subsidies cut. Other countries are affected only insofar as world prices rise. But the big, clear gainers from such price increases would be countries that are large net exporters of agricultural products – rich countries, such as the United States, and middle-income countries, such as Argentina, Brazil, and Thailand.

What about the poorer countries? For one thing, many poor countries are actually net importers of agricultural products, and so they benefit from low world prices. An increase in prices may help the rural poor, who sell the agricultural goods, but it would make the urban poor – the consumers – worse off. Net poverty could still be reduced, but to what extent depends in complicated fashion on the working condition of roads and the markets for fertilizer and other inputs, on how much of the gains are captured by poor farmers versus intermediaries, and on the poverty profile of each country.

Regardless of whether agricultural liberalization increases or decreases poverty, the impact would not be significant. Most studies predict that the effect of such liberalization on world prices would be small. The International Monetary Fund (IMF) estimates that world prices would only rise by 2–8 percent for rice, sugar, and wheat; 4 percent for cotton; and 7 percent for beef. The typical annual variation in the world prices of these commodities is at least one order of magnitude larger.

Take cotton specifically. The largest credible estimate of the impact of the complete removal of U.S. cotton subsidies on world prices is less than 15 percent. How much of an effect could this have on farm incomes in West Africa? There is actually a useful benchmark for comparison. In 1994, the member states of the Communaut Financire Africaine currency zone (in which 14 African countries have had their currencies pegged to the French franc since 1948) devalued their currency from 50 to 100 CFA francs per French franc, effectively doubling the domestic price of cotton exports. If at least some of the resulting price gain had gone to cotton farmers (and not to intermediaries or inflation), the farmers' incomes would have increased in countries such as Burkina Faso and Benin. Indeed, the price gain should have increased income and decreased poverty even more than would the complete removal of U.S. cotton subsidies. There is little evidence that a significant reduction in rural poverty took place, however. A World Bank study found that poverty in Burkina Faso remained stubbornly high and even increased in parts of the country.

Furthermore, a general reduction of trade barriers in rich countries could leave some of the world's poorest countries worse off. A substantial part of least-developed countries' exports enjoy favorable conditions of access to the markets of rich countries under various preferential trade arrangements. With the end in January 2005 of the long-standing system of quotas on apparel, for example, poor countries such as Bangladesh, Cambodia, and Lesotho, which benefited from preferential arrangements, justifiably have been fearing competition from China and Vietnam. The loss of preferential access for the poorest countries is not a justification for stopping trade liberalization in its tracks. But it is an additional reason to be cautious when estimating the magnitude of poor nations' gains from a trade-centered agenda.

Of course, if global trade and growth were to implode, as in the period between the world wars, international development would receive a serious blow. A healthy multilateral trading system is important to keep the possibility remote, and it can protect the poorest countries from unreasonable bilateral pressures. A successful Doha Round could stimulate trade among developing countries and would signal a political willingness on the part of the international community to keep the system purring and prevent an implosion – even if the actual gains for the poorest countries from trade-barrier reductions would be modest.

More money?

If not better market access, what about more aid? Boosting assistance to the poorest countries of the world is a central recommendation of the recent reports of the UN Millennium Project and British Prime Minister Tony Blair's commission on Africa, and, along with reduced corruption and better management in poor countries, it is a cornerstone of the strategy envisaged to achieve the Millennium Development Goals.

Aid has accomplished some great things. On the health front, smallpox has been eradicated, infant mortality rates have been lowered, and illnesses such as diarrhea and river blindness have been widely treated. Aid programs have improved women's access to modern contraception in Bangladesh and Egypt and helped increase school enrollment in Uganda and Burkina Faso. Aid also pays for much of the (still-limited) access to AIDS medicines in poor countries. In the last decade, aid has helped restore peace and order after conflicts in places including Bosnia, East Timor, and Sierra Leone. In addition, aid can be a vehicle for policy advice and dialogue between recipients and outsiders. There have even been macroeconomic successes, such as the $1 billion grant that allowed Poland to establish an exchange-rate stabilization fund in 1990. By stabilizing the Polish currency, this relatively small amount of financing provided valuable breathing space for the implementation of broader policy reforms.

What these successes share is that they were narrowly targeted at specific objectives. Assistance does work well, but only when the recipient countries do the right things to help themselves and have the capacity and the leadership to spend the money wisely. Some statistical evidence indicates a link between financial assistance and growth. But aid has not been associated with the sustained increases in productivity and wages that ultimately matter. During the 1990s, for example, countries in sub-Saharan Africa received funding amounting on average to about 12 percent of their GDP, while their average growth rate per capita declined by 0.6 percent per year. Meanwhile, some of today's development successes – such as Chile and Malaysia – relied little on aid. And aid to China and India has been very small.

There are many reasons for the mixed performance of foreign assistance. Donors themselves cause many of the problems. Recipient countries can be overwhelmed by the multiplicity of donors pursuing many, even inconsistent, objectives, disbursing aid to innumerable projects and imposing a plethora of conditions on its use. These factors contribute to rather than offset a poor country's lack of institutional capacity. On top of that, there is the natural volatility and uncertainty of foreign aid, which make it difficult for recipient governments to plan their budgets. For more than a decade, the bureaucracies of donor states and organizations have been unable, despite good intentions and constant resolve, to change the political incentives and constraints that impede the reform of their aid-delivery apparatuses.

Probably more important, however, are institutional deficiencies on the recipients' side. Aid is only as good as the ability of a recipient's economy and government to use it prudently and productively. Thus, the fundamental dilemma: countries most in need of aid are often those least able to use it well. That sets limits on the extent to which large infusions of foreign funds can make a difference.

The greatest example of the success of aid – the Marshall Plan – illustrates the importance of homegrown institutional competence. Because the institutions and capabilities of the United Kingdom, France, and Germany survived the war to a large extent, even their war-ravaged economies were able to exploit fully the potential of financial assistance.

This simple point addresses the view that aid is a sine qua non for African development on account of the continent's bad geography and favorable environment for diseases. A country's growth may in fact be hampered by its unsuitability for agriculture, its isolated geography, and its susceptibility to malaria and other tropical diseases. In such cases, it might seem appropriate that donors give more. But adverse geography does not fundamentally alter the fact that the effectiveness of assistance depends on the institutions of the recipient country. At its best, aid has helped nations rebuild after conflicts and assisted in achieving specific objectives. But its role in creating and sustaining key institutions and long-term economic health has been much less clear.

Sins of commission

To help developing countries help themselves, wealthy nations must begin to lift the burdens they impose on the poor. Currently, the developed world uses international trade agreements to impose costly and onerous obligations on poor countries. The most egregious example has been the WTO's intellectual property agreement, the Trade-Related Aspects of Intellectual Property Rights (TRIPS). Despite recent efforts to cushion its impact on the poorest countries, TRIPS will make the prices of essential medicines significantly greater, and this at a time when poor countries are being ravaged by one of the worst health epidemics ever known – HIV/AIDS. The price increase means that money from the citizens of poor countries will be transferred directly to wealthy pharmaceutical companies. The resulting revenue, although a significant amount of money for the poor countries, will be a relatively small part of the companies' net total profits – hardly enough to induce extra research and development.

An international community that presides over TRIPS and similar agreements forfeits any claim to being development-friendly. This must change: the rich countries cannot just amend TRIPS; they must abolish it altogether. A simple comparison makes the point clear: major industrial countries such as Italy, Japan, and Switzerland adopted pharmaceuticals patent protection when their per capita income was about $20,000; developing countries will adopt it at income levels of $500 per capita, in the case of the poorest, and $2,000–4,000 for the middle-income countries. By these standards, forcing developing countries to abide by TRIPS is about 50–100 years premature.

But costly obligations are not restricted to TRIPS. Trade agreements between the United States and countries such as Jordan, Morocco, and Vietnam have required the latter to adhere to intellectual property regulations that go beyond TRIPS, further increasing the patent holder's monopoly and restricting access to medicines. Other trade agreements have called for developing countries to open their capital accounts immediately, despite recent experience showing that doing so exposes the countries to the volatility of international capital flows.

Just as crucial for empowering poor countries is providing them with enough space to craft their own economic policy. During the last decade, economists have come to understand that economic development is at once easier and harder than previously thought. Many countries have reduced poverty and generated significant economic growth without the deep, comprehensive structural reform that has been the centerpiece for development institutions over the last quarter century. That is the good news. The bad news is that there are few general economic-policy standards that seem to apply to every country – except for such basic principles as macroeconomic stability, outward orientation, accountable government, and market-based incentives. The hard part is moving beyond these broad objectives and figuring out the appropriate specific policies for each developing country's particular needs. The many poor countries that have made progress on the general standards can better craft their own economic course if they have adequate room for policy autonomy and experimentation. The idea may sound radical, but would China have been better off implementing a garden-variety World Bank structural adjustment program in 1978 instead of its own brand of heterodox gradualism?

Almost all successful cases of development in the last 50 years have been based on creative – and often heterodox – policy innovations. South Korea and Taiwan, for example, combined their outward trade orientations with unorthodox policies: export subsidies, directed credit, patent and copyright infringements, domestic-content requirements on local production, high levels of tariff and nontariff barriers, public ownership of large segments of banking and industry, and restrictions on capital flows, including direct foreign investment. Since the late 1970s, China has also followed a highly unorthodox two-track strategy, violating practically every rule in the book – including, most notably, securing private property rights. India, which raised its economic growth rate in the early 1980s, remained a highly protected economy well into the 1990s. Even Chile – Latin America's apparently "orthodox" standout that managed to achieve both growth and democracy – violated conventional wisdom by subsidizing its nascent export industries and taxing capital inflows.

Conversely, countries that have adhered more strictly to the orthodox structural reform agenda – most notably in Latin America – have fared less well. Since the mid-1980s, virtually all Latin American countries have opened and deregulated their economies, privatized their public enterprises, and allowed unrestricted access to foreign capital. Yet they have grown at a fraction of the pace of the heterodox reformers and have been strongly buffeted by macroeconomic instability.

The contrasting experiences of eastern Asia, China, and India suggest that the secret of poverty-reducing growth lies in creating business opportunities for domestic investors, including the poor, through institutional innovations that are tailored to local political and institutional realities. Ignoring these realities carries the risk that pro-poor policies, even when they are part of apparently sound and well-intentioned IMF and World Bank programs, will be captured by local elites.

Wealthy nations and international development organizations thus should not operate as if the right policies and institutional arrangements are the same across time and space. Yet current WTO rules on subsidies, foreign investment, and patents preclude some of the policy choices made, for example, by South Korea and Taiwan in the past, when rules under the WTO's predecessor, the General Agreement on Tariffs and Trade, were more permissive. What is more, new WTO members typically confront demands to conform their trade and industrial policies to standards that go well beyond existing WTO agreements. The new Basle II international banking standards, better fitted to banks in industrialized nations, risk making it more difficult for banks in developing countries to compete.

To be sure, not all internationally imposed economic discipline is harmful. The principle of transparency, enshrined in international trade agreements and many global financial codes, is fully consistent with policy independence, as long as governments are provided leeway with respect to actual policy content. A well-functioning international economic system does need rules. But international rules should regulate the interface between different policies and institutional regimes, not erase them.

There are signs of change in the rich world's attitude. Some donors, notably the United Kingdom and the United States, the latter with its Millennium Challenge Account, are moving away from attaching explicit, heavy conditions to their grants and loans and are instead screening applicants early to ensure that assistance will be reasonably well spent. The World Bank and other organizations are designing programs with countries in which resources are disbursed not in exchange for policy reform but on the basis of pre-agreed benchmarks of progress – be it reduced inflation, more children finishing primary school, or more completed external audits of government accounts. These changes deserve to be reinforced.

Rich countries also harm their developing counterparts in other ways, most notably with their emissions of greenhouse gases. According to the growing scientific consensus, the costs of climate change will disproportionately burden developing countries. Estimates of these costs, including reduced water availability and agricultural productivity, vary from 4 to 22 percent of poor countries' incomes. Rich nations must quickly lead the way in enacting measures beyond the Kyoto Protocol. A market-based system of tradable emissions rights offers a great opportunity to combine efficiency with equitable treatment for developing countries. Poor nations would be allotted enough emissions to ensure future growth – the same right that the industrial countries have enjoyed for centuries. Market-based trading would guarantee that pollution would be cut where costs are lowest, ensuring maximum efficiency: if costs are lower in India than in the United States, for example, the United States could pay India to pollute less, and India would be financially better off in doing so.

Positive steps

Wealthy nations can also take positive steps to directly benefit developing countries – specifically, by taking action against corrupt leaders, assisting research and development, and enhancing global labor mobility.

The deepest challenge for countries in the poorest parts of the world, especially Africa, is governance. The African continent has been ravaged both by civil war and conflict and by rapacious leaders who have plundered the natural wealth of their nations. Corrupt rulers and their weak regimes have arguably been the single most important drag on African development. But with increasing democratization, the situation may be starting to improve. And rich countries can play a large role in the reform process, for the simple reason that corruption has two sides – demand and supply. For every leader who demands a bribe, there is usually a multinational company or a Western official offering to pay it. For every pile of illicit wealth, there is usually a European or American financial institution providing a safe haven for the spoils. The governments of wealthy countries need to take steps to block these activities.

There have been notable strides in the right direction: the British Department for International Development helped found the Extractive Industries Transparency Initiative a few years ago, and the UN and the Organization for Economic Cooperation and

Development (OECD) have been working together to address the bribery of officials in developing countries by foreigners. But these efforts do not go far enough.

Many institutions – the OECD and the U.S. government, for example – have laws against bribing foreign officials. But the regulations are often both narrow in scope and weak on enforcement. For example, a loophole in the U.S. laws ("deferred gifts") invites abuse. Some OECD rules damage transparency by protecting banks that hide ill-gotten wealth deposited by leaders of developing countries. Multinational companies and banks need to be more transparent in their dealings with poor-country governments. Preempting corruption must also be made more of a priority. One idea, first proposed by Harvard University's Michael Kremer, is for the international community to categorize certain regimes as corrupt or "odious." Companies that deal with such regimes would risk losing their claims to repayment if later on a lawful government decided to default on the debt passed down by its unlawful predecessor.

Wealthy countries can also spur technological advances that serve the specific interests of developing countries. Because poor countries lack wealthy markets, private companies in the developed world currently have little incentive to devise technologies for them. Hence a Catch-22 results: developing countries remain poor because of limited technological opportunities, while these opportunities remain difficult to create because the countries are poor.

The health sector provides a good example of the current problem. Pharmaceutical firms in industrialized nations conduct 90 percent of their research on diseases prevalent in the rich world – and that affect less than ten percent of the global population. There is little research on diseases endemic in the poorer parts of the world, because there are no market returns for such investments. Yet developing countries badly need medicine for preventing and curing diseases such as AIDS, malaria, and sleeping sickness. Beyond health care, developing countries also need enhanced crops that can better withstand heat, drought, and the salinization of irrigated land, as well as new energy sources that can reduce the rate of tropical deforestation.

There is already a precedent for foreign research acting to undo this technological imbalance – the "green revolution." Agricultural production in the developing world was revolutionized by new varieties of wheat developed at Norman Borlaug's International Maize and Wheat Improvement Center, in Mexico, and new strains of rice cultivated at the International Rice Research Institute, in the Philippines. Although the green revolution's impact was uneven, benefiting Asia and Latin America more than sub-Saharan Africa, the aggregate effect was nevertheless sizable. In the 1960s, southern Asia witnessed dramatic increases in productivity growth as a result of the new seed varieties. Yale University's Robert Evenson has estimated that the global return on the research on the new strains was more than 40 percent.

The international community needs to learn from this example, so that the resources of wealthy firms can be harnessed to develop important technologies for the world's poorest countries. One simple yet powerful improvement would be for rich-country governments to commit contractually to rewarding the creation of such new technologies – for example, with guaranteed purchase agreements. In effect, the international community would ensure a minimum financial return on private research undertaken for the benefit of developing countries. The Center for Global Development has devised a plan for this kind of advance-market-commitment mechanism to spark research on a malaria vaccine, at an estimated cost of $3 billion. Imagine the benefits of a $50 billion global technology-creation fund, with actual disbursement of the funds taking place over ten years or more. That $50 billion would represent only about five percent of all the financial aid that donors have promised to spend on the poor in the next decade.

Finally, to have a big impact on developing countries, trade negotiators should spend more time improving the cross-border mobility of labor – particularly of low-skill laborers, who typically are at the bottom of the pile. Current WTO negotiations on labor mobility ("mode four" in the trade jargon) focus only on high-skill labor, and even there they have made very little progress. Greater opportunities for poor and less-skilled workers to move across borders would, more than anything else, increase both the efficiency of resource allocation in the world economy and the incomes of the citizens of poor countries.

This fact is based on a simple principle of economics. The loss in efficiency due to segmented (as opposed to integrated) national markets increases with the gap in prices in these different markets, and the loss is further compounded as the gap increases. Now compare price gaps across different types of markets. In markets for goods and capital, quality- and risk-adjusted price gaps from country to country are relatively small – perhaps no more than 50–100 percent. But in labor markets, which suffer from huge border restrictions, wage gaps for similarly skilled workers are enormous – on the order of 500–1,000 percent. That is why even small relaxations of work-visa restrictions generate large income gains for workers from poor countries (as well as for the world economy). What is especially appealing is that the gains in income go directly to the workers, rather than through imperfect distribution channels (as with trade in goods) or through governments (as with aid).

Take, for example, a scheme for temporary work visas amounting to no more than three percent of the rich countries' total labor force. Under the plan, skilled and unskilled workers from poor nations would be allowed employment in rich countries for three to five years, and they would be replaced by a wave of new workers after their time ended and they returned to their home countries. Such a system would easily yield $200 billion annually for the citizens of developing nations. The returnees would also bring home far more benefits than their wages alone: experience, entrepreneurship, funds to invest, and an increased work ethic.

To make sure these benefits are realized, such a regime must generate incentives for the workers to return home. Although remittances can be an important source of income for poor families, they rarely spark or sustain long-term economic development. Designing contract labor schemes that are truly temporary is tricky, but it can be done. Unlike in previous plans, there must be clear incentives to ensure the cooperation of each party – workers, employees, and home and host governments. One possibility: withhold a portion of workers' earnings until they return home. This forced savings scheme would also guarantee that returning workers would have a sizable pool of resources to invest. In addition, there could be penalties – the reduction of worker quotas, say – for home countries with nationals who fail to return. Home governments would thus be motivated to create a hospitable domestic economic and political climate to encourage their people to come back. Of course, even with the best-designed scheme, it is inevitable that the return rate will fall short of 100 percent. Even with this consideration, however, facilitating labor mobility would bring significant gains.

Despite the obvious advantages, is a scheme like this politically feasible in developed countries? If there has been substantial trade liberalization in rich countries, it is not because it has been popular with voters, but largely because the potential beneficiaries have organized successfully and forced their agendas. Multinational firms and financial enterprises have been quick to recognize the link between enhanced market access abroad and increased profits, and they have put the issues on the negotiating agenda. Temporary labor flows, by contrast, have lacked a well-defined constituency in the developed countries. This is not because the benefits would be smaller, but because the potential beneficiaries are not as clearly identifiable. The tide has begun to turn lately as a result of labor shortages in sectors such as high-tech and seasonal agriculture, and because labor inflows would increase the tax base for financing pension benefits for retirees, thereby providing a partial solution to pension shortfalls in pay-as-you-go systems. Moreover, political realities can change – with the right leadership. In the United States, President George W. Bush has already proposed a temporary-worker program, which if designed properly could mark a useful beginning.

There are of course other ways the rich world could contribute to development. Outsiders should play an important role in preventing and resolving conflicts and humanitarian crises in developing countries. Minimizing and eliminating conflict has obvious benefits for human life – and potentially for long-term development. Just as important is stopping arms sales to dangerous governments and halting the drug and illicit diamond trades that often fund rogue groups. Another important issue is the governance of international economic institutions. The democratic deficit of these institutions has increasingly caused a corresponding legitimacy deficit. Insofar as this gap reduces the effectiveness of such organizations, rich countries would be wise to agree to reforms.

New priorities

The international community must ask itself what really matters for development, so that good intentions can be translated into real benefits for the poorest countries. To a large extent, sustainable progress is in the hands of the poor countries themselves. Internalizing this reality is important for the developing world – and also for the wealthy one, not least because doing so would check the perennial temptation to promise results that cannot be delivered.

That said, this must be clear: developed countries should not abandon the poor to their plight. If, however, rich countries truly aim to help developing countries achieve lasting growth, they must think creatively about the development agenda. If aid is increased and delivered more efficiently and trade inequities are addressed, then the two traditional pillars of development will yield rewards. But these rewards should not be overestimated. Indeed, other courses of action – such as giving poor nations more control over economic policy, financing new development-friendly technologies, and opening up labor markets – could have more significant benefits. It is time to direct the attention of the world's wealthiest countries to other ways of helping the poorest – ways that have been for too long neglected.

REVIEW AND DISCUSSION QUESTIONS

1 According to the authors, what do the development experiences of Nicaragua, Vietnam, and Mexico show? Explain.

2   To what extent would poor countries benefit from the abolition of agricultural subsidies in rich
    countries?
3   What is the authors' position in regard to how foreign aid can help poor countries develop?
4   What reforms are most likely to bring about development in poor countries according to the
    authors?
5   The authors believe that wealthy countries can take certain specific steps to help poor
    countries. Which of these steps do you believe are most likely to be effective? Which do you
    find unrealistic or unlikely to achieve the desired outcome? Explain.

Suggestions for further reading

Arslanalp, S. and Henry, P. B. (2006) "Policy Watch: Debt Relief," *Journal of Economic Perspectives*, 20: 207–220.

The authors examine in this article the likely effects of recent initiatives aimed at providing debt relief to poor countries (including the Gleneagles declaration of 2005). They argue that debt relief is unlikely to help the poorest countries but might benefit middle-income countries, which will then be likely to attract more private credit.

Collier, P. (2007) *The Bottom Billion: Why the Poorest Countries Are Failing and What Can Be Done About It*, New York: Oxford University Press.

In this book, the famous Oxford economist and Africa expert summarizes much of the research he has done over the years, often with co-authors, on the reasons why the 50 or so poorest countries in the world appear unable to achieve improvements in standards of living. Collier identifies a number of "traps" such as civil war, unfavorable geography, and bad governance. He then discusses the limitations of aid as a solution to the problems of these countries and addresses the pros and cons of alternative approaches (including military intervention).

Easterly, W. (2001) *The Elusive Quest for Growth: Economists' Adventures and Misadventures in the Tropics*, Cambridge, MA: MIT Press.

Easterly, a former World Bank advisor, takes a critical view of foreign aid and traditional development policies pushed on developing countries by the rich world. Using evidence and a wealth of anecdotes, he points out all that can and will go wrong when development policies are not thought through carefully (and especially when they do not take into account the realities of developing countries).

Easterly, W. (2006) *The White Man's Burden: Why the West's Efforts to Aid the Rest Have Done So Much Ill and So Little Good*, New York: Penguin Press.

In a follow-up to his 2001 book, Easterly criticizes economists (such as Jeffrey Sachs) who favor large increases in foreign aid to developing countries. He argues that large, top-down foreign aid programs are bound to fail, whereas small-scale, bottom-up initiatives are what it takes to remove poverty.

Rajan, R. G. and Subramanian, A. (2005) *Aid and Growth: What Does the Cross-Country Evidence Really Show?* Cambridge, MA: NBER Working Paper 11513.

In this study the authors analyze the evidence on the link between foreign aid and economic growth, attempting to correct for statistical problems that may lead to inaccurate conclusions. They find no evidence that foreign aid has helped or hindered growth in recipient countries, or that the characteristics, policies, and institutions of the recipient country make a difference.

Sachs, J. (2005) *The End of Poverty: Economic Possibilities for Our Time*, New York: Penguin Press.

Sachs makes a compelling case for an increase in foreign aid to the poorest countries in the world, arguing that these countries have geographical disadvantages that can only be overcome through substantial help from the outside. He also introduces the idea of "clinical economics," which implies a more careful approach to diagnosing development problems and designing development policies.

World Bank (1998) *Assessing Aid: What Works, What Doesn't, and Why*, New York: Oxford University Press.

In this landmark study the World Bank takes a critical look at foreign aid provision, recognizing that, on average, aid programs have not been effective at promoting economic development in recipient countries. The authors of the study, however, also emphasize that aid has helped significantly in countries with the right institutions and government policies in place (e.g., low corruption, low inflation, and trade openness).

Index

Note: *Page numbers in italics refer to data presented in table or graphic form.*